PUBLIC RELATIONS IN ACTION

PUBLIC RELATIONS
IN ACTION

SECOND EDITION

Robert T. Reilly, APR

Professor of Communication
University of Nebraska at Omaha

Prentice-Hall, Inc., Englewood Cliffs, New Jersey 07632

Library of Congress Cataloging-in-Publication Data

REILLY, ROBERT T.
  Public relations in action.

  Includes bibliographies and index.
  1. Public relations. 2. Publicity. I. Title.
HM263.R36 1987   659.2   86-30403
ISBN 0-13-738428-9

Editorial/production supervision and
  interior design: *Nancy Savio-Marcello*
Cover design: *Karen Stephens*
Cover photograph: *Geoff Gove*
Manufacturing buyer: *Ed O'Dougherty/Barbara Kittle*

© 1987 by Prentice-Hall, Inc.
A division of Simon & Schuster
Englewood Cliffs, New Jersey 07632

Printed in the United States of America

10 9 8 7 6 5 4 3 2

ISBN 0-13-738428-9   01

PRENTICE-HALL INTERNATIONAL (UK) LIMITED, *London*
PRENTICE-HALL OF AUSTRALIA PTY. LIMITED, *Sydney*
PRENTICE-HALL CANADA INC., *Toronto*
PRENTICE-HALL HISPANOAMERICANA, S.A., *Mexico*
PRENTICE-HALL OF INDIA PRIVATE LIMITED, *New Delhi*
PRENTICE-HALL OF JAPAN, INC., *Tokyo*
PRENTICE-HALL OF SOUTHEAST ASIA PTE. LTD., *Singapore*
EDITORA PRENTICE-HALL DO BRASIL, LTDA., *Rio de Janeiro*

CONTENTS

12 PUBLIC RELATIONS IN THE BUSINESS WORLD   406

13 FINANCIAL PUBLIC RELATIONS   449

14 PUBLIC RELATIONS FOR GOVERNMENT, UNIONS, TRADE ASSOCIATIONS, AND THE MILITARY   490

PREFACE

The aim of this second edition of *Public Relations in Action* is not unlike that of the original version—to present this dynamic profession of public relations in an interesting, comprehensive, and practical form. The content is intended to serve both those students who plan to adopt PR as a career and those who merely want to understand its role in society.

Increasing emphasis is being given to public relations as a management function, and that concern is addressed throughout this work, with expanded chapters on planning and management, on public relations theory and research, and on other topics that characterize the more mature practice. However, special attention is also given to those skills that are necessary to the entry-level practitioner. The written word, for example, is always going to be an important element of public relations, regardless of the delivery systems or the sophistication of the practice. Therefore, the student must perfect this skill at the same time he or she is mastering the other principles.

I have tried to provide a balance in the examples and the case problems between the large corporate role for public relations and the more modest posts that may be assigned the beginner. There are more of the former, perhaps, because those names and situations are more familiar to the student, but enough of the latter to remind readers that their initial jobs will be found in these categories. For the most part, the experience transfers easily from one to the other, even though the budgets may be dissimilar.

The changes in this edition are not cosmetic, even though nearly all the illustrations have been replaced and many new ones added. All the information has been updated, sections have been added on the new technology, extensive revisions made in the chapter on trends, and even some organizational changes introduced within chapters and in the book as a whole. At least half the text is new, and the remaining half has been rewritten, wherever that was required. Each chapter contains helpful case histories and other inserted material, along with new exercises and case problems. Chapter highlights are in a new, more readable form, and the lists of suggested readings have all been revised, with the new lists concentrating on books of the past half-dozen years.

Many of those who have adopted this text have praised its readable style; I hope that none of that has been lost. Instead, this new volume should reflect the concerns and comments of those who have used the text these past five years as a teaching tool. A number of instructors wanted to see more case problems, and these are included. Some suggested additional or expanded topics; these, too, are part of the second edition. A few opted for a more visually appealing book, and the publishers have tried to accommodate them.

In short, everything the public relations practitioner should have as a basic grounding in the profession is contained in these pages, even though some may argue about emphasis and order.

To those who supplied permission to include quoted material or illustrations, the author is grateful. This gratitude extends as well to the colleagues who read the first manuscript and contributed their suggestions: J.W. Click (Ohio University), Walter E. Griscti (University of South Florida), James F. Keenan (Robert Morris College), L.L. Mazzaroppi (Fairleigh Dickinson University), and Dennis L. Wilcox (San Jose State University). Thanks go, too, to Robert O'Neill (Los Angeles Valley College) and Adrian Headley (Arkansas State University), who reviewed the revised edition; their suggestions were, for the most part, incorporated into the final version. Of course, there have been many comments from those who have adopted the text for their classes. For these, too, the author is grateful. Special thanks to Tim Fitzgerald of the University of Nebraska at Omaha, who took many of the photos; to Bill Ramsey of Bill Ramsey & Associates, who both supplied and appeared in many of the photos; and to Dr. Patricia Leslie of Leslie Associates Inc., who also appears in several illustrations.

As anyone who has written a text can testify, it's a long, often frustrating task, with as many mechanical decisions as creative ones. The revision of such a book requires even more perseverance. Sustaining this second effort is the dictum that text revisions invariably improve upon the originals.

For the reader's sake, I hope that belief is correct.

1

WHAT PUBLIC RELATIONS IS AND ISN'T

The nature and scope of public relations are difficult to categorize. People tend to supply their own meanings to the term, interpreting its functions according to their own experience or biases. The title itself is used indiscriminately, the duties encompassed by the practice are expanding, and the many uninformed criticisms often obscure the true role of public relations.

Although many observers would deny the status of "profession" to public relations, claiming it doesn't meet the usual professional requirements of a specific body of knowledge, a unified set of standards, and an appropriate testing procedure, there are those who would contend that PR, properly practiced, *is* a profession, demanding as many skills and insights as most other professions. Increasing academic attention to public relations courses and degrees, the existence of a Code of Conduct, and the promotion of accreditation procedures seem, to these adherents, to meet professional qualifications. They point out that the practice can have a positive effect on society by presenting a deeper view of various social entities. Public relations can calm dissidents, squelch harmful rumors, promote decent health habits, argue for safety, or abet progressive political notions. It can be rewarding to the practitioner, essential to the manager, efficient for the consumer.

TOWARD A DEFINITION

"Public relations" can mean a course of action, or a state of acceptance or nonacceptance, or it can describe an entire profession. It also seems to expand or contract with organizations, depending on whether others seek to use the PR budget for their projects—which are invariably defined as "excellent public relations"—or whether they want to protect their own domain, in which case "public relations" is given its narrowest scope.

Some practitioners also point out that there is no such thing as a "PR problem." Every difficulty involves other areas.

Dave Dryden, public relations staff member for Phillips Petroleum, cited the case of his company's locating a plant near a small Texas town. The local citizens objected. "Was this a PR problem?" he asked rhetorically. "The engineers thought it was an air pollution problem; the lawyers saw a legal problem; our marketing experts considered it a logistics problem—and so on."

Given these difficulties, various organizations and publications offer their definitions, which, although perhaps incomplete, serve as guides to the practice.

The American Heritage Dictionary defines public relations as "the activities taken by an organization to promote a favorable relationship with the public."[1]

Purists would have all sorts of quarrels with that definition. It seems to ignore the research and planning functions, the evaluation aspects, and the management posture that supports these activities.

Various public relations groups and each new textbook assemble individual definitions. These get longer and longer. Among the shorter ones are these:

> . . . good performance publicly appreciated because adequately communicated. (*Fortune*)
>
> . . . the management function designed to increase profits, or the equivalent, directly or indirectly, by earning public goodwill through the adoption and continuing communication to the public of policies and procedures acceptable or beneficial to all concerned. (*pr reporter*)

Or the business-card version distributed by *Public Relations News*:

> Public relations is the management function which evaluates public attitudes, identifies the policies and procedures of an individual or an organization with the public interest, and plans and executes a program of action to earn public understanding and acceptance.

Finally, there is the definition coined at the First World Assembly of Public Relations Associations in the fall of 1978:

> Public relations practice is the art and social science of analyzing trends, predicting their consequences, counselling organization leaders, and implementing planned programs of action which serve both the organization's and the public interest.

Inherent in these definitions are several ideas that might be reviewed a bit more closely:

Management function. This stresses the fact that the public relations function within a firm operates at the highest level, helping to formulate and implement organizational goals and advising executives on strategies to be employed to reach such goals. This is not a sales responsibility or an advertising responsibility, not even strictly a promotional responsibility; it is part of management's consideration and conduct.

Public interest. These words remind practitioners that immediate and long-range considerations must be given to any actions that affect the public. Furthermore, the professional knows that public relations consists not of making something wrong seem right, but of correcting the flaw and then publicizing the results.

Evaluation. Before any plans are approved or enacted, a research phase occurs, the gathering of information to help make any later decisions as intelligent as possible. This evaluation continues through the campaign and after the campaign.

Planning. A person or an organization may accidentally garner favorable publicity. An aspiring politician might rescue a drowning child and reap consequent favorable publicity. Or a conveniently located company could shelter motorists during a sudden snowstorm and earn praise for its hospitality. Although these events constitute good public relations in the generic sense, they are not public relations in the professional sense, because they are accidental. *Planning* remains the operative word.

Acceptance. Normally, the goal of public relations efforts is acceptance by special publics or the general public. This could mean an opinion change, or opinion development, or, with regard to your friends, opinion retention. The end result may be purchase of a product, contribution of funds, support of a candidate or issue, or even a general mood of approval.

Public. Any group of people interested in an issue at any one time might constitute a public. So might any segment of society you seek to interest. Public relations campaigns, when they are most effective and efficient, concentrate on a set of publics rather than attempting to reach everyone.

Also within every examination of public relations is the formula that practitioners must teach to their infants: R.A.C.E.

"R" stands for *research*, "A" for *action*, "C" for *communication*, and "E" for *evaluation*. Some might argue for expanding that acronym to embrace *planning*, but it's a handy recipe to remember when reviewing any problem or devising any campaign. Students tackling case problems also find that short checklist invaluable.

Even within these broad limits, some professionals debate the meaning and priority of certain definitive terms. One CEO (chief executive officer) feels that counseling and communication, as important as they are, should take a back seat to the conciliatory aspect of public relations, pointing out that practitioners are uniquely qualified, because of their sensitivity and experience, to keep the internal and external company environment functioning smoothly. Edward L. Bernays wants to expurgate the word *image* from the public relations lexicon, arguing that *image* suggests "illusion," whereas public relations concerns itself with reality.

What about Advertising and Publicity?

Although it isn't possible to draw a firm distinction between advertising and public relations in specific instances, the major difference is that advertising is a *marketing* function and public relations is a *management* function. The former relates to the activities required to sell an organization's products or services and is reflective of market conditions and directed by marketing strategists; the latter attempts to sell the organization itself and initiates management decisions to achieve that goal. It's not a neat division, since there is considerable overlapping. PR can be used to sell products, and advertising may be employed for public relations purposes. Both use persuasive techniques and both have recourse to mass media. Normally, advertising has more control over time and space, since it pays for both, whereas public relations has to earn "free" coverage in newspapers, radio, and television and can't guarantee such placement. But PR does control some media items, like brochures, annual reports, films, and other promotional tools. Neither is public relations "free," since there are salaries to pay, travel, equipment, and other operating costs.

In practice, most laypersons could pick out an ad and recognize it for what it is, leaving the majority of other promotional efforts in the PR arena.

There is also much current discussion over the wisdom of merging the services of ad agencies and public relations agencies. Large advertising firms already have their PR divisions, but many of them seek added strength by acquiring very successful public relations agencies. One reason for such mergers is to provide a top-flight full-service capability; another is to prevent the potential loss of advertising clients who might be weaned away when they require certain PR expertise. The debate over such mergers centers on the relative profitability of advertising versus public relations (advertising is generally more profitable) and the tensions that could develop among people coming from different backgrounds.

Robert Schwartz, chairman of Manning, Selvage & Lee, cautions that "most senior people in P.R. come from the news side of the business where, historically, advertising and editorial were separated. Contact between the two was kept to a minimum."[2] He adds, however, that the two sides could complement each other, especially if some educational sessions are arranged for both parties.

Other ad execs recommend that care be taken to preserve the autonomy of the acquired PR firm, and that the advisory quality of public relations not be compromised by the desire for advertising revenue.

Publicity, which is often confused with public relations, is really just a tool of the larger PR concept. Publicity involves the placement of stories in the mass media and is an important element in the public relations process. However, it is possible to have wide, even favorable, publicity and still not have good public relations. The reported activities of an institution, for example, could be considered interesting, entertaining, newsworthy. Later, the public exposed to these stories may be asked to approve a zoning change affecting the institution, or a bond issue required for expansion. Their image of the organization, influenced by the news stories, could fail to support this serious request because they view the publicity as essentially trivial.

Then, too, any firm could choose or not choose to have publicity, to a considerable degree. Unless some major event occurred, like a fire or a robbery, chances are the overworked media would not be hurrying to this company to dig out news stories.

With public relations, there is no such choice. You have it—good, bad, or indifferent. As coaches say about the forward pass, "Only three things can happen, and two of them are bad." Ditto for public relations. The public may think well of you, think ill of you, or be indifferent or ignorant.

Publicity also suffers by being one-way communication, whereas public relations strives to generate dialogue and feedback. It is a more complex, comprehensive discipline.

WHO NEEDS PUBLIC RELATIONS?

Few organizations argue against the wisdom of including public relations in their plans. It wasn't always this way. Some firms used to believe they could survive on good product and fair price alone. Others thought the public could be trusted to ultimately realize the right stance in any given situation. Today, even the smallest firms try to present some sort of PR program.

Why?

Simply because public relations works. Even when a company is performing well, the public needs to be told about it. And when an organization has problems, the PR function has proved its ability to provide solutions or, at the very least, to ensure that the client firm is able to tell its version of the debate.

With the increase in corporate, even conglomerate, structure, interpersonal relations are bound to suffer. It's a long way from the person at the desk to the person at the machine, or from the nurse in the ward to the chief of staff. Communication gaps are vast, and the human touch is difficult to simulate. Public relations programs can help shorten the distance between executive and subordinate.

Externally, relationships are even more complicated. The average citizen understands less and less about government, education, space, economics, and dozens of other complex subjects. And this confusion has occurred at a time when we boast the most sophisticated and far-reaching communication systems in history.

The public relations professional seeks to cut through to your consciousness, providing you with a message you will understand and retain.

When Apple computers introduced its products, one of the firm's concerns was the reluctance of adults to learn this new skill. Giving the units friendly names, utilizing a simple logo, presenting the executives as bright young innovators—all these things tied into the ad campaign, which positioned the Apple computers as easy to operate and fun to own, making them accessible to both young and old.

Communicators like Lee Iacocca, Chrysler chairman, succeed because they seem to be able to bring business problems and decisions within reach of the average viewer or reader. A year's activities, its triumphs and failures, its profits and losses, all have to be summarized within a few pages of an annual report.

Says practitioner/editor Denny Griswold:

> Public relations actually ranks in importance with such other management functions as production, distribution, and finance. In the changing world where the actions of business, religion, education, government, and other sectors of the American system are being judged before the bar of public opinion, public relations is essential, its role assured, and its future bright.[3]

Public relations may not show up on the "bottom line" of a corporate report, as a lawsuit, tax lien, or product breakthrough might, but it's just as real and exercises similar influence on profitability. Modern managers know this. They understand that a poorly timed news story could destroy public confidence and bring down the market value of their stock. They know that an unsettled grievance may lead to a strike and subsequent loss of revenue. In a society as fragmented as ours, no company or organization can afford to ignore public relations.

However, public relations can't accomplish miracles—and it shouldn't promise any. Exaggerating one's ability to place stories in the media can have damaging results for the whole profession; so can the inclusion of celebrities as instant PR persons, and the ineptness of certain members of the vocation. Destructive, too, is the failure of management to fully trust and utilize the PR function. Practitioners often complain that the person hired to handle public relations is saddled with all sorts of entry-level communications tasks that are important in themselves, but is given no real management role.

> All too often, public relations is viewed as "firefighting" instead of fire prevention. There are countless cases where good day-to-day public relations could have prevented the need for often-unsuccessful damage-control efforts. It often takes a crisis to wake up management to the benefits of communicating with the public on a major scale.[4]

Whether the aim is to improve the sales curve or alter public policy, to raise funds or to raise issues, PR is a twentieth-century force and phenomenon.

THEN WHY ALL THE CRITICISM?

For all its efforts to project a favorable image of clients and institutions, public relations hasn't managed to successfully enhance its own image and reputation. The profession makes a handy scapegoat, and critics appear to be legion. The complaints are only rarely dangerously hostile; most are merely demeaning, like careless ethnic slurs.

Taking note of this persistent disparagement, *Public Relations News*, in an annual report issue (January 10, 1983), mentions the attacks on public relations in *Harper's*, the *San Francisco Chronicle*, and the *Washington Post*, along with accompanying negative references in everything from books to television. The article's brief defense lists the common epithets of "flacks, slaves, wolves, liars, and space grabbers" and calls for an intense educational effort to overcome the "appalling lack of understanding which is characteristic of the media."

A casual reading of the daily paper or scanning of the evening's television menu will more than justify the practitioner's paranoia:

- In the Dick Tracy comic strip, a character resembling Phil Silvers and christened "P.R. Blitz" announces he can sell anything. Fixing this self-styled "press agent" with a skeptical grimace, industrialist Diet Smith inquires, "Even something worthwhile?"
- Commenting on the high salaries of today's pro stars, Rosie Grier explains that "each guy has his manager, his lawyer, and his mouthpiece." The editor parenthetically translated that final bit of jargon as "public relations man."[5]
- A counselor for athletes characterized the NCAA's attempts to raise entrance standards as "strictly a PR move."
- President Reagan slapped a freeze on the production of government materials, claiming the Feds spend too much on PR. His deputy budget director, Edwin Harper, declared a moratorium on what he called "flicks, flacks and foldouts." There may be something about the oval office that provokes such perspectives. Richard Nixon once described some Watergate-related events as "no cover up but one hell of a lot of PR."

Few publications can neglect the opportunity to take a shot at their fellow communicators:

- "Rumor has it," hints Alan Abelson of *Barron's*, "that Mr. [Michael] Deaver is headed for a plush public relations job. In leaving politics and entering public relations, Mr. Deaver will be taking a step up professionally. We can't think of any field except politics of which that could be said."[6]
- A *Wall Street Journal* headline on declining employment opportunities reads, "DEMANDS FOR FLACKS EASES AT SOME PINCHED FIRMS."[7]

- A column in *Travel Weekly* mentions a New Orleans World's Fair executive who, "in true public relations tradition," emphasizes the positive side of the troubled event.[8]
- *Newsweek*, describing the appearance of a flamboyant politician, wrote that his dress was more like that of a PR man.
- Finally, of course, there was the *Washington Post* fiasco, in which editor Meg Greenfield wrote a stormy memo about the proliferation of releases from "flack firms" and said she didn't want any of that "damned crowd" around. Initially, executive editor Ben Bradlee supported his testy employee, but both surrendered to reality and lifted the ban on "handouts."

Everyone knows how public relations is treated in novels and on television. Like advertising, the PR profession is fictionally riddled with fast-talking, expensively clad, ulcer-prone pitchmen who have no visible ethics or scruples, and whose sinister machinations belong in a James Bond film.

"I do not believe I have ever seen a press agent sympathetically portrayed in a film or gently treated in a novel," observes *Advertising Age* columnist James Brady.[9]

(Brady, however, uses the terms "press agent," "public relations man," and "flack" interchangeably and, in an earlier column, ostensibly eulogizing a deceased practitioner, warned that you had to be careful because the dead man had not been "above putting a plug in for a client," which "was, after all, his trade.")[10]

Even the newscasts use terms loosely. A CBS Evening News anchor refers to the rebels in El Salvador who are filming the Red Cross taking government prisoners to safety:

> They [the rebels] are not without a sense of public relations.

A reporter for another network asks a representative of the Ford Motor Company if Ford's setting up of independent commissions to evaluate consumer complaints isn't really "just a public relations ploy."

Any practitioner can supply dozens of additional slurs, comments that would be considered shocking, even libelous, if applied to other professions—say, medicine or the law. People feel that public relations may be assaulted with impunity, and the defamation won't cease until the causes are better understood.

Confusion is one culprit. Public relations is constantly equated with advertising, publicity, propaganda, and high-pressure sales. Despite the efforts at drawing distinctions, the misinformation persists. One new textbook in mass communication features this paragraph:

> Public relations is directly related to advertising. In fact, there is only a very fine line distinguishing them.[11]

Publicity, too, is frequently used as a synonym for public relations, perhaps because publicity is more visible and measurable; or, perhaps, because publicity is one function of PR that can be quickly identified. Practitioners and their chief executive officers sometimes perpetuate this idea themselves. One national brewer, featured on network television, called such exposure invaluable. "That's $250,000 worth of time," he said. "That's public relations."

Adding to this confusion is the assumption of the public relations title by everyone from Hollywood press agents to athletes fronting for products. A few of these people may deserve the title, but most are totally unfamiliar with the skills and duties expected of a public relations professional. The activities of the former stars are often confined to public appearances, open houses, and periodic endorsements.

The bodyguard of one film sex symbol always billed himself as her "PR man," and a silent star, down on his luck and finding it hard to live on Social Security, entered "public relations" for a mobile-home manufacturer. Several exotic cults boast their own "public relations directors," and the 19-year-old daughter of a film and television headliner dropped out of college and wandered around Europe, finding temporary employment "in public relations at the Cannes Film Festival."

No wonder college professors continue to get students in their PR courses who are there because they "like people." Sometimes that seems the only requirement.

Even the physical image becomes a stereotype. A college public relations director remembers joining the staff of a large eastern university some years ago and being told by one of the deans that he "didn't look like a public relations man." He asked the dean what he thought a public relations man looked like. "Oh, you know what I mean," the dean responded. "Someone who goes around slapping people on the back."[12]

Besides confusion, another reason for the poor image of public relations is the inevitable adversary relationship between the practice and the media. Even reporters who have never experienced a problem with a PR person harbor the concept of the practitioner as a self-serving person who will try to interfere with a truthful encounter. Although this notion about shielding clients is overblown, it does exist, and it may be accompanied by the suspicion that the PR person is trying to sneak something past the journalist, or that the practitioner's efforts may be replete with errors or deliberate inaccuracies.

As reportorial success is measured more and more by exposé, and as media rely increasingly on the profession they criticize, you're apt to see this nagging hostility expand.

Some journalists also perpetuate the stereotype of the public relations person by the adjectives they associate with the term. For example, practitioners often appear frenetic:

"The public relations people just shrugged their shoulders and looked nervous," says a *Dallas Morning News* story about the problems of interviewing a tardy Lana Turner. And a *Sun Newspaper* column (July 6, 1983) mentions "the nervous PR flacks" rushing forward to introduce Ronald Reagan to a small businessman. The word "plush" surfaces frequently in connection with PR, and so does "shield." Dorothy Hamill is portrayed as "protected by an invisible shield of public relations people who okayed or vetoed interviews."[13]

Those who practice or teach public relations are guilty, too—guilty of not going after some of the most extravagant or devious representatives of the craft. Like the firm that a trade journal depicts, which advertises on its store front, "PUBLIC RELATIONS" and "SPEEDY 24-HOUR BAIL SERVICE." Or the practitioner who consistently violates articles in the Public Relations Society of America Code of Conduct. Or even the expensively dressed monologist who strings together 50 jokes and a few business bromides and presumes to represent the profession.

There are, too, some built-in problems associated with the practice of public relations. The nature of the function can be a form of advocacy. It should be an enlightened advocacy—the kind that corrects before it communicates, that researches before it advises. Still, it remains advocacy. And that's why an activist group protesting utility rates insists, "We want to talk to the opinion leaders; we don't want to talk to PR people." Or why the scriptwriters for "M*A*S*H" have B.J. Hunnicut talking to an army public information officer, who declares, "I refuse to lie." Hunnicut replies, "What? And you call yourself a PR man?"

There's nothing wrong with advocacy. Job applicants write résumés that emphasize their strong points. Portrait subjects choose the most flattering poses. Suitors press their causes in the most positive light. As long as this is perception rather than deception, there should be little difficulty. Like the attorney, the public relations practitioner merely wants to see that the client's viewpoint is also aired.

This effort at parity has become particularly onerous in the last two decades, when almost every public occupation, from politics to medicine, has become suspect. Confidence in former heroes has diminished, and any attempt to glorify institutions or individuals raises doubts. The negative rumor continues to have more appeal than the positive fact.

To combat this image, what can the practitioner do?

Response is difficult, because the best PR people keep a low profile. The client or company should be the star, should get the headlines. Direct communication from a background locale is awkward. However, the most effective answer to criticism is to prove by daily actions that the individual and the vocation are professional. Pushing accreditation for members is an adjunct aid. Strict adherence to codes of conduct and policing of membership follows. And there is no reason that familiar tools can't be marshaled to improve PR's reputation, pointing out, for example, the disproportionate involvement of the profession in nonprofit community affairs, as volunteers. Or explaining that public relations is, on average, a small business, but without the protection that small businesses receive.

Figure 1-1 An 1860-era "Ironhand" printing press manufactured in Chicago. This press is used by the Fine Arts Press at the University of Nebraska at Omaha.

Finally, practitioners need to occasionally counter criticism directly. They can write letters to offending sources, or speak up when orally defamed. They can be more resolute without seeming aggressive. In an article titled, "Placing Public Relations in Perspective," Dan J. Forrestal outlined the success a PRSA spokesperson had in reminding Dan Rather that his statement about "bungling by the public relations people in the White House" was inaccurate, since, at that time, there were no public relations professionals on the White House staff. Rather agreed that the "point was well taken" and promised to "be more careful." As Forrestal observed, "It was a reasonable reaction from a reasonable man to a reasonable approach."[14]

THE PAST IS PROLOGUE

Public relations has a history that argues against the contention that it is a "fly-by-night" business. Technically, the chronicle isn't nearly as lengthy as that enjoyed by, say, journalism, or religion, or the military. One measure of its relative novelty is the fact that Edward L. Bernays, considered one of the pioneers of the profession, remains active in the 1980s. Bernays and other distinguished historical practitioners are citizens of this century, but the techniques they all employed are older than written records. Man has long understood the necessity for communication, the possibility of persuasion, the value of planning, and of research, and of timing. As a concept, public relations is centuries old; as a profession, it's a recent phenomenon.

Primitive man's cave drawings, serving, perhaps, a religious purpose, also glorified the hunt and the hunter. Sumerian inscriptions dating to 5000 B.C. foreshadow agricultural-department bulletins and public-utility proposals. Most of what we know about Egypt and Assyria and other ancient civilizations comes as a result of scribes seeking to immortalize rulers. The famed Rosetta Stone, key to deciphering hieroglyphics, actually recorded the accession of Ptolemy V to the Egyptian throne. And great salesmen like the Phoenicians, realizing the complementary value of the written word, developed the alphabet that forms the basis of our 26 letters.

Greek Sophists debated the existence of truth versus personal opinion, and they gave what amounted to campaign speeches for candidates. Over 2,700 years ago, the first Olympic games were staged, requiring planning, publicizing, recruiting, organizing, and other features that remain part of the PR process. No doubt committees worked on accommodations, judging, and even such minor matters as procuring the appropriate number of wild-olive garlands for the victors.

Alexander the Great employed publicists to broadcast tales of his power and his justice to target nations, and, aware of the magic of symbols, this youthful leader adorned his helmet with white wings, marking him for ally and enemy. Julius Caesar, occupied with the subjugation of Gallic tribes half a century before the birth of Christ, took time to write letters to Rome, reminding colleagues and citizens of his triumphs. Later he composed his *De Bello Gallico* to help support his imperial ambition. In lava-encased Roman cities, we unearth Latin signs warning us against resident dogs, requesting help in locating runaway slaves, and even promoting local political aspirants.

Old Testament passages speak of spies sent to gather information in alien cities and to stir up unsettling rumors. In the New Testament, we're made aware of the missionary oratory of Christ's disciples, and their Gospel success in preserving the words of their master.

Pagan and Christian kings portrayed themselves on coinage, reminding subjects of their sovereignty, and they produced elaborate events, often in competition with each other, massaging egos and invoking authority. Celtic rulers had their bards compose flattering songs to perpetuate their accomplishments, and, in this same society, people who considered themselves wronged fasted publicly against the transgressor, creating their own ancient media event.

Medieval knights identified themselves by armorial bearings and fought under graphic standards, like the White Rose or the Red Rose, while estab-

Figure 1-2 The practice of identifying inns and taverns by distinctive signs has continued to this day, especially in Great Britain and Ireland.

lishments like schools and public houses, seeking to attract custom in an unlettered age, devised signs to depict their offerings. Monks laboriously copying manuscripts provided us with marginal ad-lib commentary and also encoded the first copyright laws. Their work gave way to Gutenberg's press in the middle of the fifteenth century, allowing the written word to be disseminated much more quickly.

In the seventeenth century, English employers, faced with a labor shortage as the result of the Black Death, boosted salaries and offered other incentives to attract workers.

We find explorers like Columbus and Magellan using basic proposal methods and some rudimentary fund-raising tactics. Swift and Voltaire satirized the existing order, often at the behest of political leaders, and helped create social change. Napoleon fretted about the editors of his day, wondering what they were saying in Paris while he was campaigning in Russia. Catherine the Great hired an art connoisseur to help her select paintings that would gain her access to Europe's cultured elite. Authors like Charles Dickens and Oscar Wilde capitalized on the value of personal tours to increase literary sales.

It's an old art. We may call these attempts crude, or lump them under propaganda (a term popularized by Pope Gregory XV in titling a council to advance the Catholic faith), or label them as unstructured, but these early campaigns were all aimed at presenting an image or influencing public opinion, and those goals remain.

Perhaps it's right that America should be credited with formalizing the practice, since this country definitely perfected the art. Our Founding Fa-

PR MEN OF THE REVOLUTION

Alfred McClung Lee calls Samuel Adams the father of the American Revolution "because he was a press agent who could dim the feats of many successors." His thesis for his Harvard M.A. in 1743 foreshadowed his future and was titled, "Whether it be lawful to resist the Supreme Magistrate, if the Commonwealth cannot be otherwise preserved." He disseminated material for American independence from 1748 to 1776 through newspapers and pamphlets. He set up Committees of Correspondence in eight towns, to which he sent copies of his paper, *The Independent Advertiser and Gazette*. His committees publicized the Boston Massacre of 1770 and the Boston Tea Party of 1773 throughout the colonies. Authorities say he did more to mold and direct public opinion in his community than any other man.

John Dickinson is called the penman of the Revolution. As a member of the 1765 Stamp Act Congress, he wrote its Declaration of Rights and Petition to the King. He authored the Articles of Confederation of the Continental Congress of 1777. He attacked British coercion and appealed to the common man with simple legal arguments.

Thomas Paine, son of a Quaker staymaker in Britain, became one of the most effective spokesmen for the Revolution. He founded the *Pennsylvania Magazine*. His famous *Common Sense*, written in simple persuasive language and published in January 1776, asked for an independent American republic. Colonial newspapers reprinted it, and authorities say that the open movement for independence stemmed from its publication date. Later, when the conflict went against the colonists, Paine's tract, *The Crisis*, with its opening line, "These are the times that try men's souls," became the rallying cry for the embattled patriots.

Patrick Henry's oratory helped mold public opinion and support for the Revolution, but only after his early difficulties with reading, writing, and mathematics, and his failure as a storekeeper and farmer. Greek, Roman, and English history gave him the impetus to become a lawyer at the age of 24, and in three years, he had 1,185 cases. He became a member of the colonial legislature in 1765 and his "give me liberty or give me death" speech rallied the colonists to the Revolution's banner.

The most effective and most famous document written by the public-relations-minded heroes of the Revolution was the Declaration of Independence, written by Thomas Jefferson. We may well owe the strength of this document to Jefferson's weakness of voice, which made it impossible for him to speak continuously. He had neither the temperament nor the ability to orate. He hated "the morbid rage of debate," believing that people were not convinced by argument, but by reading and unprovocative conversation.

In 1774, he wrote a Summary of the Rights of Americans for the Continental Congress, and it received so much visibility here and in England that he was given the honor of drafting the Declaration of Independence.

Later, in his own words, Jefferson explained the public relations reasons for the Declaration of Independence: "When forced, therefore, to resort to arms for redress, an appeal to the tribunal of the world was deemed proper for our justification. This was the object of our Declaration of Independence. Not to find out new principles or arguments never before thought of, not merely to say things that never had been said, but also to place before mankind the common sense of the subject in terms so plain and firm as to command their assent and to justify ourselves in the independent stand we are compelled to take. Neither aiming at originality of principle or sentiment nor yet copied from any particular and previous writing, it was intended to be an expression of the American mind and to give that expression the proper tone and spirit called for by the occasion."

SOURCE: Edward L. Bernays, "PR: Past, Present and Future—Men of the Revolution." Reprinted with permission from the December 1976 issue of the *Public Relations Journal.* Copyright 1976.

thers included members whose skills would be compatible with those of today's PR professionals. In particular, Samuel Adams, John Dickinson, and Thomas Jefferson have a right to that praise, and orators like Patrick Henry and philosophers like Thomas Paine are not far behind. One point to note about Adams is that he released information deliberately, according to a well-conceived plan and with the clear goal of shaping public opinion. Dickinson appreciated the advantages of writing simply but compellingly, and Thomas Jefferson, in drafting the Declaration of Independence, obviously understood the power of language to move the reader or listener.

Colonial leaders employed slogans ("No Taxation without Representation"), staged events like the Boston Tea Party, circulated printed arguments in forms such as *The Federalist Papers*, fashioned memorable titles like "Minute Men," and continually tried to beat the British to the punch with versions of current news.

In the fall of the same year that Washington was elected president, he embarked on a goodwill and information-gathering tour of some eastern states, trekking as far north as Kittery, Maine, visiting schools and factories, mending political fences, making note of commercial problems, and then returning to New York—to find a stack of unanswered mail.

In the early days of the republic, various religious sects were aided in their proselytizing by massive camp meetings featuring fiery sermons and free pamphlets. And from the initial decades of America's independence, political figures availed themselves of PR strategy. Amos Kendall, an influential member of Andrew Jackson's "Kitchen Cabinet," came to government from his editor's post on a Frankfort, Kentucky, newspaper. He ghostwrote the president's speeches, composed state papers, and made certain Jackson's views were transmitted to the press in a positive manner. Jefferson retained the services of a publicist named John Beckley, and each of the pioneer political parties included people whose responsibilities were basically public relations chores.

Popular heroes like Daniel Boone, Davy Crockett, and Buffalo Bill prospered because of the aims of land developers, politicians, or "penny dreadful" authors, whereas P.T. Barnum created most of his own favorable publicity.

During the nineteenth century, newspapers became increasingly important, touching the lives of average citizens rather than merely the wealthy. Their columns contain evidence of persuasive efforts by groups such as temperance societies and abolitionists, featuring colorful prose and specific advice. These crusading organizations also worked through established institutions like churches, and they published tracts, lobbied, and conducted rallies and demonstrations. Women in these associations often provided the impetus and acted as spokespersons.

In our Civil War, both sides had their propaganda machines, and both engaged in imaginative methods of recruiting and fund raising. The war was brought home to newspaper readers through lurid descriptions and graphic sketches. Late in the last century, some papers and magazines (*McClures, Pearson's, Cosmopolitan, Everybody's,* and others) built circulation with exposés of business and government, focusing, for example, on the life insurance field, meat-packing trusts, and partisan politics. Writers like Upton Sinclair, Lincoln Steffens, and Arthur Brisbane made their reputations dissecting hallowed institutions of the post−Industrial Age, earning themselves the collective sobriquet of "muckrakers" in a 1906 speech by Teddy Roosevelt. The president associated these journalists with the Socialist Party, referring to "wild agitators against the entire existing order."[15] The printed stories had great effect, provoking industry response. Publicists were hired (often from newspapers) to combat these unfavorable comments, and these men became the prototype advocates or press agents.

Historians are likely to date the real beginnings of public relations from the first decade of this century, when men like Hamilton Wright, George Parker, and Ivy Lee were engaged in work for various clients. Lee, in particular, expanded on the publicity concept, embracing additional means of creating favorable climates for his industrial accounts. He is responsible for convincing the American Tobacco Company to announce a profit-sharing plan, for educating citizens about the safety of flying, and, some say, for turning a cold financier, John D. Rockefeller, into a virtual saint by programming his charitable acts, from dimes for children to millions in philanthropy. Lee's reputation suffered in the early 1930s when he accepted as a client I.G. Farben, a German arms manufacturer who was close to Hitler. This lapse aside, Lee inaugurated many techniques that succeeding generations have imitated.

Other corporations, noting the advantages of Lee's approach, hired him or his emulators. Railroads, for example, began telephoning stories of disasters to editors instead of attempting to conceal them. A more open relationship developed.

People like Carl Byoir, whose firm continues to play a major role in American public relations, and Edward L. Bernays, sometimes dubbed "the Father of Public Relations," followed Lee. Bernays's career encompassed Broadway press agentry and advice to presidents. A member of George Creel's Committee of Public Information during World War I (a committee Bernays says is the first sign any government ever looked upon information as a potential weapon), Bernays used his wartime experience to found a firm he ultimately called "Counsel on Public Relations." His first client was the War Department, seeking help in finding ex-servicemen jobs. Bernays taught the first course in public relations, at New York University in 1923, and published the initial text on the subject, *Crystallizing Public Opinion.*

His accomplishments have been numerous and interesting, from pampering Enrico Caruso to cajoling Americans into bathing more frequently. He successfully promoted the notion of a big breakfast, thereby delighting a client who was having trouble selling bacon. He performed similar services for bananas and cigarettes, legitimizing the latter habit for women by convincing debutante friends to have their photos published smoking cigarettes

Figure 1-3 Edward L. Bernays, one of the profession's pioneers, with Bill Ramsey, APR, at a Public Relations Society of America Silver Anvil Award ceremony.
Courtesy: Edward L. Bernays

during the Easter Parade in major cities. Later, he worked on campaigns to discourage smoking. To present Calvin Coolidge as a less austere figure, Bernays persuaded the president to breakfast with entertainment luminaries.

Among his other written works is *Propaganda*, a volume Joseph Goebbels kept on his desk, and *The Engineering of Consent*, in which Bernays wrote:

> Evidences of the power of public opinion prove to every man the necessity of understanding the public, adjusting to it, of informing it, of winning it over. The ability to do so is the test of leadership.[16]

Besides Coolidge (and Theodore Roosevelt and Woodrow Wilson—and many of their predecessors), one president who was very conscious of public relations was Franklin Delano Roosevelt. His "New Deal" emerged complete with symbols, slogans, and promotional programs; his fireside chats were models of intimate mass communication; and his consolidation of authority during the Second World War was partially attributable to his unique penchant for mobilizing public opinion. This war also saw a rapid increase in the use of public relations by governmental and military bodies. Hitler's vast and effective propaganda thrusts were matched by the Allies. Concern for morale assumed new dimensions, and control of news escalated.

Succeeding presidents have had mixed PR success. Harry Truman, not always respected while in office, became the darling of the media and the populace after retirement. Dwight D. Eisenhower, partially buoyed by his military charisma, functioned adequately, if not spectacularly, with the public. With John F. Kennedy, Washington had its most able devotee of public relations from F.D.R. to Ronald Reagan, primarily because of his comfortable mastery of television, something Johnson, Nixon, and Ford were unable to duplicate. Critics of PR like to point out that, although Richard Nixon had the largest "public relations" staff in history, the results were dismal. Scholars insist that few of Nixon's aides had skill, training, or experience in that vocation. Jimmy Carter wasn't able to sustain the image that brought him to the White House, but Ronald Reagan, seemingly impervious to attacks, demonstrates near-flawless technique.

International public relations has accelerated as much as national public relations, both because of multiplying foreign markets and because of the complexity of global politics. During the past four decades, we've witnessed Russia devoting considerable time and money to, if you insist, propaganda. Soviet timing, aggressiveness, and commitment have sometimes embarrassed American attempts at response, and the current premier, Mikhail Gorbachev, has already demonstrated sophistication in influencing international attitudes. The Cold War warning by David Finn, president of Ruder Finn & Rotman, is as accurate today as it was 30 years ago:

> Our leaders must be increasingly alert to the reactions of the world press and keep in mind that they are being closely scrutinized by a vast international

audience. We can no longer afford to take a back seat in this critical psychological struggle. For the battle of the headlines may decide which system will emerge from the conflict with the greatest power, and thus set the pace and direction of the world of the future.[17]

Other nations, too, both established and emerging, grasp the fact that PR skills are not solely the province of business but are essential in presenting their case internationally.

WHAT ABOUT TODAY AND TOMORROW?

Although a relatively young vocation, public relations, with well over 125,000 practitioners in the United States, is becoming one of the more popular careers. In traditional journalism disciplines, increasing numbers of students are adopting the public relations sequence or degree program. Graduates of these institutions are adding a new dimension to a profession that has been, for many years, influenced primarily by media concerns and personnel.

More than 50 national public relations organizations exist worldwide, and membership in professional groups is on the rise. Company presidents indicate that they are spending more and more time on PR matters, and they have also given more authority to practitioners. In a 1981 survey of senior management by the research subsidiary of Hill and Knowlton, Inc., executives saw "great promise" for public relations but criticized practitioners for their lack of training and experience in business. Without this knowledge, they predict, PR people will have a difficult time ascending to the top company levels.

Industry continues to be a major source of public relations jobs, but areas like health, science, entertainment, education, and other service fields (law, architecture), along with telecommunications, are also strong. As in the past, more opportunities exist in the larger cities, but more competition also exists there. In general, because business is restructuring, because technology is revolutionizing our lives, communication will continue to be important, and public relations will only grow.

However, according to Chicago senior consultant and writer Philip Lesly, practitioners must be ready for the challenge:

> Changes caused by electronics will be especially difficult for most public relations people to adjust to. We tend to be essentially idea-oriented and uncomfortable with technical and mechanical things. You won't be able to practice public relations effectively in the last half of the '80's with just a local phone, a mimeograph machine and postage stamps, as the pioneers of this field did.[18]

Vice-president Philip Callanan of Hill and Knowlton puts it even more succinctly, saying that public relations professionals have evolved "from technicians who know how to get things into papers" to people concerned with "what it is we are trying to get into the papers."[19]

CHAPTER HIGHLIGHTS

- Although the nature and scope of public relations are difficult to pinpoint, practitioners insist that any definition should include its professional status, management function, public-interest component, and emphasis on research, planning, implementation, communication, and evaluation.
- Advertising is distinct from public relations because of their diverse goals and orientations, and publicity is merely one tool of public relations.
- Because of the complexity of today's world, public relations has an increasingly important task as translator and communicator, but it should not be relegated to a publicity status, or be denied access to management strategy sessions, or be expected to perform miracles. Use of public relations is widespread.
- Criticism of public relations is also widespread, fueled by confusion and misunderstanding, by stereotyping, by media antagonism, and by poor PR practice. Countering these charges takes professional and ethical conduct, accreditation, education, and occasional aggressive response.
- Although primarily a twentieth-century profession, the techniques of public relations predate history. In America, the practice has achieved its most complete form.
- Indications are that public relations will continue to grow, but some additional education or training in business and technology is necessary for today's practitioners.

NOTES

[1] ©1976 by Houghton Mifflin Company. Reprinted by permission from *The American Heritage Dictionary*, paperback edition.

[2] Jack Bernstein, "Merge Advertising and PR?—Yes and No," *Advertising Age*, May 13, 1985.

[3] Denny Griswold, "After Thirty Years," *Public Relations Quarterly*, Spring 1977.

[4] Walter W. Wurfel, "Beyond Publicity," *Public Relations Journal*, February 1985.

[5] *Omaha World Herald*, March 17, 1981.

[6] Alan Abelson, "Up and Down Wall Street," *Barron's*, January 7, 1985.

[7] Joann Lublin, "Labor Letter," *Wall Street Journal*, March 16, 1982.

[8] Charles Buffum, "View from the Business Side," *Travel Weekly*, June 3, 1982.

[9] James Brady, "Polishing the Old Image," *Advertising Age*, September 27, 1982.

[10] James Brady, "An Unpublished N.Y. Obituary," *Advertising Age*, October 9, 1978.

[11] John R. Bittner, *Mass Communication*, 2nd ed. (Englewood Cliffs, N.J.: Prentice-Hall, 1980).

[12]Arthur Ciervo, "The Poor Image of the Image Makers," *Public Relations Journal*, July 1975.

[13]*Omaha World Herald Entertainment Magazine*, November 28, 1982.

[14]Dan J. Forrestal, "Placing Public Relations in Perspective," *Public Relations Journal*, March 1974.

[15]From a speech by President Theodore Roosevelt, April 14, 1906.

[16]Edward L. Bernays, quoted in the *Washington Post*, May 23, 1984.

[17]David Finn, "Public Relations and the Cold War," pamphlet Number 21 (based on a *Saturday Review* article by Finn), issued by Ruder & Finn (now Ruder Finn & Rotman), circa 1960.

[18]Fred A. Woodress, "Public Relations Plans for '85," *Editor and Publisher*, January 19, 1985.

[19]*Publishers Auxiliary*, July 26, 1982.

SUGGESTED READINGS

ARONOFF, CRAIG E., and OTIS W. BASKIN, *Public Relations: The Profession and the Practice*. St. Paul, Minn.: West, 1983.

AWAD, JOSEPH F., *The Power of Public Relations*. New York: Praeger, 1985.

BERNAYS, EDWARD L., *Crystallizing Public Opinion*. New York: Liveright, 1961.

CANTOR, BILL, *Experts in Action: Inside Public Relations*. New York: Longman, 1984.

CUTLIP, SCOTT M., ALLEN H. CENTER, and GLEN M. BROOM, *Effective Public Relations*, 6th ed. Englewood Cliffs, N.J.: Prentice-Hall, 1985.

DUNN, S. WATSON, *Public Relations: A Contemporary Approach*. Homewood, Ill.: Irwin, 1986.

LARSON, KEITH A., *Public Relations: The Edward L. Bernayses and the American Scene: A Bibliography*. Westwood, Mass.: Faxon, 1978.

LESLY, PHILIP, ed., *Lesly's Public Relations Handbook*, 3rd ed. Englewood Cliffs, N.J.: Prentice-Hall, 1983.

LOVELL, RONALD P., *Inside Public Relations*. Boston: Allyn & Bacon 1982.

MARSTON, JOHN E., *Modern Public Relations*. New York: McGraw-Hill, 1979.

MOORE, H. FRAZIER, and BERTRAND R. CANFIELD, *Public Relations: Principles, Cases and Problems*, 7th ed. Homewood, Ill.: Irwin, 1977.

NEWSOM, DOUG, and ALAN SCOTT, *This Is PR: The Realities of Public Relations*, 3rd ed. Belmont, Calif.: Wadsworth, 1985.

NOLTE, LAWRENCE W., *Fundamentals of Public Relations*, 2nd ed. New York: Pergamon, 1979.

NORRIS, JAMES S., *Public Relations*. Englewood Cliffs, N.J.: Prentice-Hall, 1984.

ROGERS, HENRY C., *Walking the Tightrope*. New York: Morrow, 1980.

SEITL, FRASER P., *The Practice of Public Relations*, 2nd ed. Columbus, O.: Merrill, 1984.

THOMPSON, KENNETH W., ed., *Ten Presidents and the Press*. Lanham, Md.: University Press of America, 1983.

WILCOX, DENNIS L., PHILLIP H. AULT, and WARREN K. AGEE, *Public Relations: Strategies and Tactics*. New York: Harper & Row, 1985.

EXERCISES

1. Check your local paper for a story that seems to emanate from a public relations source.
2. Check for a story that constitutes bad public relations for a firm, organization, or individual.
3. Select a historical event from the last century and outline some of the public relations considerations that are involved.
4. From your own observations, what do you perceive as the negative aspects of public relations? How did you develop this perspective?
5. If you were designing a curriculum for public relations, list three courses, besides those in the public relations or journalism areas, that you feel should be part of the program. Defend your choices.

CASE PROBLEM

You are a five-year veteran in St. Luke's Hospital public relations department and find yourself at a medical conference luncheon in San Francisco. The speaker, a prominent surgeon, makes derogatory remarks about your profession.

"Public relations doesn't make money; it only spends money," he contends. "Those people are only interested in dressing things up, making them look good. They have no concern for reality. I don't trust PR people, and I see no need for them in a profession like medicine. We treat people who are ill, and that's sufficient public relations in itself."

Once the wide-ranging speech is over, there's a call for questions.

1. Do you take the floor and confront him with your views, or do you wait and write a letter? Or do you do nothing, chalking up the comments to ignorance? What are the pros and cons of each approach? Are there other alternatives?
2. If you do respond, how do you frame your reply? Outline your planned remarks or written response.

2

PUBLIC RELATIONS IS
A SOCIAL SCIENCE

For many years, Edward L. Bernays has been crusading for increased under-standing of public relations as a social science, a craft that is closer to psychology and sociology than it is to journalism. He refers to practitioners as "societal technicians" and argues for the removal of PR from the normal communications curriculum.

To a considerable degree, public relations has always been an applied social science. Practitioners have operated with a certain understanding of social response and, optimally, with a grasp of social responsibility. Perhaps this association has not been articulated well, but even a news release cannot be fashioned and distributed without some concept of the potential reading audience. Public relations professionals should be experts in divining hu-man behavior and, by extension, organizational behavior, and the source of this wisdom is in the social sciences. Bernays and others declare that be-cause public relations relies more on research, planning, and persuasion than it does on writing and graphics skills, it should be divorced from journalism.

Many practitioners disagree, asserting that hard skills are the key to entry-level employment and that they also support the veteran. Perhaps a marriage of both attitudes makes the most sense, the theory and the applica-tion. There will always be pressure to produce something—a brochure, a news release, a special event—but the results will be improved if based on knowledge of the social structure. Even the most pragmatic professional should be cognizant of behavioral theories and should be able to make them work in the marketplace.

Writes Alfred McClung Lee, " . . . the servile technocrat in either field [psychiatry or public relations] humors the patient's or client's maladjust-

Figure 2-1 As a social science, public relations requires that the professional understand and interact with others.

ments rather than helping to find a more workable and constructive social role."[1]

With the institutions practitioners serve, from business to government, under increasing scrutiny and subject to multiplying criticism, the awareness of social issues is paramount. Members of the profession understand this, and recent surveys indicate that social concerns rank high with business leaders, following economic and regulatory topics. Among practitioners, a *pr reporter* purview saw social interests jumping significantly and including everything from "intellectual freedom" and "the status of women" to "ethics" and "the impact of technology."[2]

Social awareness starts with the individual, moves to other individuals, and finally, in the mass application, takes in small and large groups.

KNOWING YOURSELF

In this guilt-conscious age, knowing yourself—understanding yourself—is often regarded as a formula for examining your own weaknesses. Not so. This admonition exhorts us to discover both weaknesses and strengths. In this context, you should know your own limitations as an understander and communicator before you attempt to counsel others.

This fact argues for the advantages of mastering psychology or, at least, mastering some of its basic principles. This discipline will teach you more about yourself and others, particularly factors concerning motivation and behavior.

Psychologists talk about our public life, private life, and "life at the center of our hearts." These terms describe the gradually deepening levels of behavior and belief.

Most of our encounters are superficial. Students and teachers meet each other this way. From this casual relationship, each party may draw conclusions that are totally inaccurate. Part of this stems from our own play acting, intentional or unintentional; we don't always let others see us as we really are. Perhaps we can't. Some marriages go sour because the spouse knows the act only too well and decides to ring down the curtain. Sales are lost, negotiations break down, and trusts are broken, all because of assumptions based on insufficient, incomplete knowledge.

Our private life relates to things we do when solitary. We may even surprise ourselves at this level, discovering that we're nervous about solitude. Instead of welcoming quiet internal reverie, we turn on television, stick a transistor plug in our ear, call a friend, pick up a magazine. Being alone with ourselves may produce discomfort, so we avoid it.

Yet what we do when we are alone is also revealing, and the astute communicator has some grasp of this phenomenon. He or she tries to ascertain what lies beneath the public life for a person or an institution.

The most private part of our person—the "life at the center of our hearts"—often astounds us. Daudet mentions his divided personality while attending the funeral of a younger brother. He observed his father weeping loudly and, while sympathizing with him in his grief, also thought how well that scene would look on the stage.

All of us arouse elements in our personality that shock us. We may find, under stress, that we are cowardly or cruel or exceptionally courageous. Deep prejudices may surface; hidden talents may emerge. It would be the rare PR person who could predict such manifestations, either in himself or herself or in others, but any communicator should be aware that they exist and that the reasons for certain actions stem from such sources.

PREDICTING BEHAVIOR

Obviously, no one can accurately forecast the way others will behave, but study and experience help in such diagnoses. For public relations professionals, it's vital that they be able to posit some solid guesses as to what a person or public might do under normal circumstances. Without such conclusions, PR could not function. A humorous anecdote written into the introductory portion of a speech is intended to produce laughs and warm up an audience; carefully selected photos in a fund appeal are meant to work on the viewer's emotions. Language and graphics are selected because of their presumed effect.

Educated conjectures can be made by applying known data to individual circumstances. To a considerable extent, all of us are products of our heredity and environment. Our genetic structure, our family background, our age, color, sex, class, occupation, living conditions—all contribute to the way we react to given stimuli.

Texts on human behavior point out common behavioral patterns, including many that are important to public relations, such as the way people select and respond to communications of all types. The practitioner should be conversant with these theories and should test them against experience. People of varying backgrounds form the audiences for the practice of public relations. The practitioner must know how to relate to such segments, as groups and as individuals.

In examining this challenge, the public relations person should remember that there are three concepts fundamental to the understanding of human behavior: motivation, perception, and learning.

Motivation, Perception, and Learning

Motivation relates to those causes that impel us toward a certain course of action. We speak of *primary motives*, which are essential to our well-being, even survival; and *secondary motives*, which are largely learned.

Primary motives encompass such ideas as self-preservation, pain avoidance, hunger, thirst, sex, and the maternal instinct. Normally these would take precedence over other motives. Although you might like to dash into the burning building and rescue the imperiled person and find your name in headlines, you are deterred by your instinct for survival or pain avoidance. People who are ravenous will quickly bypass the rules of etiquette. And the reason sex dominates so much of today's mass appeals is that it seems to work for a large percentage of its audience.

Again, these are norms. Just as it would be shortsighted to suggest that primary motives are only sporadically reliable, so, too, it would be shortsighted to deny that people do occasionally disobey what are regarded as primary dictates. People do risk their lives for others; some men and women lead celibate lives; mothers can and do reject their offspring.

In public relations (and in advertising), practitioners are equally concerned about *secondary* motives. After all, restaurant advertising is not directed at starving people, but at those whose dining routine is relatively normal. We see more promotional efforts aimed at comfort than at pain avoidance or self-preservation.

What are some of these secondary—or learned—motives?

The desire for success, for security, for peer approval. The need to acquire material things, or to obtain information. The concern for good health, for moral or religious conformity, for superior achievement.

These and other secondary motives may determine the way we dress, the vacation spots we prefer, the cultural activities we enjoy, the kind of jobs we seek. They may lure us into backpacking or karate or the Book-of-the-Month Club. They also affect our choice of companions, our political philosophy, and our attitude toward the work ethic.

Figure 2-2 Motivation to pursue a college education ranges from career choice and personal achievement to financial security and prestige.

People, and sometimes groups, are driven to accomplish things for reasons both common and private. Even though we can't always determine the latter, we can make inroads into discovering the former.

Keep in mind that no one is driven by a single motive, as in the old morality plays. We are usually impelled by several motives. On occasion our traditional motivations conflict, and we find ourselves "cross-pressured." This may result from differences between two peer groups, or differences between two personal attitudes. When this happens, we must make a choice, and would normally choose the course that seems the least difficult and offers optimum satisfaction.

A person, for example, may bristle at the notion of censorship and generally favor the principle of letting the public decide what it wishes to see or read. On the other hand, this same person may be appalled by child pornography. Should circumstances force this person into a situation in which he had to take a stand on outlawing child pornography, he would delay his decision as long as possible, then choose the course he could live with most easily.

A public relations counselor could be cross-pressured in deciding whether to accept an account that promises much-needed finances but also includes representing a cause with which the counselor is not in sympathy.

Perception, the second concept in understanding human behavior, deals with the way we see things. Individuals subjected to identical stimuli will often respond quite differently. Their mind set—a product of environment and heredity—colors their views of identifiable facts.

A large share of public relations problems are rooted in misperception. The plant manager installs a new machine that will make work easier, but the uninformed employees may consider it a threat to their livelihood. A name is inadvertently omitted from a mailing list, and the slighted party sees this as a deliberate plot.

When President Ronald Reagan took a personal role in settling the airline traffic controllers' strike, some Americans viewed this as the decisive actions of a strong leader, but others saw it as a punitive anti-union measure. And when a state government makes the wearing of seat belts mandatory, one segment of the citizenry applauds this as a safety advance and another perceives it as an infringement on individual liberty.

Because of different backgrounds and aims, some misconceptions are inevitable. Public relations programs can minimize these, however, through careful planning, anticipation, and the use of communications that are lucid and comprehensive.

As a corollary to this notion, we should remember that what people see as truth may be nearly as important as the truth itself. Just because they persist in error doesn't give the practitioner the privilege of shrugging them off. The public relations campaign must understand why such misconceptions exist and must counter them with effective and persuasive facts.

Learning, the third concept in understanding human behavior, can be defined as a somewhat permanent behavioral change brought about through experience. Reading, education, and counseling may substitute for actual involvement, but personal implication seems more commonplace. Through such contacts, you build up convictions, beliefs, and cautions. You no longer need to touch the burner or test the wet paint. You identify certain foods that upset your stomach. You learn how to relate to certain difficult individuals. Once you have forgotten to replace the ring on your carousel tray of slides and watch them fan out on the floor, you vow not to repeat this carelessness. A batch of overexposed photos will make you more cognizant of a film's ASA rating.

One needn't always learn by experience, even though that's a common mentor. The counsel of others and the tips offered by veteran authors may serve as guides. There is no reason to continually repeat the mistakes of others.

Perhaps no other profession demands as much experience as public relations. When you enter this field, you rely on the teaching of others. Then you construct your own experience, comprehending how to plan for a crowd, how to mesh conflicting newspaper deadlines, and how to minimize catastrophe.

Even an understanding of motivation, perception, and learning does not constitute a guarantee for success. Remember that psychology is a science, and it is the rare PR person who is totally skilled in its nuances.

WORKING WITH GROUPS

Even if it were possible to operate on a one-to-one basis in persuading individuals, it would be economically prohibitive, time-consuming, and, thus, ineffective. Public relations programs are directed at groups—as small as a few persons, as large as millions.

Everyone belongs to some group, either by choice (as with a church, club, union, or political party) or accidentally (according to age, sex, race, or some other denominator). We call the first group a *functional* group; the second a *statistical* group.

Each group member is influenced to a considerable degree by fellow members. Legionnaires, for example, would hold more homogeneous views on defense expenditures than would the population at large. You would expect more uniformity among Catholics on the subject of abortion than you would unearth in a random survey.

The more closely knit the group, the more the similarity of opinion. Some strict and isolated religious sects that restrict outside influence would exhibit a great kinship in attitudes. In such groups—and, really, in all

Figure 2-3 The professional PR person must be aware of small group dynamics.

groups—members are rewarded for conforming, punished for dissenting. Group norms become individual norms.

Even groups to which people do not belong but to which they wish to belong can exert a powerful influence. Teen-agers seeking admittance to some group, organized or not, will adjust their standards to qualify. Adult social climbers will develop habits that gain them acceptance in desired social circles. Newcomers in a rugged occupation will feign the sort of loud toughness that they believe impresses their peers.

Another point to remember is that individuals belong to many groups simultaneously. A male college student may also be a husband, father, veteran, Lutheran, Democrat, bowling-league member, army reservist, part-time shoe clerk, and motorcycle enthusiast. His name could appear on a dozen different mailing lists. Some part of him would respond to some aspect of each of these groups. Most groups to which a person belongs would be compatible in order that his or her life itself be somewhat harmonious. When a conflict arises, a person makes a decision, shunting aside one group and entering another.

Dealing with such diversity requires three personality traits in the individual practitioner: *reason, realism,* and *sensitivity.*

Reason

Few people admit to being unreasonable, but all of us are unreasonable at times. We curse at inanimate objects that displease us, shout at clerks, embrace an unlikely idealism in politics, stubbornly cling to views that are demonstrably incorrect.

Some major industries targeted by consumer advocates have initially denied any product problems and adamantly refused, as they saw it, to "cave in" to opposition. Instead of investigating the complaint, the company executives chose to turn on the critics and, in numerous cases, were embarrassed. A more reasonable approach would have saved them considerable grief.

Practitioners should be models of *reason,* but they are human, too. Some delay preliminary steps in the production of printed materials and then expect printers to work weekend miracles. Some overestimate the results they might anticipate from a mini-campaign. Some want fellow employees to demonstrate an energy level they can't match themselves. Some disregard the evidence that research has unearthed and persist in programs they know must fail.

Successful professionals resist such temptations. They write the speech the CEO can deliver, they plan comfortably ahead, and they consider the level of their target audiences. Their counsel and their actions are framed within the dictates of reason.

Realism

Akin to reason is the idea of *realism*. Again, the public relations practitioner must be the primary realist. The PR practitioner has to see things as they are, not necessarily as they should be, or as he or she would like them to be. Perhaps the practitioner disagrees, personally, with the "new morality." This should be a private concept then and should not blur his or her vision of the way things really are. The practitioner deals with facts and trends rather than ideals.

PR people are constantly wrestling with the shifting edges of realism, trying to find the touchstone that will make a campaign most meaningful. In battling against cigarette smoking, for example, the federal government and organizations such as the American Cancer Society have tried appeals to fear, to vanity, to social acceptability, to pride, to intellect. They've used everything from scare tactics to humor. They've promoted cigarette substitutes, espoused clinics and workshops, subsidized research, and conducted special events. All these programs seek to penetrate the reality of smoking, which involves gratification and habit. To pretend that these motives do not exist, and to consider cigarette smokers as weak or ignorant or even suicidal, would be counterproductive.

Public relations is grounded in realism. Research, experience, and common sense supplant wishful thinking. That doesn't mean that the practitioner has to surrender personal principles, or even that facts must force every decision. There are times when, in good conscience, a firm or individual must opt for an alternative that could produce troublesome consequences. The point is that these consequences should be anticipated and not erupt as unpleasant surprises.

Sensitivity

Perhaps the most important of the three qualities mentioned is *sensitivity*, a responsiveness to the feelings of others. The sensitive practitioner is alert to all the possible hurts, misunderstandings, and misinterpretations inherent in any proposed action. He or she can infer the reactions of audiences or individuals.

How will housewives perceive this banking campaign to educate them more thoroughly on financial matters? Will it be seen as a sincere effort to help, or as another demeaning putdown? When a state fair used as its symbol the comic portrayal of an American Indian, it should have anticipated the objections of Native American spokespeople. When a local television station decides to air a gubernatorial debate instead of carrying a football game, the program director should not be surprised at viewer complaints. When a farm-machinery company hosts a lavish dinner to celebrate its anniversary, executives can expect negative reactions from struggling farmers.

Sensitivity means putting yourself in the other person's place. It requires insight and a surrender of some of our own desires and prejudices.

When computer companies speak about "user-friendly" units, they are showing sensitivity to the fears of adults; when multinational industries observe alien customs and hire native executives, they are practicing sensitivity.

PR people can never let their guard down. Every action has some potential for problems to be dealt with. Speechwriters should consider whether certain words or ideas may offend a particular audience. Executives passing out honors have to be certain no one has been omitted. Before employee grievances handcuff production, the astute public relations professional has sensed this possibility, informed management, and offered suggestions for improvement. There are thousands of similar concerns in this vocation.

WHO ARE THE PUBLICS?

Every situation involves its own public. Sometimes that public may be an individual, as when dealing with a specific client, a specific legislator, a specific major gift project. In such circumstances, knowledge of psychology is invaluable, helping the practitioner to categorize the individual. Is he or she driven by emotion or intellect, by an interest in wealth or power or social equity? Is this person's style authoritative or conciliatory? When the client insists he wants to keep a low profile, does he really mean it? The more the professional understands about these essential contacts, the better.

Ordinarily, however, practitioners are working with larger groups, and with many groups at the same time. Some may be as diffuse as "the general public"; others may be defined more narrowly as "residents of the Walnut Hill Apartments." When possible, different approaches should be used to win over different groups, even though the ultimate goal remains the same. Mobil sponsors programs on public television to influence a large but mostly anonymous intelligentsia, distributes press kits to inform the media of its positions, and distributes annual reports to its shareholders. The methods and the wording may vary, but the missions are all interrelated.

In a *Public Relations Journal* article, a New York City counselor warns that PR people should not expend all their energies courting the mass media but should be more conscious of proximate publics, like employees and shareholders.

> Treat the proximate public properly—through your policies, actions and communications—and it will regard you highly; it will have a predisposition (only a predisposition, mind you, not a commitment) to discount some of the negatives the media may report about you, and you will have a core of public support.

But treat the proximate public wrong and it will be quite ready to believe almost anyone's accusation. Because, as public relations professionals have long known, people's direct experiences far outweigh what we keep trying to tell them.[3]

Influencing Leaders

The most effective way to reach such groups is through their leadership. If you can influence the opinion leaders, you will have a good chance of influencing a significant segment of the membership. It may take a little time to determine who the opinion leaders really are. Does the school board run the public-school system in your community, or is it dominated by a strong superintendent? Are the elected officers of a club or organization really the policymakers, or does a veteran cadre actually make the decisions? Advertising executives pitch their messages to audience segments that make decisions. Household-product ads are beamed at women; beer ads are directed more to men; cereal commercials have children as their targets.

LET THE PUBLIC KNOW

The Allied Pipe Company manufactured steel pipes for sewer and industrial use. In order to forge the steel used in these pipes, it melted car bodies in a giant furnace. When the furnace was operating, smoke containing a high amount of particulate matter billowed out over the neighborhood.

To complicate things further, this neighborhood was unusual. Most city planners locate heavy industry, like Allied, next to a belt of light industry, then commercial, and then residential properties. Here, Allied was right up against residential property, modest dwellings with few modern conveniences. Came the smoke, and the wash was ruined.

Area residents complained to the company and to city officials. For a time it appeared the plant might be shut down. State pollution-control authorities began an investigation. Newspaper photographers and television news crews seemed to delight in showing the clouds of smoke, particularly when silhouetted against the morning sun, making the pollution look doubly bad. Observers also failed to discriminate between Allied's controlled burning and the open burning that took place at a neighboring car-body plant. The smoke from this plant drifted over Allied and added to the complaints.

Allied hired public relations counsel, since it did not have its own department. What the PR person discovered was that Allied had been trying very hard to correct the problem and had spent half a million dollars on new equipment—which didn't function effectively in this changeable climate. Allied had told no one of its efforts. The PR counselor advised Allied to bring the neighbors in on the problem. After all, Allied was the largest employer in that community, had been a generous supporter of civic endeavors, and had once enjoyed a very favorable public image. Its loss to the city would be serious.

Three of the company's top executives went door to door in the neighborhood, introducing themselves, apologizing for the inconvenience, and inviting people to come see the problem for themselves. It wasn't easy. The officials took a lot of abuse, but the neighbors did attend an open house, along with city officials, the media, and other guests. It was a no-frills event—just coffee, tours, and discussion. The company officers detailed the problem, outlined the efforts they had made and the expense involved, and then revealed their plans for new and better equipment. There were some mutterings, but by and large, the group went away temporarily satisfied. This was the first time they had understood what was going on. All they had seen was the sooty end-result.

During the changeover period, Allied personnel were instructed to reply courteously and honestly to any complaints or inquiries. Progress reports were sent via direct mail to neighbors. The media were invited to cover installation and testing. And when the new equipment was in place, another open house was arranged.

This was a much happier affair. The "dry scrubber" did such a good job of eliminating particulate matter that Allied not only was far below the tough minimum standards set by the state's pollution-control agency but also won that agency's award as the firm doing most to correct environmental deficiencies.

Just to show that all is not roses in the PR field, the equipment that did such a beautiful job of clearing the air also emitted a high-frequency hum that drove the neighbors to distraction. A change in the smokestack arrangement finally solved this difficulty, and Allied, at last, could enjoy an industrial happy ending.

A different case, but with a similar PR approach, involved Random Oaks, a real estate development that would feature expensive residences, luxury apartments, a fashion center, tasteful commercial properties, winding boulevards, seasonal greenery, and a huge manmade lake. To bring about this miracle on the 600-acre tract, the developers had to move tons of dirt to produce the lake bed, the hills, and the parkland. Such activity would certainly result in dirt's blowing into the surrounding neighborhood, occupied by wealthy and powerful citizens. They might easily delay construction.

Solution? Random Oaks's public relations department issued a periodic newsletter to all area residents, informing them of the project, explaining that the earthmoving would be done all at once to minimize inconvenience, begging their forbearance, and holding out the promise of a posh, desirable neighbor. When part of the project was complete, the neighbors were told that 30 percent of the work had been done and that it was anticipated that the remaining 70 percent would be accomplished by such-and-such a date. Each time, the neighbors were thanked for their patience and understanding and reminded about what the beauty of this addition would add to the area.

Result? Not a single letter or phone call of complaint. Almost unbelievable. But the neighbors had been taken into partnership, had been kept informed. A simple, commonsense solution.

Think a bit about the town or city in which you live. Does the mayor or the city council actually run things? Or is there a coalition of powerful civic leaders, business and professional men and women, who influence decisions? This power may be associated with wealth, with position, or with popularity. If you can discover who these opinion leaders are and make your point with them, influencing the city at large becomes much more simple. The power structure can be a good or a bad thing, depending upon the individuals involved. But good or bad, it exists, and the wise PR person is alert to its presence.

It is possible, of course, to create a semipermanent group for a particular cause, and this group could become quite influential despite its lack of traditional strength. Small groups of individuals have blocked urban renewal, the construction of nuclear plants, the razing of historic buildings, the acquisition of park lands, and the passage of unfavorable legislation.

These groups, too, must be targets of communication, and the place to start is with their leadership. Bypassing such leadership is almost certain to result in failure.

FORMING PUBLIC OPINION

The term *public opinion* refers to the expression of an attitude on some controversial matter by some group or groups sharing a common interest, or it could be used to designate a broader population whose predispositions can be measured or inferred. In this era of rapid communication and shifting allegiances, public opinion has become a dominant factor. The late Harry S. Truman said no man could function any longer as president without the support of public opinion. We've seen public opinion cut short a war in

Vietnam, topple an American president, help oust the Shah of Iran, provoke tax reform, elect more conservative leadership, and support a growing fitness craze.

Public opinion is a bit like the wind; we observe its effects even when we can't pinpoint its source. It is also unstable, changing periodically to reflect new information, new thinking, or the result of fresh events.

"Beginning thirty years ago, the center of power in the world shifted from governments to public opinion," contended Sean MacBride, chairman of the International Commission for the Study of Communication Problems. "The process is slow, but it's continuing. Even the Russians take public-opinion polls now, on things that don't matter a lot."[4]

To substantiate his point about the Soviets, MacBride cites the case of Andrei Sakharov, whose imprisonment was widely publicized despite official moves to conceal details. MacBride claims that, two decades earlier, news of Sakharov would not have surfaced.

One can observe public opinion hardening on terrorist acts, can detect a lessening of optimism about the economic future, and can sense a growing determination to do something about drunk driving. These and other movements are fueled by public opinion.

Public opinion may shift rapidly, when shocked by some overt event, for example. Usually, however, it reverses itself very slowly—attitudes (which are really unexpressed opinions) die hard. We hate to admit that we are wrong. Besides, it is often uncomfortable to change. This means learning a whole new system, accumulating a fresh set of allies. And, too, since we tend to pay more attention to what we already believe, it is difficult to even collect data that will alter our views.

Public opinion is, after all, primarily a collection of individual opinions that, collectively, possess some weight. It is volatile, not fixed. The publics change, depending upon their interest in the matter. And attitudes move back and forth, as witness the varied assessments of presidential performance. This ephemeral nature should not blind us to its overriding influence.

Sometimes public opinion is lumped together with attitude and belief, and social scientists talk about OABs—one's opinions, attitudes, and beliefs. Attitudes are, however, really states of mind, sometimes only temporarily held, whereas beliefs are generally considered to be deeper, more permanent convictions. Neither becomes opinion until it is expressed.

INFLUENCING PUBLIC OPINION

Public relations programs seek to influence opinion in one of three ways:

1. Altering or counteracting unfavorable opinion
2. Convincing uninformed or uncommitted opinion
3. Reinforcing or conserving favorable opinion

Of these three, changing hostile opinion, or neutralizing it, is the most difficult. The most effective weapon may be the truth, but is has to be suggested rather than dictated. Remember that opinion is formed by a person's perception of some event or statement. Therefore, confrontation with objective facts *could* begin to reverse an attitude.

The trouble with this, as Jonathan Swift realized, is that you can't "reason a man out of something he wasn't reasoned into." Since emotion plays a large role in our opinion formation, logic alone may be a feeble assailant.

Perhaps change can be accomplished with relative ease in a one-to-one situation, but public relations people normally deal with the masses. That is why they may mix appeals, hoping to reach some people emotionally and some people intellectually. The messages will blend imagery with reason.

As we have seen, the problem is that not everyone is reasonable. When brought to this point, some may doubt the obvious evidence or refuse to accept it. Most people, however, will either alter their opinions or cease supporting the former opinion publicly.

Gathering latent opinion to your side is easier. It may take time, but you are working in an area in which you have fewer prejudices to overcome. Personal contacts work here, too, as do massive publicity campaigns. Consider how people have been sold on seat belts, and wall-to-wall carpeting, and smaller families, and more attention to the environment.

On a one-to-one basis, you have observed yourself how a positive suggestion, attractively presented, can move a group to your side. It may be a descriptive invitation to attend a film or a proposal to visit a certain restaurant. If the group members have no other conflicting plans, your positive lead is likely to sway them.

Because no one likes to be taken for granted, you also have to *conserve that public opinion* that is already in your camp. You can't forget old friends. The politicians who fail to visit certain wards because they consider them safe are courting defeat. If you neglect a once-loyal alumni cadre, they will move away from you.

No modern company sets out on any major program without conducting some form of opinion research (see Chapter 3). Managers and marketing specialists want to be aware of possible public reaction or more certain of public support before they present their new products or activities. Auto manufacturers, for example, know they can introduce safety features into today's vehicles, even when these add to the cost, because the public expects and approves such innovations. On the other hand, the public may be slower to okay additional antipollution devices and the resultant cost. Public opinion is also influencing legal procedures and decisions. Many Americans feel crime is out of control and favor stronger measures to curb its excesses. This attitude finds its way into local courtrooms, legislative corridors, and the halls of the Supreme Court.

Public opinion has curtailed government expenditures, aided the return of recreation vehicles, determined our television offerings, boosted the stock of health spas, contributed to the demise of large families, and supplanted crockpots with microwaves.

PERSUASION

Persuasion, like public relations, has an "image problem." Some critics react to persuasion as if it were something unnatural or contrived. Actually, not only is persuasion natural, it is virtually instinctive.

If you want people to do something for you or to pursue some specific course, you can *pay* them, *bribe* them, and even *force* them. You can also *persuade them*— and this is the most civilized and permanent method. Force may get a job done, but it doesn't convince, and it probably alienates. Money purchases services—as long as it holds out—or until the recipient gets a better offer. Persuasion, on the other hand, causes a person to do something because he or she wants to do it. Therefore it is the most effective means.

We sell ideas, concepts, products, and ourselves. The person who forgets that life is always partially a selling job will have difficulty succeeding in any profession.

Because persuasion is a powerful weapon, and because it can be misused, the public feels edgy about its effects. People wonder whether the media have too much persuasive power, or they support legislation restricting advertising on children's television, or they suspect many sales presentations.

Methods of persuasion vary according to the situation and the skills of the persuader. All of them, however, take into consideration the fact that people are both rational and emotional. Some appeals emphasize one extreme or other, but few would bet everything on either a purely intellectual or a purely sentimental response.

If your goal is to raise funds, for example, you will come to the prospective donors armed with statistics, budgets, and packages that they can afford. You will go over these factual items carefully, convincing them that the campaign is serious, well conceived, and necessary. Then, however, you will probably add the emotional appeal—their civic pride, the change to have something named after them, gratitude to their alma mater, and even guilt if they fail to contribute.

Persuasion works best when target audiences are already in a frame of mind to be persuaded. Advertising, for example, follows and reinforces consumer attitudes rather than creating them. If gives affirmation to our value system. And the best prospects for advertising are those who are already in a buying mood.

In the political arena, we see similar theories at work. Paul Duke, senior correspondent for PBS, speaking about the "positioning" of Reagan as a

Figure 2-4 The late Robert Kennedy, shown campaigning at Creighton University in 1968, possessed great personal charm and unusual persuasive powers. Photo courtesy of Bill Ramsey

Washington insider, said, "Good PR is more than just luck. It means sensing the public's mood and trying to capitalize on it."[5]

And for those who worry about such influence, Eugene Eidenberg of the National Democratic Committee commented, "I'm not troubled by the persuasion/pressure continuum. I think it's healthy for a democratic society."[6]

Persuasion is also enhanced by involvement. Those who feel they've had a role in decision making are more apt to accept the conclusions. That's one reason public utilities convene sounding-board committees, and why wise chairmen let suggestions emanate from the audience. Veteran public relations professionals know that ideas are adopted more readily if they seem to come from top executives, even when the germ is planted by someone else. One of the axioms of public relations is, "It's amazing how much can be accomplished if no one worries about who gets the credit."

Obviously, there are hundreds of special persuasion techniques. Workshops on the topic are numerous: "The Six-Step Persuasion Formula," "The Ten Most Persuasive Words," "How to Close a Sale." And social scientists are periodically coming up with fresh suggestions about the process of influence. Like requesting that a person perform a very difficult and time-consuming task in order to get him or her to agree to a less onerous assignment. Or like eliminating all but one objection, the way a good insurance salesman will do, and concentrating on the single negative to be overcome. Everyone in sales has a store of these, all designed to persuade.

There are few overnight conversions. The process of persuasion may take a long time, or it may have a temporary effect and then decline. A utility company may be able to convince water or electricity users to conserve during an emergency, but it's a more difficult chore to prolong these habits. Campaigns to promote better health through the use of less sugar, cholesterol, and salt are committed to a long siege. Movements like these, involving matters of social benefit to people, even have their own title: "social marketing." Now that we have been conditioned about diet and energy, and now that Jacques Cousteau has made us conscious of the ocean, "For Spacious Skies," a nonprofit organization, has launched a public relations program to educate us about the environmental importance of the sky.

There are no guarantees that such efforts will succeed. Many health-related campaigns have achieved only mild results: The attempts to maximize the use of seat belts, which ranged from lectures to emotional appeals, have still not achieved their goals; legislation had to replace persuasion. When this sort of forced compliance is instituted, the danger of reaction is high.

> For instance, the strong push for desegregation of the schools against the wishes of many parents led to the formation of thousands of private Christian schools. Forming them brought together many people whose consciousness of fundamentalism was heightened. That was a strong factor in creating the strong right-wing religious movement, which was a major factor in defeating Democrats who had pushed forward desegregation.[7]

Even persuasion may be viewed as a mixed blessing by some industries. The fitness craze, fervently advocated by medical, governmental, and media messages, has been a boon to diet soft drinks and chicken, but a problem for beer and pork.

> The trend isn't monolithic, or in some cases even rational. Fitness is certainly in fashion, but so once were Beatle wigs and contempt for material possessions. No two industries face the same challenges and opportunities. Concern about cholesterol and obesity, for example, have apparently induced consumers to eat fewer eggs and to swill diet soda by the vatful. Yet the candy business is booming, and sales of cheese, a product notably high in fat and cholesterol, are going through the roof. After all, eating Brie with the rind sliced off is among the most essential tokens of yuppiedom.[8]

So what do the injured industries do? They spend more on advertising, on packaging, and on new-product development. They devote their persuasive energies to recapturing their markets or creating new ones. They see that some high-calorie items, like Chicken McNuggets and its counterparts, when properly promoted, still manage to overcome resistance.

ROADBLOCKS

There is no knee-jerk certainty to the art of persuasion, the analysis of behavior and motivation, or the production of opinion change. Failures may be attributable to ineptness or false assumptions, but a large share of the defeats arise out of our complicated human nature. We know, for example, that we and others don't always act as we believe or profess to believe. Sometimes the situation induces us to act or speak contrary to our innermost convictions.

On social occasions, we may suppress our true feelings about other guests in order to avoid a scene, or we may accede to a point of view we don't share merely to prevent argument. Students who decry cheating may lapse during a tough exam. Business leaders who espouse honesty may conspire to fix prices. Adherents who are sympathetic to a cause may wilt under domestic or office pressures.

This conflict between belief and action was dubbed "cognitive dissonance" by Leon Festinger some three decades ago, and later authorities speak about "behavior modification" and other terms related to the apparent disagreement. What public relations seeks to do is not merely modify behavior but change attitudes and beliefs. People may resist this by refusing to come to terms with themselves or by responding to persuasion in an abnormal way, one that doesn't fit neatly into persuasive theory.

Defense Mechanisms

Men and women may engage in various defense mechanisms that psychologists have identified as ways of protecting themselves from frustration, or from anxiety, or from a self-perception that is in conflict with reality.

Some people may *repress* ideas that cause them pain or shame. They just won't think about them. A person may refuse to even think of death and may shield himself or herself from all reminders of it. A person may subdue sexual desires. Someone given to aggressive urges may sanely blot them out.

Others may *sublimate* these urges and desires by directing their thoughts elsewhere. They concentrate on another subject. Perhaps golf will take their minds off a failing business or a domestic quarrel. A new hobby may displace their destructive traits.

Compensation is another means of combatting reality. Rather than endure the ego-shattering effects of failure in one area, people adopt an activity that presages success. A student who can't make the football squad may excel in debate. A hopeless conversationalist may become an impressive photographer. Everyone needs some successes in life. People can't exist in an atmosphere of constant defeat and criticism. They must find something they do well and draw their satisfaction from it.

Finally, people may sometimes *rationalize* their behavior by assigning less painful motives for their behavior than really exist. A girl who has failed to make the cheerleading squad may announce that she really didn't want to be part of that silly group anyway. A hunter tells his wife he is after "meat on the table," whereas he really enjoys the thrill of the hunt. A person may buy a car because it was the cheapest thing on the lot but may then brag to friends about its economy and design.

Practitioners must understand these aberrations, at least at the functional level. The more they analyze and appreciate the variety of human behavioral patterns, the better job they will do.

STAYING ABREAST OF TRENDS

Public relations never operates in a vacuum. There are no neat textbook solutions to actual PR problems, because circumstances inevitably alter the practitioner's attempt to apply theory and experience. Professionals must not only understand human and group psychology but must also stay current on the constantly fluctuating environment around them. What worked yesterday may not work tomorrow. Since public relations, by definition, senses trends and adapts to them, the ability to take the public's pulse is a must for practitioners. They have to know where America and the rest of the world are going.

The list of trends is endless and will suffer alteration as soon as it is committed to print. Not too many years ago, futurists were predicting an irreversible migration to the big cities, a lifetime of inflation, and an untouchable status for the media. Today the focus is on movement to smaller towns near large cities, on unemployment and deficits rather than inflation, and the media continue to face increasing scrutiny.

How does the practitioner stay abreast of such changes? By reading books and articles that deal with the topic, by listening to speeches and attending workshops given by futurists, by analyzing what he or she observes and bringing a sense of logic to these findings.

"Get this image," said Larry Kaagan, vice-president and assistant to the chairman of Yankelovich, Skelly and White, Inc., speaking to a PRSA (Public Relations Society of America) luncheon. "You're looking at a Norman Rockwell *Saturday Evening Post* cover in 1938. It depicts a young man, the breadwinner; a young woman, the homemaker; and two or three children. In 1938, that illustration was true for 70 percent of America; today [1983] this image represents only 15 percent of the population."[9]

Kaagan also predicted the continued effect of women in the work force ("63 percent of mothers are now employed outside the home"), a continuing mobility among chief executives ("one in three managers has a résumé circulating"), the addition of more employees to corporate boards, the demise of "blue collar" as a term for skilled and semiskilled workers, more willingness for unions to trade job security for other goals, and the inevitable frustrations

CORPORATE CULTURE MUST MEET CURRENT NEEDS

"Corporate culture" is a term used to define a set of values espoused by company employees that govern their work attitudes, opinions, and behavior. These are instilled by management. If they are in tune with strategic planning by the administration, all goes smoothly; if not, this divergence forms a major roadblock. And when some change occurs that forces a revision of corporate strategy, corporate culture must also shift direction.

A case in point can be observed in the many smaller regional companies formed when AT&T was broken up. The parent company took two-thirds of the profit-making areas with them, notably long distance. As a result, the regional offices had to consider ways to replace that shortfall.

Traditionally, regional divisions under AT&T concentrated on cost control. As a regulated industry, they were told what they could charge for things, so the only way they could make more money was to reduce operating costs. Rewards and promotions came to those who were best at doing this, and the vast majority of employees were involved in some cost-cutting aspects. With divestiture, the emphasis changed, and these same employees had to think in terms of profits.

For example, information-type calls used to cost the regional offices money. People wanted phone numbers, addresses, the time and weather, even traveling directions, movie times, and recipes. Some of the divisions tried to check these losses by calling this service "Directory Assistance," to reduce other types of calls. It didn't work. They launched an ad campaign telling you how dumb you were if you called for help when you could have looked up the number yourself. Calls continued. They instituted a nominal charge—25 cents, for instance. No letup in the calls. Then came divestiture, and managers began thinking that, if they upped the charge to 35 cents a call and built up the volume, they might actually start making money. So they changed the name from "Directory Assistance" to "Information Services."

The president of Northwestern Bell did his part for corporate culture by setting down a series of points he felt the new company (now U S West) believed in. These included the worth of its service, its value to its customers, the importance of people in the organization, and other topics.

For three years prior to actual divestiture, Northwestern Bell had used internal publications, direct mail, and videotaped messages to prepare its employees for the change. It found these methods far less effective than face-to-face explanations conducted by a speakers' bureau. These speeches, although they center on the innovations, are worded so that they don't tell the audience members they must change. The company wants them to realize this themselves, without any notion of a threat. The goal is to make employees see how change will benefit each of them.

as a consequence of a better-educated population's failing to achieve expectations.[10]

In an article published two years earlier, Daniel Yankelovich, a principal in Kaagan's firm, wrote that "in place of the traditional ethic of self-denial and sacrifice, we now find an ethic that denies people nothing." He pointed out that self-fulfillment, a driving force in the eighties, goes beyond job and family and takes today's young person into creative styles of living. He warned that our culture and economy are on opposite courses, the former calling for freedom and the latter calling for restraint. Yankelovich finds that those who work hardest at self-fulfillment are younger, better educated professionals with liberal political leanings. For the future, however, Yankelovich looks for less self-absorption and more commitment:

> The process of developing new social signals, transmitting them, and assimilating them will take at least several decades, so that the new giving/getting compact is unlikely to reveal all of its ramifications much before the end of the century.[11]

Another prognosticator who is always stimulating is Richard Scammon, consultant and opinion researcher, who foresees a population of nearly 230 million by the end of this decade, later marriages, fewer children, more divorces, more housing units (largely because the elderly will have more options as to where they will live), and a growing fence-straddling by Americans on controversial issues. He also informs us that our Hispanic population may outnumber our black population by the turn of the century.[12]

> Hispanics come from thirty Latin American countries, plus Spain and Portugal. Ethnically and historically, Mexicans, Puerto Ricans and Cubans (the three largest Hispanic groups in the U.S.) differ from one another as much as the Irish, the English and the Scotch do. . . . Hispanics are actually white, black or Indian, or a mix of two or all three. . . . Although there is a Catholic majority, church attendance is far below that of non-Hispanic Catholics. And significant numbers are Protestants, born-agains, Jews, Baptists, and Mormons. Some, of course, don't believe. . . . Twenty-five cities in the nation now have Hispanic communities of 50,000 or more.[13]

Demographers, politicians, marketing directors—and public relations practitioners—will keep track of these changes in minority structures, since they inevitably have an impact on society.

Fads and Fashions

You can nearly follow the course of American life, especially its business life, by collecting its buzz words. Forty years ago, the key phrase was "production and distribution," whereas today's magic term is "human resources." We have "high tech" and "social marketing" and the *Megatrends*-promoted "networking." We coin words to describe our population segments, our planning tools, our persuasive methods, even our entertainment choices. Video games were supplanted by Trivial Pursuit, a board game, a trend some experts saw as a "desire for more family interaction," and light beer lost some of its market to wine coolers. Jogging has peaked, and NutraSweet and its imitators are on a roll. Crockpots have diminished, and microwave ovens will also pass, along with the building boom in tennis clubs and health spas.

> Fads, no matter where they occur, create a certain kind of status. Those who buy a Pet Rock, Cabbage Patch doll or Trivial Pursuit game often have a sense of being part of an in-group. Fads also appeal to people's desire to be part of something that is new, creative, avant garde. It seems that part of the American mentality is the idea that if there isn't constant change, something must be wrong.[14]

Some commentator is always worried about Americans, or is categorizing their life-styles. Most observers note a movement from desire ("I'd like to retire early") to entitlement ("I've worked hard and deserve to retire early"). These experts also posit a growth in "inner-directed" people, who are less likely to conform and more likely to accept social responsibility.[15] Various recent articles in *U.S. News & World Report* characterize honor as on the decline in America (owing to the erosion of family and community ties),[16] rudeness on the increase (because of intrusions into personal space),[17] and the United States in need of "moral and social recovery" to correct the "excessive individualism" of the recent past.[18]

The same publication highlighted the American pursuit of happiness in a 1985 edition, calling attention to increased tolerance for change, and to the various ways citizens seek fulfillment. Some challenge success, some opt for the bright lights of the cities, some return to nature, some battle the corporate system, some prize a quieter domestic existence, some adopt a cause, some turn to God.[19] Most of these drives, of course, are methods of achieving personal satisfaction instead of pursuing some broader social goal.

Men, Women, and Children

According to psychologists, the fears of children have changed in the last quarter century, from concerns about family and failing in school to worries about divorce, popularity, and nuclear war. Adolescents are a bit disillusioned about their futures, feeling that they may not share in the affluence now apparent. They are also more conservative, more patriotic, more religious than their parents.

We've coined names for their older brothers and sisters, those young urban professionals (or "yuppies") who are upwardly mobile and motivated by wealth and fitness, by a disdain for junk food, plastic, and traditional vacation sites.

> Yuppie meals are served on plain white plates, set down on straw place mats. The dining table, preferably butcher block, glass or marble, must never match

the dining chairs. Yuppies angle for Queen Anne service as a wedding gift, then use their half of the service for everyday flatware after the divorce. As wedding presents, Yuppies give ski wax, an ounce of saffron or a specially written home-computer program, the Yuppie equivalent of the handmade quilt.[20]

Redbook later introduced its own acronym and handbook with a guide for "yummies," or "young upwardly mobile mommies," a market segment *Redbook* woos as readers.

Another stereotype spotted by several women's magazines is the "wimp," a casualty of the modern aggressive female, a man who is stripped of his masculinity and tries too hard to please. Curt Suplee, in the *Washington Post*, asks:

> Is he the type your mother thinks is wonderful? Does he entrap you into inviting him to dinner, choosing the restaurant and then splitting the check? Bring you back to his apartment, put on Pachelbel's Canon or some Randy Newman ditty, get an oozy seepage around the eyes and then insist that you *really listen* to it? Invariably order poached salmon? Say things like, "I'm so glad you don't smoke" or "I can really *identify* with women now"?[21]

Singles have also received a lot of advertising attention in the 1980s, with hundreds of products aimed specifically at this subculture. An organization called "Everything for Singles" even packaged a special show for those engaged in the solitary life, featuring more than 200 exhibitors hawking everything from weekend ski trips, dating services, and discount tickets to water beds, tanning machines, and seductive perfumes.

> The singles market in the U.S. consists of 60 million adults over 18 (56% female, 44% male), most of whom are under 40, relatively affluent, and willing to turn over a large part of their disposable income to the hunt.[22]

People living alone, as well as the trend toward smaller families, brought down the size of the average American household to about 2.75, a decrease from 3.11 in 1970 and 4.1 in 1930, according to U.S. Census Bureau statistics. The overall median age of Americans has risen two years since the 1970 census, and now stands at 30.

Men have changed in the last decade, sharing more of the domestic and parenting chores, even to raising children as single parents. They are adjusting, although not always easily, to female success in the marketplace and learning to be more expressive, less aggressive. There are, of course, reactions against these changes, but observers see these "macho" rebuttals as fruitless against a more enduring and compassionate life-style.

Women have experienced an even greater transformation. The gender gap has closed in education, with as many women as men enrolled in college. Older women, only 10 percent of whom had completed college, are now returning to the classroom. Two-thirds of the college students over 35 today are women.

But even though women are are more visible in politics, industry, and the professions, most admit that much remains to be accomplished. Discrimination against women in elected positions and in professional fields remains. In business, too:

> Despite impressive progress at the entry level and in middle management, women are having trouble breaking into senior management.[23]

Even in communications, where feminist issues are often championed, the record is spotty. The advertising and public relations fields have generally been good areas for women, and administrative and ownership roles there are increasingly female. Broadcast has made strides, but there are still plenty of "pretty-face-versus-ability" complaints, and in newspapers, where women occupy about 10 percent of the director-editor jobs, the struggle isn't over. Dorothy Jurney, a retired journalist, writes:

> In 1977, when I first started compiling these figures, women held 5 percent of the directing editorships. Should women be satisfied today because they hold 10.6 percent overall and share a fifth of the pipeline jobs for papers over 25,000? Hardly.[24]

The female presence in industry has produced a number of changes, from daycare centers in plants to variable scheduling, and even to maternity/paternity leaves. Along with the sharing of domestic duties between spouses, studies show that more teenagers also have household roles and, consequently, have become a minor target market for advertisers.

There will eventually be a different look to business.

> Maybe because women aren't traditionally a part of the management establishment, they don't have the old-boy ethos. Therefore, I think they can be more diverse in their management styles. And I personally feel that in about 80 percent of the things that take place in a professional undertaking, any individual brings his or her own personality into the situation.[25]

As with any movement, there is a backlash of sorts. Author/journalist Susan Brownmiller, in a controversial book titled *Femininity*, catalogued evidences of a substantial return to what has been described as traditional female behavior, partly because of competition for jobs, and partly because of a shortage of men:

> This is something we never envisioned in the feminist movement. We thought we could collect our grievances and present them to men. Fifteen years later the men aren't there, and there is no one to listen to the complaints.[26]

Besides advocating caution in accepting as gospel information that may be outdated, our continuing data on female attitudes and achievements also warn the communicator that, in writing or speaking about women, he or she must be both sensitive and sensible. Advertisers are more careful in their copy, concepts, and illustrations. Although these attempts have not been wholly satisfactory from the female viewpoint, advertisers have made progress in showing women in nonhousehold, nonsubservient situations.

Most thinking people no longer consider rape a subject for humor, and spouse abuse is also something you don't joke about. A newly installed college president learned that latter fact when he mused that the advice his wife gives him is sometimes so painful he would like to "take her to the woodshed and take a 2-by-4 to her." Women's groups castigated the embarrassed administrator, calling his remarks "offensive" and "appalling." A humorous travel ad for Scandanavia made light of the Nordic pseudo-myth that a contrary wife should be chastised with a tree branch. Criticism was immediate, and the ad was withdrawn.

Language has also been a major consideration, with everything from the Bible to the daily newspaper being neutered. Some of these changes, like the use of Ms., have become standard, but others may vary with local media. The new PR person should determine what the governing stylebook in that vicinity dictates. Should there be separate "Men Wanted" and "Women Wanted" classified ads? In subsequent references, after the initial complete identification, should a woman be given a title or just referred to by her last name? Should terms like "chairman" be changed to "chairperson"? Should editors avoid descriptions of physical appearance and dress when depicting female newsmakers? Should words like "coed" be dropped?

Marriage, too, has been subject to trends, not only in terms of the details of the ceremony (or absence thereof), but also as one of several options:

> Clearly, marriage is back in style after two decades during which men and women dabbled at alternate lifestyles. Last year [1982], a record 2.5 million couples marched down the aisle, their ranks swelled by the large population in the prime marrying years of 18 to 26.[27]

Big weddings also made a return, pleasing retailers who benefit from such ceremonies, but married life is, for most Americans, different from that of their parents and grandparents. There is more flexibility, more sharing, perhaps more overt tension, but there are also some things that haven't changed—romantic expectations, the hope of permanence, and overall, a commitment to spouse and children over job.

Senior Citizens

> Over 11 percent of America's population is over 65. The over-65 population is expected to exceed 55 million within the next 40 years, and the most rapidly growing group in the country is the over-85 age group.[28]

These facts, combined with other attitudinal switches, suggest all sorts of consideration for public relations persons. Those associated with financial institutions realize that the presumably poor and lonely senior citizens are, on average, neither. They are fairly comfortable, good credit risks, and good, if cautious, consumers. A longer-lived citizenry also poses problems for those in health care, in political life, and for all who view those past retirement age as marginally productive.

Congress is becoming more familiar with the clout of the aging, who manage to send millions of letters, postcards, and phone messages to Capitol Hill on issues like Social Security. Some legislators characterize the elderly as the most potent interest group in Washington, principally because of their consistent voting patterns and their use of free time to write to or visit congressmembers.

Communication

There are many surface trends in communication—things like the growth of videotape recorders as part of the home entertainment center; the sometimes shocking nature of satellite-provided news; the increasing permissiveness in programming and advertising and its consequent challenge; the mounting pressure on news media, especially television; the proliferation in technological systems that enables us to interact faster, collect data more quickly, transmit information instantaneously, even tap public opinion in a matter of seconds.

Deeper than these concepts are the activities made possible by such hardware and the problems each creates. Will privacy be further threatened? Will gadgetry replace creativity? Will the public be able to absorb and understand these innovations?

Ben J. Wattenberg, a member of the American Enterprise Institute, argues that television news distorts reality, emphasizing bad news over good, simply because that medium lives on events and can't handle long-range trends. He cites Three Mile Island as a case in point, where a single failure obscures what he calls "the perfect safety record of the United States nuclear power industry." His book, *The Good News Is That the Bad News Is Wrong*, attempts to counteract some American assumptions with more upbeat data. Wattenberg writes, for example, that a majority of black workers are in white-collar jobs, that the proportion of under-35 married couples owning their own homes is the highest in history, and that, in the 1970s, in the middle of the energy crisis, the number of air conditioners in American homes doubled.[29]

Although findings like this may be debated, they do point out two important ideas to practitioners:

- All assumptions should be challenged.
- Alternate viewpoints should be considered.

Technology

Author Michel Poniatowski, a member of the European Parliament, claims:

> All the certainties of the industrial society in which we live are disintegrating. We are witnessing an erosion of ideologies, economic theories, and traditional culture. That is because all our assumptions, all our theories and religions come from the 19th century, from an industrial period that is approaching its end. Marxism and capitalism, for example, are 19th century doctrines, each intended as the driving force for a system that no longer corresponds to the prevailing economy or to the scientific age now being ushered in.[30]

Nuclear power. Laser-beam surgery. Robotics. Fifth-generation computers. Space exploration and the possibility of "star wars." Microelectronics at every level and in almost every phase of American life. Calculators that handicap horses, track biorhythms, provide horoscopes, and automatically program calorie intake. Ceramics and synthetics that will replace metals. Instant mail. Media texts. Satellite conferencing. Banking and shopping from home.

These few examples of scientific change are already extant, and they may soon be as passé as the initial computer games.

Conclusions

There are few conclusions—only multiplying questions, and problems, and some trends that may be magnified or interrupted. Besides those discussed, and hundreds more, the public relations practitioner looks around and ahead and sees:

- A deteriorating farm economy, with fewer family farms
- A continuing concern for the quality of life
- The increasing complication of modern society
- An escalation in terrorism, with resultant frustration
- A slight upturn in religious commitment
- The "gay rights" movement and insistence on freedom of choice in sex
- A rethinking of management practices
- A lessening of fears about communism
- A flatter economy
- Population shifts to the South and Southwest

The future promises to be exciting beyond the dreams of the wildest speculators. Some preparations may be made by surveying expert opinion and collating the responses, but this remains a list of educated guesses. For the public relations practitioner, the prudent course involves reading, discussing, thinking, and above all, remaining flexible.

CHAPTER HIGHLIGHTS

- Public relations is a social science that makes use of tenets of psychology, sociology, and other disciplines in implementing change. The more we understand about ourselves and others, the better practitioners we'll be.
- Motivation, perception, and learning are fundamental to the understanding of human behavior.
- Reason, realism, and sensitivity are key traits to possess when working with others, singly or in groups.
- Various publics must be considered, and the efficient practitioner selects those most crucial to the success of a particular endeavor. These publics are most effectively reached through their leaders.
- PR programs seek to alter unfavorable public opinion, convert uncommitted opinion, and reinforce favorable opinion.
- Persuasion is as civilized way of effecting a desired course of action (as against force or purchase), but it is not foolproof.
- Public relations is not practiced in a vacuum, so the professional must be alert to trends that affect his or her conduct of PR programs.

NOTES

[1]Alfred McClung Lee, "The Long Struggle to Make Sociology Useful," *Public Relations Journal*, July 1982.

[2]*pr reporter*, Vol. 24, No. 36 (September 21, 1981).

[3]John Paluszek, "Keep Your Eye on the Proximate Public." Reprinted with permission from the October 1983 issue of the *Public Relations Journal*. Copyright 1983.

[4]Sean MacBride, from a speech given at Stanford University, as reported by *The Press*, Vol. 8, No. 10 (1981).

[5]*pr reporter*, June 8, 1981.

[6]*Ibid.*

[7]Philip Lesly, "Managing the Human Climate," a supplement to *pr reporter*, September/October 1981.

[8]Stratford P. Sherman, "America's New Abstinence," *Fortune*, March 18, 1985. © 1985 Time Inc. All rights reserved.

[9]Larry Kaagan, from a speech delivered to the Nebraska Chapter of PRSA, January 18, 1983.

[10]*Ibid.*

[11]Daniel Yankelovich, "New Rules for American Life: Searching for Self Fulfillment in a World Turned Upside Down," *Psychology Today*, April 1981.

[12]Richard Scammon, "Social Changes: Where Will They Lead in the '80's?" *Public Relations Journal*, January 1982.

[13]Thomas B. Morgan, "The Latinization of America," *Esquire*, May 1983.

[14]Jack Santino, interviewed by *U.S. News & World Report*, "From Jogging to Trivia Games, Fads Create Status," February 11, 1985.

[15]Arnold Mitchell and Christine MacNulty, "Changing Values and Lifestyles," *Long Range Planning*, April 1981.

[16]Bertram Wyatt-Brown, interviewed by *U.S. News & World Report*, "Honor: An Ancient Ethic on Decline in America," November 15, 1982.

[17]David A. Weissler, "Why People Are Rude—Why It Hurts Society," *U.S. News & World Report*, August 22, 1983.

[18]Amitai Etzioni, interviewed by *U.S. News & World Report*, "U.S. Needs a Moral and Social Recovery," January 9, 1984.

[19]"Happiness: How America Pursues It," *U.S. News & World Report*, March 4, 1985.

[20]Review of *The Yuppie Handbook*, by Marissa Piesman and Marilee Hartley (New York: Long Shadow Books, 1984), reviewed in *Time*, January 9, 1984. Reprinted by permission from *Time*. © 1984 Time Inc. All rights reserved.

[21]Curt Suplee, "Dawn of the Wimp," *The Washington Post*, September 10, 1984.

[22]Edward C. Baig, "Making Money Helping Singles Mingle," *Fortune*, February 18, 1985.

[23]Susan Fraker, "Why Women Aren't Getting to the Top," *Fortune*, April 16, 1984.

[24]Dorothy Jurney, "More Newsroom Managers—But Nowhere Near Enough," *ASNE Bulletin*, December/January 1984.

[25]Rena Bartos, interview with *Communicator's Journal*, "Challenging Our Assumptions," September/October 1983.

[26]Susan Brownmiller, *Femininity* (New York: Linden Press/Simon & Schuster, 1984).

[27]"Marriage Is Back in Style," *U.S. News & World Report*, June 20, 1983.

[28]"Graying of America; Are Institutions Prepared?" *PRSA Newsletter*, Vol. 11, No. 3 (March 1983).

[29]Ben J. Wattenberg, *The Good News Is That the Bad News Is Wrong* (New York: Simon & Schuster, 1984).

[30]Michel Poniatowski, "The Coming Scientific Society," *World Press Review*, October 1982.

SUGGESTED READINGS

ADAMS, THOMAS B., and THOMAS D. MURRAY, *A Look at Tomorrow*. Warren, Mich.: Campbell-Ewald, 1985.

DIZARD, WILSON P., JR., *The Coming Information Age*, 2nd ed. New York: Longman, 1985.

GREER, MICHAEL E., *Perception*, a 30-minute film. New York: McGraw-Hill Films, 1984.

HANSON, JAMES, and HERBERT I. ABELSON, *Persuasion: How Opinions and Attitudes Are Changed*, 3rd ed. New York: Springer, 1976.

HARRELL, GILBERT D., *Consumer Behavior*. San Diego: Harcourt Brace Jovanovich, 1986.

LUSTBERG, ART, *Winning at Confrontation*. Washington, D.C.: U.S. Chamber of Commerce, 1985.

McCAFFREY, MIKE, with JERRY DERLOSHON, *Personal Marketing Strategies: How to Sell Yourself, Your Ideas and Your Services.* Englewood Cliffs, N.J.: Spectrum, 1983.

MITCHELL, ARNOLD, *The Nine American Lifestyles.* New York: Macmillan, 1983.

NASBITT, JOHN, *Megatrends.* New York: Warner, 1982.

REICH, ROBERT B., *The Next American Frontier.* New York: Times Books, 1983.

RYAN, HALFORD ROSS, *Persuasive Advocacy: Cases for Argumentation and Debate.* Lanham, Md.: University Press of America, 1985.

SMITH, MARY JOHN, *Persuasion and Human Action.* Belmont, Calif.: Wadsworth, 1982.

STEINBERG, CHARLES S., *The Creation of Consent.* New York: Hastings House, 1975.

American Demographics Magazine, Syracuse, N.Y.

Public Opinion Magazine, Washington, D.C., American Enterprise Institute.

EXERCISES

1. List the organizations and individuals that you feel form the power structure in your community. How would you go about reaching them?

2. What institutions in your area do you feel are most sensitive to public opinion and least sensitive to public opinion? Defend your choices.

3. List several courses in the social sciences that you think would be beneficial to a person majoring in public relations. Specify why in each instance.

4. What current trends do you feel hold most significance for your peer group? What trends do you foresee?

5. What are some of the social consequences of the scientific age?

CASE PROBLEMS

1. Because of a tax shortfall, the state legislature is considering closing the engineering school at its state university. This news unites engineering faculty, students, and alumni in opposition. They are joined by several key business leaders. The local media begin to carry charges and counter-charges. The legislators refuse to guarantee survival of the engineering school, saying only that they will "study all aspects of the issue."

   While the debate rages, the dean of a private university in the state, which also has an excellent engineering school, makes a statement that the institution can handle all the prospective engineering students the state could generate.

   "We have the space, the facilities, and the faculty," says the dean, "and we would be happy to accommodate more students."

   Reaction from supporters of the state university, internal and external, are sudden and heated. They question the ability of the private school to handle more students, point out the great disparity in tuition, contend that most of the private-school students are from out of state, and assert that the private-school faculty is too small to take on more students. The president of the private school is flooded with letters and phone calls, from engineers, state-school faculty, businessmen, and legislators. Most argue against the dean's stance.

Because of the news value, the private-school president is deluged with questions from the media. Does he agree with the dean? Has the legislature put him up to this? What about the negative reactions from local businessmen, a few of whom are on the private school's board of regents? The president decides to hold a news conference to make his position clear.

a. You are the public relations director for the private university, and the president comes to you for advice. What points would you cover with him, and what would you advise him to do?

b. You are the public relations director for the state university, and the goal of your president is to retain the college of engineering. Assuming that the private-school president merely said he supported his dean, what response, if any, would you advise your president to give?

2. Although more than 60,000 automatic teller machines are scattered across the United States, more than 90 percent of banking transactions that could be handled by the machines are conducted by the traditional methods. The typical household uses an electronic money machine only once every three months, and this despite ad campaigns, sweepstakes and bonus offerings, and staff assistance to instruct users. What do you think are the reasons for this reluctance? If you were a PR person employed by a banking association to increase usage, what things would you do, what themes would you use?

3. Tom Wellington, one of your PR clients and the owner of a chain of fish-and-chips restaurants, calls you in to show you his new ad campaign slogan, created by his advertising agency. It reads, "Tom Wellington Runs a Home for Battered Fish." Your comments to him?

3
PUBLIC RELATIONS AND RESEARCH

No intelligent person would begin a journey without a map. In fact, the seasoned traveler wants to know climatic conditions, tips for appropriate clothing, the rate of exchange for money, the political situation, perhaps even the form of electric current in use in a foreign country. These items all require some research—basic perhaps, but still valuable.

Any public relations decision or program merits the same sort of initial scrutiny. Public relations relies on the information-gathering process. It requires facts, not intuition or assumptions. You must have these facts at hand or know where to get them. To proceed without such data is unprofessional and dangerous.

Despite that truism, public relations has not been exemplary in its use of research. Frequently, clients or marketing departments supply the research data and practitioners work from it.

"The public relations practitioner in business today is about where the accountant was in the '30's," wrote PR counsel Patrick Jackson.[1]

There is also a shortage of research materials in the field of public relations, compared, for example, with marketing, politics, and other areas. Practitioners need more information on behavior, on organizational theory, on legal matters. Leaders in the public relations arena seem aware of this, and, in the past several years, steps have been instituted to correct it. A new journal, *Public Relations Research and Education*, was launched in 1984 by the PR division of the Association for Education in Journalism and Mass Communication, and the PRSA's Foundation for Public Relations Research and Education sponsors competitions for the most significant research efforts relating to the profession. In judging Silver Anvil (the top PRSA awards)

Figure 3-1 Research, formal or informal, precedes every public relations effort.

winners, PRSA committees also say more weight will be given to research-backed entries than to those lacking proof of planning or effectiveness.

About half of *Fortune*'s top 1,000 companies use research in public relations, and the list is growing. Major PR firms are also beefing up their research capacities; Hill and Knowlton's research subsidiary, Group Attitudes Corporation, is nearly tripling the research it did a decade ago, and Ruder & Finn has its own telephone research facilities and does over $1 million in this area alone. Nationally, companies specializing in marketing, advertising, and public-opinion research reported gross worldwide revenues of more than $1.5 billion in 1984—and that from only the top 94 research organizations.

VALUE OF RESEARCH

The prediction of election results, the assessment of television viewer preferences, and the solicitation of opinion on new products are familiar forms of research, but the list of uses in public relations is extensive.

Basically, PR research is used to *verify, clarify,* or *identify.*

- Assumptions about conditions affecting a company or its publics may need to be *verified* by some form of research. A public relations officer may think that the company publication is not being read very frequently or thoroughly; a survey could produce a factual basis to support or contradict this hunch.
- Occasionally, conflicting reports make decisions more difficult, or information may be incomplete, or the reasons for beliefs or behavior may be clouded. One needs to *clarify* the data. What do respondents mean when they say they favor stricter penalties for drunk drivers? Why are employees indifferent to a proposed major medical benefit package?
- Research can also *identify* problem areas or opportunities, allowing administrators to plan more effectively. A decline in enrollment is a signal to

educators preparing a budget. A general ignorance about the consumer advantages inherent in a certain new law will convince a federal agency that more communication is required.

In an article in the *Public Relations Journal*, Peter Finn, chairman of Research and Forecasts, charts four basic uses of research to support public relations:

1. *Public issues studies* "sponsored by clients as a way of making a contribution to society, demonstrating leadership, and generating favorable publicity." Such studies can support PR campaigns, and, if they are comprehensive enough, the data and the costs may be shared with several clients.
2. *Needs and perceptions assessment* research of "key audiences, such as employees; media; members of the financial community, including brokers, analysts, and portfolio managers; customers; and potential customers." These surveys, which may be repeated periodically, help PR practitioners to design or update campaigns.
3. *Program evaluation* to monitor audience perceptions, track publicity, or evaluate reactions to campaigns.
4. *Issues tracking/intelligence gathering*, which "involves monitoring key publications, regular statistical surveys of the public or opinion leaders, and periodic in-depth interviews with experts in a field of interest to a client."[2]

Editors of business publications periodically survey readership, trying to discover if they are really doing their job. Questions asked might include the following:

- What do you like or dislike in the publication?
- What would you like to see more of? less of?
- How much of the publication do you read?
- How much time do you spend reading the publication?
- What other members of your family read the publication?
- Do you discuss with others the stories you read?

You could also ask readers to categorize the style, to comment on the paper stock used, to advise on frequency of mailing, even to suggest a new publication title.

There are formal and informal methods for gathering information. The formal methods may be more statistically reliable, but the informal have real value and, in some instances, may even be preferred.

INFORMAL RESEARCH

Suppose you were hired to fill a PR vacancy at a large banking institution in a metropolitan area. Suppose, too, that you had moved to that area from another city. Obviously you would have a lot to learn. Where could you go for help?

If you needed to brush up on your knowledge of banking, you would find books in the public library, the regional university libraries, and, perhaps, the bank itself. You would want to check through the files of your predecessors to see what kind of duties they performed, and you would visit with your subordinates and with management and key bank personnel. You might want to chat with other persons in town who have similar responsibilities at other banks. You would review media lists and make the rounds of local news outlets. You would check in with the chamber of commerce to find out more about this city. You would look through past advertising, bank brochures, and the bank history, if one existed. In short, you would steep yourself in all aspects of the job so you could function efficiently and intelligently.

Although conversation may be colored by the person talking, a wide association with bank (or plant or institution) employees would be a good idea.

Perhaps you'd arrange to eat lunch with different people each day. Or you might find the bowling or golf leagues providing opportunities to chat casually about subjects of concern to your fellow employees. Some firms have internal "listening posts" to channel information to management.

You might assemble a special committee of people, externally and internally, who could help in identifying and suggesting remedies for PR problems. This *panel* should be carefully structured, should meet regularly, and should have worthwhile agenda. Its counsel should always be considered and, where possible, followed.

Research also includes *content analysis* (which may be formal or informal—the screening of printed materials for clues about existing problems or potential problems, for evidence on how the media are reflecting your institution, for information on trends and innovations pertaining to your industry or profession. Media reports, of course, may not always be accurate in terms of your needs. Simply counting column inches or television news slots is deceptive. You don't really know who read or saw the story, nor do you know how they reacted. To a degree, such analysis can measure media acceptance of your PR materials, but public reaction is harder to gauge.

Scrutinizing mail is sometimes helpful but also has its pitfalls. Negative correspondence is apt to outweigh positive response. People who are generally satisfied with a product, service, or program rarely bother to write. So the critics tend to be in the majority. Even so, their comments should be examined for validity and possible corrective action.

Similar cautions should be applied to *salespeople's comments* and *field reports*. These may be biased according to the field representative's version of business conditions. If sales are off in the cattle-feed area, for example, and you ask how ranchers are doing, you may be told money is tight, the ranchers are pessimistic, and prospects are dim. These are not really observations; they are excuses.

Variations of these techniques also surface in different places—the *in-depth* interview, for example, in which group members are encouraged to talk freely about a specific topic or a range of topics with the aim of determining reasons behind certain actions; or the related *focus group interview*, in which a moderator asks questions of specially selected publics, sometimes to aid in writing copy or selecting a campaign theme, sometimes to solve a communication problem, sometimes as a prelude to a more detailed questionnaire. These encounters are carefully structured but still have a lot of flexibility in following a subject's views. They are normally audiotaped or videotaped and frequently played out before two-way mirrors, so that observations may be made by clients or other researchers.

Typically, participants in this form of *qualitative* research are paid in advance (so as not to bias responses), and the conversation with them begins with a general warmup discussion; this is followed by broad questions ("Overall, do you feel better about your life than you did ten years ago?" "What does the word 'liberal' mean to you?") to permit participants to influence the topic choice; then a probing or narrowing of the responses, guided by the moderator; perhaps an assignment for the subjects, normally including some writing ("Put down three words you would use to describe Acme Industries"); an opinion or evaluation phase, in which judgments on statements or designs or programs may be sought; then a concluding period to wind things up, requesting any further comments and thanking participants. Sessions normally last between one and two hours.

Some methods are even less scientific. Editors occasionally check wastebaskets after distribution of a newsletter, to see how many were tossed. Or they use numerous devices, from coupons and free gifts to subscription renewal forms, to determine what the level of readership and interest might be. Farm-implement companies may buttonhole visitors to state fairs or offer prizes for those who fill out information cards.

The point is that you seek out data any way you can. Some projects don't really warrant a formal survey, and some provide insufficient time or funds for such a scientific approach. As long as you use common sense, have a goal in mind, vary the sources of information, and appreciate the limitations of the material you've collected, even these basic efforts have merit.

You should also listen a lot—and ask questions. Talented and creative people often talk too much and fail to listen enough. When you are hired to handle a public relations task, your first responsibility is to pay attention to the client's assessment of the problem and then query the client and others about its scope and details. What you are after is the *reality* of the situation. This may not be what the client sees as the reality. Causes may be obscure and hard to unearth, but you must discover them. The PR person is the impartial, levelheaded prober and assessor.

This may not be easy. Some administrators conceal facts, either deliberately or inadvertently. They may be embarrassed about their lapses or uncertain of your trustworthiness, or they may not consider certain items of any importance. You can't let this slip by. The public relations practitioner must be leveled with, must be given all the pieces if he or she is to solve the puzzle.

Library Research

Every profession has its own store of printed materials. Public relations is no exception. There are manuals, textbooks, periodicals, position papers, and other items that will prove helpful to both beginner and veteran. Some of these are listed in the "Suggested Readings" section at the end of each chapter.

In addition, PR practitioners should surround themselves with books that pertain to the particular clients they serve. Perhaps only a few of these books may be in their personal collection, but they should know where to put their hands on others.

The library (sometimes called an "Information Center") is an invaluable asset. It is surprising how many people go through life without learning how to use a library. This is a failing a PR person can't afford. Many libraries have videotapes or film strips that will introduce you to that library and its services. If such a visual aid is not available, then you should ask the librarian for help. Although librarians are stereotyped as stuffy and interested mainly in silence, they are usually generous with their time and eager to satisfy your needs and curiosity. A good librarian is challenged by a difficult assignment and will prove to be not a barrier, but an ally.

Impact, a newsletter on trends, techniques, and tools for communicators, quotes an author-librarian, Margaret Bennett, to the effect that "every library has four master keys: (1) the card catalogue; (2) the *Reader's Guide to Periodical Literature*; (3) the reference books; and (4) the reference librarian."[3]

Review the card-catalog files in your area libraries. They are usually conveniently located and contain trays of 3-by-5-inch cards, which, in themselves, provide a good deal of information. Listings are found under author, title, and subject. With many libraries becoming completely computerized, the search for material moves from card file to monitor or scanner.

The Reader's Guide to Periodical Literature, among other periodical sources, enables you to locate, by author or subject, articles published in a variety of magazines and periodicals. The references are keyed, and you can use them to track down the proper issue and volume in the library stacks.

Wander through the reference room and note the collections of books, periodicals, microfilm, and other items. There will be sets of encyclopedias in numerous categories, and in their listings you will find suggestions for additional sources. Two almanacs, the *World Almanac* and the *Information Please Almanac*, are invaluable compendiums of facts on historical, statistical, and biographical items. There are *Who's Who* volumes by geographical areas and profession, bibliographies, book review digests, cumulative book indexes, international guides to literature, Congressional Records, atlases and gazeteers, statistical abstracts, registers of manufacturers, books of quotations, directories of associations and advertisers, rhyming dictionaries, collections of synonyms and antonyms, state and federal government manuals, a choice of English dictionaries, foreign dictionaries, and countless other aids. These will save you hours of digging up facts and may also inspire related creativity.

There are, of course, specialized libraries. Law, medical, and dental libraries are part of any sizable community. Larger cities have libraries that can provide material on fund-raising sources, foundation giving, historical archives, and business topics.

The premier library is the Library of Congress in Washington, D.C., with its 55 million items, including over 14 million books, 3 million maps, over 3 million musical entries, 2 million photographs or slides, a quarter of a million reels of microfilmed newspapers, thousands of movies and posters, historical documents, and books in hundreds of languages. And that's only the beginning. It is the largest library in the world and provides reference services by mail or phone.

Keep in mind that the Library of Congress is merely one of the many research sources available in our nation's capital. There are various special bureaus, the National Archives, and the U.S. Government Printing Office, which distributes or sells more than 25,000 different publications. Researchers can also get copies of the *Congressional Record, Congressional Quarterly* (published weekly), *Congressional Directory, Public Information Guide, Consumer Information* (a quarterly catalogue of information on products and services), and other federal publications. There are also meetings that interested persons may sometimes attend, and other data that the Freedom of Information Act allows citizens to collect.

Many large cities have Federal Information Centers, and some local libraries carry a good collection of government materials. Even smaller libraries may be able to do computer searches for materials they don't possess, working with hundreds of distant databases, or making use of a network of more than 2,000 American libraries.

There are museums, old bookstores, newspaper "morgues," trade journals, files of professional associations, consulates, travel agencies, tourist bureaus, Chambers of Commerce, learned journals, private archives, and hundreds of additional information sources. Smart PR people take advantage of what's already available, paying only for research that can't be gathered any other way.

The two-dozen-member research staff at the prestigous *National Geographic*, which prides itself on accuracy, has its own translators, a backup team of subject-matter experts, and its own 78,000-volume library, as well as books owned by staffers. Still, it finds the Washington-area repositories invaluable, and researchers will call long distance to check a quote or, when necessary, take a plane to settle a dispute.

Microfilm and Computerized Retrieval

Ease of storage and ease of reading are two reasons for using such tools as microfilm or microfiche or other miniature information systems. Microfiche—a 4-by-6-inch sheet of microfilm in a cardboard or plastic frame—is handier for books, newspapers, and other, longer items.

Many libraries have these on shelves, and you ask for them by name and date or other specific. Some libraries have equipment that enables you to project the desired document on your individual monitor screen by merely pushing the appropriate set of keyboard buttons. This retrieval system is sometimes tied to other libraries and can garner information from distant sources.

In the new library technology are electronic data-retrieval systems, which allow the researcher to talk to the computer and get answers. The researcher states what he or she wants and, in dialogue with the machine, refines his need until the proper and specific details appear on the screen.

Figure 3-3 Modern technology makes retrieval of information much simpler.

Your Office Library and Files

Since you can't always be phoning the library or rummaging through its stacks, your own PR office should be the repository for certain essential information. Among these might be a good dictionary, a thesaurus, a book of familiar quotations, a public-speaking manual, government directories, a marketing-research text, fact books, a set of encyclopedias, media directories, a comprehensive atlas, a volume on grammar and English usage, a handbook of humor, and any special publications that fit your company or client needs. If you are employed in an insurance firm, for example, you would want some books on insurance. If you have among your clients a hospital or clinic, you would want books on medical subjects.

You also keep your eyes open for new volumes that could be helpful. The federal government, university presses, and a number of professional organizations and institutes issue periodic works that cover public relations topics. Perhaps you're looking for a classy restaurant to entertain a client. Two trade publications (*Sales & Marketing Management* and *Restaurant Business*) provide such a rating. The New York Stock Exchange indexes America's economic performance compared with those of other nations and with previous years. A *Consumer Sourcebook* from Gale Research of Detroit provides facts about this country's consumers. Practitioners who handle scientific accounts have a choice of periodicals, including *Science News, Science Digest, Science and Living Tomorrow, The Sciences, Science 85, Discover, Omni, Next,* and others. When you leaf through publications like *Public Relations Journal, pr reporter,* and *PR News,* you spot reviews of books covering everything from proofreading to contacting state officials. Sometimes publications print handy lists of books by subject. *In Black and White*, for example, a newsletter directed to writers and editors, may publish a list of books its editors feel most helpful for those who work in print. You'd find their recommendations for dictionaries; for volumes on grammar usage; for classics like Strunk and White's *The Elements of Style*, Roy Nelson's *Publication Design*, and Skillin and Gay's *Words into Type*; and some texts that cover effective writing for various print media.

As a practitioner, you should also get into the habit of keeping useful files—your own morgue, just like the newspaper's (another good research source). The system you adopt should be one that you and your successors can utilize efficiently. Knowing that you have something but not knowing where to find it isn't very helpful.

The usual method of filing is alphabetical, using surnames or trade names and ignoring definite articles in titles. You may also file by subject, or by geography if your clients or branch offices are scattered, and you should devise a solid cross-reference index, one that will lead you from photos to articles, or from article to related article. In addition to filing-cabinet designations, you may want a separate card index to speed things along.

To begin with, you should maintain up-to-date biographies of officers in your company or the institutions you represent. Check these periodically to see if there are new children to be listed, awards to be noted, or other changes. Such information is helpful when writing routine news stories about such principals, but even more important in cases involving accidents or death.

Photo Files

Photographs are valuable for possible use in publications or news stories, but they also serve a historical function. It is refreshing to be able to check back several years to find out who was sitting at a head table or what the decor looked like or how the plant looked before reconstruction.

Impact has some good tips for maintaining a photo and art file:

> A neat method is to affix each 8 × 10 [photo] to a 9 × 12 sheet of cardboard. This 8 × 10 becomes your master print and should never be removed from the files. Alongside the print on the file card you can identify the photo and include such data as the date the picture was taken, photographer's name, model releases, approvals, uses made of the photograph, and remarks. A negative holder can be glued to the back of the file card and the negative kept inside so that it is never separated from master print and identifying copy.[4]

Be careful in handling photographs and negatives, since smudging and cracking damage them.

File for the Future

Your files are a place to deposit quarterly and annual reports, especially those of institutions you represent and their competitors. Newspaper and

EXAMPLES OF SUBJECT HEADINGS

Accountants
Activist Groups
Advocacy Advertising
Alcoholism
Anniversaries
Annual Reports
Annual Reports to
  Employees
Architects
Associations
Awards/Contests

Banking
Bond Issues
Boycotts
Business
  Educational Participation
  Responsibility
  Small Business
  Youth and Business

CATV
Colleges/Schools
Communications
Community Relations
Comparable Worth
Computers
Consumer Relations
Conventions/Meetings
Corporate/Company
  Advertising
  Annual Meeting
  Culture
  Descriptive Brochures
  Giving/Contributions
  Histories
  Image/Identity
  Name Change
  Newsletter/Publications
  Public Relations
Cost Control
Crime
Crisis Planning
Cultural Programs

Day Care
Dealer/Distributor
Dedication/Open House
Direct Mail
Disasters/Emergencies
Drug Abuse
Drunk Driving

Economic Education
Employee Relations
  Absenteeism
  Benefits

Bulletin Boards
Communications
Courtesy
Economic Education
Evaluation
Handbooks
Incentive/Productivity
Minority Employment
Publications
Recruitment
Suggestion Systems
Surveys
Training Programs
Elderly People
Endorsement/Personalities
Energy Use
Environment/Conservation
Ethics

Fairs/Exhibits
Financial
  Disclosure
  Fact Books
  Going Public
  Investor Relations
  Merger
  Proxy
  Security Analysts
  Tender
Firefighters
Fitness Programs
Food
Foreign Companies in U.S.
Free Enterprise
Fund Raising
Futurism/Change

Gambling/Lotteries
Government
Graphics/Logos
Groundbreaking

Health Care Costs
Health Fairs
HMO/PPO
Hospitals
Hotel/Resort

Industrial Development
  City/State
Industry
  (Files maintained on many
  industries. Ask for the in-
  dustry on which you need
  material.)
Insurance
International
Issues Management

Labor Relations
Law Firms
Layoffs
Libraries
Listening
Lobbying

Management
Marketing
Media
Minority Relations
Mobile Phones
Museums

Name Change
New Products
Nonprofit
Nuclear Energy

Photography
Physicians
Plant Acceptance
Plant Closing
Police
Policy Statement
Politics
Press Relations
Privacy
Product Publicity
Product Safety/Recall
Public Affairs
Public Opinion
Public Relations
  Budgeting
  Choosing Counsel
  Client/Counsel Relations
  Counseling
  Definitions
  Education/Training
  Ethics
  Evaluation/Audit
  Fees
  Future Trends
  Job Description
  Law
  Letters of Agreement
  Licensing

  Manuals
  New Firm Establishment
  Organization of Department
  Presentations
  Professionalism
  Program Planning
Public Service
Publicity

Quality Control

Real Estate/Housing
Rehabilitation
Religion
Release Forms
Research
Restaurants
Retailing
Retirement

Safety Programs
Satellites
Seminars/Workshops
Shopping Centers
Speakers Bureaus
Speaking/Speechwriting
Special Events
Sports
Stress
Strikes

Teleconference
Telemarketing
Terrorism/Kidnapping
Topping Out
Trademarks
Trade Shows
Transportation
Travel/Tourism
TV Appearance

Utilities

Vocational Training
Volunteer Programs

Women in Business
Women in Public Relations
Writing

Youth Programs

Zoos

PRSA Public Relations
      Society of America

845 Third Avenue
New York, NY 10022
(212) 826-1776

Figure 3-4 Reprinted with permission of the Public Relations Society of America, which reminds users that there is a modest fee for use of materials from the PRSA files. Details are available from the address above.

magazine articles that may have future utility should be filed by subject. So should speech material, including jokes and illustrative anecdotes. There are government books on a variety of topics that could be handy, case histories from professional associations, and samples of your own work.

All successful practitioners also have a "swipe" file, which contains items they may someday emulate or use for inspiration. These could be chosen for their central ideas, copy merits, color choices, layout, photo treatment, or information value. Fresh ideas are rare. Most begin in stimulation from other sources. So if you admire something, hold on to it.

News stories that emanate from your office may be filed by subject or date, or they may be (and often are) pasted into a scrapbook chronologically. You may wish to cross-index these stories and provide a listing for each volume.

You should also have available any number of rosters—media, company personnel, government officials, specialty editors, and the like. These should be updated periodically and checked for spelling, address and title changes, and other factors.

Finally, correspondence. Knowing what to toss and what to save takes experience. Have a system for culling and for readily locating letters you need. Alphabetizing may not be enough. Unless you have a secretary with an unusual memory, or possess a good memory yourself, you may want additional cross-reference data, such as subject matter or dates.

The key to all informal research is careful planning. Be alert to things you can use, and organize them for instant recall. Keep them handy and keep them in good repair. Plastic covers, binders, loose-leaf folders, adequate shelf and cabinet space— all of these make for tidy appearance and prevent abuse or destruction.

Handling these chores properly marks the difference between a professional who can react immediately to a need or crisis and someone who stumbles around, falls short of satisfactory, and loses both face and clients.

FORMAL RESEARCH

Checking with colleagues and reading certain materials can be helpful, but when exact data are critical, you should opt for more formal research—for surveys conducted by professionals. Few executives today question the value of research, and most have confidence in the findings of such studies. They may not have the time or the money or the willingness to commission a survey, but the majority believe in the desirability and accuracy of such labors.

America is a survey-oriented society. Check your daily paper. Dozens of stories either contain survey details or are based on the results of surveys. People read them because they are interested in trends or concerned about conformity. It may give you vicarious pleasure to learn you are in the majority, or you may merely be curious about a public attitude.

All a survey does, however, is measure the moment. It is not a blueprint for the future. The wise PR person stays current. Presidential popularity shifts from month to month. Attitudes about capital punishment vary. So do opinions on other controversial issues, from the legalization of drugs to the ordination of women priests. Although statistical evidence is helpful—even necessary—as a temporary guide, you should never let the figures get too cold. You should also be wary about broadening the subject too much or broadening the conclusions drawn from any sampling. Research goals should be well defined, and their value should be considered in terms of the limits of the study.

Another thing to remember about surveys is that they are not substitutes for integrity, morality, or common sense. You must do things because they are right, or seem right, and not because your side has a statistical edge in the polls. Solid reasoning is more stable than the vagaries of public opinion. Should a university alter its policy on campus speakers solely because alumni opinion is slightly more conservative than campus opinion? Should decisions on matters like Mideast peace settlements be considered only on the basis of pro and con correspondence? Obviously not.

Still, when engaging in any public action, those who are prudent are aware of the tenor of public opinion, and when their actions run counter to such opinion they should anticipate the consequences.

A number of steps follow logically in the course of a survey. All are important. An inaccurate survey is worthless except, perhaps, as propaganda. And no one should attempt to research a problem unless he or she personally possesses the appropriate professional skills or can hire such skills.

Let us follow a survey from the moment a public relations counselor or research analyst has been employed to gather information or solve a problem.

The Survey

What Is the Problem?

Defining the problem seems like the simplest part of the survey. It isn't. Some executives will tell you what they *think* the problem is. Others may conceal vital information out of embarrassment, fear, or a natural affinity for secrecy. Your responsibility is to discover what the problem *really* is—and not what people *think* it is.

Management may tell you that plant dissension is caused by troublesome union leaders, but you determine that the real difficulty is faulty communication from the top. A pastor may relate financial woes to the economic level of his parishioners, whereas this problem actually occurs because of the congregation's low evaluation of parish services. It may not be as important to politicians to know they are leading in a particular precinct as it is to learn how their views are coming across.

Your first job is to listen well. Probe for straight answers, determine what has been done before to gather similar information, and solicit opinions from a variety of sources.

After you have queried and listened, allow some time for *thinking*. Let problems gestate in your mind. A little reflection often adds dimension, provokes new insights, lends perspective.

Once you have pinpointed the problem, you get into the mechanics of extracting honest and productive responses from some predetermined audience. As much as possible, you want to find out exactly how individuals feel about a certain issue. So you have to word the questions correctly, devise a means of selecting those to be polled, professionally question a sufficient number, and then evaluate the results. Each of these steps has the possibility of error, so the goal should be to keep such flaws to a minimum.

Constructing the Questionnaire

Since you want honest and accurate responses to your questions, you must be careful to ask about those things that will give you the information you need. A survey is only as good as the questions it asks. If it turns up details that really don't solve your problem, you have wasted your time.

Figure out what you need to know and then develop questions that will provide these answers. This requires both thinking and testing. Perhaps you will evolve questions that are neither direct nor explicit, but that evoke the kind of replies you seek. Perhaps the queries are simple and candid. The point is, you must know what you are doing when you frame them.

There are *open* questions and *closed* questions.

Open questions allow a variety of answers and are therefore more difficult and expensive to tabulate. An open question might be:

What things bother you most about today's advertising?

Closed questions limit the possible responses, usually to a "yes" or "no" or to a selection from a specific number of alternatives. For example:

Do you think television commercials have improved in the last five years?
Yes ____   No ____   Don't Know ____

or

Here are three suggested solutions to the commercial clutter on television. Which do you favor?
Reduce the time allowed for commercials ____
Package all the commercials in one 15-minute segment every two hours ____
Allow commercials only at hour and half-hour breaks ____

Open questions should always be asked before closed questions, since you want to target in on wider views before narrowing the focus. Related questions should also be grouped together and not scattered throughout the survey, unless you are using them to cross-check each other.

As we will see more clearly in Chapter 5, words have a number of possible connotations for individuals. That's why, in some instances, a simple yes or no may not be a sufficient answer for survey respondents. To capture the shades of feelings on an issue, a technique called *semantic differential* is used, giving the person surveyed an opportunity to rate two opposite concepts and, typically, five choices in between.

For example, people could be asked how serious they consider the energy situation in the United States to be. The extremes might range from "critical" to "not at all serious." In between these poles would be options like "very serious," "quite serious," "somewhat serious," "fairly serious," "not very serious," or whatever other terms the survey chose to define the possible responses.

Respondents could also be asked if they "completely agreed" or "completely disagreed" with a statement and would be given choices in between, like "slightly" or "strongly" or "moderately."

Surveys could have a person rate a new household appliance from "extremely useful" to "useless" and ask how often he or she uses it, giving choices from "regularly" to "never."

Whenever you present respondents with a set of options, you must be certain that all options are included. If respondents face a question whose alternatives leave no room for the way they actually feel about the situation, they will either ignore that question, respond falsely, or give up on the entire survey.

Wording the questions

The results of any survey are only as good as the questions it asks. If the wrong questions are asked, if they are improperly worded, if they are ambiguous, vague, or misleading—all these flaws will put the response in doubt.

Some questions are oversimplified. Almost everyone would like to see crime reduced, but some may not be willing to grant law-enforcement officials the power they request. Respondents who favor abortion may balk at spending federal funds for this purpose. Even nations seem to agree on the goal of peace but not on the means of obtaining it. Broad questions often produce superficial answers. As one columnist mentioned, a third of the population may respond negatively to a question about fluoride in their water, but a more meaningful and less visible statistic is that 98 percent of the people don't really seem to care one way or the other.

Wording alone can cause fluctuations of 25 percent or more. In cases where familiarity with an issue varies widely, the divergence may be even greater. The struggles in Central America are confusing to most Americans, who can't remember whose side we are on in which countries. Many would not be able to decide whether the "Contras" were the enemy or an ally. Consider these three queries:

Should American tax dollars be used to support rebels in Nicaragua who are trying to overthrow the established government?	Yes ___	No ___
Should America support the efforts of the "Contra" rebels against the Marxist government of Nicaragua?	Yes ___	No ___
Do you favor continued financial aid for nonmilitary needs for the rebels struggling against the Cuban-backed government in Nicaragua?	Yes ___	No ___

Each of the questions above would elicit a different level of response from the same people, even when taken by reputable firms in a professional manner.

Those fashioning research questions should consider language that is understandable to those who will be surveyed. You don't use "cogitate" when you could say "think," and you don't use "ritual" when you mean "event." Similarly, you must be careful that the words chosen mean the same thing to all respondents. "Stock" means different things to a rancher and a broker; "market" would be defined differently by an investor and a homemaker.

Do you own any stock?
How do you view today's market?

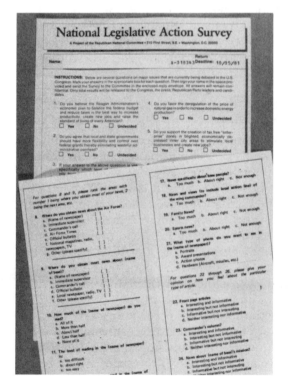

Figure 3-5 Wording of survey questions is a key element in the accuracy of response.

Terms like "often" and "seldom" also cause confusion, since they are viewed subjectively.

Do you watch television often?

What is "often"? Every night? Two hours a day? Five hours a day?
Asking respondents to "rate" something is equally difficult, unless they have the expertise or the guidelines to make a judgment.

How would you rate the management performance in this company?

The Ragan Report calls such queries "vacuum questions." And the same publication also criticizes "fuzzy" questions, ones that use vague terms, possibly because the formulator of the question doesn't have a clear idea either. It cites a readership survey that asks respondents to rate the "flow" of "company communication," and points out that both these phrasings are subject to interpretation. *The Ragan Report* suggests consulting dictionaries and thesauruses when wording questions and also advises:

> Be absolutely certain in your own mind what kind of information you want or need, for every single question you include in the survey.[5]

That means you don't clutter up the questionnaire with queries that add nothing to the information you seek. In some surveys, it might be important to know if the respondent voted in the last election, but that might have little to do with a questionnaire intended to determine after-shave-lotion preferences.

One way to correct some of this faulty language is by conducting a "pilot," or test, survey. Try the questions out on a small sample of those to be interviewed before submitting the questionnaire to everyone in the sample.

A real estate company wanted to know what recreational features should be included in a new apartment complex it was developing, so it surveyed tenants of existing complexes, asking them to rate facilities they had and to list others they would like to see added. A final question asked them if they would be willing to pay more for such additions. Respondents were wary. Who was behind this survey? How much more money would be involved? If they committed themselves, could this mean substantial increases in monthly payments? A high percentage of those responding to a pilot survey left that answer blank. The flaw was corrected by making the question more specific:

> If those additions were made, would you be willing to pay an additional monthly fee of: $10 _____ $5 _____ $3 _____   Nothing _____?

You must also avoid wording that creates bias in the respondent's mind. Congressmen and congresswomen are sometimes guilty of this in surveying their constituents. The phrasing of their queries leads voters to reply in a certain predetermined way. Here is a sample from a western senator:[6]

Are you in favor of allowing construction union czars the power to shut down an entire construction site because of a dispute with a single contractor . . . thus forcing even more workers to knuckle under to union agents?	Yes _____ No _____
Should all construction workers be forced into unions through legalized situs picketing, thus raising the cost of building your schools, hospitals, and homes?	Yes _____ No _____

Words like "forced" and "czars" and "knuckle under," and even words like "power" and "agents" and "raising the cost," make these questions suspect. To add to the problem, this survey included a letter from the senator condemning unions, referring to their leaders as "fat cats" and emphasizing the union's presumed intent to put every worker under union control. Editorials supporting these views accompanied the other items. As propaganda, the survey technique may be useful, but as a tool to collect accurate data, it is worthless.

A more valid approach is found in a questionnaire to constituents from another member of Congress:[7]

Do you favor a Constitutional Amendment allowing voluntary prayer in public schools?	Yes _____ No _____
Do you favor further reductions in federal spending even though it may affect programs that affect you?	Yes _____ No _____

Some political polls, incidentally, use variations of the semantic-differential technique. A *Washington Post*/ABC news poll makes a statement, lists some national problems, then asks respondents to give the Reagan administration a letter grade for its handling of each problem. In "improving the nation's economy," for example, 59 percent of those surveyed gave the administration a grade of A or B, 22 percent rated it C, and another 18 percent considered its performance worth a D or an F. In dealing with environmental problems, the Reagan team didn't fare as well, with 36 percent of those surveyed suggesting a grade of D or F, and only 24 percent recommending an A or B grade.[8]

Another variation involves "filter" questions, which attempt to eliminate uninformed responses by including queries such as, "Do you have any opinion on this issue?" or, "Have you ever been interested enough in this issue to take a pro or con position?" This sort of qualification does reduce the influence of responses from those who have no knowledge of or interest in the subject.

Regardless of method, the aim is always to obtain replies that are as accurate as possible. So the language should be objective, the questions as few as necessary, the level of the audience always weighed, and the "why" questions (asking respondents their reasons for taking certain courses of action or holding certain views) kept to a minimum, since these queries are difficult to answer. You should always know what you want, whom you want to survey, and what you want to ask. Then, before you proceed, you should test the questionnaire on a smaller group, even if such testing is informal.

Extracting the sample

Extracting the sample is the most complicated aspect of survey work and belongs to the research professional.

Once you know what you want to find out, and once you have put together the questions that should elicit answers, you have to determine whom you will survey and how many you will survey. There are a number of ways to approach the method of "sampling," which means gathering data from a limited segment of the population in order to draw conclusions about a much larger number.

Four kinds of sampling techniques are generally recognized:

1. *Accidental sample.*   This sampling technique is an informal means of gathering data by simply interviewing people who happen to be present in a particular place at a particular time. A man-in-the-street interviewer works this way. Perhaps the interviewer just stops folks in a shopping center and questions them about the highway speed limit. This form of survey is sometimes called a "water fountain survey" from the notion that those gathered around the office water cooler might be sampled for their opinions. Too many executives have reinforced their own convictions by using this unscientific method.

The dangers are obvious. You have no assurance that there is anything typical about the information you garner. If you stood outside a particular neighborhood bar and queried exiting customers, you might end up with a solid set of workers in one economic class, or age group, or ethnic background. Even surveying those who happen to be in a certain shopping mall has built-in defects, since it may be more heavily female, influenced by location, insufficiently representative of older persons, and even characterized by certain economic levels. With the popularity of malls for teenagers, that phenomenon could also affect results. To generalize about the entire population from any of these limited samples would be misleading.

2. *Purposive sample.*   This sampling technique deals with groups possessing known characteristics. Let us suppose you were interested only in those people who frequented the neighborhood bar mentioned above. Or that you wanted to know what American Legion members thought about the all-volunteer army. Or what female athletes thought about contact sports.

Depending on your goals, this form of survey may have validity, but you shouldn't extend its findings beyond the scope of the audience surveyed.

3. *Quota sample.*   This sampling technique attempts to include in

the group surveyed the same sort of demographic percentages that occur in the total population about whom you want to gather data.

If 52 percent of a city's population consists of female residents, then the survey response should contain 52 percent of the replies from women. If 15 percent of the population is over 65 years of age, then the sample should mirror this statistic. If blacks consitute 10 percent of the city's ethnic mix, then they should be 10 percent of the interviewees. This, of course, is the ideal—it would be impossible to match *all* demographic aspects in one sample.

You can establish quota samples by age, occupation, income levels, and other characteristics. Although such findings might be quite useful, they could also reflect the bias, conscious or unconscious, of the person who selected the categories. If you opt for surveying persons over 65, you may have selected the wrong group for your purpose. You may also tend to interview a disproportionate number of men and women who are 65 or 66, and not many who are in their seventies or eighties.

Another error that could invalidate quota sample conclusions is the extrapolation of larger data from a limited number. Suppose you sampled 1,000 people in a town and 5 percent of them happened to be Seventh-Day Adventists. It would be wrong to draw any general conclusions about Seventh-Day Adventists based on these 50 people. To develop such data, you should survey 1,000 or more members of that faith.

Accidental, purposive, and quota samples all fall in the category of *nonprobability* sampling. That leaves *probability* sampling, which is the preferred method of major pollsters and researchers.

4. *Probability sample.* The theory behind the probability sampling technique is that every unit in the universe (which could be a district, a city, a state, a nation) has an equal chance of being represented. The key word here is "chance."

Probability sampling is generally misunderstood, sometimes misrepresented, and often mistrusted. Politicians who trail in polls complain, "How can you tell anything when you ask only 1,500 people?" Disgruntled television viewers who learn that their favorite program has been canceled because of low ratings are inclined to say, "Nobody ever called me to see what I think!"

That's not the point. You may never be called. But you *could* be called. There is a *chance* of your being called. And as long as nothing interferes artificially with this chance, and as long as the survey is relatively error-free, the results derived from surveying a minuscule portion of the population can be amazingly accurate. You can test this mathematically, and you can test it against actual results, as in an election.

Everyone hears about the failures—such as George Gallup's prediction of a Tom Dewey victory in 1948—but those misses are rare among the major pollsters, and they were caused by methods that are now obsolete.

The common explanation of probability sampling involves the sack of 10,000 marbles, half of which are blue and half red. Suppose you dip in a shovel and remove 600 marbles. Chances are there will be 300 blue and 300 red or, more likely, a slight variation, like 303 blue and 297 red. It would be extremely unlikely that the shovel would contain 550 blue marbles and only 50 red. Subsequent scoopfuls should be similar to the first sample—assuming you don't peek.

In *Public Opinion and Political Dynamics*, Marbury Bladen Ogle gives a more scientific basis for such "random sampling":

> Statistically speaking, the precision of the sample increases with the square root of the number of the persons interviewed. Suppose, for example, that 900 persons are questioned in an original sample. The square root of 900 is 30. Suppose then that the size of the sample is increased to 2,500, the square root of which is 50. The measure of confidence will then roughly approximate the ratio of 5 to 3. Thus, although the size of the sample is almost tripled, the ratio of confidence is somewhat less than doubled. As a result, when working samples of relatively large size, say two to ten thousand persons are involved, the addition of reasonably large numbers of respondents has little practical effect upon its accuracy.[9]

In less-scientific terms, this means that we can achieve reliable results with relatively few people and that adding more respondents to the survey won't affect the outcome significantly. Obviously you can't reach everyone. George Gallup once figured that if he polled 1,500 persons a week (the number now used for a total), "it would take us over 1,400 years, assuming a stable population" to cover the United States.

So if people are drawn randomly, if each person has an equal chance of being represented, the odds are that the results of such sampling will be sufficiently representative to serve as a reliable barometer of opinion.

Probability sampling is usually done geographically, by population levels. People are included not because they represent any particular characteristic of the population at large, but simply because of where they live.

What is a random sample?

Probability sampling requires that people to be surveyed be randomly selected. This doesn't mean casually and indifferently pointing your finger at a phone book, or choosing every "nth" number, or having someone's baby sister throw dice. In a sense, these methods are random, but there are too many chances for conscious or unconscious "skewing" in selection.

The only way to be truly random is to use a book or list of random numbers, a computerized catalog of numbers that are guaranteed to have no sequential relationship to one another.

You match these numbers, selected at random, against some list, such as a city directory, census list, or telephone book.

Suppose you had these three numbers in a random list:

23107   09411   10110

One use of these random digits would be to apply them to a phone book and select the 107th name on page 23; the eleventh name on page 94; and the tenth name on page 101. Obviously, the number of digits you select must bear some relationship to the document you are using. In a village with a phone book whose pages number only 70, you may use only part of the five digits, or use them to count characters, or whatever.

A common use of random numbers is as a starting point for probability sampling. Once you have established this point randomly, you can build on it by using a *regular interval* number. An example will clarify this.

Assume that George Gallup wants a sample of voters in a particular state. Let us say he wants 500 respondents and 50 *sampling points* (specific geographic locations). This means he will conduct cluster interviews in ten homes surrounding each of the sampling points in order to get his 500 interviews.

Gallup begins with the census data for that state, classifying the population of each county by size. He may establish six or seven—or more—levels, or "strata." One level might be cities of a million or more population; another could be cities of over 250,000; a third could be cities from 50,000 to 249,999; next would be urban areas surrounding these larger communities; then towns with populations of 2,500 to 49,999; then villages with less then 2,500 population; then the surrounding rural countryside. Using this method, a survey of Wyoming would obviously be conducted differently from a survey of Ohio, because there are fewer strata in Wyoming.

To avoid an alphabetical bias in listing counties, Gallup would draw a serpentine line through the state and would list counties as they fall along this line.

Since he plans 50 sampling points, he would divide the state's population by 50. If he were surveying Ohio, with a population of 10,797,624 (1980 census), this division would give him a result of 215,952—which is called the "interval number." The sampling points will then be houses across the state that are listed under census-list names that are 215,952 apart.

Where does Gallup start? He starts with a random number from one of the computerized lists. Let us say he selects 84055. The surveyor would then start with the census tract for the largest city (Cleveland), beginning with the first ward, first precinct, and continue until he reached name 84055. This address becomes his initial sampling point, and he conducts ten interviews in this immediate area.

Then he adds the interval number of 215,952 to 84055, resulting in a new number of 300,007. This becomes his next sampling point. He continues to add this interval number, proceeding from the larger cities to the rural areas, stratum by stratum, until he has completed his 50 points.

As you can see, Cleveland, with a population of 573,822, might have three sampling points. Some communities of moderate size might be skipped in the counting process, and entire counties might be excluded. This is what leads to citizen complaints that surveys can't be accurate when no one in a town the size of Tiffin (population 19,549) is even queried.

That's beside the point. People in Tiffin always had the *chance* to be included if the randomizing had worked differently. The selection process had nothing to do with trying to set up some quota system, or trying to eliminate Tiffinites. Respondents were selected solely on the basis of where they lived.

Other aspects of professional surveys seem even more arbitrary, but they come about as the result of experience. Pollsters may omit corner houses, for example, because past surveys demonstrate that people who inhabit corner houses exhibit certain similar patterns of response that are not typical of noncorner neighbors. Pollsters may also give added weight to people with less education, since such persons are usually underrepresented in surveys. They may also weigh respondents based on the number of evenings that they have been out that week and, consequently, the relative odds of catching them in.

Sampling error

Chance enters into even the most careful of surveys. Some error is bound to result.

"Sampling error" is the term used to describe the degree to which the results obtained in a single sampling might be expected to vary from the results achieved by gathering an infinite number of samples. If you surveyed all 573,822 persons in Cleveland, and did it properly, your results would be almost perfect. Such a procedure is impossible. Even if it were possible, it would be costly—and unnecessary.

Four thousand samples, properly drawn, will result in a sampling error of only 2 percent, and this is close enough for nearly every purpose. A sample of 1,500—which is a common sampling number—results in an error factor of plus or minus 3 percent— again an acceptable number. The fewer the samples, the higher the sampling error. With only 100 samples, the error could exceed 11 percent, and this would be unacceptable. This would mean that in a poll that showed candidate A leading candidate B by 55 percent to 45 percent, the actual statistics could vary by plus or minus 11 percent. Candidate A might be behind, or much further ahead.

The key to keeping down the sampling error does not depend on the total population involved; it depends on the number of samples taken. The 1,500 figure works for a large city, for a state, or for the entire United States.

Another way of expressing sampling error (which can be calculated by using the standard deviation formula that extracts the square root of a number achieved by multiplying positive and negative percentages and dividing that total by the sample number) is by talking about the "confidence level." A 95 confidence level is the standard—meaning that the sampling error is no more than 5 percent.

Sampling error is not the result of sloppy work; it is the natural consequence of working with limited numbers of the population.

What Are Surveys Looking For?

The general public is most familiar with political-preference surveys or tabulated results about social attitudes. However, questionnaires can be developed around almost any topic. Women in Communications Inc. wanted to know more about internships for college students. The views of grandparents were sought by National Distillers, primarily as a tie-in to their whiskey label. "Fear of Crime" was the subject of a Figgie International survey. Sociologist Kristin Luker uses research to create profiles of female adherents on both sides of the abortion issue, and George Gallup tests changing attitudes about the abortion debate. ("Do you ever wonder whether your own position on abortion is the right one or not?") Pollsters want to know how you personally feel about the economy, whether you've purchased any stocks or bonds recently, or if you have ever volunteered your services for a nonprofit cause. Developers are looking for the pros and cons of a certain geographical location, and marketing directors want to know if they should introduce a new product in summer or fall. How do Americans view their own national spirit? Should business be governed by a stricter code of ethics?

Simmons Market Research Bureau Inc. of New York focused on the teenage market and discovered that male teens are more loyal to brands than their female counterparts are, that females are more upset with nudity in films, and that more males than females consider staying single.[10]

For Phi Delta Kappa, Gallup conducts an annual poll of the public's attitude toward the public schools:

> Suppose the local public schools said they needed much more money. As you feel at this time, would you vote to raise taxes for this purpose, or would you vote against raising taxes for this purpose?
>
> Would you favor or oppose instruction in the schools that would deal with values and ethical behavior?[11]

Corporations may be looking for problem areas within the organization, and labor unions may be seeking reasons for membership reluctance in non-union shops. Fund raisers test the merits of different types and colors of letter paper, and Public Relations Society of America chapters want to know what sort of programming their professional members prefer. The Burlington Northern Railroad asks employees how they feel about the training they've received and how they consider their chances for advancement, and about their specific job situation:[12]

> The quality of my work does not suffer because of the amount of work I am expected to do.   Agree _____   Disagree _____

A professor at the University of Wisconsin–Milwaukee is studying "influences on male identity" and asks respondents to react to various statements in terms of the influence they've had on their lives:[13]

> A man is judged by how much money he makes and how he makes it.
> Men are supposed to be brave, take risks, and have adventures.

Although the subject matter varies widely, the precepts remain fairly constant. What organizations want to know can be limitless, but the way they seek this information, if done professionally, follows a similar set of guidelines.

Conducting the Survey

The most common methods of conducting surveys are by mail, by personal interview, and by telephone. Like everything else in public relations, each route has its plus and minus factors.

Mail surveys

Mail surveys are relatively inexpensive, particularly if bulk mail rates are used. They also take less time to circulate, permit the inclusion of more questions than the typical telephone interview, and allow the recipient time to reflect.

The percentage of returns, however, may be small; the reaction against unsolicited mail, detrimental; and the source of returns, inconclusive. The last shortcoming is the most important. You may be unable to determine where the responses came from, why certain people answered, and whether these returns truly mirror the sample as a whole. Only those most interested, for example, may send back the questionnaire. Or those who agree most with questionnaire proposals may be more inclined to respond.

If you can live with questionable accuracy, slow response rates, and high margins of error, mail surveys may suffice. Some experts also suggest ways to increase the response rate—by making use of follow-up letters, by personalizing the request, or by offering incentives, such as cash, books, pens, maps, stamps.

Those opting for the mail method had also better stay current with postal regulations, remembering that, after a year has expired, mail will no longer be forwarded to an old address; that return addresses work better on the front of the letter, since the postal worker doesn't have to turn the letter over to locate it; and that, when you mail to both an address and a post office box, the mail will be delivered to whichever item appears directly above the city, state, and ZIP code.

Personal interviewing

Personal interviewing may be the best and most complete method, but it is also the most expensive and time-consuming. The plus factors are the interviewer's opportunity to display exhibits, to observe reactions, to ask a greater number of questions, and to record answers in detail. The interviewer can go over a list of possible responses with the interviewee and can show charts, graphs, photos, and other items.

On the negative side, there is the problem of getting into the home, the reluctance of interviewers to venture into certain neighborhoods, the chance of interviewers inadvertently leading responses, and the cost—which could go from $25 up per interview, depending on the locale and the relative complexity of the survey instrument.

Phone surveys

Phone surveys are more frequent than other methods. They are the cheapest and fastest, and they allow for the greatest dispersal of respondents. The problems, however, are many:

- Respondents can't pursue exhibits.
- Interviewers can't normally determine race, age, or income level.
- Respondents are less likely to venture into controversial areas over the phone. They will be more positive or noncommittal. After all, they don't know you, but you obviously know something about them.
- Questions must be few, short, and easy to understand.
- Eleven percent of households have no telephone. Poor people, minorities, the elderly—all have fewer phones.
- Since the best time to call respondents is when there is the greatest chance of catching them at home, mealtime interruptions can be an irritant.
- There is a tendency—particularly among amateur interviewers—to give up too easily on callbacks and to merely move on to the next name in a phone book rather than to the next randomly selected name.

These shortcomings can all be overcome by skilled interviewers. A pleasant introduction, a statement that this will take very little time, and anything else that will win the interviewee's confidence are excellent preludes to the survey questions. Some interviewers start by amiably giving the interviewee their name, but this ploy is beginning to pale. The interviewer may also seek to determine whether or not he or she is speaking with the head of the household, with a registered voter, or with any other person whose characteristics fit the profile needs.

Some surveys combine two or more methods and may include "catch" questions to check on the honesty of the interviewee's responses or the surveyor's recording.

One current problem faced by phone-survey users is the proliferation of sales pitches disguised as interviews. The caller begins by pretending this is a legitimate survey, asking questions about you, your family, or your home, and then turns the conversation to insurance or real estate or even to "free" dance lessons. The practice has made respondents wary, but survey teams may combat this by assuring listeners at the outset that this is not a sales gimmick.

Timing

Interviewers not only have to be careful that their calls are conducted at a time when there is the best chance of reaching people, with the least chance of competition for attention; they should also avoid asking survey questions that would be influenced by current events.

Asking opinions on airline safety after a major crash is poor timing. So would a survey on foreign-student programs be poorly timed if asked during a hostage crisis.

Who Makes the Calls?

There is always a temptation, particularly among politicians, to use inexperienced volunteers as interviewers. If this is done, these people should be gathered in a central location and their calls should be monitored by an experienced supervisor. It is preferable to stick with professional interviewers. There is less danger of their influencing responses or evading guidelines. They are also more alert to shadings in answers, to surroundings, and to negative reactions of interviewees.

Professionals are also better at making callbacks in phone interviews, and they are more likely to remain within the randomizing system.

In a "Tips & Tactics" bulletin issued by *pr reporter*, William Friedman, of Ketchum MacLeod & Grove, suggests five ways amateurs can be more effective in small-scale surveys:

- Adopt a neutrality stance. Be a third-party listener. Be objective.
- Establish rapport, then let the people talk.
- Appeal to and respect the judgment of the respondent.
- Be flexible enough to give the respondent some leeway.
- Express your gratitude to the source.[14]

Some firms hire and train their own interviewers, often people who work part-time, finding this a more economical approach, especially where there is sufficient work to keep them occupied.

> A successful interviewer is one who is articulate, has a pleasing personality and the ability to follow specific instructions. Good interviewers come from all age groups and backgrounds. Since interviewing is part-time work, good candidates may be college students, retired individuals, widows, and young mothers who prefer to work just to get out of the home. Most are women, but men also make excellent interviewers.[15]

Interviewer recruits are normally given some training in technique, instructed to obey orders regarding questionnaires, alerted to possible problems inherent in certain questions, and regularly evaluated for their attitude, completion rate, accuracy, and other qualities.

Evaluating the Survey Results

Once the information has been collected, it must be analyzed. What do these responses mean? Sometimes the conclusions can be easily arrived at; sometimes they can be deceptively complex.

Suppose, for example, that you were sampling a key voting precinct and turned up results that showed your Republican candidate leading the Democratic opponent by 56 to 44 percent. On the surface, this is cause for optimism. On closer inspection, you realize that in the last election, the Democratic candidate received only 24 percent of the vote in that precinct. The Democratic candidate's gain to 44 percent is therefore a cause for concern, not euphoria.

Every survey has some hidden elements that should be scrutinized. Accepting every finding at face value can be misleading. You must know what you are looking for; you must be able to spot subtle changes; and you must understand what this array of statistics *really* means.

Many things can go wrong in surveys. Mullen and Bishop list half a dozen difficulties in an article touting the advantages of "in-depth, unstructured interviews with a sharply limited sample of respondents":

1. The problem or problems for investigation must be defined with precision.
2. The "universe" must be accurately identified.
3. Steps must be taken to ensure that the sample will be properly representative of this universe.
4. A series of questions must be prepared, the replies to which can lead logically to inferences concerning the problem(s). These questions must be free from bias.
5. The questions must be complete—anticipating all contingencies.
6. Reliable field workers must be recruited, trained, and properly supervised.[16]

They might have added that evaluation must be thorough and precise.

One problem that leads to a poor reputation for surveys is the way some newspaper polls are taken, without adequate sampling techniques or other safeguards. Elmo Roper, one of the premier pollsters, condemns some journalists for "impressionistic thinking" in citing the way elections are going. While appreciating the pressures of their deadlines, he has harsh words for their results:

> A preference for certainty over doubt, for the plausible over the proved, for drama over accuracy, for hunch and intuition over the hard-to-assemble facts, is a common human tendency. I suspect that we all tend to believe that what we personally feel, deep in our hearts, must be true—however many times we have been disillusioned by life's errant ways. But this tendency to trust our own intuitions, or those of our pal across the street, is precisely what we must avoid in attempting to measure the opinions of millions who do not live across the street.[17]

The Editor and the Polls

The public relations practitioner may not be directly involved in sampling or in the more technical aspects of polling. He or she may, however, have some input in drafting the questionnaire and making the evaluation. The PR person should also know enough about surveys to hire a reliable firm and recognize good work.

Then, too, the practitioner could be charged with drafting a news release based on the survey data. In this likely event, the writer should be prepared for sharp scrutiny from an alert editor or news director. This person will want to know such things as the following:

- Who paid for the survey?
- How many people were surveyed—and how (mail, phone, personal interview)?
- When was the survey taken?
- How were the questions worded?
- Who conducted the survey?
- Were the extracted results based on a small number of persons within the larger survey number?

A memorandum circulated to members of the National Association of Broadcasters cautioned broadcast news departments about the judicious use of stories based on polling results, concluding with this paragraph:

> The main point to remember is that polling is both an art and a science. Wise broadcast journalists will take it upon themselves to learn where one begins and the other leaves off and maintain high standards of integrity in reporting poll results.[18]

The most suspect polls are those associated with political candidates and issues. Many are difficult to interpret and, when erroneously reported, could be damaging. Others are poorly conceived and conducted, resulting in conclusions that may be highly inaccurate.

> "If I were a publisher, an editor or reporter, I would be very reluctant to publish any polls provided by candidates, given that the motive has to be one of self-interest," [Arizona Congressman John S.] McCain said.[19]

Still, surveys generate considerable publicity, especially when the results have obvious news value—like a list of cities deemed most livable and least livable, or a study of what traits produce negative reactions in job interviews, or citizen evaluation of performance by elected officials. Companies and organizations sometimes sponsor such research and later share it with the media, settling for a mention in the story or for quotes from a company executive.

Other Forms of Surveys

Some research firms select "minicommunities," on either a quota or a random basis, and use these panels of individuals for a limited period of time—perhaps one or two years. A large city may have several panels that are available to reply to any number of queries during that time period. If they are paid, their fee is nominal.

Typically, you would submit a question (or questions) to the research firm, paying so much per question. Trained phone interviewers would then call the panel members to secure responses. These may be broken down by age, sex, and other characteristics.

This is a fast, economical, and fairly reliable way to get replies on noncomplicated issues.

Magazines sometimes include a questionnaire insert, asking readers to select their favorite domestic airline or cruise line, or getting reactions to controversial issues, or merely requesting opinions on the magazine's content. These surveys suffer from the same limitations as mail surveys, since they are not random samples and there is no way to protect against bias.

Newspapers also conduct their own interviews, sometimes employing professional firms, sometimes inserting questionnaires in the paper, sometimes asking readers to call a certain number to register their votes, and sometimes opting for the accidental sampling method of man-on-the-street interviews.

Television has also adopted the call-in technique, and cable television added the possibility of nearly instantaneous polling via electronic means.

Mass-Media Testing

Our mass media conduct many tests to determine audience interest or reaction. The results of such testing are compiled into rating books, which, in turn, influence advertising decisions and eventually the continuation or discontinuation of certain radio and television programs. Ratings have always been controversial and suspect, but until a better means of evaluation is devised, they remain the best tool for the sponsors who provide the total revenue for radio and TV programs.

Devices like the *audimeter* are attached to television sets to monitor electronically the days, times, and channels viewed. *Diaries* are also left in homes (and a small fee paid the householder) so that the viewer can record specific programs he or she watched. An interviewer could also call on people and use any one of several techniques to solicit information:

- *Personal coincidental*—The householder is interviewed during a certain program in progress or during a specific time period and is merely asked what he or she is watching.
- *Personal roster recall*—The interviewer shows the viewer a list of programs and stations and asks the viewer which of these were turned on in his or her home.

- *Personal unaided recall*—Without producing a list, the interviewer asks the viewer what programs he or she remembers seeing during a limited time period.

This same sort of variation is possible over the telephone. The interviewer may call during a program (*telephone coincidental*) or may ask you to recall programs you have heard or watched (*telephone recall*).

A number of the techniques above may be combined to deepen the sample or validate responses.

Prominent names in such media research include Nielsen, Pulse, Hooper, Arbitron, and TVQ Inc.

> In the world of TV advertising, one thing is for certain, things move quickly after the rating books arrive. It takes only two or three days for TV sales departments to evaluate the ratings, demographics, and all the other information provided and to revise their advertising rate cards.[20]

Networks also test proposed programs, screening these "pilots" before audiences in cities like New York and Los Angeles. Viewers not only fill out questionnaires after a showing, but they also have green buttons to push if they like a program, red to push if they don't, and hands off if their feelings are neutral. Pilots are also fed into selected cable television homes, after which about 100 viewers are called for their opinions. These systems aren't foolproof. The initial screening panels didn't like "All in the Family" or "Mary Tyler Moore," but they did manage to save "Cheers" and "Hill Street Blues," which took time to find an audience. Some critics protest that you can't really test creative effort, especially in the short run under abnormal circumstances, but the desire to hedge their bets on increasingly expensive production costs keeps the networks involved.

> Hit or miss, market research will continue to play a crucial role in commercial TV, where the stakes are high and the success ratio low. Whether such efforts stifle creativity or merely help the networks give the public what it wants is something not even the Nielsens can know for sure.[21]

If anything, testing continues to get more sophisticated. British "people meters" are being experimented with in some American cities. These devices, which are attached to all sets in cooperating households, automatically record station viewing information and also have a device to single out (by ultrasound or infrared signal) the particular person watching. Even when you watch a show at a neighbor's house, you can record these data when you return home. Some 128 channels can be identified, along with eight different viewers. (Incidentally, as a public relations note, when the system was introduced in Boston, the sponsor was characterized as "a major international research company" rather than a British company, because of fears of possible Irish-American antagonism toward an English firm.)

Printed Media

For printed media, both aided and unaided recall are used, with an interviewer leafing through a magazine or newspaper with a subscriber, checking on his or her recollection of certain articles or advertisements.

The print ads are graded for reader awareness, sponsor indentification, and amount of copy read. The results of such surveys are often supplied to the advertiser, sometimes as a promotional campaign by individual publications.

Editors of internal company publications may also survey their readers, using a questionnaire to determine reading habits, preferences, omissions, irritants, and other opinions. Some editors merely check wastebaskets to see how many of their publications are unceremoniously dumped. They also enlist panels of experts to assist them and submit their work to professional judges, enter contests, save letters to the editor, or make deliberate errors to see if anyone notices.

CRITICISM OF RESEARCH

There is much criticism of research—not merely by the people who suspect the accuracy of the results but also by those who worry about the whole principle of predicting the future based on the present or the past.

Most of the problems with research, in terms of public acceptance, focus on skepticism about the sample numbers, confusion because of varied predictions, personal reluctance to accept the conclusions, and concern about the influence of published polls. From the pollsters' vantage point, the issues are escalating costs, the difficulty of achieving objectivity, and the proliferation of research firms, some of which are notably unprofessional.

Even though we are more cognizant of the highly visible polls, especially on political topics, we must remember that most of the survey research in the United States is done for commercial clients, and the results may never be made public.

Our penchant for devouring statistics also produces satirical observations by writers and humorists. When Ann Landers printed a survey finding that 72 percent of the female readers prefer cuddling to sex, Mike Royko, tongue in cheek, responded with his figures contending that two-thirds of American men preferred sex over bowling, drinking, golfing, and cuddling.

THE FUTURE OF RESEARCH

The only certain thing about the future of research is that many of the items discussed in this chapter will be radically altered. Computers will provide the major changes. They will be used to store and retrieve data, make comparisons, draw conclusions, total statistics, and write and edit news releases. All these tasks are being done at the moment by some companies, and when computers get within the range of even smaller PR departments, the effect will be dramatic.

Other electronic tools have direct or indirect meaning for research, from computer graphics, which allow last-minute changes in charts and data, to monitors in supermarket checkout stands, which not only provide price lists but also enable manufacturers to instantly check sales trends. Electronic mail speeds information, and public databases hooked to an office computer provide details about everything from the sale of canned peas to the forecast for corn production in 1990.

CHAPTER HIGHLIGHTS

- Research is an essential starting point in public relations programs, enabling practitioners to verify, clarify, and identify issues. The subjects researched are multitudinous, and public relations firms, after a slow start, are making increasing use of information-gathering techniques.
- Informal research methods include the use of libraries and printed materials, other archival collections, interviews, panels, content analysis, mail scrutiny, field reports, focus groups, and other techniques.
- Practitioners should also build their own libraries and devise an efficient way to store printed material and photos.
- Formal research refers to surveys, which require professional consideration of the problem to be solved and the questions to be asked.
- Survey samples may be accidental, purposive, or quota samples (all of which are nonprobability choices), or probability samples, which require geographic randomization. A confidence level of 95 percent is considered necessary.
- The common ways to conduct surveys are by personal interviews, telephone polls, and mail questionnaires. Media testing may use these means plus electronic aids. In all forms, the people preparing, conducting, and evaluating the project are the key.
- Editors should regard all polls critically and check to be certain they are news and not propaganda.
- Although subject to suspicion and criticism, polls remain popular, and electronic innovations will make them more efficient, effective, and accurate.

NOTES

[1]Patrick Jackson, *Communication Briefings*, a monthly newsletter, 1985 sample issue, Blackwood, N.J.

[2]Peter Finn, "In-House Research Becomes a Factor." Reprinted with permission from the July 1984 issue of the *Public Relations Journal.* Copyright 1984.

[3]"The Keys to Library Research," *Impact,* No. 106 (1969).

[4]"How to Build a Morgue," *Impact,* No. 182 (1976).

[5]*The Ragan Report,* May 17, 1982.

[6]Senator Orrin G. Hatch, January 1975.

[7]Congressman Hal Daub, January 1983.

[8]*Washington Post*/ABC telephone poll, conducted January 11–16, 1985.

[9]Marbury Bladen Ogle, Jr., *Public Opinion and Political Dynamics* (Boston: Houghton Mifflin, 1950).

[10]"Simmons Study Finds Male Teens Are More Brand Loyal Than Females," *Adweek,* September 28, 1981.

[11]George H. Gallup, "Gallup Poll of the Public's Attitude toward the Public Schools," reported in *Phi Delta Kappan,* September 1981.

[12]*BN News,* April 1984.

[13]Ian Harris, School of Education, University of Wisconsin–Milwaukee.

[14]William Friedman, "A Basic Training Document: Guidelines for Small-Scale, Do-It-Yourself Telephone Surveys," "Tips & Tactics," *pr reporter,* Vol. 19, No. 19 (October 5, 1981).

[15]Elnora W. Stuart, "Hiring and Training In-House Interviewers," *Public Relations Journal,* July 1984.

[16]James J. Mullen and Michael E. Bishop, "Clinical Interviewing in Public Relations Research," *Public Relations Quarterly,* Spring 1975.

[17]Elmo Roper, "A Plea for the Polls," *Columbia Journalism Review,* Fall 1962.

[18]Richard V. Ducey, "Public Opinion Polling as a Newsroom Resource," *National Association of Broadcasters Research Memo,* February 1984.

[19]M.L. Stein, "Relying on Polls," *Editor & Publisher,* October 6, 1984.

[20]Dave Rhein, "The Ratings Game," *Des Moines Sunday Register,* January 9, 1983.

[21]Louis Weisberg, "Audience Reaction Steers TV Pilots," *Advertising Age,* February 28, 1985.

SUGGESTED READINGS

BABBIE, EARL, *The Practice of Social Research,* 3rd ed. Belmont, Calif.: Wadsworth, 1983.

BACKSTROM, CHARLES H., and GERALD D. HURSH, *Survey Research,* 2nd ed. New York: Wiley, 1981.

BAILEY, KENNETH D., *Methods of Social Research,* 2nd ed. New York: Free Press, 1982.

BLALOCK, H.M., Jr., *Conceptualization and Measurement in the Social Sciences.* Beverly Hills, Calif.: Sage, 1982.

COZBY, PAUL, *Methods in Behavioral Research,* 2nd ed. Palo Alto, Calif.: Mayfield, 1981.

GALLUP, GEORGE, and CRAIG NORBACK, *America Wants to Know: The Issues and the Answers for the Eighties.* Madison, N.Y.: A & W Press, 1983.

KRIPPENDORFF, KLAUS, *Content Analysis: An Introduction to Its Methodology*. Beverly Hills, Calif.: Sage, 1980.

Marquis Who's Who, nearly 60 different volumes covering the United States and foreign countries and surveying a variety of occupations and professions. Chicago: Marquis, annually.

PATTON, MICHAEL QUINN, *Qualitative Evaluation Methods*. Beverly Hills, Calif.: Sage, 1980.

RIVERS, WILLIAM L., *Finding Facts: Interviewing, Observing, Using Reference Sources*. Englewood Cliffs, N.J.: Prentice-Hall, 1975.

SUDMAN, SEYMOUR, and NORMAN M. BRADBURN, *Asking Questions: A Practical Guide to Questionnaire Design*. San Francisco: Jossey-Bass, 1982.

WIMMER, ROGER D., and JOSEPH R. DOMINICK, *Mass Media Research*. Belmont, Calif.: Wadsworth, 1983.

1980 U.S. Census: Population and Housing Characteristics. National Decisions Systems, 1983.

Public Relations Review. College Park, Md.: University of Maryland.

EXERCISES

1. Interview one of the veteran employees of a local firm or institution, concentrating on some past events—plant opening, addition, anniversary, new president, or whatever. Check this person's recollections against contemporary accounts to be found in the local newspaper files.

2. Locate four stories in your local paper that either quote the results of surveys or are based on the results of surveys.

3. Select a current issue and see how many references you can locate on this subject in your college or local library.

4. Select a current national or international figure and research his or her background, using the library.

5. You are the public relations director for your university, and you want to determine whether students at this university can *afford* a $25 per-credit-hour tuition increase, whether they are *willing* to consider such an increase, whether they would *remain* in school if such an increase were instituted, and what sort of *expectations* they would have as a result of this increase.

   a. Write a questionnaire to achieve these goals.

   b. Decide on a sampling method.

   c. Conduct the survey.

   d. Evaluate the results.

   (This would be most effective as a class project, with students agreeing on the final form of the questionnaire, sharing the interviewing load, and, as a class, discussing the findings.)

CASE PROBLEMS

1. A 1985 *Travel Weekly* study claimed that an eight-day recreational-vehicle trip for a family of four was far cheaper than a similar trip using car-hotel, train-hotel, bus-hotel, or air-hotel combinations, "regardless of distance, duration, or regions visited." Assuming you are the PR director for a national bus line and wanted to respond to this assertion, what sort of information would you gather? What sort of things would you want to know about the original study?

2. Howard Johnson's, in a 1985 print advertisement, called attention to a "recent independent survey of business travelers" that stated that "our guests rated us a good deal higher than Holiday Inn (for room decor), than Ramada (for staff efficiency), than Best Western (for wake-up and message service) guests rated them." Assuming you were the public relations director for Holiday Inn, Ramada, or Best Western, what observations would you make about these survey statements?

3. A national brand of cigarettes advertised its product as having "less tar than the average of the ten other leading brands." Where is the flaw in this statement?

4. Here is a question asked in a survey: "When a movie or entertainment star endorses a candidate, does it have any effect on the way you vote?" Any comments on this question?

5. This question was asked of 593 people: "What maximum speed do you set for yourself when highway driving?" Of those interviewed, 52 percent stated that they drove 55 miles per hour or less on the highways. What other means would you use to validate or contest these data?

4

PUBLIC RELATIONS PLANNING AND CREATIVITY

Once the public relations practitioner has assembled the raw data—the product of research—and has considered the modifications dictated by the current environment, he or she is ready to enter the planning stage.

Planning is nothing more than the determination of goals for an organization and the outlining of means to achieve these goals.

Fund raisers have a slogan: Plan your work, then work your plan. This is sound advice. No one would lay carpeting or cut out a garment without a pattern. And a contractor doesn't pour a foundation without studying the architect's blueprint. If the pattern and the planning are accurate, the work goes smoothly; if not, the project founders.

Planning encompasses every phase of a business or organization, and it involves personnel at every level. Public relations professionals not only employ planning in their work but must also be cognizant of the planning of others that affects their function.

Planning may be positive, preventive, or remedial. A PR person may want to originate a salutary project or may anticipate a negative situation and take measures to prevent it, or may have to correct an already harmful condition.

A cable TV company ran a full-page advertisement in the Sunday paper, promoting its security service. The response was good, but when the interested customers phoned the number given in the ad, they heard a recording; the cable company was closed on Sunday. Eighty percent of the callers hung up without giving their names.

Conversely, New College, Oxford, founded in the late sixteenth century in England, discovered a few years ago that the oak beams in its great dining hall were being eroded by beetles, a fate common to oak beams everywhere. The disconsolate College Council, certain that no oak beams of that caliber were available nowadays, summoned the College Forester, the person responsible for tending College lands. He said he was expecting their call and was able to reassure them. When the College was built, a grove of oaks was also planted, against the day when beetles would ravage the original beams. Now 400 years old, these oaks were ready for "harvesting" as replacement beams. This plan had been passed down from Forester to Forester from the time of Queen Elizabeth I.

Planning affects the large picture and the small picture. Some economists are arguing for international government intervention in economic planning as mass production becomes more flexible and supply and demand more imbalanced. At the same time, luncheon hosts are discussing the menu with a caterer and invitations with the printer.

STEPS IN PLANNING

Although each plan has its own unique features, the steps taken in planning are rather similar:

1. Gathering of data
2. Analysis of data
3. Identification of problem or opportunity
4. Examination of past experience
5. Examination of the experience of others
6. Consideration of future developments
7. Evaluation of alternatives
8. Selection of the best alternative
9. Weighing of positive and negative factors
10. Implementation of plan
11. Monitoring of plan

Gathering of Data

All the information necessary to a thoughtful and thorough consideration of the subject should be assembled. Collecting such data may mean the employing of both formal and informal research methods. Many companies have their own research divisions that can produce such details and thus ensure more reliable decisions.

Planners must also know their own organization well, understanding who they are and who they are not, what their strengths and weaknesses are, where they are going, and who their target audiences are.

Once derived, this research information should be organized into easily understood units so that participants in planning may have ready access to what they need.

Figure 4-1 Every intelligent program begins with planning.

Analysis of Data

The facts are examined—realistically. This takes an open mind and more than a little skill. Each piece of evidence is sifted for meaning. Each element is examined for potential harm or help to the institution. Future developments are postulated, and relationships to organizational goals are studied.

Identification of Problem or Opportunity

After sufficient discussion, the problem or opportunity should emerge. The company may discern that it is falling behind the competition in certain sales areas. The public relations director may isolate a rumor that is destroying employee morale. A news bureau chief senses a publicity coup.

Whatever the focus becomes in this planning facet, every attempt should be made to produce a conclusion that is both specific and clear.

Examination of Past Experience

If history repeats itself, then so do problems. Faced with a difficulty, practitioners should review their own experience for similar situations and should check the records to determine the root causes. Success or failure with related situations in the past may exhibit clues for future conduct.

Suppose a financial public relations adviser is proposing a breakfast meeting of all regional financial analysts. In checking past records, he or she discovers that a similar breakfast held four years earlier was poorly attended, and there were complaints about the early hour. This should lead to the adviser's contacting a sampling of analysts to see if this situation still exists. If it does, a change in time should be considered.

When one of the newly created telephone companies reviewed its hiring practices with an eye toward attracting applicants with broader backgrounds, it examined its past record on bias in selecting interviewees, its testing routines, the entry-level jobs it had offered successful candidates, recurring deficiencies it had noted in applicants, its integration of women and minorities into various departments, and its record of conformity with national norms.

Examination of the Experience of Others

Few topics in public relations are unique. Chances are that all PR problems have been experienced somewhere else and that all innovations have precedents.

Many associations maintain lending libraries of case histories. CASE (Council for the Advancement and Support of Education), for example, an amalgam of collegiate fund raisers, alumni officers, and public relations directors, keeps elaborate files on all sorts of subjects, from class picnics to multimedia recruiting tools. Other associations may incorporate case histories as part of their regular publications.

There will be others, who can be reached by phone or mail or in person, whose counsel may save the practitioner from costly error. Those conducting an anniversary celebration for their company or organization would certainly want to review the printed or oral record of those who have managed a similar event; those assembling their initial PR plan would be aided by a look at an existing plan.

Consideration of Future Developments

Planners always consider the effect of the future on the programs being inaugurated. Although the future cannot be predicted with certainty, there are observable signs that may indicate caution or encourage optimism. This is where the knowledge of trends helps.

"In reality," states planner Lyle D. Reed, vice-president of Burlington Northern Railroad, "the long run is just a series of short runs, [and] we try to look beyond the short run to examine the long-run inputs of our plans and directions."

Evaluation of Alternatives

Every problem has more than one solution. In planning sessions, alternatives are laid on the table for consideration. Most of these suggestions have plus or minus features. Frequently, they will compete with one another. Anything from the selection of a date to the introduction of a new product will have its list of choices. The greater the number of options one has (up to a point), the greater the likelihood of a prudent, effective recommendation.

Selection of the Best Alternative

After the alternatives have been weighed, a decision must be made. Sometimes planners get bogged down in the process itself, convinced that the very act of planning is the end and not the means. This cannot be allowed to happen. Ultimately some proposal must win acceptance and some method must be adopted.

Weighing of Positive and Negative Factors

When a specific alternative has been embraced, there should be further discussion about the consequences of this choice. What harm could result? What publics might be adversely affected? What future difficulties might arise? Can we afford it?

If we allow employees a discount on the automobiles we manufacture, will this action irritate the stockholders? If we institute a fringe benefit offering tuition-free scholarships to the children of employees, will we be able to handle the escalating college costs in the years ahead?

Implementation of Plan

At an appropriate time, the plan is launched, and its dictates are pursued until the goal is reached or until the planners are convinced the attempt is a failure. In the latter case, it's back to the drawing board and the process repeats itself.

During the implementation phase of any plan, cooperation and commitment are required. This suggests that key people should be involved early and their support won, and that all others should be indoctrinated as soon as the plan is operable. If important personnel drag their feet, if funding dries up, if too little time has been allowed, if significant publics have been ignored—these and other lapses could doom an otherwise satisfactory plan.

Monitoring of Plan

As the plan is being implemented, the professional practitioner makes observations, obtains feedback from participants, and draws preliminary conclusions. If results look questionable, some adjustments may be required. If, on the other hand, the plan is working out better than expected, this may be the time to commit additional money and personnel to exploit the success. Conversely, if the implementation phase if faring badly, this may counsel cancellation. There is no sense in waiting until disaster strikes.

PUBLIC RELATIONS PLANNING

Just as with other divisions of a company or organization, public relations personnel have to compose, implement, and evaluate their own specific plan. As they do so, the overall goals of the employer or client must be considered, along with the possible effect on society.

One technique used by practitioners in developing their plans is called the "communications audit," which is described by Joyce F. Jones as "a broad-scale, loosely structured research study exploring a company's public relations both internally and externally. The purpose of the external phase of the audit is to use key members of key publics, in effect, as consultants for the company."[1]

Jones characterizes the process as discovering any disparity between what the company's administrators think and the way key publics perceive the company, and then recommending a program to close the gap. She considers an audit advisable when there are changes in management or in public relations, when earnings are dropping, whenever PR or advertising practices are studied, and whenever the public relations director seeks a clearer mandate from management.

STRATEGIC THINKING

Burlington Northern's long-range strategic plan calls for the successful implementation of the company's basic strategy: to prosper in a competitive low-growth environment.

BN's strategy is based on four premises:

- *Cost Reduction*. The company, facing intense competition from low-cost owner/operator truckers, plans to continue to be profitable by emphasizing consistent service, while meeting or beating the price charged by the competition.
- *Marketing Strategies*. The company's aim is to focus on growth through new markets designed to maximize the present value of freight markets. In other words, reduce activity in areas that are unprofitable while expanding in more attractive ones.
- *Asset Productivity*. Plans call for a gradual reduction in the railroad's roadway base without sacrificing revenue from secondary feeder routes.

- *People.* Plans are to further create a working environment in which each person can perform to the fullest of his or her abilities. The importance of each job will be stressed, along with a more participatory management philosophy to create incentives for higher productivity.

BN's strategic plan—projected out to the year 1999—is the company's most tangible product of the planning process. Its purpose is to identify and understand the forces which will affect the company's future.

Although projected over the next 15 years, the plan is not overly rigid. Instead it is a tool in a continuous process, updated annually.

Personal and departmental goals are developed for the coming year—complete with objectives and methods of measurement. They are forged into action plans for the future that support the company's short- and long-range objectives and strategies.

BN's overall plan also lists indicators for measuring progress by describing the present environment and projecting the future.

The plan anticipates that future years will continue to be highlighted by a challenging competitive environment for the railroad. Although 1984 was a strong recovery year, the outlook for 1985 and the years beyond is for slow economic growth and intensified competition—from both motor carriers and other railroads.

Projecting future economic conditions, the plan anticipates that any substantial traffic volume increase will come from increasing BN's market share—not from an overall growth in the market.

Charts and graphs outline anticipated revenue, ton miles, diesel fuel prices, changes in the prime interest rate and the consumer price index and indicate the limited economic growth in volume over the next few years.

While a financial section deals with such concepts as revenue forecasts, work force projections, capital expenditures such as track programs, and budgets and earnings, the plan's strategic section lists actions to be taken—particularly in the area of competition.

Heightened competitive pressures in 1985 are anticipated—the first full year of the Chicago and North Western coal operation in the Powder River Basin. Intense competition is expected to exert downward pressure on prices, and in most cases prevent full recovery of inflationary cost increase.

Ultimately, the plan calls for BN to be THE competitive leader in the transportation industry by serving markets aggressively, attracting traffic from competing modes, capitalizing on intermodal capabilities, and penetrating markets beyond rail lines while retaining profitable BN traffic susceptible to diversion.

SOURCE: Courtesy of *BN News,* January/February 1985.

When things are going fairly smoothly, public relations practitioners are often reluctant to examine their programming, even though it may be operating under guidelines fashioned years earlier, when the company was substantially different.

Writing in *Public Relations Journal*, Elaine Goldman concludes, "It's amazing how many corporate communication departments are outdated, even in *Fortune* 500 companies."[2] She poses a series of questions to help professionals determine whether or not the communications system needs overhauling:

1. Have the corporate objectives been delineated in terms of such factors as your company's business, markets, capital needs, growth plans, industry, and, most significant, the vision of the chief executive officer?

2. Is your company in a business that is becoming increasingly more affected by such external factors as government regulation, industry maturity, increased competition, changing structures of capital markets, new technologies, and public attitudes? Does your company need more representation on Capitol Hill?

3. If your chairman is fairly new, how are his or her methods different from those of the previous chairman? Does the chairman want high visibility or prefer to function internally? How does the chairman perceive visibility as a corporate tool? How does the chairman perceive the role of communication in marketing?

4. Have the capital-market needs of the company changed? Does the company need to be better known to the financial community?

5. Have the relationships between internal and external communication changed?

6. Is the communication strategy for positioning the company supported by all divisions, and in all published materials (including advertising)? Does the communication department structure support this concept?

7. Do communication employees have strong skills?

8. Have orientations changed? For example, has corporate presence become more important than marketing presence? Should investor relations have a higher profile? Is product exposure becoming more of a factor than institutional visibility?

9. Should the company participate more in debates on issues that affect its business climate?

10. Are departmental lines of reporting and responsibility responsive to the needs of the company?"[3]

While these elements are being weighed, the PR person must also be considering what affect various publics, including competition, may have on the organization; must be aware of what the media are saying about the company; and should be up on new legislation that could alter the way the firm does business.

Like any other plan, the public relations plan starts with fact gathering, pays attention to the publics involved and to the competition, sets down realizable goals, delineates ways of reaching these goals, and builds in a system of evaluation. Wise planners also make sure they don't commit all their time to the new regimen. Some unforeseen circumstances are certain to crop up and will require immediate action, so the practitioner should have some contingency time to be used for emergencies. The planner must also keep things in balance, remembering all the tasks at hand and allotting appropriate amounts of time for each.

Communicators must persevere in their planning, even though they know that an organization's future plans may not always give public relations the billing it deserves.

> Managements always have been obliged to identify first with their marketing and profit responsibilities. The emphasis may vary, but not the priority.[4]

Perhaps there is some consolation in the recognition that a company's plans rank first in terms of what employees read in company publications, scoring higher than personnel policies and job advancement. And there may be some adjunct psychic benefits.

> Giving the public relations staff the opportunity to participate in management—to see its own thoughts help form program plans—can increase creativity, efficiency and the overall effectiveness of the public relations function.[5]

ELEMENTS OF A PLAN

Any plan involves six elements:

1. The reason for the plan
2. The goals or objectives of the plan
3. The current status of the organization vis-à-vis these objectives
4. The methods of implementation to be used
5. The target audiences
6. The cost

Every plan should have a purpose, or *reason for being*. Manufacturers want to increase sales; promoters want to build attendance; politicians want to ensure elections. A hospital public relations director may want to correct a misinterpretation of hospital charges, or expand publicity coverage, or blunt the attack of an opposition group.

Goals and *objectives* will also vary. These are not interchangeable terms. Goals are usually described as the end result of a campaign (or a series of campaigns), whereas objectives constitute the things that must be done to reach these goals.

An advertising campaign for a brand of hand soap might seek to increase its share of market by 5 percent. The objectives would then include a strong advertising campaign, increased dealer participation, new marketing techniques, additional shipping schedules, pricing considerations, and other factors.

The current *relationship* of the organization to the goals and objectives must be determined. Perhaps only slight adjustments must be made, because the institution is already close to its goal. This plan may be short and simple. If, on the other hand, the goals are far removed from present reality, considerable planning will be mandatory.

Actions to be taken or *methods* to be employed are spelled out. These are specific activities under each objective. Now that the planners have decided what they want to do and why, they must wrestle with "how."

Let us assume the need is to neutralize a group of neighborhood protestors who are blocking a proposed low-income housing site in their area. The goal in this case is to provide low-income housing for deprived citizens, and the objective is to remove the roadblock of protest. Should the issue be forced through the courts? Should the objectors be invited to a public forum? Should literature be mailed to all dissidents? Should a media campaign be waged to discredit the motives of the neighborhood group? Should the poor be mobilized to hold a counterprotest?

One or more of these alternatives may be selected, weighed, and implemented.

Also requiring consideration is the *audience* for communications. Who are the people who must be reached? Where are they located, and what is the most effective and efficient way to reach them? When is the best time to make contact?

Careful planners list all possible target audiences, perhaps breaking them into primary and secondary publics. No relevant group should be omitted. It is safer to err on the side of encompassing too broad a public segment than to take the chance of missing a vital group.

The trick, of course, is to personalize the approach to each group as much as possible. In a hospital, the physician might receive a different message than the nurse, and the nurse a different message than the trustee or patient. Faculty, students, and alumni would be treated in different ways, since their interests and information vary. Military units would have unique communications for legislators, senior officers, junior officers, enlisted personnel, and hometown newspapers.

The more the practitioner knows about each group, the better the message he or she can design.

Budgeting

Obviously, *cost* enters into nearly every plan. When you are examining the accepted plan for weaknesses, you must consider the budget requirements. Perhaps the most effective way to communicate with a specific audience is via prime-time television—but can you afford it? The price of paper, printing, and postage may limit your direct-mail appeal to a smaller segment of the populace than you initially intended.

Although dollar amounts may be important in themselves, even more important is the effectiveness of those dollars. Television, for example, may still be the best solution, even though it costs much more, because it reaches more of the people you want to reach at a lower per-unit cost.

Planners must know what things cost and must not guess at prices. They must also be realistic and not let their desire for a solution cloud their reason.

Some plans start with a set budget figure and everything is tailored to fit. ("You have ten thousand to spend on this party and that's it.")

Others first outline things to be accomplished, then put dollar figures on them, and then request a commensurate budget.

Too much of the budgeting for public relations (and for advertising) is haphazard. Some figures are virtually pulled out of a hat. Others are extensions of a previous year's expenditures, or a match for a competitor's expenses, or the result of someone's reading that a certain percentage of profits should be allocated to advertising and promotion.

There is no magic percentage that covers all situations. It is not 5 percent or 10 percent. It could be more or it could be less.

The sanest concept is to match the budget to the need. What will it take to do the job properly? An organization just starting up may need to commit a higher percentage of its profits than one with an established reputation. A firm with nationwide clients is going to find it more expensive to communicate than will a local company.

"There are two approaches to managing a public relations operation," declares Jack Tucker, senior vice-president and director of public relations for Keyes, Martin & Company in New Jersey. "A business approach, or a gamble. The former rests on sound principles of budgeting and cost control; the latter doesn't. . . . Any effort lacking these two cornerstones will fail for one of three reasons:

1. The program has to be stopped at a critical point because there isn't enough money to continue.
2. The original program has to be drastically altered in order to stretch the remaining dollars.
3. The program ends up so expensive that benefits cannot justify the cost."[6]

Intelligent budgeting takes into account not only the more easily tracked items, but also the cost of staff time and of local services (phone, photocopying, and the like). These costs have all been escalating in the 1980s. Printing, envelopes, professional dues, and paper have risen most, with postage not far behind. Salaries have tended to grow more slowly. But they are all cost items. Some nonprofit organizations have been hardest hit, having to slash their personnel and services to accommodate federal and state cutbacks.

The budget for any activity is both a "goal" and a "control." You strive to stay within the amount originally determined, and you use this figure to decide on and to monitor expenses. That's why careful attention should be given to this factor in the early stages of planning and why it also needs constant administration.

As with any other aspect of public relations, you first do your research, ascertaining what expenses are likely to be and what objectives will be realized. Then you approve or cut, communicating the budget figures to others and monitoring their use.

It's a smart practice to list all conceivable expenditures for any PR activity and to talk these over with others who might provide input. Make certain that you have included all possible expenditures and that you've left a cushion for emergencies. Succeeding chapters mention some specific applications of the budget to items such as advertising, production, special events, and political campaigns. Regardless of the variations, good budgeting technique involves common sense, detailed analysis, experience, and administrative courage and ability.

No one can escape budgeting; this is obvious. Even when you plan a personal vacation, you include transportation; lodging; meals; fees for entertainment; tips, perhaps, if you are a careful budgeter; even airport taxes, luggage transfers, refreshments, and gifts. Planning for a major public relations event is similar—only the items are different.

PRIORITIES

One plan usually gives rise to another. If you are to accomplish *this*, you must do *this*. Some plans will have priority over others, and some activities must take precedence over others.

According to a veteran public relations executive, John F. Budd, the key words in any PR program are *priority* and *discipline*:

> Priority demands that your common sense recognize that any program must have a realistic, achievable goal. . . . By discipline, I mean the guts to stick to the plan and the program and not be seduced by peripheral projects, the spontaneity of which is always more appealing than the drudgery of programmed commitments.[7]

Budd cautions the practitioner to weigh one assignment against another, and to orient the program to the objectives of the corporation. He suggests allocation of time on a percentage basis, and the listing of priorities as primary, secondary, and optional:

. . . you can't spend all of your time writing stories; you can't spend all of your time being available to the "drop-in" trade, visiting plant managers for internal good will purposes, or sitting in on interminable meetings.[8]

MAKING THE MOST OF YOUR TIME

According to management consultant R. James Steffen, most people in business could increase their productivity by a third or more if they would learn to control their activities, expend their energies wisely, and concentrate on the most important and immediate task. He advocates writing goals down weekly, then daily, then checking them each evening to see what has been accomplished.[9]

Harvard professor John Kotter argues with the notion of listing everything, preferring a looser agenda, "more like a big complex map constructed over time." Kotter's analysis of good managers convinced him that they accomplished more by talking to others than they did by cranking out reports or shouting orders.[10]

Figure 4-2 Planning calendars are a necessity. This one serves as a guide to advertisers during a newpaper's centennial year.
Courtesy: *Omaha World Herald*

There's a cottage industry devoted to helping people make better use of their time. Books abound on the subject, and periodic conferences promise to teach you "How to Get Things Done!" In these sessions you learn how to say no, how to cope with interruptions, how to deal with superiors, how to avoid doing everything yourself, and how to recognize when you should let well enough alone.

Other experts counsel short vacations to refresh the mind; the setting of time limits on each working day; developing the ability to laugh at your mistakes; getting more mileage out of each thing you do; and learning what you must do, what you can defer, what you can delegate, and what you can forget.

"Work smarter, not harder," they advise.

DECISION MAKING

All the research and planning go for naught if the person who controls the implementation process can't make a decision—or won't make a decision. Some executives can't stand being wrong, or they fear reprisals, or they don't want to chance losing any friendships. They may appeal to higher authority, try to find a safe, standard solution, pass the buck to a subordinate, clutch wildly at an apparent solution, or do nothing and hope the problem will disappear.

The informed and confident executive, however, is not cowed by a challenge. Having diligently passed through the planning process, this exec selects and blesses one of the options. The ability and willingness to do this is one characteristic that sets good managers apart.

TYPES OF PLANNING

Short- and Long-Range Plans

Short-range plans are intended to meet a somewhat immediate need, whereas long-range plans attempt to forecast future trends or state future goals. The latter may have a scope of five, ten, or more years.

Chief executives are likely to spend a high percentage of their planning time on long-range matters, whereas departmental supervisors or shop supervisors may concentrate more on plans for that day, week, or month.

Short-range planning takes less time to create and is specific. Long-range planning takes longer, is more general, and, because of the time lag, is more prone to error.

Every organization should have a long-range plan. This is the only way to exhibit corporate leadership, to integrate individual and departmental efforts, to act rather than react, and to enjoy the relative luxury of some deliberation time in periods of crisis.

From the public relations viewpoint, long-range planning prevents myriad headaches. Unless there is a plan, it is difficult to assess daily chores properly, or to measure results, or to document efficiency for a client or supervisor, or to convince a comptroller of the need for funds.

With proper planning, new programs can be boldly formulated instead of being timidly defended. Real needs can be demonstrated and a sense of direction established.

Strategic and Tactical Plans

Strategic plans, somewhat like long-range plans, deal with the establishment of organizational goals and the development of policies to achieve these goals, whereas tactical plans refer to specific methods for reaching these goals. In military parlance, the strategic aims would be to win the war or a certain campaign; the tactical maneuvers would focus on specific battles or engagements.

Assume that a large insurance company wants to move into the malpractice insurance field and, within a given number of years, intends to dominate this field. All of this it wants to accomplish without reducing the profitability of existing programs. Those are goals, or strategic plans. The tactics, then, would describe ways to move toward dominance—a competitive rate structure, augmented sales force, attractive printed materials and sales tools, exhibits at health-related conventions, and wide publicity—particularly in medical journals, personal communication with medical leaders, and a massive advertising campaign.

One-Time Plans and Standing Plans

Some plans have a single, limited purpose—to celebrate a centennial or to produce a documentary film. Once the end is attained, the plan may be dissolved. Thus the one-time plan serves no ongoing function.

Standing plans, on the other hand, encompass management policies, standard operating procedures, and institutional or company rules.

Policies are general guidelines to assist in decision making. They could cover anything from proper attire to emergency leave.

Procedures explain how things are to be done—particularly things that occur with some frequency. Public relations departments may have a regular system for answering complaints, acknowledging donors, or typing a certain executive's speech.

Rules define what should and should not be done in a given situation. A publicity director may have an office rule that all envelopes to media outlets must be individually typed. A company may insist that all news items and brochures must clear through the PR office—a good rule, incidentally. Rules may be discarded on occasion, and they are often suspended to meet a unique situation.

OBSTACLES TO PLANNING

Despite the logic and necessity of planning, it is common for communications and events to be poorly planned. The reasons, or excuses, are numerous:

1. *Not enough time.* There may not be enough lead time to plan an event properly. Or the practitioner may be so busy "executing" that he or she takes no time to look ahead.

2. *Lack of confidence.* The practitioner may take a dim view of the planning process, or of the organization, or of his or her own abilities.

3. *Fear of failure.* Some PR people live in fear of having their ideas shot down. They play it safe, insulating themselves against complaints by continual busywork or by failing to bring plans to measurable fruition. This type of person cannot last long in such a visible profession.

4. *Resistance to change.* A number of executives enjoy the comfort of familiar routines. Their goals are outdated and their methods unimaginative—but they squeak by.

5. *Too much red tape.* Steering new concepts through channels may be so complicated that the practitioner doesn't even try. He or she could also be naive about organizational structures and ignorant of the way corporate actions are accomplished.

6. *Failure to understand the present environment.* Plans go awry because facts external to the organization were not considered. Several recent advertising campaigns had to be scrapped because they proved offensive to minorities or because they seemed "sexist" to female consumers.

7. *Not enough money or personnel.* Overworked executives may conclude that initiating any new program will simply add more work for them, so they sit on innovations. PR persons may feel, too, that the money to support their ideas will never be released, so they drop them. The situation could be real or imaginary. Increasing the mail contributions to a charitable institution won't work unless more personnel are added to process the increased returns.

8. *Vague company goals and objectives.* Unless the practitioner knows where the company intends to go and how it plans to get there, he or she cannot come up with satisfactory subplans.

9. *Exclusion of PR person from key meetings.* Some practitioners are summoned to the executive suite only after a crisis has arisen. No public relations program can function under these conditions. The PR director should insist on being part of the strategy team.

VARIATIONS IN PLANNING

No two circumstances are exactly alike. Organizational structures dictate some differences. So do such things as the nature of the business and the size of the institution or corporation. Small organizations obviously require less-complicated planning than large ones do. The whole gamut of extant internal and external conditions also influences planning.

Managerial styles vary. Some executives are cautious, even secretive, and confine planning tasks to relatively few people. Others possess a more open, liberal style, involving people at all levels and disseminating results widely.

Subject matter constitutes another variation. The purchasing officer's plans will differ from those of the public relations director. The former will be considering such elements as inventory, unit cost, availability, and future need, while the PR director will be studying target audiences, media response, and communication roadblocks.

There are also differences of opinion on "central planning" versus a design constructed at a lower level. Tom Peters, author of the very successful *In Search of Excellence*, comes down in favor of the latter regimen.

> . . . large, central corporate staffs that generate 35 notebooks, each 300 pages long, are a waste of time. Many give lip service to "the right stuff," like decentralized, bottom-up planning. But look at their apparently innocuous corporate "planning-guidance document," and you'll see that they have carved up space which should have been left to divisions. I'm in favor of sound strategic thinking and a well-drawn strategic plan—at the division level.[11]

Flexibility

Some flexibility should be built into every plan. Nothing will work exactly as diagrammed. Costs may escalate, people may stumble, the environment can alter drastically, and goals may change. Instead of becoming upset when such cogs appear, the professional should be able to shift gears and save at least part of the plan.

Timing

An otherwise good plan may be ahead of its time; people aren't ready for it. It may also be too late; the mood has passed. Knowing exactly when to inaugurate a program takes considerable skill.

Timing in planning is like training in athletics. The runner and the boxer attempt to peak at the race or bout. In the same way, plans are most effective when they reach a somewhat conditioned audience.

Another timing caution is that planners must always allow sufficient time for their objectives to be realized. You can't decide to raise $4 million on Thursday and schedule a kickoff breakfast for the following Monday.

Appropriateness

Plans should be appropriate to the organization or institution. They must be able to win management's support and should be matched to the resources of the sponsor.

More than that, they should also be appropriate in themselves, and in terms of the image and goals of the institution. A downtown treasure hunt may be properly sponsored by a merchants' group but may be inappropriate for a cancer-research institute. Establishing a scholarship fund for underprivileged students could be good public relations for a corporation but a questionable move for a private hospital.

SOME PLANNING TECHNIQUES

A couple of decades ago, the magic word was *brainstorming*, a tactic that was employed primarily by advertising agencies but that made inroads into all kinds of institutions. This formula demanded that, at planning meetings, no one interrupt the flow of positive ideas unless it were to "hitchhike" on the original thought with another positive suggestion. Every proposal, brilliant or naive, was laid on the table. Only after these offerings were exhausted was any evaluation made. Although this practice has virtually disappeared, it did have its good points.

It can be maddening to listen uncritically to suggestions that are patently impractical, have been tried and discarded, or far exceed the budget. On the other hand, it can be equally frustrating to have potential solutions shot down by those who consistently react negatively. Brainstorming gave all ideas a chance.

Variations on this technique encourage a reasonable amount of openness but install a strong chairman, who eliminates the obviously unworkable ideas.

More in vogue, but not as strong as it once was, is the *management by objectives* (MBO) concept detailed by Peter F. Drucker in a 1954 book entitled, *The Practice of Management*. Many companies still employ this planning technique, although surveys show that only about 10 percent of them find it totally effective.[12]

Management by objectives focuses on opportunities rather than problems. Each subunit within a corporation or institution develops its own clearly defined objectives. These must coincide with and enhance the corporation's or institution's overall goals. Objectives and accomplishments are reviewed periodically to ascertain whether goals are truly being met.

It takes time to effect an MBO plan, and a lot of paper is generated. Those two things alone stop a lot of managers. Others worry about getting locked into notions that can suddenly change.

The trick is to avoid setting goals that contain variables beyond the person's control. You don't want to promise impossible sales figures or count on 100 percent company loyalty. Goals should be practical but should require effort, and should be compatible with the super goal. Management must support the idea and must agree to reward performance. Each organization should construct its own MBO version, since imposing another's blueprint doesn't usually work.

Public relations departments may aim for goals as general as improved readership of the company newsletter and as specific as the placement of features in a select publication.

Another current method designed for initial planning stages is *issues management,* which involves the assigning of pertinent internal and external issues to institutional task forces. These groups analyze issues that could affect the company, and they recommend strategy to comply with these findings.

Obviously, the issues may vary. Energy conservation might be paramount at one time, then worker displacement, company takeovers, the information overload, terrorism, plant closings, foreign competition.

"My job is to see that management doesn't get any surprises. I alert them to issues that will affect them," said John Snow, director, corporate public affairs, research and planning, Sears, Roebuck & Company. "Keep it simple. Fancy language is the kiss of death."[13]

Practitioners should be in on issues management planning from Day One. They help identify those individuals and groups that Australian issues-management expert Tony Stevenson calls "stakeholders," and they assist in surveying this group for attitudes that conflict or coincide with management goals. Finally, they implement methods of reaching these "stakeholder" publics.

A strong issues-management team combines members with varied experience and personalities. Many older and successful managers are less sympathetic to the human issues that pervade today's thinking, and they should be balanced by others for whom human needs are a priority. While they search for problems, they also look for opportunities. Rafael D. Pagan, Jr., an issues manager for Nestlé, cautions:

> Reliance on simple techniques won't work for business and can only end by hurting our profession. We must make sure that issues management is not viewed by others in the corporation as a business-management fad, but as a dynamic, synergistic political force—a necessary ingredient in all long-term corporate planning and strategy.[14]

Some public relations practitioners recommend the *top-down* method of planning, where the company begins with a clear objective and builds on it, almost the way it would compile an organizational chart (see Figure 4-3).

Another planning system is PERT (program evaluation and review techniques). This consists of planning communications and events so that they

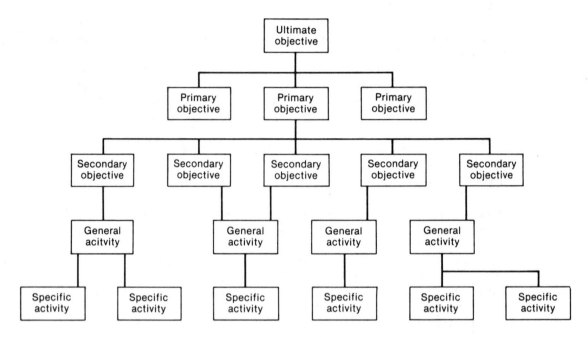

Figure 4-3 Top-down planning chart.

are accomplished on time. PERT charts are drawn up to calendarize sequential events leading up to the final result.

For example, a bimonthly company publication could use the PERT device by establishing a date when it wants the magazine to be in the hands of the readers. Working backward from that date, it determines dates when copy must be completed, when art and illustrations must be done, when the initial layout must be rendered, when copy and art will be delivered to the printer, when envelopes are to be addressed, when proofs are due for review, when the printer will ship the magazines, and when stuffing and mailing will take place.

In establishing such a chart, all contingencies should be included. Weekends would ordinarily be eliminated; complicated artwork would be given more time than simple black-and-white photographs; such things as the availability of certain paper stocks and type, or the use of color separations, or the number of pages to be printed would affect the delivery date.

PERT charts are handy when scheduling special events, too, and the more complicated the event, the more necessary the strict adherence to a calendar.

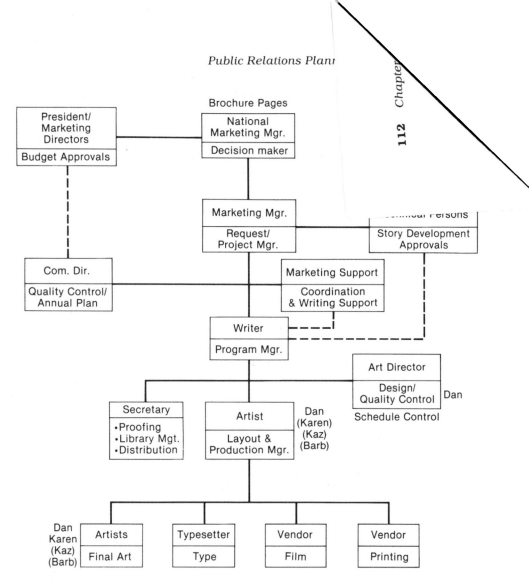

Figure 4-4 A flow chart from an architectural firm delineates the routine for approval and production of brochure pages.

PUBLICATION PLANNING

Just as political strategies and special events need their own blueprints, so does every printed piece, particularly those that are issued regularly. The PERT example stressed the need for a complete and realistic schedule to carry a publication every step of the way from concept to distribution. The magazine, brochure, or newsletter shouldn't be thrown together in a panic; it should be planned.

Impact lists seven advantages of publication planning:

- More creative time to prepare feature articles
- Avoidance of deadline pressures and hangups
- Less trauma over clearance time lags, story kills, and other problems
- Greater editorial depth in articles
- Time to think out and achieve editorial objectives
- More balanced coverage of all editorial objectives
- Advanced planning of special issues and special publication promotions[15]

Publication planning also considers goals, determining what the magazine or newsletter is intended to accomplish. Is this a mouthpiece for management or an employee morale builder? Does it have an external as well as an internal audience? Are you after some specific things, like increased production, contributions, attendance at special events, a less hostile work environment?

Editorial content supports these goals, with the fact in mind that, unless the publication is interesting enough to be read, the other aims fail. Will workers plough through a long and boring article on safety, or could the same information be communicated in a briefer, livelier manner? Do external readers want to see pages of bowling scores and engagement announcements?

Editors often plan at least a year ahead, assigning articles that come out of editorial conferences or, if they wear several hats, scheduling their time so they can produce the copy. There is always room to insert a late-breaking important item, but it is comforting to have all the material plotted, balanced, and in some state of completion.

COMMUNICATION PLANS

As part of the public relations plan, organizations may develop a specific communication plan, dealing solely with the messages they will create and circulate during a certain period. In some firms, this planning is very formal and detailed, starting with research, encompassing internal discussion, then feedback from management, then drafting and publication of the plan, a review by all concerned, and constant monitoring.

When Chevron U.S.A. shut down its New Jersey plant in 1983, it prepared the way with a well-defined communication plan that released information first to employees, then to elected officials, and finally to the media and general public. Special sessions were conducted with union leaders, and the company's public-affairs manager made a personal visit to the state capital in addition to notifying state, local, and federal officials by letter or phone. Some 400 letters were also dispatched to suppliers, contractors, and customers. A midafternoon news release through Business Wire was complemented by a hand-delivered release to the local paper.

Touted as the product of years of research and market analysis, the new Coca-Cola entry into the soft-drink market achieved a remarkable awareness ratio among Americans. It also raised the gustatory ire of original-formula devotees. A Seattle-based organization of "Old Coke" drinkers claimed a membership of 60,000, many of whom lobbied by phone or letter for the company to return to the 100-year-old formula. In less than three months, Coca-Cola announced that the familiar taste would be back, as "Coca-Cola Classic," prompting some skeptics to assert that the whole scenario was planned, to increase Coke's share of the cola market.

A more persistent and annoying problem dogged Procter & Gamble for more than five years. Its man-in-the-moon logo, a hundred-plus years old, combined a motif of 13 stars, representing the original colonies, with a humanized crescent. Rumors connected this design with satanic worship, and a whispering campaign alleged that P&G administrators admitted on network television ("Phil Donahue Show," "Merv Griffin Show," "20/20") that their profits were channeled to the support of devil cults.

At first the company treated the few queries lightly, and even when the calls totaled thousands per month, P&G officials felt that the crisis would fade. Instead, the number of calls grew to 12,000 – 15,000 per month, asking if the rumors were true, and Procter & Gamble was obliged to go on the offensive. It secured statements from television producers and executives to the effect that no P&G spokesperson had ever discussed the logo and/or Satanism on national TV. It sent thousands of letters to Southern churches and enlisted the advocacy of the Rev. Jerry Falwell to combat what research revealed as fundamentalist sources of the charges. The company also hired investigators to trace the origin of these rumors and initiated legal action against those responsible.

The questions and complaints diminished, and Procter & Gamble officials breathed more easily. Then, in 1985, the rumors started again, this time not in the South, but on the populous East Coast. Company research was unable to detect the origins of the fresh accusations, nor could it explain the phenomenon of the protests when most people surveyed couldn't even identify the logo and thought little about it. In March and April 1985, P&G received more than 15,000 calls, all asking if the rumors were accurate.

The Cincinnati-based firm gave in and announced a plan to gradually phase out the trademark as its packages are redesigned. This was no easy task, since P&G has hundreds of product lines, including Sure, Prell, Crest, Scope, Charmin, Pampers, Bounty, Cheer, Biz, Duncan Hines, Zest, and others. A spokesman said the move was made to kill the malicious stories and because the logo was not an important element on the product package. The logo is retained as a company symbol, however, for use on literature and stationery.

Besides helping to alleviate the pain of a negative story by communicating to all interested parties within a 24-hour period, the communication plan also enabled Chevron's administrators to package the story in their terms, emphasizing adverse economic conditions, their long and detailed study of the problem, and their efforts to handle employee and community concerns evenly and sympathetically.

EMERGENCY PLANNING

Emergency planning is sometimes called "planning for disasters." The object of such planning is to minimize unfavorable results and to permit rapid reaction to crises.

Every organization must anticipate adverse conditions, but those institutions whose nature involves risk must be especially conscious of emergency planning. The military, police, hospitals, mines, chemical plants, transportation agencies, and large entertainment centers would be examples. Every institution, however, has some crisis potential. In an article on emergency planning, H. Zane Robbins lists some of these:

- *Financial emergencies*–proxy fights, tender offers, disruption of annual meeting
- *Civil disorders*–riots, sabotage, unlawful picketing
- *Labor union trouble*–attempts to organize plant and office employees, contract negotiations, strikes
- *Natural disasters*–fires, floods, tornadoes, explosions
- *Robbery*
- *System malfunction*–power outage, outbreak of food poisoning in the company cafeteria
- *Government action*–unexpected action by Congress, the SEC, FTC, or some other federal or state government body
- *Demonstrations*–peaceful picketing, sit-ins
- *Legal emergencies*–litigation initiated for or against the institution
- *Executive death*
- *Scandal*–embezzlement, misuse of funds, etc.[16]

All these contingencies should have well-developed responses, and these responses should be worked out at some relatively quiet time before the emergency erupts.

"A crisis is marked by these characteristics," writes Donald R. Stephenson, director, corporate communications, Dow Chemical Canada. "It is sudden; it is urgent; it is instantly visible to and involves top management.

"Those conditions ensure that problems of territoriality, politics, and foot dragging, which often mark other issues, will not arise. Moreover, the severity of the problem creates opportunities, because a crisis does three important things:

- It focuses everyone's attention on one concern and calls for cooperation.
- It gives the company a chance to demonstrate its capabilities and its concern for people affected and for the interests of the community involved.
- It gives those managers who deal with the crisis and resolve it a chance to impress their superiors. Because it focuses the attention of top managers, it automatically makes them aware of what is done and who does it."[17]

Because crisis situations cause people to labor under great pressures, the more simple and complete the emergency plan is, the better. You need credible spokespersons, who are informed, articulate, and unflappable. Other employees should be trained to refer questions to them. Language used by these spokespersons should be free of technical jargon and clear to the layperson. Information should be circulated fast and frequently, to squelch rumors and to remove any suspicion of guilt. Those releasing details should not recite optimistic platitudes but should try to explain what the situation really is and why they make such assertions. And, of course, they should be cognizant of media needs and deadlines.

Alert companies and organizations attempt to locate potential trouble spots in advance, and they have material on these areas, perhaps even kits of information, that can be rapidly disseminated. They also train management to deal with crises, sometimes subjecting them to "ambush interviews" to gauge their reactions and responses.

Charles M. Rossie, Jr., senior vice-president, Foundation for American Communications, suggests this *Pre-Crisis Checklist*:

- Designate in advance who will speak to reporters.
- Prepare an emergency plan.
- Conduct rehearsals and provide spokesmanship training sessions.
- Update your plan often.
  Include:
- *Emergency notification system.* Procedures for security people to provide internal notification of emergencies.
- *External notifications.* A public relations function for media, a security or even a legal-department function for protective agencies, insurance, and other parties.
- *Protective agency procedures.* Prearranged procedures for liaison and cooperation with fire, police, and others.
- *Fact finding.* A procedure to gather information and centralize it is a must during the emergency.
- *Management briefings.* Before information is disseminated, it should be provided to the executives and managers internally to give everyone the same set of facts.
- *Media notifications.* You need an advance plan of action to notify media. You may decide to limit your response. You may initiate contact with all news agencies, whether they inquire or not.
- *Information center.* In conjunction with protective or government agencies, at a location under your control, it can be useful to have a predetermined

information center that reporters and editors know will be the focal point of your information efforts.

- *Background information.* During the chaos, who will remember the background information? If you have background packets prepared in advance, you can save everyone time and trouble.[18]

Crises come in all shapes and sizes. McDonald's has survived rumors of worms in its meat and a tragic massacre at one of its franchise operations. In the former case, the firm tracked the rumor to its source, had its management team eat in the accused restaurant, and relied on the generally strong reputation of the company. In the latter instance, it reacted swiftly, publicly sympathizing with the aggrieved families and shutting down the restaurant. It later turned the site into a monument.

Occidental Petroleum experienced the wrath of an entire area over the Love Canal issue, when one of its subsidiaries dumped chemical waste. The Three Mile Island nuclear station was permanently handicapped, not only by the accident, but also by the inept handling of the media. Johns-Manville has been battling lawsuits for years over charges of cancer-causing asbestos.

Wise administrators take immediate action to correct problems before engaging in any communication. Rely Tampons were withdrawn from retailers' shelves as soon as evidence pointed to a possible link with toxic shock syndrome. McDonnell-Douglas grounded its DC-10s for over a month of rigid inspections following the Chicago crash that killed 273 people. In the aftermath of the Kansas City Hyatt Regency disaster, where an overhead walkway in the hotel collapsed, killing and injuring dozens of patrons, the KC health

---

CAPSULE CRISIS

On September 30, 1982, Johnson & Johnson learned that one of its major products, Tylenol, was linked to a cyanide death in Chicago. The company went public immediately with whatever information it had, canceled Tylenol advertising, urged retailers and pharmacists to remove suspect containers from their shelves, cooperated fully with the Food and Drug Administration, and conducted its own investigation. Even though $400 million in sales volume was at stake, J&J officials never considered any course other than full disclosure.

More deaths were reported. Johnson & Johnson laboratories inspected over a million bottles and determined that the contamination was confined to the Chicago area. In their search they recovered two additional contaminated units. Police named a suspect. Concern was expressed about copycat killings. News broke rapidly, with surveys showing that 90 percent of Americans were familiar with the Tylenol danger.

To handle the fast-developing events, J&J Chairman James E. Burke met twice daily with a select group of seven advisors. The company established a consumer hot line that registered more than 30,000 calls in two months. Ads inviting customers to exchange capsules for tablets were given full-page treatment in mid-October, and later that month, television spots advised of the return of Tylenol in tamperproof containers. Employees received a pair of letters in the same month, updating them and thanking them for their cooperation; four videotaped reports to past and present employees followed. Members of the company's corporate relations staff made visits to 160 congressional offices, and J&J execs appeared on network shows like "Donahue," "60 Minutes," and "Nightline." Articles in *Fortune* and *The Wall Street Journal* gave a positive impression of all the company was doing. A 30-city teleconference was held. One of the company's outside PR consultants estimated that more than 80,000 separate newspaper stories and thousands of electronic hours helped convince Americans that Tylenol was a victim rather than a villain.

When Tylenol reappeared in a new tamper-resistant package, the public accepted it in record numbers, and professionals were calling Johnson & Johnson's crisis communication a lesson for the public relations practitioner.

After surviving that disaster, however, Johnson & Johnson found itself facing a similar situation again in February 1986, when a young woman in Westchester County, New York, died from taking a poisoned Tylenol capsule. Again, the parent company reacted swiftly, approving regional and, finally, complete removal of the product from suppliers' shelves. Johnson & Johnson purchased ads in 400 daily newspapers, offering consumers an opportunity to trade capsules for caplets, a solid form of pain reliever. Mailgrams were dispatched to more than 100,000 physicians, pharmacists, and hospitals, promoting the caplets. At a February news conference, J&J chairman James Burke was a bit testier, blaming local television coverage for part of the panic and insisting that the caplets were an acceptable, safe substitute.

In general, Johnson & Johnson was again perceived as victim rather than villain, and many observers praised the company's social concern, which overrode any financial considerations. However, the repeat tragedy had some different elements this time. Competition was greater, and these competitors did not hold back in deference to J&J's problems. Soon Tylenol had to begin advertising in order to hold its share of the market, even though it preferred to let the shock waves subside before going public commercially. Surveys showed serious damage to the Tylenol brand name, and the company ceased manufacture of the capsules, accepting losses in excess of the $100 million that accompanied the 1982 deaths.

In a sense, Tylenol unwittingly provided a second classic crisis case, demonstrating that, even when the company is not really held culpable, irreparable damage may be done.

agencies were praised for their efforts, but architects and hotel executives fared less well, with spokespersons being criticized for their scapegoating excuses and their initial lack of attention to safety.

Few tragedies have received the scrutiny accorded the January 1986 shuttle explosion that took the lives of all seven astronauts, including a civilian schoolteacher. Millions watched as this occurred, adding to the tragic impact and the angry response. NASA spokespersons did not handle themselves or the situation with sufficient skill. The media and the public seemed willing to delay comment or criticism until the facts were in, but once the details began to unfold, the onus fell on space-agency officials, who, many claimed, had opted for a launch despite warnings of potential danger by technical experts. Executives were relieved of duty, the entire program was suspended, agency funds were placed in jeopardy, and both the credibility and viability of the future launches were injured. Much of this reaction was inevitable, but more astute public relations response could have averted some of the negative factors. You can't hide, you can't dissemble, you can't shift the blame. Tragedy must be faced squarely and honestly.

When 48 workers were reported lost on a Mobil Oil Canada Ltd. oil rig off Newfoundland, the company public relations officer had an immediate statement, clarifying the nationalities of those working at the site, describing the type of rig involved (semisubmersible rather than the anchored jack-up model), the details of the rescue efforts, the fact that workers had earlier been ordered to leave the rig, that they all had on survival suits, that this unit had been drilling for a year and a half without incident, and that other Mobil rigs in the areas were safe. Given the circumstances, Mobil probably came out of this as well as it could.

Tylenol (see box) suffered through a crisis in 1982 that became a classic example of correct and courageous response, but a repeat of the problem four years later, although met with equal skill and candor, showed that even honesty, reputation, and responsibility have limits in protecting an image.

Smaller companies and institutions, too, have their crises. An expensive piece of new equipment fails. Employees vote to strike. Food poisoning disrupts an open house. A senior executive officer for a financial institution is charged with suspicious loan practices. A campus speaker draws legions of protestors. In all these instances, remedies must be found quickly and the reporters briefed as completely and openly as possible.

Media representatives praised the Clark and Shroeder artificial-heart implant cases for the cooperation shown by the chief physician and his staff, who were always available, always professional, and always able to detail the situation in lay language. Less complimentary were the comments by newsmen about the Baby Fae baboon-heart-transplant operation, in which they considered the chief physician unavailable or uncommunicative, his staff not members of the team and therefore not up on the case, and some of the news releases from the hospital inaccurate.

TRAGEDY IN BHOPAL

Even more catastrophic and far more complicated than the Tylenol disasters was the crisis that hit Union Carbide when its plant in Bhopal, India, experienced a deadly chemical leak that eventually took more than 2,000 lives. It became the worst industrial accident in history, and opinion is divided as to how well Union Carbide's management team handled the resultant publicity. Company officials feel they were as open as they could be, and they were certainly demonstrably caring and sympathetic. Some public relations experts view the chemical firm as being less visible once the lawsuits started to mount.

The whole affair was a PR nightmare. Initial reports of a few dozen deaths soon zoomed to hundreds, then thousands. Facts were garbled, because only two open phone lines existed between Bhopal and Union Carbide's Indian headquarters in Bombay. The key executives in Bhopal were arrested and held incommunicado. Company chairman Warren Anderson, who flew from the United States to India, was denied access to the plant and its officials. Meanwhile, the media bombarded Union Carbide for answers, and it wasn't able to supply them.

Like all progressive organizations, Union Carbide had an emergency plan, and it quickly gathered two-score communications personnel to implement it. Anderson participated in daily press conferences. Still, the firm was hampered by the lack of definitive information, the magnitude of the casualty list, international media pressure, and, on top of the Bhopal crisis, the revelation that Union Carbide's West Virginia plant had experienced similar chemical leaks.

Union Carbide and its Indian subsidiary donated nearly $2 million in relief funds, but this was characterized as insufficient by victims and their families. American attorneys descended on the stricken village, and one lawyer claimed he would sign up 20,000 clients, while two others talked about $15–$20 billion class-action suits. Chairman Anderson publicly acknowledged his company's moral responsibility but denied any criminal liability for conditions supervised by Indian nationals. He wanted the cased tried in India, whereas the American attorneys argued for an American venue.

The lawsuits curtailed much of the company's communication, adding to its image problem. For a time, the price of Union Carbide stock dipped, but it eventually recovered, and product sales were not adversely affected. In July 1985, Union Carbide shut down its Bhopal plant.

Part of the reason for the minimal negative effect on Union Carbide, considering the extent of the catastrophe, was, no doubt, the conviction that a disaster like this might happen to any multinational firm.

CBS faced a crisis of sorts, battling the takeover attempt of Ted Turner. Pan American Airlines, running in the red, was also plagued by strikes and other employee problems. And there are the numerous corporate confrontations with dissidents, demonstrators, even would-be terrorists.

In combatting activists, those who have survived such encounters intact advise making certain you are familiar with all the legal ramifications, especially the rights of both sides, and they counsel against giving the "enemy" any ammunition it can use against you. According to them, the company or organization should be more aggressive, not letting the activists dictate terms or control publicity. The activists should not be allowed to concentrate on a single issue but should be forced to face the total picture, and arguments against them should blend both reason and emotion. Since only a small percentage of the activists are hard-core protestors, the opposition should do its best to neutralize that segment, exposing its weaknesses.

Others remind communicators that they must be honest and open, that they should examine protests for legitimate complaints, that they should confront activists at an early stage and, wherever possible, beat them to the punch with the media.

When Public Service Company of New Hampshire took on the activists at its Seabrook plant, it made the mistake of exerting political pressure. One state senator tried to introduce a bill to make nuclear protests illegal; state police planted an informer in the activist camp—and were caught at it. The company worked more covertly, but the protestors made certain all their plans and activities were public. The utility executives helped create sympathy for the underdog by their sub rosa methods and their defensive strategy.

Some crises can be anticipated better than others. If your plant uses toxic chemicals in manufacture, you know the possible consequences and can prepare for them. If you build vehicles, you consider the possibility of recall. But Mexican tourism wasn't ready for the loss of revenue created by the kidnapping and killing of American travelers, and multinational firms are often caught unawares by a sudden political shift.

You do the best you can, calculating all imaginable risks and formulating the steps you will take to recover. Some proposed remedies are general and comprehensive, like what to do in the event of a flood; others are as specific as suggestions on the method of confronting shoplifters.

If there is a potential problem, there should be a plan.

WRITING THE PLAN

Once a plan has been agreed upon, it must be committed to writing and distributed to all those who will be concerned with its implementation. This means that accurate notes must be taken during the discussion phase, that these notes should be concisely stated but completely clear, and that the chief executive must approve the content before dissemination.

The way a report is written is significant. The language must be factual but must capture the imagination and enthusiasm of the reader. The plan should be unfolded logically, starting with the problem or idea and then branching into its various components. Goals and objectives have to be explicit, and items like the budget and the means of evaluation should be included.

First, the writer should *outline* the plan, organizing minor items under major headings. Second, he or she should flesh out the report, putting the *objectives* close to the beginning. All important details should be included, and transitions between paragraphs and subjects should be easy to follow. Long, distracting information may be relegated to an appendix. Key words and phrases should be emphasized. *Conclusions* and/or *recommendations* should follow the expository section, and a brief *summary* is usually helpful.

Rereading and rewriting are essential. The writer must be certain that nothing is left out, that nothing is ambiguous or misleading, and that the conclusions derive naturally from the logical sequence of the preceding material. The writer also anticipates questions and describes as much of the planning phase as is needed to convince the reader that all alternatives were soberly considered.

A well-written plan is something like the closing argument of a trial lawyer. The situation is summarized, the evidence capsulized, and the conclusion clearly stated.

Practitioners must remember that it is not only evaluation that must be built into planning, but also the proposed communication. Plans themselves must be communicated to those who have a role in their implementation and success, and the "action" phase of planning invariably involves communicating with target audiences.

THE CREATIVE PROCESS

Plans may be formulated without creativity, but the ability to fantasize, to originate, is usually helpful. This talent may be hidden because, to the employer, it may seem unbusinesslike or unprofessional. PR practitioners don't want to appear too esoteric, so they talk in the business vernacular. Even when the practitioner wants to fly, he or she knows that a feet-on-the-ground appearance is essential.

Still, the payoff is in innovation.

Without the research for new ways to do and say things, we become mechanical and stale. Communications are dull; events are repetitious. When imagination is brought into play, the ideas sparkle; more important, they provoke attention and interest.

An Ohio practitioner, Dr. Tom Kuby, who did his doctoral dissertation on "Creativity in Public Relations," calculates that only one PR person in twelve excels in creative abilities, a fact that intrigues him.

"Since creativity is valued by the public relations practitioner," says Kuby, "and encouraged and rewarded by top management, it follows that there is a need for public relations professionals to learn to develop their creative potential."[19]

Then why aren't more professionals creative?

"One of the chief roadblocks to creativity stems from physical, perceptual, and mental habits that build up over time," says R. Donald Gamache, president, Inotech Corporation. "These habits tend to tune out things."

Some practitioners like things tidy, or they feel the need to conform. Others fear failure, or being wrong. Still others impose constraints that aren't really there, or they shy away from abstruse problems, or they are locked into single-track solutions. Some practitioners have lost faith in their ability to devise truly creative responses, and some are draining themselves by a debilitating life-style. There are those, too, who consider creativity a rare and delicate gift, and they are frightened of its imagined fragility.

"Creative people are usually curious, and this curiosity leads to knowledge in many areas," writes John M. Keil, in an *Advertising Age* article dispelling common myths about creativity. Keil finds creative people no more intelligent or witty than others, and, although they may not be neat, they are organized.[20]

Highly creative people are, however, a bit more intuitive, and they demonstrate a preference for complexity and novelty. In the currently popular "right-brain, left-brain" terminology, the "right brain," which houses the emotional and creative abilities, is constantly being checked by the "left" or analytical side. Instead of fantasizing, the PR person may quickly move to familiar territory and sacrifice something complex and imaginative for something documented and workable.

Figure 4-5 The visual impact of printed materials is critical in this age of communication overload, so a unique approach helps.
Courtesy: The Minnesota Chapter of PRSA and IABC/Omaha

Break your habits, experts tell us. Tolerate more ambiguity. Break a few rules; become a child again. Associate with creative people. Know what rituals enhance your creativity. Postpone evaluating your ideas.

With Ernest Hemingway, we might confess that we "don't know anything about imagination except that it's something we get for nothing." We don't know why some people have it and others don't, and we're not sure exactly how it works.

But we do know a few things.

1. *Creativity can rarely be forced.* In fact, the creative idea often comes when the mind is open or fallow. You can sit at your desk all day without a single productive idea occurring, and then, on the way home in your car, a brilliant thought pops into your mind. Creativity is like that. It seldom follows logical steps; it goes by leaps and bounds. It is not organized; it is intuitive. This is one reason why good ideas are hard to charge for. They may take minutes, whereas the dawdling and dreaming and probing and scratching took hours.

2. *The creative mind often begins slowly.* As a manager, you may be merely interested in getting something done, in seeing *a* result, *a* product. The creative person wants *his* or *her* result, *his* or *her* product. This process takes time, and the creative person rarely shares the executive's temporal pressures. He or she may stand by the window or sit tapping a pencil. If you trust this person, based on past performance, you suffer these long dry spells and hope for rain.

3. *The creative mind can be primed.* Even though you can't force creativity, you can nudge it. Every creative mind works this out for itself. Some walk, some read, some listen to music. Some drink, smoke, or doze. Some need an inspiring setting; others opt for a familiar desk and chair.

One helpful tip to PR persons writing about products and companies and finding themselves dried up is to revisit the plant, or bring the product home, or listen to comments of customers or employees. These will get them thinking again. Reading or viewing what others have done may also stimulate the creative juices.

4. *The creative mind needs direction.* This is tricky. If you put too many constraints on the creative person, he or she rebels or will turn out a perfunctory piece of work. On the other hand, if you set no limits, this person may spend $1,000 on a piece of artwork for which you have budgeted $100. Meet with the creative person early and often if you are supervising these efforts. Set some reasonable goals in terms of money, time, and the campaign objectives. Make sure you are in agreement. Then give that person some freedom. Let his or her fancy roam—always with the realism of the situation in mind.

Unless you do this, these creative persons may eventually evolve a brilliant but useless solution. Once this point is reached, it is nearly impossible to redirect their talents. They are stuck on this result—*their* result.

5. *The creative mind is rare.*   Real creativity is hardly commonplace. The truly original thinker or designer forms a minute segment of the public relations cadre. For most of us, it may be enough to recognize and use genius when it surfaces. And, at other times, it may be enough to score high at a functional level of creativity, producing messages that are clear, interesting, and effective. We do this by observing the efforts of others and by thinking through our own needs and resources. It is fruitless, for example, to try to impose the successful Volkswagen and Alka-Seltzer campaigns on a product like industrial elevators. Each problem, each project, has its own special needs and opportunities.

MAKING IT WORK

Planning, then, is a combination of research, thinking, and creativity. You blend this trio into a set of actions that looks promising. You always hope for the truly great idea—"the golden gimmick" that is pursued in advertising circles—but you usually settle for something workable, sensible, and marketable.

"A new idea, however good, isn't enough," declares Robert Rosenfeld, head of Kodak Research Laboratories' Office of Innovation. "Ideas have to connect.

"Creativity refers to the generating of new and novel ideas, usually by an individual, whereas innovation refers to the application of an idea and is generally a collective process."[21]

CHAPTER HIGHLIGHTS

- There are eleven steps in planning: research; analysis; problem identification; examination of past experience, the experience of others, and future effects; evaluation, selection, and weighing of alternatives; implementation and monitoring of the plan.
- Public relations planning often starts with an audit of key publics and their current status vis-à-vis the firm or organization.
- Every plan involves six elements: reason, goals, current status, methods of implementation, target audiences, and cost.
- Priority considerations and maximizing the use of one's time aid in the decision-making process.
- There are short- and long-range plans, strategic and tactical plans, and one-time and standing plans.
- Obstacles to planning include lack of time or confidence, fear of failure, resistance to change, red tape, insufficient funds or personnel, vague objectives, insufficient information, and failure to analyze trends.

- Planning techniques include brainstorming, management by objectives, issues management, top-down planning, and program evaluation and review techniques.
- Various types of crises call for detailed emergency planning.
- Creativity complements planning, but is fairly rare because of numerous habitual and psychological roadblocks. Creativity can't be forced, may be slow, but can be stimulated. Eventually, in public relations, it must result in something tangible.

NOTES

[1]Joyce F. Jones, "Audit: A New Tool for Public Relations," *Public Relations Journal*, July 1975.

[2]Elaine Goldman, "Dinosaur or Rocket?" Reprinted with permission from the October 1984 issue of the *Public Relations Journal*. Copyright 1984.

[3]*Ibid.*

[4]James A. Files, "RACE," *Public Relations Journal*, July 1982.

[5]Kerry D. Tucker, "The PR Team—A Fresh Approach to Planning," *Public Relations Journal*, May 1978.

[6]Jack Tucker, "Budgeting and Cost Control." Reprinted with permission from the March 1981 issue of the *Public Relations Journal*. Copyright 1981.

[7]John F. Budd, Jr., "Priority and Discipline Keys to Programming," *Public Relations Journal*, November 1967.

[8]*Ibid.*

[9]R. James Steffen, "On the Job: Stick with Priorities," *U.S. News & World Report*, January 25, 1982.

[10]Walter Kiechel III, "Beat the Clock," *Fortune*, June 25, 1984.

[11]Tom Peters, "An Excellent Question," *INC.*, December 1984.

[12]Fred E. Schuster and Alva F. Kindall, "Management by Objectives: Where We Stand—A Survey of the *Fortune* 500," *Human Resource Management*, Vol. 13, No. 1 (Spring 1974).

[13]"Issues Management; Linking Decisions to the Environment," *Speechwriter's Newsletter*, April 15, 1983.

[14]Wes Pedersen, "Challenges and Concerns of Issues Management," *Public Relations Journal*, February 1984.

[15]*Impact*, No. 189 (1977).

[16]H. Zane Robbins, "Do You Need Emergency Plans?" *Public Relations Journal*, September 1971.

[17]Donald R. Stephenson, "Are You Making the Most of Your Crises?" Reprinted with permission from the June 1984 issue of the *Public Relations Journal*. Copyright 1984.

[18]Charles M. Rossie, Jr., "Now Is the Time." Courtesy of *Communicator's Journal*, November/December 1983.

[19]"Developing Creative Abilities," *PRSA Newsletter*, Vol. 10, No. 3 (March 1982).

[20]John M. Keil, "Popular Myths about Creativity Debunked," *Advertising Age*, May 6, 1985.

[21]Sarah Ban Breathnach, "Making the Connections," *Washington Post*, November 5, 1985.

SUGGESTED READINGS

ANDREWS, KENNETH R., *The Concept of Corporate Strategy*. Homewood, Ill.: Irwin, 1980.

ARGENTI, JOHN, *Practical Corporate Planning*. London: Allen & Unwin, 1980.

BERNSTEIN, ALAN B., *The Emerging Public Relations Manual*. New Brunswick, N.J.: Pase, 1982.

CORNELL, ALEXANDER H., *The Decision Makers Handbook*. Englewood Cliffs, N.J.: Prentice-Hall, 1980.

DARROW, RICHARD W., and DAN J. FORRESTAL, *Public Relations Handbook*, 2nd ed. Baldwin, N.Y.: The Professional Development Institute, 1985.

GRUNIG, JAMES E., and TODD HUNT, *Managing Public Relations*. New York: Holt, Rinehart & Winston, 1985.

HAIMANN, THEO, WILLIAM G. SCOTT, and PATRICK E. CONNOR, *Managing the Modern Organization*. Boston: Houghton Mifflin, 1978.

JONES, HARRY, *Preparing Company Plans*. London: Gower, 1974.

KING, WILLIAM R., and DAVID I. CLELAND, *Strategic Planning and Policy*. New York: Van Nostrand Reinhold, 1978.

LESLY, PHILIP, *Overcoming Opposition: A Survival Manual for Executives*. Englewood Cliffs, N.J.: Prentice-Hall, 1984.

LINNEMAN, ROBERT E., *Shirt-Sleeve Approach to Long Range Planning*. Englewood Cliffs, N.J.: Prentice-Hall, 1980.

LORANGE, PETER, and RICHARD F. VANCIL, *Strategic Planning Systems*. Englewood Cliffs, N.J.: Prentice-Hall, 1977.

LYLES, RICHARD I., *Practical Management: Problem Solving and Decision Making*. New York: Van Nostrand Reinhold, 1982.

MAKENS, JAMES C., *The Marketing Plan Workbook*. Englewood Cliffs, N.J.: Prentice-Hall, 1985.

NADLER, GERALD, *The Planning and Design Approach*. New York: Wiley, 1981.

NAGER, NORMAN R., and T. HARRELL ALLEN, *Public Relations Management by Objectives*. New York: Longman, 1983.

PITZ, GORDON, F., and JACK McKILLIP, *Decision Analysis for Program Evaluators*. Beverly Hills, Calif.: Sage, 1984.

RADFORD, K.J., *Strategic Planning: An Analytical Approach*. Reston, Va.: Reston, 1980.

REUSS, CAROL, and DONN SILVIS, *Inside Organizational Communication*. New York: Longman, 1984.

ROSS, ROBERT D., *The Mangement of Public Relations*. New York: Wiley, 1977.

SIMON, RAYMOND, *Public Relations Management: A Casebook*. Columbus, O.: Publishing Horizons, 1986.

EXERCISES

1. Outline a public relations plan to attract industry to your community. Consider what industries might make the most likely target audiences,

what assets your community can offer them, and what means you will use to reach and convince them. Public relations advertising may be used in addition to other elements of the PR program.

2. Create a new magazine for a reading audience not currently being served. Come up with a title, logo, and table of contents. Specify the audience, the price, the method of distribution, and the kinds of advertisers this publication might attract.

3. Check with a local firm, organization, or government entity about the existence of an emergency plan for employees. Ask if you may have a copy. Check to see how often the plan is updated. Bring the plan to class for discussion.

CASE PROBLEMS

1. You are the public relations director for an East Coast railroad line that has been struggling for ten years to make its freight hauling pay. Most years are, at best, breakeven, and the company hasn't shown a profit for shareholders in the last four years. As a consequence, railroad bridges and crossings are poorly maintained and the subject of citizen complaints. Several local newspapers have run editorials complaining about the condition of railroad property. Late one night, you are called at home and told that one of your company's trains, traveling at an excessive rate of speed for that stretch of track, had derailed and struck a bridge abutment. That wasn't the worst news. The weakened bridge subsequently partially collapsed, dropping a passing car to the tracks below and sending the driver to the hospital in critical condition. Your informant on the telephone says, "There's more. The engineer had been drinking before he went on duty, but he insists he wasn't drunk, He's in the hospital, too, but with minor injuries."

    a. What action do you take, and in what order?

    b. Once the initial crisis has been handled, what further actions would you suggest to superiors?

    c. What type of directives should have been written into the railroad's emergency plans to cover situations like this?

2. You are the public relations director for a 60-bed hospital in Red Fork, Colorado, a town of 29,000 people. Typically, the hospital treats the normal community illnesses, maintains a maternity ward, and has a pretty good medical staff of orthopedic surgeons because of the high incidence of climbing, skiing, and chain-saw accidents. Patients requiring treatment for heart ailments, cancer, and other problems are generally transferred to Denver, 180 miles away. Rod Lightner, rock music idol whose records have been at or near the top of the charts for three years, is injured in a fall while hiking, and is carried on a stretcher to your hospital. His back injury dictates that he not be moved for at least six weeks. His

agent and climbing partner sends for Lightner's own physician and two specialists this doctor recommends. They will arrive the next afternoon. In the meantime, word has spread locally about Lightner, and soon the hospital switchboard is alive with calls, including those from media all over the United States and Europe.

a. How do you handle the immediate problem?

b. What things must you consider for the next month and a half?

c. What sort of information relating to this sort of event would you hope to find in the hospital's emergency planning manual?

3. As the public relations director for a medium-sized industry, you find you need some additional creative assistance and suggest the hiring of an outside agency. Your employers, descendants of the company's founders, are a conservative group, and they worry about the expense and about the intervention of new people. You convince them the experiment will be worth the investment, and they give their approval. One thing worries you, however. The creative staff of this outside agency, although capable, highly respected, and successful, is flamboyant in speech and dress, and may not interact well with your employers.

How would you make this relationship more compatible?

5
THE COMMUNICATION PROCESS

Eventually, all the research and planning lead to implementation. In public relations, something has to happen. The result may be a special event, a new union agreement, a donation to charity. Most often, the execution of a PR plan takes the form of communication. News releases, films, booklets, photos, letters, and other tools are tangible evidence of communication.

If communication were perfect, there would be few problems in the world. We would all understand one another. Unfortunately, there are many communication lapses, from censorship to overkill. The public relations practitioner must be expert in communicating in order to minimize these errors and create understanding. This involves a combination of specialized skills: "There is the myth that communication is a fairly common phenomenon which involves a fairly common set of skills," writes author Leo Rosten. "I submit to you that communication is extremely rare; that we really don't know very much about how to get an idea from one head into another."[1]

Although communication skills may be unique, the need and urge to communicate are not. Nearly all our waking hours are spent in some form of communication— listening, speaking, reading, viewing, writing. Even our silence speaks to others. When communication is absent or distorted, we assume or suspect or become frustrated. We react unreasonably when we aren't told something. We become confused when a memo is obscure or a phone call ambiguous. That's what makes communication such a challenging discipline.

HOW COMMUNICATION WORKS

There are numerous models, some complex, some simple, but all concerned with the way ideas and information are effectively transferred from a source to a receiver. The most basic communication system looks like this:

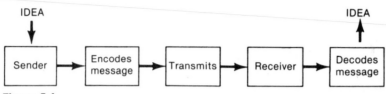

Figure 5-1

The sender has a message he or she wants to communicate to another person or group. The sender has an idea, a concept, which must be relayed accurately. This sender then chooses the symbols or language (words, pictures, sounds, really anything that appeals to the senses), arranges them in some order, and prepares a "package." This package must be transmitted by some means—a telephone call, letter, personal visit, five-screen slide presentation, print ad, brochure, or even skywriting. The receiver gets the message, in whatever form, and must translate it according to his or her own interpretation. If the message has been carefully worded and properly transmitted, and if the receiver is in the proper frame of mind and reference, the concept envisioned by the sender emerges in pretty much the same fashion in the receiver's mind.

If the sender and the receiver share a common background or experience, this makes it much easier to establish understanding. The executive makes more immediate sense to subordinates who are familiar with him or her than he or she does to subordinates who are reacting for the first time to this executive's statements. The first group knows what to expect and how to interpret various aspects of this message. The second group is more typical of the mass audience, however, since many PR programs must be aimed at segments of society whose unifying characteristics are only superficial.

For some messages, communication is simple. Military commands, for example, are succinct, and the response automatic. If a parent yells at a child to turn down the stereo, the meaning is clear. It would be difficult to confuse the intent of a label that reads, "If contents are swallowed, call a doctor." Most messages, however, are tougher to decipher, and even presumably safe messages can be misinterpreted.

If it's possible to exchange ideas with the receiver, or to respond to questions or suggestions, this sort of conversation improves communication, refining the content and getting rid of many misconceptions.

In this model, the communication is circular, allowing for feedback, but also hampered by "noise" or "static" or "interference," meaning the introduction of any outside element that can flaw the message (Figure 5-2).

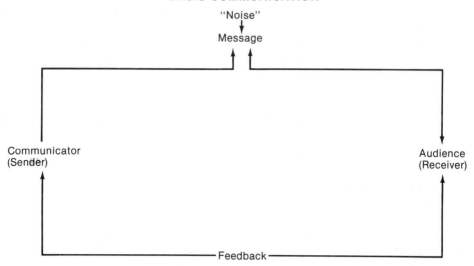

Figure 5-2 Courtesy: Richard Kramer

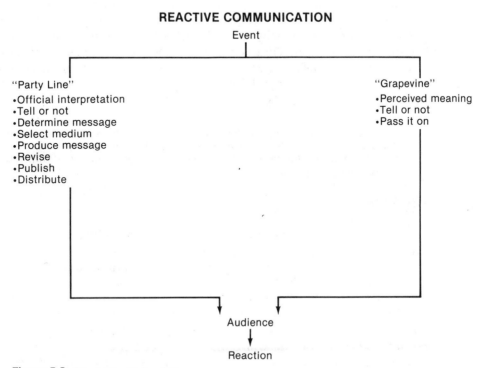

Figure 5-3 Courtesy: Richard Kramer

Even a telephone call, which is a two-way communication, can leave the caller or receiver baffled, wondering what the other person meant by a certain phrase. Letters sometimes prompt requests for clarification, or they cause responses not intended. When communication can fail in cases involving only a pair of people, it's easy to understand why mass communication, which characterizes most PR efforts, is so difficult to achieve.

Another PR problem associated with the transmittal of information is the fact that rumors move much more swiftly than the truth—or at least the company's version of the truth. The reasons may be glimpsed in this next model; there are just more steps to consider in the more formal "reactive" communication (Figure 5-3).

The Sender

The relationship between sender and receiver is significant. The way messages are accepted or rejected depends to a considerable extent upon who is talking to whom. If individuals view the government as one giant bureaucratic mess, then even the most bland communication from a government office will irritate them. The same speech delivered by a member of your political party and by a member of the opposition party will evoke contradictory responses. A playful remark by a friend may be enjoyed, but the same comment from an enemy will be resented.

If you know, like, trust, and even admire the sender, his or her message is more likely to move you or change your opinion. Every good public speaker knows this, and that is why he or she tries to warm up an audience at the beginning of a speech. That is why the same speaker does a little research into the audience before appearing. And that is why he or she also knows the subject and discusses it candidly. These are the ways you project credibility.

What is true of speaking is true of writing:

> Writing skill is a tool used to manipulate a reader. It gets him to think and feel as you want him to. In this sense, all writing for an audience is argumentation; that is, an attempt to persuade. It is a public act with the social consequence of changing other people.[2]

The Receiver

Audience predispositions are also important. Individuals and, to some extent, groups seek out information congenial to their beliefs and shy away from data that run counter to these beliefs. Liberals and conservatives prefer columnists who match their political philosophies, for example, and many company executives hear what they want to hear and shun those messages that diminish their perceptions. All this goes back to the psychology of the individual. There must be something in it for the receiver, some sort of reward, before he or she will bother to decode the message, or greet the message with an open mind. It is not as simple as drawing a diagram and

Figure 5-4 Communication can be complex—or it can be crudely simple.

pointing the arrows in the right direction. The communication must always be expressed in the language of the audience rather than that of the sender.

Since we can rarely be certain that our mass-communication messages reach the receiver, we must be prepared to repeat the messages over a period of time, perhaps in a variety of ways. Advertising campaigns are built on this thesis. If we miss them with radio, we catch them with billboards. One of the messages will get through. Incidentally, when this happens, the recipient, if interested, is also more likely to note future messages on the same topic or recall past ones.

Even when public relations practitioners work diligently at communicating, they may still fail—particularly if they are careless or inexperienced. There are many ways a communication can go awry.

ROADBLOCKS TO COMMUNICATION

Ralph E. Frede, director of development and public relations for the Baylor College of Medicine in Houston, Texas, has developed a series of a dozen "roadblocks" to communication.[3] They are worth examining:

1. *Censorship.* This is the suppression of what people see, hear, or read. This can be natural and unavoidable, as when distance, language barriers, or mental capacity isolate a person from certain knowledge. Usually, however, we are concerned with *artificial* censorship, which occurs as someone in power decides to stop or alter a message. We needn't think only of foreign dictators in this context. An overzealous editor can perform the same function, or a corporate executive who demands to read all copy emanating from that firm. If the message is halted or substantially changed, the receiver can never know what the sender intended.

2. *Absence of a clear purpose.*   The sender isn't certain as to why he or she is delivering this message. Some companies issue reports or sponsor events simply because they have always done so. The reasons that created the original report or event may be altered or absent. We should always ask, "Is this communication necessary?"

3. *Audience not clearly defined.*   This roadblock is related to the communicator's failure to picture the receiver properly. If you prepare a speech for what you assume is a young college crowd and find instead that you are speaking to middle-aged stockbrokers, you're in trouble.

4. *Faulty language selection.*   Given our choice of various sensory appeals— primarily words, images, and sounds—we make a poor decision in terms of the audience we have defined. A highbrow position paper is lost on those with only a high-school education. Rock music may be a poor background for a slide show at the Chamber of Commerce.

5. *Conflict of message and action.*   This roadblock reminds us of the old adage, "Actions speak louder than words." It has to do with integrity. If you mouth certain principles and enunciate them in communications but belie them in practice, your message will be suspect. Your client firm advertises itself as an "affirmative action" employer, but there are actually no women there above the level of secretary. A plant that advertises its environmental concern but continues to pollute destroys its credibility.

6. *Lack of semantic knowledge.*   We will have more to say about this shortly, but it simply means that if senders do not understand the connotation of words they use, they may easily offend an audience they are trying to impress. A foreign visitor, addressing a businessmen's breakfast, was trying to convey his admiration of America's competitive spirit, but referred to his audience as "aggressive people." Some company PR directors object to the use of "reindustrialization" to describe our economy, protesting that it sounds like a return to the assembly lines and sweatshops. Those who are shaky about the overtones of a word should look it up. If still uncertain, they should use a synonym.

7. *Faulty arrangement.*   When language has not been arranged in proper sequence, it is difficult to follow. Perhaps the emphasis is in the wrong place, or the central idea is buried in a long paragraph. The reader or listener should always have a sense of making progress, and, if guideposts are necessary, they must be supplied. Presidential spokesman Larry Speakes, in replying to a reporter's query about whether or not his boss had read the House Intelligence Committee's report on the bombing of the U.S. embassy in Beirut, could have selected a better sentence sequence than, "I don't think he's read the report in detail. It's five and a half pages double-spaced."

8. *Choosing the wrong channel.*   Each medium has its strengths and weaknesses, and one may be more appropriate than another in a given situation. Instead of a letter, we should have made a phone call. Instead of a brochure, we should have used slides. Instead of a newspaper ad, we should

have used direct mail. Instead of trusting to the mass media, we should have used our own internal publication. These are all judgment calls, and we try to choose that method—or channel—of communication that seems to offer the best potential for reaching the largest number of our target audience with the most effective message. The budget, of course, may sometimes force us into secondary decisions, but even these may be enhanced with a little thought.

9. *Unattractive packaging.* If you have no skill in a particular medium, either hire someone who has or leave that medium alone. You may know nothing about paper stock, color selection, typography, art, or layout, and yet you set out to design and produce an expensive brochure. Madness! Even worse are the pitiful examples of television documentaries produced by those with no aptitude for or experience with this technical medium. The result of these gaffes is that your message is counterproductive. Instead of winning friends, you manufacture critics.

10. *Bad timing.* When we transmit and *with what frequency* is crucial. Soliciting parishioners for membership in your church organization will fall quite flat if the calls are made on a Saturday afternoon when the local university is playing football on network television. Printed pieces sent during the heaviest vacation periods or during the heaviest mail periods lose their effectiveness. Scheduling your special event in conflict with the major social event of your community dooms you to reduced news coverage.

A related sin consists of sending out too many messages. Recipients get the feeling that they have read this before or that you have nothing better to do with your time and money than to pile mailing upon mailing. Incessant phone calls may be a real irritation factor. And a surfeit of news releases may cause a newspaper to toss all your stories into the wastebasket.

11. *Lack of useful information.* Because we live in a busy society, replete with communications, we become increasingly selective. We read and attend to those messages that promise us some benefit. We save and discard our third-class mail on this basis. We read or ignore newspaper inserts because of what they mean or do not mean to us.

Some communicators, caught up in the enthusiasm of their cause, assume that their audiences are equally turned on. Most unlikely. It is safer to assume that they are apathetic and that their attention is focused on other things. You must win them away.

In the advertising field, they talk about benefits from the manufacturer's point of view and from the consumer's point of view. The manufacturer may like to brag that its car is made of the finest, triple-riveted, double-coated tungsten steel. What the consumer wants to know is whether this car will last longer, ride smoother, save gas, impress the neighbors. Wise copywriters address themselves to the consumer and talk the consumer's language. So do successful PR persons.

12. *Incorrect premises or assumptions.* If communication is based on false premises, it cannot succeed. You may assume that the audience

received an earlier memo and therefore fail to provide background data. You may overestimate the enthusiasm for a particular program. Some CEOs still apologize to female colleagues about discussing finances at a luncheon, assuming that such topics are dull to them.

Frede's list focuses primarily on errors made by the sender, but there are also problems of external interference, things the sender can't control; and communication can also be short-circuited by hostility on the part of the receiver, or inattention, or inability to understand, or similar factors.

SOME MODERN COMMUNICATION PROBLEMS

Perhaps the most serious problem in American communication is "information overload," the proliferation of messages that makes comprehension more difficult. The channels of communication are simply overloaded, and practitioners who toss one more message into the stream are contributing to the clutter without solving their problems.

One answer is to send fewer messages to fewer people. Audiences should be segmented, if possible, with only target audiences receiving communications. That would result in less waste coverage and more impact. Personalizing the message also helps, but not in the crude way of some national lotteries or magazine subscription appeals. Communicators should take a lesson from the successful advertisers who first get our attention and then submit the information. Letters, speeches, even memos, can begin with a salutation or lead line that pulls readers and listeners in. Some experts also argue for fewer statistics and more emotional examples to support the salient points.

Accompanying this plethora of information is a concurrent disinclination on the part of Americans to listen, and especially to read. More accessible forms of communication have reduced the number of people who rely on print for information, both because they are not good readers and because they really don't want to read. Moreover, we've become used to having things packaged for us—like 30 minutes of news, weather, and sports; and magazine digests; and film and TV synopses; even shortened versions of the Bible and *Moby Dick*. Graphics are increasingly important for teasing us into copy and retaining us once there. Few people care to confront pages of solid type.

This phenomenon of increasing source material combined with less desire to wade through it has been dubbed "discommunication," and it has made the role of the public relations communicator even more vital. Someone has to translate the more complicated pronouncements, and someone has to make the prose more attractive and accessible, and someone has to do a better job of defining the audiences, and someone has to package the materials in a more efficient and acceptable manner. The PR practitioner is trained for these tasks.

Philip Lesly calls our attention to another communication change—the decentralization of communication. He reminds us that technology pulled

Figure 5-5 SOURCE: Anonymous

never try to teach
a pig to sing.
it wastes your time
and annoys the pig.

America together and centered its communication in Manhattan, "with specialized segments in Washington, Los Angeles, and Chicago." But the latest technology is splintering our communication, with special-interest publications supplanting general-circulation ones; with cable the fastest-growing television sector; with small-city and suburban papers growing faster than big-city dailies. Lesly sees the demise of our media monopoly, with a consequent reduction in citizen conformity:

> The climate of attitudes is different in various locales, in spite of the homogenizing effects of the networks, press services, mass magazines and book publishers—all centered in one place. When the impact of those mass media wanes, the local differences will probably be accentuated. Mobility will have a further effect: More people are likely to choose the human climate they like, just as many have been choosing the weather climate.[4]

Professionals cannot afford to regard the public as monolithic. It is composed of smaller groups, each with different needs and concepts, each needing to be addressed a bit differently. These publics will respond to available information, but they must have the information. When they can't distinguish messages easily, based on their interests, communication suffers. Again, good public relations provides such clarification.

Some Further Psychological Considerations

We can't know too much about communication. Serious public relations practitioners not only avail themselves of the mechanical "how-to" information but also scan the literature for details on how the process works.

Berelson and Steiner, in their book *Human Behavior*, devote an entire section to mass communication.[5] Among their findings are these provocative statements:

1. The spread of rumors is directly related to audience predispositions; rumors tend to be heard by people to whom they are congenial; they are changed into more personally satisfactory forms; and they are best countered by the circulation of objective information that is not explicitly tied to the rumor itself.

2. People are especially likely to seek out congenial information on a [controversial] matter just after coming to a decision on that matter. [Religious converts experience this; so do those who switch political parties. Even in noncontroversial matters, this can be true. The best readers of Ford ads, for example, are those who have just purchased a new Ford. The ads provide positive reinforcement for their decision.]

3. People interested in a topic tend to follow it in the medium that gives it the fullest and most faithful treatment.

4. Anticipating subsequent use increases retention, even of uncongenial material. [Students who anticipate a certain question in an upcoming exam will pay more attention to that part of the lecture. If you hear a good argument for or against a position you take, and foresee a future debate with a colleague, you will remember these bits of data.]

5. Strong appeals to fear are less effective than minimal appeals to fear. [What the authors are saying here is that a strong threat may cause you to balk, or to submit without changing your attitude. A mild threat may cause you to rethink your whole situation and decide to change your opinion or conduct of your own accord.]

6. Presenting only the favored side of an argument is more effective than presenting both sides in persuading less-educated audiences and in reinforcing the already persuaded. Presenting both sides is more effective with the better educated and the opposition and is also more effective as inoculation against subsequent propaganda. ["Propaganda," of course, is applied most often to communication the receiver rejects. The receiver's own side, however, can be guilty of the same single-minded messages, but he or she prefers to see these as positive. In a sense, all public relations—or a good part of it—could be classified as propaganda. Apologists would be quick to point out that there is a vast difference between propagandizing for an essentially evil cause, using distortions and lies, and propagandizing for a good cause, making certain the client's views are aired.]

7. The higher the education, the greater the reliance on print; the lower the education, the greater the reliance on radio and television.

8. People tend to misperceive and misinterpret persuasive communications in accordance with their own predispositions, by evading the message or by distorting it in a favorable direction. [Witness the stated skepticism of intelligent smokers against the findings of cancer specialists. Note how

grade-school children will misquote their teacher if they can turn this teacher's remark into a more favorable suggestion.]

9. In cases where the audience approves of the communicator but disapproves of his conclusions, it tends to disassociate the source from the content.

10. Arousing audience predispositions in favor of the intended message early in a communication will increase the likelihood that the message will be accepted and decrease the chances of later attrition. [This explains why speeches, letters, and articles should get off to a good start. If you alienate an audience at the outset, or leave it with the impression that you don't know the topic, it is virtually impossible to reroute its thinking.]

Much research is currently going on in the field of communication. Scholars seek to learn how visual language, like that of television and the films, is affecting this generation. They want to know more about words as symbols, and about audience attitudes, and about environmental interference and other topics. Following their discoveries forms another area of special interest for the dedicated public relations person.

NONVERBAL COMMUNICATION

Much has been written in recent years about nonverbal communication. Even though some studies may have overreached in arriving at questionable theories, the idea that the way we look and move conveys impressions, and colors communications, is solid:

> How well the public relations practitioner recognizes the consequences of such basics as body language, what people really mean when they give you their opinions, is important. How to perceive true attitudes from impressions may sound like an inconsequential consideration. Far from it. It can be the basis for recognizing the essence of a communication problem and how to deal with it.[6]

There are obvious examples. People can show boredom by yawning, dozing off, shifting from one foot to the other, looking around, cupping their chins in their hands. The speaker who notices members of the audience checking their watches realizes it is time to sum up. People may also show interest by the way they lean into a conversation, by their mobile faces and alert eyes. There are numerous ways to indicate grief, happiness, disagreement, confusion, and other conditions.

A good salesperson doesn't slump back in his or her chair when in the act of closing a deal. An unconvinced client, however, might slump back, fold his or her arms, and frown. No sale.

In *Body Language*, author Julius Fast calls *posture* "punctuation for a conversation," pointing out that different positions are related to varying emotional states:

> The ordinary citizen who understands body language very well, and uses it, has a grasp of these postures, though he may be unaware of it, and he can relate

them to the states of people he knows. In this way he can actually keep a step ahead of other people in his dealings with them.[7]

Experts have categorized about 125 nonverbal signals—raising the eyebrows, crouching, hunching the shoulders, tilting the head, folding the arms, crossing the legs—and they claim that many of these signals cross national and language barriers. Very often these movements give away a person's true feelings, regardless of what is being said. Sometimes an executive relates some optimistic news to employees, but nervous gestures of the hands and feet suggest he is lying. Attorneys watch jurors and judges, attentive to frowns or tightening of the lips.

Body language really deals with relationships. Handshakes, for example, betray insecurity, caution, stubbornness, or the need for acceptance. Posture can signal dominance or subservience.

> When a respected executive talks to a subordinate, the lower-ranking person will listen intently with his eyes riveted to the executive's face. To look around would be a sign of disrespect. On the other hand, when the subordinate is speaking, it is considered perfectly appropriate if the boss looks about or gazes at his watch.[8]

There are questions of invasion of space, with most people preferring a distance of two feet or more during conversation, and there are some acculturated signals, like the V-for-victory gesture, which may fade, or the "Number One" sign that is a fixture in football. There are the various flirting routines that are understood by denizens of the singles bars, and the staredowns in the boxing arenas. Some of these are learned or deliberate, but a lot of our body language is involuntary. We can't really *not* communicate; our speech or our bodies are always conveying some message.

Extensions of body language are noted in touches, which may be affectionate, reassuring, threatening, tentative, or any number of other expressive forms. David Alan Safer even extends body language to include institutions and organizations, contending that their actions speak considerably louder than their words. He cites instances of firms that provide bonuses for executives in years when wages and shareholder benefits are limited, or hospitals that complain about the low use of their facilities by minorities but do little to attract such groups.

> For although the public relations professional may manage all the company's overt and formal communications functions—publicity, media relations, executive speech writing, public and community affairs, organizational communication and the like—the public perception of such actions as hiring, retention and promotion, marketing and pricing policies, occupational safety, and health and waste-disposal practices may negate and defeat previously stated objectives and cause the credibility gap to yawn ever wider."[9]

Whether dealing with individuals or institutions, the practitioner must become sensitive to these nonverbal signals. The system isn't foolproof, but it's an interesting and helpful adjunct to other forms of communication.

THE WRITTEN WORD

Many skills are desirable to possess in public relations, from graphics to elocution, but the handiest—almost indispensable—talent is writing. "Show me the public relations person proud of his independence from the tyranny of the typewriter and I'll show you a person estranged from the reality of his profession," writes John F. Budd, Jr. "The soundest plans, the noblest intentions are fundamentally rhetoric until understood—or, at least, acknowledged—by those whose approbation is important. If you can't close the communications loop, you're lacking an essential dimension as a compleat public relations professional."[10]

You may land a post in which you are able to hire writers, or where tasks are sufficiently departmentalized that you are relieved of such work, but this would be a unique situation. Even then, you still have to write letters, memorandums, proposals, and other communiqués.

Budd is taking note of a trend among public relations professionals to make light of the writing skills, to assign them to a less-skilled, lower-echelon

Figure 5-6 Of all the skills the practitioner will find useful, the ability to write ranks first.

employee. Professionals may consider themselves above such mundane chores; they are the planners, the visualizers, the philosophers. As Budd says, "Pity! It will undo us yet."

This lack of attention to writing was noted by a survey showing that younger public relations professionals may not possess the crisp writing skills of their PR elders. The study attributed the difference to the journalistic backgrounds of the veterans as against increased marketing preparation by newer members.[11]

Of course, this is a national trend. For years, critics have been bemoaning the state of writing in American schools, claiming that too few English teachers are prepared for their jobs; that the emphasis is on literature or, as some contend, esoteric courses stressing gender awareness in literature or fantasy or some other genre; and that students are not convinced that writing skills are important. Hugh Kenner, author and chairman of the English department at Johns Hopkins University, suggests we present writing as "an arcane skill, with many interests and awards, like computer programming" in order to make it attractive to young people.[12] Many companies have been forced to include training sessions in communication, especially writing skills, for their executives who are bright but not very literate. These people find themselves unable to prepare proposals or reports, write letters, construct a speech. The process is largely remedial. Robert Pattison says:

> Almost all Americans can read and write. Thus we seem to be equal. But very few Americans possess discipline in the habits of language necessary for its advantageous use, and those few who do so effectively control the many who do not.[13]

Among those who exercise such control are those in the public relations field—if they can write. "To me," writes Georges Carousso," PR writing is the most challenging and creative writing ever discovered."[14]

Understanding the Language

Just as color is the painter's tool and the musical note is the composer's, so is the word the tool of the writer. The more the writer—and the public relations person— knows about language, the better he or she will do in terms of communication.

To begin with, the writer must understand that words have origins, ancestors, relatives—just like people. Our English language is composed of words derived from the Indo-Germanic, Anglo-Saxon, French, Latin, Greek, Spanish, and other languages. It is constantly changing, annually adding hundreds of new words. It is *alive*.

Words have an atmosphere surrounding them that we can't always explain. We get a different feeling about the use of *saliva* and *spit*. *Grief* is much stronger than *sadness*. *Abhorrence* has less impact than *loathing*, and *fear* looks weak beside *terror*.

In writing—and speaking—we must choose our words carefully. They should be just the right words to produce just the right effect. One false step can bring down the entire communication.

There can be a considerable gap between the denotation of a word and its connotation. Perhaps the most embarrassing writing lapse (next to mis-spelled words and grammatical errors) is the lack of understanding about the connotation of words.

Denotation refers to a dictionary definition—the *meaning* of a word. *Connotation* has to do with what the word suggests or implies—the other echoes that differentiate a word like *grief* from a word like *sadness*.

Denotatively, *aid* means to "help." But when we are in trouble, we don't yell "Aid!" The reason for this choice probably goes back to the root of these words. *Aid* comes from *aider* in Norman-French, which is a more courtly, proper, polite language. *Help* is an Anglo-Saxon or Old English word, and when in trouble or otherwise emotionally upset, we generally rely on the more earthy Anglo-Saxon.

There may be occasions when a more ornate style would be preferred, but these are rare. All great writing is simple writing, from Scripture to Michener. Public relations writing must be simplified, so we opt for a vocabu-lary that is clear and colorful. That is why a knowledge of linguistics is helpful. Appreciating why one word will evoke greater response than another comes from experience and sensitivity.

Words Have Meaning

Because we ordinarily use words as our communication tools, we are limited by what they may convey to others. *Home* can mean a pleasant memory, a happily forgotten jungle of frustrations, an orphanage, a country, a structure, a summer retreat, a distant city. *Love* can be a deep commit-ment, a banner slogan, infatuation, or a religious experience. Every abstract word, and many concrete ones, permit a variety of personal interpretations.

Practitioners must make sure their terminology means essentially the same thing to an intended audience. They can't behave like Humpty Dumpty in Lewis Carroll's *Through the Looking Glass*:

> "I don't know what you mean by 'glory,'" Alice said.
>
> Humpty Dumpty smiled contemptuously. "Of course you don't—till I tell you. I meant, 'there's a nice knock-down argument for you.'"
>
> "But 'glory' doesn't mean 'a nice knock-down argument,'" Alice objected.
>
> "When *I* use a word," Humpty Dumpty said, in rather a scornful tone, "it means just what I choose it to mean—neither more nor less."
>
> "The question is," said Alice, "whether you *can* make words mean so many different things."

"The question is," said Humpty Dumpty, "which is to be master—that's all."[15]

Although it's true that the PR professional must be able to forge prose to serve a specific purpose, the fact remains that the message must have meaning for the recipient. If it doesn't, it fails. Cricket seems as inane to an American sports enthusiast as does American football to his English cousin. Highly technical jargon is lost on the uninitiated. Even a cartoon's humor may be lost on us unless we understand the basis of the joke. When a music critic compares a composer to "giants" like Messiaen, Elliott Carter, and Pierre Boulez, the compliment means nothing unless you're into the modern idiom. Even a Doonesbury cartoon, showing rock musician Thudpucker in Ethiopia, requires the reader's knowledge that Hall and Oates are white in order to smile at the Ethiopian guide's comment that they are considered across Africa to be America's greatest black band.

Edmund Wilson once compiled a partial list of more than 100 words denoting drunkenness, from "lit" and "stewed" to "loaded" and "lathered." Besides the familiar "said" to indicate speech, there are dozens of more attractive substitutes—added, disclosed, cautioned, replied, stated, volunteered, corrected, whispered, quipped, emphasized, confessed, claimed, cracked, and so on.

We are also creating new words constantly, in a variety of ways. We lop off portions of words, forming "gas" from "gasoline" and "edit" from "editor." We abbreviate, making "stage properties" into "props," and "flat tire" into "flat." We also add on or alter, following "hamburger" with "cheeseburger," "ranchburger," "charburger," and other forms. Nouns become verbs, as we "elbow a shopper" or "stomach a remark." The reverse is also true when we experience a "close shave" or attend a "Broadway hit."

Words also enter our vocabularies from science, from the media, from the infusion of foreign terms. Slang and jargon supply words and phrases that may be temporary, and every new fad or occupation hurries to develop its vocabulary. The drug culture created dozens of euphemisms, from "grass" and "pot" to "narc" and "dust." Even break dancing added its dictionary entries, from "home slice" for "best friend" to "word up," which means "speak the truth."

Jargon is effective only with limited audiences, and it can be useless if practiced on the wrong group or if perceived by the right group as an attempt to hypocritically enter its camp.

No communication may be understood by all possible audiences. The job of the practitioner is to make sure the target audience is able to deal with it. Someone once called writing the process of telling stories to strangers, and PR exec Philip Lesly defines it as "a form of courtship," with the suitor using "logic, ardor, charm and persuasion to overcome the reticence of his intended."[16]

There's no such thing as a captive audience; the professional has to capture it. There is rarely anything in a message that the receiver absolutely must hear (with the exception of a lifeboat drill or a tornado alert), so it is the responsibility of the communicator to prove the importance of the message. Being open, honest, and clear is essential; all literary skills are adjuncts.

When you strip writing to the basics, you really go through a process of deciding what you want to convey and then choosing the language that will best express it. Then you may select images or examples that add clarity and force, and then determine whether your prose is fresh and compelling.

The Color of Language

Why do all mountains have to be "snowcapped" and all valleys "peaceful"? As one wire service editor reminded his reporters, does every police chase have to be "bullet-punctuated" and every fire exude "acrid" smoke?

Not all clichés are bad, of course. Some serve a purpose, like "bottom-lining" a report. And some may also be resurrected by a change of a single word in a group of words, or by presenting the phrase in an unexpected context. Even placing the word in quotes may help, letting the reader know the writer understands the senility of the phrase.

Overwriting

Akin to this weakness is the penchant many people have for overwriting. One of the good writer's greatest traits is the courage to cut deftly and mercilessly. All the verbiage that precedes, interrupts, and drags out sentences should be eliminated. If it's "needless to say," why say it? If something "defies description," then don't try. All this, plus such baggage as, "I would like to say that . . ." or, "It was at this time in my life that . . . ," and, "What I am trying to say is . . . ," deserves a decent burial. Even words like *seriously* and *rather* and *quite* merely weaken your language. Use them sparingly. Keep sentences as short as possible, but vary for effect. You do this by throwing away all the stale and unnecessary words you have allowed to creep in and by replacing them with colorful words that generally move people.

THE INTANGIBLE WRITING PLUS

Although many practitioners can learn to do a better job in their writing, there is no doubt that the exceptional public relations writers have a special gift, a talent for that medium. It manifests itself in a confident style that features imaginative expression, compelling examples, and even a bit of humor.

Consider a pair of travel brochures. Both have identical goals—to entice readers to book an African tour. One is replete with photos and is slickly, professionally written. The other has line drawings instead of photos. The copy for the former is good, but the copy for the latter is outstanding. What makes the second brochure distinctive is that it sounds warm and personal, as if it were written by a real human being.

Given the time and money, which tour would you rather go on?

> Africa, the storied continent of contrast, is awaiting your discovery right now! Big game reserves teeming with wildlife . . . lions and rhinos . . . cheetahs and zebras . . . giraffes and gazelles. Ngorongoro Crater, home of huge herds of wildlife. Colorful native markets where bartering is still very much in vogue. [17]

Good, punchy copy, but not exactly personal. It reads too much like advertising talk. On the other hand, the second brochure develops a question-and-answer style that exudes personality and humor.

> DO NOT SHAVE IN THE TEA—A dreadful custom in East Africa is early morning tea. It is automatically brought to you at 6:30 A.M. every morning in the lodges. When one of our safariers asked on the first day of his trip about shaving facilities in tents, we told him hot water would be brought to him in the morning, but we forgot to mention that morning tea comes first. When he got his tea, he shaved in it. It never occurred to him to drink it, but this is really what you are supposed to do. [18]

To write like this isn't easy. It requires skills similar to those that produce memorable literary works, but the goal is more pragmatic. Some communicators suggest that the PR writer should think like an advertising copywriter. Those who create the nation's advertising know that they must get attention quickly, that they have a short space in which to make an impression (meaning they must write and edit tightly), that the copy must flow, and that they have to earn the reader's interest and commitment.

A pair of young film makers, in thanking a foundation for the money that made possible their documentary on rural village life, could have copied the standard letters of gratitude that repeat the familiar phrases and contain all the polite expressions. Instead, they chose to describe to the foundation board the excitement and pleasure the villagers exhibited when they previewed the film, detailing their request for an immediate second showing, and explaining that the last people left the hall in the early morning hours, having shared photos and recollections throughout the night. Instead of reading a formal response, the board members were made part of the event.

Good writers know that imagery has a power to move that statistics do not. Both are helpful, but the imagery is more compelling, more memorable. Reading and practice help hone a literary gift, but it remains a gift.

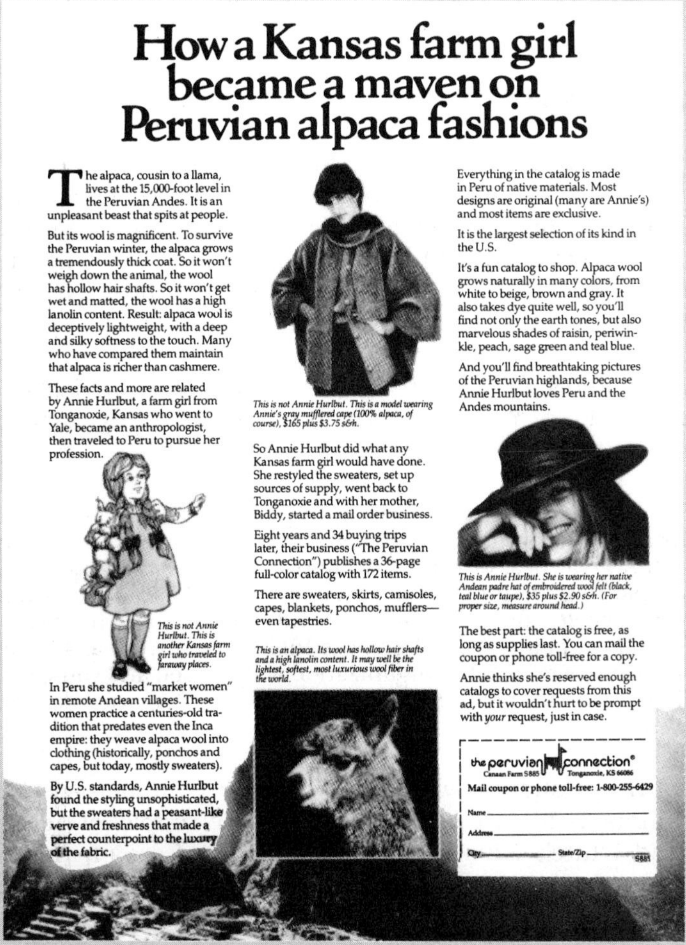

How a Kansas farm girl became a maven on Peruvian alpaca fashions

The alpaca, cousin to a llama, lives at the 15,000-foot level in the Peruvian Andes. It is an unpleasant beast that spits at people.

But its wool is magnificent. To survive the Peruvian winter, the alpaca grows a tremendously thick coat. So it won't weigh down the animal, the wool has hollow hair shafts. So it won't get wet and matted, the wool has a high lanolin content. Result: alpaca wool is deceptively lightweight, with a deep and silky softness to the touch. Many who have compared them maintain that alpaca is richer than cashmere.

These facts and more are related by Annie Hurlbut, a farm girl from Tonganoxie, Kansas who went to Yale, became an anthropologist, then traveled to Peru to pursue her profession.

This is not Annie Hurlbut. This is another Kansas farm girl who traveled to faraway places.

In Peru she studied "market women" in remote Andean villages. These women practice a centuries-old tradition that predates even the Inca empire: they weave alpaca wool into clothing (historically, ponchos and capes, but today, mostly sweaters).

By U.S. standards, Annie Hurlbut found the styling unsophisticated, but the sweaters had a peasant-like verve and freshness that made a perfect counterpoint to the luxury of the fabric.

This is not Annie Hurlbut. This is a model wearing Annie's gray mufflered cape (100% alpaca, of course), $165 plus $3.75 s&h.

So Annie Hurlbut did what any Kansas farm girl would have done. She restyled the sweaters, set up sources of supply, went back to Tonganoxie and with her mother, Biddy, started a mail order business.

Eight years and 34 buying trips later, their business ("The Peruvian Connection") publishes a 36-page full-color catalog with 172 items.

There are sweaters, skirts, camisoles, capes, blankets, ponchos, mufflers—even tapestries.

This is an alpaca. Its wool has hollow hair shafts and a high lanolin content. It may well be the lightest, softest, most luxurious wool fiber in the world.

Everything in the catalog is made in Peru of native materials. Most designs are original (many are Annie's) and most items are exclusive.

It is the largest selection of its kind in the U.S.

It's a fun catalog to shop. Alpaca wool grows naturally in many colors, from white to beige, brown and gray. It also takes dye quite well, so you'll find not only the earth tones, but also marvelous shades of raisin, periwinkle, peach, sage green and teal blue.

And you'll find breathtaking pictures of the Peruvian highlands, because Annie Hurlbut loves Peru and the Andes mountains.

This is Annie Hurlbut. She is wearing her native Andean padre hat of embroidered wool felt (black, teal blue or taupe), $35 plus $2.90 s&h. (For proper size, measure around head.)

The best part: the catalog is free, as long as supplies last. You can mail the coupon or phone toll-free for a copy.

Annie thinks she's reserved enough catalogs to cover requests from this ad, but it wouldn't hurt to be prompt with *your* request, just in case.

the peruvian [**connection**®
Canaan Farm 5485, Tonganoxie, KS 66086
Mail coupon or phone toll-free: 1-800-255-6429
Name _____
Address _____
City _____ State/Zip _____

Figure 5-7 The copy in this ad tells a story that you can read again and again.
Courtesy: The Peruvian Connection

Read to Improve

One of the best ways to improve writing is to read good writing. For the public relations practitioner, this means reading other PR materials that have style and power. Richard Burton, in a promotional piece for a TV special on Winston Churchill, described the prime minister's effect on a room full of people as "like a blow under the heart." Churchill himself said of a rival politician that "he seldom deviates into accuracy." And you occasionally find telling prose in as unlikely a place as a corporate annual report, especially when the writer is attempting to explain a financial downturn or a new social achievement.

Construction and Style

Some public relations writers, brought up on Vonnegut and Brautigan, seem to think that anything goes. What they are not aware of is the tough internal discipline that underlies what sometimes looks like the freest stream-of-consciousness meandering. What could appear more unstructured than James Joyce's *Ulysses?* And yet this book is one of the most tightly written, heavily plotted novels ever penned. One part of it was even written to a stopwatch!

Even if you could get away with it as literature, disjointed prose has no role in public relations. You must organize your thinking, arrange your ideas, build your story:

> The keys to effective, economical writing are planning and organization. This is true of *any* kind of writing, be it news story, magazine feature, novel, or speech. . . . A great deal of time and effort can be saved through the simple process of "plotting" your text, just as a novelist would. Take a few minutes to outline your article, key point by key point, working out the best possible sequence for those points. You'll be amazed at how much time and labor you will save in the actual writing. The organization will be good and you will find that second thoughts really aren't necessary, as they so often are with unplanned, unorganized efforts.[19]

The practitioner should own a good book on grammar—perhaps several. Some grammar books are merely catalogs and examples of rules; others, like Strunk and White's *Elements of Style*, concentrate on the common errors; still others anthologize examples of style. Although this is not the place to resurrect forgotten rules, it might be worthwhile to look at some points on style that can save or damn a piece of copy:

Important ideas come at the end of sentences and paragraphs.   They are not buried inside. Think of a joke. The punchline comes at the end. You don't say, "That was my wife, that was no lady," but the reverse.

Say, "Public relations is not publicity, graphics, and glad-handling; it's a management function." That's stronger than saying, "Public relations is a management function, not publicity, graphics, and glad-handling."

Even worse are those sentences that hide the important idea in a forest of words: "We are talking about a decline in profits of 7 percent, which is, more or less, after you add in the allocation for depreciation, comparable to the off year we experienced when the plant was first expanded, during the Vietnam years and the years that followed."

Ideas should be arranged in order of climax. Again, like the joke or anecdote, you build to the finish, or a climax. Speeches or articles or reports that wander all about, dropping key elements here and there, are impossible to follow. Organize thoughts and parade them out in logical order.

Don't be afraid to repeat. Repetition enhances clarity. You may want to vary the repetition for a more pleasing style. Remember that you are conveying information or persuading, and not dazzling the reader. If there is a chance some vital details may elude the reader, repeat.

Use the active voice. In the passive voice, the subject becomes the object. It is a duller way of phrasing things, particularly news. Not "The doors to the new wing were opened by the hospital administrator, Roger Forbes," but "Robert Forbes, hospital administrator, opened the doors to the new wing."

Work on verb strength. Too many writers rely on adjectives to color their prose. Verbs can do a better job.

Instead of saying, "Inflation is a menace to the entire supermarket industry," or, "Inflation has a menacing effect on the entire supermarket industry," how about, "Inflation menaces the entire supermarket industry"?

The verb "to be" is static and has little power. Rather than, "The horse was in the field," think, "The horse patrolled the field," or, "surveyed the field," or, "ignored the field." Make the verb do some work.

In news releases, of course, you don't want to get too clever or poetic, but in other types of public relations writing, imaginative verbs really help.

Provide decent transitions. When you move from one thought to another, the passage should be smooth. The reader should not have to check back to see how and where he or she arrived. Transitions can be handled mechanically, with words like *so* and *but* and *since*, or via content when it is obvious you have logically extended a previous idea.

Create a compelling opening and a memorable close. Busy people need a reason to begin reading any written piece, and they should take something away. Writers seem to be more adept at producing the interesting lead; they fail at producing a suitable conclusion. Either may consist of an appropriate quotation, but the conclusion should usually be a form of punctuation or summation. It gives the reader the feeling of completeness.

Write to express, not impress. Forget your exalted position. Relax. Keep in mind that the average person has a vocabulary of fewer than 10,000 words and may regularly use only 10 percent of these. Avoid what Westbrook Pegler used to call the "out-of-town" words, those multisyllable words that writers like William Buckley use.

Columnist James J. Kilpatrick cites Buckley's use of "opsimathy" in praising Nelson Rockefeller, and he confesses his own fondness for words like "limicolous": "I have had such love affairs," Kilpatrick told an audience of newspaper publishers in December 1977. "I have been in love with *oxymoron*. I had a fling with *alembic*. For quite some time I've been enchanted with *troglodyte*. But in the name of clarity, I beseech you, let us contemplate these lovely, alluring words and let us say a small prayer: 'Lead us not into temptation.'"[20]

Avoid jargon.   Every profession has its own jargon. The military talk about "nuclear deterrents," which sound like peaceful defenses instead of bombs. Educators have their "methodologies" and "underachievers" and "nonlinguistic thinking." Physicians and scientists exchange Latin banalities; sociologists worry about "culturally deprived" people and "infrastructures." Even journalists, who protest most about such failings, are not without their own jargon.

Writing in the *Columbia Journalism Review*, Ernest Havemann reminds his fellow journalists of their sins:

> On the front page of almost every newspaper every day, we find words like "reconnaissance," "logistics," "interdict," "infiltration." . . . On the financial pages, we find words like "preferred," "common," "yields," "discount rate," "prime rate," "debenture," and "convertible debenture," not to mention "subordinated debenture."[21]

Havemann analyzes terms like "red dog" and "blitz" on the sports pages, and the ridiculous titles given to magazine articles. All are examples of jargon.

Edwin Newman has written two books—*Strictly Speaking* and *A Civil Tongue*—that deal in depth with the problems of language, assailing writers, politicians, advertising copy writers, teachers, businesspeople, and others who are debasing English. Newman's favorite targets are the "ize" words, like "prioritize," and the "wise" words, like "energywise" and "languagewise."

There is something suspicious about an "Anger Reduction Workshop" led by a "facilitator" who promises to "maximize the learning dynamic." Or a swimming pool that's called an "aquatic therapy facility." Or a wholesale firing that becomes a "planned reduction in force," or, even worse, "a resizing of the operation to the level of profitable market opportunities."

People now no longer "meet," they "interface." And the brain becomes a "cognitive hemisphere," and a plane crash in Chicago is caused by "the captain's failure to exercise positive flight management."

These errors occur primarily because writers think they sound more impressive, or because they are deliberately cloaking their meaning.

A military newspaper, satirizing this style, rendered the tale of Little Red Riding Hood into service jargon. The story began:

> Once upon a time there lived a female, whose nomenclature was Hood, Red Riding, Little. She was a girl, happy. Her duty uniform consisted of the following

items: (1) dress, red, cotton, shade 76, 1 each; (2) cap, red, w-hood, 1 each. Her duty AFSC was food handler.[22]

We might add "networking" and "resourcing" and "impact" and "state-of-the-art" and "cash flow" and "double-digit" and "self-destruct" and "photo opportunity" and a legion of other phrases we read in PR materials.

Avoid redundancy.   Economy is the key to good writing. When you've made your point, move on. Do we need to say, "advance planning," "honest truth," "small in size," "plain and simple," "carbon copy," or "at the present time"?

Avoid euphemisms.   These may resemble jargon and are more palatable substitutes for the more direct expression. A parish bulletin heads a column on parishioners who have died with, "Departures from the Faith Community." Sounds like a train schedule. Dead people also "cross over," "pass on," or "move to a happier existence." One journalist said a person "demised." Bankruptcy can become a "downward readjustment," and what used to be called "wife swapping," then "mate swapping," is now "expanding the circle of love."

Give readers the score.   It's a common experience to tune in late to a sports broadcast or telecast and hear minute after minute of play-by-play or commentary, but no score. You want to scream at the announcers, *"What's the score?"* In writing you must also keep the reader in mind. Make your point and keep reminding the reader where he or she is and how things are going.

Don't explain too much.   Although we have stressed score-telling and repetition, it should be stated, too, that a surfeit of explanatory material becomes boring. If you feel you have made your case, move along. Don't punish or insult the reader.

Many writers find it helpful to overwrite and then cut. But they should remember to cut. In your company magazine, for example, will the employees get four pages of type detailing how management came to its conclusion on the state of the economy, or will they read how these decisions affect them?

Be sensitive.   Don't let your bias show in your writing. Ask yourself if what you have written could be misinterpreted by women, or blacks, or Hispanics. Will the translation you commissioned work for Mexicans *and* Puerto Rican citizens? Have you ignored the Native American in your list of minorities?

In an *ASNE Bulletin*, copy editor Lucille deView asks, rhetorically, whether Geraldine Ferraro's dress size should be reported when Walter Mondale's suit size isn't; whether we should use ethnic origin to describe a person when that fact isn't relevant; whether we shouldn't focus on a person's accomplishments and not his or her accompanying handicap; whether we shouldn't abandon ethnic stereotypes, like "cool Swedes" and "fiery Greeks"; and whether we shouldn't also scrap "sneer" words like "so-called" and "self-styled" and "would-be."[23]

There are those who argue against the neutering of our language to avoid charges of sexism, and they present such exhibits as "craftspersonship" to buttress their arguments. It is true that some extremes wrench the language, but the principle of sensitivity and evenness still holds.

Keep sentences short—but vary for effect.   When sentences get up to 30 words long, they are tough to read. Seventeen words is standard, and anything below that makes for easy reading. The reading skills of the audience must be considered, of course, but when your sentences average in the mid-twenties in word count, you lose a majority of readers.

Watch punctuation.   Some flexibility in punctuation is possible, and some stylebooks prefer one method over another. We also know that the trend today is toward fewer hyphens and fewer commas. There are some decent one- or two-page guides to punctuation that capsulize the common forms. Writers should also be aware that punctuation may serve other purposes besides clarity and correctness; punctuation may also emphasize, or retard, or alter the meaning.

Consider a narrative style.   Studies show that readers are attracted more to a narrative writing style, such as found in magazines, than they are to a summary style, characteristic of newspapers. The project dictates some choices. You don't normally use a narrative style in a news release or a proposal, but there are lots of options in other forms of writing, and the anecdotal approach is simply more appealing than the factual statement.

Master a conversational style.   Experts advise writers to write as they talk, meaning that there should be a personal touch to the prose rather than a stilted, unnatural feel.

Keep it simple.   Prefer the simple sentence to the complex, and the familiar word to the unfamiliar. Keep the paragraphs short. Condense the language rather than setting down everything you know about a topic. The whole story of creation is confined to 100 words in Genesis. Aim for compact prose that involves the reader.

Revise and rewrite.   Jack Kerouac declared that he never rewrote his prose. The same claim was once made for Shakespeare, that he had never "blotted a line." His contemporary, Ben Jonson, said he wished Shakespeare had blotted a few. Even genius can stand revision, and those writers with far more modest talents can always benefit from a second or third look, and a fourth or fifth rewriting. In these further readings, you catch errors, shorten sentences, gain new insights, alter a phrase for the better, remove clichés, improve communication.

Remember that the test of public relations prose is that it has to work. The point must be made, the information transmitted, the change provoked. Without preaching, the writer must show how such communication will benefit the reader.

CHAPTER HIGHLIGHTS

- Communication involves a sender, receiver, and message. It works best when feedback is possible, but the formal reactive method moves more slowly than rumors.
- The perception of the sender and the mood of the receiver both affect the acceptance of the message.
- There are many roadblocks to communication, including censorship, lack of purpose, poor audience definition, faulty language selection, lack of credibility, lack of semantic knowledge, faulty arrangement, inappropriate timing, lack of useful information, incorrect assumptions, information overload, decentralization, and inattention.
- Communication has numerous psychological aspects, including the disposition of the receiver, interest in the topic, and the perceived use of the information.
- Nonverbal communication may augment or counter the spoken word, and PR professionals should become expert in reading the 125 common body-language signals.
- Writing, although important for practitioners, is getting less attention within and without the profession.
- The communicator must understand the history of language, the connotation of words, the need for clarity, and the possibilities of imaginative prose.
- Many elements affect construction and style, from the building of sentences to the elimination of jargon and clichés. Writers should write simply, adopting a conversational tone, with the aim of expressing rather than impressing. The final test is whether or not the written word achieved its goal.

NOTES

[1]Leo Rosten, "The Myths by Which We Live," *Vital Speeches*, April 15, 1965.

[2]James Howe, *The Making of Style* (Philadelphia: Chilton, 1972).

[3]Ralph E. Frede, speech prepared for the Summer Academy of ACPRA (now CASE), Notre Dame, Indiana, 1973.

[4]Philip Lesly, "Managing the Human Climate," a supplement of *pr reporter*, No. 65 (November/December 1980).

[5]Bernard Berelson and Gary Steiner, *Human Behavior* (New York: Harcourt Brace Jovanovich, 1967).

[6]James B. Strenski, "Where Does Communication Begin?" *Public Relations Quarterly*, Spring 1977.

[7]Julius Fast, *Body Language* (New York: Evans, 1970).

[8]Interview with Allan Mazur, "What Your Body Language Tells Others," *U.S. News & World Report*, August 8, 1983.

[9]David Alan Safer, "Institutional Body Language," *Public Relations Journal,* March 1985.

[10]John F. Budd, Jr., "The Last Writes?" *Public Relations Quarterly,* Summer 1978.

[11]*Adweek,* September 28, 1981.

[12]Hugh Kenner, "Writing Is an Abnormal Act," *U.S. News & World Report,* February 14, 1983.

[13]Robert Pattison, "The Literacy of Power," *Communicator's Journal,* September/October 1983.

[14]Georges Carousso, "In Praise of Public Relations Writing," *Writer's Digest,* November 1976.

[15]Lewis Carroll, *Through the Looking Glass* (New York: Random House, 1946).

[16]"Reaching Your Reader: Keys to Effective Communication," *Impact,* No. 186 (1976).

[17]Courtesy of Park East Tours.

[18]Courtesy of Percival Tours.

[19]Wesley Pedersen, "Effective Writing—With Economy," *Public Relations Quarterly,* Spring 1976.

[20]James J. Kilpatrick, speech delivered to the annual conference of the Associated Press Managing Editors, New Orleans, December 1977.

[21]Ernest Havemann, "Journalists and Jargonists," *Columbia Journalism Review,* Summer 1966.

[22]*Space Sentinel,* November 11, 1971 (reprint from *Vietnam Log*).

[23]Lucille S. deView, "Test Your Bias IQ," *ASNE Bulletin,* September 1984.

SUGGESTED READINGS

BERGER, ARTHUR ASA, *Signs in Contemporary Culture.* New York: Longman, 1984.

CHENEY, THEODORE A. REES, *Getting the Words Right: How to Revise, Edit and Rewrite.* Cincinnati: Writer's Digest Books, 1984.

CORRADO, FRANK M., *Media for Managers: Communication Strategies for the Eighties.* Englewood Cliffs, N.J.: Prentice-Hall, 1984.

DEFLEUR, MELVIN L., and SANDRA BALL-ROKEACH, *Theories of Mass Communication.* New York: Longman, 1982.

HALL, EDWARD T., *The Silent Language.* Westport, Conn.: Greenwood, 1980.

HIEBERT, RAY ELDON, DONALD F. UNGURAIT, and THOMAS W. BOHN, *Mass Media IV.* New York: Longman, 1985.

JASSEM, HARVEY, and ROGER DESMOND, study on mass communication and the new technology in the anthology, *Information and Behavior.* New Brunswick, N.J.: Transaction Books, 1985.

KNAPPER, ARNO F., and LODA I. NEWCOMB, *Style Manual for Written Communication.* Columbus, O.: Grid, 1983.

KREPS, GARY L., *Organizational Communication.* New York: Longman, 1986.

LONGYEAR, MARIE, ed., *The McGraw-Hill Style Manual.* New York: McGraw-Hill, 1983.

MCGUIRE, JOHN F., *Words in Action: The 5 C's Approach to Good Writing.* Lanham, Md.: University Press of America, 1984.

MONTGOMERY, MARTIN, *An Introduction to Language and Society*. New York: Methuen, 1986.

NEWMAN, EDWIN, *A Civil Tongue*. New York: Warner, 1980.

NEWSOM, DOUG, and TOM SIEGFRIED, *Writing in Public Relations Practice*. Belmont, Calif.: Wadsworth, 1981.

PASSEL, ANNE, *Your Words: Public and Private*. Lanham, Md.: University Press of America, 1982.

RICE, RONALD E., and ASSOCIATES, *The New Media*. Beverly Hills, Calif.: Sage, 1984.

ROCKEY, EDWARD H., *Communicating in Organizations*. Lanham, Md.: University Press of America, 1985.

ROMAN, KENNETH, and JOEL RAPHAELSON, *Writing That Works*. New York: Harper & Row, 1981.

SAFIRE, WILLIAM, *On Language*. New York: Times Books, 1981.

SCHMIDT, BARBARA, and NANCY SCHMIDT, *Communication: The Non-Verbal Agenda*. 30-minute film. New York: McGraw-Hill Films, 1984.

STRUNK, WILLIAM JR., and E.B. WHITE, *The Elements of Style*, 3rd ed. New York: Macmillan, 1979.

WHITMAN, DIGBY, *The Road to Readability*. Chicago: Lawrence Ragan Communications, 1983.

Communication Concepts, monthly newsletter, Washington, D.C.

Written Communication, quarterly. Beverly Hills, Calif.: Sage.

EXERCISES

1. Select two print ads that contain good examples of language that evokes positive images and persuades the reader. Select two print ads that fail to do this.

2. Using direct mail only—third-class advertising mailed to your house—illustrate three of the roadblocks to communication listed in this chapter.

3. Observing friends and strangers for a day, make a list of nonverbal signals you detect and indicate what each probably means.

4. Here are some words that have changed meaning in popular jargon: *trip, hooked, fix, fuzz,* and *scene*. List ten more words whose meanings have altered in recent years.

5. Select five words and list one synonym for each; then show how the word and its synonym differ in *connotation*.

6. Make a list of five words whose spelling always gives you trouble; five grammatical errors, clichés, or sayings that bother you; five problems you yourself have in grammar or punctuation.

7. Write a one-page description of your college and university, directed toward high school seniors in a state at least 500 miles away, with the aim of getting them to enroll. What unique features will you emphasize? What colorful language will you use to create images and persuade?

CASE PROBLEMS

1. A large manufacturer of food products (breakfast cereal, flour, cake mixes, frozen pizza, and other items) employs two dozen scientists, all with specialized doctoral degrees, in the company's research and development division. The money to fund their research must be approved by the firm's accounting division, presided over by three persons holding M.B.A. degrees. Problems arise when those in the accounting department can't decipher the proposals by the scientists, and they insist that the scientists make clear why the money is required and how it will be used. The scientists insist that the accounting-department executives should be more familiar with their terminology. The company president tells you, the public relations director, to settle this dispute. How would you handle it? Who's right and who's wrong? If you initiate some specialized training, be specific about the personnel involved and the detailed program and goals.

2. The state police in a western state are anxious to improve their public image. Citizens complain that the police are ticket-happy and that their presence is more oppressive than necessary. One specific item that surfaces is the way a state trooper deals with a motorist who is ordered to pull over. "They stand behind you outside the car so you have to twist your head backwards and look up at them," one man charges. The commander of the state police agrees but explains, "The officer never knows what he or she is going to come across. That driver could be armed. We tell them to stand that way to protect themselves." The governor asks you, her aide, to look into this. "I'm sure some sort of compromise is possible," she tells you. What solution might you propose?

3. In a survey conducted by the public relations office of a large insurance company employing 3,000 people in its home office, there is a question asking what the major problem is, in the eyes of employees. Over 70 percent of those responding identify "communication" as one of the two major company shortcomings. As PR director, you're trying to analyze this response. What are some of the specific complaints it might include? What would you do to correct these lapses? How would you go about refining the responses a bit more, to discover what particular things are bothering employees? To get this information, write out the questions you would ask.

6
PUBLIC RELATIONS AND PUBLICITY

The most counterproductive attitude a PR practitioner may entertain relative to the media is to accept the conclusion that the two vocations are necessarily adversarial. A more realistic and effective reading of the relationship might regard public relations and the press as complementary. Both have individual tasks; they sometimes conflict, but more often, the generating of news and the gathering of news coincide. Reporters and editors may not want to admit it, but upwards of three-fourths of the stories published or broadcast emanate, not from investigative reporting, but from the sources themselves—often prompted or channeled by PR specialists. On their side, practitioners are too quick to criticize the few negative encounters with the media and reluctant to recall the many positive experiences.

In working with reporters, the PR professional must accept several premises:

1. The public has a right to know.
2. The mass media are the ordinary channels for communicating this information.
3. The First Amendment to the Constitution protects the media in their news-gathering and dissemination processes.
4. The individual reporter is charged with unearthing and writing the news that will later be published or aired. The reporter would also like to get this news first.

The First Amendment has been vigorously upheld by the media and the courts. Even when some abuses surface, the prospect of limiting press freedom inevitably looms as more onerous than accepting the occasional injustice. Newspapers are supposed to be impartial in their presentation of the news, although their opinion pieces and editorials may adopt an obvious bias. Networks operate similarly and are also subject to the Fairness Doctrine, which dictates that contrasting and conflicting views should be aired in an equal and equally forceful manner.

Despite these safeguards, controversy continues. Mobil Oil Company, committed to a more aggressive advocacy stand than most industries, took on NBC for a special the network did on gasoline pricing, and Shell responded to the same network for what it perceived as an inadequate time frame for its viewpoint on the safety of offshore rigs. General William C. Westmoreland engaged in an expensive libel suit against CBS, claiming his reputation was injured by the network documentary, "The Uncounted Enemy: A Vietnam Deception." The National Council of Churches demanded time to respond to a "60 Minutes" program on fund raising; members of the Reagan administration have publicly criticized newspapers and television news for their "biased and one-sided" stance on the government's Central American policy; the Rev. Jerry Falwell, Ted Turner, and organizations like Fairness in Media all express their desire to temper the "liberal bias" they perceive in CBS, by either purchase or protest.

Many communicators see the media as being under siege and the First Amendment as threatened. Some attribute the complaints to a public distaste for bad news; others see it as a question of balance; still others as a sensationalizing of news, precipitated by fast media, like television.

> A 1966 study by the Newspaper Advertising Bureau showed that 79 percent of adults in the U.S. read a daily newspaper. In 1984 that percentage had dropped to 66 percent. Meanwhile, the Harris Survey showed that confidence in the press (including newspapers) plunged from 29 percent in 1966 to 14 percent in 1982. Thus, said [Tom] Holbein, the decline in credibility in the press has paralleled the decline in newspaper readership.[1]

Although the public perception of television news rates higher than that of newspapers, both sources face credibility problems. Practitioners have a dual stake in this issue. First, the PR professional should be equally concerned about any erosion in First Amendment freedoms, and second, the practitioner has an opportunity to provide some of the balance that critics find absent.

"We write about airplanes that haven't crashed," explained one PR spokesperson.

From the editor's or news director's viewpoint, the danger from the public relations arm comes from increased dependence on the source it criticizes. Pierre Berton, writing in the *Financial Post* of Toronto, laments:

> Handout journalism . . . dominates the media. I don't mean that everything you read, see or hear is the result of a printed handout. I mean that much of it *arrives*, more or less unsolicited, at the media's doorstep. Only a small part of

what we receive as news is the result of a tough-minded, hard-nosed investigation by aggressive journalists.[2]

Some editors boast that they toss out 90 percent or more of the news releases they receive. This is unlikely. Veteran publicists contend it's almost too easy placing material, adding that some of their releases aren't even edited and sometimes appear under by-lines of staff members. That doesn't mean that inept practitioners will attain the same results.

INDUSTRY GOES ON THE ATTACK

On November 25, 1979, "60 Minutes" aired a segment on "uncontrollable construction costs" at Illinois Power's nuclear plant in Clinton, Illinois. While CBS was filming, the power company duplicated the footage with its own cameras. After the program was broadcast, Illinois Power claimed a number of inaccuracies existed, errors of fact as well as of omission. To counter these, they produced their own videotape, counterpointing the "60 Minutes" program with their own film footage. Company officials took issue with CBS on "misstatements or distortions" centering on daily construction costs, the purpose of Illinois Power's rate-increase request (the company said it was to cover inflationary cost increases, whereas the documentary alleged it was for the nuclear plant), the contentions that Illinois Power's expenses were far above the norm and that the managers of the new plant were inexperienced, and other points of difference. On January 27, 1980, "60 Minutes" corrected two of its statements but insisted the other allegations were true, based on its investigation. Illinois Power prepared another point-by-point rebuttal, again using the mass media. Its public affairs office began circulating 1,000 copies of its videotape, concentrating on business, education, communication, and civic groups. The tape can be obtained from the company by mailing a blank tape that the public affairs office then dubs and returns. A more complete package was made available by the Media Institute, which interested itself in the case, including the Illinois Power videotape, the complete transcript of the original CBS broadcast, copies of correspondence between the two parties, and documents filed with the Illinois Commerce Commission.

Mobil Corporation, stung by what it regarded as deliberate falsehoods about oil-industry profits, launched an advertising campaign promoting industry viewpoints from its perspective. The copy was written by Mobil's PR staff and defended company profits, examined the costs of discovering and tapping oil reserves, and even took a few swipes at politicians and the media. Often the print ads ran in major newspapers opposite the editorial

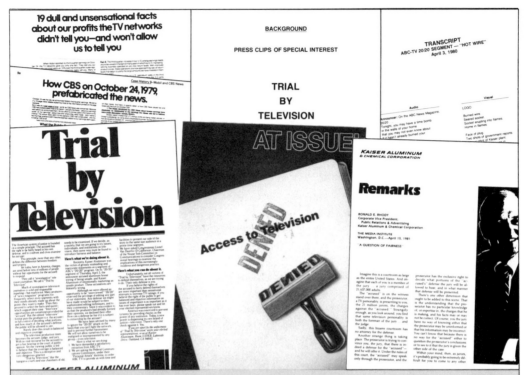

Figure 6-1 Starting in the 1970s, a number of American firms took a more aggressive stance against reporting they felt to be biased, especially in the television medium.
Courtesy: Mobil Oil and Kaiser Aluminum & Chemical Corporation

page, but when Mobil tried to place these issue-oriented commercials on television, two of the three networks refused them on the grounds that they would produce demands for equal time. Mobil offered to pay for the equal time, but the networks still refused, so Mobil took out ads detailing these denials and showing a storyboard and script of the proposed TV spot.

A few years later, in 1982, the *Washington Post* ran a story hinting that the son of Mobil's president, William P. Tavoulareas, was aided in his shipping-business career by paternal influence. Tavoulareas sued and was awarded over $2 million in damages, but later had that finding overturned by a higher court, which declared it found no "actual malice" grounds for the verdict.

In the interim between these two judgments, Mobil and Tavoulareas brought their case to the public. When *The Wall Street Journal*'s executive editor criticized the original decision, saying, "It's a great commentary on our times when a jury finds for an oil company against a newspaper," Mobil ran a print advertisement headed by the quote and asking whether oil companies were to be deprived of their civil rights and maligned with impunity.

To protect its executives against the cost of mounting libel suits in the future, Mobil has taken out special defamation insurance policies on them.

When Geraldo Rivera anchored a "20/20" broadcast on aluminum wiring on April 3, 1980, Kaiser Aluminum, which was singled out in the telecast, cried "foul." It objected to Rivera's use of language like "a ticking time bomb . . . lurking behind the walls of more than 2 million homes," his taking of quotes out of context, his use of discredited witnesses, his failure to point out that some statements had later been disavowed, and the juxtaposition of visuals used to illustrate the report. Like other companies that faced similar situations, Kaiser fought back with threatened legal action, requests for redress, publicity, speeches, and advertising. Calling the actions of ABC-TV "trial by television," Kaiser spokesperson Ronald E. Rhody, corporate vice-president in charge of public relations and advertising, condemned the blurring of journalism and entertainment, the lack of balance in some newscasts, and the hapless predicament of the accused. However, he also criticized American business for its "timidity . . . the unwillingness to risk controversy, the almost catatonic clinging to the blanket of corporate invisibility. . . ."

In its campaign for equal time, which ultimately ended with a four-minute rebuttal opportunity on ABC's experimental new program, "Viewpoint," on July 24, 1981, Kaiser put together a kit that was mailed free to opinion leaders. It contained the "20/20" script, reprints of ads, press releases, a letter from the corporation's attorney, the annual report, a collection of press clippings, copies of speeches by Rhody, and a special magazine-format publication giving the company's views on access to television.

Combat is rarely as effective in public relations as compromise, but there are times when a tough stance may be necessary. Determining when to take this risk is one of the trickiest calls in the PR profession.

Besides lack of skill in the news business, which, as one editor points out, is also the public relations person's business, the media may also fault public relations for shielding clients or impeding their search for the truth. At times this is a legitimate complaint. But if so, it results from shortsightedness on the part of the public relations officer. It is bad practice to try to conceal facts. The PR person's job is to reveal information, making certain the boss's or client's side of the story is also told. Successful public relations is built on reputation, and once this reputation is lost, the PR person cannot function. The easiest way to lose it is to lie.

The road to media respect is via honesty, accuracy, and professionalism. The practitioner must know the requirements of each medium and make every effort to accommodate them. Treating media people openly and expecting the best may occasionally be naive, but more often than not, it will provoke a professional response.

PERSONAL RELATIONSHIPS

Personal friendships are advantageous, and so are the chats at the local press club. When the chips are down, however, a good reporter won't let friendship stand in the way of a story. Practitioners should understand this—and be disappointed if a reporter acted otherwise. The reporter should, conversely, expect practitioners to represent to the best of their ability the people who pay them.

When it comes to relationships between the boss or client and the members of the press corps, the PR role is always that of mediator. If a client suggests that the practitioner call up a reporter or editor and blast this person for something he or she has said or written, the practitioner should refuse. The practitioner may have other clients, and there will be other days. These ties must be amicable. What the practitioner should do is reconcile the disagreement, perhaps by explaining the reporter's job to the client, or even bringing both parties together. But you don't saw off your PR limb.

SOME MEDIA RULES TO LIVE BY

Always treat the news media equally.   This might be amended to say, "as equally as possible," since you can't really apply the same standards of cooperation to a small weekly as you do to a major metropolitan daily. The deadlines are different, for one thing, and you can't regularly hold news for one certain day to give the daily and the weekly a simultaneous scoop. However, you should not play favorites. Perhaps you have a close friend who is on the news staff of one of the four local TV stations. You constantly leak the big stories to this friend. Your name will be mud with the other stations, the radio outlets, and the newspapers.

What you aim for is an equal break in release times. It is impossible to satisfy everyone, but a decade or two ago the wire services, meeting in convention, worked out a rather good rule. Stories released for the afternoon edition of the newspaper are fair game for the noon news on radio and television. Morning releases may be used on the preceding night's 10:00 P.M. news segments. This does not always set well with the daily paper—particularly when it is a strong paper. And it shouldn't. Any news gatherer wants to be first. And this is a compromise—but it is a compromise that makes the PR job possible.

When reporters uncover a story themselves, that's a different matter. If they check with you on it, you owe them the courtesy of allowing them to break the news first. After all, they could have used it without alerting you. After they have their story out, you may send a general release.

Be helpful to the media.   You should be helpful to the media, particularly when it hurts. If you get up at 3:00 A.M. and rush to your office to get some factual data for an inquiring reporter, he or she won't forget it. If you give reporters a lead on a story that has nothing in it for you, they will appreciate it. And they will also be grateful for stories that are on time, in a usable form, and totally accurate. Your photos, too, should be professional and with sufficient contrast to make for good printing in the paper; or with the proper axis (horizontal) for television.

Get the name right.   When addressing a news release to a particular desk, be sure you get the name right—and the title, if any. There will be many changes over a year's time. Stay abreast of these, check spelling, and watch for other errors. All media lists should be checked at least every other month.

Don't try to peddle weak stories.   Peddling weak stories is unprofessional and unproductive. Above all, don't try to exert pressure to get these stories in, or resort to tears. You don't threaten to pull ads if the story isn't used, and you don't remind the reporter that you bought the drinks at the press club last Saturday evening. The story must sell on its own merits.

Nor should you ask a reporter to kill a story you view as damaging to your firm or a client. All you should ask for is a chance to include your side of the story. The best advice to a PR person facing a disaster is to get the story out honestly and completely. Any use of subterfuge is certain to backfire. If you live by the principle that the public has a right to know, you will succeed.

Don't speculate.   This practice is dangerous from two angles. It may hurt your client or company, and it may destroy your credibility with the media. Be certain of your facts before you make any statements. Guessing at reasons or amounts or consequences is unprofessional.

Be aware of deadlines.   A story delivered past deadline (or even on deadline, if this is avoidable) is a strike against the PR person. Newscasts are aired at set times, and newspapers are printed at specific times. These may vary, but the local PR person must know all of them.

Understand media requirements.   The PR person should be aware of the mission of the various media, should be conscious of their special needs and regulations, and should understand the nature of news. This means the practitioner shouldn't cave in to the vanity of a client or CEO, but should exercise news judgment *before* the story is written. The style books of the media should be studied and followed, and specific instructions about mechanical details should be obeyed.

The practitioner should understand that interests and audiences may change for certain media and that this presents a new set of story guidelines.

Be accurate.   Every news release should be examined for incorrect or incomplete information, for spelling or typographical errors, for inconsistencies, repetitious facts, and other lapses—*before* it is allowed to leave the PR office.

Be accessible.   This may be especially true when the news is bad, but practitioners should always be available to the media, to clarify, or add, or verify. Accessibility, particularly when the going gets rough, is a quality admired by the media, as is the PR person's ability to also make company executives accessible.

Be consistent and professional.   As a PR person, one must earn the trust of the media, and this comes about by being honest, reliable, thoroughly grounded in details of the organization you represent, careful in gathering and writing news, and as quick and open with negative items as with positive ones. Good practitioners don't stage phony events, don't pout or gloat, and don't pester editors after the story has been delivered.

THE OTHER SIDE OF THE COIN

There are times, of course, when the PR practitioner must stand up for what he or she knows to be right. These instances will be rare, but the practitioner could be confronted with unfair or debasing treatment from an individual member of the news media. Practitioners are not obliged to roll over and take this injustice. They should make their point with the reporter as forcefully as possible. If this doesn't work, as a last resort they may appeal over the reporter's head. This tactic is risky, since there is an understandable fraternity among news reporters who work together, and practitioners may alienate more than just the offending journalist.

The PR person shouldn't look upon his or her job as being subservient but should be slow to exhibit anger or make a complaint. The good reporter is just as remorseful about an error as is the practitioner.

> In my view, if you have positively concluded that you have a case, present it. If the media clearly are wrong, tell them. Most journalists today respect you for giving them your point of view. Journalists' memories on misdemeanors are long. And I believe in human nature. As a minimum they'll be much more careful next time.[3]

Practitioners are also critical of the media's tendency toward sensationalism, their failure to provide enough skilled reporters to cover such emerging areas as the environment and the elderly, and their continuing hostility toward the PR sources of news.

Some aspects of the media produce problems that are part of the hazards of modern communication. Short deadlines, limited space and time, and the competition among media sometimes result in the airing or printing of news that is incomplete or inaccurate. The assigning of inexperienced reporters, especially from local electronic media, to complicated and special-ized stories may create errors. So may sloppy editing or the desire to increase circulation or win awards.

Neither profession is free of mistakes, but the practitioner normally has a bigger stake in keeping relations solid, so he or she treads more respect-fully.

THE ETHICS OF THE RELATIONSHIP

There are no national rules defining what the relationship shall be between the reporter and the PR person, but many newsrooms have their own pub-lished code. Some of these are quite stringent. The *Milwaukee Journal*, for example, includes the following guidelines in its statement of editorial policy:

> Free tickets or passes to sports events, movies, theatrical productions, circuses, ice shows or other entertainments may not be accepted or solicited by staff members.
>
> A staff member who needs to attend an event for background purposes should buy a ticket and turn in an expense voucher.
>
> Gifts of insignificant value—a calendar, pencil, key chain, or such—may be accepted if it would be awkward to refuse or to return them. All other gifts should be declined. Staff members may not accept any gifts or liquor, wine or beer.
>
> Junkets, free trips and reduced rate or subsidized travel may not be accepted.

The list goes on to state that books and records obtained for review will be turned over to deserving organizations and not retained by the reviewer. Free memberships cannot be accepted, or reduced-rate merchandise, and political activities are forbidden, even volunteer activities.

Some papers—and radio and TV stations—are less specific. Books and records are kept, and sometimes sold, by reviewers. Junkets on military or Hollywood assignments are common. There are no prohibitions against Christmas gifts. Actually, from the PR point of view, this situation is harder to deal with.

In the Code of Professional Standards issued by the Public Relations Society of America, this statement is made:

> A member shall not engage in any practice which tends to corrupt the integrity of channels of communication.

Individual PSRA members, however, disagree over the interpretation of these words. Besides, the variety of possible "corrupting" situations is large.

What about placing a reporter on your company payroll as a consultant? Or taking a reporter to lunch? Or asking him or her to volunteer for a nonprofit organization? Or approaching a public relations firm about spon-soring a cocktail party at a media convention?

Even the apparently innocent practice of awarding prizes to journalists has become suspect. David Zinman, a *Newsday* staffer, returned his $500 Empire Award for medical reporting, stating:

> What I was reacting against is a subtle, sometimes difficult-to-pinpoint public relations technique whose influence extends far beyond my insignificant award. *Editor and Publisher* lists more than 130 prize contests for newsmen, and this is not an all-inclusive list. The names of the award-giving groups read like a national lobbyists' convention. Prizes are given by doctors, truckers, airlines, travel associations, insurance agencies, lawyers, osteopaths, shoe firms, dog food manufacturers, religious groups, scientists, and tax-exempt foundations— to name a few. They offer awards ranging from a plaque to $2,500.[4]

Zinman suggests that editors scrutinize such contests more thoroughly, eliminating those that seem imprudent, and that they, rather than the sponsoring company, pay a reporter's expenses to go and pick up an award. In particular, he feels, writers should never accept cash prizes from groups about which they regularly report. Instead, he opts for writers' making their own awards, free, as he puts it, "of the green umbilical cord of public relations."

There are other issues—from "payola" or "plugola" payments slipped to broadcasters for mentioning a product name to "background" sessions with government officials in which all comments are off the record. There are also the staged or pseudoevents—the press conference called by some militant group, the demonstration, the press release from the Defense Department.

> All are a way in which a salesman for a point of view may present his case. The problem in this fast-moving society is to put hundreds of these pseudoevents, staged daily, into a context that bears a relationship to their importance.[5]

Caution and prudence are the best policies in all such matters. It may be OK to give a yuletide present to some special friend in the media if the gift is obviously a token of friendship and cannot, in any way, be viewed as a bribe for past or future favors. Even thanking a reporter can be touchy. Will the reporter think the PR person extended this gratitude because the story seemed to be so one-sided in his or her favor? Perhaps such applause should be saved for those stories that were outstanding and that had nothing to do with either the practitioner or the practitioner's firm or clients.

> The role of public relations, as it pertains to the news media, is to provide us with factual information, either self-generated or upon our request, dealing with the products or services of their employer. That has to be about it. You provide the information, you provide the facts.[6]

That counsel may be a bit too limited to function within comfortably, but it is certainly safe, and certainly paramount.

With some justification, representatives of the media say they sometimes feel used by public relations people who are relying on them to publicize an event or a cause that should be supported by advertising or other promotional means. They cite cases of fund-raising affairs for which publicity is forced upon them, sometimes by a community-conscious publisher. They bring up the staged media events, such as demonstrations or sit-ins or mini-parades. Local newspapers and electronic media feel particularly pressured by organizations that enjoy local favor, even when these organizations are commercial ventures. Every reporter is expected to be kind to the county fair and the zoo and the children's home.

But the problem is deeper than this. Political leaders, including presidents, have lured reporters to news conferences to garner publicity for their favorite programs, some of which never materialize. Some of the 200 reporters who covered the sensational Claus von Bulow trials were guests or hosts at dinners and cocktail parties involving the defendant, the judge, and the defense and prosecution teams. Von Bulow, on trial for the attempted murder of his wife, courted the media, as did his children, who sought his conviction. The children hired their own publicist and offered exclusive interviews to certain outlets. Von Bulow's companion, Andrea Reynolds, distributed her own handouts and also phoned reporters to critique their copy.

In an article by staff reporter Jeanne Saddler, *The Wall Street Journal* (April 2, 1985) scored the PR practice of circulating television news clips that contain subtle and not-so-subtle commercial plugs for clients. Some of these are aired without identifying the source, claimed the *Journal* article, leading to the impression that they were actual news. Some filmed segments allow local stations to insert their own announcers, live or voice over, and some allow users to employ their own typefaces for superimposed interview identifications. Almost all are soft-sell, quietly and unobtrusively introducing a product or a point of view.

There are, too, the package deals that some smaller newspapers and trade journals accept, or even solicit. These tie an ad to a news story. Some pairing of advertising and news can be accidental or even legitimate. When cellular telephones were introduced to a city via a full-page print ad, it made sense that the local paper also ran a news story, with a local angle, explaining how these mobile phones worked and what they cost. Although the product name was used in the story, the information had sufficient news value to justify inclusion, but the proximity of story and ad still raised eyebrows.

Reporters and practitioners won't always agree on what is news and what is "space grabbing," but the sensitive PR person will avoid those news releases that are blatantly self-serving. They inevitably destroy credibility and relationships.

RECOGNIZING NEWS

Erma Bombeck once declared that no group in the United States was as committed to rejection as are publicity chairmen. That may be true, but if so, it's because most of them are inexpert in divining news and writing the subsequent release.

Opinions differ, of course, as to what constitutes news, and editors are paid to exercise judgment on what shall appear in the paper or on the air. And changing values also alter the perception of news importance. Still, there are far more constants than variables.

A 1982 survey conducted by Michigan State University for the American Society of Newspaper Editors and Newspaper Readership Project sought newsroom attitudes about news. Leading the list as most significant were stories that directly affected readers—news that educated, or informed, or changed the status quo. Next came news of interest—something entertaining, unusual, unknown. These two categories accounted for nearly three-fourths of what journalists defined as news. Less critical, but still important, were news stories that were timely, current, trendy. Proximity and prominence made up the final two choices, focusing on items that were local or involved famous people or events.

Everyone's interpretation of what news is may differ, and therefore the topic must be defined broadly. News is really anything that interests people in general, or any smaller audience within that overall public. Many women think too much space and time is given to sports. Some critics laugh at society news. But these items are meant for someone, and there is sufficient interest or they wouldn't be carried.

Famous people make news.   The media don't cover kindergarten entry for everyone's children, but they may be out in force when Jackie Onassis drives her youngsters to school. A minor operation sets no typewriters clicking, unless it involves a person of stature, like a president. You may tire of magazine covers featuring rock stars or television personalities, but they sell publications. Fame is relative; local citizens may also have reputations sufficient to provoke coverage of their more mundane activities—their parties, vacations, retirement.

Good stories are popular.   Everyone likes to read about romance, or about humorous incidents; everyone sometimes attends to gossip, or follows the progress of a trial or crime. News that has a bit of a plot attracts readership, and so do stories that have style.

Readers are interested in the new and different.   Sports notes and scores, movie and television listings, plans for future construction—all attract attention. So do stories with a twist, like the indigent man who returns a wallet full of money to the person who lost it, or the beauty queen who declines her crown. Appointments and promotions fit into this category, as do the announcements of any fresh plans.

Figure 6-2 Famous people always make news. Here, Mother Theresa visits with Father Robert Hupp, former director of Boys Town.
Courtesy: Father Robert Hupp and Boys Town, photo by Bill Ramsey

Importance lends significance.   Weathercasts, health tips, ways to save on taxes, methods of conserving energy—all succeed as news because they benefit the individual. So may publicity concerning legal matters, or a plant closing, or even the rerouting of traffic.

There are other categories as well, and experience should reveal these. What interests you could interest others, but there are also subjects and events beyond one person's purview that may be news to a separate audience. PR people with publicity responsibilities should develop the proverbial "nose for news," should learn to circulate within an organization to unearth possible stories, should have a cadre of employees who provide story tips, and should be alert to possible tie-ins with other news.

THE NEWS RELEASE

Most publicity is delivered via the news release (or press release) route, by mail, by hand, or by computer. Consequently, these news releases should be written as carefully as if they were produced directly for the medium itself. Even though they may often be rewritten, particularly to fit space and style, the better the job the practitioner does, the better the chance of the practitioner's deathless prose surviving. If the release is riddled with errors and obvious "puffery," it won't even get a rewrite; it will be discarded. If it is salvageable but confusing, the writer may get an embarrassing phone call. If it is wordy and disorganized, the writer may witness the demise of his or her favorite lines.

Learn how to write a good news release, one that the media cannot ignore. Once you develop a news sense, the rest comes easy. Here's how:

1. *News releases should by typed and double spaced, and they should contain generous margins.* Don't write releases by hand. This is an immediate giveaway that you are an amateur. Besides, even though you have excellent penmanship, some of this will be difficult to read.

The spacing allows the editor to make various emendations, corrections, or additions.

The margins (which should be about $1\frac{1}{2}$ inches on either side) are useful for the same purpose.

The news release should be on good-quality white paper and typed on only one side.

2. *Don't send carbons.* The media should get originals, or machine or mimeographed copies. Carbons tell the newsperson that someone else received the original. The other methods indicate that everyone was treated alike.

3. *Avoid flamboyant letterheads.* You know the kind sometimes favored by military units and sport publicists? Large splotches of color and giant angular words like "Flash!" and "News!" take up a third of the sheet. Not only does this restrict your writing room, it also suggests to the editor that you may be trying to pass off a weak product in a glittering package.

Many editors prefer receiving a release with *no* printed letterhead occupying space they might use for editing purposes. The requisite information can all be typed as part of the release.

4. *Indicate the source.* In the upper left-hand corner (normally), put the name, address, and phone number of the person writing the release. If you are PR director for a specific company, the company address and phone number should be used here. If you are an independent public relations counselor, give your firm name and phone and, after skipping a few spaces, list below the name of the company, institution, or organization for whom this is being written.

Listing your home phone along with the business phone is a PR plus. It tells the newsperson you can be called at home, and it shows an added willingness to be helpful.

5. *Provide release instructions.* This line, which is usually in caps and often underlined, indicates your preference of release time. Unless there is a compelling reason to do otherwise, just put "<u>FOR IMMEDIATE RELEASE</u>" in this space, which should be several spaces below the name, address, and phone. If you have a specific time and date in mind, write, "<u>(HOLD) FOR RE-</u>

LEASE, MONDAY, MAY 2, P.M." If you do this, don't leave too long a lead time, because that increases the danger of the release's being lost or the deadline broken. If you know what a city room looks like, you know that most reporters don't have the space to keep neat files of future stories. If you don't know what a city room looks like, make that visit a top priority.

6. *The headline.*   This is optional. Many editors prefer to write their own headlines, partly because of characteristics of style, but primarily because of mechanical requirements. Keep in mind that a good headline written by you may be ignored, but a bad headline may keep the entire release from being read. For small-town papers with limited staffs, prepared headlines may be helpful—*if* you're good at it.

The headline comes between the release information and the body of the story and fits into an area of about two inches. Leave this space open when you omit writing your own heads.

7. *Every release should be dated.*   Sometimes this is included on a line just below the information on the writer of the release. More commonly, it occurs in a "dateline" that precedes the story's lead sentence, thus: (SCRANTON, PA., May 2—). Note that the place *where the story originates* is also given. Perhaps your PR firm is located in Hammond, Indiana, and your letterhead says so, but you are covering a story for a client in Scranton, and that's what should be in the dateline. The story runs right on from here.

Some publicists prefer to date their stories at the bottom, and this, too, is acceptable.

When you use a date *within* a story, it is wise to spell the whole date out. Don't say "The band will perform next Monday." Say "The band will perform next Monday, May 2." Unless the reporter has these dates as a guide, it will be impossible to tell how long that story may have been around.

8. *Write concisely.*   Remember that your story may be cut anyway. If you get used to writing tightly, you will save most of the copy because it is all necessary. You must be clear and absolutely accurate. Don't leave out essential facts. Come to the point quickly, and avoid superlatives and anything that reads like the stereotypic work of a "flack."

Although the *inverted pyramid* style—a format that moves important news-release facts to the beginning of the story—is the oldest and most common journalistic method of handling news, there are other ways to write leads. Remember, however, that the practitioner doesn't have the latitude of the journalist. Anything too cute may be scrapped. Daily papers, at least, rewrite most stories, and editors are looking for facts, not style.

The inverted pyramid, nearly the opposite of the short-story technique that culminates in a surprise ending, requires that the lead paragraph contain the *five W's*—who, what, where, when, and why. Sometimes *how* is added to this list. An example of a *five-W* lead paragraph follows:

> Plans for a $7 million addition to the Douglas Community Hospital were announced today at a news conference held in the hospital cafeteria. Spokesper-

son Linda Kurth, marketing director for DCH, said the new wing will increase capacity by 200 beds.

Following this opening paragraph, the story might spell out other details, such as proposed completion date; sources of funding; identities of contractors, architects, and suppliers; description of design and materials; information on other services to be housed in the new unit; and additional facts that would enhance the report.

Besides the *five-W* lead, the practitioner may occasionally opt for starting with an interesting quote, a bit of humor, a summary statement, an attention-getting claim, or some other literary ploy. However, the PR person should know the editor to whom this variation is directed.

News releases are frequently paragraphed, indenting about eight spaces instead of the usual five. Each paragraph would normally be composed of four or five sentences. Avoid long, involved sentences, but vary the structure to eliminate monotony.

Professionally written news releases are not literary exercises, even though the writing should be as crisp and compelling as possible. Space and time are limited, so every word should count.

"Most stories do need to be trimmed," according to Jack Smee, associate editor of the *New York Daily News*, "to fit available space and to make room for others readers are entitled to see. . . . A news story should be written to convey information or belief in the most direct and intelligible form the writer can create. And the writer should stop writing when that job is done."[7]

Other news release tips:

- Localize the story when you can, providing the home addresses of those involved to permit further checking by an editor.
- Avoid technical terms if you can, and if that is not possible, explain them succinctly and in lay terms.
- Provide a good lead and a logical conclusion.
- Leave nothing out that is essential.
- Do your own editing before sending out the release.
- Spell names correctly, giving the full name the first time it is used, and also the person's title. The style books of local outlets should be checked to determine their preferences in terms of titles, abbreviations, and other usages.
- Don't begin your release with the name of the CEO.
- When using a quote, identify the speaker as soon as possible in the sentence or paragraph.
- Remember, you are writing news, and not an ad, letter, or brochure. Stay away from opinion, editorializing, or puffery.

9. *Numbering pages and other mechanical details.* If possible, you should keep your release to a single page. However, if it runs to multiple pages, put "——more——" at the bottom center of the page that is to be continued. (Incidentally, it's a good idea to complete sentences—and, if

possible, paragraphs—before indicating a move to the next page. Otherwise, if the pages get separated, you could end up with a strange quote.) Succeeding pages should be numbered and "slugged" with an identifying headline or subject reference. This is usually done like this:

hospital wing —— 2

Some style books prefer "Add 1" for the second page and so on, and still others opt for "2-2-2-2" and the release title. "Page 2" is rarely used.

When you come to the end of your release, use any of the following:

—30—
####
—END—

"—30—" is preferred. The origin of this usage is clouded, but if you are curious, ask your local wire-service bureau chief. This person's myth is as good as any.

10. *Additional information.* If you want to add additional information about accompanying photos or a subsequent open house, or about some story detail that needs amplification, put this in a note to the editor following the end of the story:

PHOTO ENCLOSED: (Caption)

or

ARCHITECT'S RENDERING OF NEW WING ON DISPLAY IN LOBBY OF FIRST NATIONAL BANK. COPIES HEREWITH.

Keeping in mind the fact that a relatively small percent of releases submitted actually get used, not only does it make sense to do as effective a job as possible in writing the news release, but it also seems logical to keep costs reasonable. Keeping releases to one page saves money and pleases editors, and you might even use a little larger paper (like $8\frac{1}{2}''\times14''$) rather than go to a second sheet for a few extra lines. Economy also dictates that media lists be kept current so that postage isn't wasted on undeliverable mail, and that publicity people might be more selective, eliminating outlets where interest will be minimal. Figures 6-4 through 6-7 contain samples of news releases.

WRITING FOR THE ELECTRONIC MEDIA

Writing for the electronic media should be different from writing for the print media. Realistically, however, most PR persons send the same releases to all media. It just happens to be a case of time and economy. If you have the time, however, you should write a different release for radio and television, keeping it short, and couching it in a more conversational tone. Difficult words should be given phonetic pronunciations:

Today anti-war activist Sinead (SHINADÉ) Morrison . . .

And, since the listener can't hear quotation marks, be sure that any direct statements are understood as such:

These are her words, and I quote . . .

Spell everything out—dates, dollars, numbers. Remember that these have to be read. In fact, if you suspect that the "rip and read" newsperson for a small radio station may have trouble with anything, spell it out.

As for the television news release, you could write it in the audio-video form shown in the next chapter—*if* you have sufficient visuals to accompany it. Otherwise the broadcast form is fine, and you can indicate what art (photos, film, charts, and so on) you are supplying.

Obviously, a story with visual possibilities has more appeal to television news directors, and they favor local angles. Language should be simple and brief. You must also know the right people to reach in the stations; you must learn how to approach them in person or on the phone, and, with stories that have no immediate deadlines, you should be persistent without being annoying.

Many major corporations supply networks and local stations with newsclips, 16-mm sound footage usually a minute or less in length and accompanied by a printed script. Often, these do not involve fast-breaking news but serve as features or support materials. Firms turn out clips on safety, or travel, or ecology, or research and development, or new products, or special

---

ACME INDUSTRIES
1111 North 52nd Avenue
Lincoln, Oregon 00000

CONTACT: Ron Smith
503-000-0000

FOR IMMEDIATE RELEASE

Lincoln, OR (June 3, 1987)—Acme Industries of Lincoln, Oregon, today signed a multi-million-dollar contract with the Department of Transportation to provide a fleet of road graders for the government's new air strips in Oregon and Idaho.
Acme spokesperson Arnold Grebeaux (GREY-BO) said 40 graders will be sold for the work at Maxim Field (Salem, Oregon) and Trent Field (Moscow, Idaho).
Grebeaux said exact figures for the sale will not be available until mid-June.

—30—

Figure 6-3 Shorter release for radio and television.

The Coca-Cola Company

news release

Media Relations Department
P.O. Drawer 1734 Atlanta, Ga. 30301
Telephone (404) 676-2121

CONTACT: CARLTON CURTIS
(404) 676-2678

FOR IMMEDIATE RELEASE

COCA-COLA TO BE SOLD
IN SOVIET UNION

ATLANTA, JANUARY 23, 1985 -- Coca-Cola, the world's most popular soft drink, is going on sale in the Soviet Union, it was announced today by Donald R. Keough, president of The Coca-Cola Company.

"We are delighted that Coca-Cola will soon be available to a potential new market of 275 million people," said Mr. Keough who recently completed a week of meetings with Soviet officials in Moscow. "The people of the Soviet Union are joining the people of more than 155 countries in the world who enjoy the delicious and refreshing taste of Coca-Cola."

Coca-Cola will first be available through the shops which serve tourists, the diplomatic corps and other foreign visitors to the Soviet Union.

Consumers will be able to purchase Coca-Cola on the Soviet domestic market in Moscow and in additional cities by summer. This availability will coincide with the 1985 edition of the FIFA/Coca-Cola Cup for the World Youth Championship, an inter-

-more-

ENTERTAINMENT TONIGHT

THE LIPPIN GROUP
8124 West Third Street · Suite 204
Los Angeles, California 90048
213-653-5910/212-838-6140

"ENTERTAINMENT TONIGHT" TO PRESENT SPECIAL SERIES
"THE REAL MEN OF ROCK," APRIL 28 - MAY 4
FIVE MAJOR ROCK STARS TO BE FEATURED

LOS ANGELES, APRIL 15 -- David Lee Roth, Rod Stewart, Bob Seger and Little Richard will be among the top male rock stars profiled as "Entertainment Tonight" presents a special six-part series entitled "The Real Men of Rock," the week of April 28, it was announced by Producer Jack Reilly.

The series, hosted by "Entertainment This Week" co-host Leeza Gibbons, will include candid interviews with several stars and will provide a revealing look at the private personalities behind their public images.

"The Real Men of Rock," begins Monday, April 28, with a preview of the week's upcoming segments and a look at a number of rock legends, including Elvis Presley and Bruce Springsteen. On Tuesday, April 29, Gibbons interviews veteran rocker Bob Seger. Wednesday, "Entertainment Tonight" visits the home of the outrageous David Lee Roth, while Thursday's interview focuses on the legendary Little Richard. On Friday, Gibbons talks with British superstar Rod Stewart who, at the age of

(more...)

TELEVISION DOMESTIC DISTRIBUTION

Figure 6-5
Courtesy: *Entertainment Tonight*

Figure 6-4 News release formats differ but basic elements are always present.
Courtesy: The Coca-Cola Company

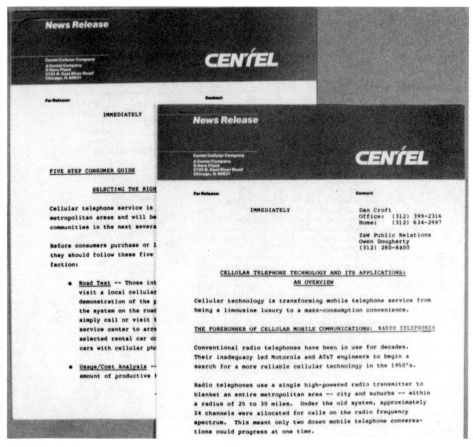

Figure 6-6
Courtesy: Centel Cellular Co.

events. These are invariably produced by a sophisticated internal audiovisual department or by outside professional cinematographers.

With the advent of cable television and the subsequent expansion of the available channels, new opportunities opened up for publicists in terms of news releases, film, and guest appearances. Cable television has far fewer rules, not too many editorial regulations, an opportunity for airing issues, and no external imposition of the Fairness Doctrine.

Radio newscasts are frequent and require short copy that can be read without major difficulty, except when proper names and technical terms must be included. Radio stations are also happy to get a mix of voices and live sound instead of only a studio announcer. "Actualities," which are audiotapes supplied by news sources, are blended into broadcasts.

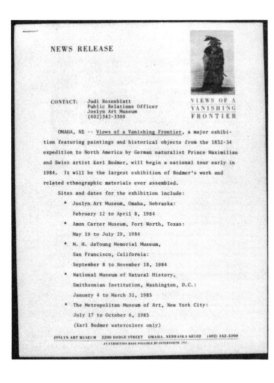

Figure 6-7
Courtesy: Joslyn Art Museum

PROMOTING THE OLYMPICS, AN OLYMPIAN TASK

The 1984 Olympics got off to a troublesome start. After keeping the planners of the Games guessing for months, the Soviet Union announced it would boycott the events in Los Angeles. Most of the communist-bloc nations followed. On top of that, rumors circulated that parking, driving, and housing in L.A. would be a nightmare, and that crime would get out of hand. Despite all these omens and misgivings, the 1984 Games turned out to be one of the best-run sporting venues in history, and, except for some reportorial gaffes that came off sounding exceedingly chauvinistic, the Olympics were also a PR success.

None of this happened automatically.

A year and half before the Games began, President Reagan addressed the Olympic Committee via videotape, assuring them that all would be in readiness. A public-opinion poll was conducted to ascertain attitudes of Los Angeles residents. This survey showed them to be ignorant of many aspects of the planning, so the Olympic Committee drew them in to serve on groups like "Olympic Neighbors." Former Olympic athletes formed an

Figure 6-8 An important part of the 1984 Olympics was the extensive media coverage, backed by guides and other materials from the Olympic Committee.
Courtesy: Michael Moran, U.S. Olympic Committee

"Olympic Spirit Team," which spent two years prior to the Games visiting schools, civic clubs, hospitals, and sporting events to plug the 1984 spectacular. Dozens of major U.S. corporations were contacted about sponsorship, and even the torch relay—the longest in history—raised $12 million. When the Games were completed, their director, Peter Ueberroth, turned over the financial surplus to the International Committee.

Every aspect of the Olympics involved hundreds of details—the housing, food, security, ticket sales, transportation. One of the most complicated was the media coverage.

Advance publicity consisted of, among other things, more than 35 major news-release packets targeted for 1,170 American outlets. The total number of pages in these releases (biographical sketches, performance records, rundown on the Olympic Trials, and so on) was nearly 1,000 per outlet. A 208-page *Olympic Press Book*, featuring biographical sketches on every athlete and coach and an extensive historical section, was mailed in advance to 1,100 outlets, and another 5,000 were distributed to the world media at the Games.

During the Olympics, some 345 individual news releases and bulletins were issued by the press staff, and 30 major press conferences were conducted over a three-week period. Some of these conferences attracted more than 500 journalists.

Those responsible for the media also had to issue passes, arrange for individual interviews, provide facilities for the media, and handle any problems that arose. These 20 members of the USOC Media/Public Information Division also had to look after parking permits for journalists, check on equipment needs and supplies, and attend to any complaints initiated by media reps.

An intricate transportation system moved people from the Forum to the Velodrome to Lake Casitas to Dodger Stadium to the Long Beach Convention Center to campuses at UCLA, Pepperdine, USC, Fullerton, Loyola, and elsewhere, including the Los Angeles Coliseum.

Photographers were instructed as to lighting conditions at each venue and given details on how film could be speedily processed.

Sandwiches and soft drinks were available to the media, along with a number of gifts and some recreation options, including tours of Disneyland, film studios, and the Olympic villages; nightly movies; baseball; concerts; and parties.

Special requirements, such as microphones, camera platforms, electrical outlets, copying machines, and dozens of other items, were anticipated and provided.

Despite the absence of the Soviets and the Eastern Bloc nations, the 1984 Games were later praised as the most thoroughly planned and smoothly executed of all the Olympics. The media effort was singled out for special commendation by Olympic reviewing teams, citing the outstanding facilities for the media, the reliable equipment, the cooperation by everyone involved, the selection of experienced PR personnel and a sufficient number of them, and, added the reviewers, luck.

> . . . good traffic, good weather, good people, good attitude, lots of medals, lots of flags, no controversy to speak of, a happy press corps with good housing, good press transportation, lots of seats and interviews, etc.

There's little doubt that the 1984 Olympics, in terms of public relations, set the standard by which future Games will be measured.

Information provided in part by Michael Moran, director of public information and media relations, U.S. Olympic Committee.

releasse Monday, November 1o at 5:15p.m. (DO NOT BREAK RELEASE TIME)

DO NOT (REPEAT, DO NOT) RUN IN LOCAL SECTION

        Tledo,0 — Nove —— One of the greatest discovries of this century was announced last week by Rayomnd Wilson of InCalda Bakeries Inc., a holy-owned subsidary of Marathon Bakeries.
        Triple density unleavened flour ∅used in baking breads and cakes xxx is now available to housewives at what spokesmen say is a very effordable price∅. The characteristics of this flour are improved viscosity and twice the wedge capacity in singular chamber units.
        Housewives are certain to enjoy this new product.
        The flo∅ur comes in 5# sacs.

EDITOR: Please send four clips of this article to me at above address.

Figure 6-9 How NOT to write a press release.

Other Publicity Tips

Veteran practitioners realize that, if the media cover an event themselves, the chance of the story's being used is infinitely greater than if it came via the mails. Sometimes a news release alerts them to a story, or a phone call or visit might serve that purpose. Even if the media show up, they are normally supplied a news release, to save their asking for information that could be provided in advance.

Certain media services will circulate news and features to their list of outlets for a specific fee. Companies often use these services to reach specialized editors or specialized journals.

There is really no end to the stories an active publicist might generate. Besides the timely news stories, there are interviews, predictions, polls, public statements on controversial issues, national tie-ins, features, and other ways to achieve publicity. However, the professional always asks how an activity benefits the client or organization and how it fits into the overall goals.

As important as publicity may be, some public relations executives caution against its overuse. Such preoccupation may detract from other managerial tasks the practitioner should be performing, or it may focus attention on some narrow aspect of the business, or it may result in a surfeit of "vanity-type" news, which does little but flatter the company officials.

Once the news release has been delivered, a few more cautions are necessary. Don't bug the editor, asking if the story was received and whether or not it will be used. Don't ask the editor for "tear sheets" or copies of the story when and if it runs. Don't overkill any one story, sending multiple copies to different people at the same newspaper or station.

Above all, don't nurse a grudge because your story wasn't used or because it was handled in a way you didn't quite agree with. If there is actual error, point that out, but don't dispute a question of news judgment or emphasis. The publicist and the editor sometimes see things differently.

When Continental Bakers was exonerated by the FTC on eleven of twelve counts of misleading advertising, the company naturally featured this statistical triumph in a subsequent news release. A wire service, however, focused on the one case involving guilt. Was this unfair? Probably not, since this case, centering on the claim that Wonder Bread built strong bodies eight ways, was far more familiar to the public than the eleven blameless examples. Both sides, from their viewpoints, were right.

INTERVIEWING

When the practitioner is conducting an interview that may lead to a news story or feature, each situation may be different. Some subjects are so colorful and quotable, the stories nearly write themselves. Others are more reticent, or cautious, or simply dull. The interviewer, by experience, learns to be flexible and to treat each assignment as a new challenge. Here are some standard procedures:

1. *Research the subject.* Know the personality and his or her field. Do a mental dry run on how you are going to conduct the interview. Prepare a list of questions.

2. *Decide on the method to be used.* Notes? Tape recorder? Memory? Memory is rare, risky, and too subjective. Tape recorders are common, but the interviewer should be flexible. If the recorder is bothering the subject, or turning him or her into an actor, it should be turned off. A combination of notes and recorder works well and saves time when assembling the final story.

3. *Learn to listen.* If the subject begins to talk about a Canadian fishing trip, the interviewer should not interrupt with tales of somebody else's fishing exploits. The interviewer is there to learn.

Even though there is a prepared list of questions, the good interviewer will be ready to deviate from it to follow an interesting lead.

4. *Probe for the best material.* As some experienced interviewers suggest, you must touch a nerve without losing the subject. Get the subject's confidence, then ask questions that will reveal his or her deeper convictions and ideas.

5. *After the interview,* thank the interviewee, then return to the processor and get the information down while it is fresh. Normally the subject would not have the right to review the story before it is printed. However, you may have to oblige some people in order to get the interview. In the public relations business, you will probably have to permit more copy review than you would in the preparation of media news.

Media Interviews

On some occasions, public relations practitioners may be required to solicit an interview for a client, or they may be instrumental in preparing the client for a session initiated by the media. In either case, control has passed to the reporter/interviewer.

Many executives do not understand or trust the media. Their sense of what is newsworthy is often unconsciously biased, and their methods of communicating with employees or even with peers may make poor television technique. They take a long time to say things, say more than they have to, and can't distinguish between remarks for attribution and those "off the record" or for background. Executives may get nervous, even hostile, or, in a state of panic, may emerge looking far less intelligent than they are.

Some firms specialize in training executives for such encounters, teaching them how to dress, how to gesture, how to respond. Stephen C. Rafe and Walter J. Pfister own New York's Executive Television Workshop, where CEOs

Figure 6-10 Handling television news conferences is a skill the PR person must master, then communicate to clients and superiors.

learn how to deal with the modern media. They remind subjects that they have rights, too, including these:

- Sufficient time should be given to prepare.
- Length of time and names of other guests, if any, should be provided.
- Notice should be given if the interview is being recorded and, if so, whether a copy of the tape may be requested.
- Introductions should be accurate and editing fair.
- Setting and personnel involved should ensure physical comfort.
- The subject should be allowed a reasonable amount of time to respond without constant interruptions.
- The person interviewed is entitled to know the credentials and background of the interviewer, and, if these seem weak on the specific issue to be discussed, the subject may request an opportunity for a background session prior to any live interview.
- The ground rules should be reviewed and agreed to by both parties.
- Pfister and Rafe suggest a live or live-to-tape interview rather than a taped one, to avoid editorial distortion of comments. They also advise having the public relations person present.
- They tell their clients that, if the two parties can't agree on ground rules, the CEO should decline the interview and ask that the reasons for doing so be aired.[8]

Training sessions for execs also include instruction on the way they should handle rhetorical tricks, like hypothetical questions, assumptions, baiting, needling, putting words in the subject's mouth, and even pauses. Interviewees are advised to remain cool and to present their case positively. No one should lie, but neither should he or she chatter on aimlessly or falter under the questioner's pressure. A quick wit helps here, enabling the gifted speaker to defuse or translate a loaded question. Some subjects are so skilled, they actually take charge of the interview.

Refusing to deal with the media is a poor solution, since the resultant story may make the CEO appear secretive or uncooperative. Besides, a good interview may be very beneficial to an individual or organization.

> The press can also be a corporation's ally in bad times. When a corporate executive says publicly, "Our subsidiary is having a tough time right now. We missed the market, failed to anticipate a change in consumer mood, and here's how we're regrouping," that kind of candor begets credibility. Few reporters can resist that kind of honesty, not only because it is refreshing, but because it shows respect for the reporter's intelligence and a trust that he will present the information accurately and in context.[9]

Fortune magazine states things another way, admitting that "strategies for handling routine requests from the press differ widely," from silence to stalling to cooperation.

> For all these perversities and confusions, though, a management choosing among policies might do well to settle on opening its doors—almost all the way—when coping with the press. Companies of that persuasion can adduce as evidence occasions—often crises—when an open policy has led to a happy ending. Where keeping the doors shut would have led, no one knows.[10]

When a reporter calls for an interview, the practitioner should try to be of assistance without seeming to interfere. This may involve convincing reluctant administrators that granting such an interview would be beneficial. Some people shy from the press out of fear; some just feel they are not newsworthy. The public relations person has to show them how their cooperation is in their own best interests.

When a reporter calls requesting an interview, the PR practitioner should make every effort to be accommodating in terms of date and time. The practitioner should also have background material—like biographical data—available and should supply any other materials that would be helpful.

The PR person may also want to rehearse the interviewee in advance, particularly if the interviewee is nervous or wary. This lesson should not be devoted to ways of being deceptive and evasive, but to means of understanding the probable questions and supplying the correct answers.

Should the PR practitioner sit in on the interview?

This is a tricky question. If the reporter has no objection, the matter is simple; there is an advantage to having the PR person on hand. If the reporter objects, the best strategy is to agree to this restriction, although there could be cases where the PR person might insist. This would depend on the competency of the interviewee, the nature of the subject matter, and the reputation of the reporter or publication. If present, the PR person should maintain a low profile and should avoid interrupting or interpreting.

It might be added that businesspeople form only one professional subject to interviews. Politicians, entertainers, scientists, educators, and many others, including volunteers for nonprofit institutions, may find themselves on camera, before a mike, or facing a row of print journalists. The same rules apply to them, along with an added caution for politicians not to filibuster and obfuscate, and for scientists and educators to use the language of the layperson.

Finally, if the practitioner has a hand in selecting a spokesperson to meet with the media, the chief executive officer may not always be the best choice. Carole Howard of AT&T Information Systems, lists five qualities of a good spokesperson:

- A knowledge of the topic.
- An understanding of the organization's overall objectives and strategies.
- An ability to "tell and sell"—in everyday English and from the point of view of the reporter's and the publication's or station's audience—not your organization.
- The confidence of top management. . . . You do not want to choose someone who is not well respected by those within.
- A desire to do the interview. If a spokesperson demurs beyond what normal modesty and apprehension would explain, back off.[11]

If the CEO possesses these attributes, fine; if not, shop around. The PR person, however, should resist the temptation to play this role, except when the subject centers on the public relations area.

PHOTOGRAPHY

There seem to be so many good photographers around. Every year, the ad-agency execs and other business leaders scan hundreds of portfolios. Most of them have something to recommend them. Still, when you want a certain kind of photography, you realize how rare are the creative, versatile geniuses.

Photographs help sell stories, or they can stand on their own. They can be decorative, supportive, or individually compelling. Note the tremendous reliance on photographs in most media, from the newspaper to the internal company publication.

In a *Public Relations Journal* article, free-lance photographer Mel Snyder asks rhetorically why photos should be used, then responds:

Three very good, simple reasons: to communicate information quickly; to create excitement without easily recognized bias; and to offer graphic proof of intangibles, such as market acceptance, style leadership, quantity production, modern manufacturing techniques, dynamic management, etc.[12]

You almost assume technical competence in the photographer. Real photography starts from here. It's like playing tennis. If you have to think about your strokes, you can't really play.

Newspapers require photos with sharp contrast. Those grainy pictures that impress contest judges are virtually useless in the newspaper because of the printing process and the paper quality. Magazines using a slick-coated stock are much better for reproduction and can handle the more subtle contrasts. Television stations prefer slides or film, and the slides should be horizontal in order to fit the requirements of the home screen. The proper ratio of width to depth, for television visuals, is 4 units wide × 3 units deep. Tape, however, is used almost exclusively.

Good subject matter is a must. Candid, interesting, unretouched shots seem to work best. The "grip-and-grin" photos of two people exchanging a check and the posed ground-breaking shot of four men poised on shovels are both visual clichés. In an attempt to move beyond these graphic sins, photographers have invented further clichés—the check gets larger, the shovels turn to bulldozers, and the static quartet of social planners is depicted clustered around a sterling silver tea set.

Figure 6-11 Sometimes a simple idea makes a good photo. Two schoolchildren give their own weather report (writing backwards for the sake of the camera).
Photo courtesy of Bill Ramsey

Perhaps a different angle will help—from above, or obliquely. Or a radically different setting—perhaps even the locale that will be affected by the check, such as a new hospital wing or a children's playground. Close-ups, or the arranging of heads at different levels, or the creation of dramatic lighting effects also make for variety.

Most photographers counsel against using more than five people in a group photo. This rule may be broken at times, but it isn't a bad formula to live by. The more people the photo depicts, the less likely the readers are to look at it.

> When it works, photojournalism is the art of making two-plus-two equal eight. When the words and pictures are expertly chosen, matched and displayed, they have far greater impact than they would if viewed separately.[13]

The cheapest thing on any photo assignment is the film. That is why even the best photographers take plenty of pictures—so they can make an intelligent selection. Besides, it is embarrassing to run out of film and miss that final—and, inevitably, best—opportunity for a picture. You really don't save money by holding back on film; you only limit the potential.

The same principle applies to photographic equipment. If the practitioner is also going to serve as photographer, he or she should have a couple of decent cameras, certainly a twin-lens or single-lens reflex camera or two and,

Figure 6-12 Composition makes this picture, one which appeared all over the country. A nun at Duchesne Academy uses a stepladder for her daily flag raising. Photo courtesy of Bill Ramsey

perhaps, a press or view camera. There should be a supply of lenses for regular, telephoto, wide-angle, and other shots, and correction and contrast filters—perhaps a pale yellow, yellow-green, and deep red. The professional will want a camera case, a lightweight tripod, an extra exposure meter, and, perhaps, some lighting equipment for portraits and other uses.

There are plenty of photo courses and photo books. Some show the photographer how to bring out a subject's personality, or how to infuse life into a group portrait. Some demonstrate creative ways to get unusual prints. Some even have specific tips, like shooting men from medium distance or close-up and women from the waist up or further away—ostensibly because men's emotions are revealed more by their faces, whereas women add more clues by their body language.

If public relations practitioners possess photographic skills themselves, and if they have the time or the small-shop necessity, this can be a plus. Without such talents, they are wise to employ someone who can take decent pictures. Even then, it's a team effort:

> A man with a good inventory of ideas, who thinks on his feet, is the best public relations photographer. But he does his best work when the public relations man who employs him has done his own homework . . . and takes the time to communicate with him. That's the only way to get 100 percent delivery from a good photographer.[14]

In illustrating a story for newspaper or television, you will probably select your best photo to accompany the news release. Sometimes, if you have several good pictures, you may send them all and let the editor choose. If you are lucky, you could end up with an impressive picture story.

When photos are used for publicity purposes, timing also becomes a consideration, not merely in meeting deadlines but also in anticipating

Figure 6-13 The practitioner may accompany the photographer on photo missions, to make sure the coverage matches the illustration plan.

seasons and events. A picture that might make a good Fourth of July feature may be passé in August. An old file photo of a celebrity visiting a local plant might get new life when that person makes national news.

Some Photographic Do's and Don'ts

When posing a group shot, be sure to keep the people together until you get all the identifications so you can list them, L(eft) to R(ight) on the caption. *Never write on the back of the photo with a hard pencil or ballpoint pen.* This could cause damage to the photo and could show through in reproduction. The best system is to type the identifications—or other caption—on a sheet of paper and attach it to the back or bottom back of the photo with rubber cement.

As long as we are on photographic "don'ts," *don't use a paper clip to attach anything to a photo.* If it sits around awhile, the impress of the clip may become visible. Or the clip may tear the picture when being removed.

Figure 6-14 Crop marks should be made on the margins of the photo and not run through the picture.

Don't run crop marks through the photo. (See Figure 6-14.) If you intend to have the photo cropped (particularly for publications you are producing yourself), indicate the crop marks on the margin of the photo, using a grease pencil, and repeat these measurements on the back of the picture, along with any reduction or enlargement directions, like this: "Crop to 24 picas wide by 10 picas deep; blow up to 48 picas wide and 20 picas deep." (Picas are easier to work with than inches, as will be discussed in Chapter 8.)

The reason for not drawing crop marks through the entire photo is that you may want to use the picture again, with different dimensions. Besides, improper crop marks limit the engraver's work.

Cropping not only helps the designer meet a mechanical need but also makes a more dramatic effect possible, and it can eliminate distracting details.

The cropped photo—or the original, if no cropping is done—may need to be scaled down to fit a certain space. The easiest way to accomplish this is by using a circular slide rule and setting up a length/width ratio.

If, for example, you had a typical 8″-by-10″ photo (or 48 picas × 60 picas) and needed to fit that photo into a column that was 12 picas wide, you would set up this ratio on your slide rule. (See Figure 6-15.) A quick reading of your slide rule shows you that the depth of the printed photo will be approximately $9\frac{1}{2}$ picas.

There is also the "scaleograph," which combines two L-shaped elements that can be adjusted to show larger or smaller proportions of a photo. And there is the much older method of triangulation, whereby the person doing the scaling lays tissue over the photo, draws a diagonal on the tracing paper across the photo, and then adds the horizontal or the vertical line, depending on which is critical in the layout. From the point where that line intersects the diagonal, he or she adds the complementary line to complete the rectangle, and these are the dimensions.

Photographs will usually be captioned. *Caption* and *cutline* are terms now used interchangeably to describe copy that appears below a photo. In the past, the *caption* appeared above the photo and the *cutline* below.

> Cutlines should help the photograph tell its story. It should guide the reader's eye and indicate what is worth noting. It should serve as a linking device to maintain continuity when pictures appear in a series. It should supplement the text and add new information.[15]

Stock photos may provide the publications editor with a variety of graphic styles, or they could save the company travel and other expenses to a distant locale. Such pictures may be available directly from a photographer, or from an agency, library, or stock-house. Subject matter varies from history and industry to portraits, sports, travel, and popular culture. At least 100 agencies operate in major cities, and some have branches in smaller communities. Cost of the service depends on the photographer, the desired size, the length of time the picture will be in circulation, the distribution area in-

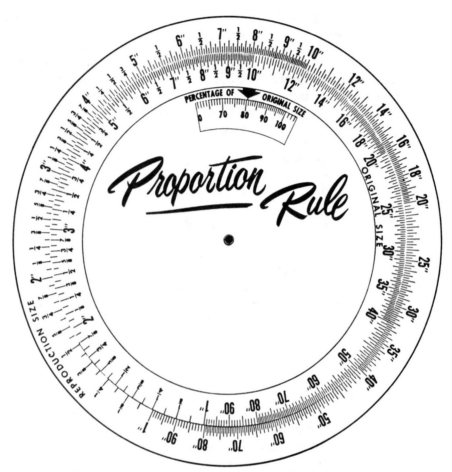

Figure 6-15 The proportion wheel or circular slide rule.

volved, and other factors. Catalogs spelling out these details and listing the photo areas on hand are available.

> Stock photography is one solution that even the most experienced public relations people often overlook. By definition, stock photographs are file photographs that may be licensed for use or reuse. They may have originated as commercial assignments for advertising, works for photojournalism, or fine-art photographs.[16]

Photos should be mailed flat, protected with cardboard, and marked "PHOTOGRAPH: DO NOT BEND" on the envelope. Slides may be protected in plastic sheets with pockets, encased in cardboard, or mailed in tray containers.

THE NEWS CONFERENCE

"News conference" seems to be a better label than "press conference," since the word *press* has strong overtones of the print media, and this may offend some of the more sensitive electronic reporters.

Perhaps a good rule for the news conference is, never hold one if you can handle the news some other way, or unless something will really be added. It may make you or your client feel good to assemble all these illustrious scribes, but they are not that keen about running off to conferences with marginal news value. A brief visit by an important figure would be an adequate reason; or an announcement with strong pictorial possibilities; or a major story that is going to provoke questions—such as a plant closing or a political withdrawal.

Print journalists are usually less enthusiastic about news conferences than are those attached to radio or television. They sometimes complain about the abundance of electronic equipment and the lack of specialized knowledge among members of the other media, making it more likely that the print journalist will ask the most incisive questions in more technical fields. This argument has lost some of its force as television equipment has become more compact, and as the larger television and radio stations also hire or train specialists.

If you do hold a news conference, be sure you invite everyone who would have a legitimate news interest. Sometimes this means reporters from ethnic and religious newspapers and, on occasion, editors of local college or high school papers.

Pick a convenient place to hold the conference, but avoid the suite in your own office. It always looks bad when the reporter deliberately writes that the press was called to such and such a PR office. Pick a hotel, or if you have press-club facilities in town, use them. For the brief stopover, a convenient airport room should suffice. Be certain there are outlets for the electronic equipment.

Pick a time for the conference that allows the media to meet their deadlines. Holding a conference at noon, for example, rules out coverage in a P.M. newspaper and also excludes noon newscasts.

If you have maps, schematics, photos, or other exhibits, have them available. Mount them on easels if you can. And consider a backdrop—and even a sign for the lectern. Why should you advertise the hotel? Put the sign for your client across this logo. Don't have too busy a backdrop, however, or it will detract from the speaker.

It is not a bad idea to phone the principal media the afternoon before a morning conference, as a reminder (assuming you notified them by mail or phone days earlier). And having coffee and, perhaps, rolls is a nice little courtesy.

Each news conference may present some fresh problems. Those multinational firms that hold such meetings in foreign countries advise flexibility, calm, a grasp of the native language, a willingness to accede to local customs, the possession of impeccable credentials, and an avoidance of any behavior likely to characterize sponsors as "ugly Americans."

Companies wishing to reach a number of communities with a single news conference may televise the event and beam it via satellite to other cities. Reporters in these distant areas may relay questions to the source or to live company representatives on hand in each locale. Each place would receive similar press kits, copies of charts used, and perhaps photos or film clips. Backup equipment and alternate spokespersons would also be involved, since the possibility of something going wrong is increased, and technical experts should be consulted at every stage. Although the cost of such a structure is not inconsequential, if it is properly planned and managed, it is not prohibitive, even for relatively small corporations.

PRESS KITS, PRESS ROOMS, AND PRESS PARTIES

Press kits may be simply a news release and photograph or an elaborate imitation-leather folder like those dispensed by the Rolls-Royce people. These kits usually combine a current news story with background information and visuals. For example, you might find the following items in the press kit announcing a fund-drive dinner to build a new hospital:

- Biography of the dinner speaker
- Photo of the speaker
- News release giving details of the event
- Drawings of the proposed new hospital
- Location map for the hospital
- Fact sheet on hospital, health needs, etc.

Industrial firms might include their annual reports, aerial photos, pictures of new equipment, map showing worldwide offices, and the like.

The folder containing these should be attractive but need not be expensive. A simple folder with inside pockets usually suffices.

Press kits may be handed out at news conferences, delivered personally to reporters, or even mailed as background materials.

The *press room* is a special area for the press, set aside permanently, as in the case of such space in government centers, or temporarily, in times of crisis or as an adjunct to a special event, such as a convention.

Actually, two rooms are now normally reserved for the media—one that can be used for interviewing or relaxing and another to serve as a more functional area. Each room should have sufficient electrical outlets and telephones, media kits, handouts (like biographies of speakers), perhaps coffee or soft-drink dispensers, ashtrays, and appropriate furniture. Typewriters

WORKSHOP CHECKLIST: SETTING UP A NEWS CONFERENCE

By Alvin M. Hattal

When planning the time for setting up your news conference, always be aware of media schedules. Afternoon papers are at work generally by 6:30 or 7:30 A.M., and morning papers by 10:00 or 10:30 A.M. So if possible, the conference should be scheduled for about 11:00 A.M., or 2:00–2:30 P.M., preferably on Tuesday, Wednesday, or Thursday, when reporters are usually more readily available to attend. Special attention should be paid to the special needs of television, the technical and trade press, and photo assignment editors.

Preliminaries:

____ Make a complete list of prospective media attending, such as: print media, including photo assignment editors; TV and radio assignment editors; separate conference for technical press.

____ Mail or telephone invitiations to reporters.

____ Notify photo assignment editors.

____ Notify TV and radio assignment editors.

____ Have event listed on city wires' calendars.

____ Compile information on interests of reporters invited.

____ Get outside and staff-backup photographers.

____ Invite government officials, as appropriate.

____ Send news releases and advance material.

____ Notify interested members of Congress.

____ Assign employee to supervise physical arrangements of news conference.

____ Brief public information staff, including secretaries.

____ Develop anticipated questions and suggested answers.

Briefing spokesperson:

____ Brief the spokesperson on media attending, interests of individual reporters, and format of conference.

____ Determine who should be available at conference to assist the spokesperson in responding to detailed questions.

____ Hold practice session with prepared Q&As.

Physical arrangements:

____ Check: room size; acoustics; accessibility; PA system; electrical outlets.

____ Have standing or table lectern.

____ Reserve room.

____ Prepare diagram of room.

____ Inspect physical setup (tables, chairs, podium, etc.).

____ Have electrician on hand.

____ Have extra chairs available.

____ Reserve some seats.

____ If luncheon, reserve table near lectern.

____ Have available: pencils; paper;

coat racks; typewriters; telephones; charts; blackboard; easel; projector; tape recorder and back-up machine; extra tapes; batteries.
____ Arrange for stenographer.
____ Check signs showing way to: conference; restrooms; telephones; coat check.
____ Decide where to set up signs and easels.
Other:
____ Notify guards.
____ Meet with banquet captain and review luncheon service schedule; i.e., when bars open and close, when food service begins.
____ Provide escorts and guides at entrances and parking lot.
____ Provide parking for reporters and TV and radio representatives.
____ Brief photographer.
Releases, handouts:
____ Opening statement
____ Press release(s); press kits
____ Photos
____ Necessary clearances
____ Advance copies for spokesperson and top staff
The conference:
____ Recheck immediately before conference to make sure tape recorder is working.
____ Have assigned public-information staff member(s) present.
____ Check off names at door against RSVP list.
____ Distribute releases, etc.
____ Place staff at the doors.
____ Monitor tape recorder.
____ Introduction: establish ground rules re attribution.
____ Set up Q&A period.
____ Make formal close.
Follow-up:
____ Send releases to media not attending and to press club rack.
____ Transcribe tapes, if any and if necessary.
____ Stimulate follow-up interviews.
____ Monitor wire services, TV, radio. Order transcripts, if any.
____ Provide other corporate officers with any appropriate material developed at conference.
____ Send clippings to top executives and staff.
____ Prepare and review file on conference.

Alvin M. Hattal is executive vice president for Paul S. Forbes and Associates, Inc., in Falls Church, Va. SOURCE: Alvin M. Hattal, "Workshop Checklist: Setting Up a News Conference." Reprinted with permission from the May 1985 issue of the *Public Relations Journal.* Copyright 1985.

(primarily electric, but with a manual or two) or electronic editing terminals should be supplied. Access to these rooms should be limited, and PR staff members may be assigned to these areas to exercise some sort of control, to answer questions, or to provide other help.

If the media are not always enthusiastic about news conferences, they are even less thrilled about the so-called *press party*. This is an event at which you get the media together to, more or less, thank them or cement relationships. Generally, there is no news value and none is intended. A number of newspapers—like the *Milwaukee Journal*—counsel their reporters to boycott such sessions.

Some practitioners devise their own methods of disseminating news. Regis McKenna, who specializes in high-tech PR, rejects the notion of news releases and news conferences, relying instead on an unorthodox system called the "multiple exclusive," in which McKenna gives simultaneous access to different parts of a single story to several selected media.

PUBLICITY SOMETIMES SELLS

When Coca-Cola announced its new Cola taste, more than 80 percent of Americans became aware of the product—before a single ad was run or a single product placed on retailers' shelves. Publicity created this awareness, just as it fueled the phenomenal demand for Cabbage Patch dolls in 1983. Books, movies, travel, new gadgets—all may prosper with strong promotional campaigns, with or without advertising. These efforts also buttress the efforts of salespeople and are much cheaper than a comparable amount of advertising.

You can't count on this, however. As stated earlier, the newspapers are suspicious of PR releases (and they should be, as professionals) and will usually indicate a public relations source if they think it necessary. If the matter is controversial, they should also gather data from the opposing side. You often see stories that, at first glance, look like news stories but are outlined by a border that carries the word *advertisement* over and over.

Publicity not only is less expensive but may also get you into sections of the paper (like the front page in most papers) where you could not place ads. And readers tend to place more credence in a news story—albeit a PR-created one—than in an ad for the same company or product.

OTHER OUTLETS FOR PUBLICITY

Besides the daily newspapers and the local and national electronic media, there are many other markets for news releases and photographs. Thousands of weekly papers are anxious for local items, and the trade journals snatch up stories in their specialties. The college press consists of newspapers often ignored by those outside academe, but they offer an opportunity to reach an important target audience. Thousands of newsletters accept features of interest to their readers, and hundreds of publications with ethnic circulations take items that are sensitive to their audiences' needs.

The alert publicist tries to get maximum benefit from any news release,

Fomenting a Revolution

When Weight Watchers International, the largest company in the weight reduction and weight maintenance field, developed a new diet including champagne, wine, beer, peanut butter, popcorn and honey, the idea was revolutionary. Never before had dieters been able to say "yes-yes" to such traditionally "no-no" foods. Called the New Food Plan, the diet was designed to make weight loss easier by increasing taste, variety and menu flexibility.

To introduce and explain the new diet program, Weight Watchers International retained Ketchum MacLeod & Grove Public Relations.

Diet Emancipation

Weight Watchers New Food Plan was created with an eye towards reconciling today's active lifestyles with optimum federal Recommended Daily Allowances. The idea was to free dieters from weight control drudgery, making traditionally taboo foods a thing of the past.

Marketing objectives were bold. Weight Watchers wanted to reach record numbers of people with its New Food Plan information. They also wanted to increase attendance at Weight Watchers classes, and let people with as little as 10 pounds to lose know that they were as high a priority to Weight Watchers as those with many more pounds to shed.

To accomplish these goals, Ketchum MacLeod & Grove Public Relations developed a publicity program designed to capture the attention and enthusiasm of Weight Watchers franchisees and to attract media coverage. Publicity efforts were both local and national in scope, and they were timed to complement the New Food Plan's national advertising schedule.

Launch was set for the three-month period following the Christmas holidays—historically a "food indulgent" season.

Divide and Conquer

Local media coverage began with a "Do It Yourself" publicity kit that Ketchum MacLeod & Grove Public Relations created and distributed to Weight Watchers franchisees across the country. Packaged in a wicker picnic basket, the kit contained foods permitted on the new program, tips for media placement, sample letters for editors and radio and TV producers, suggestions for local New Food Plan press debuts, press releases and photographs.

For the national campaign, KM&G PR arranged a black tie affair at America's oldest fast food eatery, Horn & Hardart's Automat in New York City. Fast food being the antithesis to weight control, the Automat provided a perfect setting to reveal a diet plan allowing sugar, salt and alcohol.

To generate editorial interest, the day before the formal introduction waiters, dressed in black tie garb, delivered a glass of champagne, a black tie and a media advisory to key editors and radio and TV producers in the New York City metropolitan area.

On January 6, 1981, over 300 media representatives flocked to Horn & Hardart's for their first taste of the New Food Plan. Amid the art deco atmosphere of the Automat, guests played "Guess What You Can Eat On The Weight Watchers New Food Plan." Instead of the usual fast food fare, the Automat's vending machines dispensed portion controlled servings of the New Food Plan menus.

The Fruits of Victory

More than 375 million people were reached with information of the New Food Plan following its introduction at the Automat.

Led by the New York Daily News, the world's largest circulation daily, which ran a seven-day diet series on the New Food Plan that included front page mention. Weight Watchers New Food Plan information appeared in newspapers in every state in the continental U.S. Cover articles also appeared in The Star and The Globe, two of the largest circulation national weekly newspapers.

Newsweek Broadcasting helped spread the news to 70 television stations across the country. National Public Radio beamed the story to 47 states in the U.S. and Puerto Rico.

The revolution was fanned by extensive coverage in leading consumer magazines, including cover stories in Family Circle, Mademoiselle, Ladies' Home Journal and Women's Day Diet and Exercise Guide.

National syndicates also publicized the New Food Plan. United Press International distributed a photowire story to 1,017 newspapers, 44 television stations and 3,238 radio stations. Newspaper Enterprise Association, Cox News Service and College Newspaper Network also filed features.

Finally, People Magazine readers voted Weight Watchers New Food Plan as diet of the year.

Weighing the Results

The successes of Ketchum MacLeod & Grove Public Relations efforts on behalf of Weight Watchers International New Food Plan are most clearly documented by the dramatic increase in Weight Watchers classroom attendance. Following the introduction of the New Food Plan, classes doubled and membership increased. Extra sections had to be added to accommodate the influx of hungry dieters.

Ketchum MacLeod & Grove Public Relations, using publicity as the major communications tool, helped Weight Watchers International to both successfully introduce an unprecedented diet plan and to realize specific marketing goals and objectives.

The introduction of the New Food Plan proved that a well planned and carefully executed publicity program can revolutionize public perceptions of dieting and weight control.

Figure 6-16 As detailed in this brochure, publicity can have a decided effect on marketing products and services.
Courtesy: Ketchum Public Relations

Figure 6-17 Articles carried in trade magazines often serve double duty as reprints.
Courtesy: Skinner Macaroni Company

trying different angles for different editors—like a straight story for the local daily and a religious slant for the Catholic weekly. Features may also be reprinted in a variety of periodicals, and photos can be moved on the wires or mailed to selected journals.

In this era of change, those responsible for publicity must realize that, as the nation's press becomes more and more electronic, the old news-release delivery system may be phased out. Only those stories in the computer may make it past the editor's terminal.

Other advances, some of which are detailed in Chapter 9, alter the traditional reporter/publicist relationship, meaning that, in order to continue as a credible professional source, the practitioner must possess the knowledge and the hardware to stay current.

CLIPPING SERVICES

Many public relations firms and major business, professional, and educational institutions use a clipping service to keep track of the print stories about them. Bureaus exist in all large cities, and through their national (sometimes international) network of readers, they supply all these items at so much each. This can be good, just to keep abreast of what is being said about you or, perhaps, to be aware of how many of your news releases are being printed. It is helpful, in fact, to supply the clipping service with a copy of the release you would like checked out, making it easier to spot.

Some corporations—Mobil and Phillips, for example—have their own staffs of "clippers" in addition to the service. These people arrive early, go through a stack of newspapers, then prepare a report for executives, including items on the company or relating to the industry.

Burrelle's Press Clipping Service employs nearly 800 people and serves more than 4,000 clients. Its brochure explains that its employees read more than 1,700 daily papers, every Sunday paper in America, more than 7,600 weekly papers, some 6,200 magazines and trade journals, 215 religious and ethnic papers, and more than 200 publications for black readers. They even clip from college papers and the underground press; monitor network radio and television news, and the local news in 35 American cities; cover Dow Jones, Reuters, and United Press International wire services; and read all the major daily papers from foreign countries. With the aid of its computer banks, Burrelle's also issues an early-morning news roundup bulletin to subscribers, compiling items from nearly 50 newspapers, magazines, and network newscasts, assembling these by categories, then transmitting $8\frac{1}{2}'' \times 11''$ montage sheets electronically to office facsimile machines.

Other clipping services perform similar functions, charging different sorts of fees, but reflecting the extent of use. To curtail costs, companies and organizations must be specific about their needs, requesting that the press-clipping bureaus exercise a certain selectivity. A corporation may not want to pay for multiple copies of its listing on the New York Stock Exchange, and a university may eliminate the line scores on hundreds of sports pages.

Many public relations offices keep a clipping scrapbook, or transfer newsclips to microfilm. Clips may not measure the success of a PR campaign but do provide some indication of media acceptance and also serve as a showpiece for clients.

LISTS AND DIRECTORIES

In addition to the lists the PR person may compile of local and regional media, there is often a need for wider distribution of information. The practitioner should have one or more publicity-type directories in his or her office and know where others may be available in the local library. The more popular directories include the following:

- *N.W. Ayer Directory of Newspapers and Periodicals*
- *Bacon's Publicity Checker*
- *Editor and Publisher* directories
- *Standard Rate & Data* directories for all media
- *National Directory of Weekly Newspapers*
- *Writer's Market*
- *Protestant Publications Rate and Data Book*
- *Catholic Press Directory*
- *Broadcasting Directory*
- *Publisher's Weekly*
- *The Newsletter Yearbook Directory*
- *Working Press of the Nation*
- A variety of other national, regional, and local directories

CHAPTER HIGHLIGHTS

- In working with the media, the public relations person has to understand and support the First Amendment rights of reporters and editors.
- There are some areas of disagreement and conflict between the media and the practitioner, but many areas of accord.
- Publicists should be fair and even-handed, helpful, accessible, accurate, and professional.
- Both practitioner and reporter have their own goals and their own ethical codes, and neither should do anything to compromise the other.
- News may be of widespread or narrow interest, and can involve famous people, unusual events, current happenings, or important information.
- The news release should be technically correct, complete, concise, and focused on significant events rather than puffery.

- Radio and television news departments require different forms of news releases.

- Interviewing calls for research, tact, attention, and probing. When a client or employer is the subject of an external interview, the PR person should prepare this individual, work out ground rules, and try to be present at the interview.

- Photography is a special skill. If PR people possess this skill, they should still be alert to the special graphic needs of the media; if they are inexpert, they should hire professional photographers.

- The news conference should be used sparingly and should be planned in detail, like any event. Equal care should be spent on staging press parties, organizing the press room, or assembling the press kit.

- Publicity may be equally effective in the smaller, lesser-known media, and it may also be extended via reprints and other methods.

- In-house clipping departments or clipping bureaus may be used to keep track of media use of stories, or of published information in certain fields of interest.

- Media directories provide specific information on publications and staffs.

NOTES

[1]Tom Holbein, Belden Associates, quoted in a report from the American Press Institute J. Montgomery Curtis Memorial Seminar on "The Public Perception of Newspapers: Examining Credibility," November 1984.

[2]Pierre Berton, "Journalism's Achilles' Heel," reprinted in *Atlas*, April 1977.

[3]Thomas E. Burke, "Advice for PR Folks Facing Reporters," *ASNE Bulletin*, September 1984.

[4]David Zinman, "Should Newsmen Accept PR Prizes?" *Columbia Journalism Review*, Spring 1970.

[5]James McCartney, "Must the Media be 'Used'?" *Columbia Journalism Review*, Winter 1969–70.

[6]Bos Johnson, news director of WSAZ-TV, Huntington, West Virginia, quoted in Lane Talburt, "Personal Favors and the Press," *Public Relations Journal*, February 1974.

[7]Jack Smee, "Saving Words—and Saving Readers," *ASNE Bulletin*, March 1983.

[8]Compiled from news items in *pr reporter*, May 18, 1981, and March 22, 1982; and *Communication Briefings*, April 1983.

[9]Dorothy Lorant, "Can We Talk?" *Washington Journalism Review*, July 1985.

[10]Walter Guzzardi, Jr., "How Much Should Companies Talk?" *Fortune*, March 4, 1985.

[11]Carole Howard, "When a Reporter Calls. . . ." Courtesy *Communicator's Journal*, May/June 1984.

[12]Mel Snyder, "How to Get the Best in Pictures," *Public Relations Journal*, March 1969.

[13]Egon E. Weck, "Photography's (Not So) Latent Image," *Public Relations Journal*, March 1975.

[14]Allan B. Starr, "How to Get Top PR Photos," *Public Relations Journal*, April 1971.

[15]*Impact*, No. 162 (1974).

[16]Michael Heron, "Imagination Unlimited through Photographs in Stock," *Public Relations Journal*, April 1985.

SUGGESTED READINGS

Bacon's Media Alerts. Chicago: Bacon's Publishing Company.

Bacon's Publicity Checker. Chicago: Bacon's PR and Media Information Systems, annual.

Cable Contacts, Radio Contacts, Television Contacts, TV News Contacts (media guides). New York: Larami Communications, 1986.

FRIEDMAN, SHARON M., SHARON DUNWOODY, and CAROL L. ROGERS, *Scientists and Journalists: Reporting Science as News.* New York: Free Press, Macmillan, 1986.

HOWARD, CAROLE, and WILMA MATHEWS, *On Deadline: Managing Media Relations.* New York: Longman, 1985.

HUTCHISON, EARL R., *Writing for Mass Communication.* New York: Longman, 1986.

The IMS Directory of Publications (formerly Ayer Directory). Fort Washington, Pa.: IMS Press, annual.

JONES, CLARENCE, *How to Speak TV: A Self Defense Manual.* Marathon, Fla.: Video Consultants, 1984.

KLEPPER, MICHAEL M., *Getting Your Message Out: How to Get, Use and Survive Radio Television Airtime.* Englewood Cliffs, N.J.: Prentice-Hall, 1984.

LEVEY, JANE FREUNDEL, *If You Want Air Time.* Washington, D.C.: National Association of Broadcasters, 1984.

Media Resource Guide. Los Angeles: Foundation for American Communications.

MENCHER, MELVIN, *Basic News Writing.* Dubuque, Ia.: William C. Brown, 1983.

NEWSOM, DOUG, and JAMES A. WOLLERT, *Media Writing: News for the Mass Media.* Belmont, Calif.: Wadsworth, 1985.

NOLTE, LAWRENCE W., and DENNIS L. WILCOX, *Effective Publicity.* New York: Wiley, 1984.

Professional's Guide to Public Relations Services, 4th ed. New York: Public Relations News, 1984.

Public Relations Guide. Cincinnati: Procter & Gamble Educational Services, 1983.

RUBIN, BERNARD, ed., *When Information Counts.* Lexington, Mass.: Lexington Books, 1985.

SIMON, RAYMOND, *Publicity and Public Relations Worktext.* Columbus, O.: Grid, 1983.

Standard Rate and Data Services, media guides for advertising in various media. Skokie, Ill.: Standard Rate and Data Services, Inc.

TUROW, JOSEPH, *Media Industries: The Production of News and Entertainment.* New York: Longman, 1984.

WATTENBERG, BEN J., *The Good News Is That the Bad News Is Wrong.* New York: Simon & Schuster, 1984.

WEINER, RICHARD, *Professional's Guide to Publicity*, 2nd ed. New York: Weiner, 1978.
Working Press of the Nation, 5 vols. Chicago: National Research Bureau, annual.
YALE, DAVID R., *The Publicity Handbook*. New York: Bantam, 1982.

EXERCISES

1. The U.S. Postal Service turned down a request from the town of St. Joseph, Missouri, to issue a stamp commemorating the 100th anniversary of the death of Jesse James, contending that his notorious life made him unfit to grace a stamp. There are a lot of angles a reporter or publicity person could have taken in writing up the story of this action. Assume you are doing PR for the St. Joseph Chamber of Commerce and write a headline and lead sentence for this story about the rejection of the James commemorative stamp.

2. Select from newspapers or magazines three photographs that you consider good, from a public relations and general-interest viewpoint. Explain why for each.

3. Write a trio of news releases about a special event of your own choosing. It can be an actual event or one you create. The first release should be written a month ahead of the event, giving the general details. The second release should be more specific, including such things as biographical details on the speaker (if appropriate) and program notes. The third release should be written immediately after the event as coverage for the media that failed to show. Remember that the second release should advance the first release and not merely repeat the same data in a different way. And the third release cannot be couched in glowing advertising terms; it must be objective. (If the reporter writes about it in such language, that's OK, but you can't.)

4. Take the final release written above and convert it to a news release for a local radio station.

CASE PROBLEMS

1. After nearly a year of work as PR counselor for a consortium of private state colleges, you have finally succeeded in getting a bill approved by the legislature that will provide a maximum of $500 to any student in the state who elects to attend a private institution. Total funding will amount to several million dollars in the first year alone. Because of the controversial nature of the issue and the tax dollars involved, the consortium has to agree to a court test on the constitutionality of the bill before any funds will be released. You announce that you will select a legal firm and arrange for a friendly suit by the first week in September. However, when that time comes, the selection process has not been quite completed, and the con-

sortium members have not yet had an opportunity to vote on the choice. You explain this to the legislative committee, and the members grant a two-week extension. You then issue a news release to all media detailing what you have done. Driving home from work that evening, you are listening to the radio and hear your story, except that it has been twisted to sound as though the consortium has reneged on its promise. Concerned about the possible loss of a lot of money, you phone the station immediately. The news director informs you that his announcer merely read the wire-service story, and suggests you call the local wire-service office.

You do so, explaining to the young man who answers the phone that you are the sole source of that release and that the rewrite job he did gives a false impression. He reacts with hostility, asserting that he wrote the story the way he saw it and that he doesn't have to take orders from any "PR flack."

    a. What arguments do you use to try to convince him to change his mind?

    b. If he refuses to change his mind, what further steps might you take?

2. You are the public relations director for a meat-packing plant in a medium-sized Minnesota town. The farm economy and other factors have caused the plant to lay off nearly half of its 400 employees, and there is talk that the company may have to shut down. One of the stated conditions of remaining open is that employees agree to take a pay cut. The union balks at this, and the president closes the plant, stubbornly refusing to consider reopening until the union leaders agree to the proposal. "There can be no negotiations on this," he says.

While the whole situation is in litigation, awaiting the possibility of forced negotiations, the local newspapers and television stations have been covering the story with daily reports. Most of these have portrayed the president in a negative light, and several of the stories do contain erroneous information or incorrect assumptions. The president is furious, phones the publisher and the station managers personally, and demands retractions. They agree to rectify any mistakes and they do print and air corrections. However, the overall thrust of the stories continues to irritate the president, and he doesn't forget them, even when the reduction in pay is accepted and the plant reopens. Several months later, the president, as a member of the local Chamber of Commerce economic development committee, is asked to speak on the progress in trying to attract new industry to this Minnesota community. Instead of following this script, the president launches into a tirade against the media, showing slides of the erroneous newspaper stories and playing tapes of the offending radio and television broadcasts. He ends by saying that the media have ruined this town and that he will no longer attempt to bring any new companies to a city with such irresponsible journalists. There is some applause, but most of the listeners appear stunned. Local media representatives are incensed and call you immediately to protest.

a. What do you say to the media? (Incidentally, you were not aware that the president was going to deliver this speech, so you are caught by surprise.)

b. What do you say to the president?

c. What might you do to turn this situation around?

3. You have promised a weekly paper with a circulation of 20,000 that you would hold a story for release until Thursday, the day the paper is published. However, on Tuesday, after the weekly paper has locked up its presses, you get a call from the daily paper, circulation 300,000, indicating that it has picked up certain pieces of the story and wants your confirmation. What action should you take?

4. One of your clients insists on holding a news conference when you know that there is little real news to communicate. You are afraid the media will be unhappy with you both for summoning them to such an event. What might you say to the client to talk him out of this move?

5. You have submitted a story to a trade magazine on behalf of a client. It is a legitimate news story that stacks up well against the kind of articles this magazine usually carries. The editor phones you and suggests that your piece will have a better chance of being published if you also buy some significant advertising space. What should your response be?

6. The president of your town's largest bank wants to produce a brochure that will convince the public that this bank is really personalized. He wants it to convey a warm, individualized image. What specific photos might you suggest?

7
OTHER FORMS OF PUBLIC RELATIONS WRITING

The news release is merely one form of written communication; the public relations director must master several. One never knows when an anniversary celebration will call for a slogan; or when a corporate name change will demand facility with language; or even when a client may request an original toast. Not everyone can accomplish all these tasks. There is writing that is functional and acceptable, and writing that is rare and imaginative. The practitioner must be capable of the former, at least. One good argument for strong writing demands on the entry-level PR person is that the work provides the opportunity to write a variety of different things, adding experience and style.

THE FEATURE STORY

The news release may suffice for most news stories, but some demand more complete treatment. The reasons for such extension can be human-interest appeal, an abundance of information, or an incident that lends itself more to storytelling than to straight news.

Many such "feature stories" are also free of deadline requirements. Unlike "hard news," they may be released at any time. The feature may—and often does—stem from a regular news item or from the inspiration of another feature.

> Someone once said there are no uninteresting subjects, only dull and uninteresting writers. It is the responsibility of a good writer to make a seemingly dull subject glow and shine. . . . If you begin to look carefully, you will find that

article ideas are knee-deep around you. You begin to sense that there is a story in this or that and begin to see life around you from the standpoint of the writer.[1]

The advantages of features include the opportunity to get additional space for your firm, the possibility of greater reader interest, and the chance to humanize a sometimes pedestrian subject.

There are many kinds of features, all of which may be explored within the confines of a single company or organization. Some grow out of news items, but many may be created with a little thought, a little imagination. There are, for example:

- *Personality profiles.* Most people have a story to tell, if you probe deeply enough. This type of feature requires decent interviewing skills, curiosity, and style.
- *How-to articles.* These features are increasingly popular, especially when they center on step-by-step ways to save time or money, or accomplish difficult tasks.
- *Tie-in features,* which use a current event and give it a local angle. The death of an international statesman may give rise to a story about a company vice-president who visited him the previous year. An earthquake in a distant country may lead to a feature by an employee who once worked there.
- *Trend stories* may result from internal research on a specific topic or may adapt a national story on trends to the local situation. If statistics show that college students are more interested in business careers than ever, as a university PR director, you may want to see how this theory works on your campus.
- *Seasonal articles* may deal with methods of celebration, or reminiscences, or the effect of the holiday on the workplace. Some companies, for example, have contributed features on employees who must work on New Year's Eve, or a newly naturalized worker who has a fresh way of viewing the Fourth of July.

There are dozens of other feature types, designated as human-interest, enterprise, even personal-experience formats.

Let us say that the practitioner sends out a routine story on a retirement party at his or her firm. While attending this party, the practitioner discovers that the retiree has some unusual plans for the ensuing years. This leads to an interview and a longer feature story. The same event could also spark a story about retiring, about selecting retirement gifts, about the retiree's wife's outlook, or any number of variations.

More creativity will go into a feature story, but it must still be accurate. You work within the facts, involving more of the reader's emotions. The news story might tell of the fire at the plant, giving details of injuries, cost of replacement, the number of alarms, probable causes. The feature might focus on the destruction of some ancient furniture that once graced the home of the firm's founder, or it might tell of an employee who had a narrow escape and how he had previously survived a plane crash and a bombing in Vietnam.

First, of course, you have to recognize a potential feature. Then you do your research. If, for example, you decided to do that piece on gifts for retirees, using your plant's retirement party as the focal point, you might want to survey other companies to see what they do, or interview firms specializing in executive gifts, or talk to several people who are retired to get their opinions of such gifts. When you have all these facts in hand, you decide what slant the feature will have, draw up an outline, and then begin writing to this outline.

Features require strong leads—something to get you hooked on the article. A headline or a photo may help, but the first sentence or two should be compelling:

> The reporter has a wide repertoire of leads to choose from; some are designed to startle and shock the reader, others to tickle his curiosity, others to stir his imagination, and still others to succinctly inform him about the nature of the story.[2]

Many forms of leads are possible, but they should be compatible with the general style of the publication you intend to interest. Some writing texts offer two dozen or more ways to get the features started. Here are a few of these:

- *Ask a question.* "Why do some employees rise rapidly in a firm and others remain locked into their jobs for years?" or, "When was the last time you checked your furnace filters?"
- *Begin with a quotation.* "'We don't mind spending a million dollars to straighten half a mile of track,' said railroad spokesperson Dodd McCartney."
- *Address the reader directly.* "If you are one of those people who hate soap operas. . ."
- *Use a narrative lead.* "Tom Reynolds parked his car in the company garage, in the same spot he'd used for the past four years. He was late; the meeting must have started already."
- *Provide some description.* "Nugent is a small town, with a single bank, a new bowling alley, and the water hydrants still displaying their bicentennial colors."
- *A summary lead* that capsulizes the whole feature. "When Albin Chemical opened its Dorset plant last week, two of the spectators were veteran employees with over 100 years of experience between them."
- *First-person lead.* "I never imagined I'd be seated on that airplane next to one of America's legends. . . ."
- *Contrast lead.* "Marriages may be made in heaven, but mergers have more mundane origins."
- *Teaser lead,* using a line that drags the curious reader into the body copy. "There was no other way to explain those noises coming from the storage room."
- *A simple statement.* "Americans use more energy per capita than any other people on earth."

DERUS MEDIA SERVICE, INC.

8 WEST HUBBARD STREET
CHICAGO, ILLINOIS 60610
312-644-4360

CCK-35

Figure 7-1 There are media services available to handle feature releases and placement. Courtesy: Derus Media Service, Inc.

Heroism Can Be Found In Any Dog

If you own one of the 51 million dogs in this country, you may want to take a fresh look at your canine friend. Just like the nine finalists of the 1984 Ken-L Ration Dog Hero of the Year Award, your furry pooch may have the makings of a hero extraordinaire.

Dog experts across the country agree that there is no way of predicting if your dog has hero potential. And the variety of finalists for the Ken-L Ration Dog Hero of the Year prove that any type of dog can demonstrate the courage that it takes to save a life.

Five of the nine finalists are all-American mixed-breeds, followed by two German Shepherds, one Doberman Pinscher and a Standard Poodle. Six of the finalists are male dogs. Regardless of breed and gender, all the finalists have shown that they are their owners' best friends.

- "Bandit," an eight-year-old male Shepherd/Border Collie, chased away an attacking bear to save the life of owner Ed Tafelski of Mellen, WI. Thanks to Bandit, Tafelski escaped more serious injuries than the broken ribs and leg scratches he received before Bandit's rescue.

- "Lady," a two-year-old female German Shepherd, leaped between master Burnice Wilson of Asheboro, NC and a 600-pound charging hog when Wilson fell and broke his arm during a shoat roundup. Blocked from view by tall grass, Wilson was unable to attract attention to his plight. By distracting the irritable sow, Lady provided valuable seconds for Wilson to make his trouble known to friends.

- "Leo," a four-year-old male Standard Poodle, threw himself between 11-year-old Sean Callahan of Hunt, TX and a striking 5½-foot diamondback rattler. Leo saved the boy from injury, but not before receiving several snake bites himself. The veterinarian who saved Leo speculated that young Sean would not have survived the massive dose of snake venom injected into the canine hero. Leo is owned by Sean's parents, Bud and Lana Callahan.

Six-month-old "Budweiser" is a finalist for the 1984 Ken-L Ration Dog Hero of the Year Award for saving the life of two-year-old Erica Ferber.

- "Leica," an eight-year-old female German Shepherd, rescued owner Rebecca Counsellor of Hubbard Lake, MI when the accomplished horsewoman was thrown from her horse. Suffering a fractured pelvis, collapsed lung and torn esophagus, Counsellor managed to remove her belt and tie it around Leica's neck, and commanded the dog to "Go home!" The heroic canine responded and led a rescue party back to the fallen woman.

- "Budweiser," a six-month-old male mixed-breed puppy, braved howling winds and bitter cold to find his owner's two-year-old daughter, lost in the woods near the child's Hortonville, NY home. Budweiser stayed with diaper-clad Erica Ferber, keeping her warm, until help arrived.

- "Sheba," a female Labrador-Irish Setter mixed-breed owned by Gary Vittori of Truckee, CA, saved her 27-year-old owner from drowning when he was suddenly gripped by cramps while swimming across a reservoir. By paddling alongside Vittori, Sheba kept her owner's head above water and towed him to shore.

- "Max," a 15-month-old male Doberman Pinscher, led owner Kathy Yaunk to an injured elderly resident in a nearby apartment in Columbus, OH. Although Yaunk had been told by another resident that someone was crying for help, she couldn't find the right apartment until Max led her straight to the distressed man. The dog wouldn't leave the side of the 70-year-old man until help arrived.

- "Rags," a five-year-old male Poodle-Lhasa Apso mixed-breed, ran for help when owner Jim Grieco of East Moriches, NY slipped into a diabetic coma. By barking, Rags roused Grieco's mother and led her to where Grieco lay.

- "Puppy," a male Pekingese-Poodle stray, had just been adopted by three-year-old Tiffany Fugett's family when he saved the Stillwater, OK tot from drowning. The youngster had climbed a fence and fallen into a neighbor's swimming pool. Puppy dived in after her and, by latching onto her sweater with his teeth, held her face above water long enough to enable two neighbors to help. Once the girl's rescue became news, Puppy's original owners, Bryan and Brenda Thomason, came forward to claim Puppy as their lost dog, "Frodo."

These nine dogs were selected as finalists from hundreds nominated for America's oldest and most prestigious dog hero award. For more than 30 years, Ken-L Ration's Dog Hero of the Year program has nationally recognized those dogs that demonstrate outstanding bravery, loyalty and intelligence by performing deeds leading to the saving of life or property. The 1984 Ken-L Ration Dog Hero of the Year will be announced in the May issue of Consumers Digest magazine.

Ken-L Ration has already begun seeking nominations for the 1985 Dog Hero. If you know of an heroic rescue by a canine, please share it with Ken-L Ration. To nominate a canine hero and receive a free booklet on how to care for your dog, send a detailed description of the heroic act, along with your name, address and telephone number to: KEN-L RATION DOG HERO OF THE YEAR, P.O. Box 10446, Kansas City, MO 64111

Leads may be poetry, or jokes, or trivia questions, or they might be composed of lists, or foreign phrases, or they could be combinations of several types. Their common denominator is the ability to pull the reader into the feature. Leads should also be varied, especially in company magazines, where a repetitious way of beginning articles would soon lose readers.

Like all good writing, the body of the feature story should carry the reader along, maintaining interest, sprinkling the prose with quotes, adding a few anecdotes, and including sensory detail. The best feature writers *show* rather than *tell*, letting the reader become part of the story instead of the object of a lecture.

Nearly every writer finds it easier to come up with a good lead than to provide a strong close. The ending of every feature should come about logically, should seem natural and definitive. It might provide a twist or surprise, or it could confirm the promise of the lead, or it could merely summarize the conclusions advanced by the article.

> Tom Reynolds eased himself back into his Phoenix. After 7 already, and his proposal didn't fly. Still, he felt the day had been worthwhile. He'd learned a lot about Amalgamated—and about himself.

Every article will be different, depending on the subject, the anticipated audience, and the skill of the writer. Reading the work of others is a good way to learn, but the best way is to practice writing such articles yourself.

The feature may be directed to some special editor at the daily paper or at the magazine. A query to such people in advance would be in order. Or perhaps you may wish to plant the idea with them and let them supply a staff person to write the piece. Either way should be acceptable, as long as it results in producing extra and favorable coverage for the client firm.

LETTER WRITING

The public relations person doesn't often get a sense of progression in his or her work. Not like a mechanic, for example, who can rattle off the types of engines he has learned to fix over the years. PR practitioners have a more difficult time appreciating their own skills—until they see the letters written by presumably intelligent businesspersons. They realize the average business or political leader can't write a simple letter and can't express things succinctly, interestingly, and in a way that will persuade or motivate. Practitioners realize that, yes, after all, they have learned something. They would never write a letter like that.

The ability to write a good letter shouldn't be downgraded. Some fundraising experts receive thousands of dollars for a single, effective direct-mail letter. Exceptional letters have won brides, obtained contracts, changed lives, sold properties, landed jobs, stalled bill collectors, and drawn both tears and laughter. Every letter is an opportunity, and the way you use that opportunity depends on how much skill you have and how much you really care.

Direct mail has become a very sophisticated tool in political campaigns in the last decade. In a losing campaign in 1982, New York gubernatorial candidate Lewis Lehrman sent out eleven different mass mailings to residents of the state, including 3 million mailed in the last week of the campaign. Computers allowed him to target audiences with positive and negative messages, designed to upset Mario Cuomo. This million-dollar effort by Lehrman nearly won the election for him. In the same year, in order to ensure that Republicans got out to vote, the Republican Senatorial Campaign Committee sent a Reagan "election-gram" to 8 million voters at a cost of $1.3 million. By mailing letters directly to certain voting blocs, you can target in on the worries, fears, and prejudices of varied groups. And, as one campaign manager pointed out, people may disregard TV spots as politics, but they tend to pay attention to letters.

Direct mail may make up a large portion of the letters produced in this country, but, for the practitioner and his or her boss, the job of writing a decent message may be a one-at-a-time chore. There are guidebooks to help with this communication task, and they're worth reading. However, after seeing what they have to say, the letter writer should put them aside. You don't write a good letter out of a book; you write it from your heart and mind. Letters should be simple, honest, natural, and free of the stodgy style that begins:

> Yours of the 16th instant received and contents duly noted . . .

or that wanders around like this:

> It has come to my attention that a luncheon might now be appropriate and I wonder if I might be bold enough to request that you check your calendar and see if, hopefully, the date of September 15 is free and clear for you, as it is for me?

when you could say this:

> Lunch on September 15?

Your correspondence must be complete and clear, and sound as though a person, not a machine, wrote it.

> Writing effective business reports, proposals and letters takes a little know-how. Many of these communications have become less formal and more conversational, because business is beginning to recognize that doing business does not preclude the fact that real human beings actually talk to other human beings. For example, letters are now (to quote a computer term) "user-friendly" and sound natural. The guideline is simple: If you wouldn't say it, don't write it.[3]

Salutation and Close

Most *salutations* could be less rigid, especially in a mass-produced letter that will go to thousands of strangers. Calling them "Dear Friend" may not be appropriate, and "To Whom It May Concern" is too cold. Whenever possible, use the proper name of the person addressed, looking it up or calling that person's office when in doubt. If you must use a mass approach, consider something other than "Dear Sir or Madam." Many direct-mail pieces start with a narrative hook, a little line, almost like the lead in a feature, that brings you into the letter.

> Last night the temperature hit 42 degrees below zero.

That sentence would get more attention for the needs of a Dakota tribe than a greeting to "Dear Friend of the Native American."

Even "Good Morning!" is better than a formal opening—except, of course, for those occasions that call for formality.

The *complimentary close* of a letter, on the other hand, is best left alone. Exotic innovations, like "Fondly yours" or "With deepest and most sincere affection," may provoke strange reactions from your business associates. Stick with the traditional closes, like "Sincerely."

If you could riffle through the letters in the file of any major business office, you could eliminate the first and last paragraphs of 90 percent of its correspondence. The writers don't know how to get started, so they pile on the clichés. And they loiter on the page long after they have delivered the message. Get right into the story and quit when you are finished. The reader will appreciate it.

The Body of the Letter

With regard to the body of the letter, here are some brief tips:

1. *Be careful of slang and humor.* Slang is outdated fast, and a phony will be exposed quickly. Humor, too, can be misunderstood. You can be genial without trying to be funny. Of course, if you can really handle humor, this approach might be used—but sparingly.

2. *Be careful what you say.* Your letters may be saved and the contents used against you at a later date.

3. *Don't get too familiar.* "Hi, John baby" is no way to greet a new correspondent—or even an old one.

4. *Don't write in a white heat.* When we are angry, we sometimes dart to the table or typewriter and blast the offending party, marveling the whole time at our own ability to turn a clever, penetrating phrase. OK, write the letter—but save it, don't mail it. The new dawn may find you in a more reasonable mood. Otherwise you may have made a terrible error, and your bitterness is there in writing. Besides, you could run afoul of the libel laws.

5. *Don't stew over crank letters.* If criticism if going to bother you, you have no business being in public relations. Your mistakes—and triumphs—are all out in the open. If you get an anonymous crank letter accusing you or a subordinate, read it for any kernel of help it might offer and then toss it into the wastebasket. Don't fret and worry over the opinions of someone who hasn't the courage to sign his or her name. And don't get into a paper war with kooks who do sign their names. You will regret it.

6. *Avoid obvious fraud.* You know those letters that tell you that you have been selected to receive a free dance lesson? And they even spell your name wrong!

7. *Remember the rules for good writing.*   Use short, clear sentences. Get rid of such awkward clichés as "the aforementioned" and such unnecessary verbiage as, "Would you kindly be good enough to send me. . . ." And watch your English. Misspelled words and poor grammar jump out at the reader and damage your effectiveness.

Perhaps the best rule to remember in writing letters is to put yourself in the place of the recipient. So many letter writers are so full of what they want to say that they spill it out without any regard for the condition and mood of the receiver when he or she slits the envelope. Imagine a real person opening this letter—even a form letter. If you can draw an honest and accurate picture of this individual, you are on your way to writing a decent letter.

The Office Memo

A word might be said here about the office memo. This, as *Better Letters* points out, can be a "deadly weapon." Some people use it as a protective device, carefully constructing the message to absolve them of future blame. Other people write "mean." They aren't even aware of it, but their memorandums come across as blunt and angry.

Follow the same procedures you do with other correspondence. Be clear, factual, and honest. Don't put anything in the memo that you wouldn't want unfriendly eyes to see. And be certain that everyone who should get a copy does get a copy, and in the proper "pecking order," meaning that top executives are listed above junior officers on the routing list.

The memo can have a number of purposes—to communicate information, solicit information, serve as a reminder, praise, criticize, or simply commit to writing details that have been communicated orally.

The format may vary, although most memos contain the firm name at the top, followed by spaces for the names of the recipient and sender and the topic.

Memorandums should be carefully thought out, organized, and written when the writer is in a controlled mood. The language should be simple, concise, direct, and friendly. Before you circulate the memo, it is wise to give it a final reading.

REPORTS AND PROPOSALS

Another form of writing expected of the public relations practitioner is the compiling of reports and, perhaps, the preparation of proposals.

Reports

The emphasis in reports is on clarity, logic, and comprehensiveness rather than on imaginative language. Some reports are written almost open-ended, just laying out the facts and allowing the reviewing parties to draw their own conclusions. Most reports, however, are written with a point of view, even though they also marshal facts in a readable fashion.

In preparing a report, the writer should first collect all the data he or she wishes to include. This may entail a study of past correspondence, interviews, reading, and perhaps even a survey. Having collected these data, the writer makes a rough outline of contents and decides on a method of approaching the report. Will it be strictly chronological, moving from one date to another, or will it begin with a problem and present either an accomplished or a suggested solution? The nature of the report will help decide this. Whatever format the writer chooses, he or she should proceed logically from one point to the other, being careful not to leave gaps in thinking or include misstatements of fact. If there is a conclusion, it should be reasonable and unmistakable.

Charts and diagrams help, of course, and it is often beneficial for the preparer of the report—or some knowledgeable spokesperson—to go through it with the reviewer.

Proposals

Proposals are a bit different. Here you obviously want something, so, although reason and accuracy are still important, you must always be aware of the need to persuade. Perhaps you are seeking a federal grant, a budget increase, more personnel in your division, a change of policy or procedure, a plant addition, a new college curriculum, a special event—any number of things.

Usually the proposal starts with where you are at the moment, sometimes preceded by a brief history of how you got there. Then state the problem or opportunity, followed by a detailed solution, and then the cost, and personnel time factors involved. The final portion of the proposal could contain exhibits if these help.

Remember that the busy executive may not share your enthusiasm or vision. The more cogent and appealing you can make your presentation, the better the chance of its success. Don't tell this executive how nice this is going to look, show him or her a sample.

When preparing proposals for private foundations or federal agencies, you are often given guidelines and sometimes provided with a specific form or format. Even within these rather rigid limitations, there is room for some "sell." Certain people gain a reputation for "grantsmanship" because they know how to prepare an interesting and exciting proposal. They get attention—and they get money.

Departmental plans, including those for the communications department, are similar to proposals when they must be committed to written form and presented to management. To do this effectively, the drafters must be familiar with the power structure in the company, must be sensitive to the best time for submission, and must couch the plan within the language and goals of the organization. The "action plan" should cover objectives, strategies, personnel involved, and budget.

> The easiest way to become part of the organization's planning process and to gain credibility for yourself and your plans is to volunteer to coordinate, write and polish your department's operating plans. Chances are if your department director is not much of an organizer or writer, you'll be greeted enthusiastically. Once you've seen the process from the inside out, you'll be ready to do your own communication planning and sell it more effectively to the real decision-makers.[4]

SPEECHWRITING

One of the most difficult forms of public relations writing is the speech. In the first place, a good speech is a tough assignment for anyone. It becomes even more arduous when you have to turn your work over to someone else for delivery. If, as some communications experts contend, the speaker and the speech are one, then your challenge becomes the creation of a star from a lump of oratorical clay.

You should always work within the limits of reality. If the person for whom you are preparing the remarks is good with statistics but socially shy, you'll want a short speech, built on his or her strengths, with short sentences and an absence of poetic phrasing. If the speaker has a weak sense of humor, defer the jokes. If your assigned speech will be given by a person who is a poor reader, don't furnish pages of flowery rhetoric. In other words, *know your speaker.*

Every speechwriting assignment should begin with a session or two with the person for whom the speech is being written. At these meetings you want to ascertain what sort of a person he or she is, what the person would like to say, what the person feels comfortable and uncomfortable with, what the person can handle and can't handle. You don't leave this phase until you feel confident you know how to proceed. Otherwise, you are in for a lot of rejection and rewriting.

Following these initial consultations, the speechwriter does all the necessary research, using, ordinarily, many of the informal methods of gathering data. This research should encompass not only the subject to be discussed but also the audience, environment, organization, equipment, and other aspects of the talk.

Regarding the audience, you'll want to determine how many will attend, who they are (in terms of age, interest, occupation), and what they expect. Your approach should suit the audience, playing upon its most responsive chords and steering clear of any taboos.

If the arena or dining hall has any built-in problems with acoustics, sight lines, speaking systems, or other architectural peculiarities, consider these in preparation. The environment may also suggest some opportunities for humor.

Whatever it takes, you want to produce the right speech for the right person to give to the right audience.

Most speechwriters make several drafts, checking with the speaker when they feel the talk is nearing its final form, getting this person's input and blessing. The speech should reveal something of the speaker's character along with the message, and should evoke not only interest but trust, respect, acceptance.

Executives may not always cooperate. Some don't want to go through the consultation stage, claiming they haven't the time; some force their bad ideas on the speechwriter and receive a bad speech in return; some don't know whether a speech is good or bad, so their critical comments are not helpful. The speechwriter wants involvement on the part of the speaker, but the writer must also make the speaker better than he or she really is.

Once the material is assembled and the rough drafts have been approved, the speechwriter should settle down to a final version. Each writer has a different way of proceeding. Some like to work closely with an outline from the outset; others like to write freely and gather elements together later; still others use a tape recorder and dictate. Some do first drafts in pencil, and others punch their thoughts into a computer, enjoying the ease of editing. Whatever works, works, but for the majority who prefer an outline, here is a sample. One caution: It's merely a guide and should not be followed slavishly.

  I. Decide on general purpose of speech (inform? entertain? persuade?).
  II. Decide on general subject.
  III. State your specific subject.
  IV. State your specific purpose (combine I and III).
  V. Central idea (a concise idea that gives the audience a key to the general ideas in the speech).
  VI. List the *main points* as developed from the central idea:
   A.
   B.
   C.
  VII. Develop the main points:
   A.
    1.
    2.
   B.
    1.
    2.
    Etc.
   (Write main points in complete sentences. Supporting materials may be written in phrases.)
  VIII. Develop conclusion (use an outline form).
  IX. Transitions (write a sentence to connect each main point).
  X. Develop the introduction (use an outline form).

XI. *Then order the elements above into a basic outline, as follows:*
Introduction
Main Point 1 and supporting materials
Transition
Main Point 2 and supporting materials
Transition
(*Other main points in order*, with appropriate transitions)
Conclusion

Introduction

Not every speech has to start with a couple of jokes, although, if the speaker can handle humor, this is an acceptable way to begin. What you want to do is arouse interest, set the tone for the remarks, and warm the audience up to the speaker's personality. You could begin with a question that the speech will answer, or surprise the audience with a statement or quotation that has a bite to it. A comment about the location (especially the town itself) or the occasion or some of the other guests may work. If you know for sure what will be said prior to the speaker's talk, you might hitchhike on those words.

> I'm delighted to find myself in San Diego again. It's always been one of my favorite cities.
> This is the first time I've ever addressed a group of educators. The last time I talked to a teacher I had to stay after school and clean the erasers.
> The preceding speaker mentioned that more and more is being said about less and less. I'm going to try to make a liar out of him.
> There is no farm crisis. That's what the Secretary of Agriculture said. And I agree with him.

Body of the Speech

The important thing about constructing the central portion of any speech is that it should flow logically, moving effortlessly from point to point, making it easy and interesting for the audience to follow. The choice of language should fit the theme and the audience, and should be written to be heard, not read. Here are some tips:

- Break up the speech into sections. Number and time each section. This will aid memory and timing.
- Punctuate frequently, assisting the speaker with pauses that produce certain desired effects.
- Use statistics sparingly, and make them pay off.
- Strive for clarity above all else. The speaker *must* be understood.
- Tie in to local people and events when possible.
- Develop a rhythm for the speaker, one that complements the content— making sure the speaker can handle this technique.

- Use "nouns that bleed and verbs that sting and rattle."[5]
- Personalize the speech with experiences from the speaker's life.
- Sprinkle in appropriate quotes—but not too many.
- Avoid words that are difficult to pronounce. If such words must be used, as with names and titles, give the speaker the phonetic pronunciation, as one would in a news release for radio.
- Incorporate colorful imagery whenever it fits.
- Stay away from potentially offensive material, whether humorous or otherwise.
- Use contrasts to make a point. ("The total endowment at Windsor College is less than the monthly interest on Harvard's endowment.")
- Underline or capitalize words you want emphasized. Use dashes to indicate pauses. If you intend any physical directions, like "(HOLD UP CITATION)" or "(WAIT FOR LAUGH)," write these in, perhaps in capital letters and in parentheses.
- Don't be afraid to repeat important points. Some speakers say, "Tell 'em three times." But vary the ways you repeat.
- Maintain a conversational tone throughout.
- Be honest. Don't exaggerate, or unfairly criticize, or force a phony emotion.
- Write in some places where the speaker *must* establish eye contact. Even gestures may be suggested, if they come naturally.
- Provide good transitions.
- Involve the audience when you can. Sometimes a speaker may solicit responses, or request questions, or ask for acknowledgment. Some speakers like to walk down into the audience, carrying a portable mike.
- Keep in mind passages that may be quoted by the media. In fact, the PR person should provide the media with a copy of the speech immediately in advance of the talk.
- Prepare the speech the way the speaker wants it—completely drafted or merely cue lines? On cards, $8\frac{1}{2}'' \times 11''$ sheets, in a notebook? Large type or regular type?
- Time the speech.
- Allow ample time for review and rehearsal by the speaker.

Anecdotes and Examples

Everyone likes a story, and you can see an audience perk up when a speech text is humanized by a personal experience or pertinent anecdote. Numerous books catalog anecdotal materials, and these may serve in a pinch, but the best stories are the ones that have involved the speaker, even if indirectly.

Instead of citing statistics on the incidence of cancer deaths from smoking, a speaker would probably get more attention with a paragraph that began:

> Two nights ago, I visited my father in the hospital. I hardly recognized him. Dad was a two-pack-a-day man, and the habit finally caught up with him. . . .

Figure 7-2
Courtesy: *Speechwriter's Newsletter*, Lawrence Ragan Communications, Inc.

Writing and coaching at Florida Power & Light

Van Forrestor, 39, speechwriter for Florida Power & Light Co., has been writing speeches since he was 16 years old—not, however, for Florida Power & Light. He joined that company last May after years of public relations and speechwriting work for agencies and corporations, including Burson-Marsteller and General Electric. He has also been a member of Toastmasters International for 18 years. He competes yearly, but so far unsuccessfully, for its international speech championship. He majored in speech and was a debater at the University of Miami.

"I'm good at it [speechwriting] because I give them [speeches]," he told *S/N.* "I know what the guy's going through and can write for it. I can write around or through problems. I don't write technical papers for the nuclear society. A speech is for the ear. The audience must get the point the first time around. A speech must be clear and to the point."

Forrestor has also been a speech coach. He still is, in fact, for any executive at Florida Power & Light who wants help. "I set the videotape machine and critique and help the executive. If the executive asks me, I will work with him for a month or even years. Speaking takes practice." [Florida Power & Light has its own training program for speakers. Forrestor's help is offered in addition to that.]

When it comes to writing a speech, Forrestor begins not with a videotape, however, but with an audio tape and recorder. He sits down with the speaker for 15 or 20 minutes, turns on the recorder with its unobtrusive condenser microphone, and, in effect, turns on the speaker. "I ask the same question four ways," he says. "We laugh and joke. I ask him what he wants to say, how he wants to approach the audience, how he wants to leave it. Through free association of ideas, the guy starts talking, and beautiful quotes come out of his mouth. I use those quotes and ideas, and then the speech looks vaguely familiar to him when he gets it back."

In free association and a tape recorder lie truth for the speaker, in Forrestor's book. From the taped session he goes to the company computer, with its access to four data banks, and searches out the data that's needed for the speech. This is the easy part, Forrestor says. It's "matching the mood and audience" that's tricky. The taped session is crucial to that goal.

He types up its results, hearing again the speaker's words. Then he has before him the transcript and the facts from the data banks. He reads it all over, then goes home and sleeps on it. At 4 or 5 a.m. the next day, he's back at the office, in the pre-sunrise Florida quiet. It's "gut-out time" then. By early afternoon he has a draft.

Forrestor is the only full-time speechwriter for the 12,500-employee company. Many more speeches ("hundreds") are given than he writes, Forrestor says. Testimony before regulatory bodies and presentations to analysts, for instance, are done by "technical people." And the company's lawyers write their own, of course.

Forrestor's schedule for the next month indicates a year-long projected output of 70 to 80 speeches for Florida Power & Light executives. He also does slide and video scripts and other speeches for the company's speakers bureau, called the Community Information Program (CIP).

CIP is coordinated by Melodie L. Womble, who becomes Forrestor's client when he writes for the 200 speakers who fan out into the community for the company, enlarging on its central theme and focus of an ad campaign, "Working Hard at Being the Kind of Company You Want." The nine-year-old CIP has 30 films at its disposal, and six to ten speeches. A speech is given to a speaker with the understanding that he or she can personalize it, said Womble, but "a lot give it verbatim." In any event, these CIP speakers do not sit down with Forrestor and his tape recorder before they go out. That's for executives only. [Florida Power & Light Co., P.O. Box 529100, Miami 33152]

LAWRENCE RAGAN COMMUNICATIONS, INC. PUBLISHER
THE RAGAN REPORT   SPEECHWRITER'S NEWSLETTER   THE REPORTER'S REPORT   407 SOUTH DEARBORN, CHICAGO, ILLINOIS 60605

Examples and analogies are also useful speech tools. Instead of just saying that inflation has taken its toll on the prices of household goods, you might say, "A jar of peanut butter that cost $1.69 in 1970 now sells for $3.39."

Humor

If you opt for the use of humor, and the speaker is able to deliver your jokes or one-liners, you still want to be certain the material is relevant to the occasion, that it won't be familiar to this audience, and that it won't offend listeners.

Very little ethnic humor is appropriate to use, and so-called "blue" material, which may work at the corner bar, is a risk at almost any kind of formal gathering. Good taste should dictate the course of comedy in speeches.

Some audiences like jokes and may sit still for a string of them. Most groups, however, expect a little meat in the talk and will be disappointed if the entire speech is a stand-up routine. Topical one-liners are more difficult to write, but more effective with most crowds. These relate to some news event, or local personality, or some topic recognized as current and colloquial.

There are people who specialize in writing gags for speakers, and books and services that provide such bon mots. Again, these are handy, but a lively comic imagination still surpasses them. Besides, you spend a lot of time leafing through joke books and comedy services before you find the line or lines that fit both speaker and topic.

Timing

How long should a speech be? Stephen Leacock once said that an audience tires of a speaker in ten minutes and that a good audience could do it in five. Facetious, yes, but good advice on brevity. You rarely hear anyone complain that a speech was too short. Twenty minutes is a good time to shoot for, meaning that the speechwriter may prepare between ten and 15 pages of double-spaced copy, depending on the nature of the material and the speed of delivery.

There is, finally, a comfort level that should be reached by the speaker in cooperation with the speechwriter. The speech should be one that is easy to master, so it can be delivered in a manner that appears extemporaneous. If

Figure 7-3 Both speechwriting and speech making are tools of the PR professional.

the speaker is so wed to the manuscript that he or she can't look up, it makes for a dull evening. A relationship has to be established between speaker and audience at the outset, maintained throughout, then capped with a well-wrought conclusion.

Close

The final words of a speech should be every bit as compelling as the opening words—perhaps more so. You want to leave the audience with a thought, or move it to action, or sum up your argument. What you must avoid is the feeling that the speaker has run out of steam and doesn't know how to end the talk. Make the ending deliberate and potent—like Churchill's famous conclusion:

> Let us therefore brace ourselves to our duty and so bear ourselves that if the British Commonwealth and Empire last for a thousand years, men will still say, "This was their finest hour."

Many types of closes are possible. Most give the listener a sense of finality, but some indicate a course of action to be followed, and others pose a problem and leave the audience thinking of a solution.

Other Speaking Assignments

PR persons not only may be asked to write the standard speech; they may also be required to write introductions of speakers, invocations, toasts, remarks for chairpersons. Again, some books may help, but an even better solution is to listen to other people who do this successfully, and practice, practice, practice.

Robert Lehrman, in a *Public Relations Journal* article, suggests that corporate executives (and their speechwriters) can learn something from the politicians about public speaking. He cites half a dozen traits of the better political speeches and speakers:

1. *Politicians use a basic speech*, one that can be used over and over, with a few variations for the locale and occasion.
2. *Politicians are concise.* They know the limits of an audience and try to accommodate the listener.
3. *Politicians relish Q and A.* This goes back to what was said about audience involvement.
4. *Politicians speak concretely.* Well, some of them do, using short sentences and word pictures.
5. *Politicians speak vividly.* The good ones use anecdotes, humor, imagery, analogies. They reveal themselves.
6. *Politicians practice.*[6]

INTERNAL COMMUNICATIONS

A lot of thought, effort, and money go into employee communications. Even so, much of this effort is dissipated because there is no real communications plan, no overall goals except for a vague notion about morale and efficiency, and few specific ideas about what each item in the communication chain is expected to accomplish. So much of the material that is published within companies is poorly conceived, even if well-designed and well-written. Any printed piece should have a clear intent to reveal the firm or organization in a positive but honest manner, and without the usual clichés of corporate prose and portraits.

A solid communication program requires the commitment of management, sufficient funds and personnel, a clear line of authority, short- and long-range planning, and a method for evaluation. The PR person may have to take the lead, convincing management of the necessity for a well-structured system. This must include means of disseminating management directives and philosophy to employees (magazines, newsletters, closed-circuit television, bulletin boards, and so on), methods for achieving employee input (complaint boxes, internal surveys, telephone hotlines), and opportunities for group or one-on-one meetings.

In covering the publication phase of its communication program, General Motors had to implement activities that reached the editors and public relations directors at its 150 major locations across this country. The company was determined to accomplish this on a regular and timely basis. The plan included:

- A daily tape-recorded telephone newsline summarizing GM and industry news
- This same information in a hard-copy newswire form through GM's time-sharing computer system
- *Information Briefs*, published every two weeks, consisting of six to eight pages of bite-size printed and graphic materials that did not duplicate other materials
- Special mailings of major news releases, speeches, and prepared articles
- A series of two-day editors' conferences hitting hard on skills training and idea-sharing activities
- A *GM Editors' Resource Guide*
- *Inside Information*, an idea-sharing monthly newsletter to communicators.[7]

All these items require writing at corporate headquarters, and they will be adapted to local needs, again requiring the skills of the writer.

Company Magazines

One common communications tool is some kind of publication aimed at staff members. This could be a daily or a periodic newsletter, or it could be a more elaborate public relations periodical. The object is pretty much the same—to inform the "internal" audience of company policy and actions, to provide a forum for employee ideas and activities, to boost morale.

Even though the PR periodical is generally a management tool, it should not be an obvious one. If the copy is too propagandistic, the employee reader won't bother with it. The writing should be useful, informative, colorfully presented, and amply illustrated.

> No matter how carefully planned a publication may be, it will end up in the circular file instead of employees' minds if it is dull, full of jargon, or loaded with long words. Good writing style is really invisible. But it makes the material easy—and fun—to read.[8]

The most effective company magazines have the ability to define and explain the organization to those who work there. They have the added task of introducing change and converting readers to it. To accomplish this, top management has to cooperate by articulating policy, and editors must move beyond the superficial and provide publications that meet employee needs.

Figure 7-4 Company publications exhibit a variety of cover designs. Courtesy: Exxon Corporation, New Jersey Bell, Ralston Purina Company, E.I. du Pont de Nemours & Company, Shadyside Hospital, Boston University Alumni Association, and Burlington Northern Railroad

Figure 7-5 Exxon's internal/external publication, *The Lamp*, features an open look, large photos, and an exciting graphic design.
Courtesy: Exxon Corporation

How do you know what the employees want?

For one thing, you can survey them. Many firms run periodic reader-ship surveys, and although these are often less than satisfactory, they do provide some clues as to interest and preference. Southwestern Bell in St. Louis gathers employees in focus groups, presents them with recent company magazine stories in different forms, and requests their opinions on which works better for them. Using this technique, they discovered that text and sidebar (a short piece of copy adding an independent bit of information to the story) were favored over text alone, and that photos of employees were popular, and that readers wanted by-line identification of authors rather than anonymity.

Large companies sometimes use a system involving reporters for various departments or divisions. The publications editor can't be everywhere. Even if the editor has time to write the entire publication, he or she cannot be expected to know about a humorous incident in the traffic department, or wedding plans for a couple in Warehouse #3. An efficient network of reporters—preferably people who can at least recognize a story even if they can't write it—fills this gap.

One trend in recent years, especially with larger companies and organizations that have vital public ties (like hospitals), is the creation of a publication that serves both internal and external readers.

> Businesses around the world are discovering that the company magazine is the endlessly flexible medium. Your magazine is the pipeline to employees, the door opener for the sales force, a lead producer, the best way to explain the hundreds of ways your product can be used.[9]

The magazine can be a way to attract or soften up prospects, or to promote a long-range favorable image of the institution. It may accomplish this with fairly direct copy, or the slant could be more subtle, as when hospitals produce magazines devoted solely to health tips and without any hard sell for their particular services. Nonprofit institutions that subsist on charity use their publications as appeals, sometimes bluntly, sometimes with finesse. Missionary societies feature articles on the more dramatic work of their members. A few companies even publish bilingual company magazines, accommodating their non-English-speaking employees.

Graphically (and this subject is covered in more detail in Chapter 8), company magazines are characterized by bolder design; larger format; larger typeface; shorter articles or ones broken up by subheads, boldface, or other devices; fewer but larger illustrations; more white space; a richer blend of stories, including some that would not have been acceptable years ago, either because they were controversial or because they didn't represent a strong enough corporate identification; more reader involvement—trivia questions, crossword puzzles, photo identification, anecdotes from readers; additional charts and graphs to illustrate statistical matter; and even the retention of the more popular features, such as sports news, recipes, and engagements.

A quick glance at a table covered with company publications is sufficient to illustrate the fact that budgets and talents vary. Money isn't everything in producing attractive printed pieces, but it helps. There's no magic formula for determining what a company magazine should cost. Even if there were, too many organizations are already limited by a ceiling figure and couldn't aspire to the desirable norm. Despite this wide-ranging financial differential, every publication should have a budget—a realistic budget—that includes salaries, free-lance fees, cost of photography and artwork, paper, typesetting, platemaking, printing, binding, distribution, and other overhead costs, from Social Security to utilities.

Figure 7-6 Architectural brochures have come a long way from rough blueprints and skeletal design. Today's materials are invariably clean, crisp, and attractive. Courtesy: HDR, Inc.

Partially to reduce costs, partially to present a different look, and partially to achieve a closer match with certain types of readers, a number of firms and organizations use a tabloid newspaper format for their internal magazine, occasionally giving it a magazine look with large illustrations, or structuring it to resemble a regular tab section. Newsletters in a smaller size are popular, too, especially for those companies with small PR staffs and tight budgets. Some corporations publish slick magazines, tabloid newspapers, and newsletters, all with different audiences and goals. These same firms may include employees on their lists for brochures directed to external publics.

BROCHURES AND PRINTED MATERIALS

Brochure writing is something like writing a short story. You begin with a provocative lead (aided by a headline and illustrations) to entice the reader inside. Once you have the reader's interest, you unfold the story in logical, colorful portions, often separated by short "subheads" that break up the gray look. You must be terse in this writing. Every word should count.

When the end of the presentation is reached, a summary close should be used, or a call to action, or an offer of further information. A booklet on the danger signs of cancer, for example, might advise the reader about seeing a physician. A brochure soliciting aid in defeating a piece of legislation might conclude with names of elected representatives and suggestions for contacting them.

Any short printed piece can be tough to write. It looks easy, but the writer must condense a substantial amount of material, satisfy the boss or client, and anticipate the reactions and questions of the eventual reader. It's a difficult assignment.

Direct Mail

Under "Letter Writing" we discussed the proper way to handle the letter portion of direct mail, but there are other considerations. Most direct-mail appeals contain several items—typically, a letter, a brochure, and a return card or envelope. There may be additional inserts, but it isn't too hard to get cluttered, so you should aim for as few items as possible.

Since direct mail has the potential to irritate people, the sender should struggle to make the prose credible, the message personal, the name correct, and the mailings not too frequent.

> Of the 50 billion or so pieces of junk mail the post office handles (or mishandles) annually, I receive about half. Or so it seems. . . . I think I'd buy more stuff through the mail if there wasn't so much awful prose to gag on. . . . I also don't enjoy the childish allurements booby-trapping the mailings—meaningless membership cards in gleaming plastic to stroke our egos, gilt-edge certificates of specious value aimed at our latent greed, stickers to transfer, numbers to rub off, stamps to lick, cards to punch.[10]

Direct-mail pieces must have instant appeal. The writing should be clear, factual, and surfeited with self-interest messages for the prospect. These mailing pieces are generally heavily illustrated, and they should anticipate everything the reader would like to ask.

Direct mail of a public relations nature may solicit funds, but it is more likely to be an invitation to attend certain programs or a reminder about wills and bequests or a statement of company policy. It sells in a less obvious way.

Depending on the nature of the mailing and the strength of the mailing list, responses to mail appeals can run high or low. A "cold" mailing to a general, unknown audience might garner returns of 2 percent or less. A similar mailing to regular customers or prime prospects could run to 33 percent or more responses. If the mailing promised something unique, replies would also increase.

The attractiveness of the mailing itself will aid returns. So will the inclusion of a self-addressed envelope (particularly one that is stamped), a return card, or a coupon. The easier you make it for the person to respond, the greater the number of responses you will get.

The mailing envelope itself often has a brief message to interest readers enough so that they will open the letter or package and not merely discard it. Sometimes the return address will lack a company name so that recipients will be curious as to the sender and open the mailing. Individually typed or handwritten envelopes—or those that look as if they were—will have a better chance of being opened than those that seem to be mass-produced.

There are hundreds of tricks to direct mail that experienced practitioners can explain to the newcomer. Periodic seminars in this specialized area are held in major cities, and mail-order houses and paper companies often issue brochures outlining these techniques.

Miscellaneous Communications Tools

Even within a company, the public relations department may be overseeing a variety of print assignments—daily news summaries, sales bul-

Figure 7-7 Major firms issue numerous internal and external publications. Courtesy: Adolph Coors Company

letins, dealer magazines, shareholder or corporate mailings, production schedules and manuals, citations, catalogues, handbooks, programs, invitations, announcements of internal radio or television broadcasts, even book-length company histories. Each of these forms presents its own challenge.

Bulletin-board copy, for example, should be attractive and legible, and should be located in well-lit and well-traveled areas. It should also be changed or updated frequently to preserve timeliness, and the boards should be cleaned periodically to avoid clutter.

Information racks, with employees' pamphlets, should also have a good location and should be colorful and attractive enough to make employees want to sample the contents. Reference materials on pay scales, vacations, fringe benefits, sick leave, and other policies may also be here—or they could be distributed to new employees as they check in.

FILMS, SLIDES, RADIO, AND TELEVISION

Writing scripts for films, slide shows, radio, or television requires a special talent. This doesn't mean that public relations practitioners cannot become reasonably adept at writing all four (they may, in fact, *have* to do so), but they must realize there is no easy transition from the more familiar print to these media. If they can afford the services of an outside expert, they should hire one. Then they might work with this professional person, picking up the techniques and later applying these techniques themselves.

Films

Films are the most specialized of the visual communication methods, primarily because the PR person has so little chance to practice. Some firms—like major insurance companies—may have their own film departments and do a number of films each year. Most of these films will be training films without much attempt at art. When firms plan a more ambitious movie—for public relations purposes, perhaps—they will probably bring in an independent film maker. Someone in the PR department might still be expected to write the script, so it's a good idea to be as versatile as possible, as long as the writer is conscious of his or her limitations.

An award-winning entry by General Motors in 1984 was an eight-minute industrial film that paired scenes in its robotic factory with a sound track featuring classical music. Northwestern Bell offers dozens of films from its library, dealing not only with telephone etiquette but also with science, safety, sports, social science ("The Black Contribution"), history ("A Most Notable Century"), travel, and other subjects. Phillip Morris captured a Whitney Museum exhibit of American folk art on film, later transferred it to videotape, and has been showing it for ten years, attracting a live audience of more than half a million, as well as the television viewers. The cigarette manufacturer calculates that this and other films (including ones on other museums, on children's art, on state or private collections) have been seen by more than 7 million people, in addition to the commercial and PBS audiences.

Since film is a visual medium, the beginning scriptwriter must become picture-oriented. One director suggested that writers be charged $10 for every word they put in a script. If such penalties were imposed, we wouldn't have the wall-to-wall narration that plagues many scripts. Writers should *see* the film play in their minds and write from that vision. They should let the pictures carry the weight of their message, speaking only when they must.

Each public relations film should have a theme, some one idea the viewers can carry away with them. That idea must be compellingly portrayed, infused with the same vision and enthusiasm the creator intended. The writer must not be heavy-handed, however. Film is a subtle medium, so underlining every point will offend an audience. Let the audience *experience* the film.

> . . . film is a corporate medium. No matter how brilliantly you write the script, you're dependent on a bunch of other people to bring it to life. This can come as a shock to the writer accustomed to creating in solitude. . . . So learn from the filmmakers you'll be working with . . . the director, the crew, and the film editor. . . .[11]

For this reason, the scriptwriter will not put in every camera direction, angle, or optical effect, such as dissolves or cuts. Usually it is safer to describe the effect you want and allow the technicians to experiment with ways to achieve it. Of course, if there is some special technique you need in a specific spot, you could write this in.

Each film is self-contained. You can't accompany it as you might with your home movies, explaining what was intended and why particular shots didn't work. The film is its own emissary. That is why adequate thought must go into the script, into production, and into ultimate distribution.

The plus factors for film are many. Film offers a chance to reveal a company or a cause in a more complete and interesting way, combining sight and sound. Since viewer retention of film messages is high, it is also a superior teaching tool.

The drawbacks are obvious. Films are outdated rapidly. Clothing and car styles change, and so do city skylines, people, and even editing techniques. Alterations in the finished film can be costly. Then, too, films require a projector and an experienced operator and can malfunction during a showing.

The major shortcoming is cost. Although the per-unit cost may not be high, considering the potential audience, the initial outlay is often enough to discourage the prospective sponsor.

A good color film with lip-sync sound (meaning that the people shown sometimes speak their own dialogue rather than relying entirely on an off-camera narrator) will run a minimum of $2,000 a minute. Some filmmakers will consider this figure ridiculously low. They could charge double or triple that for some of their less-difficult endeavors. Because of this high cost, a good advance script is a virtual must. If you have to play around with ideas while all that expensive equipment and talent are on location, the budget zooms upward. Give the director something he or she can shoot to, leaving some leeway for the director's creativity and for unseen opportunities that may arise.

The timing of a film may be critical or it may be optional. If your distribution plans are limited to showings to small groups, it doesn't make much difference whether the film runs 18 minutes or 22 minutes. For television, however, you must produce a film that works within the half-hour or hour format, including commercial interruptions. In this case, you may be shooting for a film that runs $28\frac{1}{2}$ minutes or less. Remember, too, the other opportunities for films, from trailers in movie houses to continuous showings in airport lounges. You may want to make a movie that is adaptable to a number of time demands.

Filmmakers can brief you on the amount of footage each time length will require. Using 16-mm film, for example, a 30-minute film would consist of just under 1,100 feet of film; using 35-mm film, you would need 2,700 feet. And, in 30 minutes, at a normal reading pace, you *could* get in about 3,600 words, but you would be foolish to have anything like this many.

One overriding consideration that should precede even a rough draft of a script is how one will attract an audience and how large and of what character that audience will be. Too many filmmakers pour a lot of cash and talent into a movie without spending sufficient time thinking about distribution. Some films may have built-in audiences, as with firms that have myriad branches, or universities that possess dozens of alumni clubs, or organizations like Rotary that have units all over the world. For those who must construct their own audiences, a little research and a little correspondence might help, but there are also companies specializing in such services. For a fee, they agree to market your film to schools, churches, commercial theatres, television, resorts, and other centers, along with maintaining the film, keeping track of attendance, even supplying collateral printed materials.

Writing the Script

There are many ways to write a script. The model shown in Figure 7-8 is only one way, but it is one of the most preferred. Numerous books on the market give alternate forms and also go into more detail than this text allows. (They may even get so specific as to tell you to "keep your boss out of the film." This, by the way, may not be easy, and you could miss that exceptional executive thespian. However, this is generally a good rule.) These books will also help you with such problems as integrating sound, locating props, selecting performers, adding humor and suspense, and avoiding difficult dialogue.

	SOUND: AIRPORT NOISES. SNEAK IN URGENT MUSIC WITH MODERN TEMPO.
LONG SHOT OF AIR BASE, SHOW AIR FORCE DESIGNATION. CU ADMIN BUILDING.	
DISSOLVE TO TWO AIRMEN—ONE ON RADIO, THE OTHER READING MANUAL. RADIO OPERATOR IS FEMALE.	OPERATOR: Come in X-627. Three-0 calling X-627. Come in.
BOMBER IN FLIGHT	PILOT: (Off camera; filtered mike) This is X-627. Over.
CUT TO RADIO OPERATOR	OPERATOR: Give us your location. Over.
INT BOMBER	PILOT: (Off camera; filtered mike) Flying at 26,000 feet. Over South Korea. Map gives it a place called Mopko. Over.
CUT TO RADIO OPERATOR	OPERATOR: Roger. Out. (Removes earphones)
TWO SHOT	AIRMAN: (Sets manual down) Mopko! What's Mopko? OPERATOR: (Stretches) Who cares?
AERIAL VIEW OF VILLAGE	SOUND: SNEAK IN ORIENTAL MUSIC
SUPER TITLE: WHO CARES ABOUT MOPKO?	

Figure 7-8 One version of a film script.

Television

Television is the glamor medium at present, the new toy we have not yet tired of playing with. Its power is undisputed. Both addicts and critics attest to this. Even federal regulations regarding political expenditures seek to restrain the advantages of excessive television exposure. For public relations purposes, too, it is a useful tool.

As with film, television relies to a large extent on visual images. You "watch" television; you "listen" to radio. On TV the "audio" supports the "video," but the two should work together effortlessly.

Remember that television is an in-home medium, a low-brow and middle-brow medium (with notable exceptions), an entertainment medium (again, with exceptions), and a competitive medium. Whatever you write, keep these factors in mind.

The PR person should provide each television station with a script, film clip, slides, or other visual or audio aids, plus any instructions or requests that apply to the item to be telecast.

Figure 7-9
SOURCE: From the article,
"TV: The Essence of
Communication," by
John F. Budd, Jr.
Courtesy: *Communi-
cator's Journal*,
January/February 1984

10 Commandments

If you have something worthwhile and relevant to say and have identified your audience, you will be more successful if you follow the communications commandments we have developed.

The Ten Commandments of Communications:

✔ Thou shalt not use "talking heads." The animation of face-to-face conversation does not transfer to celluloid. Further, the body language we all use is lost. It becomes boring to watch talking heads.

✔ Thou shalt not patronize. Do not be condescending. Employees are smarter than that.

✔ Thou shalt not be phony-casual. If the chairman never takes his coat off, don't tape him in shirtsleeves.

✔ Thou shalt not robotize. Do not force your subjects into canned, robot-like commentary. If you must use a teleprompter, use it as one applies garlic . . . judiciously. Better to always let the subject say in his own words what you've agreed should be the basic thrust of the commentary.

✔ Thou shalt not obfuscate or waffle. Remember, you are trying to communicate, not to further confuse. Discuss issues in clear, understandable language no matter what the lawyers advise.

✔ Thou shalt not be arty. Leave the fancy dissolves and flashy picture manipulations—shrink, rotate, and zooms—to the commercial shows. Preserve the integrity of your subject by harnessing the naturalness of television.

✔ Thou shalt not be wordy. Keep it tight; edit, edit, and edit! Remember, although we speak at the rate of 180-200 words per minute, the brain can process speech sounds at rates up to 400 words per minute, and visual images augment this.

✔ Thou shalt not be a snob. Hiring celebrities to narrate may help your ego, but they will overpower the program and add artificiality, not realism, to the messages you are communicating.

✔ Thou shalt not be a cheerleader. Nothing is perfect. Be candid and, where it is relevant, let your programming bring out problems or negatives. Employees know there are two sides to all questions and issues. Reflect this—it adds to your credibility as a programmer.

✔ Thou shalt never be satisfied. Every program can be improved. The questions can be more specific, the answers more direct, and the picture tighter. Be your own severest critic.

The most commonly used format for television is the two-column approach, with the left-hand column for the "video" or picture portion, and the right-hand column for the "audio" or sound portion. Room is always left for directors and producers to enter technical directions or to time the performance.

Public relations assignments for television could vary, although the dominant format is likely to be the short public-service announcement (PSA). In addition, the writer could be asked to tackle a longer documentary or to counsel an executive scheduled for a news or panel show. Each is a separate challenge.

To most corporate communicators, television was just a new generation of film—somewhat more flexible, thanks to cassettes, but film (on tape) nonetheless. It was, to them, no more than a relatively modest evolution, similar to that they had experienced when companies outgrew house organs and began to publish readable tabloid publications. More of the same, but in a different package. How wrong they were![12]

Even though the changes may be more technical than literary, every scientific advance, from satellite to interactive TV, also affects the script-writer. The more the equipment can do, the more the script can suggest. Lightweight cameras, compact recorders, and computer editing make possible things that were not envisioned a decade ago, and the next ten years will introduce more mini-stations, revolutionary graphics techniques, and other innovations. Some location effects can already be duplicated inexpensively, and the speed with which a videotaped production may be assembled has been drastically cut.

Besides the obvious internal uses for closed circuit and videotape, such as teleconferencing and sales training, these devices have sometimes re-placed film in the production of external programming. Phillips Petroleum videotaped "Petroleum Geology for the Non-Geologist," and Kodak produced a short videotape on sports and hobbies. McNeil Pharmaceutical Company, Johnson & Johnson, and the PR firm of Clarke & Company used satellites and Picturephones to launch their program aimed at curbing the use of such gateway drugs as alcohol, marijuana, and cocaine. Elanco Products Com-pany created a 30-minute television special that was aired in prime time over more than 100 farm-area television stations on Agriculture Day, March 18, 1982. The program, with a primary aim of building goodwill among farmers, pushed the commodity check-off program as a boon to exports. Radio and television promotional spots were integrated into this campaign, as were printed materials and standard news releases. Elanco's followup research showed that more than half the farm homes in America watched the special, and that the viewers' response was overwhelmingly positive.

Another innovative use of videotape for PR purposes is the producing of internal news programs.

The Tucson Medical Center employs videotape to boost morale, often building a feature into its monthly show to explain a problem area. Staff people are used as reporters (with appropriate credit), an anchorperson ties the 15-minute show together, and the in-hospital telecast even includes commercials for things like the gift shop, an on-site blood drive, or a special event.

Mutual of Omaha offers a twice-monthly ten-minute "People" show that blends news, sports scores, and a feature. Recent segments explored elevator courtesy, the internal messenger service, the common cold, interviews with employees competing in a national bowling tournament, an employee fash-ion show, a review of local black history, and a chat with the company magazine editor, who moonlights as a bizarre rock singer. The producer says his audience is predominantly young, female, and single, and sometimes difficult to program for. The programs are telecast over a battery of 24-inch monitors in the employee lunchroom.

Regular print channels of communication have been augmented by videotape by Pennsylvania Power & Light. To reach its 8,100 employees in 19 different locations, the utility firm created a monthly news-format show called "Focus," and it also airs periodic specials on topics like nuclear radiation, energy costs, safety, transportation, and employee benefits. All viewing is scheduled on company time.

Those who write and produce such shows urge that management approval is essential, that the PR department or the audiovisual department have sufficient time and personnel, and that the program look professional. They further stress that the video must be honest and free of obvious propaganda, and that it be considered as a supplement to other communication, not a replacement.

Another television-writing chore that may be handed to the PR practitioner is the preparation of an executive for a TV speech, interview, or panel. The writer keeps in mind the intimate nature of this medium, counseling against any flamboyant oratory (which comes across as too extreme), advising against excessive reading, inserting natural gestures for the speaker or accompanying him or her with visual exhibits, and incorporating any other

VIDEO	AUDIO
MAT WITH LARGE EYE IN CENTER; SUPER "WHAT THE EYE SEES."	SOUND: THEME MUSIC. THEN UNDER.
ZOOM IN ON EYE AND SHOOT THROUGH HOLE IN CENTER. FOCUS ON MAGICIAN AT TABLE DOING COIN TRICK.	NARRATOR: Ladies and Gentlemen— Marvello the Magician! Keep your eyes on him, ladies and gentlemen—keep your eyes on him! Have you spotted the coin? You say it's in his right hand? Sorry. There it is, inside his coat pocket.
CUT TO BIG MODEL EYE	Proving once again the hand is quicker than the eye? Well—maybe. At least, here's the culprit that keeps folks like
CU EYE	Marvello in business. The star of our show—the human eye.
WIDEN SHOT TO INCLUDE NARRATOR, WHO POINTS OUT AREAS OF EYE.	We're going to concentrate on what the eye does rather than on what it is, but perhaps we can spend a moment looking at the . . .

Figure 7-10 TV script format.

STOP DRUG ABUSE BEFORE IT STARTS

ANNCR: You're raising a family. You know the joys and the problems. The good times and the bad.

And more than anything you want your kids to grow up to be happy.

But problems do exist growing up isn't easy.

And sometimes kids get involved with drugs and later wish they hadn't.

Yet some problems don't have to happen;

they can be stopped (FOOT STAMP) before they start. That's prevention

and you may have already begun when . . . You listen to them and help them to make decisions.

When you encourage them to develop new interests.

And when you help them to understand themselves and others.

You're not alone. There are teachers, friends, clergy, coaches, employers . . .

2ND ANNCR: (VO) or local tag: Learn how you can stop drug abuse before it starts. Send for this

new booklet today. Write: Family Box 1701 Washington, DC

PORTER, NOVELLI & ASSOCIATES, INC.

Produced for the National Institute on Drug Abuse

Figure 7-11 Storyboard on drug abuse.
Courtesy: Porter, Novelli & Associates, Inc.

aids that will result in a convincing appearance. Supplying stacks of notes and folders, for example, may be detrimental. When a television guest sorts through these seeking a fact, he or she merely looks confused rather than careful or scholarly.

Radio

Radio is, of course, meant for the ear. Preparing copy for this medium requires the full and imaginative use of the possibilities of sound. Consider the emotions readily awakened by a distant train whistle, a marching band, a scream, a jungle drum, a baby's cry, thunder, a rock beat, and the entire galaxy of musical and natural effects. Upon hearing these sounds, the mind takes over and conjures up the images that film and television overtly convey. The human voice, too, unfettered by visual distractions, can be a powerful sales tool.

Writing for radio is challenging—and can be fun. All kinds of situations can be created at very little cost. Radio stations and sound studios have record libraries that offer thousands of musical selections and sound effects. With a little flair for creativity, you can concoct a message that will attract attention. If, of course, you want original music and a group of top recording artists to play it, the outlay of cash will be much higher.

Almost anything your mind can envision can be adapted to radio. Humor, brief drama, synopsized operetta, man-on-the-street interviews— the list is long. Whatever you do should be something you, as a writer, can handle. Humor, for example, is tough for a beginner. It requires both writing skills and top talent—and decent production.

It is unlikely that you will ever find yourself writing anything lengthy for radio. Today's formats rarely have room for this. Your assignments are more apt to be public-service announcements for nonprofit institutions or regular public relations ads for your firm or your clients' firms (see Figures 7-12 and 7-13). The PSAs are aired without charge, and the stations may also cut the tape for you. The stations don't *have* to do either of these things. Even though the Federal Communications Commission will take into consideration a station's public-service contribution at license renewal time, this doesn't mean that stations must use every PSA that is given them—including yours. Therefore you should make the spot as professional as possible; you should ask; and you should thank the stations that use them.

SOUND: CAR ENGINE, MOVING QUIETLY. NATURAL SOUND OF BIRDS, ETC.

ANNCR: At 55 miles per hour, you not only save money on gasoline, but you also may hear
the birds—instead of a police siren.

SOUND: CAR ENGINE FADES, BIRD NOISES UP.

Figure 7-12 10-second radio PSA.

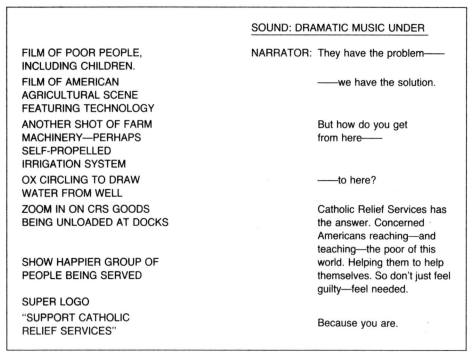

Figure 7-13 30-second PSA for television.

Radio PSAs (and commercials) are usually ten seconds or 30 seconds long, rarely 60 seconds, and very rarely longer than that. When writing your spot, you must absolutely adhere to these time limits. An eleven-second PSA or a 33-second one will be tossed aside. They don't fit.

Here are some tips for writing for radio:

1. *Have a strong opening.* Remember that radio is a "background" medium, and you have to arrest the individual's attention. A strange sound effect, along with music and unusual wording, can produce this effect.

2. *Keep it believable.* Even the most bizarre spots have some thread of sense to them.

3. *Avoid words that are difficult to pronounce or understand.* The talent will appreciate the first virtue; the listener, the second. Remember that *chief* may sound like *cheap*, and *plight* may sound like *flight*. Avoid confusion and always keep words in a context that is unmistakable.

4. *Use a conversational tone.*

5. *Make full utilization of sound.*

6. *Don't be afraid to repeat.* Repetition aids memory, and radio is one of the best media to use as a memory device.

7. *Focus on one idea.* Don't burden your brief message with too

much copy; the listener can't take it all in. Decide on one thing you would like the listener to take away, and be sure you have included this.

8. *Have a strong ending.* You should conclude with some call to action, even if it is only to reflect on what Smokey the Bear said about forest fires. You may want people to attend an open house or contribute to a worthy cause. Give them all the facts; remind them of the facts; close with an appeal.

9. *Read scripts aloud to time them.* In figuring length of scripts, try to keep ten-second PSAs under 30 words; 30-second PSAs under 70 words; and 60-second PSAs under 130 words. Normally all three will occupy less than one typed page.

As mentioned in the preceding chapter, radio is a good medium for "actualities," recorded news messages that have an immediacy to them. Companies or individuals may tape these brief statements, which can then be introduced by the station announcer as if they were live reports from the scene (but without categorizing them as such). Several short comments may be recorded on a single tape and supplied to stations. Small stations are usually happy to receive these, and regular producers of actualities claim they get a higher percentage of usage than does the typical printed news release.

Public-service announcements may be national or local, with the latter becoming more common in recent years. The chief complaint some stations have about the local spots is that they are poorly written and clumsily produced—although there are exceptions.

Business is not normally able to avail itself of this free air time, but some firms and organizations have found ways to circumvent this prohibition. Utility companies may successfully market PSAs for safety; food companies have broadcast and telecast tips on nutrition; Avon produced a spot to persuade young women to remain in school; and Johnson Wax distributed a PSA on roach control, without any sponsor identification.

Slides

With every medium you choose, you will discover strong points and weaknesses. Film, for example, has a compelling effect and great versatility. Slides, although lacking some of this visual and storytelling power, are less expensive and more flexible, and they usually have a stronger production schedule.

Slide scripts should also be sparse, although you may require a bit more explanation than in film. It is awkward and dull to merely describe each slide as it pops up, the way your neighbors do with their Grand Canyon 35s. Sometimes an individual slide is so provocative that you must stop and give it a caption. Generally, though, you write the narration and fit the slides to your story.

If you were doing a slide series on a university, for example, you wouldn't need to say, "This slide shows a student in a biology class. And this shows young woman in the library. And this is a picture of a football game." Perhaps all those slides could be shown over the narrator's comment that the students at the university enjoy a well-rounded curriculum.

Sometimes a script is written to slides you already have, although the opposite procedure is preferable. In either instance, a good photographer is a must. Again, unless this is your forte, get someone else to do it. Your cousin Ralph may be cheaper, but the results will make you cringe every time you see his efforts on the screen. You want pictures that are not only in focus and properly exposed but also dynamic, appropriate, and interesting.

Whether you use one or two screens, or an entire barrage of images, depends on the subject of your show, the budget, and the mechanics of transporting and erecting the multiscreen jobs. It can easily take half a day to set up and sync a complicated show involving five or more screens and projectors. Practitioners must ask themselves whether this is workable for their salesperson in Pocatello. Such computerized extravaganzas are also expensive, requiring more slides, more equipment, and more personnel.

The subject, too, may rule out the more sophisticated approach. A program announcing a downtown renewal project may wish to dazzle the audience with visuals, but a slide show intended to dramatize the plight of delinquent children may suggest a slower-paced, lower-key concept. In this latter case, perhaps a two-screen show with a dissolve unit (as discussed in the following chapter) may suffice.

As with film, the practitioner should consult an expert in the field, particularly for the more complicated shows. Some exposure to the mechanics will give the writer a better feel for the rhythm of the show, the length of time a slide should be on the screen (probably an average of four seconds for a "normal" pace), and the number of words needed to provide for a smooth flow. Once you understand a medium, it is much easier to write for it.

Slide scripts resemble television scripts, but there are variations. What they all contain, however, are the following:

1. Identification of slides
2. Identification of music or sound effects
3. Narration
4. Cues for slide changes

Some scripts use four columns: the first for the number of the slide, the second for the description of the slide, the third for narration, and the fourth for sound or music instructions. Cues are marked in, using a dot or an asterisk, probably in color.

This format becomes a bit clumsy, since the columns are very tight. With narration in particular, this causes problems. A little more freedom is provided by the two-column format shown in Figure 7-14.

The asterisk in the slide script signals a slide change. This may be done manually or automatically.

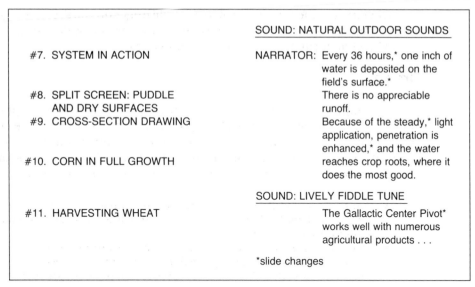

Figure 7-14 Script for slide show.

Many writers find it much easier to insert both the cues and the slide numbers *after* the script is written. This allows more flexibility. You may discover, for example, that the show seems to drag in spots; this can be remedied by adding a few more slides. When the program seems too episodic, you may add more words or cut a few slides.

Some writers also work from a storyboard of some kind—perhaps a large sheet with cartoonlike panels, or a series of 3-by-5-inch cards. These would indicate the story line in rough form, even before you begin shooting the slides.

One commercial enterprise that uses multimedia very effectively is the real estate industry; brokers, contractors, and developers find the multi-image audiovisual presentation a prime selling tool.

Michael O'Rourke, director of marketing for Sanctuary Realty, Florida, claims that his slide program, shown to more than 1,000 brokers in a matter of weeks, deserves credit for high traffic and closings.

> In my opinion, a well-done multimedia production is an awesome selling vehicle that promotes the company using it as high-standard professionals.[13]

Film Strips

Instead of the more cumbersome slides, many companies use a continuous-loop film strip (16 mm or 15 mm), which can be programmed for more than thirty minutes of sound and over 200 separate frames. Typically, such a presentation will run ten to twelve minutes, using about 150 frames or less. Obviously some frames (or pictures) will linger on the screen longer than others, depending on their visual quality and the script demands.

The slide format also works for film strips.

Timing

It is impossible to give an exact number of words to fit any script—films, slides, radio, or television. Word lengths differ, and so does the pace at which they should be delivered. "Hurry on out to the Baltimore Race Track for ten exciting races" can be said in about the same time as ". . . delicious, appetizing, mouth-watering salads." However, some *general* guides may be helpful:

- You can get slightly more than two words into each screen second. A 60-second spot might have as many as 130 words. A 30-second spot would contain under 70 words.
- Figure that each page of a film script will time out to less than a minute—perhaps 50 seconds. A 28-minute film will run about 30 script pages. Again, this may vary widely. A complicated production scene might take two lines of a script but play for three minutes.
- The two-column TV-style script runs about half as long per page as the film format. Thus the 28-minute TV documentary, using this format, would total about 60 script pages.
- The number of slides used in a presentation depends on the pace of the message. A ten-second PSA would normally involve no more than three slides; a 30-second PSA, ten slides or less. Long slide programs vary widely, depending on pace and the number of screens used.
- Read your message aloud at a normal pace, timing it with a stopwatch or sweep second hand.

CORPORATE ADVERTISING

Writing advertising copy is a specialized area, and writing corporate advertising copy is even more demanding. Authors whose prose appears in the slick journals probably couldn't turn out a decent print ad, and some agency copywriters who handle products well can't come to grips with the requirements of the corporate campaign. By extension, this suggests that the average public relations person will also struggle with this communication form. The best solution would be to hire a person who has corporate advertising experience. The next best route, and one many firms employ, is to enlist the cooperation of the firm's advertising agency. Without either of these alternatives, the PR director with a small staff and budget probably tackles the assignment alone.

There is no question but that corporate advertising (called "advocacy advertising" in some of its forms) has improved considerably in the last ten to 20 years. Even so, much of it remains dull or heavy-handed, possessing little credibility and merely stroking the executive bias.

TEN COMMANDMENTS OF CORPORATE IDENTITY

1. Honor your company's philosophies, goals and marketing objectives.
2. Do not take the name and identity of your corporation, its products or services in vain.
3. Do not covet your competitor's package design, brand name or trademark.
4. Do not bear false witness against your own corporate or product capabilities, features and promises.
5. Subsidiaries and divisions shall honor the parent company through a corporate identity program.
6. Do not allow individual suppliers to institute, modify or change your corporate identity.
7. Do not use promotional advertising campaigns and promotions to represent the corporate image.
8. Do take advantage of free advertising space and other cost-saving measures in creative and memorable ways.
9. Do not pollute the landscape with bad design.
10. Respect your company's image.

Figure 7-15
SOURCE: Elinor Selame, "Guidelines to Identity—Ten Commandments of Corporate Identity." Reprinted with permission from the November 1984 issue of the *Public Relations Journal.* Copyright 1984.

Advertising copy is very pragmatic. It is also terse. You use short sentences. Often incomplete sentences. The ad must produce results, probably not alone but in combination with other elements in a total advertising campaign. Unlike most advertising, which sells a product or service, public relations advertising is usually concerned with building a company image or addressing a certain issue—a plant strike, an anniversary, pending legislation, industrial philosophy.

In a brochure devoted to corporate advertising, *Business Week* attempts to define corporate advertising:

> Corporate advertising is an imprecise umbrella term for a dozen or more kinds of advertising done for as many reasons and directed at very different audiences. . . .
>
> For all the variety in purpose and execution, there are really only three basic *functions* corporate advertising can perform:
>
> 1. Increase *awareness*
> 2. Extend *familiarity*
> 3. Influence *attitudes*
>
> And in that order. Only when people have heard of you, and also have some notion of what it is you do and how it relates to them, can you attempt to influence their attitudes with any reasonable prospect of success.[14]

Initially, corporate advertising had many specific, temporal goals. A new plant was being opened; a strike needed to be explained; some interruption had occurred in utility or transportation service; the firm's name had been changed. Later, as corporations learned that these campaigns could succeed, they tackled subjects a bit more complicated, like the work ethic, or First Amendment freedoms, or the causes of the energy crisis. Advocacy advertising has diminished a bit (because, say some observers, the present government has been more understanding of business), but the use of corporate advertising for investor relations or marketing purposes is on the increase. Although only 2 percent of the money spent by companies for advertising goes into corporate advertising, this is also going up. The top ten corporate advertisers spent $222 million in this area in 1983, led by AT&T and Ford Motor Company. Generally, oil companies seem to fare best with readers and viewers in terms of recall of messages, and for a time, they were among the leaders in corporate advertising.

Weyerhaeuser employs corporate advertising to explain its ideas about conservation; U.S. Steel stresses its community involvement; Union Pacific Railroad, aiming its ad campaigns at employees, assures readers and viewers that they "can handle it"; IBM focuses on its human resources; Ingersoll-Rand strikes back at foreign competition; and McDonnell Douglas announces a breakthrough in computer graphics.

Periodically, the attitudes toward corporate advertising, especially advocacy advertising, are surveyed, and the responses are generally positive, with 90 percent of the respondents being able to remember a corporate ad they read or watched in the previous two years, and with two-thirds of those surveyed approving the practice and stating they found the ads believable. Better than half the respondents admitted these ads changed their minds on certain issues.

Some public relations advertising is of the gift kind. A local school or other organization asks you to contribute an ad in its program or newspaper insert. Such space has marginal value but is often necessary to maintain good community relations.

The Telephone

Even though the telephone is a departure from *written* communication, it does belong in this section because it is a common tool for good or evil. The switchboard operator and the receptionist—and the secretary—are key public relations personnel whether they know it or not.

Fortunately, there are training sessions for such people at local telephone-company offices, or the telephone company will supply you with a sufficient number of brochures on telephone etiquette. These are succinctly written pamphlets that list the do's and don'ts of handling this delicate instrument.

Keep in mind that the person responding to a telephone call is, for that moment, the entire company. The caller may never have visited your plant, met your executives, or read your literature. His or her impression may revolve around this call. Therefore, a good receptionist can be invaluable.

Some people have the knack of answering a phone in a way that says they are happy you called, will process your call efficiently, and will handle any problems that arise. If they can remember your name based only on the sound of your voice, that's a bonus. And they may even manage to instill an unseen smile in their delivery.

As with everything else, it seems, the modern era provides the means of altering your voice to be more assertive, sensitive, credible, or what ever quality you aspire to. You can get exercises to develop your voice, and tips on how to rehearse with a tape recorder or friend, on methods of breathing, even on the ways of handling noise (by talking into it, rather than above or below it).

Although a pleasant or authoritative voice is handy, the first require-ment for one who answers the phone is to get the details right. If a return call is necessary, be sure the person who answers gets the name, the correct spelling, the phone number, and any other facts, such as the time the call should be made. When the person is put through to someone in the company, this should be done quickly, with apologies for any delays. Try to avoid switching from one person to another, and don't leave anyone on "hold" without periodic updates on the situation.

There can be many irritants in phone conversations. When you call another person and, before telling you whether he or she is there or not, the receptionist asks, "Who's calling?" you may subsequently wonder whether or not your identification was the reason the person was "out." If screening is necessary, the caller should be told first that so-and-so is in and then be asked, "May I say who's calling?"

Curt responses, rude behavior, carelessness, indifference—all are taboo on the telephone. Try to be helpful, personal, and polite. Let the caller hang up first, and don't forget your manners in such matter as "Thank you" and "You're welcome."

Why unload these courtesy tips on the PR person? Well, even though you may not answer your own phone (and, by the way, it is impressive when you do), you must still monitor the performance of those who do. This is a ticklish situation, and you may have to struggle with other executives to convince them of the importance of phone behavior. A periodic refresher course, put on by the phone company or yourself, would be a good idea for all personnel who handle the telephone.

The telephone has also become a vital marketing tool, primarily because of its cost-effectiveness and because of our changing life-styles, in which convenience influences many buying decisions. A whole new type of script-writer has emerged, the one who puts together the "telephone sales package," incorporating product promotion and sales psychology. At one time, only siding and dance lessons seemed to be pitched over the phone, but now the listener may hear about everything from politics and insurance to vacation homes and computers. Some telephone sales are recorded, allowing space for a reply.

A Kansas City public relations firm (TEL-A-PR) even offers consultation over the telephone, especially to smaller companies with limited budgets. The cost is $15 for ten minutes of advice and can be charged to a credit card.

Since the breakup of AT&T, the various phone companies in competition with one another have designed new services—computerized switchboards, interconnecting telephones and private radio systems, solar-powered microwave transmission, improved answering devices, teleconferencing, satellite transmission, facsimile transmission of papers and documents, and, with more interfacing with computers ahead, the widespread use of picturephones.

Whether oral or written, communication in public relations should be as polished and professional as possible. It should come naturally, because it's been made part of the practitioner. The serious PR person reads, listens, practices, experiments until skill, flexibility, and versatility result.

CHAPTER HIGHLIGHTS

- A variety of feature-story possiblities offer the practitioner an opportunity to expand on news or to develop another form of corporate or organizational promotion.
- Most letters are overwritten or poorly written. The adept correspondent is able to sound personal, clear, and convincing. The key to a good letter is writing for the recipient rather than satisfying a personal need.
- The ability to write concise, accurate, complete, and compelling reports and proposals aids the PR person in selling plans and raising funds, among other things.
- Speechwriting requires a knowledge of the speaker and audience, research, and skill with language that sounds good to the ear. Outlining invariably helps, as does listening to and reading other speeches. Anecdotes and humor spice up such presentations.
- Internal communication takes many forms, from printed pieces to closed-circuit television. The company magazine is a common tool and should deliver what the employees want, based on editorial research.
- Direct mail, because of its poor image and capacity for irritation, must be written well, must meet postal requirements, and must get the recipient to open the package.
- Few PR professionals have experience with scriptwriting; they should assign this chore to the experts. Many companies use films for training and for promotion, with much of the technical work being farmed out.
- Television and videotape are common communications tools, serving internal audiences for training and morale building, and serving external

publics as information sources. Writing for both film and television demands a strong visual sensibility, brevity, and a sense of timing.

- Radio scripts are written for the ear, and the writer should take advantage of all the possiblities of sound, from music to special effects.

- Public-service announcements, although more common for nonprofit organizations, may sometimes be produced and distributed by corporations, with minimal identification or none at all. Care should be taken to make these as professional as possible.

- Slides, although static, have the advantages of being cheaper and more flexible than film or videotape, and, with the use of multi-images, they can have considerable impact. A two-column script, similar to a TV script, is used.

- Corporate advertising continues to grow, but there are few expert copywriters for this genre. Corporate advertising seeks to make readers aware, then familiar, so that their attitudes may be affected.

- The telephone is an often-ignored public relations tool that has a variety of uses, from conferencing to marketing, but it may also affect callers negatively when handled without finesse.

NOTES

[1]John Paul Jones, "As Exciting as Dishwater," *Writer's Digest*, February 1974.

[2]Daniel R. Williamson, *Feature Writing for Newspapers* (New York: Hastings, 1975).

[3]Adele Greenfield, "User-Friendly Correspondence," *The Executive Female*, September/October 1984.

[4]Angela D. Sinickas, "How to Sell Your Communication Plan to Management," *Communication World*, November 1983.

[5]*Impact*, No. 180 (1976).

[6]Robert Lehrman, "Lessons from Campaign '84." Reprinted with permission from the December 1984 issue of the *Public Relations Journal*. Copyright 1984.

[7]Cliff McGoon, "More Publications, Better Editing, Mark GM's Emphasis on Communication," *IABC Journal*, Vol. 8, No. 1 (1978).

[8]David R. Yale, quoted in Elizabeth Howard, "More Than a Bulletin Board," *Public Relations Journal*, July 1982.

[9]Don Picard, "Magazines Communicate," *Communicator's Journal*, November/December 1983.

[10]Gerard McTigue, "Opening Mail Can Be Hazardous to Your Psyche," *Advertising Age*, May 20, 1985.

[11]Barry Hampe, "How to Write the Film Documentary," *Writer's Digest*, September 1975.

[12]John F. Budd Jr., "TV: The Essence of Communication." Courtesy *Communicator's Journal*, January/February 1984.

[13]Michael O'Rourke, quoted in *Public Relations Journal*, September 1984.

[14]*Corporate Advertising*, brochure produced by *Business Week*, 1984.

SUGGESTED READINGS

ADLER, MORTIMER, J., *How to Speak: How to Listen.* New York: Macmillan, 1983.

BEACH, MARK, *Editing Your Newsletter.* Portland, Ore.: Coast to Coast, 1980.

BRADY, JOHN, *The Craft of Interviewing.* Cincinnati, O.: Writer's Digest, 1976.

BRENNER, ALFRED, *TV Scriptwriter's Handbook.* Cincinnati, O.: Writer's Digest, 1985.

COLE, ROBERT S., *The Practical Handbook of Public Relations.* Englewood Cliffs, N.J.: Prentice-Hall, 1982.

Communication Briefings, monthly newsletter, Glassboro, N.J.

D'APRIX, ROGER, *Communicating for Productivity.* New York: Harper & Row, 1982.

Decker Communications Report, Madison, Wisc.

DEGEN, CLARA, ed., *Understanding and Using Video.* New York: Longman, 1985.

DOUGLAS, GEORGE A., *Writing for Public Relations.* Columbus, O.: Merrill, 1980.

Editors' Workshop Newsletter. Chicago: Lawrence Ragan Communications.

FRIEDLANDER, E.J., *A Concise Guide to Newspaper Feature Writing.* Lanham, Md.: University Press of America, 1982.

GARVEY, DANIEL E., and WILLIAM L. RIVERS, *Broadcast Writing.* New York: Longman, 1982.

HILLIARD, ROBERT L., *Writing for Television and Radio,* 4th ed. Belmont, Calif.: Wadsworth, 1984.

KLEPPNER, OTTO, *Advertising Procedure,* 9th ed. Englewood Cliffs, N.J.: Prentice-Hall, 1986.

LEE, ROBERT, and ROBERT MISIOROWSKI, *Script Models.* New York: Hastings House, 1978.

MAYEUX, PETER E., *Writing for the Broadcast Media.* Rockleigh, N.J.: Allyn & Bacon, 1985.

POE, ROY W., *Handbook of Business Letters.* New York: McGraw-Hill, 1983.

RODDICK, ELLEN, *Writing That Means Business: A Manager's Guide.* New York: Macmillan, 1984.

SAMOVAR, LARRY A., and JACK MILLS, *Oral Communication: Message and Response,* 5th ed. Dubuque, Ia.: William C. Brown, 1983.

SCHOENFELD, A. CLAY, and KAREN DIEGMUELLER, *Effective Feature Writing.* New York: Holt, Rinehart & Winston, 1982.

SIMON, MORT, *How to Write a Successful Report.* Brookfield, Vt.: Business Books, 1984.

Speechwriter's Newsletter. Chicago: Lawrence Ragan Communications.

SWAIN, DWIGHT, V., *Scripting for Video and A-V Media.* Stoneham, Mass.: Focal Press, 1981.

VAN NOSTRAN, WILLIAM, *The Non-Broadcast Television Writer's Handbook.* White Plains, N.Y.: Knowledge Industry Publications, 1983.

VERDERBER, RUDOLF F., *The Challenge of Effective Speaking,* 5th ed. Belmont, Calif.: Wadsworth, 1982.

Advertising Age, Chicago.

IABC Communication World, San Francisco.

EXERCISES

1. Write an outline for a speech to be delivered on any national holiday. Write both the introductory paragraph and the closing paragraph. Have a specific speaker in mind to deliver this speech, and a specific audience to receive it. Identify both.

2. Select a nonprofit institution in your locality, or a cause that interests you, and write a 30-second public-service announcement to be aired on local radio stations. Subject matter may involve fund raising, a special event, or general image building.

3. For the same institution or cause, write a 30-second PSA for television.

4. Select three company publications and critique them for content, appearance, and audience appeal. Be specific in your comments.

5. Write *one* of the following letters:

   a. Selecting a local nonprofit organization or a cause that interests you, write an appeal letter for funding to your area's small business firms (restaurants, pharmacies, grocers, etc.), keeping in mind the special audience, the reasons for giving, and their method of response. Describe the total mail package.

   b. Your local newspaper recently ran a series of editorials critical of what it called "the materialism of today's youth." The editorial contended that young people of college age are interested only in their own welfare and that the idealism of past generations has disappeared. Write a letter to the editor expressing your views on the subject, remembering that your aim is to *persuade*, not be outraged, sarcastic, or vaguely argumentative.

   c. You work in an office that contains a number of heavy smokers. You are allergic to cigarette smoke and ask them not to smoke around you. There are no rules at this company about smoking on the job, and your fellow employees think you are overreacting. They continue to smoke. Write a letter to the company president, who is also a cigarette smoker, explaining the situation and suggesting some way to achieve relief.

CASE PROBLEMS

1. As a private consultant with a reputation as a speechwriter, you are called to the office of a corporate president who has been in office only three months. His aides have already told you that the president is not a very dynamic speaker, feeling more at home in smaller groups. However, he has to address the annual meeting of the company's executives from more than 60 branches scattered across the United States. About 300 people will be there.

The problem is that the man whom a majority of the executives thought should be president will also be there. Stung by the rejection, he decided to take early retirement, and this annual meeting is also an occasion to bid this man adieu. To further complicate things, this disappointed rival happens to be an excellent platform speaker, with charm and humor, and he is scheduled to speak right before the new president.

"I know the crowd will be with him," says the president, "and I also know he's a far better speaker than I am. But I'm the chief executive, and I can't just run away and hide. I have to let them know I'm in charge. I can't afford to fall on my face."

a. What counsel would you give the president?

b. What sort of speech would you write—in terms of length, general content, delivery?

c. Write the first and last paragraphs of this speech.

2. As part of a complete turnover in management, you are brought to a large insurance company as public relations director. The company employs 2,000 people in its home office, has 20 branch offices scattered across the country, and has some 600 salespeople on the payroll. One reason for the change in management was the deteriorating morale of the employees at all levels. Among their complaints was the failure of management to tell them what was going on. All communications came to them via memo or bulletin-board notices, and these invariably contained decisions that were already operative. Your new boss wants to run a more open administration where things are done by cooperative effort rather than fiat. He instructs you to prepare a communication program to help him meet these goals. How would you proceed? What kind of materials would you envision? What would their individual purposes be?

8

PUBLIC RELATIONS AND PRODUCTION

A public relations director who is fortunate enough to have a supporting staff—or a budget sufficient to employ free-lance help—may need to know very little about production. Others will handle that chore. Even then, however, it would be helpful to know how things are produced and why, and what options are open in the creation of various messages.

For public relations practitioners who must wear many hats, a knowledge of production is a great asset. They may be obliged to try their hands at layout, photography, typography, copy fitting, and other mechanical details. They may be assembling the television shows and producing the public-service announcements. Besides, production can be exciting, and a knowledge of it improves their standing with those professionals who do this for a living.

The first thing the practitioner should learn is to ask and listen. Printing and paper salespeople are often excellent mentors. They have a stake in the PR person's education. Not only may this increase their sales, but they will also receive materials that are properly prepared, thus saving them time and resulting in a better product. A good printer is as desirous of creating an excellent printed piece as is the practitioner. They share a similar professional pride.

In addition, practitioners can take courses in design and production, or they can read the many good books now available on these subjects. Once they learn how a thing can be done, they will discover numerous possibilities for innovations. They should save and analyze brochures they admire. Later they can improvise from these models.

Few public relations people are also artists, but many develop at least a workable flair for design. Don't tell yourself you can't draw a straight line. You can! You may not become an illustrator, but you will be able to put together a blueprint that an artist or a printer can follow. That in itself is an accomplishment.

LAYOUT AND DESIGN

Much of what we do in layout or design is instinctive. If you have ever shifted plates on a table to create a more aesthetic appearance or arranged pictures on a wall to achieve balance, you are moving in the right direction. All that *layout* means is the organization of various elements into an attractive and unified whole. In advertising, for example, you might begin with a photo, a headline, some body copy, and the signature and address of the sponsor. You then put these together in a way that will attract attention and invite reading. In developing a brochure or publishing a house organ, you adopt similar techniques to capture and interest your audience.

Much attention has recently been paid to "visual communication," or "visual literacy." Communications scholars are examining the language of pictures and symbols to determine how they affect people independent of the written or spoken word. Our own experience tells us that images on a television screen, paintings in a gallery, and even the crude figures carved centuries ago on cave walls—all have meaning for us, independent of descriptive phrases.

Figure 8-1 The first row of visual symbols is probably more familiar to Americans than the second row—unless they have driven a lot in Europe. The symbols indicate Ladies Room, Telephone, No Smoking, No Vehicles Allowed, Traffic Roundabout, and Resume Speed.

This trend finds its way into communication, where graphic symbols have been used to convey a whole range of abstract ideas, from trust to strength. Considerable effort and money are lavished on the creation of corporate logos and other identifying devices, in order to reproduce visually what the words are conveying on the written page. A majority of the publications issued by corporations are well designed, but that can't be said of the products of smaller companies and organizations. More and more, however, the graphic designer is serving a consultant's role, improving the quality and look of the print media.

> Successful graphic design can be said to serve several purposes. It captures attention, drawing the reader into the total message; it supports that message by organizing it in a clear and easily accessible manner; and it lends to the printed communication a feeling, a visual *gestalt*, that conveys an essential something about the company. Graphic design is not to be thought of as just decoration, or something to be considered only when copy runs short or needs to be enhanced or clarified. Today, design is an integral part of the communications effort, as inseparable from it as words and thoughts are from content and meaning. And though the value of good design is difficult to measure at the bottom line, most organizations today would rather work with it than without it.[1]

Although the graphic work of corporate designers may be the most artistic and arresting, an observer can see the results of visual literacy everywhere. Television playfully rearranges images, tabletop books heavy on photos are increasingly popular, and, following the lead of *USA TODAY*, newspapers across the country have added more graphs, more color, more illustrative materials.

The *USA TODAY* staff produced a special section for the American Society of Newspaper Editors, explaining how they achieve their effects, how much time they take, and what purpose they serve. They also passed along some general tips to editors and designers:

- Establish your own style.
- Be consistent—in terms of typefaces and screens.
- Make graphics personal—incorporating human figures when possible.
- Practice restraint. Don't overdo the visuals.[2]

THE BASIC ELEMENTS

All aspects of design, from fine art to commercial layout, incorporate three basic geometric elements—the circle, the rectangle, and the triangle. These geometrical figures, sometimes elaborated into cubes, pyramids, cones, and other variations, may be found in combination in paintings, advertisements, and brochures and in the whole range of visual communications (see Figure 8-2).

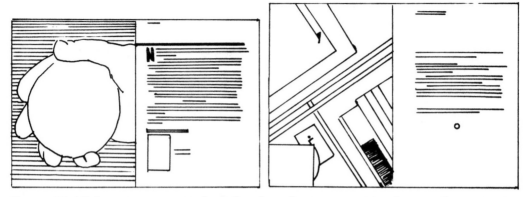

Figure 8-2 All layout is composed of the three basic geometric shapes—the rectangle, the triangle, and the circle. Check any group of ads and brochures and you'll find a combination of these three elements.

Each of these three shapes is capable of endless adaptation, and each has visual properties of its own. The triangle, for instance, represents solidity. It would make a good symbol for a bank or an insurance company. Note how many paintings of the madonna and child rest within the comfort of the triangle. The circle suggests motion, action, focus. Its curves are generally more appealing to the eye than the bulky rectangle or stolid triangle.

All of these forms, of course, rely on the line, the basic element (unless you count the dot). Lines may be vertical and majestic, horizontal and restful; they may be piled up neatly to suggest order or staggered to suggest variety; they may be curved upward to indicate growth; they can show speed, power, conflict, beauty (see Figure 8-3).

Another aspect of design and layout is *tone*, the intensity of lightness and darkness in whatever is depicted. If you imagine a scale of values moving from white to black, you realize that there are all kinds of shades of gray in

Figure 8-3 Even the simple line exhibits variety: It can be monotonous, interesting, stately, tense, sensuous, alive, dynamic.

between. These gray shadings have the possibility of bringing life and dimension to a line drawing. These tones can also mute the harsher aspects of line. If you want to see the value of such tonal qualities, make a Xerox copy of a nice subtle photograph and compare it with the original.

There are many ways to use tone qualities in printed pieces. You can "model" illustrations, provide a gray background for headline type, or screen back bold type.

COLOR

Color is light, a form of energy that travels in waves, and each color we see has its own wavelength. The human eye has sets of "receptors," which are able to distinguish among these wavelengths and assign a name to certain "colors."

What happens when we see color is that light waves are reflected off an object into our eyes. If the object were a lemon, we would see yellow. The waves could also pass through some transparent substance, such as a stained-glass window or a color transparency, and all light except that belonging to the particular color would be absorbed. Our eye picks out the waves that are not absorbed and assigns them spots on the spectrum.

We could also see light directly, by staring at a neon sign or the sun, but that has little application in public relations.

Red, yellow, and blue are usually classified as *primary* colors, with their combinations being classified as *secondary* colors. Red and yellow, for example, give us orange; red and blue give us violet; yellow and blue produce green. There are various combinations possible from these six colors, and, theoretically, a combination of the primary colors would result in white or colorless light. (Some specialists, incidentally, regard red, blue, and *green*, as the primary colors.)

Color is not merely decoration; it has the capacity to produce various effects. Men, for example, respond best to the color blue, whereas women favor red. But these are generalizations, and the color employed should be appropriate to the message.

Red, which suggests warmth and excitement, seems to emerge from a page, whereas blue and green are most restful and recessive. Red may also denote anger or danger, and blue, in some of its hues, can be depressing. Yellow may brighten a printed piece, mirroring the sun, but it can also become garish and sickly. Spring and growth and youth are conveyed by green, which may also connote immaturity. Lavender makes one think of flowers or perfume or watercolor paintings, and a deeper purple conjures up royalty. Brown recalls leather and wood to men, furs to women.

Note how carefully advertisers choose colors in accordance with the product or the season. Fall calls for browns and oranges; Christmas is red; spring is green. The Marlboro cigarette ads, focusing on the macho aspects smoking, utilize many reds. Kool cigarettes, emphasizing milder taste, work with greens.

Public relations brochures, too, must use appropriate color combinations. "Wills and Bequests" booklets should not be pink, and a program for the local ballet company should avoid industrial gray. In addition, producers of such materials must understand how colors function in terms of clarity. Solid red type would be difficult to read for very long. Pastel lettering would also be hard on the eyes. Photographs printed in green make people look sick and unnatural.

The sophisticated practitioner learns what colors clash and what colors blend, what color combinations make for more facile assimilation, how colored paper changes the appearance of printed colors, and how the juxtaposition of certain colors alters the look of each.

Those who might guess that black on white is the most legible combination would be wrong; according to psychological tests, it is in fifth place, preceded by black on yellow, green on white, blue on white, and white on blue. However, when colored paper is being used, unless you or your designer is very good at this, it's generally safer to use black ink on a lighter-colored stock. Colors also require balance. Some colors—red and black, for example—are heavy, and could overpower the yellows and greens. Over the years, the astute PR person, even if not a graphics specialist, develops a sense of what works and what doesn't.

To appreciate the basic properties of color and how they relate to one another, go to your local paint store and ask for a color wheel (see Figure 8-4).

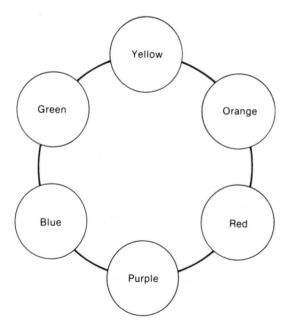

Figure 8-4 A simple color wheel.

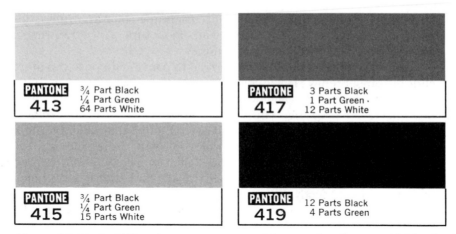

PANTONE 413	¾ Part Black ¼ Part Green 64 Parts White
PANTONE 417	3 Parts Black 1 Part Green · 12 Parts White
PANTONE 415	¾ Part Black ¼ Part Green 15 Parts White
PANTONE 419	12 Parts Black 4 Parts Green

Figure 8-5 Each PMS color can be selected by number from available sheets of individual swatches.

You might also ask your printer to provide you with a PMS color chart, consisting of a page (or catalog) of postage-stamp-size colors with hundreds of varieties, each keyed with its own code number (see Figure 8-5). When you spot the exact color you want, you detach the little swatch and affix it to the printed piece near the area to be imprinted. The printer then selects that specific ink, by number, for use on that area. It is the most foolproof way to achieve the effect you want.

There are at least 7,500 different colors, all of them combinations of the primary and secondary colors. As mentioned, the subject affects the choice, but so do tastes, and colors have their trends just as do customs and conduct. Color adds reality and prestige, and helps capture readers.

Hue, Value, and Chroma

Color has three dimensions—*hue*, which refers to the dominant wavelength (such as red, lavender, yellow); *value*, which relates each color to the black-and-white scale, giving us light reds or dark blues, and so forth, depending on the amount of "grayness" added; and *chroma*, which means the intensity or purity of color.

When transparent inks are printed on paper, the paper becomes the light source. Printers refer to the "primary printing" or "process" colors as yellow, magenta (red/blue), and cyan (blue/green). These three colors, along with black for definition, give a four-color or full-color look. The addition of each color, however, means an added cost.

The use of one color is relatively simple. You choose the color and inform the printer; the printer selects the matching ink and runs the paper once through the presses. Two colors means two press runs (except in a few specialized presses that can run more than one color at a time), and three means three, and so on. Each run means more time, since the previous color must have time to dry, and more money.

How are colored photos transferred to paper? Suppose you start with a slide or transparency. These colors must then be "separated" so that you can prepare the four plates (yellow, red, blue—or yellow, magenta, and cyan—plus black) for printing. The transparency is placed in a special camera, which isolates the blue by using an orange filter that absorbs the red and yellow and allows only the blue to be projected. Other filters are used to separate the other colors. A plate is made for each color, and they are printed one on top of the other, starting with yellow and ending with black. Each plate must be perfectly matched with its predecessor in order to prevent a fuzzy look. When the resultant printed photo is sharp and clean, it is said to be in perfect "registration."

The paper on which such photos are printed affects the appearance, just as it affects color. A glossy-coated paper causes pictures to reproduce more clearly; papers with a dull finish soften such photos. Newspapers, for example, have their limitations in reproducing color, although they are improving.

From a practical public relations viewpoint, some caution should always be exercised. Color should be added when it serves a special function, as, for example:

1. Highlighting critical portions of a black-and-white illustration or emphasizing portions of the text. Soft colors can also be used to subdue.
2. Creating a mood for an article, feature, or abstract illustration, perhaps by use of tint block.
3. Differentiating or separating visually what is being said editorially.
4. Adding interest to heads or subheads. Bold sans-serif type in color is eye-catching; screen panels or reverse blocks are real "blockbusters."
5. Making diagrams, charts, or formulas easier to follow and understand.
6. Pinpointing and keying locations on maps. Arrows or wedges can also be used in the copy.

In illustrations or text, the skillful use of color can add cheer, better understanding, more readership, and greater popularity to public relations material. Color breeds success![3]

HARMONY, SEQUENCE, AND BALANCE

Both fine and commercial art, including layout, share a concern for the three principles of design—harmony, sequence, and balance. These elements, when properly blended, result in atractive composition (see Figure 8-6).

Harmony means a unity that exists among the various parts of the whole. In music, this would mean the blending of notes without creating dissonance. In art, it means that color and line and shape and tone—and even subject matter—work together to create a single effect. In layout and

Figure 8-6 Every layout possesses harmony, sequence, and balance—like this brochure cover, which is informally balanced, with all elements working together and the eye directed through the illustration to the copy. Courtesy: Merton House Travel and Tourism Publishers, Inc. From "Instant Travel Art," by Louis Mercurio

design, it involves the harmonious relationship among colors, type, art, and composition.

Sequence refers to the flow that exists among elements in a composition. Music has a melody line, and fine art uses line and color and flat shape to direct your eyes through a painting. Even the comic strip moves you along, panel by panel; and printed advertising will carry you from the headline or illustration through the body copy to the signature and address or to the coupon. Brochures should take you, easily and almost unwittingly, from the front cover to the back cover.

Balance requires that the various parts of a composition combine to provide a feeling of equilibrium. You experience disorientation when you lose your physical balance. It is an uncomfortable feeling. Looking at a printed piece that is not in balance results in similar discomfort.

There is *formal* and *informal* balance, with the latter being much more interesting. Where you have formal balance, you can draw a line through the center of the page and the items on one side will exactly balance those on the other. It is almost like a mirror image. In informal balance, the appearance is more subtle. You still have the feeling of balance, but it is accomplished by the juxtaposiion of variant items. A weighty mass can be balanced by a bright color. A large object can be balanced by a more interesting smaller object. The positioning of dissimilar masses can bring them into balance.

Think for a moment of a scale or seesaw. You can achieve balance by placing two identical objects equidistant from the center. This would be "formal" balance. You can also achieve balance by placing two smaller objects to balance a larger, or by moving a larger object closer to the center than a smaller one. These would be examples of "informal" balance.

LAYING OUT THE PRINTED PIECE

When you are ready to design or lay out the printed piece, you have line, shape, tone, and color to work with, and you employ these within the guidelines of harmony, sequence, and balance. Your job is to utilize their properties in some combination that supports the copy and enhances interest.

There are several ways to start work on a printed piece. Many artists like to do small, rough sketches, called "thumbnails." Such a technique is prevalent with print advertising. These are quick drawings that merely assemble the elements in different combinations. Artists may do many of these until they settle on one that seems the best for their purpose. Then they will do a more complete sketch (or "comprehensive" or "comp"), which they will show to the client. If it is approved, they get the artwork or photo, have the type set, paste it all together, and have the plate made (see Figure 8-7).

Public Relations Magazines

In laying out a company (or other) magazine, the designer works with a "dummy," a mockup of the magazine as it will look in its finished form. This dummy may be smaller than the final product, but it is usually the same size. On these blank pages, the designer pencils in ideas for the way the type and illustrations will go together.

Often the layout will begin with prelined sheets that indicate the columns, usually in light blue, since this color will not photograph. The layout designer can then take the elements and move them around to provide a pleasing appearance. These elements—type, headlines, photos, artwork—may be enlarged, reduced, cropped, or eliminated.

A majority of magazine layouts conform to the "grid system," in which the page is divided into grids, the way a map might be divided for easier location of geographical sites. Employing a grid system is like putting up the framework of a house and then deciding on where to put panels and windows for different effects. Some publications use two columns, some three or more, and these may be divided vertically into four equal sections, thus forming rectangles. These rectangles define the space to be used for placement of copy, graphics, photos, charts, headlines, and sidebars. Although the grid system is workable and safe, it can also get dull, so the good designer considers ways to provide variations.

In recent years, magazines have tended to be more open, to have more white space. Crowded pages are discouraging to the reader and do not look modern.

All the pages in the magazine should work together. This is particularly true of those that are adjacent to each other. On occasion, two pages opposite each other will be considered as a unit. Called a "spread," these pages present a special problem for the layout person, but, as with all layout problems, there are a number of solutions. Sometimes a headline will move across both pages, or a motif will be repeated on the opposing pages, or a tinted background will tie them together, or a photograph will lap over. The important thing is that the result appear unified.

How do you get more satisfaction out of life?

How do you get more satisfaction out of life?

By expanding your ability to help others. That is why University Hospital is important to you. It is a teaching hospital, a patient referral center where, as a nurse, you will find a great variety of patients.

Here scientific research and the human aspects of medicine combine to create a togetherness, a spirit of sharing, enjoyed by staff and patients alike. It is a stimulating, refreshing atmosphere in which to work. You will like it at University Hospital.

For more information about nursing at University Hospital mail the coupon below. We will send our brochure: "together, we step into tomorrow."

REQUEST FOR FREE ILLUSTRATED BROCHURE

Name _____

Address _____

Phone _____

City _____ State _____ Zip _____

Mail this coupon today to: ▶ Miss Carol Wilson, R.N.
Director of Nursing Service
University of Nebraska Medical Center
42nd & Dewey Avenue
Omaha, Nebraska 68105

Figure 8-7 Ad in comp and print.
Courtesy: Holland Dreves Reilly Inc.

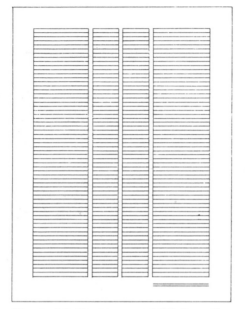

Figure 8-8 Designers establish patterns, or "grids," to simplify their layouts. This horizontal grid is adaptable to two or three columns for a company newsletter. Layout sheets are prepared in advance, in grids, and copy and pictures then laid over the grids.
Courtesy: *The Ragan Report* and Raymond Dorn

Designers learn by experience and by examining the work of others. They know they have many options and that content should influence their choices. Perhaps they want an antique effect or a mechanical effect, or perhaps they want the magazine to have an aesthetic quality. Everything they do—type, color, illustrations—should work to this end.

They also know they can decide on the numbers of columns they will have on each page, and how wide each will be. Most designers advise keeping columns under 40 characters wide, since wider columns make for more difficult eye movement. Designers can break these columns up any way they choose, using large two-column illustrations or longer one-column ones.

Articles may be confined to a single page of a two-page spread. Or they may flow through to more pages. Sometimes a front-page story will be continued inside for either space or interest reasons.

With a number of firms and organizations adopting the tabloid newspaper format instead of the magazine or newsletter style, other possible layouts suggest themselves, although the grid system works well here, too. Again, a little ingenuity helps. Most newspapers have the banner, or logo, at the top of the front page. Some, however, move this to the center of the front page, and a few even run it vertically along the side.

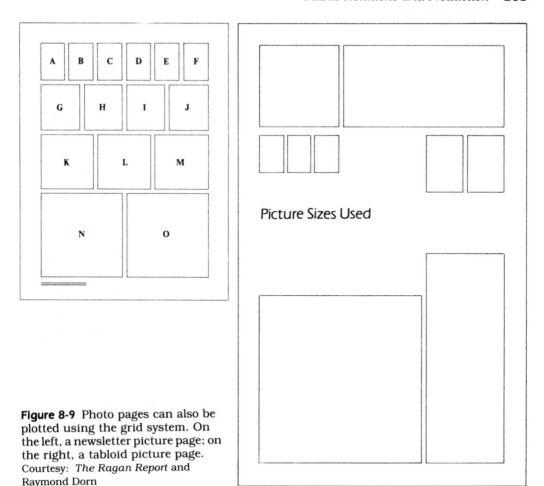

Picture Sizes Used

Figure 8-9 Photo pages can also be plotted using the grid system. On the left, a newsletter picture page; on the right, a tabloid picture page.
Courtesy: *The Ragan Report* and Raymond Dorn

When breaking the pages into grids or modules, the designer should vary the size of the photos and other graphics, stretching some across two or three columns, elongating others. Squares are the least interesting rectangular form and should be avoided, but the layout person should also make certain that one grid dominates the page, and that there aren't too many shapes cluttering up the design. Sometimes borders may be used with the photos; sometimes white space sets off graphics and type. Large photos, especially on the front page, are in vogue.

What has been said about other forms of communication also applies here. The graphics should fit the message and the audience, and not merely be imposed because they looked good elsewhere.

The design cannot be any better than the information it tries to communicate. You must understand your readers before you create devices to speak to them.[4]

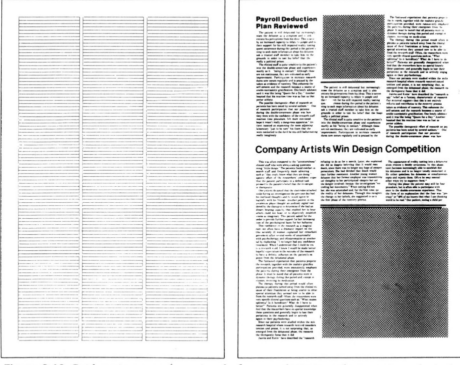

Figure 8-10 Grid systems work, not only for newsletters and magazines, but also for other printed matter—like tabloids. Here is a three-column grid system in use.

Courtesy: *The Ragan Report* and Raymond Dorn

Brochures and Booklets

When you come to brochures and booklets, it might be good to start by folding paper. Make up the type of piece of you want, using, if possible, the kind of paper you have in mind for printing, and then rough out the elements after you have the paper folded.

There are various ways to fold paper—single fold, which gives you four panels to work on; a double fold, which provides six; an accordion fold, which can provide six or more. You can decide on a vertical or a horizontal fold. In magazines, you may have a "gatefold," which is a full or partial page that folds out from the bound or stitched magazine.

Off-size brochures add an element of interest (because they are different), but they can also cause problems in folding and mailing.

Examples of paperfolds are given in Figure 8-11.

The design of folders and brochures follows the same principles as other forms of layout. You have to worry about how the piece will be mailed, meaning that you have to consider in advance whether it will fit a normal #10

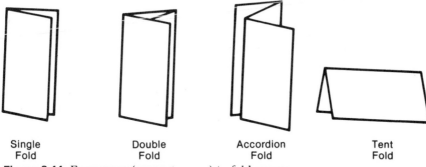

| Single
Fold | Double
Fold | Accordion
Fold | Tent
Fold |

Figure 8-11 Four ways (among many) to fold paper.

envelope or require some other means of delivery. You also have to be conscious of where the paper is folded, so that it doesn't impede reading or destroy the appearance and effect. And you have to envision how the reader will read the brochure, so that the copy and graphics follow sequentially.

The Direct-Mail Package

Direct mail often includes several printed pieces, as described in the preceding chapter. Some of these are more difficult to print than others, so the time allowed should be based on the most complicated item. Planning ahead should also include such chores as assembling, addressing, tying, and mailing. If you are aiming for a specific date—such as Christmas or an election day or an annual meeting—planning becomes even more imperative.

In general, printers should be allowed two weeks to print a relatively simple job (even though they can do it in less time) and twice that long to handle a more difficult assignment. If the project is really challenging, either because of size or because of the quality of illustrations or some other factor, even more time should be allowed. What sometimes happens is that the PR person fails to figure lead time properly and must ask the printer and printer's staff to work at nights and on weekends, resulting in escalating overtime charges. It is better to start too early than too late. Having some breathing room permits more accurate proofreading and makes changes more feasible. It also protects against sloppy and unacceptable work.

> The time to work with your printer may be a lot earlier than you think. And when you enter into a "partnership" with one or more good printers, you will find that a printer can, and must, do a lot of things for you besides print ink on paper. Of course, some printers do nothing but printing. But today's better companies can help you from the earliest stages of conception and design, through the selection of paper and color schemes and formats, all the way to production, folding, binding, and sometimes inserting, shipping and mailing.
>
> Your printer can offer you advice all along the way on how to save yourself

time, money and headaches. He may even have some ideas about marketing and promotion, gleaned from his work on hundreds of similar projects. And if he's unable to economically meet your specifications, or if he's unable to do the work by the date you need it, then he will generally be able (and willing) to work with or refer you to another printer who can.[5]

A major contribution of printers is to alert PR people to the size restraints of certain printing projects, remind them of economical cuts of paper and envelope requirements and postal restrictions. (See "Paper," below.)

The person preparing mailings not only should be familiar with printing schedules but should keep up on postal regulations. Since these change periodically, it is a good idea to post current regulations near the postage meter, in the mail room, or in some other logical place. In general, the practitioner will be concerned primarily with first- and third-class rates and will have less to do with second-class or fourth-class (parcel post) rates.

Given sufficient volume and time, a mailing house may be used to handle all the mechanical chores, from stuffing and labeling to posting. If you do your own mail work, here are a few tips:

- Use the ZIP codes. The 9-digit system (sometimes called "ZIP plus 4") went into effect in 1981, and even though it is voluntary, postal authorities insist it will speed up your mailings. For a nominal fee, the post office may ZIP your mail.
- Presort your mail and bundle it by local and out-of-town, or by ZIP code areas, or metered and nonmetered, or first class or third class.
- Be certain you have sufficient postage to cover delivery.
- Check into a bulk-rate permit from your local post office if you do volume mailing. It will save you money.
- Check into the special fourth-class rate, which includes books, films, manuscripts, catalogs, records, and similar items.
- Even though first class *should* reach its destination faster and with greater effect, this is not always true. Third class, besides being cheaper, can also have considerable pulling power, particularly if the piece itself is attractive.
- At least once a year, run a check on your addresses by requesting the post office (for a fee) to notify you about undelivered mail and address changes. After a year, the post office will no longer forward mail.
- Keep in mind that mail will be delivered only to the address immediately preceding city, state, and ZIP. This comes into play when both an address and box number are displayed. The latter one will get the mailing.
- Certain envelope restrictions apply, like the elimination of those minuscule envelopes and the appearance of the green "teeth" markings on large-size first-class envelopes.

When preparing the total package, you must know whether or not you want responses and how you will tabulate them. You must also be aware of any stuffing and mailing difficulties caused by unusual size or weight. And be certain the envelope you plan to use will hold the enclosures.

Perhaps you have your own regular audiences for these mailings—employees, alumni, government officials, and the like. There will be times, however, when you will want to purchase lists of various kinds. These are available through mailing houses or list brokers. You can procure people's names by occupation, geographical location, age, sex, race, buying habits, and many other characteristics. You can work with owners of certain cars, or those who buy Christmas cards, or all types of magazine subscribers, members of all religious denominations, opera buffs, and even rock collectors. The more specialized the list, the more it usually costs. You may pay anywhere from $15 per thousand names to $50 per thousand and up.

It is a good idea to buy a portion of a large list and experiment with it. If returns are good, buy another portion. If they still hold up, then buy the whole thing. Make sure these lists are regularly checked for changes.

If the firm or organization maintains its own list, there should be a simple method of keeping it current and a way to easily extract portions of the list for limited mailings. If the practitioner wants to reach just implement dealers west of the Mississippi, this should take only minutes.

There are various methods of addressing, from hand-addressed and personally typed envelopes (usually limited to small groups and formal occasions) to metal or plastic plates and, more and more, the use of high-speed computers. Batteries of computer-driven printers may be used to personalize letters and provide copy inserts, and so may interlocked electric typewriters fed by cartridges but allowing for manual inserts and addressing.

Direct mail provides an interesting challenge, and experts are always experimenting with messages, enclosures, teaser material on the envelope, varied types of lists, typefaces, size, even paper stock. Some companies divide their identical messages into batches employing index stock versus offset stock, white versus blue, salmon, ivory, lime, gold, and other colors, and then measure results. Indications are that colored stock—at least some kinds of colored stock (blue, gold, lime)—and a textured finish enhance returns.

More experimentation is inevitable, as higher postage rates force professionals to target audiences better and prepare packages more carefully. Costs have caused many organizations to be less generous in mailing free brochures to people (the American Cancer Society once received 500,000 requests from a single Ann Landers column!), and they probably curtail the reminder mailings to volunteers.

Direct mail, which is used for everything from fund raising and campaigning to bill collecting, boasts its own institute, educational foundation, magazines, and two major national organizations, Direct Marketing Association (DMA) and Mailing List Users & Suppliers Assocation (ML/USA). Even though it has been around a long time, this means of communication (thanks to computers) is enjoying a renaissance.

PHOTOGRAPHY AND ARTWORK

The old proverb about one picture being worth a thousand words has never been more true than in this visually oriented generation. Consequently, most public relations pieces rely heavily on photography or other forms of illustration.

If you can afford the services of a staff or a free-lance photographer, do so. If you are reduced to taking your own photos, do your best to learn this profession. Use a good camera, drill yourself in composition, follow the book on settings, experiment where you can, and take plenty of photos. A basic course in photography would be a great asset, or, failing that, a book that takes you step by step.

When you are after realism, credibility and immediacy, the photo is usually superior to the illustration. For style, whimsy, contrast, and other factors, a drawing or a painting may serve better. Ordinarily a photo might be cheaper, unless you are involved with a difficult trick shot or expensive models. In these cases, look into artwork.

With all the modern developments in darkrooms, you can do many things with the reproduction of pictures. You can produce the *square half-tone*, which is the way your prints come back from the laboratories. Or an *outline halftone*, where the background is dropped out, leaving only what you want; or a *vignette*, which supplies an old-fashioned look by framing the subject in an ellipse with soft edges (see Figure 8-12). You can create a poster effect, use the harsh black and whites of "solarization," lay screens over the print to give it a grainy finish or an antique finish, and dozens of other varieties.

You may be located in a place where these many options are not available, or you may not have the budget to afford them. If you *can* work with

Figure 8-12 Photo types (square halftone, vignette, and outline).

Figure 8-13 One solution to a tight budget or to the lack of an art department is "Instant Art," available in dozens of categories and styles. Courtesy: Merton House Travel & Tourism Publishers, Inc.

different reproduction methods, you extend the possibilities for sensory effect.

Certain subjects—like children and animals, for example—are virtually guaranteed to provoke interest. Even a poorly conceived photo featuring these subjects will draw some attention. Of course, in most public relations assignments, you don't have much leeway in subject matter. You select those photos that work into the story you are telling.

If you tried to copy a photo directly onto a piece of paper, you would get the dark, muddy appearance you get from copying machines. So a screen is laid over the film when the halftone is reproduced, and this screen breaks the photo into myriad dots. (Take a magnifying glass to a photo in a newspaper or magazine and you can easily discern this dot structure.) The individual dots pick up the ink and prevent it from puddling up in one spot. These screens are fine or coarse, depending on the type of paper you are using. For newsprint, which is very absorbent, you use a coarse screen—large dots and not too close together. This would probably be from a 55 to an 85 screen, which means there are 55 or 85 of these dots to the linear inch. When you work with richer, glossier paper, you can use a finer screen—120 or more. The dots are smaller and closer together. This results in better, truer reproduction. The resultant plate created by this tone gradation process is called a "halftone." You can combine line drawings with halftones or add an extra color to produce a "duotone."

Simple line drawings don't require this screening process, but when you add tone to them, they have to be treated like photographs. There are many forms of artwork—pen and ink drawings; wash drawings, which have tone values; scratchboard, which removes ink instead of putting it on; combination line and halftone; pencil sketches; paintings; water colors; and even magic-marker drawings. And the styles, too, range from serious and heavy to light and frivolous.

Trends affect art styles. With the return of "nostalgia," typefaces and illustrations aped the 1920s and the 1950s. We've also had "punk graphics," which essayed a garish, random look; and the conservative bent of the nation has also influenced designers, who have returned to more traditional format. Ivan Chermayeff, international designer specializing in corporate identity, says:

> A symbol is only a short and quick way of saying a great deal more. It is extremely important that it be recognized and read clearly in our competitive environment. We are bombarded with millions of images all day long, and thousands are graphic images because of the pervasiveness of advertising. The things that are quick, short, memorable and demand attention add up to something that works.[6]

In public relations projects, pragmatism normally dominates. Everything, including the graphics, must lend itself to the mission of the communication. You select the right photograph or piece of art, with the right feel to it, something that at least complements the printed word, or, better, something that may extend and enhance it.

Computer graphics is the newest kid on the block, but most art directors aren't yet ready to abandon their pens and easels. For one thing, the equipment to produce these graphics can be very expensive—as high as $7 million or more. That makes the cost of developing a computerized television spot cost between $1,000 and $3,000 a second. The process is fast, however, and versatile, with the ability to create slides, video, overheads, and hard copies. Architects build structures within the computer, saving them the cost of constructing a model and allowing them to test for stress and other potential problems. Geologists employ computer graphics to examine soil erosion, and flying buffs can enter a simulator in Dallas and, thanks to computer graphics, recreate a flight into any airport (at a cost of about $1,500).

For advertising and public relations, the potential is great. In preparing an annual report, the designer can feed in figures, convert them to bar graphs, turn them sideways, change colors, enlarge or reduce, create shadowbox effects, fill them in, switch to pie charts—with changes taking less than two minutes. Flow charts and maps may be produced in multiple copies, and hundreds of logo variations may be studied. You simply describe the variables to the computer (surface, texture, light source, and other graphic considerations) and the instrument takes over. As this form of art becomes more reasonable and popular, additional applications will be possible. Right now, thousands of colors are available, and hundreds of different type selections. Existing programs feature animation, slide film, color prints, layout, and other graphics needs.

For those wanting to make a modest investment in hardware and software with limited capabilities, there are systems available for between $50,000 and $100,000.

Practicing Layout

A good way to practice layout is to take some pages (print ads, magazine pages, brochures) and trace them, rendering all the elements into basic shapes. See how they overlap, abut, balance each other. Or you can try to sketch such things freehand, again just working with the rectangle, triangle, and circle to see how these layouts come together.

To go further into this subject in such a brief section is impossible, but there are numerous guidebooks (see "Suggested Readings" at end of chapter) that cover everything from advertising design to magazine design. These guidebooks will present the endless variety of designs available to you.

TYPOGRAPHY

Selection of type can have a definite effect—either positive or negative—on the reader, since type is not merely a set of alphabets but a part of the design, with almost a life of its own. The PR person may never become an expert in this area, but he or she should be familiar enough with this skill to distinguish one type family from another in order to make a sensible and appropriate choice.

First, remember that type is part of the layout. If you tack a brochure or page of a magazine to a wall and step back, you will immediately discern that the blocks of type fit into the overall design. That is how they should be considered when a printed piece is conceived.

Second, look through some books of type. Note how the different typefaces have the potential for creating various effects. Some are happy; some are sober. The cursive scripts seem right for invitations and fashion advertising. The classic look of some of the roman faces fits stock offerings, expensive automobiles, and chapter headings. The bold modern lettering reminds us of newspaper headlines and sale merchandise. There are also offbeat alphabets for everything from square dances to Greek restaurants. All of these establish a mood in addition to conveying a message.

There are five general classifications of type:

1. *Text.* This is the Old English look we still see on shop signs and parchments, but it is not used much today for other PR purposes. (*Text* is also a term used to designate the body copy in a brochure, book, or other printed piece.)
2. *Roman.* This typeface grew out of the fact that straight lines, when carved on columns, give the optical illusion of being more narrow at top and bottom. To compensate for this, the Romans thickened both extremities a bit. These eventually developed into "serifs," little strokes placed at the ends of the larger strokes. Roman faces are further subdivided into Old Style, Modern, and Transitional, based on the relative differences between the thin and thick strokes. The serifs make reading easier, particularly in the smaller sizes, and there are more roman alphabets than any other kind.
3. *Gothic.* This is a modern-looking typeface without any serifs and with straight strokes of equal value. It is functional in appearance and second only to roman in popularity. Sometimes a thick serif, the same width as the gothic stroke, is added, and the result is called "square serif" type.
4. *Script.* This typeface resembles handwriting and has a graceful look to it. Usually the letters slant to the right, although some are erect, and they are joined together, or appear to be. When the letters are obviously not joined, this is called "cursive script."
5. *Ornamental.* This is a catchall category for those typefaces that have a specialty or a novelty look—P.T. Barnum type, balloon letters, Broadway, Hobo, and hundreds of others. These may not be as readily available in all typesetting shops.

There are many variations of the typefaces listed and, of course, thousands of other effects that are the result of special hand-set type or artwork. The local printer may not have an endless supply of faces, however, so the practitioner should become familiar with what is available and should know the source and cost of other type that must be ordered elsewhere. Figure 8-14 illustrates the five main type classifications.

Within the five classifications listed, there are "families" with names like Garamond or Bodoni or Cheltenham. A family is a group of typefaces with the same basic design but with differences in the width of characters, boldness and lightness of strokes, and so on.

Within each family are a number of "series," or a complete range of sizes in one specified face.

The series in turn, is made up on "fonts." A font is composed of one type size within the series (see Figure 8-15).

For example: Cheltenham might be the family; Cheltenham Wide the series; and 10-point Cheltenham Wide the font.

Within this 10-point Cheltenham Wide you would still have some variety—caps and lowercase, small caps, italics, numbers, and punctuation marks. You could also see condensed and extended type within each font, and both lightface (the normal type look) and boldface (a darker version of the same type). Not every family would have all these options, but many do.

abcdefghijkl mnopqrstuvwxyz
ABCDEFGHIJKLMNOPQRSTU
VWXYZ&   1234567890$$¢

ROMAN

**abcdefghijklmnop
qrstuv   ABCDEFG
HIJKLMNOPQRST**

BLOCK OR GOTHIC

*abcdefghijklmnopqrstuvwxy
ABCDEFGHI
JKLMNOP2R*

SCRIPT

abcdefghijklmnopqrstub
wxyz ABCDEFGHI
JKLMNOPQRST

TEXT

*abcdefghijklmnopqrstu
vwxyz ABCDEFGH
IJKLMNOPQRSTU*

ORNAMENTAL

Figure 8-14 Five type families.

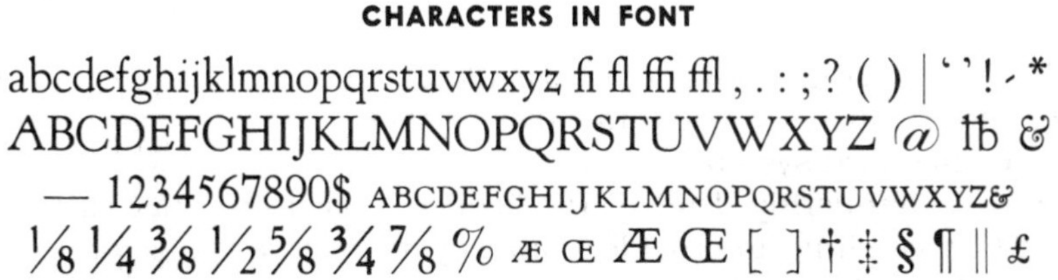

CHARACTERS IN FONT

abcdefghijklmnopqrstuvwxyz fi fl ffi ffl , . : ; ? ( ) | ' ' ! ⌐ *
ABCDEFGHIJKLMNOPQRSTUVWXYZ @ ℔ &
— 1234567890$ ABCDEFGHIJKLMNOPQRSTUVWXYZ&
⅛ ¼ ⅜ ½ ⅝ ¾ ⅞ % æ œ Æ Œ [ ] † ‡ § ¶ ‖ £

Figure 8-15 One font of type.

   Just because a number of type styles are available, they should not be mixed indiscriminately. In putting together any printed piece, it is best to stick to as few type styles as possible. If you do mix styles or families, be sure they are compatible. If not, you will achieve the same effect as clashing colors. Readers may not be able to discern why they feel negatively about the printed effort, but they will have a genuine sense of discomfort.

   Although compatibility and common sense are desirable, these goals shouldn't make cowards of typographers. A little innovation in typefaces and arrangement will attract and divert readers. Scan the type books and try to envision improvements that will bring pages to life. Look at the distinctive work of other designers—the way they use headlines, or the way they stack headline extenders, or the treatment of cutlines and captions, or the judicious inclusion of subheads. Even typewriter type may be improved by varying size and spacing.

Some cautions about type should be observed:

- Anything less than 10-point type will be inaccessible to many readers. If it comes to a choice of cutting copy or reducing type size, cut the copy.
- Lines set in all CAPITAL LETTERS are hard to read. Practitioners may think they are adding emphasis, but they are only courting confusion.
- Also hard to read are long passages of copy set in sans-serif type. For headlines or ads, sans serif works fine, but not for longer articles or brochures.
- Reverse type, like white on black, is tough for most eyes, and so are types that are overprinted on too dark a screen, or on colored paper that obscures the print.
- Some exotic types, including text and circus and others, are not good for longer communications or for messages that must be read quickly, as on a billboard.
- Reproducing type at some odd angle—slanted, vertical—rarely works. Our minds and eyes are conditioned to left to right reading, and although other placement may surprise, it can also perplex and irritate.

Measuring Type

The height of letters is measured in "points." It takes 72 points to make one inch, so a 72-point typeface would approximate an inch. A 36-point face would be half an inch; an 18-point letter would be about a quarter of an inch, and so on.

The measuring is not perfect because of white space above and below all letters and because some letters vary in design. For all practical purposes, however, the point system works.

Type is frequently "leaded" (or "ledded"), meaning that extra space is allowed between lines to provide a more open effect. If you saw a line of type marked "10 on 12" (or "10/12"), you would know that this was 10-point type with two extra points of "ledding."

The width of lines is measured in "picas." There are six picas to an inch. This is simply an easier division to work with than fractions of inches.

Reading is enhanced by three things—the choice of typeface (with roman easier to read in lengthy messages than gothic, script, text, or ornamental), the size of type (with 10-point common), and the length of the line (under 40 characters).

Edmund C. Arnold, who chaired the graphic art departments at Syracuse and Virginia Commonwealth universities, suggests an optimum line length, which is $1\frac{1}{2}$ times the lowercase alphabet being used. In the font of Cheltenham shown in Figure 8-15, the alphabet length is approximately 13 picas wide. According to Arnold, the line length (or column width) easiest to read would then be 19–20 picas wide.

Hot and Cold Type

When Gutenberg revolutionized printed communication in the fifteenth century, he relied on hand-set type—type that had to be picked out of a rack, a letter at at time, and set into a frame for printing. Until the nineteenth century, when the first typesetting machines were invented, hand-set type was the only method available. It is still used, although normally only for headlines and finely printed books.

The typesetting machines are like miniature foundries, which cast letters (monotype) or entire lines (linotype) from molds. The letters or lines ("slugs") are then locked into a frame that is used on a letterpress for direct printing, or to produce a proof that can then be made into a plate for offset printing.

"Cold" type is a name given to the method whereby typefaces are "imaged" directly on paper. This could include transfer and paste-down letters, electronic composition, photocomposition, and hard copy from computer-generated type. It might also include the use of special typewriters (IBM Selectric, Varityper, Justowriter), which make a "direct impression" that can be photographed and made into a printing plate. These typewriters may also type the message onto a coded magnetic tape, which can then reproduce it, using another machine.

Photocomposition utilizes a machine with a keyboard that prints typefaces onto paper (or film) by allowing light to penetrate through a film negative. The size of the letters may be varied by changing the focal length of the internal camera or performing a similar function. These machines are hand-operated (producing three or four lines per minute) or automatic, using perforated tape from a regular typewriter (and producing 14 or 15 lines per minute).

Keep in mind that type can SCREAM or be *very subtle*. It can create effects by using ALL SMALL CAPITAL LETTERS or by u n u s u a l s p a c i n g. It can be **bold** or lightface. After a while you get a feel for these possibilities and use them wisely.

Remember, too, that these observations about type merely scratch the surface. Typography has a fascinating history, from Egyptian hieroglyphics to computer symbols. Typography's hundreds of mechanical secrets are learned through experience, and new looks in type are invented every year.

COPY FITTING

When you are planning a brochure, a magazine, or a public relations ad, you are faced with the question of how much type of a certain size you can fit into an allotted space. "Copy fitting" has several solutions.

One quick solution is offered by many type books that print a pica rule at the bottom of their pages (see Figure 8-16). By looking up that page, you can readily see how many characters of each size of typeface will fit within the column width you have chosen.

To measure depth, you can work from the point size, remembering to allow for the leading, which is normally one or two points. You could also use your ruler to measure a page of the preferred type to see how many lines there are to an inch.

You can employ the *square-inch* method, drawing a square-inch block around copy in the typeface and size you want, and then counting the characters within that square inch (see Figure 8-17). Then determine how many square inches you have to work with (in the ad or brochure) and multiply this number by the characters per square inch. This will tell you how many characters you can get into the allotted space. After that, you set your typewriter for the appropriate characters per line and count lines. Admittedly, this is an awkward and not-often-used method.

A fast and accurate method is provided by charts that are coded to match each typeface and size. By checking the coded number for each family and size against a pica width chart, you can find out the number of characters of that face and size that will fit comfortably into the predetermined space.

Let us say, for example, that you wanted to use Cheltenham Wide typeface, in 10 point, and wanted to know how many characters would fit in a company publication with a column width of 12 picas. A glance at one chart shows the figure 128 under the 10-point column for Cheltenham Wide. Matching this number against a second chart, and reading over to the 12-pica column, you would find the number 32, and that is the number of 10-point characters that would fit your magazine column line (see Figure 8-18).

Figure 8-16 Some type books include a pica rule at the bottom to facilitate measurement of width.

12-pt. Bookman Italic (Lino)

He was at the zenith of his power when the officials began making an inquiry in regard to his prejudice against the single tax movement. Counsel having du
abcdefghijklmnopqrstuvwxyz
ABCDEFGHIJKLMNOPQRSTUVWXYZ
1234567890$

Bookman available in 14-18-24-30-36-pt. Monotype

Picas   5   10   15   20

Methodology. The technique of ranking cities was used as a basis for evaluation. Two approaches were employed to rank the cities. First, a final city standing was computed from the aggregate score of the city for all 80 indicators separately ranked. This method assigns equal weights to each factor, i.e., high electrical rates and dirty air have equal weights. This approach, while straight-forward and simple, produces a measure that may be criticized as not taking into consideration the fact that many basic statistics measure the same conditions and that some conditions may be more or less important than others. For comparison, a second ranking approach was used. This approach gives equal weight to four categories of conditions or concerns (economic, demographic/environmental, crime, recreational/educational).

The ranking technique permits only an approximate measure of city differences at one point in time. The emphasis on the city as the unit for measure has in some cases led to underrecognition of the extent of the interaction between nearby cities in large metropolitan complexes such as Los Angeles. Despite these limitations the City Index can assist city planning and administrative decision makers by providing a picture of many functional areas of city life. Exhibits can also be prepared for any of the 100 cities in the study. Any city not included in the study could develop its own index and compare its own conditions with the specific values provided in this report or with other available data.

There are 119 characters fit within this square inch. Take the number in your copy (multiply the number of characters per line by the number of lines) and divide by 119 to find how many square inches your copy block will be.

119 Characters

12 lines

Assuming you are fitting copy to a column 40 characters wide, count over to 40 characters and draw a line (light blue, so it won't reproduce) and count characters left over on right. Divide this number by 40 to see how many more lines this block will take.

216 Characters

$$\begin{array}{r} 5+ \\ 40\overline{)216} \end{array}$$

$$\begin{array}{r} 12 \\ +5+ \\ \hline 17+ \text{ or } 18 \text{ lines total} \end{array}$$

Figure 8-17 Two copy fitting methods.

CHART 1

	6	7	8	9	10	11	12
Cheltenham Wide	90	103	109		128		154

The number 128 is the code number found beneath 10 pt. in this face.

CHART 2

	8	9	10	11	12	13	14
128			27	29	32	35	37

Reading across from 128 on the second chart, under the 12-pica column we discover that this line will contain 32 characters.

Figure 8-18 Charts for measuring widths.

When you are working consistently with the same type size and the same column widths, as you might with a regularly issued PR publication, you can merely count the number of characters per line in a previous issue and then set your typewriter for that number of characters and type the article.

Counting the number of lines to the inch in the previous issue and matching these against the number of lines you have typed will give you the depth of your piece.

Some PR people like to cut out columns from previous issues—columns with the same number of lines as their newly typed copy—and paste this section of type into their dummy. This gives a clear idea of the way the finished product will look.

Depth charts are also available. These have a column of point sizes across the top (horizontally), and a column of line depths running vertically. Suppose we had Cheltenham Wide in 10 point, with two points of leading. We would look under 12 point, then read down until we came to the number of lines in our article—say 29. We would then lay a ruler against this column and see that 29 lines of 12-point Cheltenham Wide will take 27 picas.

Copy fitting should remind practitioners that they may also serve as publication editors, whether they bear that title or not. In this role, they must not only worry about whether the proposed copy meets mechanical requirements but also check it for accuracy, spelling, grammar, balance, newsworthiness, and other factors. Since the buck stops at the desk of most PR people, careful and sensitive editing must be virtually instinctive.

PAPER

Paper receives far less attention than it deserves in the printing process. And yet its color and texture have much to do with the way the finished product looks and feels. Public relations practitioners should have sample books of paper on hand so that they can select the right weight, finish, and color for a specific printing job.

In recent years, with the high cost of paper and the shorter supply of many stocks, the wise PR person checks with the printer or paper salesperson to see what is immediately or readily available. You can't show up at the printer's with the copy of a brochure you like and say, "Print it on paper like this." This particular stock may no longer be in use, or it may require months to make delivery. Try to live within what is practical.

Weights of paper are calculated per ream, and obviously, the heavier the weight, the thicker the individual sheet. Normally, for example, you would use a heavier-weight cover stock for the outside of a brochure or booklet and a lighter-weight stock for the interior pages. It is cheaper, of course, to use the same weight for the cover as for the inside, but this doesn't give your printed piece as much body. One-sheet folders and flyers might fall in between the page weight of 50 and 60 pounds and the cover weight of 80 and 100 pounds. What you try to do is make the printed piece appear substantial without causing too many folding and mailing problems.

As everybody knows, paper comes from trees. The process involves the cooking and screening out of cellulose to create chemical wood pulp, then bleaching and refining, blending and drying. In this process, you can lay different finishes on the sheet. There are uncoated or "plain" papers, such as the rough *antique* surface, a smoother *machine-finish* paper, and the smoothest uncoated surface, the *English* finish. Coated papers have more gloss and serve better for sharper photo reproduction. In this category we have *coated* paper with dull, glossy, and embossed finishes; *matte* paper; and *cast-coated* papers. Within these broad divisions are many varieties, from mirror finishes to ripple surfaces, as well as a growing number of reprocessed *ecology* papers.

Each paper comes in its own large sheet, and when you are planning the size of your brochure or magazine, you should ask how many pages of your specified size you can get from one sheet. Rather than have a lot of waste from each large sheet, you might redesign your brochure or move to a different-size paper sheet. The standard-size sheet, for example, is $25'' \times 38''$, which would accommodate eight $8\frac{1}{2}'' \times 11''$ pages per side, or 16 pages per sheet, using both sides.

Sometimes you may wish to "bleed" a photograph or illustration off one or more edges of the page. This is done by running the art over the normal edge of the $8\frac{1}{2}'' \times 11''$ (or other) area and then trimming it to the proper dimensions.

Each sheet also has a "gripper edge," a strip one-half inch or less that is gripped by the printing cylinder press or sheet-fed rotary. Nothing is printed on this strip.

Some reminders:

- The color of the paper affects any color laid on it.

- The paper's finish affects the appearance of halftones.
- The paper's weight and texture have their own tactile appeal.

PRINTING PROCESSES

Although there are several ways of transferring an image to paper (or to other materials), the public relations practitioner will normally be concerned with *letterpress* and *offset lithography.*

In letterpress printing, ink is applied to a raised surface and transferred to the paper by pressure (see Figure 8-19). If you have ever used a stamp to mark a package "fragile," that is the same principle. These metal plates with raised surfaces are, of course, much larger than your tiny stamp, and they can be used on platen presses, flatbed presses, rotary presses, and other less-common models. Before the discovery of "cold type," letterpress used "hot metal type" from monotype and then linotype machines. Cold typesetting is a less expensive process, and letterpress often has the type set by the "cold" method and then makes a plate of the entire page.

Offset lithography (sometimes called planographic printing) is based on the principle that oil and water don't mix. The metal plate used here is thin, and, at least to the naked eye, the image is not raised. This plate is wrapped around one cylinder on the offset press, after being treated chemically so that the images accept ink, and the blank places repel ink. A second cylinder receives the impression of the plate and then transfers it to a third cylinder that carries the paper.

In a majority of cases, offset turns out to be a cheaper process. It is also a handy process in terms of your being able to judge appearance before printing. The offset plate looks like the finished product, whereas a letterpress form is harder to relate to the ultimate result.

What you or your publications department usually supplies to the offset plate maker is "camera-ready copy," which means that you have pasted up all the copy and artwork on the same size sheet as you want produced, and you have left windows (by using black ink or, more commonly, red acetate, which photographs as black) the proper size and location for your halftones. You make a negative from this camera-ready art, and these windows then come up clear. You slip the negative of your photo, already screened, behind this window and then make your positive.

Whoever edits the publication may also oversee the pasteup, unless the company is large enough to have its own art and layout department or is able

Figure 8-19 Letterpress and offset plates.

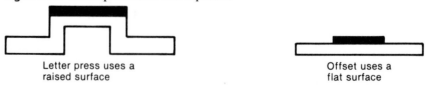

Letter press uses a
raised surface

Offset uses a
flat surface

MARK	EXPLANATION	EXAMPLE	MARK	EXPLANATION	EXAMPLE
ℓ	Take out character indicated.	ℓ The proof.	⌐	Raise.	⌐ ⌐The proof.⌐
∧	Left out, insert.	∧ Te proof.	⌣	Lower.	⌣ ⌣The proof.⌣
#	Insert space.	# Theproof.	[	Move left.	[The proof.
℧	Turn inverted letter.	℧ The ploof.	]	Move right.	] The proof.
X	Broken letter.	X The proof.	∥	Align type.	∥ [Three men. Two women.
⊥	Push down space.	⊥ The proof.	=	Straighten line.	= The proof.
eq#	Even space.	eq# A good proof.	⊙	Insert period.	⊙ The proof∧
⌣	Less space.	⌣ The proof.	,/	Insert comma.	,/ The proof∧
◠	Close up; no space.	◠ The pro of.	:/	Insert colon.	:/ The proof∧
tr	Transpose.	tr A proof good.	;/	Insert semicolon.	;/ The proof∧
wf	Wrong font.	wf The proof.	∨	Insert apostrophe.	∨ The boys proof.∧
lc	Lowercase.	lc The Proof.	⌄⌄ ⌄⌄	Insert quotation marks.	Marked it proof.∧ ∧
sc	Small capitals.	sc The proof. (The)proof.	=/	Insert hyphen.	=/ A proofmark.∧
c+sc	Capitals and small capitals.	c+sc The proof. The proof.	∧ 2	Insert inferior figure.	∧2 Water. HO∧
caps	Capitals.	caps The proof. (The)proof.	∨ 3	Insert superior figure.	∨3 A²=B²=C∧
P	Capitalize.	P The proof.	/	Insert exclamation mark.	/ Prove it ∧
ital	Italic.	ital The proof. The proof.	?	Insert question mark.	? Is it good ∧
rom	Roman.	rom The(proof.)	(?)	Query for author.	(?)was The proof read by
bf	Boldface.	bf The proof. (The)proof.	[/]	Insert brackets.	[/] The Jones boy...∧ ∧
stet	Let it stand.	stet The proof. The proof.	(/)	Insert parentheses.	(/) The proof 1 ∧ ∧
out sc	Out, see copy.	out sc He proof.∧	/¹ₙ/	Insert 1-en dash.	/¹ₙ/ The proof ∧
spell out	Spell out.	spell out King (Geo.)	/¹/	Insert 1-em dash.	/¹/ The proof ∧
¶	Start paragraph.	¶ read. The	/²/	Insert 2-em dash.	/²/ The proof ∧
No ¶	No paragraph; run in.	No ¶ marked The proof.	☐	Indent 1 em.	☐ The proof.
			☐☐	Indent 2 ems.	☐☐ The proof.
			☐☐☐	Indent 3 ems.	☐☐☐ The proof.

Figure 8-20 Common proofreader's marks.
Courtesy: *Public Relations Quarterly*

to turn this task over to other professionals. If the pasteup is done internally, the editor (who could be the PR person) must check the copy thoroughly, perhaps with a magnifying glass, to make certain there are no breaks in the type, or misaligned paragraphs, or copy running uphill, or blurred words. The mechanical aspect of the printed page must be as clean and accurate as the content.

Plates can also be made from proof sheets (clean, glossy sheets that have been printed or photographed) or, really, from any page or image that will reproduce. You can't, however, reproduce a printed photo very successfully. Screening a print that has already been screened results in a dark, muddied reproduction.

Other printing processes include *screen printing* (sometimes called "silk screening"), an old and versatile method that employs a fabric (nylon, polyester, cotton organdy, silk) that is blocked by a stencil that defines the areas to be printed or eliminated when ink is laid on the screen and forced through by a squeegee; *gravure*, the opposite of letterpress, since the image is etched below the surface of the plate (lasers may now be used in this engraving); *flexography*, a simple process for printing on cellophane, tags, milk cartons, and the like; and *web offset lithography*, which is similar to regular offset printing except for being roll-fed and using oven-dried inks. No doubt *computer printing* will one day be added to this list when the cost and quality are more competitive.

No one can learn about printing just by reading. Ask your local printer for a tour of the printing plant to see how they strip negatives, make plates, adjust for color, run the various presses, cut, stitch, bind, assemble, and perform all the other functions required to produce a printed piece.

RADIO PRODUCTION

Normally, radio production is a relatively simple process. Many commercials and public-service announcements are recorded with a single engineer who spins the records or cues the tape, integrates the live talent, and then runs off "dubs" or copies.

A practitioner serving as a volunteer for a local charity might want to record a 30-second radio spot for its fund-raising dinner. All he or she needs is a script, a record or tape of music or sound effects (if any), an announcer or actors to read the lines, and a studio or station with a sound engineer. Sometimes the station may supply the background music or effects from its own library, and might even offer a booth announcer as talent. The engineer starts the opening sound, cues the announcer, fades the sound underneath, and brings it up again when appropriate. The spot will be timed to see that it conforms to the 30-second limit, and additional takes will be done if the recording lacks anything in quality or timing. The voice and music could also be recorded separately and mixed together later by the engineer.

Recording for radio can also be complicated. If you bring the college orchestra and glee club to a recording studio to cut a record for sale to alumni, there are problems with sound and balance, with sour notes and retakes, with timing, and other factors. The engineer or engineers would have a large board with many "tracks" they can lay over each other, building up the total sound.

Since the normal public relations use of radio, outside of news, would be public-service announcements or public relations advertising, your main concerns should be with a good script, proper timing, decent talent, and production quality that satisfies you.

You may also save studio time by rehearsing your spot thoroughly in advance, perhaps on an inexpensive tape recorder.

FILM PRODUCTION

Again, the public relations person's regular role in the creation of films is probably confined to scriptwriting (or co-writing) and approval of the product in its fine-cut stage.

Once the script has been written, revised, and approved, the film company will begin its shooting schedule. Depending on the complexity of the film, it will organize the sequences to save time and money, filming all scenes that occupy a certain location, instead of jumping from one to another as the script may indicate. On occasion, the company may find some shots impossible or not resembling what the scriptwriter (or PR person) envisioned. This may call for some rewriting on the spot.

The film company gathers ample footage, taking some scenes from many angles, and adding extra shots to be used when it cuts within scenes. This raw film is developed, and the company then screens what it has, in no particular sequence. After that, providing the company has everything it needs, the editor or editors go to work and begin to assemble the film according to the script. They make a rough cut of the film, without the optical effects (such as dissolves, cuts, fades, and the like), add a rough sound track (sometimes called a "slop track"), and play this on a special machine that is

Figure 8-21 Filming on location presents some difficult logistical and mechanical problems.

able to match up, in somewhat crude fashion, the sound and visuals. You get your first glimpse of what the film might be like. At that point, you may wish to make changes. Something may not look the way you had hoped. You may cut and add scenes, change dialogue, move scenes into a different sequence, add or subtract music and sound effects, and do anything else that seems called for to improve the production. This particular screening probably involves all the people who have a stake in the film, including executives of your firm or client firm. This is the place to get all the suggestions, since the more finished the product becomes, the more expensive and time-consuming it is to make alterations.

There may be other interim "rough cuts" and then a "fine cut," which is close to the way the final film will look, and close to the desired length. (Most film producers find that PR films should run between ten and 28 minutes, with the latter time designed for television.) If this fine cut is approved, the print is then sent to a film laboratory, where the sound track or tracks are laid on and optical effects are added. These effects include *fades*, where the scene moves in or out of a dark screen; *dissolves*, where one scene is married for a moment to a new scene before the second scene emerges; *cuts*, where one scene stops and another starts; plus many other technical devices, from split screens to "freeze frames." The experts will worry about how to achieve the effects; all you need know is what you want and why.

The final print is then made. Actually, there are a number of steps along the way, with terms like "answer print" and "work print," but the process is much as described above. The wise PR person stays with the editing, checking periodically without becoming a nuisance. This is the one way to exercise control and avoid unpleasant surprises.

You will want to obtain a number for prints for distribution purposes. This number depends on the size of the audience you anticipate. The cost of additional prints is not high, but the initial cost of producing a film can be quite expensive. Therefore, before you ever commit yourself to film, you should be certain the potential audience warrants the investment.

TELEVISION PRODUCTION

Involvement of public relations practitioners in television is usually at the local level, rarely at the national level. If you do happen to become part of a network program, you will probably find that your role is so minor you won't have to worry much about production aspects.

At the local level, however, this could be different. Most programs produced by local institutions for public relations purposes have small budgets, small audiences, and viewing hours that are rarely in prime time. You will probably catch them on a Saturday or Sunday morning. Because they must normally be produced inexpensively, the local TV crew may not be able to give them as much attention as they would a more lucrative assignment. This means you will have to take a fairly large role in pulling things together.

Figure 8-22 Some production knowledge is an asset to the practitioner.

In addition to the scriptwriting, perhaps, you may be expected to assemble all the props, supply the slides and other visuals, produce camera cards, locate or take film, line up actors and announcers, submit live or recorded music, run off a sufficient number of scripts, and stand by to assist with anything else.

For the shorter public-service announcement, you may even want to design a "storyboard," which is something like a comic strip with captions. You can buy specially designed paper for this and either draw in the panels or use photographs. The storyboard is something like the print layout—a visual guide to what you would like to see on the TV screen. It is also of invaluable help to the director who will produce the show.

Once the show is being taped, however, the director, who will be operating from a control booth, doesn't want you tapping him or her on the shoulder every few minutes and making suggestions. This is the director's show when it is under way. You should go over everything initially, focusing on script and storyboard. Later, if you don't like the results, explain why and ask to have it done over again.

If you represent a nonprofit organization, the television studio may provide its facilities and personnel free. If not, there will be a charge for studio use, including the crew, at so much per hour. That is another argument in favor of good planning. Have everything ready to go—and adequately rehearsed—before you get to the studio. That way, you don't mess around while the meter is ticking.

In the early days of television, everything was live. Today, virtually everything is taped. This way, you can immediately review a production—or a PSA—and make changes. Videotape also allows you to do all sorts of visual tricks, like popping objects in and out as if by magic or, through the use of two cameras and a chromakey area, making it seem as if a real person were sailing in a toy boat. And that's only the beginning. There is rear projection, which is used on many news programs but can also create a realistic-looking setting for any show; and front projection, which has similar features; and a whole series of "wipes" and "dissolves," which cause the screen to explode, to be wiped clean, to divide into parts.

You should visit a television studio and watch how the experts work. This will educate you on the amount and type of equipment they have and what they can do. Notice how they alternate long shots, medium shots, close-ups, and other effects. See how the zoom lens can be used for dramatic reasons as well as practical ones. In a few visits, you can learn enough to do your part in the production, even though you don't understand everything about how and why the equipment works.

Remember, too, that even though you may be a novice, you do have an idea of what you want. If you find any part of the program dragging, or any of the acting unbelievable, or any of the music inappropriate, speak up. After all, you are the one responsible, and you should get it right.

Videotape, once a technique to make television programs more error-free, more flexible, and more versatile, now has a life of its own. Although still the basis of most TV shows, videotape has become part of the home entertainment center and plays a major role in business communication. Produced in television studios, film studios, or company studios, videotapes are used for a variety of purposes, as noted later in this chapter. Some productions blend video with computer graphics, creating products that are part of this generation and therefore good tools for reaching an internal corporate audience.

Many companies, even when they have their own facilities, rely to a considerable extent on outside production companies. Practitioners may write or co-write the script, help determine audiences, make certain the proper playback units exist within the firm, set deadlines, and supervise shooting and editing.

A number of systems are in use, notable VHS and Beta, and four basic tape widths, with the half-inch tape most popular in the home and the three-quarter-inch tape preferred in business. One-inch and two-inch tapes offer even finer quality, but the cost of equipment has slowed their adoption.

One current debate centers on the virtue of videotape over multi-image slide shows. Those who champion slides point to lower costs—which may or may not be realistic. A good slide show and the equipment and personnel to program it may run from $50,000 on up. Advocates of videotape tout the instant-playback feature, which permits the producer to check each shot, and the fact that slides may be transferred to videotape. True, but a multi-image show is generally sharper on a large screen and, overall, may cost only a

Figure 8-23 The audio-visual room is a standard fixture in most firms and organizations.

third of the budget for producing a similarly conceived videotape. As with advertising, all forms of visual communication have their strengths and weaknesses, and the wise PR person plans for a combination of media.

Multi-Image/Multiscreen

Before you undertake one of these multiscreen shows, consider why you are using this medium and how you will package it. This goes for the overall show and for segments of it. For example, it makes sense to move from screen 1 to screen 2 to screen 3 when you are comparing things. It might be very effective to go from screen 1 to screen 3 when you are demonstrating opposite ends of something, like populations in California and New York. And hitting all screens at once is good for visual effect, like showing all the new buildings in a revitalized downtown area. The trouble with many multiscreen slide shows is that they throw images on the screen with no real connection to mood or purpose. The gimmickry has taken over the message.

One- and two-projector shows can be produced very simply. All you need is the equipment and the slides, and you can get someone to make the tape that will provide the music and narration as it cues each slide into place.

For the larger productions, you need help. You may still be involved in the script and even in providing slides, talent, music, and advice. But the assembling of all this material is a professional's job, so leave it to him or her. If you can afford it, you should have the same professionals accompany you each time you set up the show. These are delicate programs, and the slightest alteration in sound synchronization, for example, can throw the whole thing

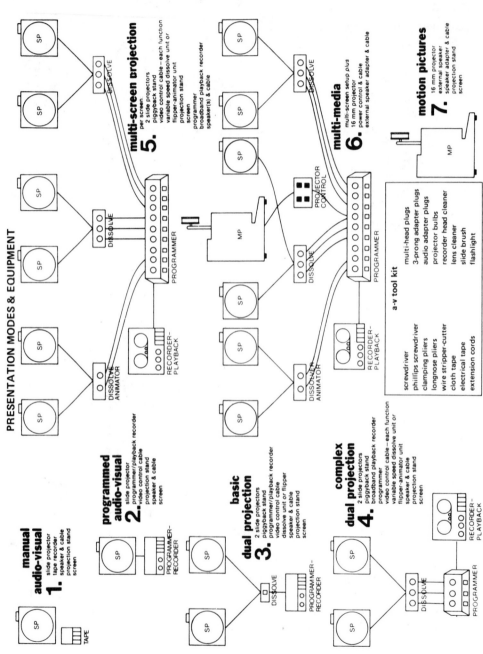

Figure 8-24 Diagrams demonstrating various audio-visual setups.
Courtesy: Sight & Sound, Inc., Omaha, Nebraska

off. You need someone on hand who can spot the problem immediately, correct it quickly, and get things moving again—like a pit crew at Indianapolis.

Whether you are working with two projectors or a battery of two dozen projectors, the principle of the multi-image program is that one slide dissolves into another, pulsed electronically, accompanied by a soundtrack, and cued to dissolve slowly or rapidly to fit the subject and mood. Rapid changing can create the illusion of motion. Sometimes a narrator ties the show together; sometimes the background consists of people pictured making their own comments, giving the presentation a documentary immediacy.

Obviously, the slides must be good, must be done professionally, should have the potential of working together (calling for shots from slightly different angles), should be on the horizontal axis, should be strong on people rather than static objects, and should suggest action rather than portraits.

Like any other form of communication, the multi-image show should have clear goals, should interest and entertain instead of preach, and should be technically perfect. Length may vary, but a 10-minute slide program can seem very long. Graphics must be readable and on the screen long enough to register. Music and sound effects should not overpower speech.

OTHER PRODUCTION CONSIDERATIONS

Many other items may be ordered by the public relations practitioner during his or her career. Perhaps a letterhead must be designed, or a company logo created, or a business card put together. Perhaps the practitioner is in need of a trophy, or a matchbook, or an engraved pen, or a plastic keychain. The list is endless. Ordinarily, the PR person would work with a graphics specialist and with the salespeople representing these individual items. You will find these people listed in the Yellow Pages of your phone book. Technical requirements and limitations, unit costs, delivery schedules, and other matters should be discussed in advance.

PR practitioners are not expected to know as much about production as the specialists do, but they should know what responsibilties exist for them in each medium. That's the way to earn respect, please clients or bosses, and win new clients.

PUBLIC RELATIONS IN THE HIGH-TECH AGE

An honest introduction to any discussion of high-tech communication might admit that much of the material may be obsolete before it sees print. This is true, but practitioners must still be aware of the changes that will affect their profession. Some of these advances come in the form of equipment and delivery services; others touch PR people indirectly, through the needs and activities of clients. All these innovations have a human dimension as well, reflecting on morale, ethics, interpersonal relationships, and other personal areas.

Computers

The principle of punched cards that predated the floppy disks may be over a century old, but the real revolution in computers can be localized to the last decade. Nearly 300 different manufacturers vie for the computer business, and they market more than 5,000 different software programs. Although the practitioner shouldn't discard the typewriter and file cabinet just yet (after all, there are power outages and downtime), the modern PR office has to be thinking computer. John F. Budd, Jr., writes:

> Those who do not change or adapt not only will have relegated themselves to second-class corporate citizenship—down from management or staff (policy) to line (implementation)—but equally significant, they will have defaulted on the opportunity to harness the single greatest innovation in communication since Gutenberg introduced movable type.[7]

With all the hardware and software available, some professionals, reluctant to change habits, declare they'll wait until the field settles down and the prices stabilize and the units are at maximum efficiency. Experts advise that there may never be a "right" time to buy and that, while waiting for this ideal, the professional gives up time, effectiveness, and other benefits the computer allows.

There is also the concern about the difficulty of switching from old habits, and about the time necessary to become comfortable with the new communication tool. All the stories about the competence of children or the case histories of peers may not suffice; the practitioner finally has to come in contact with the equipment.

Over $80 billion a year is spent on computers in America, with 20 percent of that money going to software purchases. America still leads in the software area, but Japan is making inroads. After developing programs that will perform functions from games to the writing of wills, manufacturers are now working on expanding the capacities of single disks, linking up personal computers, speeding up communication between units, and other cooperative uses.

One of the chief PR uses of computers is in word-processing capability. Since much of public relations has to do with communication (speeches, news releases, letters, proposals, brochure copy, scripts, and so on), the possibility of expediting these functions is especially appealing. Deletions, additions, and corrections are all simplified, and some practitioners insist that not only is the quantity of work expanded, but the quality improved.

> Writing and editing become so much easier that you'll have more time to polish your prose. In fact, you may find it so easy and—yes—fun that you may have to

put a self-imposed limit on how many times you'll let yourself revise a document.[8]

Along with this supposed "fun" may come problems. Getting used to commands can be frustrating, and watching the screen may be tiring, and there is the ever-present fear of losing some valuable prose in the machine. The plus factors more than compensate for the debits, according to author Peter A. McWilliams, who says that "word-processing computers are sufficiently wonderful to forgive science for its two-and-a-half millennia of foot-dragging." He lists a few ways word processors can assist the writing process:

- Effortless change.
- Elimination of retyping.
- Perfect spelling. (There are also programs to correct grammatical errors and punctuation.)
- Lack of noise (although some writers enjoy the clacking of keys).
- Portability. Some, weighing about ten pounds, fit in a briefcase.
- No bells and carriage returns.
- Ease of correspondence, enabling you to write letters that are essentially the same to a number of people in just a few minutes.
- Research is simplified.
- New programs offer variety—to satisfy a writer's curiosity.[9]

McWilliams also salutes the pleasure he gets from his word processor, something he says he never received from any previous mode of communication.

Publishers are fond of the word processors and may convince authors in their stables to purchase compatible units. The writer may submit a floppy disk to the editor instead of a typed manuscript. This disk can then be transmitted over a telephone line to a computer typesetter. Similar arrangements are certainly in the near future for news releases and feature stories.

If you wish to produce hard copy from the word processor, you'll require a printer of some type, and public relations people should be certain they find one that meets their need. Many professionals advise against the dot-matrix printers, which are cheaper but may not look as good as the poorest typewriter type. Letter-quality printers are favored, with emphasis on those with speed, flexibility (like justifying margins and properly aligning decimal points), and dependability. Practitioners in the market for a printer may wish to take their most difficult and technical assignments with them when shopping, just to be certain the unit can handle it.

Computers may also be invaluable in other areas of public relations. In bookkeeping, for example. To make money in this profession, accurate records must be kept so that charges can be quickly and properly traced and assigned to the correct clients. Computers can handle the accounting procedures, maintain ledgers, invoice clients, address mail, keep time sheets on employees, and do dozens of other chores that now demand more time and personnel.

Scheduling, trafficking, insertions and work orders are done by the computer, which also maintains project budgets and is interactive with the accounting program. For example, if we try to enter a media bill into the accounting system and the bill does not agree with the insertion order, the computer rejects it.[10]

Computers may be used to compile and evaluate publicity clips, keep a source file of magazine articles and technical information, even shop for clients' Christmas gifts. They can record donations to nonprofit organizations and provide breakdowns on volunteer talents. Office inventories may be monitored and photos sized and audiovisual projects timed, all in a matter of seconds.

Research

Every phase of public relations, from research to evaluation, has high-tech applications. The revolution in research capabilities may have provided the most valuable current asset, however. The capacity for storage, instant retrieval, and speedy analysis of data make computers an enormously helpful PR ally.

Whole libraries are committed to a relatively few disks and may be summoned by the touch of a key. Individual computers may be locked into a larger data-retrieval system capable of supplying details on an almost endless variety of topics.

Compuserve, for example, began in 1980, sponsored by a combination of newspapers and wire services, to provide technical information on a shared basis. NEXIS advertises that it lets users research the world's most important publications in seconds.

NEXIS finds the stories, displays them on your video screen, and lets you zero in on the facts you need. You're left with a lot more time to do what really counts: think, analyze, react, decide.[11]

The Public Relations Society of America introduced PRLink, a 24-hour national computer network and database, in 1985, making it accessible through a computer terminal and telephone modem. In addition to news and other services, subscribers get a look at award-winning case studies, seminar schedules, and professional ideas.

A number of other acronymic services each promises a slightly different blend of information. ERIC (Educational Resources Information Center) emphasizes scholarly research; PR Aids allows professionals to audition and select media; Select Information Systems specializes in locating documents. Thousands more extend, duplicate, or parallel these services.

Public-opinion sampling is far easier, far cheaper on the computer. Existing programs consisting of randomized samples of opinion on a variety of current topics are available. Interested persons can tap into the data, ask questions, perform analysis. New data can also be fed into the computer and new conclusions drawn. Such techniques may save weeks of time and thousands of dollars.

Programmers devise solutions to almost every computer need. In an article for *Communication World*, author/consultant Allan Kennedy lists some specific uses, like direct-mail selectivity by background and interest; followup letters to people, internally and externally, who complain about any matter; and even a series of communications to give progress reports on trouble areas—potholes, for example:

> When a complaint comes in, whether by letter or by telephone, the basic information—name, address, nature and location of problem, date of complaint—gets entered in the system. Each repair project is then assigned a target completion date and a person or sector responsible for its execution. A letter then immediately goes out to the complaintant, acknowledging the complaint in detail and giving the target repair date: "Thanks for letting us know about the pothole at 5th and Vine. The combination of warm days and freezing nights has produced a record number of potholes this spring. We plan to have that hole filled by next Thursday.[12]

The computers also kick out other letters in the event that the target date is not met, explaining the delay; and the same system produces work orders for inspection and, finally, a note telling the complaining party that the hole is fixed and that the organization appreciates the tip.

This system has any number of PR applications. So have other programs. Database systems that scan hundreds of newspapers and magazines can be tapped for the tracking of a firm's own news releases—by category, if desirable—and can even print the results on special forms for circulation to interested departments. Combining computer information with the results of supermarket scanners at checkout counters may marry market analysis to behavioral profiles.

Supercomputers can run structural tests on buildings, materials, and machine parts that don't yet exist. Photographs may be stored on disks and called back with a single command. And there is much more to come, like the imperfect but improving "artificial intelligence" that may one day write those news releases and speeches that occupy entry-level practitioners.

Electronic Mail

The big news in postal circles isn't the nine-digit ZIP codes or even the overnight delivery of materials; it's the use of computers to transmit messages electronically. Some national and international services link up a network of cities and promise to move mail in less than a minute, even picking up and delivering. Many offices now have their own desk computers tied into other computers so that messages may be exchanged.

> Electronic mail makes the post office and even private delivery services look like the pony express when it comes to whisking notes, letters, or documents

Figure 8-25 Computer enhanced graphics provide speed and flexibility.
Courtesy: Morin Advertising Art

crosstown, cross-country, or across oceans. The young business— some of the major players like MCI and Western Union began offering mail services in the last two years—is expected to grow rapidly in the next few years. Companies like MCI, Western Union, GTE, and ITT are spending millions of dollars developing and marketing computer-communication services for individuals and businesses.[13]

There may be as many as 5 million subscribers to the electronic mail services by 1988, making it an even more practical system. Users are assigned their own "electronic mailbox" within the parent company's main computer and can now communicate with others listed in a printed directory. Some service firms (Telemail, Easylink, MCI, ITT Dialcom, GE Quik-Comm, Sourcemail, and others) charge initiation fees, set minimum rates, and base charges on time or message length, with varying costs for evenings, weekends, and holidays. Some of them also offer additional services, from data banks to dating services.

Phone companies are meeting this sort of competition with innovations of their own. Mobile phones have long been an asset for the frequent traveler, and teleconferencing cuts down on travel bills. They also offer "voice mailboxes," where callers can deposit messages to be picked up later by clients or associates. Picturephones, already in use, may soon be more affordable, and fiber optics are guaranteeing economy and quality of transmission to metropolitan areas.

Cameras

Although the cost is currently prohibitive for the weekend shutterbug, newspapers and magazines may move more and more to the use of electronic cameras. These cameras store electrical charges on microchips and allow almost instantaneous viewing, cropping, and color correction. No darkrooms to equip or chemicals and paper to buy. The images can move from the initial scanning to page makeup. Through telephone hookups, pictures may even be transmitted from the scene of a hot news story or sports event, reassembled by the page generator, and then sent out over a Videotext or turned into hard copy. Electronic cameras may take up to 60 pictures per second, at speeds as high as 300,000 ASA, whereas today's films may be rated only as high as 1,000 ASA, with most photographers using speeds only as high as 400 ASA. Initially, the quality of the images was not good enough for newspapers, but that is changing. The cost, too, is being reduced.

Other Video Innovations

The number of communications satellites is triple that of a few years ago, greatly influencing the nature and cost of meetings, putting distant corporate branches within easy reach, and undoubtedly influencing the way we think about the world. Networks employing satellites have been established in a number of areas affecting public relations. Hospitals, for example, may subscribe to any one of a number of satellite networks that program medical news, health tips, information aimed at physicians, upbeat movies, and even a special comedy hour with a wellness format.

Cable television, although regarded by many PR practitioners as having high potential, is not used extensively by professionals. Limited audiences, clutter, the inferior quality of much programming, and their own ignorance of the field have kept cable PR use at a minimum. Practitioners also feel that cable television should cut back on its attempts to reach mass audiences and concentrate more on "narrowcasting," the pinpointing of specific target audiences. When that is accomplished, they say, cable will be more in tune with the needs and plans of public relations.

Even public-access cable is not getting the attention from PR people that it deserves. Some of this is attributable to their own failure to promote themselves. The cable stations that do a good job on their own PR also seem to attract the most public relations projects.

Videotapes are now channeling annual reports to shareholders, training salespeople, launching new products, and expanding the results of meetings. As learning tools, videotapes have long been admired, but they are only beginning to make themselves felt as communication tools.

Figure 8-26 Mobile satellite dishes enable television stations to do newscasts from remote areas.
Courtesy: WOWT

The Automated Factory

Even though some technological changes may not be located within public relations offices, they will still make themselves felt in the PR practice. Those engaged in political public relations, for example, will want to stay current on the use of closed-circuit television to monitor and testify at legislative hearings. PR persons for other corporate products may want to analyze the success of some major car manufacturers in introducing their latest models via satellite. And they'll want to check the marketing, budgeting, and personnel implication of FMS—flexible manufacturing systems—which consist of:

> . . . computer controlled machine centers that sculpt complicated metal parts at high speed and with great reliability, robots that handle the parts, and remotely guided carts that deliver materials. The components are linked by electronic controls that dictate what will happen at each stage of the manufacturing sequence, even automatically replacing worn-out or broken drill bits and other implements.[14]

Expensive to install, these flexible systems eventually save money, not only in personnel but especially in replacing several larger machines, reducing plant size, and allowing smaller volumes of certain goods at lower prices. The Japanese have been leaders in this area; they have one factory, the Yamazaki plant, that links 34 robots and 65 computer-controlled machine tools via fiber-optics cables to a headquarters design center. By telephone, a person in a distant office can direct the robotic plant in the manufacture of machine parts. American firms have been a little slower to introduce these methods, sometimes because of concern for quality control, sometimes because they fear that certain delicate operations can't be handled automatically. Eventually, because of foreign competition, some adjustment to robotics must be made. The automobile industry is already heavily into automation, and textile firms are trying to revive their fortunes by adopting new techniques, adding air-jet looms and computers.

The Personal Factor

Unions may worry about loss of jobs in the face of high-tech equipment, and they may wrangle over who shall have jurisdiction over these innovations, and workers may feel even more alienated from management. The narrowcasting aspect of television may further fragment audiences—delighting manufacturers, perhaps, but extending the differences between the haves and have-nots, here and around the world. A new bureaucracy of experts will arise, taking many of the decisions away from management, and especially from on-line personnel. There is even the whole question of incentive and the reward for production, when the actual work may rely on the efficiency of machines.

Many firms (and this includes newspapers) have been reluctant to change to new systems. There are fears and concerns that must be allayed. Author Carol T. Gaffney posits five stages employees go through when automation is introduced: self-pity, denial, anger, compromise, and finally, acceptance, with past worries forgotten.[15] These fears are not confined to secretarial and blue-collar jobs. Executives want to protect their own turf, may worry about their dexterity, may not want to vary their work habits. Some say office problems will not be solved by automation, but will be highlighted.

Steps are being taken to reduce resistance to change. Training sessions and tangible rewards are offered. "User-friendly" computers are touted. Interactive video allows a person to almost talk to the computer. Flexible work schedules, sabbaticals, shorter workweeks, earlier retirement—all these are attempts to compensate for a business life-style that gets increasingly complicated, impersonal, and frustrating.

Because of such problems, it appears that there will always be a need for the translator, the negotiator, the communicator; for the sensitive person who can anticipate, plan, and implement; for the public relations specialist.

CHAPTER HIGHLIGHTS

- Understanding design and production can be a necessity in a small office, an asset in a large office, and an addition to any PR person's list of talents.
- Graphic sensibility, which is partly instinctive, enhances communication, especially in this visually literate world.
- The line, circle, rectangle, and triangle are the basic design shapes, augmented by tone and color.

- Color, a form of energy that travels in waves, has the capacity to evoke various reactions, from anger to serenity. Using the more than 7,500 colors properly requires taste and experience but brightens up any publication.

- Harmony, sequence, and balance (formal and informal) control layout and design, working together to produce an effective printed piece.

- Company magazines are often designed around a grid system, but imagination and variation divide the arresting from the routine.

- Brochures and booklets also call for layout skills, but begin with folding paper, and direct-mail packages require, in addition to graphic knowledge, an understanding of postal regulations, lists, and recipient response.

- The simple photograph may be reproduced in a number of ways—square halftone, outline halftone, vignette, posterized, or screened in a number of attractive patterns. Artwork, too, has its styles and techniques, and computer graphics are just beginning to have an effect.

- Type, too, can create certain responses, and within the five general classifications of type (text, roman, gothic, script, and ornamental) are hundreds of type families, even though the practitioner may find a limited selection at the local printer's. Type, divided into hot and cold versions, is measured in points, with 72 points to an inch, and width of typed lines is measured in picas. Understanding the mechanics of typography is necessary for fitting copy.

- The practitioner must be aware of the properties of paper and their effect on printing, and should also know the assets and liabilities of the principal printing techniques (letterpress, offset lithography, gravure, screen printing).

- Radio production can be simple or complicated, depending on the results desired, but the key to maximum use of this medium is to take full advantage of the characteristics of sound.

- Film is normally farmed out to professional studios, but many corporations have their own in-house television departments to produce internal programming and videotapes. The PR person's responsibility here, except in cases of necessity or specialized skills, is normally reduced to scripting and supervision.

- Multi-image slide shows are not cheap but are flexible and work well on large screens. Again, the simplest shows may be handled within a company or organization, but the more complicated ones require outside assistance.

- Computers have revolutionized communications, affecting everything from the computer-compatible news release to research and public-opinion polling. Electronic mail is also expected to replace the regular system to a considerable degree, once cost and universality are conquered.

- Videotext is supposed to replace the current printed newspaper, but many experts now think the two forms will coexist.

- Electronic cameras may make the traditional darkroom obsolete because of their speed and their in-camera potential.
- As automation and high tech continue to change our lives, public relations people must be alert to the human adjustments required. Since their job is communication, their futures should encompass not only the latest hardware, but also the philosophy and planning to reach others in a high-tech age.

NOTES

[1] Rose DeNeve, "The Graphic Edge," *Public Relations Journal*, July 1985.

[2] *ASNE TODAY*, special tabloid, May 10, 1983.

[3] Alphons J. Hackl, "Color as a Communicator," *Public Relations Journal*, August 1968.

[4] Robert Lockwood, "Newspaper Design: Did We Miss the Revolution?" *ASNE Bulletin*, March 1983.

[5] Sandra Friedlander, "Mailers and Printers Unite!" *ZIP*, November/December 1980.

[6] "The Cutting Edge of Chermayeff," interview in *Communicator's Journal*, January/February 1984.

[7] John F. Budd, Jr., "Are We Communicating More and Saying Less?" *Public Relations Journal*, January 1984.

[8] Sheri Rosen, "How to Hire Your New Computer," *Communication World*, November 1983.

[9] Peter A. McWilliams, "The Word Processor." Courtesy *Communicator's Journal*, September/October 1983.

[10] Edward Reed, "The Computer and Accounting," *Public Relations Journal*, January 1984.

[11] NEXIS brochure, 1985.

[12] Allan Kennedy, "Back Fence Conversations: New Tools for Quality Communication," *Communication World*, November 1983.

[13] Michael Cooper, "In the Stretch: Electronic Mail," *Public Relations Journal*, January 1985.

[14] Gene Bylinsky, "The Race to the Automatic Factory," *Fortune*, February 21, 1983.

[15] Carol T. Gaffney, "Crisis in the Workplace," *Computerworld*, September 28, 1981.

SUGGESTED READINGS

BUDD, JOHN F., *Corporate Video in Focus*. Englewood Cliffs, N.J.: Prentice-Hall, 1983.

BURROWS, THOMAS D., and DONALD N. WOOD, *Television Production: Disciplines and Techniques*. Dubuque, Ia.: Brown, 1978.

Communication Illustrated, monthly newsletter, Bartlesville, Okla.

COMPESI, RONALD J., and RONALD E. SHERRIFFS, *Small Format Television Production*. Rockleigh, N.J.: Allyn & Bacon, 1975.

Corporate Showcase, annual. New York: American Showcase Inc.

COWAN, ROBERT A., *Teleconferencing: Maximizing Human Potential*. Reston, Va.: Reston Publishing, 1984.

CROY, PETER, *Graphic Design and Reproduction Techniques*. New York: Hastings House, 1972.

Graphic Arts Monthly, New York.

Graphis Annual, Bethesda, Md.

HILL, MARY, and WENDELL COCHRAN, *Into Print*. Los Altos, Calif.: Kaufmann, 1977.

How to Do Leaflets, Newsletters and Newspapers. Boston: PEP, 1982.

HUDSON, HOWARD PENN, *Publishing Newsletters*. New York: Scribners, 1982.

KEITH, MICHAEL C., *Production in Format Radio Handbook*. Lanham, Md.: University Press of America, 1984.

KENNY, MICHAEL, *Presenting Yourself*. New York: Wiley, 1982.

LANGFORD, MICHAEL, *Basic Photography*, 4th ed. New York: Hastings House, 1978.

LAZER, ELLEN, A., ed., *The Teleconferencing Handbook: A Guide to Cost-Effective Communication*. White Plains, N.Y.: Knowledge Industries, 1983.

MCCAVITT, WILLIAM E., *Television Technology: Alternative Communication Systems*. Lanham, Md.: University Press of America, 1983.

MURRAY, RAY, *How to Brief Designers and Buy Print*. Brookfield, Vt.: Business Books, 1984.

NELSON, ROY PAUL, *The Design of Advertising*, 3rd ed. Dubuque, Ia.: Brown, 1977.

RAND, PAUL, *A Designer's Art*. New Haven, Conn.: Yale University Press, 1985.

RUEGG, REUDI, and GODI FROHLICH, *Basic Typography*. New York: Hastings House, 1972.

SMITH, PEGGY, *Proofreading Manual and Reference Guide* and *Proofreading Workbook*. Alexandria, Va.: EEI Books, 1981.

TURNBULL, ARTHUR T., and RUSSELL N. BAIRD, *The Graphics of Communication*, 3rd ed. New York: Holt, Rinehart & Winston, 1975.

WARFORD, H. STANLEY, *Design for Print Production*. New York: Hastings House, 1972.

WHITE, JAN, *Designing for Magazines*. New York: Bowker, 1982.

———, *Editing by Design*. New York: Bowker, 1974.

———, *Mastering Graphics*. New York: Bowker, 1983.

———, *On Graphics: Tips for Editors*. Chicago: Lawrence Ragan Communications, 1983.

WIEGAND, INGRID, *Professional Guide to Video Production*. White Plains, N.Y.: Knowledge Industries, 1984.

ZINSSER, WILLIAM, *Writing with a Word Processor*. New York: Harper & Row, 1983.

The S.D. Warren paper company produces a number of booklets helpful to practitioners, covering company publications, annual reports, and a number of production topics, such as:
The Company Catalog
How to Plan Printing
Ghosting
Paper Estimating
Paper Surface Comparison
Printing Elements and Methods
Business Management and Printing

EXERCISES

1. Cut out from magazines or newspapers four photographs, preferably black and white, which represent different styles or techniques. Discuss the effect created by each.

2. Trace four print ads, rendering the forms, including type and illustrations, into the simple shapes of circle, rectangle, and triangle.

3. Design a brochure for a local bank, with the aim of attracting young married people to open and maintain savings accounts. Write the copy, prepare a dummy, indicate illustrations and headlines, and specify size and family of type (check typebooks at printers or in your library), color of paper, and other factors. Consider this ready to go to a production staff, which will then have the type set, do the pasteup, and get it to the printer. Your job is to make your design wishes as concrete and complete as possible.

4. Select a current television commercial that you will be able to view several times over a period of a few days. Identify the commercial, describe what occurs in it, and list all the production considerations for the producer—talent, music, sound effects, props, special effects, and other items. What did they need to make this work?

5. Using your own or a borrowed tape recorder, tape a public-service announcement for a local nonprofit agency. This means you must write the script (10 seconds or 30 seconds), get the music or sound effects, select talent, and record it. Bring the script to class with the tape, along with any other supporting data you need.

6. If you were laying out a magazine column that was 12 picas wide and you knew you could fit thirty-six 10-point characters into that width, how would you go about typing up the copy? And how would you determine how many lines or how much space this would take? (Don't *do* this—just tell *how* you would do it.)

7. Describe a computer program or activity you feel might be helpful in the performance of a specific communication duty within a specific industry or organization.

CASE PROBLEMS

1. You are the public relations director for a large health insurance firm. An integral part of your operation centers on the crew of about 80 people (mostly female, mostly young) who work the telephones fielding questions and complaints. In front of each person is a computer terminal that allows them to call up the file on any particular person immediately. The problem with this job is that the workers are constantly busy, often repeating the same information over and over, sometimes fielding abuse

from customers (which they are told to politely turn aside). Eyes are glued to the screen and movement restricted. To add to the problems, no smoking is allowed except on breaks (which are sometimes impossible to take), the salary is fairly low, and those working here are considered at the lowest rung of the corporate ladder—and they know it. As a consequence of all these things, morale is shot and turnover is high.

Your boss instructs you to talk first with the supervisor (who spot monitors the employees' answering techniques) and then with the staff.

a. What sort of information would you be after? What questions would you ask of the supervisor? Of the staff?

b. Assume you learned through these interviews that conditions were as stated above, perhaps worse, and that boredom and low esteem were the main problems. Devise a plan for your boss that would improve morale. Be specific.

2. One of your corporate public relations responsibilities is the supervision of the audio-visual department in this multinational diversified manufacturer of automobiles, trucks, farm machinery, lighting standards, and sewer pipe. Over the years, the AV department has acquired a huge inventory of equipment, plus a large studio within the headquarters building, and a small but able staff. Up to now, this staff has only been doing training tapes for the corporation's sales force, which doesn't begin to make use of equipment or personnel.

Assuming you want to correct this situation and make more efficient use of what you have, how would you proceed?

a. Whom would you talk with, and in what order?

b. Assuming these talks were productive, draw up a plan, with as many specifics as possible, covering other uses for the equipment and staff.

9

PUBLIC RELATIONS AND SPECIAL EVENTS

Special events, in one form or another, usually involve the public relations person. These events are staged occurrences calculated to attract public attention. They may be as complicated as a national convention or as relatively simple as a private luncheon; they may attract thousands of people or a handful. Yet they share some things in common—they require detailed advance planning and constant checking.

Unfortunately, many events also share the common condition of being poorly conceived and clumsily executed. Instead of running so smoothly that they seem effortless, they expose to the public every shortcoming of the sponsors.

Not every mistake is the fault of the planning team. The oft-quoted Murphy's law states, "If anything can go wrong, it will." Although facetious, this remark has an element of truth. Even careful attention to detail cannot always provide for the unforeseen—the sudden illness, the abrupt shift in weather, the fire in the kitchen. However, the PR practitioner should begin planning for each event by cataloging each area of concern and listing all items that could go awry. This will minimize error.

Keep in mind that a special event is just as much of a communication tool as a news release or an annual report. In this case, a social function is used to convey an image or message about the institution, and poor packaging of the event distorts the message every bit as much as a poor print job or an amateurish public-service announcement. The audience is usually a specialized audience, chosen for its presumed interest in this affair. This special event may be your best chance to reach it.

The event may be a backyard barbecue for a board of trustees or an elaborate multimillion-dollar day-and-a-half conference staged every five years by Coca-Cola for its 400-plus American bottlers. The former may involve only invitations, menu selection and preparation, space considerations, and a modified agenda. Coke's 1984 soiree for its bottlers, an important target audience, was held at Atlanta's Hyatt Regency Hotel and featured games, prizes, a country western band, a live cow, a 70-foot indoor hot-air balloon, a symphony orchestra, a chorus line, tumblers, jugglers, bagpipers, clowns, a high-wire act, animals constructed out of Coca-Cola cans, a laser light show, commercials flashed on huge video screens, headline entertainers, a robot, a spaceship, and fireworks. The meals, served by 200 waiters to the overall crowd of some 3,500 people, included an eight-foot mound of Maine lobsters, and the drinks, offered by 55 bartenders, emphasized the sponsor's product. Desk personnel sported Coke T-shirts, and there were numerous speeches— introducing new products, attacking the competition, stimulating the participants.

Obviously, a lot more time, effort, personnel, and money went into Coca-Cola's special event, but even the backyard barbecue requires some thought and some planning.

PARTY PLANNERS

Because of the complexity of some modern affairs, the occupation of party planner has moved from the salons of high society to the corporate milieu. For a fee, the people specializing in such events will review the invitation lists, suggest themes and decorations, help select entertainment, arrange table settings, supervise publicity, and accomplish a majority of the chores ordinarily assigned to public relations staff members.

> A major national publishing company recently hosted a reception for their advertisers. They greeted guests with "aloha" and placed leis around their necks. As the guests headed for the buffet table they discovered a Texas barbecue with all the trimmings. Each dinner table was visited by a Gypsy fortune teller who read palms. . . . An international oil company invited its managers to a conference. Two French Pierrot mime characters stood frozen like statues on display boxes. As the attendees registered, the mimes came slowly to life, winked, blew a kiss, and, using an invisible camera, took a photo of the guest.[1]

Party planners may suggest placement of certain guests, separating those who will probably talk business from those who will only party, or managing compatible groupings.

Selection of a party planner should be as thorough as the choice of a fund raiser, interior decorator, or key employee. References should be sought and checked, fees discussed openly, duties spelled out, and company approval garnered from the highest levels.

On average, party planning, although growing as a vocation, will not be available to most public relations persons for most events. They must do their own planning, execution, and evaluation.

Figure 9-1 Meetings may be conventions that attract thousands or a small luncheon with a handful of participants. Both take planning.

PLANNING

In any kind of planning, "details, details, details" is a good start. Write them down and check them off. Don't rely on memory, no matter how quick. Was everyone notified? Did we stay within the budget? Has the equipment arrived? Do I know the rules of etiquette required at this occasion? Where are the plaques? Did the programs reach the hotel? Does our Tool and Die Plant Orchestra know the national anthem? Ad infinitum!

Think of the stage plays you have enjoyed. If you heard and observed scenery being shifted, if you were aware of muffed lines, if light cues evoked tardy responses, if you could see the flimsy set shake—all these things detract from enjoyment. When they don't occur, your concentration is where it belongs—on the action and dialogue.

That's how a well-run special event should seem—so smooth that you are never conscious of the machinery.

Why Are We Holding This Event?

There are many reasons for producing a special event. Some celebrate an occasion, like an anniversary or a grand opening; some raise funds or promote political careers; some cultivate the audience's loyalty or reward its industry; some merely continue a tradition, whether or not there is any longer a viable purpose. Some, like a number of Washington gatherings, have a goal known only to the hosts.

There must be a reason for assembling. Special events take time and money, stealing personnel from other important tasks, so they should be initially scrutinized for relative merit and periodically checked to see that they continue to serve a specific function. Sometimes an event begins with a stated purpose, which then becomes lost in the minutiae of execution. Some fund-raising dinners actually lose money. Some affairs that are intended to win friends alienate a majority of those attending.

Several years ago, a major hotel successfully attracted the city's elite to its open house but had incorporated no greeting, no tours, no speeches, no brochures. Guests showed up, ate, drank, looked at each other in bewilderment, and left.

Just because some administrator thinks a dinner would be a nice idea, or just because you did something last year, this is no justification for taking on the onus of a special event unless the purpose is evident. The PR person should insist on definite goals or should courageously reject or discontinue the event.

Clearing the Date

In the initial stages of planning, the PR person, if involved, considers the date of the event.

The practitioner may be somewhat flexible at first (unless the date falls on some predetermined anniversary), but he or she should get early acceptance for a specific day and time. This should be far enough away to permit adequate planning and should also fit neatly into organizational or institutional plans.

The practitioner must consider what other events may conflict and thereby curtail attendance. A major football rivalry or prime social affair could be too strong to ignore. Certain seasons may reduce participation by some segments of the audience. Although there is no way to avoid every conflict, the practitioner should steer clear of serious competition.

Once the practitioner has settled on a workable date, this date is cleared with others who may be involved. If possible, the practitioner gets responses in writing from those affected. This will spare him or her later complaints about thoughtless scheduling.

Securing the Facility

The next step is the location of an appropriate site. If the event is a groundbreaking or ribbon-cutting ceremony, that decision may be automatic. For many events, however, the PR director must review some options. Factors like anticipated audience, nature of the event, budget, and availability come into play. If the PR director decides to hold a dinner at his or her own plant or campus, can the people there cater it, and are cocktails a problem, legal or otherwise? If the director opts for a hotel, he or she must know what is available and what the strong and weak points are of each. Some cities have a limited number of choices, particularly for large crowds. And some may be booked years ahead, especially during such popular months as June and December.

In addition to the mere ability to hold a specific number of guests, the wise planner looks at such areas as parking, reputation of hotel employees for cooperation, hidden costs, cuisine, and even the architectural character of the structure. If guests are invited, for example, to a fund-raising dinner, a shabby facility may reduce donations. On the other hand, a charitable organization like the Red Cross or the United Fund may want to avoid the appearance of luxury and may settle for a more modest setting.

All first-classs hotels will supply planners with detailed information on their facilities.

The coordinator of any event should pay a personal visit to the facility to be used. During this visit, he or she may observe that the renovation promised in a brochure hasn't been accomplished or that it will not be completed by meeting time. Many planners like to make the visit unannounced, perhaps taking a room at a hotel and checking its room service or sampling its dining fare. They will also look into such features as the swimming pools or adjacent shops. Serious planners may order from room service, sit in the lobby and observe how the desk handles guests, and order drinks at the busiest hours and check the time elapsed before delivery. They may sample the highly touted restaurant fare, visit the city's famed attractions, record the costs of items from theater tickets to cabs. They'll stop in at beauty shops and barbers, tour the golf courses and other sport facilities. When they return to headquarters, they may quietly assess the pros and cons of this and other sites before making a decision.

The site should be checked again when the program is set and room assignments established, and again just prior to the event, and again before each day's program. This constant surveillance guards against surprises and ensures against untidy facilities, loss of equipment, too few chairs, missing notepads and programs, and similar shortcomings.

The planners will want to know where light switches and control panels are located, whether there are sufficient outlets, and where the engineer resides in the event of a need for extension cords or first-echelon repairs. They should be familiar with the amount and nature of the public-address equipment and where to go to tend an ailing microphone.

If sliding panels separate some rooms, noise levels should be checked. Avoid putting a loud film, for example, next to a quiet panel discussion.

If the rooms are not well marked—or even if they are—signs indicating the direction of specific meetings are welcome additions for strangers. These should be attractively lettered and not relegated to a busy assistant with a flair for magic markers.

Be certain guests can readily find the restrooms, elevators, checkrooms, and other service areas.

Obviously, such considerations as price range, convenience, employee attitudes, and general reputation also influence site decisions.

Members of the planning team should draw up a report for management, listing assets and liabilities, and should make their recommendations and sell their choice to their superiors. It must be a place they can all live with.

> Site selection is setting a stage. It should create the proper atmosphere, but not overwhelm the players. The psychological effect on the audience should produce the proper frame of reference for the business to be transacted or the benefit expected from a learning experience.[2]

The practitioner should work closely with facility personnel, making certain they understand each other. Large hotels, auditoriums, and convention centers have "event coordinators" whose primary responsibility consists of assisting the planner.

The coordinator will usually offer scale drawings of meeting rooms, a timetable for arrival and departure, a checklist for special equipment, and other similar aids.

A major health-insurance firm constructed a multistory underground facility covered by a glass dome and has permitted limited use of it by outside organizations. Events are held to no more than two a week and should involve no more than 350 people. Event planners sign a contract; agree to a fee structure based on space, time, services, and the nature of the occasion; arrange for all catering; and supervise cleanup. Other restrictions involve lighting arrangements, smoking, and the clearing of all publicity by the insurance company.

Banks sometimes supply meeting rooms for local nonprofit groups, and shopping centers build in space to handle small meetings, primarily to accommodate tenants. Many airports promote their conference facilities, expanding on the earlier small space allotted to news interviews of traveling dignitaries. They offer parking, AV equipment, phones, decorations, food and drink, even entertainment. One major terminal lists menus for all three meals, ranging from a continental breakfast under $3 to dinners (seafood a la Newburg, beef Wellington, Cornish game hen, and so on) from $15 up. Even hors d'oeuvres are divided into cold (prawns on ice, 100 pieces, $150), hot (tenderloin brochettes, 50 people, $100), and snacks (mixed nuts, bowl, $10).

For royalty and the top celebrities or the conspicuously wealthy, hotels may provide unusual foods, extra security, interpreters, rare wines, exotic flowers, oversized bathtubs, baskets of fruit native to their countries. For the Duke and Duchess of Luxembourg, housed in Washington's Vista Hotel's 25-room presidential suite, the management provided a special box of American and Belgian chocolates and decorated with a marzipan Luxembourg flag.

Every abnormal meeting situation suggests a deeper study of the proposed site. No practitioner should, for example, schedule a meeting overseas without having inspected the facilities first. In fact, employing a reliable local person to look after things while the staff member is absent is advisable. New hotels and newly furnished hotels may also be risky and should be examined with current needs in mind. Sometimes such facilities need a shakedown year to get them in proper shape. Holding special events in resort areas adds a touch of class but also presents distractions and, perhaps, raised eyebrows from the IRS. The hotel, motel, or conference center should be a source of support for the planner and not an additional headache.

Major-Convention Sites

Major conventions require even more planning because of the complications caused by numbers and space allocations. For some of the nation's largest organizations, the selection of a convention site may be limited to a relative handful of cities. Other cities have no facilities large enough to handle their general meetings, or they cannot house them in one or more adjacent hotels, or they have inadequate personnel or attractions.

On the other hand, one problem at conventions is keeping the delegates around for meetings. San Francisco's Chinatown or Fishermen's Wharf beckons them. They drift toward the roulette tables in Reno. In New York it could be the theaters, and in New Orleans, the night life. Granted, these locales also boost attendance, but if you want the delegates to stay closer to home, you might settle on places like White Sulphur Springs, West Virginia, or Mackinac Island, Michigan. The amenities are here, but the temptation to wander from the hotel is reduced.

Notifying the Participants

Those who will have principal roles in the special event—company executives, local dignitaries, and the like—should be notified by phone or letter, and adequate time should be allowed for their response. Four to six weeks might be the ordinary lead time unless the participant is distant from the site and of sufficient importance to have an abnormally busy schedule, or unless the event itself is of unusual magnitude. One week's—or even two weeks'—notice is too short a planning space for all but the social outcast.

For events open to the general public, mass-media invitations may suffice, but whenever possible, it is better to issue individual invitations by mail.

Meetings that are held at a regular time each month would of course require a shorter time period. A reminder the preceding week would be acceptable.

As with advertising, each form of meeting notification has its plus and minus features. The telephone is a rapid medium of communication but

Figure 9-2 Most hotels provide planning guides. Courtesy: Hyatt Corporation

Hyatt Regency Vancouver

British Columbia and the great Pacific Northwest will never be the same again. Neither will your conventions. We've brought every shining facet of Vancouver and Northwestern living into one very unconventional convention hotel.

It's everything you could wish for. Plus a little more.

A little bit of sea. A little bit of mountains and a little wilderness. It's Canadian. It's American. And it's totally exhilarating.

When you get together at the Hyatt Regency Vancouver, your convention standards promise never again to be the same.

There are meeting rooms and board rooms, banquet rooms, sample rooms and still more meeting rooms. We offer as much as 15,000 square feet in a single private dining area. Use it all. Or just a portion.

Our meeting rooms and board rooms are more than just meeting rooms and board rooms. They were knowledgeably designed for people who conduct meetings for a living. People in advertising. Public relations. Insurance. People in the stock market. Wholesalers. And retailers.

The Hyatt Regency Vancouver dedicates three complete levels to convention and meeting needs. On the Plaza Level is the Plaza Ballroom with 5,000 square feet of space. Use all 5,000. Or divide the Ballroom into three sections, according to your needs.

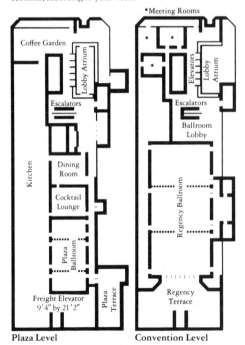

Plaza Level   **Convention Level**

On the Convention Level is a second ballroom. The beautiful and spacious Regency Ballroom. With more than 15,000 square feet of space, it accommodates 1,500 people for a banquet. Or 2,000 people auditorium-style. It, too, divides into three sections.

In addition to the Regency Ballroom and its terrace and foyer, there are three extra meeting rooms, convention offices, or whatever, on the Convention Level. That makes

a grand total of more than 25,000 square feet of meeting space.

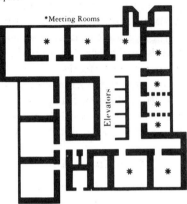

Terrace Level

And on the Terrace Level are seven rooms for displays, meetings or seminars. These rooms, when set up for seminars, will accommodate groups of 75 to 120 people comfortably.

All of the meeting rooms provide the latest audio-visual equipment, and instant-access walls containing a movie screen, chalk and tack boards and ample storage space. They are designed to be used. Thoroughly. And an experienced staff stands ready to make everything run right—from major initial planning through last-second changes.

But in case you think the Hyatt Regency Vancouver is all work, read on.

The spacious lobby is every bit as exciting as the interiors of the famous Hyatt hotels in Atlanta and Chicago. But we have our own Canadian flair. It's the most exciting and airy lobby north of the border.

What's more, there's a cocktail lounge, plus a restaurant called "Truffles" that's a true gourmet's paradise. It sets the tone for some of the most enjoyable dining you'll find on the West Coast. For something lighter, come into the coffee shop that's more than a coffee shop...glassed in from top to bottom, with a sparkling view. Enjoy relaxation in our downstairs bar, that's got a beautiful streetside view of one of Vancouver's busiest thoroughfares. And that's just on the inside. Step outside into a garden, and in the garden, a beautiful outdoor swimming pool.

Also on the outside, our extra elevator, the Polaris, that takes you **34** stories straight up to the Odyssey, a rooftop **supperclub** and cocktail lounge that offers one of the most spectacular vistas on the West Coast...Burrard Inlet, the North Shore mountains, Lions Gate Bridge, Stanley Park ...the works!

Come stay with us—convene with us—at the Hyatt Regency Vancouver. You'll never again have a conventional convention.

Connie Williams - Director of Sales
655 Burrard Street
Vancouver, B. C. V6C 2R7
(604) 687-6543

lacks the ability for later reference. A telegram is fast and relatively inexpensive but must be short and has minimum information. A brochure provides the best reference material but can be costly and slow. A letter is cheaper but contains little information. Each audiovisual means, from recordings to videotape cassettes, has its strengths and weaknesses. The practitioner weighs all factors in exercising his or her choice.

Although the mass media will not normally replace personal invitations, they offer the opportunity for both publicity and advertising, and they serve as excellent reminders.

It is hardly fair, however, to place paid advertising in one medium while soliciting public-service time or space from others. Be consistent.

Compiling the Calendars

Deadline Calendar

No planning is really complete until you have compiled a calendar that works backwards from the date of the event. Give that target date the familiar "D-day" designation and work backwards, beginning the calendar at "D minus 60" or even earlier.

This calendar should be large enough to allow the lettering in of one or more chores for appropriate dates. Many planners put together their own huge wall calendar, with spaces for each date measuring six to eight inches square.

As far as possible, the planner should live by this calendar. If the planner ignores one day's admonitions, he or she may find that duties are piling up and there is no time to fulfill them. Systematic completion of the required chores makes life easier for all concerned.

More manageable versions of this deadline calendar (like 8″ × 10″ sheets for each month) could be supplied to associates and co-workers.

Entries should include such things as securing the facility, lining up program participants, visits with the caterer, organizing program copy, getting copy to the printer, and mailing invitations.

Publicity Calendar

Along with the calendar for program details, many organizations also compile a publicity calendar.

Assume, for example, that the event is a college commencement. The publicity calendar might include such items as preparation of hometown news releases on graduates, securing the speech from the speaker, feature stories on unusual graduates, honors to be awarded, and graduation lists. The wise publicist spreads these out to garner more space and time and to avoid media overload.

This publicity calendar must be coordinated with the deadline calendar, and it should also fit into your overall media plan. You can't ignore everything else just because you are hosting a special event.

Establishing the Budget

Someone has to pay for the special event. It's the rare situation in which management says, "Just run the thing and send us the bill." Even the wealthiest of organizations wants an estimate of costs. The planners must either (1) start with a predetermined amount of money and tailor the expenses to fit, or (2) establish all foreseeable costs and submit a budget for approval.

To structure a budget properly takes experience. Don't be afraid to counsel with others who have run such events and with service personnel at hotels, restaurants, auditoriums, or exhibit halls. They can provide accurate estimates.

All possible costs must be anticipated. Even if tickets are sold, there will be nonpaying guests, and their expenses must be included. The planners must print tickets and programs, provide travel expenses and honorariums, decide on gratuities, and handle such publicity charges as photos and mailings, as well as dozens of other expenses from awards to entertainment. The practitioner should always leave a cushion for the unknown.

Even when the organization pays all the expenses itself—as at a groundbreaking ceremony or an open house—it still needs to know what financial target it is aiming for.

The biggest error is to underestimate costs. Some sponsors with a deep but misplaced faith want to keep ticket prices within the reach of the average person while offering a gourmet spread. They end up remitting the difference. All reasonable costs must be built into the ticket price—or someone must determine in advance how they will be paid.

THE SPEAKER

Every PR person seems to have a specific technique for attracting prominent speakers. Many work through friends; some use speakers' bureaus; others merely contact the person directly.

The first thing to consider is the appropriateness of the speaker to the occasion. Many organizations have committees that help select speakers by collecting information on possible candidates and making recommendations to the chief executive. Prudence should always be exercised, particularly if the sponsoring organization has any religious, philosophical, or political taboos. Don't line up a speaker and then have to renege because something in that person's background makes him or her unacceptable. Check first.

Prominent people who are asked to speak should be approached at least six months in advance of the date. Some popular platform artists may require a full year. If acceptance is tentative, you may want to have a local substitute waiting in the wings.

Many popular speakers have their own agents or are affiliated with speakers' bureaus. One New York bureau has hundreds of America's biggest names in its stable—Dan Rather, Barbara Walters, Mike Wallace, F. Lee Bailey, Dick Clark, Ann Landers, Ed McMahon, Gloria Steinem, David Brinkley, Gary Hart, Jane Pauley, and dozens of other notables. Many carry a hefty price tag, but they also spur attendance and provide an aura of success to the event.

Some organizations react against the paid performer and prefer to work with the gifted amateur (who should also be compensated). Every community has a few local speakers with ability, and others may be located within easy flying or driving distance. Obviously, the demands of the occasion and the extent of the budget influence the options.

The organization's chief executive should issue the speaker's invitation, but the PR planner may want to augment this with a call from a mutual friend. If there are other compelling reasons for the speaker's attendance— such as local ties, alumni status, political gain—use these.

What to Tell the Speaker

Once the speaker accepts the invitation, he or she should be given all the information necessary to ensure a superior performance. These details might include the following:

What is the event? Is this an anniversary, an open house, an awards dinner? Make certain the speaker understands the history of the occasion, its significance, and its character.

Attendance? An estimate of the attendance helps the speaker in the composition of his or her remarks. There is a difference in concept when preparing a speech for a crowd of 1,500 or an intimate assembly of 25 people. It also helps to know who these people are. Male or female, or both? Age? Professions or roles in life?

Past speakers? This detail may not be necessary, but it is sometimes helpful to know what kind of speakers handled this assignment in the past. Particularly when the previous speakers have been a distinguished set, the upcoming speaker may feel appropriately flattered and challenged.

Program? The speaker should be given an outline of the program, detailing other talks, presentations, or entertainment. The main speaker ordinarily concludes the program and may be interested in what precedes the speech.

Length of speech? Although this could be a sensitive issue, there are ways to let the speaker know what time frame you expect. You can tell the speaker that such speeches have averaged 20 to 30 minutes in past years, or merely say that "about 20 to 30 minutes would fit nicely into the program." Make it a suggestion, not a command. A long, windy speech can devastate your event. The setting of limits protects against this.

Taping and press conferences? Common courtesy dictates that the speaker be asked if the speech comments may be taped. The speaker's permission should also be secured for a press conference.

When and where?   The speaker needs to know the time and place of assembly, parking arrangements, and other physical details. If you are located in one of this nation's lesser-known communities, the speaker may welcome information on the best way to get there. Midwesterners are now inured to the fact that coastal residents may telescope their entire region. ("You're from Iowa? Well, I have a cousin in Cleveland.") If the speaker is unfamiliar with the location, spell out travel arrangements. This sort of common sense also applies to communities where there are facilities that sound alike—the Chicago Club, the Greater Chicago Club, the Chicago Athletic Club, and so on. If you anticipate any sort of confusion, take the risk of being explicit.

Honorarium?   To avoid future misunderstandings, it is wise to spell out the financial arrangements. Obviously, expenses should always be covered. An *honorarium* is a sum of money above expenses that is offered as compensation for the speaker's time and talents. The speaker may decline the honorarium, but this should be his or her decision. To a wealthy industrialist or a politician traveling at government expense, such considerations may seem trifling. To a faculty member, or a minor civil servant, or an impecunious artist, the matter is important. The fee should be paid immediately after the event; the expenses may be paid later. Above all, don't leave this detail until after the event and make it an embarrassing point of controversy between host and guest.

Miscellaneous?   The speaker should also be told whether dress is formal or informal, whether his or her spouse is invited, what arrangements have been made for accomodations and for local transportation, background information on the sponsoring organization or institution, names and titles of persons seated at the head table, and anything else that will add to the speaker's understanding and comfort. Finally, don't let the speaker overindulge at the pre-event cocktail party.

What You Need from the Speaker

Planners should ask the speaker to provide them with his or her speech title, a biographical sketch, and a recent photograph. As the event nears, they may also request a draft of the speech that they can use for a news release or that they can reproduce in part or in whole for the attending media.

Ask the speaker if he or she has special needs, such as a screen and slide projector, chalkboard, or other item of equipment.

THE CHAIRPERSON

Every event needs someone who will help it run smoothly. This person bears the title of chairperson, master of ceremonies, toastmaster, or some other appellation. Duties differ depending on whether the event is a luncheon, an outdoor dedication, or an annual meeting of stockholders, but the overall role is the same. The chairperson introduces the various program segments much as a television host presents succeeding acts—but with more class. The chairperson sets the tone, warms up the audience, keeps things flowing.

This responsibility can be the most difficult program assignment. The chairperson must be good, but not too good, and should not normally overshadow the main speaker. He or she must know *everything* that the speaker knows about this event, *plus*:

Rostrum lineup. Since the chairperson handles introductions, he or she needs the list of those seated on the dais or at the head table. The chairperson also needs their titles and, when necessary, the phonetic spelling of difficult names. For example: Eoin (OWE-UN) Mason, President, Willamette (WILL-AM-ET) University. These people should be lined up on a chart according to the seating arrangement so that the chairperson can introduce them in a proper sequence, such as from left to center, then right to center. The audience location should be indicated. The chairperson should also be told who will line up the honored guests in the assembly area for the procession to the rostrum. Normally, the person in charge of the affair—perhaps the public relations director—should handle this duty personally, sparing the chairperson this responsibility.

Dr. Thomas	A
Ms. Ellis	U
Rev. Turner	D
Gov. Reed	I
Mr. Carson	E
Dr. Wright	N
Mrs. Thomas	C
Gen. Dacey	E
Mr. Ellis	

Complete program. Every item on the program, from grace to benediction, from the national anthem to the unveiling, should be given to the chairperson (or M.C. or toastmaster). This includes all speeches and presentations. There should be no surprises and, except in emergency situations, no last-minute changes or additions. Such alterations interfere with the smooth flow of the program. ("Say, Ralph, why don't you call on Chuck Jones for a few words? He's been with the company 43 years. He may not want to say anything, but give it a try.") Introductions from the audience should be kept to a minimum, and program planners should be certain that if they initiate this practice, no one is left unannounced. This is particularly annoying to political figures, and the chairperson may be interrupted by waving hands and shouts from their adherents. ("Hey! You forgot City Councilman Blodget! No, over here!") Unless the planners are sure of the attendance, a safer practice would be to ask all the political leaders to rise in a group for audience applause. Ditto for any other identifiable set, such as former presidents or reunion classes. Entertainment can also be a problem. Should the band play before dinner, during cocktails, during the meal, or after the meal? Should the chorus sing prior to the main address? When do we show the new company film? There is no set formula for answering these questions. As a guide, however, the entertainment should be placed where it fits most naturally, where it provides balance, and where it does not delay the program. The point here is that the chairperson should not have to worry about this segment.

Miscellaneous.   You may wish to pass along to the chairperson any local taboos that could cause embarrassment, any opportunities for humor or personal references (although these are not too helpful to a stranger), or any aspect of the physical setting that may affect his or her performance.

What You Need from the Chairperson

What you need from the chairperson is related to his or her importance. If a local person, you may need only his or her title and the correct spelling of the name. A popular TV or Hollywood star should be treated like the speaker and both a photo and biographical sketch requested.

An exception might occur when the chairperson, although local, is still the main attraction.

PUBLICITY

Some stories on events may be prepared in advance and held for release (by you) at the appropriate time. Since you can anticipate a number of items, having these stories ready may save you grief during the busy period. Each story should be significant, however, and should have a genuinely new slant rather than containing a mere rehash of previous releases.

The announcement story generally comes first. Then, perhaps, a more detailed rundown on the principal speaker. Award winners make a separate story. And even anticipated attendance figures or other details may be legitimate news.

The media are more skeptical of crowd estimates than they used to be. Estimates for political figures are often the most suspect, as are any by those promoting a cause. Attendance at an event in a closed arena is easier to manage, since there is a published seating capacity, but the parade, the rally,

TOURING EXHIBIT REQUIRES DETAILED PLANS

Managing any special event requires continuous attention to detail, but when that event is taken on the road to a number of cities, the duties and the problems multiply.

In 1985, Internorth (now ENRON), a Nebraska-based energy firm, collaborated with Omaha's Joslyn Museum to create, transport, and market an exhibit of paintings by the nineteenth-century Swiss artist Karl Bodmer, along with other related art objects and artifacts, all related to the early American West. The collection was titled, "Views of a Vanishing Frontier," and after opening at the Smithsonian, it toured five American cities. By the time the year was up, some 350,000 people had seen the exhibit, including 3,500 who had attended special exhibit luncheons. Sponsors tallied more than 250 feature articles in national magazines and newpapers and figured that total news coverage across the country amounted to more than two solid hours.

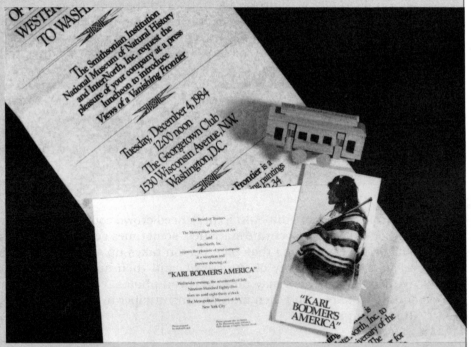

Figure 9-3 When Internorth Inc. took its exhibit of Karl Bodmer's paintings on the road, invitations to special luncheons and receptions took different forms—a traditional card for New York, a long scroll for Washington, D.C., and a press invitation in San Francisco accompanied by a wooden cable car. Courtesy: Enron Corp.

All this required planning.

While appropriate people were working on technical aspects, such as organizing the displays or assembling dioramas or attending to crating and arranging transportation, public relations specialists were contacting the museums that would host the exhibit, reminding them that the show must be noncommercial, and discussing with them the responsibilities for promotion and promotional materials.

In general, the local museums handled local promotion, aided by materials from Internorth's PR department. Included in these materials were a press kit, an exhibit catalog, a selection of posters, a portfolio of reproductions, a gallery guide, and a promotional brochure. Planners also designed banners and produced videotapes of varying lengths, allowing for an introduction by the host museum. Maps, a teachers' handbook, a slide program, and discussion outlines were part of an educational package.

There were local receptions, personal invitations to shareholders living in host cities, and even time for the company's financial-relations personnel to talk with brokerage houses in the same cities.

Preview breakfasts were scheduled for prominent educators, and one city used the occasion to launch a Community Day, which attracted 5,000 people. Planning even contemplated possible inclement weather and provided rain checks.

As the response grew, small knapsacks with materials from Indian reservations were added to the teaching tools, and the sale of reproductions exceeded expectations.

For the museum and its corporate partner, the touring exhibit was a real coup, but it succeeded because of the extent and concern accorded the smallest detail.

the protest are more difficult. Experienced crowd counters devise their own methods of getting accurate statistics, sometimes getting a blueprint of the mall or street, figuring that each person takes up six or eight square feet, calculating the density of the crowd, and then applying the appropriate mathematics. Others may take overhead photos, count those in a certain square-foot area, and then multiply this number by the total number of the units occupied.

POTENTIAL PROBLEMS

Working with Volunteers

Before the practitioner recruits any volunteers to assist with special events, he or she should be certain that there are specific tasks for them to accomplish. Planners should determine their own needs well in advance, then secure good, reliable people to handle the assignments.

Directions to volunteers should be complete and explicit, and the planners should conduct periodic checks on their progress. It helps to delegate authority, but someone—probably the public relations planner—must coordinate the overall effort.

One caution: Don't overload yourself with volunteers whose eagerness to serve (but with nothing to do) becomes a burden.

Whenever possible, volunteer efforts should be publicly recognized and rewarded. No volunteer should fail to receive thanks from the chairperson within a few days of the end of the event.

Registration

No one likes to register for a meeting or conference. Even waiting in line to sign your name at a funeral can seem endless. Consequently, the experienced person in special events makes this exercise as painless as possible.

Once again, prior planning is the key. Conference delegates, for example, should be encouraged to register in advance. Perhaps a discount might be allowed for early-bird registrants. When the delegate arrives, his or her kit should be ready, containing program, meal tickets, name tag, and other materials.

Many cities find the local chamber of commerce helpful in providing personnel and typewriters for the registration desk. It may also supply name tags. In any event, there should be sufficient people assigned to registration to make it run efficiently and to allow for occasional breaks. Someone familiar with the overall conference should be available at all times to respond to such difficult questions as the following:

"Can I get a refund on my dinner ticket? I'm staying with my cousin."
"May I bring a guest to hear the president?"
"Where do I store these exhibits?"

Locate the registration desk close to the normal flow of traffic, but with sufficient room to operate effectively.

If you have to make change, have a cash drawer and plenty of coins and small bills. Also have handout materials, city maps, convention papers, a bulletin board for messages, and any other items that aid the process.

Name tags should be typed as large as possible or neatly handlettered. Don't forget their purpose. You might, in fact, encourage wearers to place them on their right sides rather than the traditional left. In this way, your eyes go naturally to the name tag during a handshake, and you avoid the embarrassment of craning your neck to read a name you should have remembered.

All registration policies—single-meal admissions, reentry checks, refunds—should be established in advance and publicized to eliminate rude haggling with guests.

Decorations

Decorations are a good job for an imaginative and dedicated committee. If the event has some theme, this helps. If not, the planning committee may want to invent an appropriate one. Decorations may involve flowers, table favors, wall hangings, lighting effects, napery, and even elaborate items like false ceilings, trellis gates, and live fountains.

Naturally, there are specialists in decorations. The party planners may do this, or interior decorators, or, for the do-it-yourself practitioner, there are services that suggest items for all occasions. For a fall event, they might propose an Oktoberfest, complete with steins, beer-barrel centerpieces, German flags and posters, Tyrolean hats, cutout beer-garden figures, balloons, colorful vests, and dozens of other items. A Western Chuckwagon Roundup features Stetson hats, cotton bandanas, aprons, sheriff's badges, toy guns, fake saloon fronts, reward posters, and sets of famous-place signs.

Imaginative organizations have transformed their local halls into Irish villages, French art colonies, or turn-of-the-century casinos. These innovations can be expensive and need to be worked into the budget. Happier still is the use of facilities that are so innately attractive that they require no adornment.

Select a motif, establish a budget, appoint a committee—that's the way to start. This committee should be allowed ample time and funds to complete its work, keeping in mind that much of the decorating may be left until the day of the event. If left in place too long, decorations can be torn, become dusty, or otherwise deteriorate.

If flags are used, be sure the committee chairperson understands the protocol for placement of the American flag and other standards. In general, the American flag is placed to the right of the audience if on the floor and to stage right (audience left) if displayed on the stage. Posting and hanging procedures should be checked with some local military unit.

What goes up must come down, and that certainly is true of decorations. If donors want to save certain items—such as school colors or a company banner—someone should be on hand to retrieve them. If they want to make gifts of the floral arrangements, there should be procedures for carrying this out. Unless some person or persons look after these details, the decorations will be discarded. The best solution is to have the same committee responsible for putting up and striking the decorations. The latter task is less fun but will save future headaches.

Food and Drink

If the person in charge is a gourmet cook or connoisseur of fine wines, that's a plus. Short of these gustatory abilities, however, it pays to read, to profit from experience, to meet early with the caterer, and to use a little imagination.

The type of function may be a determining factor. A formal dinner suggests a formal menu; for an open house or an anniversary, punch, coffee, and cake may suffice.

The theme may also suggest a menu. If the gathering is an annual Saint Andrew's Scottish Banquet and you can't come up with haggis, how about "Angus beef wi' skirlie and marled greens wi' trimmings," which translates into roast beef and and salad. Many a March 17 table features corned beef and cabbage, despite the fact that it is not really a traditional Irish dish. And a Santa Lucia Festival would be unthinkable without pasta. There are many ethnic, regional, and commemorative reasons for certain bills of fare, and some fund-raising events have even set out a sparse Third-World meal to remind guests of the cause they espouse.

Menus should be tastefully selected and tastefully printed or written. A gift for describing food in colorful prose is a plus. Here's a menu from a restaurant-association dinner:

Soup en Grouté
Fresh garden vegetables with barley
and beef in beef consommé with puff pastry

Salad
Tossed Romaine, spinach, and iceberg lettuce
with a tarragon vinegar dressing, garnished
with toasted almonds and mandarin oranges

Entrée
Roast tenderloin on a bed of wild rice, marchand sauce,
with seafood kabob and julienne zucchini and carrots in
a sweet basil sauce and fruit garnish

Dessert
Cocoa Cinnamon Supreme

The budget, as always, is a factor. Very seldom is the sky the limit. This calls for consultation with the caterer and the selection of a menu that meets both taste and price. Sometimes you can improve an ordinary meal by including a clever dessert or some innovative preparation. The day is past when luncheons for women inevitably consisted of chicken in a patty shell and luncheons for men featured roast beef, mashed potatoes, and peas. Guests expect a little more. Many want to avoid heavy luncheons, and luncheon desserts are often eliminated.

Since this is a specialized area, expert opinion—such as that of the catering or banquet manager—should be enlisted.

The number of guests affects food to a considerable degree. Serving steak to 500 people is difficult, because some of the steaks must be "held" and kept hot. This could result in their being dry or too well done. For large numbers, fowl is easier to handle, cold appetizers should supplant hot ones like soup, and potatoes make a better choice than peas or carrots.

A caterer can pass along numerous other tips. If you absolutely must have beef, then ask the caterer how you can serve prime ribs (or other cuts) to this huge gathering without ruining the entree. The caterer will probably suggest that all get their meat medium in this instance. He or she may also dictate a choice of vegetables and help assemble a balanced menu.

Such decisions may seem far from the managerial aspects of public relations, but they are nevertheless important. *Someone* has to worry about them. Someone, too, must supply the hotel or convention center with an estimate of attendance. Crowd estimates may be plus or minus 10 percent in many situations, but the planners should be certain the facility managers approve of such arrangements. Otherwise the event chairperson will be charged for the estimated number even though fewer show up.

Planners must discuss with the caterer how gratuities will be handled, how wine will be served, whether dishes will be cleared before the program begins, where the kitchen is located (in case you must hunt up some tardy entrees), and other facets that involve the caterer's services.

When you are planning a cocktail party or a cocktail hour, adequate personnel and space should be secured. Opt for professional bartenders. Willing volunteers often spill more than they save, ineptly mix drinks, or tend to be overgenerous with friends. Professionals are worth their pay, and they look a lot better.

Locate the bars in a place where the attendees have room to move, and if dinner is to follow, consider the proximity to the dining facility. Establish some method of payment—cash, tickets, or free bar. If a free bar, set time limits, not out of economy but to reduce the temptation to overimbibe.

If the sponsors plan to supply their own liquor, this detail should be cleared with the hotel or restaurant. Some do not permit such substitution or, if they do, they may impose a corkage fee.

Occasionally, a party will feature only wine and cheese. Others have just a few drink choices. If this works, it makes things easier and more economical, but most cocktail parties must offer a more extensive choice. Bourbon, scotch, gin, rum, and vodka are musts, with wine and beer by the container. Since trends also affect drinking, today's parties may stock wine coolers and after-dinner libations.

Most planners figure on about two drinks per person, and they know a quart bottle supplies from 30 to 32 drinks, so they can estimate the amount of liquor required. Simple or elaborate hors d'oeuvres may be served, and, again, there is a trend toward less-fattening and more-healthful snacks.

If you supply the bar, remember that some liquor may be left over. If it is not claimed, the hotel personnel may confiscate it for themselves or the hotel. You paid for it, so you should claim it to use for future parties or hospitality suites.

Table Arrangements

There seems to be no standard book of etiquette for table arrangements at banquets. There are, however, some goals to be met. Head tables should locate guests in order of importance, should be functional in terms of program participants, and should present a pleasing image to the audience.

The more important the guest, the closer he or she sits to the center. Husbands and wives are usually separated, and it is unwise to cluster any group, such as three clergymen or three admirals or four women.

If the number at the head table is uneven, the chairperson usually occupies the center chair, with the main speaker or honored guest on the chairperson's right and the organizational president or other dignitary on his or her left. If the table has an even number, the chairperson will usually be on the left and the speaker to the right of center. From then on, the list moves left and right according to position or title, remembering that you want to spread out spouses and not bunch up look-alikes—religious, military, and the like.

Planners find it helpful to put the names of head-table guests on 3″ × 5″ cards and then shift them around until they arrive at a suitable arrangement. Then the final seating chart can be made.

Figure 9-4 Tables should be arranged for comfort, efficiency, and ease of seeing and hearing the program.

Avoid a long head table. Just scanning these huge tables is enough to tire an audience. For most occasions, ten to 15 people are enough. When there are many honored guests, two head tables may be set, one below the other. In this case, the top table has precedence.

Legible place cards should be located by each plate, and these should be checked right before the meal to make certain they are matched correctly with the seating chart. There is a tendency to mix left and right when setting the cards, and that leaves the chairperson in the awkward position of looking left when introducing someone on his or her right.

Floral arrangements at the head table should fit the theme, if any, and should not obscure the guests.

Normally, head-table guests will be asked to report to a specific room, preferably near the dining area. After the other guests have been seated, these persons must be lined up in keeping with the seating chart. They then progress into the dining room, with the person seated at the far end of the table leading.

Before this entourage is given the go-ahead, make a final check to see that their route is unimpeded. Someone may have locked a door or moved a table since you last checked. Also, tape down any electrical cords that could be hazardous. And be on hand to assist head-table guests if the dais is too high. This procedure may be required only for the elderly or for women wearing long dresses.

It is a good practice to arrange with a few people, scattered throughout the dining area, to begin the applause when the head-table guests march in. Otherwise the audience may be occupied in conversation, and the honorees are ushered in sans recognition. Such applause also helps alert the crowd to the fact that the program is about to begin.

Try to avoid platforms that are too high or too narrow. Guests will appear ungainly trying to master the tall step, and when not enough seating space has been provided, guests may push back their chairs and summarily disappear. Besides causing confusion, such accidents could lead to legal action.

As soon as the head-table guests have found their places, the chairperson should take over. If the first few items on the agenda naturally tie together, the chairperson must verbally coordinate them. It looks clumsy, for example, to have the audience stand as the head-table guests come in, then sit, then be asked to rise for the invocation, then sit, then be asked to rise for the advancement of the colors. It would be simpler to move directly to the podium and say: "Would you please stand (or remain standing) for the invocation and for the advancement of the colors that follows?" If they need direction at the end of this pageantry, ask them to please be seated.

A buffet dinner, which is visually appetizing, creates a special problem. Most chairpersons find it advantageous to have the head table served rather than struggle through the food line. And the invocation should be given, perhaps, when some of the guests are seated and others are still in line.

Otherwise the early eaters will be finished a long time before you pronounce the grace before meals. Just say, "Will those of you who are seated remain seated and those of you in line just remain standing for the invocation by————.''

Media Table

Arrangements for the media may not be necessary, but if sponsors elect to invite them as guests, they should provide a table, appropriately designated, and located (1) close enough to the head table to permit easy access to photos, and (2) close enough to an exit to allow early departure to meet deadlines.

If there is live coverage of an event, there may be the added problem of camera placement. Put the cameras where they can get the best and most varied shots without intruding too much on audience comfort. After the members of the decorating committee get used to the cameras interfering with their virgin decor, they will find that these cameras add excitement to the proceedings.

The media may be provided with press kits on this occasion or may have received them at an earlier press conference. If the program features someone who is newsworthy, the media are not going to be satisfied with a news release and speech copy. They will want to interview this person.

If some of the media show up and others do not, the publicity chairperson should deliver some sort of news release to the absentees—or, at least, to the wire services that feed their newsrooms.

Exhibits

Exhibits are of two major kinds—those from entrepreneurs who purchase booth space to display their wares, and those consisting of voluntary exhibits that may be part of a competition.

For the former, be sure you allocate adequate space in a readily accessible area, with good lighting and sufficient electrical outlets. Be sure, too, that you charge enough to cover costs and that you do not locate fierce competitors next to one another. A sensible procedure here would be to check with someone locally who has experience with exhibits and ask this person the tough questions about booth sizes and equipment, assembly time, various charges, and the like.

You may sometimes be involved in preparing a traveling exhibit, or a permanent one, for your own firm or clients. This requires a solid idea, one that will involve a transient audience; adequate planning and financing; a knowledge of fabrication, illumination, and installation; perhaps copywriting and photography skills; a consideration of transportation and security; and even a concern for temperature and humidity at the site. Normally, the public relations person would be instrumental only in the design concept stage and, perhaps, in the writing phase. Construction is probably handled by experts. But the problems of transportation, placement, and security would then fall back on the PR staff.

Exhibits to be judged can also be a headache. Many arrive at the last minute and must be uncrated, carried to the exhibit area, and tastefully displayed. When the meeting concludes, all exhibitors should know that any materials they fail to remove will be scrapped. Don't get into the hassle of mailing back tons of brochures, pamphlets, slides, and TV cassettes. Once again, visiting with someone who has suffered through this routine will spare you hours of agony.

Security

For large gatherings, you may want to hire the services of law officers for crowd control. Members of the fire department could also be on hand. Such officials should be unobtrusive and, perhaps, in civilian clothes—except where the uniform is intended as a deterrent.

Sometimes you have no options on security. If your main speaker is the president of the United States or another key government spokesperson, the matter of security may be taken out of your hands. Secret Service personnel will tell you what they require, and you must comply. Their dictates could change exit and entry plans, decorations, and other items.

For such political VIPs, clearance will be necessary for media representatives, transportation provided for traveling reporters, extra typewriters and electric outlets arranged for, media kits prepared, and you could even be involved to an extent in airport and parade-route security. Having distinguished national leaders appear at a function may garner publicity and boost the corporate image, but it also causes many special problems for planners.

DETAILS AND CHECKLISTS

Many other aspects of special events must also be considered. Ushers for special tables, for example; ticket takers; parking—including reserved spaces for special guests; accounting procedures; local recreational opportunities for convention spouses; hotel accommodations; and perhaps baby-sitting availabilities.

Chairpersons could be faced with the problem of an unruly member of the audience, possibly as the result of too long a cocktail hour. Rather than cause a scene, some chairpersons tolerate such rude conduct, hoping it will go unnoticed. They should not. Obnoxious guests make the evening a disaster for the speaker and the audience. Arrange for a few people to see that the offender is gently but firmly ushered out.

Avoid interrupting the program with announcements about car lights left on and similar diversions. Summoning physicians used to be a necessary chore, but today's electronic beepers make this obsolete.

Drawings for prizes can also be a drag. Put some lively person in charge of this, along with an assistant who can dispense gifts rapidly. Don't continue to repeat numbers that go unanswered. Move on. Keep the number of prizes within reason, and save the best for last.

Another awkward moment can arrive when the dining room has to be cleared for dancing and the chairperson is obliged to announce to an entire section that they must depart for the bar or corridor while their tables are being removed. If at all possible, reserve another room for dancing, or set the dining room cabaret style. The same principle applies to eating and meeting rooms—keep them separate.

Entertainment may enliven the evening, but it can also kill it. Keep it short unless it is the main feature. Some amateur choral groups, for example, may not know when to quit, and they will go through their entire repertoire. Caution them about time limits and, if you can, catch their rehearsal to see if they are conforming. One courageous chairperson, faced with an organ duo consisting of players who were notorious for performing beyond their welcome, simply pulled their plugs after 20 minutes! Be certain entertainers are properly lit and miked, and work out cues in advance. Finally, fit them into the program effectively so that you avoid paying scale to musicians who are merely sitting around waiting to perform.

It bears repeating that all mechanical details should be constantly checked. After you have placed the awards by the lectern, the head waiter removes them. Some oaf kicks out the slide-projector plug. A waitress adjusts the screen. The lectern bulb blows. The microphone whistles. Even after you check, a fuse can still malfunction or a film break, but planners must anticipate as many failures as possible.

There are a number of checklists available for special events. Crain Communications Inc., publishers of *Advertising Age, Advertising & Sales Promotion,* and *Industrial Marketing,* publishes periodical "Business Meeting Selector" inserts that contain both checklists and articles. Hotels and organizations sometimes reproduce their checklists. An extremely comprehensive "Checklist to End All Checklists," consisting of 16 pages and several hundred entries, appeared in the May 1972 issue of *Public Relations Journal,* and *pr reporter, Communication Briefings,* and other trade publications have contributed their lists.

A MINI CHECKLIST FOR SPECIAL EVENTS

A. *Purpose*? Goals?   B. *Audience*? Interests?
   Working plan   How to reach
   Coordinator   How to prepare

C. *Date*
Relatively clear of conflict?
Reasonable in terms of
preparation?
Appropriate?

D. *Facility*
Type
Location
Image
Staff
Transportation to and from
Nearby entertainment;
in-house amenities
Restaurants
Guest rooms
Meeting rooms
Sound level
Any complimentary rooms for
guests?
Method of payment?
Any other groups in hotel?
Decoration or table-
arrangment needs

E. *Promotion*
Invitations
Publicity
Radio and TV interviews; news
conferences
Posters
Public-service announcements
Marquees and billboards
Advertising

F. *Registration*
Advance or at door?
Personnel
Cash drawer
Information kits
Name tags
Direction signs
Potential problems?

G. *Equipment*
Ashtrays, wastebaskets, pens,
pencils

Scissors, glue, staplers, paper
clips
Stationery, news release
forms, scratch pads, labels
Typewriters, phones,
sufficient outlets
Pointers, shovels (for
groundbreaking), lecterns
Etc.

H. *Printed Materials*
Signs
Programs
Menus
Awards and citations
Placecards

I. *Volunteers*
Number needed? Duties?
Supervision?
Cost?

J. *Audiovisual Materials*
Power supply
Screens
Tape recorders, slide and film
projectors, TV monitors
Videotape recorders
Cassettes, slides, films
Photo coverage
Special audiovisual needs?

K. *Food and Drink*
Available menus
Number of meals and
anticipated attendance
Cuisine
Any dietary, ethnic, or
religious problems?
Number of waiters
Gratuities
Hors d'oeuvres
Bar locations
Liquor required
Bartenders
Purchase system for drinks?

L. *Guests and Speakers*
How invited, and when?
Transportation needs
Accommodations
Welcome
Honoraria
Copies of speeches; any
   problems?

M. *Entertainment*
Type, placement, and timing
Equipment and staging needs
Union regulations
Dance band and dance floor?
Recorded music?
Special musical needs—
   national anthem, school
   song?
Contracts and costs

N. *Exhibits*
Space
Charges
Shipping
Solicitation of and judging
Lost pieces?
Return?

O. *Security*
Police and fire fighters
Ushers and staff members
Health personnel
Insurance

P. *Miscellaneous*
Activities for spouses
Notes for review and evaluation
Budget by events and total
Checkrooms; assembly room
   for head table

The PR planner should devise a personal list to fit the event, checking with some of the standard lists in making the catalog of items. A shortened version combining ideas contained on many lists appears as an insert in this chapter.

MEETINGS

Some linguists claim that the most beautiful words in the English language, phonetically, are "cellar door." There are those who would argue that the most beautiful words are, "The meeting has been canceled."

As a nation, we seem to be mad about attending meetings. With no problem at all, the average American can tie up three or more nights and an equal number of luncheons a week. Some meetings are productive; most are not. There is a significant amount of wasted effort and time, poor organization, weak leadership, trivial agendas, and restless membership.

More planning should go into meetings. In the first place, they should have a specific goal, or they should be postponed until there is something worthwhile to discuss. If you are placed in charge of a meeting—as may often happen—make sure there are some teeth in the agenda. If possible, send the agenda out to members in advance. Give them a chance to study it. You might even add some special readings as a homework assignment. This way, people will be primed for discussion.

Put someone in charge of the meeting who will move things along. This takes skill and tact. You don't want this person to appear authoritarian, but you need someone who can summarize, proceed speedily toward votes, cut off senseless discussion.

Also, pick a suitable meeting place where speakers can be seen and heard and where members feel free to participate. Hot, crowded conditions make for a surly audience, and even the most reasonable proposals may be shot down.

Despite the obvious shortcomings and the myriad quips about meetings, they are one of the most preferred means of communication, next to face-to-face sessions with one or two individuals. There are numerous complaints that these meetings contain too much top-down information and not enough upward communication from employees or members.

Xerox public relations staffers contend that meetings not only provide clues to employee thinking but also humanize company executives. At Chase Manhattan Bank in New York, every exec who can make it (including out-of-town visitors) attends a Friday meeting to exchange ideas and to listen to speakers discuss financial topics. A weekly newsletter extends news of these meetings to other Chase Manhattan offices around the world. At Pitney Bowes, they post the minutes of their bimonthly departmental meetings.

Corporate meetings like this will be most successful when thoroughly planned, probably by the PR officer or by employees assigned this task, and when they involve a real commitment by management to listen and to act. Often the participatory meeting is seen as a gimmick to provide the illusion of democracy, whereas the decision makers are not prepared to be open and flexible. They may not have any procedure for assimilating and implementing the ideas proposed. The practitioner performs a definite service when he or she counsels management about the necessity for actual reflective attention. The executive must participate, not manipulate, and the PR person helps get this attitude accepted.

Meetings should not be used as a substitute for doing something concrete. Neither should they be burdened by problems beyond the scope and control of the members. When properly organized, correctly chaired, and adequately informed, attendees may be very helpful, especially in solving somewhat complex and controversial problems, and, in the process, they will make a stronger commitment to the eventual solution.

There are also sales meetings, some of which are more glitter than substance, and so-called marketing meetings where prospects for certain services are invited to special seminars, often at a reasonable fee, and while being informed, are subtly sold on the sponsoring firm.

Even public relations agencies conduct their own meetings. Practitioners Bob Dorf and Alex Stanton ask:

> How often do we carve out time in our hectic schedules to share new ideas with others in our management group? How often does management exchange ideas with employees? And how often do we provide clerical and professional staffers

an opportunity to learn from one another? Probably infrequently at best. One way to overcome this chronic neglect of the "shoemaker's children" is through professional development seminars.[3]

Dorf and Stanton's agency meets away from the office, presenting a state-of-the-company address and seminars of specific interest to employees. They counsel advance planning (at least two months), having something for everyone, using outside speakers, and holding the meetings at regular yearly intervals.

With executives spending between 50 and 75 percent of their time in meetings, many companies are opting for teleconferencing, although some face-to-face meetings are still required, because the human dimension adds to the meeting. Since information exchange rather than decision making characterizes most meetings, the electronic system may be satisfactory, and it is certainly easier on personnel and the budget. These sessions may utilize audio only; audio plus some graphics; one-way video permitting only the presenters to talk; two-way video, allowing for audience response; multilocation video, with cameras and monitors set up in a number of sites and cities; or computer teleconferencing, in which the compatible computers are linked.

Boeing, Exxon, the American Bar Association, the American Dairy Association, and the American Medical Association use teleconferencing. So do Aetna, Atlantic Richfield, and many of the major hotel chains. Merrill Lynch employed the technique to brief its representatives on new tax laws, and 3M instructed its sales force on its new marketing plans via teleconferencing. The state of Alaska, handicapped by distances between cities, uses the method for education, and the Catholic Telecommunications Network of America brought together, via satellite, some of the top authorities on nuclear disarmament. Continental Airlines reached more than 200 commercial stations with a satellite-aided telecast following a "60 Minutes" segment on the carrier's safety record.[4]

Miscellaneous Meeting Tips

A knowledge of parliamentary procedure is a help. You may not want to invoke Robert's Rules of Order at every opportunity, since this may cow some members and irritate others. When things threaten to get out of hand, however, parliamentary procedure can be used to restore discipline.

Always announce meetings well in advance, and if time and numbers permit, use a calling committee for last-minute reminding. If you know that the agenda will not require extended discussion, you should set some target hour for dismissal and work toward it.

Be familiar with each association's bylaws and constitution, particularly sections that describe the number of mandatory meetings, the attendance required to constitute a quorum, and similar items.

Table 9-1 Parliamentary rules at a glance.

Motions	Purpose	Vote Required	Requires a Second	Debatable	Amendable	May Interrupt Speaker
Privileged Motions (arranged from bottom to top in order of precedence)						
Adjourn to specific time	To set time of next meeting	Majority	Yes	No	Yes	No
Adjourn	To end meeting	Majority	Yes	No	No	No
Recess	To dismiss meeting for specific length of time	Majority	Yes	No	Yes	No
Question of privilege	To make request during debate	Majority	No	No	No	Yes
Special order of business	To force consideration at a specified time	2/3	Yes	Yes	Yes	No
Call for orders of the day	To force consideration of a postponed motion	None; 2/3 to postpone	No	No	No	Yes
Incidental Motions (no order of preference)						
Appeal decision of chair	To reverse decision of chair	Majority	Yes	No	No	Yes
Call for division of house	To get accurate vote		No	No	No	Yes
Point of order	To correct parliamentary error	Decision of chair	No	No	No	Yes
Object to consideration	To suppress consideration	2/3	No	No	No	Yes
To suspend the rules	To take action contrary to standing rules	2/3	Yes	No	No	No

Subsidiary Motions (arranged from bottom to top in order of precedence)

Lay on table	To defer action	Majority	Yes	No	No	No
Previous question (stop debate)	To force into immediate vote	2/3	Yes	No	No	No
Limit or extend limits of debate	To modify freedom of debate	2/3	Yes	No	Yes	No
Postpone to a definite time	To defer action	Majority	Yes	Yes	Yes	No
Refer to committee	To get information or recommendation	Majority	Yes	Yes	Yes	No
To amend an amendment	To modify amendment	Majority	Yes	Yes	No	No
To amend	To modify a motion	Majority	Yes	Yes	Yes	No
Postpone indefinitely	To kill	Majority	Yes	Yes	Yes	No
Main Motion	To introduce business	Majority	Yes	Yes	Yes	Yes
Main Unclassified Motions						
Take from table	Consider a second time	Majority	Yes	No	No	No
Reconsider	Consider a second time	Majority	Yes	*	No	Yes
Rescind	Consider a second time	2/3	Yes	Yes	Yes	No

*Undebatable when the motion to be amended, reconsidered, or rescinded is undebatable.

SOURCE: This table is based on Robert's Rules of Order.

THOSE OTHER EVENTS

Although we have concentrated primarily on dinner and meeting events, it should be obvious that numerous other events also have their own public relations opportunities and problems.

Plant Tours

Tours of plants or other institutions may be periodic or regular functions. A newspaper, for example, may hire guides to conduct visitors such as schoolchildren through the plant daily. Other institutions may schedule tours only when they open a new facility.

One problem is estimating the number of people who will attend, particularly if the invitations are open to all who want to come. You are uncertain whether to expect 300 or 3,000. This affects such things as parking, in-plant traffic, refreshments, and personnel. Some institutions have minimized this by issuing invitations alphabetically and assigning *suggested* visiting hours to each alphabetical group. When the invitation list is controlled, of course, the problem may disappear.

There is also the question of how the tour will be conducted. Will guides be assigned to groups and take them throughout the plant? Or will the visitors progress from station to station, to be met there by different guides for each locale? Whichever method is used, it is mandatory that the guides and other personnel be thoroughly briefed so that they can respond to any questions. Other considerations include:

- Direction markers and signs
- Parking
- Exhibits
- Safety precautions, such as barriers and glasses
- Special insurance for visitors
- Traffic control—police
- Information kits or brochures
- Souvenirs
- Play area for children
- Area for refreshments
- Cleanup crews before and after tour
- Press coverage

To this list could be added many of the things discussed under banquets, such as speeches, equipment, and the handling of special guests.

A different kind of tour is one that puts a PR person and, perhaps, a client on the road, visiting a planned number of editors and news directors.

The client, who will probably serve as spokesperson, may be an entertainment celebrity, a sports figure, a political hopeful, or a corporate executive. As with everything in PR, planning is the key. A reasonable schedule, enough money (preferably in travelers' checks), sufficient kits and news releases, constant checking with the home office, and accurate lists of the people to be visited—these are essentials. Joan H. Wood of Richard Weiner, Inc., also suggests monitoring local media as you travel, critiquing the spokesperson's presentation, collecting information en route, and keeping the client rested and healthy.[5]

Open House

You could have an open house without a tour, bringing the guests to a central location in the company or institution and presenting a program that would show them some elements of the building. Usually, though, at least a limited tour would be involved.

The main concerns about an open house are to make certain that all who should be invited are invited; that provisions are made for handling different size crowds; that the event moves smoothly, without crowding or confusion; that the purpose of the open house is realized; and that those present have something to take away with them.

Dedication

A key question at any dedication ceremony is the rationale for holding it in the first place. Not every building addition or decorating change calls for a ceremony. Dedications require effort and expenditures; they should be worth it.

When dedications are held, every effort should be made so that the site, the audience, the speakers, and other details will be appropriate to the occasion.

For example, if an air force base were dedicating a new museum featuring military artifacts, you would want an air force band on hand to warm up the crowd and play the national anthem. You would want some top brass on the dais along with government officials and local citizens. The decorations would suit the event, and there might be a red, white, and blue ribbon to be cut at the entrance to the museum.

When Citicorp dedicated its new San Francisco office, company officials and local dignitaries signed the final steel beam before it was hoisted into place. Other firms haul a fir tree to the top of the structure for a "topping off" ceremony. Capsules are buried in cornerstones, containing artifacts from the current period, with hot-air balloons marking the locale and, normally, guided tours of the facility. The trick is to find new—but fitting—ways to handle such special events. Innovations make these occasions memorable instead of dull.

Groundbreaking

Since groundbreaking ceremonies will be held outdoors, weather is a major consideration. Perhaps you will need to rent a large tent or provide wooden pathways across muddy areas. You will have to be certain that the public-address system is keyed to the outdoor needs, including the competition from surrounding sound. You will probably keep the program short. After all, the big moment comes when the first spadeful of dirt is unearthed.

If you can, create a new way of breaking ground. The executives with shovels at the ready is old hat, and so is the gimmick of the president in the tractor cab. A playground dedication had several small children take out the first scoopfuls of dirt with beach pails and shovels. A farm-implement company used a parade of its machinery to dig the dirt. A university hospital employed the oldest living alumnus and a medical-school freshman to perform this chore.

With groundbreaking and all outdoor events, practitioners should consider weather or cancellation insurance, especially when financial losses might be significant. Not every insurance company provides this form of protection, but sponsors should check around until they come up with a reputable firm that writes such coverage.

Anniversaries

As with dedications, not every anniversary is worth commemorating. Greatest attention is given to twenty-fifth, fiftieth, and hundredth anniversaries, with some smaller emphasis placed on dates like the tenth and twentieth and so on.

Some anniversary celebrations run that entire year, but most focus on a limited period, perhaps a week, and confine the events to that time slot. This is more economical and saves wear and tear on the personnel and facilities.

One midwestern university recently reached its hundredth birthday and successfully spread the commemoration over a year by tying into existing events—like ball games and commencement—while encouraging students and faculty to come up with others. The planning committee launched a film, published a history, played host to dozens of seminars, featured several dinners, ran student contests, sold mementos, sponsored a European charter tour, dedicated a new building, and underwrote a series of scholarships. The calendar published each month was full, and the resultant publicity was unusual and continual.

Candy manufacturer Luden's Inc. of Reading, Pennsylvania, maker of 5th Avenue chocolate bars, augmented the usual anniversary dinners and printed materials with a campaign to mount "5TH AVENUE" signs, in the

THE HARTFORD COURANT *CELEBRATES ITS 200TH*

When the *Hartford Courant* began preparations for its bicentennial in 1964, two years were allotted to the planning. The objectives were:

- To commemorate a significant event in history
- To establish clearly the *Courant*'s right to the title of America's oldest newspaper in continuous publication
- To improve the national and statewide image of the paper, with special emphasis on central Connecticut
- To heighten the pride of those who produce and distribute the *Courant*

Dozens of events were scattered through the anniversary year, with many of them calling for detailed and extensive preparation. Among these were:

- Publicaton of a history of the *Hartford Courant*, titled *Older Than the Nation* and written by a Trinity College professor. Four thousand copies were printed.
- Staging of a symposium built around the theme of "the enduring American press" and involving some of the nation's top editors, publishers, and writers. Among the thousand-plus in the audience were journalists and editors from numerous East Coast papers, and teachers and students from a dozen area colleges. A booklet containing the texts of the talks was later printed.
- The evening prior to the symposium, a banquet was held for 500 Connecticut opinion leaders, with Yale's president as speaker.
- Publication of seven special anniversary sections of the newspaper, totaling 312 extra pages, which helped the *Courant* exceed 200,000 circulation for the first time in its history. Nine thousand of these were mailed across the country and abroad, and copies were flown to some 48 editors of major dailies.
- A 12-page booklet in miniature newspaper format, capsulizing the paper's history, was distributed to civic leaders, libraries, schools, advertisers, and the media.
- To supplement its long-time slogan, "Start Every Day Right," the *Courant* added a special anniversary slogan, "Older Than the Nation . . . New as the News." This appeared on stationery, printed materials, calendars, bumper stickers, banners, and the newspaper masthead.
- Employees were given emblem pins with "200" surmounting the paper's name, and paper boys were supplied their own specially designed pins. All employees were invited to a family outing, where 1,200 people found rides, games, food, and door prizes.
- A special cancellation for stamps going through the Hartford post office was used, until a rival newspaper complained and the practice was halted. The newspaper's own stampmeter repeated the anniversary slogan.
- A New England States Exhibition at the 1964–65 World's Fair contained

a blowup of the front page of the first edition of the *Courant*. And three major *Courant* exhibits were located at the Eastern States Exposition and in prominent Hartford display areas.

- Several local and national organizations saluted the *Courant* during 1964, and newspapers, magazines, and radio and television stations carried news stories, features, and interviews that achieved worldwide coverage. The newspaper also purchased some national advertising space.

- One imaginative project involved a horsemen who was to carry a facsimile of the Declaration of Independence to the *Courant*, just as a rider had in 1776. Fourth of July traffic promised to be too dangerous, so a new route had to be laid out. The same message was bounced off a Telstar satellite and picked up by a Dataphone machine in the *Courant* lobby. The horseman, attired in Colonial garb, timed the ride to appear in front of the *Courant* offices at exactly 3:00 P.M. on the Fourth, where a fife and drum band greeted him.

A budget of $30,000 was allocated to the anniversary, and it was not spent completely. Of course, some of the events were hosted by others, and a number of items (the special sections, some giveaway items, hours of volunteer labor) were not figured in the cost. At the same time, two anniversary editions, which included advertising, realized over $100,000 more than comparable editions the preceding year.

The events were all run in-house; the *Courant* had considered the offer of help from a local public relations firm but had decided to go it alone.

Courtesy: Bob Eddy, retired editor and publisher, *The Hartford Courant*, who planned and directed this program.

candy-wrapper colors, above the "5TH STREET" markers in downtown Reading. Company officials gathered support of merchants, political leaders, and area residents, provided the signs, decorated invitations with a reproduction of the candy bar, and distributed mini-bars to those attending the name-change ceremony. In addition to achieving the goal of solidifying community support, the company reaped far-reaching publicity.

On its seventy-fifth anniversary, Pace University in New York City commissioned a special logo; published a history of the school; tied in existing cultural events, like a performance by the Joffrey II Ballet company; and had students duplicate old university building portraits, taking photos from the same vantage points decades later.

When the James Bay Energy Corporation of Montreal marked its tenth anniversary, employees were invited to fly free to the worksite of their choice, to enter a golf tournament, to enjoy an exhibit of painting and sculptures by other employees, and to attend a brunch on the anniversary date. A film festival featuring company productions during the decade ran twice weekly, and memo pads and pens bearing the new logo and slogan were distributed to all workers, along with calendars incorporating key dates.

Conventions

Some 25 – 30 million Americans attend conventions annually, and they spend in excess of $15 billion. In addition, more than 6,000 organizations spend over $400 million annually in convention expenses. That's the major reason why attracting conventions is a prime goal for communities of any size in the United States.

Most organizations look for a locale that includes all the advantages and amenities mentioned earlier in this chapter, but sites may vary from the metropolitan centers and resorts and include Caribbean cruise ships or Mississippi stern-wheelers.

Planning for a convention may be a massive responsibility, especially for large groups. Getting people to and from the convention site, reserving sufficient numbers of rooms, building a program that pleases a majority of delegates, calculating menu requirements and head count, providing adequate entertainment opportunities—all these and a hundred other details give PR planners fits. Someone has to promote the event, see to concurrent publicity, babysit some of the guests, oversee photo coverage, get the tons of printed materials completed and delivered.

Conventions are exciting for those attending, but most of the practitioners involved derive their reward from the happy departure of the guests.

Miscellaneous Events

Only the imagination limits the number and kind of events that may be scheduled. New products are sometimes launched amid a carnival setting at a local mall. Lorimar Productions took its popular TV show, "Dallas," to the public, employing a traveling van packed with memorabilia from the series. The mobile museum, constructed at a cost of $100,000, tours shopping centers across the country.

A presentation is also an event, an occasion when a PR firm pitches an account. Bozell and Jacobs, making a bid for a large airline's advertising account, reconstructed the airline's board room so they could rehearse the meeting perfectly before the event. These sessions come at the conclusion of many weeks or months of research and creativity and are tense gatherings, especially for the presenters. There must be substance, sufficient excitement, graphics, and a careful choice of words, and, even though the event is highly organized and expertly staged, there must also be a sense of sincerity and commitment. Clients want to know who the people are who will work on their public relations account and what they can do to improve image and sales.

There are sports luncheons to kick off a season, emergency board meetings to tackle a crisis, annual assemblies of shareholders, class reunions, fashion shows—all different, all somehow the same, demanding careful planning and attention to detail.

Sponsored Events

Corporate sponsorship of events, from jazz festivals to the Olympic Games, has become an $850 million industry. Special-event sponsorship, or event marketing, links a product or service to a leisure pursuit—usually in sports or the arts. Sponsorship allows a company to target demographic groups and communicate with them on common ground—participation in the event. While communication through advertising tends to be one-sided, events create opportunities for two-way communication between consumers and sponsors—a powerful tool for persuasion.[6]

One thinks of STP and auto racing, Wheaties and athletics, Mobil and the arts. Dairies may sponsor Little League, Virginia Slims promotes a tennis tourney for women, Volvo is identified with the Grand Prix circuit, Fleischmann's is into cross-country skiing. We find Colgate-Palmolive engaged in sponsorship of sports competition in all 60 of the countries where its products are sold, and Clairol places on tour an exhibit featuring mother-and-child paintings. Companies and organizations are into marathons, bike races, concerts (including rock concerts), artistic competitions, public-television specials, award banquets, and other events. They use them to focus on a new, related product, or to sustain an image, or to win community acceptance. Obviously, there should be some relevance to the firm's choice of activity, and the tie-in shouldn't be blatantly commercial. Moreover, the corporation must know it can afford the event and that it can do a good job with it. Failure is expensive and damaging to reputations.

A Final Note

Always have a "Plan B" to replace your original plan if something goes wrong. And this alternate plan should be as well thought out as the original—just in case a snowstorm clogs the parking lot, or the groundbreaking is rained out, or the main speaker is circling O'Hare. Try to anticipate all possible emergencies. This is one way to prevent their ever occurring!

Assemble procedure books for each special event, listing the duties of everyone involved. Include sample letters, programs, checklists, citations, and any other information that will make things easier for your successor.

Many organizations provide such books to new officers or new branches. They are essential for continuity and efficiency.

And once an event is concluded, conduct an evaluation of it, using, perhaps, forms distributed to guests or delegates, soliciting their appraisal of speakers, program, accommodations, and other details. Planners can determine whether events ran smoothly, whether they started and finished on time, whether they remained within the budget, and whether they were properly publicized and adequately attended. What the sponsors want to find out is whether it was all worthwhile and how they might improve future events.

SPEECHMAKING

The writing of a speech is one possible public relations duty, but you might also be called upon to deliver a speech yourself. Now that you know how to write one, the delivery shouldn't be all that bad. If you need help or encouragement, join a group like Toastmasters, or take some speech courses at a nearby college. You don't have to become a skilled orator, but having the ability to make a decent presentation is a great asset.

Ordinarily, a speech is communication and not a performance. Your job is to convey information, not to dazzle the audience with style or extraneous tricks. Enthusiasm masks a lot of deficiencies. Listen to someone with deep convictions, solid content, and a firm, honest delivery, and you will forgive things like a weak voice or awkward manner. If the speaker believes in the message, the audience will probably follow.

Every speech requires thorough preparation. At least three rehearsals should be arranged, duplicating actual conditions as much as possible. Reading a speech quietly in a recliner doesn't simulate the later experience. It isn't necessary to memorize the text, but you should be comfortable with it, marking places where you need to pause or to pronounce or emphasize correctly. You needn't have the thing by rote, but you should be able to work free of the manuscript at times.

Even expert speakers must deal, occasionally, with stage fright. The feeling is natural, and it can be controlled. Rehearsal and practice are assets, and so is a realistic assessment of the situation. Your career will not be over if you don't match Kennedy's inaugural address. You must appear relaxed, look the audience in the eye (perhaps selecting one or two of the most interested and friendly faces), concentrate on the message, pause if you get addled, and never mention that you are nervous. Some experts suggest a balanced stance, gesturing to relieve tenseness, and even a few steps on stage before speaking, to eliminate trembling knees.

There are also aids a speaker can rely on. Jim Westberry, president of a Dallas communication group, suggests three techniques:

- Live video projection
- Magazine format
- Dramatic reinforcement[7]

The live projection gives an audience a closeup look at the speaker on a large screen; the magazine format surrounds the speaker with interrelated graphics that allow him or her to move easily from subject to subject, like turning pages. Dramatic reinforcement could be anything from taped interviews to slides, film, or video. Although these add dramatic effect and perhaps a certain comfort level, they also give the speaker something else to think about, and something else that could break down. Audiovisual adjuncts condense the delivery of information and help audiences remember

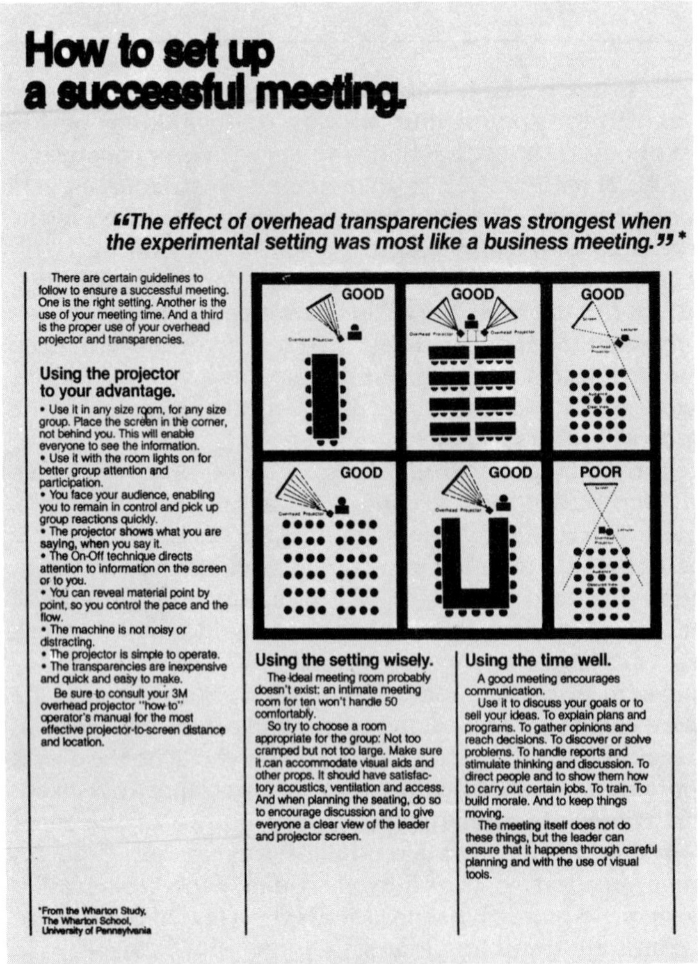

How to set up a successful meeting.

Figure 9-5
Courtesy: AudioVisual
Division/3M, 1986

"The effect of overhead transparencies was strongest when the experimental setting was most like a business meeting." *

There are certain guidelines to follow to ensure a successful meeting. One is the right setting. Another is the use of your meeting time. And a third is the proper use of your overhead projector and transparencies.

Using the projector to your advantage.

• Use it in any size room, for any size group. Place the screen in the corner, not behind you. This will enable everyone to see the information.
• Use it with the room lights on for better group attention and participation.
• You face your audience, enabling you to remain in control and pick up group reactions quickly.
• The projector shows what you are saying, when you say it.
• The On-Off technique directs attention to information on the screen or to you.
• You can reveal material point by point, so you control the pace and the flow.
• The machine is not noisy or distracting.
• The projector is simple to operate.
• The transparencies are inexpensive and quick and easy to make.

Be sure to consult your 3M overhead projector "how to" operator's manual for the most effective projector-to-screen distance and location.

GOOD GOOD GOOD

GOOD GOOD POOR

Using the setting wisely.

The ideal meeting room probably doesn't exist: an intimate meeting room for ten won't handle 50 comfortably.

So try to choose a room appropriate for the group: Not too cramped but not too large. Make sure it can accommodate visual aids and other props. It should have satisfactory acoustics, ventilation and access. And when planning the seating, do so to encourage discussion and to give everyone a clear view of the leader and projector screen.

Using the time well.

A good meeting encourages communication.

Use it to discuss your goals or to sell your ideas. To explain plans and programs. To gather opinions and reach decisions. To discover or solve problems. To handle reports and stimulate thinking and discussion. To direct people and to show them how to carry out certain jobs. To train. To build morale. And to keep things moving.

The meeting itself does not do these things, but the leader can ensure that it happens through careful planning and with the use of visual tools.

*From the Wharton Study, The Wharton School, University of Pennsylvania

details, but you have to know who the listeners are, and what the situation is, and what you expect from the presentation. Merely superimposing graphics on a talk makes no sense.

Not all critics agree with the incorporation of visuals. Some, pointing out that the eye is more sensitive than the ear, claim that graphics overpower language and that a speech, which is meant to be heard, is diminished by attractive visuals.

One other mechanical device, used primarily in television, is the Tele-Prompter. It could also be utilized to advantage in regular speechmaking situations. Once the speaker adjusts to the location and pace of the rolling lines, the appearance of ease and fluency may be generated. Like every other item of equipment, it is only as valuable as the skill of the user makes it.

Panels

Besides appearing solo at the lectern, practitioners (or their bosses or clients) may find themselves as panelists at meetings or on television. Many of the body-language and oratorical tips apply here as well. Gestures may be more subdued; nervous habits more pronounced; continuity more haphazard. Responses should be direct, not too long and involved, and may include points you intend to work in when you get the chance. Panelists should maintain eye contact with fellow panelists and the audience, should stay within time limits if the presentation is formal, and should learn how to package their ideas in memorable sentences.

Help

Aside from the associations one can join to improve speaking abilities, help can be obtained from publications (like *Speechwriter's Newsletter* and *The Executive Speaker*) and speech coaches. Some of the latter may be instructors at a local university, or sales trainers at a nearby corporation; others make a profession out of preparing people to meet the press or the public.

FUND RAISING

Special events can include fund raising, and chances are the PR person will become involved in this activity at some time during his or her career. If the organization for which you work doesn't mount a campaign, you are likely to be drawn into local fund-raising efforts for various charities and building drives. It helps to know a little about how these campaigns work.

The first thing to remember is that fund raising is a highly specialized profession. Perhaps you worked on your parish fund drive and it didn't seem all that hard. Fine, but don't forget you had a captive audience, and one that was uniformly motivated and whose generosity or lack whereof would have been highly conspicuous.

Fund raising is difficult. Some institutions, unequipped for such efforts, look jealously on the successes of similar institutions and conclude that they can reap the same benefits. They are kidding themselves. Even a modest sum like $250,000 can become impossible unless you have someone aboard who knows how to corral this kind of money.

Another thing to remember is that many of the principles of fund raising are mechanical. If you carefully follow certain routine steps, you may do quite well—provided the potential is there. If you organize properly, have rapport with your workers, create an environment conducive to giving, and provide top leadership, you have a fighting chance.

Sometimes it seems that, in fund raising, "them that has, gits." It seems that way because it's true. Why is this? It's because they have an "image of effectiveness" in the public mind. They *deserve* such support; they successfully publicize this need and merit; and they take time to organize their campaigns, beginning with a massive public relations blitz.

Conducting a Fund-Raising Campaign

Before you can expect people to support your cause, you must demonstrate that you are worthy of their help. Some otherwise sane organizations sometimes begin fund-raising campaigns without establishing themselves as meritorious. The excuse might be their current great need or their upcoming anniversary. Not good enough. People should feel favorably toward you, understand your benefits and your desires, and *then* they should be asked.

The way fund-raising professionals operate is by, first, surveying needs and potential. They usually conduct a survey among prospective donors in the constituent audiences. They are asking, basically, three things:

1. What do you think of this institution and its leadership?
2. If it has a campaign, will you work in it?
3. If it has a campaign, will you contribute?

There are other questions, too, but they all lead up to the prediction about success or failure and the probable amount that could reasonably be raised.

If the go-ahead is given, the professionals then help build the "case." Why does the institution need this money? What does it plan to do with this money? What will this mean to the donors and to others whom the institution serves? Does it deserve such support? From hours of discussion and compilation, a "case statement" is evolved, and this becomes the bible for the campaign. Proposals to individuals, companies, and foundations look to this case statement for their copy platform. Campaign brochures and visuals borrow from the contents. Special gift appeals are packaged from its list of projects. The case statement helps everyone in the campaign to speak the same language.

After building the case, the professionals help build the team. Again, working with the institution, they try to recruit the very best people, people who can both give and influence others to give. They build down from them, in paramilitary fashion. If the top leaders are designated "generals," then these generals have a number of "colonels" under them, and these colonels have "majors," and so on. This pyramidal structure includes hundreds of workers, or "lieutenants," in the lowest echelon.

Fund campaigns are heavily calendarized—they work by the calendar, assigning different tasks to each day. Publicity sets the stage for the campaign, and then the top leadership goes out after major gifts. Sometimes these are called "pattern" gifts, meaning that other donors will follow the lead of these givers. If the community's largest bank gives $50,000, for example, the smaller banks may give $25,000 or $15,000. But if the largest bank gives $25,000, then the others will scale down their gifts accordingly. Consequently, every effort is made to bring in pattern gifts at a high level.

Large industries will also be solicited in this early phase, along with wealthy individuals and foundations. Success depends on people who know how to prepare proposals. Personal contacts and persistence are also aids. For the most part, however, foundations do not react to need; they support interesting people and programs, particularly those that may have broad application elsewhere. To some extent, the same is true of government grants.

Once the big money is in—usually more than 80 percent of the total sought—the general campaign is launched, involving hundreds of workers and thousands of prospects. These prospects could be small businesses, individual householders, employees, alumni, and the like. They would receive some mail notices, perhaps, and also be subject to publicity and advertising barrages. The key, however, is the personal call, made by a fellow employee or a volunteer worker.

There are many theories about fund raising, and many techniques for achieving success. Some fund raisers claim that the most effective pitch is one based on guilt. Others assert that personal recognition is the font of large gifts. Still others see the chance to be involved in some potentially great program as the spur. One thing is certain: The weakest argument for giving is the fact that an organization is going under and needs the money to prevent total collapse.

When the fund raising is tied to a special event, especially when the campaign isn't after megabucks, the approach may be less serious. There are celebrity roasts, walkathons and swimathons, car washes and tailgate parties, bed races and egg tosses, selling of services (like cleaning or résumé writing), raffles, flower sales, even the hawking of cookies or candy. These activities may have more promotional value than monetary value, but they may accomplish limited goals, like refurbishing a clubhouse or sending people to a convention.

Direct-Mail Appeals

In addition to personal fund raising as described above, there are many direct-mail appeals—as your own postal accumulation will attest. These range from crude begging to sophisticated presentations. Millions of dollars are raised annually in America via this medium. Because of scandals in recent years, the federal government has tightened up on such fund-raising efforts, and full accountability is now expected.

As in every other field, there are also direct-mail experts, people who can counsel you on lists, write the letters, prepare the package, and evaluate the responses. Most companies that do volume mailings employ one of these people, probably on a consulting basis.

Some fund raisers also use the telephone to good effect in soliciting funds. They call for pledges and then follow up with a reminder letter. And, of course, there are telethons, auctions, fund-raising dinners, and many other ways to gather needed funds. But none of them is easy!

Some Final Fund-Raising Points

First, how and when should you choose a fund-raising firm? You should choose such a firm whenever it is obvious that you can't raise the money yourself. When you are talking about large sums, that's nearly always. The professional brings not only skills and experience but also authority and an extra pair of trained hands. As to how you choose, the best advice is to ask to see the person who will work on *your* campaign. Fund-raising firms might send their best person to get the account and then supply you with one of their lesser lights to run your campaign.

Fund-raising firms—reputable ones—do not charge a percentage for their work. They set a fee and get that fee whether they raise more or less than the stated goal. Percentages are considered unethical.

Second, *once a campaign is under way, it is total war.* Everyone participates. you may be very jealous of this fund-raising interloper and resentful of the high salary, battery of phones, number of secretaries, and seemingly absolute power. You may decide to be uncooperative and balk at requests for publicity help. That's foolish. You will only hurt yourself. Keep in mind that this person will eventually leave and if the campaign is successful, you will be better off. Then watch what goes on; you might learn something.

Philanthropy Today

Giving habits and methods are rarely stable; they change with other aspects of American life. Donors today are more sophisticated, more wary, but their combined philantrophy continues to rise, topping $70 billion annually. Middle-income givers seem to be giving more, whereas the more affluent donors, affected by the 1981 Economic Recovery Tax Act, which reduces the tax benefits of charity, have curtailed their generosity somewhat. With the drying up of support for some social and cultural programs at the government level, the hope is that private financing will fill the gap, but thus far, despite more professional appeals and considerable publicity about the shortfall, corporate and individual donations have not made up the difference. Proposed new tax laws are expected to further reduce private giving, perhaps by as much as 25 percent. Affected will be higher education, the arts, social and health organizations, and religious groups. All this points to more competition for the charitable dollar and more expertise on the part of fund raisers. It also emphasizes the requirement of a solid PR program to precede requests for funds, and the need to make a commitment to effective business practices and complete disclosure. Those institutions—like private colleges and hospitals and various homes—that rely on gifts for survival will increase and improve PR staffs or they won't be around.

BOARD MEMBERSHIPS

Special events may revolve around decisions by boards of directors. These directors or trustees can be extremely valuable to an institution's public relations function; they can also be a problem.

In forming a board—if you have that happy chance—aim for the top people in your community. Start with a small, prestigious group, and the members of this group will be able to recruit others. If this is an advisory board, formed for a specific purpose, you may want broad and varied representation. A Citizens' Council or a Public Relations Advisory Committee might be examples. Where you are creating a board for a large or nonprofit organization (educational and charitable organizations, for example), you may want to stay with peers, with community leaders who can raise funds, commit personnel, and direct public opinion.

Also, have set terms for rotation. This is a source of great difficulty. If you have no rules for rotation, you may be stuck with board members who never come to meetings and who never contribute anything to their roles. The trick is to ease out useless members while retaining active ones. The way around this is to set a term of, say, three years, with possible reappointment for three more years. After that, the member must resign and cannot be brought back until three years have elapsed. This way, weak board members are never asked back.

Board members should have clear lines of authority. If they are to be merely advisory, be certain they understand this. Even then, it is poor practice to go against their advice too often. Many important people will no longer sit on boards where they have no real power. They are used to making decisions, and they expect to make them here as well. In granting this, you may surrender some control, but it is usually worth it.

CHAPTER HIGHLIGHTS

- The secret to success in the staging of special events is attention to detail.
- Party planners may be employed to manage special events, but most functions still remain the responsibility of members of the public relations or community relations staffs.

- The first stages of planning include determining the purpose of the event, clearing the date, securing and inspecting the facility, compiling the calendar, establishing the budget, and notifying key participants. Then the program is arranged, including speaker, chairperson, and entertainment.

- Hundreds of details are part of any event—registration, decorations, menu, seating, and exhibits. That's why complete checklists are essential tools.

- Meetings should be held only when they respond to a definite need, and should be well organized and directed.

- Miscellaneous events include plant tours, dedications, groundbreakings, open houses, anniversaries, conventions, and presentations for new business.

- Sponsorship of special events by corporations and organizations is increasing, partly owing to the favorable relationship between cost and effect, partly because of the opportunity for publicity, and partly because of the positive effect on the community.

- Speakers, including practitioners, must conquer their fears, practice their craft, and take advantage of the audiovisual aids at their disposal.

- Fund raising is becoming more competitive, more sophisticated, and more professional. PR persons must work closely with fund raisers, setting the stage for solicitation and publicizing needs and success.

- A solid board of directors is a tremendous asset to any firm or organization, but it must be chosen wisely and given concrete direction.

NOTES

[1] Joe Jeff Goldblatt, "How to Produce Special Events," *Public Relations Journal*, June 1985.

[2] Rea W. Smith, "How to Select Your Meeting Site," *Public Relations Journal*, May 1978.

[3] Bob Dorf and Alex Stanton, "The Shoemaker's Children," *Public Relations Journal*, October 1983.

[4] Janet Cote-Merow and Jeremiah L. Goldstein, "Teleconferencing: Everything You Wanted to Know," *Communicator's Journal*, September/October 1983; and Alvin M. and Daniel P. Hattal, "Video-Conferencing," *Public Relations Journal*, September 1984.

[5] Joan H. Wood, "How to Arrange Successful Media Tours," *Public Relations Journal*, May 1985.

[6] Lesa Ukman, "The Special Event: Finding Its Niche," *Public Relations Journal*, June 1984.

[7] Jim Westberry, "Enhancing Your Speech," *Ad Week*, October 5, 1981.

SUGGESTED READINGS

BENTLEY, C.F., *How to Run a Meeting*. Toronto: Coles, 1979.

BISHOP, ANN, *Slides: Planning and Producing Slide Programs*. Rochester, N.Y.: Eastman Kodak, 1984.

GARD, GRANT, *The Art of Confident Public Speaking*. Englewood Cliffs, N.J.: Prentice-Hall, 1986.

KENNY, MICHAEL F., and RAYMOND F. SCHMITT, *Images, Images, Images*. Rochester, N.Y.: Eastman Kodak, 1983.

LIEBERT, EDWIN R., and BERNICE E. SHELDON, *Handbook of Special Events for Non-Profit Organizations*. New York: Association Press, 1972.

McMANUS, ED, and BILL NICHOLAS, *We're Roasting Harry Tuesday Night*. Englewood Cliffs, N.J.: Prentice-Hall, 1984.

Meeting News, monthly newsletter. New York: Gralla.

Meeting Robbers, 20-minute film. Del Mar, Calif.: McGraw-Hill Films.

SPINRAD, LEONARD, and THELMA SPINRAD, *Speaker's Lifetime Almanac*. Englewood Cliffs, N.J.: Prentice-Hall, 1984.

ZENKER, ARNOLD, *Mastering the Public Spotlight*. Boston: Dodd Mead, 1984.

EXERCISES

1. Select a national holiday, anniversary, or other special occasion and write out a menu that is both appropriate and appealing.

2. Using one of the major firms in your city as an example, consider how you would conduct a tour of its plant or office. Visit the place yourself and walk through the facility, making notes on how you would conduct a tour. Draft a proposal for this tour by the company's management, including route, days of the week, approximate attendance, refreshments, program, and other considerations.

3. Come up with a theme for the following events:

   a. Diamond Jubilee of your college or university

   b. Groundbreaking for the first senior-citizen high rise in your community

   c. Grand opening of a posh restaurant featuring Austrian dishes

4. Prepare a letter to a potential convention group, inviting the members to your city and working into the letter the various amenities you feel this city offers—especially those not available elsewhere.

5. Select a local charitable or nonprofit institution or organization and prepare a one-page case statement, merely listing the items that should be included in order to motivate a donor.

CASE PROBLEMS

1. A major religious denomination is agreeable to holding its national convention in your city, but expresses concern about accommodations. The convention is expected to attract 5,000 members and guests; your hotel space amounts to only 4,000 rooms, and many of them, of course, would be occupied by other people. Your city would like to host this gathering, since it would mean millions of dollars in new revenue.

   What other avenues might you explore to meet the needs of the

conventioneers? How would you solve other problems that these alternative solutions might create? What would you do to ease the likely complaints about your city's not being big enough to do a decent job?

2. After you have managed to secure this convention, one of the members of
   the city council makes a jest having religious connotations, and this
   tasteless comment is printed in the paper. Convention planners read it,
   are irate, and call your Chamber of Commerce, threatening to call off the
   entire event. What can you do?

3. You handle public relations for your state chapter of United Cerebral Palsy
   and recently completed a telethon that raised nearly a quarter of a million
   dollars in your state. A week after the telethon, the local newspaper, in a
   major story, reveals that almost 35 percent of the money raised went for
   expenses—telephones, microwave transmission, entertainers, and postage. The newspaper article compares this with less than 5 percent in
   expenses incurred by the local United Way campaign. The obvious innu-
   endo is that your costs were exorbitant and that the money contributed to
   the victims has been siphoned off.

   In responding to this story, what sort of information would you
   gather, and why?

4. The board of trustees at Saint Patrick's Hospital is composed of physicians and both professional and business persons. One member of the
   board, a successful business leader, is continually and openly critical of
   hospital administration and board activity. He frequently leaks stories to
   the news media about hospital situations he considers detrimental. Moreover, he refuses to assist in fund raising and takes little part in any board
   matters that do not interest him. He is a thorn in the side of the administration and an irritant to other board members. He is in the second year
   of a four-year term. There are no real grounds for removing him, and
   besides, such a step might result in further damaging publicity.

   What steps might the administration or the board take to neutralize
   this person's effect on public opinion?

10

EVALUATION OF
PUBLIC RELATIONS
PROGRAMS

The most ignored aspect of public relations is undoubtedly the evaluation phase. Both clients and practitioners are often willing to close the books once the news release is mailed or the special event concluded. This is especially true when success attends the venture. Little reflection is given to the plus and minus factors of a completed campaign.

Evaluation must be continuous. In the planning stage, alternatives are evaluated; in the implementation stage, actions are evaluated; intermittently and ultimately, results are evaluated. This means that the elements of evaluation have to be built into every plan. You have to know what you intended to accomplish before you can determine whether you succeeded. Every program deserves and requires analysis. If planning is important, so is the consideration of how the planning worked. This is the way to benefit from errors and triumphs, avoid repetition of mistakes, reduce costs, concentrate on courses of action that work, and plan more fruitfully in terms of time and personnel.

This evaluation phase may be informal or scientific. It may involve a few people seated around a table or a massive survey. It can take hours or weeks. Basically, it seeks to answer the question, *How did we do?*

You really want to determine, with as much objectivity as possible, whether or not the program achieved the results you anticipated, whether it was worth the expenditure of money and personnel you committed to it, and whether you might have done better with another project.

Some institutions repeat a program annually, simply because they did it last year. They become hypnotized by the numbers adding up. "Our Thirty-first Annual Conference!" Someone needs to sit down and ask, Why are we doing this? You may discover that attendance is falling off, that the discussions are stale and repetitious, and that even those who attend are doing it

Figure 10-1 Evaluation is built into every program, project, and event, and occurs during and immediately after the occasion.

out of some sense of loyalty to the organization. At this point, the program should be dropped or severely altered. Instead, however, most organizations plunge ahead to the "Thirty-second Annual Conference," investing considerable funds and time in a hollow activity.

A company gathers all its employees for the traditional Christmas party on December 24. The boss assumes that all the smiling employees and their families love this little gesture. Actually, these people find it cold, uncomfortable, and hypocritical. They would rather spend this time at home or doing some last-minute shopping. They resent this forced participation. The PR person should have sufficient courage—and prestige—to be able to suggest change or elimination to his or her superiors.

In conducting an evaluation, a strong checklist is a must. This list could be compared with the original plan so that the outcome could be measured against the vision. Where there are discrepancies, these should be pursued until a reason emerges.

Perhaps you failed to properly indoctrinate or inform those you hoped would help or participate. Did they understand what was going on and why they were needed? If they did and still failed to come through, is there an underlying reason for the lack of cooperation?

Perhaps you selected the wrong team to begin with. Or gave them incomplete instructions. Or failed to make periodic checks on progress.

Perhaps you aimed your communication at the wrong audience or failed to include audiences that should have been contacted. You may, too, have failed in one of the communicative ways mentioned in Chapter 5.

During lengthy projects, regular meetings may be held to discuss progress. These gatherings allow leadership to assess each activity or communication. Problems surface, opportunities evolve, budget commitments are reviewed, and weaknesses are exposed. Money and personnel may be shifted from an area that is stagnant to one that shows promise.

LEVELS OF ANALYSIS

Not every project or program deserves the same intensity of measurement. Those that are vital to image or sales, those that consume personnel and funds, and those that are, by their nature, complicated rate more time and attention. Rarely does any PR area get too much analysis; the opposite is probably true.

Evaluation can range from none to adequate. Kalman B. Druck, president of Harshe-Rotman & Druck, talks about four levels of evaluation:

1. *Intuitive judgment*, where it appears that everything worked properly, but there are no hard supporting data.
2. *Visibility*, which occurs when clippings of a news release or airing of a TV special follows your initiating steps.
3. *Observed behavior*, where some of the campaign goals are concretely realized.
4. *Ultimate action*, which is the culmination of all goals, including sales, behavioral change, passage of a law, and the like.[1]

STEPS IN EVALUATION

There are numerous ways to conduct your own public relations audit. Since institutions and programs differ widely, some will focus on checklist items that others lack. Some factors, however, are pretty constant:

1. *How did I do personally?* Practitioners must ask themselves how they functioned, whether they fully understood the program, whether they put sufficient effort into it, whether they worked well with others, how well they dealt with the machinery and services available, how thoroughly they counseled management, how efficiently and economically they conducted the program.
2. *How did others do?* Were they properly informed? Did they perform up to expectations? Were sufficient numbers involved?
3. *Did we reach the intended public?* Did they properly identify those individuals and groups that they wished to reach? Were the programs to accomplish these goals realistically planned and executed? Did these target audiences receive and understand the communication? Did they act on the message?

4. *Were the short- and long-range goals of the program met?* Did the program or programs, for example, result in an opinion change, altered conduct, membership, contributions, legislation, electoral success, or whatever other aims the planners contemplated?
5. *Did we stay within the allotted budget?*

The more specific the goals, the easier it will be to measure results. If a university seeks to increase enrollment by 5 percent and actually increases it by 7 percent, that is measurable. If a company wants to trim a budget without loss of efficiency and does so, that is measurable. Firms can evaluate advertising results, membership quotas, sales, safety, and other areas.

MEASURING PUBLICITY

Publicity is one of the easier aspects to measure. At least the *use* made of your promotional efforts can be checked. You know what news releases you issued and can get an idea about which were printed or aired. Some radio and television stations give periodic reports to PR persons regarding the stories they used. Without such a document, you must keep your own records, using a clipping service or your own office personnel and assigning people to monitor radio and television news.

What you can't easily measure is the effect of these stories, or even the total audience reached. You have to estimate and assume. Despite the flaws in evaluating publicity, recordkeeping is a good idea, since publicity is often the scapegoat for programs that do not succeed. Some kind of roster of numbers of stories used and total linage helps to quiet critics.

EVALUATING COMMUNICATION

In addition to research mentioned in Chapter 3, certain tests can be applied either to static documents to determine readability, or to groups to assess results.

The more common readability tests are these:

- The Flesch Formula
- The Gunning Formula
- The Dale-Chall Formula
- The Cloze Procedure

The first three formulas focus on such items as sentence length, word difficulty, number of personal words used, verb force, familiarity of vocabulary, or, in the case of Dale-Chall, the number of words used that appear on their select list of 3,000. Theoretically, the more understandable the language and the easier your communication is to read, the more success you will have with readers.

The Cloze Procedure is a "missing word" test, in which you see how well you can understand a communication when every "*n*th" word is removed.

The Gunning Formula may be the simplest to use. To check copy using this formula, you begin by selecting a passage of approximately 100 words—but not less. Complete each sentence when making this count.

Then count the number of sentences in this passage and divide this number into the number of words. This will give you an "average sentence length."

Next, count the number of words in this passage that have three or more syllables. Try to eliminate from this tally the easier compound words, certain verb forms, and proper names.

Next, add these two numbers—the number of words in the average sentence length and the number of words of three or more syllables. Multiply this total by a factor of 0.4, which will give you the approximate number of years of education a person would need to read this passage easily.

Let's suppose we have a passage of 121 words containing five sentences. This would make the average sentence length 24 words. The number of words of three or more syllables in this passage turns out to be 22. Adding these figures together we get 46, which we then multiply by 0.4, giving us a result of 18.4. This means that reading skill equivalent to that of a person holding a master's degree would be required to read this passage *easily*. This does not mean, however, that the passage is appropriate for the person with a master's degree; it may be too simple.

A score of 15 is usually considered "easy" reading, and anything above 35 gets into the "difficult" range, with 55 and over constituting a "very difficult" degree of reading. Many scientific articles would fall into this last category, because it is virtually impossible to find a simplified form of certain technical words.

Keep in mind that these tests—sometimes lumped together under the term "Fog Index"—are meant to serve as a check on writing but should not be regarded so rigidly that they inhibit writing.

Keep in mind, too, that audiences differ in ability, and you should know what educational level you are shooting for. A college alumni magazine would have a higher index than a high-school yearbook, and a professional journal should score higher than a company newsletter.

Admittedly, these formulas may get more use from scholars than they do from PR practitioners. Too few PR persons apply this kind of test to their copy before disseminating it, although they should. These procedures are more likely to be used after the fact. The in-house publication should be submitted to the Gunning test, for example, to see how well it will communicate to readers. In the long run, then, it has a practical value. On a day-to-day basis, however, these tests simply don't get used.

The Company Publication

Reading levels are only one aspect of internal communications. Something may be readable and still not be read. Editors who are on top of their jobs always allow for some form of feedback. This may come in a visible way through suggestion boxes, guest columns, letters to the editor, and other response devices, but they merely scratch the surface. The editor—and management—should know whether or not this important internal tool is really effective. Checking this out requires some method of soliciting reader opinion along with a brutal personal analysis on the part of the staff.

Bill Cunnea, of Cunnea Strategic Communications, advises:

> Rip the hell out of it. Look at your own past performance as if it were done by a predecessor on the job that you want. Criticize yourself in terms of how the publication *doesn't* relate to the firm. See what *isn't* there connecting each employee to the overall industry and to your company.
>
> As painful as it may be, keep on asking yourself if you would subscribe to your own publication. After all, that's what your company is doing, and they do so not only by paying for the printing costs and paper, but also by paying for you. A publication written for the editor eventually has only a circulation of one.[2]

After this surgery, Cunnea suggests examining the "wreckage" and seeing what can be pulled together from it, with the cooperation and understanding of management.

Some editors devise a long list of questions they want answered, from whether the editor and staff continue to have a clear idea of the publication's mission to whether they have stayed current with developments in copywriting, editing, design, and production.

Impact listed 45 benchmarks for editors, including these:

- Do you know how to stimulate creative thinking, both your own and your staff's?
- Do you use your time effectively?
- Have you developed a personal approach to writing?
- Do you periodically gauge reader attitude and reaction?[3]

Besides reviewing the results of a readership survey, another way for an editor to stay humble is to realize that tests show employees rating company publications, as a source of information, somewhere in the middle of the list of possibilities. The immediate supervisor leads the roster, followed by the grapevine, handbooks, bulletin boards, small group meetings, general employee publications, and annual reports. Most employees seem to feel frustrated about any communication moving from the ranks to management. Incidentally, even though the grapevine is ranked second as an actual source, it places dead last as a preferred source.[4]

Communication Is Merely One Tool

It's a mistake to assume that communication can do it all. Look at the millions who, for one reason or another—but not lack of communication—ignore warnings of the surgeon general about cigarette hazards. Numerous advertising campaigns have won national awards but failed to increase product sales. Conversely, sales sometimes rise despite poor ad campaigns or ineffective communication. Communication and sales *should* go hand in hand, but they don't always do so.

When you test communication, then, you may discover that your copy is hard to read, or find out how many people could have read it, or even how many people *did* read it, but it is very hard to find out what they thought and what they did *after* reading it. Hard, but not impossible. An in-depth survey may be the appropriate tool to use here.

The final step in evaluation is to ask yourself how the lessons you learned will help with future projects. If you merely throw up your hands and say, "What can I do with so few people and such a limited budget?" that becomes counterproductive. If this is really the problem, then your evaluation should document a request for more personnel and more money. If these are not forthcoming, then you either quit or learn to live within the restrictions established. Even in this latter category, you will discover ways to economize, activities to drop or trim back, and ways to make people and dollars stretch.

Evaluation techniques are being discovered, refined, and tested all the time.

In advertising, for example, firms like Starch test the number of people who (1) noticed an ad, (2) read most of it, and (3) could identify the sponsor. One might probe further, determining which sources of information were most effective and whether the action suggested in the ad produced a sale, an inquiry, or a change of attitude.

Some magazines offer reprints of feature articles about certain companies or products. The number of requests for reprints will tell you something about the effects of the publicity, and some firms even try to reduce the cost per inquiry to a formula, dividing production costs by the number of magazines in the market divided by the number of inquiries from the market.

Salespersons are also evaluated. Firms keep charts on performance, and they adjust for such items as territory, length of time on the job, and local conditions. Sometimes quotas are assigned in advance and the salesperson is measured against the percentage of quota achieved.

Mailing pieces can be evaluated in terms of coupons returned; trade ads can be measured in terms of dealer response; share of market can be examined before and after a campaign; field trips may be made to involve personal evaluations; expense accounts may be analyzed; and a hundred other tests performed.

SPECIAL EVENTS

With the rediscovery of special events as strong marketing and image-building tools, more attention is being paid to the value of such activities—especially where corporate sponsorship is involved. Increased competition among sponsors also makes tough assessment necessary.

In the past, special events were adjuncts to PR programs, something you did to commemorate a milestone or launch a new structure. Today these happenings are considered in a more positive light. They are planned, even when there is no immediate impetus to stage them. Most companies spend time researching the relevance of the event to their particular goals, the probable costs involved, the likely effect of the event or association, and the problems that might arise.

It's not enough to merely feel good about the relationship, or to congratulate yourself that you are doing something significant for American youth or local morale. More and more, planners are trying to determine what effect such events will have on traffic and sales.

If a motor oil lends its name and financing to the Indianapolis 500, the company certainly intends for this gesture to increase the market for its product. Ditto for a breakfast food tied to the Olympics, a Macy's parade, or the Virginia Slims Tennis Tournament. Al Guerrara, of the Pabst Brewing Company, advises:

> You have to figure out just what it is you want out of the event, and not go in cold and hope something good turns up.[5]

Image building remains a by-product, but when the results are tabulated, sponsors still expect to hear some cash-register noise.

MEETING IS OVER—IT'S EVALUATION TIME
By Martin J. Bell
President, Comart Aniforms

New York—You've just had your meeting and now you want to know how effective it was. How do you judge whether it was worth the time and expense?

Easy. You ask the same question you would for any other type of communication—from a simple memo to a multimillion-dollar ad campaign. Did it accomplish its objectives?

Then again, maybe it's not so easy. Because some funny things can happen to objectives on the way to a meeting, any of which could make the question inoperative.

One of them is failing to set specific objectives in the first place. Companies that pride themselves on the comprehensiveness of their marketing, sales, and media objectives may plan an important business meeting with only the vaguest generalities in mind. If you haven't tried beforehand to pinpoint the relative importance of such goals as motivation, information, and excitement, you can't expect to pin down their effectiveness later on.

Then there's the other extreme: measuring effectiveness in terms of unrealistic objectives that are beyond a meeting's inherent capabilities.

The typical example is the sales meeting. You've pinpointed your sales goals in elaborate detail—down to the smallest territory, with action plans for every region. Is it valid to withhold or revise judgment on the meeting, pending the ultimate outcome of those sales goals?

Basic marketing fundamentals clearly say "no." But somehow they can become clouded where a sales meeting is concerned. Companies forget that it's only one vital tool in the overall communications mix and as interdependent as any other. It should never take more than its share of the credit or the blame.

To use an advertising analogy, a meeting is like a single magazine ad or one 30-second TV commercial. Except in the case of direct response, you can't attribute a specific share of the ensuing sales to that one ad alone. But you *can* test how well your ad gets its message across and how many people remember it. In short, did it communicate?

That's a question you can—and should—ask about any meeting, whether it's for salespeople, staff employees, or customers. Positive communication should always be an objective, whether your other goals include excitement, motivation, training, information, or recognition. Communications is one of several quantitative objectives whose effectiveness can be tested with a very high degree of accuracy with the use of questionnaires.

How elaborate should this research be? It should keep a logical relationship to the total budget and objectives. We have created meetings for companies such as American Airlines, American Express, and Caterpillar—for audiences ranging from 50 to 16,000 (on a rotating basis)—and in many cases, extensive evaluation tests were considered good investments by the companies involved.

Such evaluation might include an advance questionnaire, another directly after the meeting, and perhaps another three to six months later. The questions should be as specific, easy to answer, and goal related as possible.

One client wanted to hold a corporate sales meeting that would bring together two recently merged companies for the first time. As a secondary objective to the sales content, the client wanted the meeting to emphasize the groups' common bond. So it mailed, in advance, a three-page quiz about both divisions with an attractive prize structure for "good marks."

Since it was necessary for each paper to be identified, assurances were given that no personal stigma could attach to a below-average showing. Everyone knew in advance that a separate organization would handle the grading, name the winners, summarize the results, and then destroy the papers.

Where the respondent's identity isn't an evaluation factor, don't ask for it. You'll get far more reliable opinions about such objectives as excitement and motivation if you eliminate the employee's temptation to impress management. Try to get reasons, not just ratings. Why was the meeting valuable? Where did it fall short?

This kind of audience reaction should be sought as quickly as possible after the meeting—ideally, before attendees leave the meeting site—and then again a few weeks later to compare reactions.

If your meeting ends in taking orders from customers, it's as reliable a measurement as a coupon ad or passing the plate after a sermon. But other types of on-the-spot reactions can fool you. Questions can reflect healthy curiosity—or mere confusion. Silence can indicate concentration—or boredom.

To help insure measurable, effective results, don't lose sight of the human touch. There's a realistic limit to the information people can remember, so don't overload them. Instead, concentrate on a few major concepts and save the details for follow-up discussion groups.

Reprinted with permission from the April 23, 1979, issue of *Advertising Age*. Copyright 1979 by Crain Communications, Inc. Source: Martin J. Bell.

BACKCASTING

A new term that entered the evaluation lexicon recently is "backcasting," simply a way to describe the process of scientifically measuring trends over the past several years. Such exercises enable users to get a clearer picture of income and expenditures, to see whether or not one department has been fiscally favored over another, to locate problem areas in sales, and even to chart progress in the PR area.

> An annual review of public relations programs for cost–benefit ratios can help establish clearer program priorities. Backcast statistics can identify those programs which work hardest for the dollar, based on standards expressed as quantity (number of publicity placements), quality (how well the story angle focuses on identified audience needs/concerns/interests), time (hours budgeted) and cost (expense budgeted).[6]

Solid facts may justify a budget increase, shift funds and personnel from one department to another, expose an unprofitable client relationship, substantiate a suspected gap in media coverage, or alter the direction of a campaign.

THE BUDGET

Except among those rare institutions for which money seems to be no real problem, most programs must function under a tight budget. You establish this at the outset, try to live within it, and then determine how well you did. Failing to stay within these monetary confines can be painful.

For many years, political campaigns were notorious for spending more than they had. Advertising agencies, public relations counselors, and all sorts of suppliers, from hotels and caterers to limousine services and airlines, found themselves holding worthless IOUs after a candidate had suffered a defeat. To protect against this, most suppliers require cash in advance from candidates. The media operate this way when a political hopeful wants time or space. This may work a temporary hardship on the candidate, but it eventually helps him or her by preventing campaign bankruptcy.

Cost overruns in private industry are no more acceptable than they are with taxpayers upset about federal spending. Film directors have been fired, even blacklisted, for bringing in features that greatly exceed the proposed budget. Some of these films, like "Heaven's Gate," have become legend because of the excessive costs. Even a company banquet or a sponsored cross-country race must not go beyond the dollars committed. Other goals may be met, but a budget deficit puts a damper on all allied success.

The budget must also be related to results. Even though you stay within a budget, you may still arrive at an excessive per-unit cost for the people reached.

EVALUATING THE PR FUNCTION ITSELF

Many PR activities receive scrutiny—and *all* of them should. That includes periodic analysis of the public relations firm or department itself. Checks should be made to see how efficient personnel are in their assigned roles and how effective communication and other internal policies are for staff and superiors.

Among the operations most often evaluated in PR shops are the following:

Internal relations. Management wants to know how successful it's been at communicating policy; how morale is faring; what concerns are paramount among employees; how effective company publications are; and what more can be done to ensure two-way communication and shared goals.

Community relations.   Through opinion polls, analysis of mail and phone calls, sponsorship of activities, and presence in the community, the firm may ascertain how the neighbors view it and its conduct.

Shareholder relations.   Although many factors affect an increase in the value of stock, there are ways to measure the success of communication to shareholders and the financial community, and to assess attitudes of those who are participants, to a greater or lesser degree, in the financial health of the company.

Customer relations.   This evaluation may have many facets, from the simple counting of product sales to the surveying of dealers and distributors. Often numbers dominate, but there are times when attitude toward the product and the corporation may be equally important.

Government relations.   No company is free of government regulation, and some have greater, more frequent contact with government at all levels. Evaluation may apply to programs and laws, those supported and those contested; to an investigation of communication effect; and to an examination of friendly and unfriendly legislators.

Sales and marketing.   Gathering data on sales is relatively easy, especially with computer help, but the assigning of reasons for gains or losses, or the solving of geographical or product-line declines, is tougher.

Publicity.   Communicators want to know what stories were used and where, whether they were successful in cracking some targeted media, and, if possible, what results the publicity achieved.

Advertising.   For several decades, advertising has been scientifically measured, based on responses, awareness, sales, and other considerations. The techniques remain imperfect, but this is one area where evaluation has been fairly constant.

EVALUATION PERSISTS THROUGH CALM AND CRISIS CONDITIONS

Sometimes evaluation may be conducted through periods of relative quiet, when officials have the luxury of somewhat serene introspection. They may calmly examine performance and potential. On other occasions, evaluation must be conducted on horseback, with decisions called for in a tight time frame.

Public relations or communications audits—used to set priorities or make programming more effective—are often considered part of PR staff routine. Professionals compare their perceptions of client reality with the views of those they serve and those of the audiences affected. Any differences are addressed in a new set of programs and communications.

While this sort of evaluation has some time element attached, it is normally less frantic than evaluation in periods of crisis.

In the summer of 1985, TWA faced 17 days of hostage negotiations following the hijacking of its Flight 847. An operational planning group composed of TWA staff members, including those in charge of corporate communication, was the first to learn of the situation and began a vigil at their posts, round the clock, for a few days before four-hour respites were feasible. Fortunately, the TWA handbook outlined the steps to be taken in such emergencies, though, of course, no crisis goes exactly by the book.

From a special control center, the planning group analyzed each bit of incoming information from Athens, Algiers, Beirut, Washington, and elsewhere. They were in constant touch with the State Department, the FBI, the FAA, the Department of Transportation, and other federal bodies. They also communicated with other corporate members, often through computers, with the media, and with relatives of the hostages. The latter chore alone took days—building a hostage list from the flight manifest, finding relations, making at least daily contact with these relatives. Reservations agents helped with this phase of the operation; reservation desks were staffed 24 hours a day. Travel agents also had to be notified as well as passengers. All other TWA PR efforts came to a standstill during these two and a half weeks as the planning group concentrated on the major problem.

Relations with the press were delicate. As the planning group uncovered bits of information, it had to evaluate each in terms of accuracy and impact, and also had to decide whether release of these details endangered those held captive. Even TWA's private conviction that security at Athens was adequate had to be measured against the government's caution about traveling through that airport. The result was that no statement was made.

Although there was really no time to evaluate the negative impact on the airline's future, the planners were able to keep track of expenses related to the crisis and found the costs in excess of half a million dollars. Even the final days required all sorts of discussion, evaluation, and decision making: How would the released hostages be transported back to the United States? What stops would be made en route? What controls would be exercised regarding those allowed to greet them? How would the media be handled at all these junctures?

Once the captives were safely back in American hands, the staff had to turn its attention to the impact on regular operations—and the return of the plane, still held in Beirut.

Administrators—including communicators—who can quickly analyze a situation, coolly appraise alternatives, thoroughly sift information, and courageously make decisions are invaluable—and all too rare.

Special events.   As mentioned earlier, each staged event requires analysis, even when it will not be repeated. As this PR tool grows in use, measurement will become more sophisticated.

Managerial skills.   Good companies check out the success of managers at all levels in achieving pre-established goals, including production quotas and communication.

Trends.   Chapter 2 discussed trends and the need to adapt to them. Whether issues management or some other form of analysis is applied, the environment must be regularly reviewed and programs adjusted to meet its demands and opportunities.

MANY USES FOR EVALUATION

Agencies that rely heavily on volunteers could extend the research done by Gallup about why volunteers stop (too busy, project completed, moved, work conflict, relative or friend no longer involved, lost interest) and evaluate their programs on the basis of negating some of these objections.

A Minnesota bank is currently evaluating the success of sponsoring Halloween parties for children of prospective customers, and it is reaching a blue-collar audience through direct mail rather than newspapers because this population segment scores low on newspaper readership.

More and more companies employ exit interviews when employees leave, to help the firm evaluate working conditions and personnel policies. In higher education, teacher evaluations are common, and evaluations of collegiate administrators are also in vogue. Corporations may do likewise, rating executives on communication skills, leadership, planning ability, development of new markets, interpersonal skills, and other attributes.

Savvy employees, who understand how the evaluation system works within their companies, learn how to relate their accomplishments to organizational goals and objectives. Public relations practitioners often have a more difficult time doing this, since their accomplishments may be less concrete than a sales manager's, development director's, or maintenance chief's. The way around this is to establish objectives early, spell out their fulfillment, and tie these successes to other, more visible company activities.

NEW FORMS OF MEASUREMENT

Most systems of evaluation are standard—surveys, panels, questionnaires, sales charts, and the like. Some companies regularly read published results of public-opinion polls on subjects of interest to them. Others utilize computers to monitor and analyze news. Many conduct mini-polls by telephone, or distribute questionnaires to employees.

There has been considerable criticism of the usual methods of measuring public relations achievement. Increases in sales, passage or cancellation of legislation, increased awareness of a company or a product—all may be desirable, but they do not necessarily correlate with the PR effort. Other factors may have exerted influence, and separating out the public relations effects may be impossible. Clippings may accumulate as public opinion erodes. Communication may meet all the stated goals, but sales don't follow.

Advertisers took a long time to learn that their research on emotional versus logical appeals on television was misleading. Since most of their evaluation has been based on day-after recall, advertising execs assumed that the logical message was more effective, because it was remembered better. Recognizing that emotional appeals are more difficult to verbalize, ad analysts developed a new testing technique, requiring respondents to supply missing information rather than describing content.

Some evaluators also borrow techniques from academic researchers, using Q-method testing, in which the emphasis is not as much on numbers of respondents as it is on a broad spectrum of questions.

Whatever the procedure, the bottom line remains: How well did we do, and why?

CHAPTER HIGHLIGHTS

- Evaluation, the most neglected step in public relations programs, basically answers the question, "How did we do?"
- Areas of concern in evaluation include internal relations, community relations, shareholder relations, customer relations, government relations, sales and marketing, publicity, advertising, special events, managerial skills, and current trends.
- Evaluation may move from intuitive judgment to visible evidence to behavioral modification to the execution of the campaign's desired results.
- In evaluating, the practitioner asks, How did I do? How did others do? Did we reach the intended public? Did we meet our goals? Did we stay within budget?
- Publicity may be measured by tabulating stories and by assessing their effect. Communication can be tested by applying one of a quartet of readability tests: Flesch Formula, Gunning, Dale-Chall, or Cloze Procedure. Company publications may be analyzed internally or by soliciting reader opinion. Special events are measured against their initial goals.
- "Backcasting" involves a historical look at a specific subject area to help establish guidelines for the future.
- Evaluators need to know that testing communication is merely one part of the equation, and they should also be aware of the various methods that might be employed.

NOTES

[1]Willard Bailey, "Program Evaluation." Reprinted with permission from the September 1968 issue of the *Public Relations Journal.* Copyright 1968.

[2]*IABC/Omaha Newsletter*, March 1985.

[3]*Impact*, No. 148 (1973).

[4]IABC Survey, cosponsored by Towers, Perrin, Forster and Crosby, 1981.

[5]Mary McCabe English, "Seeing That Special Events Measure Up," *Advertising Age*, October 25, l984.

[6]Robert F. Smith and Kerry Tucker, "Looking Back," *Public Relations Journal*, December 1984.

SUGGESTED READINGS

CARO, FRANCIS G., ed., *Readings in Evaluation Research*, 2nd ed. New York: Russell Sage Foundation, 1977.

KOSECOFF, JACQUELINE and ARLENE FINK, *Evaluation Basics*. Beverly Hills, Calif.: Sage, 1982.

PATTON, MICHAEL QUINN, *Practical Evaluation*. Beverly Hills, Calif.: Sage, 1982.

ROSSI, PETER H., and HOWARD E. FREEMAN, *Evaluation*, 2nd ed. Beverly Hills, Calif.: Sage, 1982.

RUTMAN, LEONARD, *Evaluation Research Methods*, 2nd ed. Beverly Hills, Calif.: Sage, 1982.

———, *Planning Useful Evaluations: Evaluability Assessment*. Beverly Hills, Calif.: Sage, 1980.

STRUENING, ELMER L., and MARILYNN B. BREWER, eds., *Handbook of Evaluation Research*. Beverly Hills, Calif.: Sage, 1983.

EXERCISES

1. Apply the Gunning Readability Test described in this chapter to one of the following and determine the level of readership:
   a. Your campus newspaper
   b. One of your textbooks
   c. Your local daily or weekly newspaper
   d. A magazine to which you subscribe
2. Many colleges and universities have evaluation instruments for faculty members, and there seem to be complaints about all of them. Some instructors contend charisma plays too large a role, that class size and content affect appraisal, that students often don't appreciate teaching until they graduate, and so on. Devise a brief survey that could be distributed to your classmates that would contain ten questions you feel should be asked in evaluating an instructor.

CASE PROBLEMS

1. You are the public relations director for a soft-drink company that ranks about tenth in sales in the United States. The president calls you in and tells you he's been approached by organizers of the Baja California auto race, a grueling week-long affair over some of this continent's roughest terrain. Sponsorship will cost about $1 million and must come from the existing advertising and public relations budgets. In evaluating this special event as a possibility for your firm, what sort of questions would you ask? What things would most help you decide? How would you gather these answers? What sort of evaluation would you build into the plan, if you go ahead with it? How will you conduct this evaluation?

2. Midtown's public power district used to spend a considerable portion of its advertising and public relations budget on selling electrical appliances and all-electric homes. Following consumer reaction to the energy crisis, however, the company shifted to advertising that tried to accomplish three things: (a) promote conservation of energy, (b) promote safety (warnings about kite flying, indiscriminate digging, etc.), and (c) educate the public about the uses and value of nuclear energy. Several board members are complaining that this kind of advertising is doing no good at all, and you, as a public relations director, are expected to respond to their criticisms. How would you go about evaluating these campaigns? What facts and results would you look for? How would you present this report to the board?

11
THE PRACTICE OF PUBLIC RELATIONS

Understanding what public relations is and how it functions is merely the beginning. Even the most comprehensive course under the most experienced and talented instructor cannot teach certain aspects of the profession.

Among the more difficult lessons to learn in a classroom situtation are these:

1. *What things really cost.* Things rarely cost anything in school. A poorly written assignment, a spate of typographical errors, an error in an annual-report balance sheet, a mistake in case-problem judgment—these may merely reduce the grade. In the world of public relations, they can cost a great deal of money, cause a program to collapse, or lose a client.

2. *What real deadlines are.* Despite the instructor's best efforts and most adamant demeanor, excuses are frequently accepted for work that is late. Illness, a clutter of exams, basketball practice, and other reasons may be proffered and acknowledged. The media are not so gracious. If you miss a deadline, you miss the opportunity for publicity, legal notification of stock-holders, proper notice for a special event, or reservation for space or time for a public relations advertisement.

3. *Working with noncreative people.* In a classroom situation, the student really has only the teacher to please. The student's work is measured, to a considerable extent, against the performance of others in the class rather than against some publishable norm. Unfortunately, things will never again be that simple. Instead of dealing with an instructor who may be both creative and sympathetic, the practitioner's efforts are arrayed before a client or a committee. This can be a humbling experience, since the client may be uncreative and skeptical.

CHARACTERISTICS OF THE PR PERSON

Every professional and public relations educator has had the experience of asking a young person why he or she wants to enter the field. The response is often stereotypic: "Because I like people."

Liking people may be an asset in many professions, from salesperson to receptionist, but it is no special advantage in gaining entry into public relations. Neither is a winning smile, a charming personality, or a handsome countenance. All these qualities may be desirable, but they are not at the heart of public relations.

Experts differ on what traits they would prefer to see in those embarking on a public relations career, but most lists would include the following, although not necessarily in the same order:

1. *Organizational ability.* Unless the aspiring entrant possesses an organized mind, unless he or she can benefit from past experience and put together a cogent plan, success is unlikely. Lack of organization is much more fatal than a limp handshake.

2. *Judgment.* Even though judgment is thought of as a quality belonging to the more mature, that doesn't always hold true. Some youngsters have excellent judgment, whereas some of their elders exercise poor judgment. Still, experience should be an aid. The active PR practitioner makes dozens of important decisions every week. Some of them involve reputations; others involve large sums of money. Practitioners can't score 100 percent, but they had better have a solid record for being right most of the time. Good judgment tells the practitioner when to send a message and when to hold it. Good judgment helps word the message. Good judgment acts like a conscience to leaven planning.

3. *Communication skills* (preferably writing). Public relations is communicating, so the practitioner should be adept at it. Perhaps great writers are born, but some training and adequate practice can make a good communicator out of a fair one. Again, if the practitioner has absolutely no flair for communication, he or she will have a hard time finding a PR niche.

4. *An open mind.* Public relations holds to certain basic principles, but the externals change all the time. The practitioner has to be ready to change with them. Practitioners can't edit publications the way they did in 1960, and practitioners can't approach audiences—women, minorities, young people, and others—the way they did in the immediate post–World War II era.

5. *Understanding.* Understanding is difficult to describe. It isn't merely sympathy, or curiousity or charity. It is these virtues and more. It is a drive to really know, at the deepest possible level, just what makes individuals and society tick. If practitioners meet this challenge only superficially, it won't be nearly good enough.

6. *Originality.*   People may function pretty well without originality, but all the exceptional public relations people exhibit this rare asset. They are original thinkers. They can construct conclusions from the combination of two old ideas. They can let their minds soar, and they can devise fresh solutions rather than old by-the-book answers.

7. *Integrity.*   Integrity goes beyond the mere prohibition against dishonesty. People should, of course, always be ethical. Not only is this the decent thing to do, it is also the most profitable in the long run. But, beyond this admonition, integrity means having the courage to advance your ideas forcefully and the courage to strongly oppose your boss or client when you believe he or she is wrong. Some weak PR persons cave in once their premises are attacked. They nod whenever the VIP speaks. Such people are nearly useless, because they have no convictions of their own and they can do virtually nothing to prevent catastrophe.

8. *Leadership.*   Leadership is related to integrity but has other aspects. In some situations, the PR director is not made part of the management team. He or she is called in when there is a problem or some onerous task to be performed. The way out of this impossible situation is via the vigorous demonstration of leadership, which should entitle a person to attendance at these high-level gatherings. Don't forget, too, that the PR professional must persuade people all the time—and not only the external publics but also his or her own peers and superiors. The professional has done the research and has the plan. He or she must be able, diplomatically, to cause others to follow.

9. *Broad knowledge.*   The PR person can't know too much to begin with and must never lose his or her thirst for further education. Certain basic subjects—psychology, sociology, economics, history, political science, English, and various areas of the humanities—should be in every professional's background. Management and marketing courses are essential to the student who plans to enter corporate public relations. As practitioners add new clients or move to another PR post, they may discover they need to know something about science or agriculture or music. They may need to learn a new language or imbibe a new culture. The ability to do these things separates the practitioners who merely get by from those who truly excel.

10. *Patience.*   There are many frustrations in public relations and many deadlines and demands. The job is often a pressure cooker. If you are impatient with others, or with your own performance, this could be disastrous. You have to attack your job on a day-to-day basis, assuming that there will be disappointments and a certain amount of unavoidable error. The sun will come up the next day.

Other observers might add dedication, discretion, optimism, a talent for research, self-confidence, poise, and problem-solving abilities.

WHO ARE THE PROFESSIONALS?

The response to this question, seeking to develop a profile of the average PR person, changes considerably over a ten-year period. Both the Public Relations Society of America and the International Association of Business Communicators survey their memberships, usually annually, as do individual professional chapters, colleges and universities, and various private organizations.

The IABC Foundation, in its 1985 *Profile*, said this of its typical member:

> She's 34 years of age, the manager of a corporate communication department in the finance or banking field where she spends at least 25 percent of her time on management functions, including supervising at least one employee. She's been in the field eight years, with her current employer four years and in her current job at least two years, where she earns $29,608.[1]

The same survey catalogued a sharp increase in salaries over a two-year period but a continuing imbalance between earnings of men and women

Figure 11-1

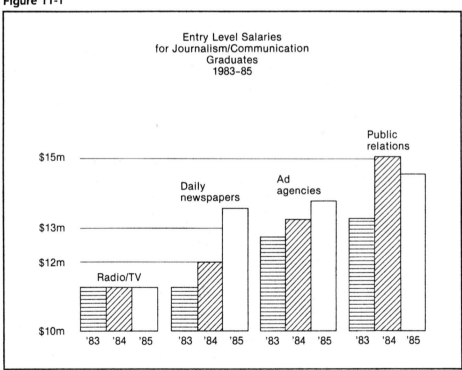

practitioners. Corporations were the major employers, and a third of the jobs occupied by members were newly created positions. Nine out of ten respondents were college graduates.

The prototype PRSA member is generally older than his IABC counterpart, is male, may have an advanced degree, and averages about $10,000 a year more than his younger counterpart. Discrepancies between male and female salaries remain at this level as well.

The highest salaries at all levels are found on either coast, with industry, utilities, and private consulting all compensating PR principals at about the same rate. Women are entering the profession at a considerably faster pace than men (and some studies show them to be more trusted as spokespersons), and minority businessmen and businesswomen (especially blacks) account for up to 10 percent of those in the field.

A survey conducted by former Ohio State University professor Walt Seifert in 1984, using members of the Central Ohio PRSA Chapter, revealed:

> . . . most respondents enjoy what they are doing; the average practitioner performs 19 different functions per year; most majored in journalism; more men than women are policy counselors; men tend to stay in the field longer; practitioners with graduate degrees earn considerably more than those with only bachelor's or high school degrees; accredited practitioners earn more than those who are not accredited.[2]

Like salaries and duties, the issues current in PR also change periodically. Once professionals identified topics like energy, the environment, and inflation as among the key areas requiring communication skills. In 1985 (according to the IABC survey), the leading issues were employee morale, cost containment, competition, productivity, technology, and government relations. Topics like ethics and professionalism and social responsibility also received more attention.

Figures on the number of practitioners are hard to come by. Some settle on 40,000 professionals as an accurate count, but most analysts would find this too low. More than twice that number is a more likely total, even without bringing in some of the questionable vocations. From a fourth to a half of those active in PR belong to some professional organization, notably PRSA and IABC, if you arrive at a conservative overall estimate.

Revenues for the nation's top 50 public relations firms were nearly $450 million in 1984, an increase of 24 percent over the preceding 12 months. The number of employees also showed large gains, an optimistic omen for college graduates.

In 1984, based on gross billings, the top five public relations firms in the United States were Burson-Marsteller, Hill and Knowlton, Carl Byoir & Associates, Ruder Finn & Rotman, and Ogilvy & Mather. All reported a sharp rise in income.

As the nation's business press has noted, public relations has finally arrived. Denny Griswold, founder and editor of the 43-year-old *Public Relations News*, says:

> If you study the history of American business, you'll see that the leadership always responds to the needs of the time. There was a time when production was king. When marketing grew in importance, the salesman took over. During the antitrust era, the financial man and lawyer were on top. Today, public relations skills are what's called for, and public relations is achieving status in the corporate world comparable to production, marketing, finance and law.[3]

With this improved status, public relations now becomes an avenue to the corporate board room, a route heretofore confined to those with financial or marketing credentials. Professional aspirations, broader backgrounds, and the advantages of spokesperson skills have vaulted PR people to the top in a number of national firms.

BREAKING INTO PUBLIC RELATIONS

Entry into public relations is hardly uniform. According to the *Public Relations Journal*, the two most common avenues for beginners are these:

- Entering the profession right out of college, with a degree in journalism, English, public relations, or business administration forming the academic background
- Transferring to public relations from another media post

Eight out of ten people come from the categories above. Corporate public relations claims most of the beginners, with counseling firms ranking second, and schools, government, and associations competing for third place.

Like any profession, public relations has its assets and liabilities. The work is challenging, varied, and service-oriented, and the compensation is generally good. Hours can be long, some relationships can be difficult, and the necessity of providing continual solutions can be taxing.

Advancement may come rapidly to those in the profession who can make a real contribution. That is why it makes sense to take an initial PR job that may not offer a staggering salary but does promise experience and exposure. If the work is good, the practitioner will be noticed and job offers will follow.

Selection of new employees may not always be so scientific: "The majority of employers still use intuition to hire people and don't rely on any kind of testing mechanisms such as editing and spelling tests."[4]

Beginners will probably find themselves working in press relations or information services, helping edit publications, handling public affairs, or assisting with audiovisual presentations.

Well-known counseling firms rarely hire untrained personnel. Their recruits come primarily from communication posts of some five or six years' duration.

EDUCATIONAL PREPARATION
FOR PUBLIC RELATIONS

A survey conducted in the fall of 1980 by Professor Paul V. Peterson of Ohio State queried journalism students in 243 of the nation's colleges, and it discovered that public relations led the way in terms of career interests. Scholarships for PR majors have increased; business-administration schools have added courses in public relations to their curricula, or have recommended that their students pick up the course elsewhere; and the number of degree opportunities in PR has expanded.

Overall, despite the continuing emphasis on "skills" within the curriculum in order to prepare students for entry-level positions, there has been an increase in theory courses, a greater involvement of professionals as guest lecturers, an expansion of internship or other practical experience, and an insistence on a diverse array of liberal arts and business courses as background. For the serious professional, education beyond the bachelor's degree is desirable.

Course names are dissimilar, but most univesities offering a degree in public relations require a principles course, one in case problems, several writing courses, some form of graphics, and courses in organizational communication, persuasion, research, corporate communication, public opinion, editing, and related subjects. Some mandate economics and other business subjects, psychology, sociology, and, if the student intends to specialize in some area of public relations, courses in that specialty. Some programs include advertising, statistics, media history, communication law, radio and television production, and some form of practicum.

Although the debate continues over whether or not the PR sequence should remain within a communications or a journalism department (as against the business curriculum, for example), the fact is that communications is the home for a majority of the programs. Even so, practitioners and educators have been emphasizing for years the need for the professional to understand more than the techniques of good communication. They insist that a greater knowledge of business and theory is essential, especially if the PR person is to fill an advisory role.

Among other areas of contention, arguments are made for the employment of more veteran PR personnel on university faculties instead of a surplus of those whose training is primarily academic; for the existence of a mandatory master's degree; for the development of an exit exam in college to test capabilities. Periodic professional committees have wrestled with curriculum suggestions, but progress has been slow. Some blame the ambivalence among educators and professionals; some accuse accrediting associations that have emphasized journalism; and some point to the low status of public relations programs in liberal-arts curricula—a sort of academic snobbery.

> . . . professionalism will not be served properly until there is general agreement among educators and practitioners on precisely what professional standards the beginning public relations person should be required to meet. In short, what is needed is a synergy of education and expectations.[5]

Internship programs define another area of disagreement. Educational accrediting associations restrict credits in this area and tend to regard such activities as of questionable academic value. Practitioners, on the other hand, applaud the internship for its realistic associations, and they promote an increase in the number and kind of internships.

Some internships carry stipends, often the minimum wage, and others are offered without pay. Credit also varies, from zero to three hours, and the number of required internship hours, the addition of term papers, and similar stipulations are not standardized.

Large cities offer more opportunities, since large and small businesses, PR firms, government agencies, nonprofit institutions, and other internship sources are apt to be located there. For the employer, the internship also provides help with a specific task, an extra pair of hands, or a vacation replacement.

Graduates generally appreciate the internship experience. For many, it leads to the first job. For the rest, it adds practical experience to their résumés and job skills.

Another means of gathering experience is with the student-run public relations company, tied perhaps to the campus PRSSA (Public Relations Student Society of America) chapter or a specific PR class. The students create an agency setup under faculty supervision, solicit and service clients

Figure 11-2 Internship experience is both a valuable learning experience and a help in finding that first job.

(often not-for-profit firms and agencies with small budgets), and either divide up any net income or place it in a special fund.

Many other innovations are due in public relations education, including the formulation of more standard graduate degrees that will emphasize theory, research, and management. There is also talk about the institution of more master's degrees that combine PR with another discipline, like science, medicine, law, or business administration.

THE FIRST JOB

Locating a job in PR isn't simple. There are a number of roadblocks. One problem is that many positions advertised under the heading of public relations are not PR jobs at all. A typical ploy is to advertise sales work as public relations, but one also sees receptionist posts, bartender jobs, and hostess work listed under PR headings.

Another problem is that many public relations openings are never advertised. Word seems to just get around, and the positions are filled via grapevine connections. This means that making the rounds of firms and agencies and staying in touch with public relations professionals will be helpful.

Internships are a plus here, as is membership in a student chapter of PRSSA or IABC. Any way the student can tap into the network of professionals is an advantage. Generally, the college placement bureau is not conversant with PR jobs, so the communications-department faculty may be a better source of leads.

When starting from scratch, the applicant might use the Yellow Pages of the local phone book or a city directory, a Chamber of Commerce business list, or some other tool, and should make a roster of prospective employers, starting with major companies with large PR staffs, then graduating to smaller firms with smaller staffs, then considering nonprofit agencies, government agencies, and others.

Starting salaries for those with limited or no experience beyond the college degree may range from $11,000 to $15,000, with a few lower and higher. As with salaries of veteran practitioners, salaries of beginners also fluctuate according to area or type of firm or organization.

THE JOB SEARCH

Looking for a job *is* a job. Even though opportunities in public relations are expanding, the competition is also expanding, and the person who knows how to position himself or herself will more likely get the nod.

Dr. Frederick H. Teahan of PRSA calls job hunting "the ultimate marketing campaign," and urges applicants to be serious and scientific about it.

Among his suggestions are determining your objectives, researching the field, identifying prospective employers, learning how to promote yourself, and tailoring the résumé and letter to the specific job opening.

Teahan also believes in direct mail to numerous prospects, following up quickly on those that reply, and registering with all possible job clearing-houses. All professionals recognize that timing plays a part in hiring, so the only way to ensure that you'll be considered is to have your name and résumé circulating.

People looking for work must know their own strengths and weaknesses, and should try to match their strengths to certain job openings. This calls for a bit of creative research—looking up the prospective company in Dun & Bradstreet or Standard & Poor's Registry; checking local and national news files; calling the Better Business Bureau; talking to someone who works there; collecting material such as annual reports or company brochures; reading up on company execs in *Who's Who* volumes; phoning the firm or paying a visit. Some aggressive job seekers solicit interviews by asking employers how they got into that field themselves.

Initially, looking for work can be depressing, but you must be ready for a certain amount of rejection before you hear the words of acceptance. That makes patience and persistence twin virtues in the job search.

The Résumé

There are three types of résumés:

- The traditional chronological résumé, which provides information on the applicant's personal background, education, military record (if any), and interests, and a list of jobs and employers, with the most recent listed first.
- A functional résumé, which features skills mastered rather than an orderly list of job titles. This works especially well for someone who may have learned to do things as a volunteer, or whose company affiliations are not impressive. This form of résumé lets prospective employers know what you can do rather than where you've been.
- A targeted résumé is one tailored to match education, skills, and experience with a specific position. Sometimes the résumé may be broad enough to fit a number of jobs in a certain field, but it is often made up for a single post.

Résumés should be typed, and many of them are now being printed. They should be limited to a page and a half or less, with ample spacing, no fancy lettering or other visual gimmicks, and normally no photograph. Résumés must be complete and accurate, without typos or misspelled words or missing information.

Chronological résumés generally begin with personal data—name, address, phone. Federal guidelines recommend that résumés not carry statements on age, height, weight, general statement of health, marital status, and other items that may be prejudicial.

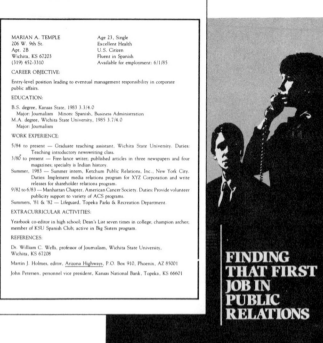

Figure 11-3
Courtesy: Dow Chemical
U.S.A., from its brochure,
*Finding That First Job
in Public Relations*

Then educational background is added, starting with the highest degree earned and moving backward in time. Jobs are listed in the same way, from the current to the earliest. Unless the applicant's job list is slim, the least-important positions might be eliminated. There should not, however, be wide gaps in career information.

For the more imposing positions held previously, more detail may be given so that the interviewer will fully understand the responsibilities handled by the applicant.

Awards, honors, and professional memberships may be included at this point, and items like hobbies or athletic interests may be added.

References generally end a résumé, although some résumés just state that references will be furnished upon request. When references are given, those listed should be asked first and their approval given. Make this a short (three or four names) and varied (teacher, employer, counselor) list.

For public relations openings, a strong portfolio is a great advantage. Prospective employers would like to see what you have done. News stories, magazine articles, brochures, and other printed pieces can be collected in a folder chronologically, with your most recent work last. Each item should be dated and identified. If you have visual items like films or TV programs you have written the scripts for or produced, be certain you supply the means to screen them. Never let your original "clip file" out of your hands; supply prospective employers with photocopies.

Special factors, like fluency in a foreign language or extensive overseas travel, should be mentioned, as should any posts that had management responsibilities, including volunteer offices. Since this is also a writing exercise, use action verbs and, if you can do so expertly, tune in on the particular jargon of that profession.

Job applicants have used oversized playing cards, stock certificates, audiotapes, and even a pizza box with wedge-shaped résumé sections—all to get attention. Sometimes these may work, but they may turn certain personnel people off.

There should almost always be a cover letter accompanying the résumé. This is another chance to show your writing style; this letter may contain facts that didn't fit the résumé, especially when they are specific to the job opening, and may also subtly demonstrate what you know about the company and its needs.

Keep in mind that the main purpose of the résumé and cover letter is to secure an interview.

The Interview

College seniors should take advantage of campus interviews, learning how to respond to questions, how to dress, how to establish rapport with the interviewer. For each of these they might prepare in advance, learning what they can about the firm or organization. As any counselor will tell you, questions about vacations and Christmas bonuses are hardly material for initial queries; stick with a discussion of your career plans and the way they might merge with company goals.

For employment in public relations, consider the attributes listed earlier in this chapter as the virtues interviewers will concentrate on. The secret in any competitive job situation is to spotlight some essential "plus" factors not possessed by other applicants. If all have college degrees and all have written for the campus paper, then an internship could be a plus. If the others have internships too, then other job experience or published work or special skills could constitute an advantage. Everyone has some edge for certain posts; the trick is to find and exploit it.

During the job interview, the person doing the hiring may ask for clarification of some résumé items, may request more details on job performance, may probe to learn more about the applicant's personality and goals. The way a person presents himself or herself may be scrutinized, along with the person's knowledge of the business or organization, imagination, professional attitudes, even enthusiasm and sense of humor. Interviewers could try to pinpoint salary demands, if appropriate, and they could check out what appears to be a plethora of job moves.

Companies like Dow Chemical U.S.A. and Metropolitan Life Insurance Company have issued helpful booklets on the job search, as have *Quill* magazine, *Changing Times*, *Public Relations Journal*, and other sources. They all include specific tips, like preparing thoroughly, not smoking or fidgeting, asking intelligent questions, anticipating interviewer questions, looking interested, dressing properly, and following up with a note, whether or not you get the job.

JOBS IN PUBLIC RELATIONS

The variety of titles alone would nearly convince you that opportunities in the field of public relations are many and diverse. To begin with, there is the choice between serving as an internal public relations person or opting for the public relations counseling firm. Both have their assets and liabilities.

The Internal Public Relations Director

The internal PR person is salaried, part of the management team, and responsible to his or her specific organization for all (or part of) the duties usually associated with this profession.

Titles may vary widely. Even in a limited area like college and university public relations, there are 50 or more titles describing essentially the same function: director of public relations, vice-president for university relations, director of community relations, vice-president for communications, and so on and on. There are also news bureau directors, publications specialists, and a host of other subordinate titles.

The staff PR director operates within a specific budget and in cooperation with both management and other department heads. His or her duties may be all-encompassing, or there could be a PR team to share some of the responsibility. On occasion, outside help might be retained for a specific project, or counsel might be employed permanently on a part-time basis.

Duties of the internal public relations person vary according to the nature of the institution and the size of the staff. A public relations director with a large staff, for example, would spend more time in planning, management, and counseling than in writing, editing, or placement of stories. The person working alone or with a small staff may have the writing and editing responsibilities, and also photography, placement, and production.

Among the other duties assumed by internal PR people are community relations, lobbying, the training of others to represent the organization, institutional advertising, the designing of programs to achieve goals, the management of special events, and the all-important advisory function to top management.

The obvious benefit of a staff person on the premises is his or her intimate knowledge of the organization. This person is around to catch the day-to-day PR signals, to advise associates, to spot possible stories, to move fast on possible problems. Some would claim that a staff person is also more economical. That depends. If you have a modest-sized business and are faced with the outlay for a good PR person, a secretary, office space, and other costs, you might well consider the benefits of part-time counseling.

The shortcomings of "inside" persons may also be obvious. Lack of objectivity is a big danger. When they are close to a situation and must work alongside the same people, their vision may become a bit insular. They ignore potential problems because such problems involve difficult personal relations.

They may also have tried certain remedies and failed, so they pretend the problem doesn't exist. Or they may not even recognize the problem.

Internal PR persons often find it harder to say no when they disagree. This, after all, is their home, and they like to keep it relatively happy. Because the PR person anticipates the barriers, he or she may not even try to scale them.

Another syndrome that can affect staff PR people is too long an association with a job, which may make them stale. They are comfortable and know how to get by, so there is no need to push things. They may become bored, compliant, and lazy.

Sometimes staff people are so overburdened with work—work that should be shared by associates—they just figure there is no sense in inventing new programs or even doing their utmost on old programs. If the organization won't give me any more help, the staff person says, it can't blame me for the way things are.

Even the general advantage of team membership and closeness to the organization can be a drawback. This person can be used. Associates drop all their problems in the PR person's lap. "After all," they declare, "it is public relations, isn't it?"

The Public Relations Counselor

The PR counselor is a person employed by one of the approximately 2,000 public relations firms, or as a member of a PR department in an advertising agency, or as a private free-lancer. In general, this person would be a bit older on the average than the staff practitioner, would be more experienced, and would be better paid. He or she would handle one or more clients and could be in a strictly advisory role or could also execute some programs, either alone or in cooperation with staff PR members.

A majority of the PR firms would offer a full range of services, from news releases to special events, but some specialize in graphics or financial affairs or other limited areas.

Although advertising agencies were initially reluctant to incorporate the public relations function in their shops—primarily because advertising promised more return for effort expended—many now have their own PR departments, and some large ad agencies have merged with major public relations firms. The reasons are simple. Even though the commission on advertising may come in big chunks, whereas PR fees are earned more slowly, the fees are steady and they are income. Moreover, having this added capability adds to an agency's reputation and prevents other agencies with PR departments from stealing its clients. Some advertising agencies claim that their PR accounts bring in a third or a fourth of their revenue.

Smaller firms may attempt to counter the clout of the larger PR firms by affiliating with other small companies here and abroad. This type of network provides the opportunity for local service for a client (like photo coverage of an event distant from the home office), more sensible media placement, research (including sharing and combining the results of surveys and focus groups), specialists in certain areas who can tackle a difficult project, and the sharing of information or case histories on certain industries or operations. Medium-sized companies often network, and the large firms also take advantage of this tactic to expand their capabilities, especially abroad. Some of these networks are formalized, having stockholders, officers, and annual meetings.

The individual consultant may enjoy a certain amount of independence and autonomy and prestige, but the consultant also gives up a bit of security, some company fringe benefits, and perhaps the sense of belonging.

Some of the benefits of the outside counselor are the reverse of the internal person's shortcomings.

Objectivity is the main asset. The counselor arrives with fewer prejudices and, most likely, with no experience, good or bad, with that particular company or organization. The counselor should be able to see things more as they are, free of the nuances that come with close association.

Another thing the counselor brings, perhaps, is a wider variety of experience. If the counselor has been in the business longer and has had many more clients, his or her backlog of cases, both successes and failures, should be invaluable in applying past experience to new problems.

The outside person could offer both breadth and depth. The breadth comes from his or her staff, perhaps branch offices and wider relationships with the media, perhaps outlets in New York, and perhaps a number of specialized skills. The depth comes from the addition of another person to the problem-solving team.

An outside expert may or may not be more economical, but is usually listened to a lot more closely. This may not be fair or even wise, but it is true.

On the negative side, there can be many clients clamoring for the counselor's time. Priorities must be set, and some clients will be lower on the scale than others. Every successful PR counselor contracts for more time than he or she can reasonably spend. The counselor lives in dread of the day when all clients might call at the same time and want something. Fortunately, this rarely happens. Still, no single client is the one true love, and each may have to wait his or her turn.

This outside expert can rarely duplicate the loyalty and attention provided by a good staff person. The counselor is not on the site and cannot be expected to know all the little shop gossip. It may also take some time to become acquainted and be accepted. Then, too, the counselor's limited contacts with each firm might not allow a deep enough knowledge of that particular business or organization. The counselor may be skimming the surface and relying on general skills.

There is a key human relationship involved in private counseling, besides the ability to relate to numerous publics. The prime relationship is with the firm's client.

The client and the public relations counselor must trust and respect each other, must share confidences, must work toward similar goals. The client should avoid feeling that he or she knows as much about public relations as the practitioner, and the practitioner should not assume that the client knows nothing. The counselor should be honest and objective in relaying advice, and self-critical in reviewing his or her own performance.

If counselors had one universal plea, it might be that clients come to them earlier—before they get into trouble. Many clients arrive with headaches in hand, and some of these illnesses are terminal.

Obviously, the best way to obtain and retain clients is by doing consistently good work. Even then, there is no guarantee that something may not intervene to cause the client to depart. That's why the alert PR firm is always on top of the account, always seeking new and better ways to do things, always in touch with the client, always alive to signs of dissatisfaction. A company that wants to keep an account services it with good people (and enough of them), communicates regularly and openly, discusses fees honestly, and tries to match the client's interest in the particular product or service. You listen and you talk, just as you do in any relationship, and you try to anticipate needs.

Sometimes the relationship breaks down, and, with over 2,000 PR firms to choose from, the client may decide to look elsewhere. What sort of things will the client be looking for?

1. *Financial stability.* Check credit rating and bill-paying reputation.
2. *History.* How did the firm originate? What is its rate of turnover in accounts? Has the organization grown? What about staff turnover? and profitability?
3. *Peer recognition.* How involved in professional societies are firm members, and how are they regarded by counterparts in other PR firms?
4. *Related experience.* Has the firm under consideration handled any similar accounts? What is its track record with present accounts?
5. *Editorial recognition.* What is its reputation with the media?

TAKING MYTH OUT OF PR
By A.C. Croft

Ever since Ivy Lee was a trusted adviser to John D. Rockefeller, much of the perception of PR counseling companies has rested loosely on a number of myths. Passing time and events have added to those myths and deepened the misperception. A few of those myths—arbitrarily deemed to be most pervasive—need to be dispelled.

Myth No. 1: They don't know my business.

Fact: No public relations company is going to know the day-to-day operation of your business as well as you do. But major companies offer a wealth of specialized and general knowledge and an objective perspective that is a major part of the contribution they make to your public relations effort. They also can learn the basics of your business quickly. Remember, you're retraining PR experts, not experts in *your* business. It's realistic however, to expect that a large PR agency will have people on its staff who know enough about your business to be helpful quickly.

Myth No. 2: I can do it cheaper inside.

Fact: It depends on what you need done. The more simple, basic tasks you can handle inside, the better. If all you need written are production releases and personnel announcements, why retain a PR company? For less than $20,000, you can hire a junior person who will perform perfectly adequately. (But don't forget the cost of that person's office space, equipment purchases, and fringe benefits. Personnel people estimate that overhead costs add at least another 100 percent to the cost of hiring. Of course, you'll also need someone on your staff with enough time and ability to train and supervise the junior person.)

If you need broader, more demanding services such as strategic planning, overcoming a poor image, establishing a leadership reputation, providing broad marketing support, producing an employee publication, an annual report, or a multiple-screen slide show, counseling the CEO or other executives on sensitive community relations, labor relations, or consumer relations problems, you have two choices. Build a large internal PR staff with the varied skills and experience—and cost—to handle a variety of needs. Or retain a PR company with the varied talent and experience to meet your needs.

And remember, with a PR company, your hand is always on the faucet handle. It's much easier to slow down or—perish the thought—stop a PR company's activity than it is to lay off permanent employees.

Myth No. 3: Public relations companies that are part of an advertising agency don't provide broad professional public relations services; they just do product publicity.

Fact: Not true. Ten of the 20 largest PR companies in the U.S. are owned by advertising agencies. They operate as independent, autonomous, full-service divisions or subsidiaries of the parent company.

Alliance with an advertising agency provides access to such resources as research, databases, art direction, audiovisual and print production capabilities, and helps sharpen PR people's marketing insight.

Myth No. 4: Public relations companies promise more than they deliver.

Fact: Some do, but not for long. You should, however, expect results that are more meaningful than clippings or TV time: Measured attitude or awareness changes; an increase in qualified inquiries; a jump in sales, or a specific action by a target audience. The company also should be held accountable for cost-efficiency.

Myth No. 5: If you're a small client, you'll never see any of the company's top people after the new-business pitch.

Fact: Also true, occasionally. However, most well-regarded companies believe that every client, no matter what its size, deserves its "fair share" of the agency's individual and collective time and minds. The quantity of service you receive—the number of individual hours invested in your behalf—will naturally be determined by your budget.

However, the *quality* of the service . . . the thinking behind it . . . will always be at the top of the scale. (Successful agencies recognized long ago that small clients can very easily grow into larger ones.)

Myth No. 6: A public relations company's primary job is to produce lots of publicity.

Fact: Wrong. Purposeless publicity tends to be next to valueless. Generating editorial coverage for a newsworthy product, or staging a media event to attract coverage when real news is missing, requires professional skill and creativity. However, every publicity tactic or special event must contribute to an over-all objective, help establish a specific position for the client or communicate a targeted message to a precisely defined audience.

Myth No. 7: Always retain a PR company that has lots of "contacts" in your field.

Fact: Baloney! The theory that "contacts" are essential to the proper practice of professional public relations is possibly the most woebegone myth of all.

Today, for the most part, if you have an interesting story that an editor or broadcaster believes will appeal to his readers, listeners or viewers, chances are it will get used. If it's a bad story, all the "contacts" in the world won't get it published or will, in some instances, keep it from being published.

SOURCE: Courtesy of the author, A.C. Croft, senior vice-president and Midwest general manager, Bozell, Jacobs, Kenyon & Eckhardt Public Relations. Excerpted and reprinted from the May 27, 1985, issue of *Advertising Age.* Copyright 1985 by Crain Communications, Inc.

6. *Specialization.* If the client requires certain specialized services, he should check on the ability of the PR firm to deliver them.
7. *The service team.* Who are the people who will work on the account? Are they professionals? How will they mesh with staff members? How well are they supervised?
8. *Programming logic.* Do they build their programs on adequate research, or do they communicate by intuition?
9. *Measurement.* What are the public relations firm's accountability procedures? How does it report progress? Will it supply periodic reports?
10. *Executive interchange.* Is the PR firm's management available to the client organization's leadership? How does it stay in touch? Are the people leaders in public affairs, communication thinking, and techniques?[6]

FEES AND CHARGES

The outside counselor sells ideas, experience, and expertise, but most of all, he or she sells *time.* Whatever fee arrangement is arrived at, it ordinarily relates to the time spent or to the time the counselor estimates will be spent.

Because of the nature of creativity, it would be impossible to pay people otherwise. You can't compensate them per idea—or for the time each good idea takes. The practitioner may have to discard hundreds of bad ideas before arriving at the good one, and someone has to pay for that time.

Let us take a concrete example. You represent a major banking institution in your city, and you are phoned at 10 A.M. and asked to read a small item in the morning paper. It comes from a neighboring state, which your bank services with credit-card programs. An ambitious candidate for governor in that state has accused three of his state banks of "usury," since their credit-card interest could amount to "over 18 percent a year," more than the legal limit in that state. In the brief story, he names your bank as being equally culpable, since it is the supplier. Your bank president has phoned friends in the neighboring state, and they say it will all blow over, that this is merely campaign rhetoric and the complaining candidate has no intention of following up. The bank president says, "I think perhaps we should just ignore it. What do you think?" You reflect a moment and reply, "Well, there are two terms I don't like in that story: 'usury' and '18 percent.' Both are misleading. I think we should issue a release for the evening paper, which has quadruple the morning circulation." The president agrees, and you write the story, bring it to the bank for approval, and have it at the news desk and wire-services desks before the noon deadline. Elapsed time: two hours. On the basis of $60 an hour, you earned $120. Was this effort worth $120? It was probably worth much more. In a sense, you are like the auto mechanic who replied to a critic, "You're not paying for the time I took finding the trouble; you're paying because I knew where to look."

Fees vary from place to place, with larger fees more common in places like New York and Los Angeles and smaller ones the rule in many midwestern and southern communities. Coastal clients are used to paying such fees; those in other sections of the country are not.

Reputation also influences costs of services. Firms that employ experienced and talented personnel and handle prestige accounts usually have a minimum billing they will accept before agreeing to represent a client. Hill and Knowlton, one of the nation's two largest public relations agencies, starts any relationship with a "retainer" from the client, much as an attorney would request a similar fee merely to represent someone exclusively. Most large firms have such an arrangement.

The story may be apocryphal, but a prospective client was said to have inquired of a Hill and Knowlton executive, "How much do you charge for your

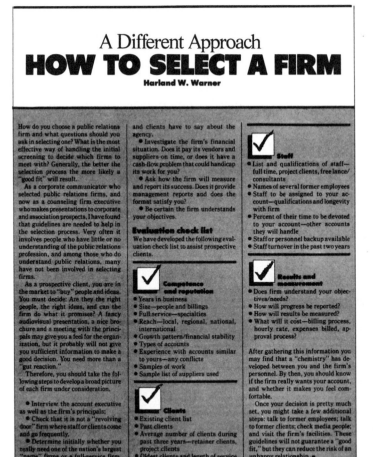

Figure 11-4

SOURCE: Harland W. Warner, "How to Select a PR Firm." Reprinted with permission from the October 1983 issue of the *Public Relations Journal.* Copyright 1983.

services?" Without blinking, the PR executive said, "Four thousand dollars per month." "And what do you do for that?" asked the businessman. "We think about you," said the PR executive. He added that if they did anything beyond that, there would be an additional fee.

A less-prestigious firm could not operate like this. There would be some negotiating with the client until they arrived at a suitable fee arrangement.

Generally, fees fall into one of four categories (although there are many variations):

- *By the day* (per diem). Consultants average over $500 a day, and a few make upwards of $2,000 a day.
- *By the hour.* Rates vary, but they probably average about $50–$60 per hour, with a few on either side of this average. PR firms may also have different rates for different consultants, with senior consultants earning the higher figure.
- *By the project.* This is often arrived at when services are sporadic, or when a major event will occupy the time of numerous personnel. The consultant tries to estimate in advance the time involved and quotes a figure based on that calculated guess. Like a house painter, he or she must be accurate in order to satisfy both the client and the PR firm.
- *By retainer.* A monthly or an annual amount of money is provided to the consultant, either to cover all anticipated costs or, in many cases, merely to retain the exclusive services of this consulting firm. One of the three rate structures above could then be added to this retainer.

Other forms of compensation are a minimum monthly fee plus actual costs and a reasonable markup on contracted services, a retainer plus net costs, and other variations. Discussion of these matters should always be up front and open. The consultant should be properly compensated, and the client should get value for his or her investment. No good PR person likes the feeling of accepting money without performing a commensurate service, and no client relishes the notion of surrendering funds without an appropriate return.

Sometimes, perhaps when a PR firm is beginning a relationship with a small or unknown company, the consultant may ask for some money in advance, especially if the PR firm must make some cash commitments to other suppliers. Client and consultant may also agree to a six-month contract, subject to review after that period, with the consultant reducing the fee if the work proves to be less than anticipated, and with the client increasing compensation if the task takes more time. There is a give and take in the business of fees, and no set amount is established nationally, like a union pay scale.

The fees are also based on "billable" time, those days or hours when the consultant is actually working on the account. Time spent seeking new business, having lunch, on vacation, doing volunteer PR chores, or handling other office tasks are "non-billable" hours and produce no direct revenue. Still, they occupy time that must be balanced by the productive hours.

Keep in mind that there are other expenses besides the particular counselor's salary. His or her office employs secretaries, clerks, accountants, and other auxiliary personnel who must be paid, even though they do not work directly on the account. The company is also entitled to some profit, and, if it is publicly held, so are its stockholders. Then, too, there are always some costs that are not billable, or that the counselor forgets to bill—the copy machine, phone calls, the rent and utilities required to support an office.

The best ways to avoid debates about charges are these:

- Have a clear understanding with the client before accepting the account, and keep him or her regularly informed. No surprises!
- Keep accurate time sheets and other records.
- Work hard at the job and at client relationships.

One other source of income for the public relations firm is the markup allowed on what are called "collateral" materials. These include photos, printing, research, secretarial help, and other services that are contracted out. The traditional markup is 17.65 percent. If a photographer takes a photo and bills the PR firm $100, then the firm would bill the client $117.65. If you have ever tabulated the time it takes to instruct a photographer, review his or her proof sheets, select, perhaps call or visit, and do whatever else is necessary to get the pictures, you will agree that some compensation is justified. Time spent with printers is even longer, and if you supervise such things as research or the use of your secretaries for stuffing and mailing, you are entitled to some return. The client, of course, should always know in advance about this arrangement, and it is a good practice to itemize these amounts in billing.

Money can be made fairly easily by a good firm, but it can be lost just as easily. Counselors who fail to keep records, who forget to apply a collateral charge against a specific client, who neglect to notify the accounting department of special billings—all these lapses mean losses. A public relations firm can fail in other ways as well. Sometimes it extends credit and gets burned. Sometimes it goes out on a limb with an expensive printing piece and the client fails to pay. Sometimes it makes an error and has to make good its mistake. Any one of these flaws could wipe out the profit in an individual account.

BIG FIRM VS. SMALL FIRM

When people are considering the prospects of aligning themselves with a large or small corporation or PR firm (assuming they have such an option), they must decide which life-style suits them best.

The major companies offer more extensive benefits, greater prestige, and more staff help with projects. Smaller firms promise closer client—

consultant or client–boss relationships, more variety, and the satisfaction of seeing the enterprise grow. In the larger organization, the creative person could get locked into a single function for a single client or department (like handling trade-show exhibits), whereas the creative person in the smaller firm may be awash in detail for several accounts and without appropriate backup support. The large operation may be more stable; the small one can be severely wounded by the departure of one major client. Those who thrive on risk and diversity and autonomy may prefer the small shop or industry; those who admire order and prestige and permanence may see themselves with the corporation or comprehensive PR firm.

THE ETHICS OF THE PROFESSION

Ever since Watergate, the subject of ethics crops up more frequently at professional conferences and occupies more media space and time. The issues are sometimes complicated and controversial.

Should Geraldine Ferraro, after running for the high office of vice-president, cash in on that notoriety by accepting half a million dollars to star in a soft-drink commercial? Should Sam Ervin, made famous by his Watergate lectures on morality, serve as a spokesman for American Express?

What about the old media questions on the use of a photo showing a grieving parent? Or the practice of sports reporters accepting free meals, reduced rates at hotels, rides in the team bus, and other considerations? What about the refusal of many editors to participate in polls taken by outside firms while they criticize those who decline to be interviewed for their own polls? And what about those writers for numerous publications who lift items from other sources without attribution?

Business seems especially vulnerable. Twenty of the nation's largest corporations were cited in 1985 for a variety of violations in fulfilling their defense contracts, ranging from price fixing, bribery, overcharging, and bid rigging to subcontractor kickbacks, product substitution, duplicate billing, and falsification of performance. Others are in trouble because of their machinations abroad—falsifying company records, providing lavish gifts to prospective clients, bribing officials, and interfering in the internal affairs of a foreign country.

There are more subtle sins, like the refusal to take seriously complaints about environmental hazards. Or the manipulating of published earnings, using new accounting methods, or reallocating costs, or changing the parameters of the reporting period. Or the granting of loans and extension of credit by banking institutions to poor-risk friends.

Some of these activities constitute illegal conduct, but many of them fall into that gray area that may be defended as "just business" or "common practice" or "necessary when you're working with certain people." These

---

AVOIDING CONFLICT OF INTEREST

Even the most reputable public relations firms sometimes make mistakes.

In 1974, Mrs. Jacob Javits, wife of the then senior senator from New York and ranking Republican on the Foreign Relations Committee, proposed to the Shah of Iran, through his advisors, that she do public relations on behalf of that Mideast nation. This lobbying effort was cloaked as a relationship with Iran Air and was channeled through the prominent PR firm, Ruder & Finn, for whom Mrs. Javits had done occasional consulting work. Critics contended that all parties involved understood the true nature of the contract, which was to be funded to the tune of $500,000.

In the spring of 1979, after the Shah was deposed by the Ayatollah Khomeini, the papers detailing the public relations arrangements came to light. But the whole matter had been resolved three years earlier.

In 1976, when word of Mrs. Javits's role was revealed and the public learned she was receiving money for her consulting work, pressure forced her to resign. Shortly thereafter, the account with Ruder & Finn was canceled, and the public relations firm voluntarily returned part of the money paid to them before the contract was terminated.

The concern, of course, was that the wife of a top government official had a secret contract with a foreign power for the purpose of representing that country in the United States. No laws had been violated, but the relationship was, at the very least, imprudent.

The speedy resolution of the problem by Ruder & Finn, and their long history of ethical conduct, saved the firm from extended embarrassment.

---

aberrations go beyond the salesman's padding his expense account or the clerk's stealing pencils and paper clips, but they represent the same form of thinking.

Public relations people face the same temptations. They may want to conceal a truth or mask a failure, to stretch a point or bend a principle. Ethical practitioners resist these urges.

In the immediate post-Watergate era, a government official who had served under President Richard Nixon was discussing the presumed difficulty of remaining honest while enjoying high public office.

"It really isn't that hard," he said. "If you would only ask yourself this one question before taking any action: 'Would I do this if I knew my actions would be publicized in all media tonight?' If you cannot face that, then don't perform the action. It's that simple."

In a way, it *is* simple. We generally know when something we are about to do is a bit shaky. That's the time to follow your better judgment. Perhaps this means passing up a fast dollar or losing a shot at a wealthy client. However, you will benefit in the long run, and, more important, you will be able to live more comfortably with yourself and your associates. After all, making money is only one of the rewards of public relations—and it is not even the prime reward.

To begin with, public relations practitioners should properly identify themselves and the work they perform. Unless they truly offer specialized services (lobbying, financial relations, labor negotiating), they shouldn't advertise them. Experience and backgrounds should be neither falsified nor exaggerated. No promises should be made to clients that cannot be fulfilled— such as guaranteeing publicity or an increase in corporate earnings. Every client should be treated fairly and communicated with honestly. Business practices within the department or agency should be above reproach. Don Bates writes:

> Our ethics as practitioners are complicated by the "middle-man dilemma." Probably more than any other profession, we hold special our obligation to perform in accord with the public interest. On the other hand, we also hold special our obligation to serve the interests of our employers and clients, many of whom often think or act contrary to the public interest. As a result, we find ourselves in the uncomfortable position of talking out of both sides of our mouths in order to survive.[7]

Although this conflict may present a problem, it provides no excuse for unethical behavior.

> One of the realities that the public relations practitioner must face is that conflict often arises in a society when the individual's need is measured against the corporation's need.[8]

Good companies recognize their social responsibilities; they have corporate consciences. Like Johnson & Johnson, they stop advertising a tanning agent that may have encouraged excessive exposure to the sun, or, as with Tylenol and tampons, they speedily withdraw suspect products from retail shelves. Good PR people encourage such actions.

One of the benefits of an ethical approach is that, in the long run (and often in the short run), it works. An institution must have some values, some articles of faith, some code of ethics. Adhering to these establishes reputation, attracts good staff members and clients, and makes life much simpler. Sticking to these principles may occasionally hurt, but it pays off.

Three-fourths of the *Fortune* 1,000 companies have corporate codes of conduct, often including general statements of company philosophy, conflict-of-interest clauses, a ban on the giving or receiving of gifts, prohibitions against the misuse of corporate assets, reminders about laws affecting the business, and other such sections. Most of these codes involve formal acceptance by employees and have some sort of regular review. Sanctions,

These are some of the things we do. If you'd like to know more about our capabilities, contact the public relations director at any of these offices listed below.

Figure 11-5 This ad lists some of the varied roles played by public relations professionals. Courtesy: Ketchum Communications, Inc.

although not universal, are becoming more common. Some corporations, like Caterpillar Tractor, even provide worldwide editions of their ethics statements, standardizing practices wherever they do business.

The Public Relations Society of America drafted a Code of Professional Standards in 1954, then revised and strengthened it in 1977. It appears in the appendix to this volume and covers the practitioner's relationships with clients, the media, and the public. It stresses honesty and fair dealing with all segments of society, including one's competitors.

Even with this document as a guide, there are numerous lapses within the profession. A *Wall Street Journal* article addressed this issue:

> Pressure to produce, even if it means compromising personal moral standards, is perhaps greatest at the middle-management level. But nowhere do the ethical conflicts come into sharper focus than in the corporate public-relations departments. . . . "As a PR man," one of them explains, "you are at the point of disclosure. You are the mechanism of disclosure. So you can't hide behind the corporate veil like the lawyer and the accountant."[9]

Practitioners may sometimes delude themselves about a questionable ethical practice, but they usually know that such behavior is not consistent with professional conduct. When that twinge of conscience arises, it is best to review the situation, with an eye to rejecting the suspect course.

Here are some tips on ethical behavior:

1. Never accept a client whose character or conduct does not match your own standards. But if you do take on a client and later become concerned about the client's ethics, don't abruptly abandon him or her. You should make your concerns known and gracefully ease out of the relationship, but you should no more ditch your client in a crisis that a lawyer should turn his back on a client in the courtroom. If your PR client's conduct is criminal, of course, that's a different matter, and you should have no part of that.

2. Never handle two clients who compete directly with one another unless both clients agree to this arrangement. Even so, it is not a good idea. If you develop a successful campaign for one and a so-so campaign for the other, the second client will accuse you of giving your best efforts to his or her rival.

3. Always level with the media.

4. Conduct all your financial activities on an open basis, concealing nothing from client or public.

5. Keep the public interest in mind at all times, even when you are acting as a special advocate for your client.

6. Avoid unfair comments or criticism of competitors. These remarks come back to haunt you.

7. Respect any confidences that come about as the result of your client–counselor relationship.

8. Follow the guidelines established by the Public Relations Society of America, and build your own standards on top of these.

Admittedly, some cases are complicated, and practitioners can innocently diverge from the strict ethical code. They may even argue that they are acting in the best interest of their client. But it is always better to err on the side of ethical conservatism than to stretch the moral interpretations to their limits.

To aid the practitioner, the Public Relations Society of America not only offers its Code of Professional Standards in printed form but in 1984 produced a 35-minute videotape incorporating the 14 basic articles of conduct, the statement of principles, interpretations, examples, and case problems.

PUBLIC RELATIONS AND THE LAW

Besides ethical considerations, there are legal considerations to be observed in the practice of public relations. Even though the PR person is not a lawyer (and shouldn't try to perform like one), some basic knowledge of the laws that affect the practice is helpful. Not only will this save the practitioner from making some disastrous mistake; it can also be helpful in dealing with attorneys. Lawyers tend to be cautious. If they were writing advertising or public relations copy, either nothing would emerge or it would be so intricately worded as to be unintelligible to the layperson. Knowing how far you may safely go and being able to substantiate your conclusions is a definite asset.

There are two general points to remember: First, the law is always changing, and what may have been permissible a year ago may not be permissible today—the new, more stringent copyright laws are a case in point. And second, public relations practitioners can be legally liable when they condone, participate in, conceal, or otherwise involve themselves in unlawful actions committed by people they represent.

It is the rare PR person who deliberately flouts the law. Most problems occur because of carelessness or ignorance. The penalties, however, can be just as severe. Although practitioners should not allow a company's legal counsel to infringe on matters that are strictly public relations issues, they should not ignore legal advice concerning actions that could bring sanctions on them, their companies, or the clients they represent. As with other aspects of this profession, a good working relationship between lawyer and practitioner is desirable.

The most common areas of concern in public relations law are defamation, privacy, copyright, and contractual negotiations. However, many other legal matters affect the practitioner.

Our income tax laws, for example, may be important to the individual counselor who operates out of his or her residence and who lists a number of deductions as a cost of doing business.

Product publicity must conform to regulations set down by the Federal Trade Commission and other government agencies. Many of those rules center on false claims about the product, or a failure to live up to a warranty, or the negligent promotion of an item known to have unrevealed risk factors.

A political public relations consultant may be guilty of concealing information, making irresponsible statements, falsifying records, and other misdemeanors or crimes.

Daniel J. Morgan, a Florida practitioner, invoked the First Amendment guarantee of free speech when he was evicted from a county commissioners' meeting as he was advancing the case of his developer client. The Public Relations Society of America issued a statement supporting Morgan's stand.

Many other cases involving public relations people may surface in the future, especially as the practitioners push for professional status. More will be expected of those who claim to be professionals, but that doesn't protect PR people from the lies clients may tell them or from the results of their own ignorance.

Defamation, Libel, and Defenses against Them

Defamation is a word whose definition always seems imperfect. It can be construed as anything that tends to damage a reputation in the popular sense. This embraces conditions ranging from loss of esteem or respect to outright hatred, contempt, isolation, and hostility.

To be actionable, defamation must be communicated in some form to a third party and the person defamed must be identified, although not necessarily by name. If the person can be recognized from a description, such as "the bald-headed, bearded guy who always sits in the corner of the lunchroom," that would be sufficient identification.

Usually defamation is divided into slander and libel, with *slander* being classified as oral defamation and *libel* as written defamation. These distinctions limp, however. Radio and television caused all sorts of problems. Was it libel or slander when a commentator made a remark considered defamatory? Did it make a difference if he read from a script or ad-libbed? If there is any trend, it is toward considering such utterances as libel, no matter what the source.

Phelps and Hamilton, in their book *Libel: Rights, Risks, and Responsibilities*, list eight defenses against a charge of libel:

1. *Consent or authorization.* The person claiming he or she was libeled gave permission for the libelous remark to appear.
2. *Self-defense or right of reply.* Assuming that a drama critic made a nasty remark about an actor's performance (as the critic could do because of the "fair comment" privilege below), the actor might retaliate with a statement questioning the critic's credentials.
3. *Privilege of participant.* This would rarely affect a PR person. It applies rather to the protection given legislators, judges, and others when they make statements in official proceedings.
4. *Statute of limitations.* In most states, there is a one-, two-, or three-year limit after which claims of libel cannot be made. Arkansas, Delaware, Hawaii, New Mexico, and Vermont have no such statute. The practitioner should be aware of the law in his or her state.
5. *Truth.* This means that the statement you made was true—but you had better be able to prove this in court.
6. *Privilege of reporting.* Journalists (and PR persons, when acting as journalists) have the right to report on what was said at public meetings.
7. *Fair comment and criticism.* This protects critics and reviewers when writing about an artistic event or product. "Fair" is a broad term, however, and could be interpreted tightly or loosely. Panning a performance might be one thing, but suggesting that this poor showing resulted from some strictly personal source (drinking, drugs, and the like) could be construed as unfair.
8. The New York Times *"actual malice" rule.* This deals only with libel actions brought by public officials or public figures. These people have less protection against libel than an ordinary citizen has and must prove either "actual malice" in the so-called libelous statement or "reckless disregard for truth."[10]

Sometimes a retraction may help mitigate damages in a libel suit but is not really a defense.

Most of the defenses listed above are not absolute. They are subject to interpretation, and different juries may see things in different ways.

Several cases in recent years have sought to define the extent to which a public figure might sue for libel. In 1974, the *Gertz v. Robert Welch, Inc.,* case narrowed the privilege a publication might have in defaming a private citizen:

> Prior to the *Gertz* decision, a publication making false and defamatory state-ments about an individual was generally protected from liability by the United States Constitution's First Amendment guarantees of free press and free speech, as long as the libeled party was engaged in an activity of general "public inter-est." Under a series of United States Supreme Court decisions starting in 1964 with the case of *New York Times* v. *Sullivan,* and culminating in 1971 with the case of *Rosenbloom v. Metromedia,* a defamed individual could not succeed in an action against a publication for libel on a matter of "public interest" unless he proved that the publisher or writer knew the facts when published were false or should have entertained serious doubts regarding their truthfulness. Since courts tended to consider any "newsworthy" materials a matter of public inter-est, libeled plaintiffs found themselves with the burden of having to prove that the defamatory article was published with "knowledge of reckless disregard of the truth."[11]

Gertz, a Chicago attorney, sued Robert Welch, Inc., because one of Welch's publications had referred to him as a "Communist fronter." What is significant about Gertz's victory is that Gertz, who was generally regarded as one of the finest and most active attorneys in Chicago, was labeled a "private citizen" by the court.

Two years later, in *Time, Inc. v. Firestone,* the court characterized a Palm Beach socialite who held press conferences and subscribed to a press-clipping service as a private individual.

Lack of a precise definition of "public figure" continues, with even the U.S. Supreme Court sidestepping some of the cases brought before it. Some categorize public figures as (1) those who involve themselves in a temporary public controversy and are thus labeled "limited-purpose" public figures, and (2) those whose positions automatically bring notoriety, called "all-purpose" public figures. Both have to prove "actual malice" in order to win their cases, whereas private individuals do not have that added burden of proof.

Public relations practitioners could be involved in libel actions in two ways: One of the practitioner's clients might be libeled, or, more likely, he or she could be accused of libel in a news release, speech, or other communi-cation.

Many cases never reach the courts—often because the size of judg-ments sought is so large that it may make sense to settle earlier.

In 17 libel cases in 1984 and 1985 studies by the Libel Defense Resource Center, three awards exceeded $1 million and another exceeded a half million. A survey by the center last October found that the average affirmed award in 63 cases studied between 1982 and 1984 was a relatively low $60,000—still a staggering sum for a weekly or a small daily.[12]

Or, it might be added, a small company or small PR firm.

Privacy

Invasion of privacy may occasionally involve the media and public relations communications. Rights of privacy are also somewhat vague, but they center on four areas:

1. *Intrusion*—actual invasion of a person's seclusion or solitude, or into his or her private affairs
2. *Disclosure*—the revealing of embarrassing private facts about a person
3. *False light*—publicity that places a person in a false light in the public eye
4. *Appropriation*—using some person's name or likeness without his or her permission

The "newsworthy" test is applied to privacy, meaning that a story that was of public interest, or involved a public figure, or was already a matter of public record, or had some "social value" would not normally be considered an invasion of privacy.

Time may be a factor here, too. Resurrecting a criminal charge against a private person who served time for the offense could be an invasion of privacy in later years, even though that crime was a matter of public record.

Anyone who deals with communication must be wary. A gossip column in a company magazine may stray into error, perhaps printing something the writer considers funny but the party involved sees as injurious. False light may occur when a photo is miscaptioned, when a fictional character comes too close to a real person, when a writer "embellishes" a story with "facts" that never happened, when editorial selection of certain details presents a person in a deceptive or incomplete fashion.

> A "false light" publication can be literally true, yet still be actionable. *Saturday Evening Post* found this out some years ago when it published a photograph of a girl who had been struck by a car. A newspaper had published the same photo two years earlier, but as timely news, and therefore no libel or invasion of privacy suit resulted. But when the magazine used that photograph to illustrate an article about careless pedestrians, the courts held that the blameless child had been placed in a "false light."[13]

The point here is that the original photo could be defended as legitimate news, but the later reuse falsely suggested that the injured child was at fault in the accident.

Some of the cases involving "appropriation" are interesting, encompassing everything from a human cannonball performer who successfully sued a television station that carried his complete act on the air, to stars like Woody Allen who blow the whistle on look-alikes appearing in TV commercials. A California statute even makes the commercial use of a deceased person's name, voice, signature, photograph, or likeness a "transferable property right," meaning that anyone who owned this right could sue another person "appropriating" the deceased persona.

Privacy Journal, a monthly newsletter, published an 80-page compilation of state and federal privacy laws in 1981. This volume gives details on laws pertaining to public records, telephone solicitation, credit reports, even computer crimes. Practitioners who conduct business nationally should have this information, and everyone in public relations must be conversant with the pertinent state laws.

Securing Releases

To avoid the charge of appropriation, PR practitioners must get into the habit of obtaining permission for the use of a person's name, likeness, or statement. You can't, for example, photograph a group of shoppers walking through the downtown section of a city and later use that picture with a cutline suggesting that they are headed for a mid-city bank. You can't reach an agreement with a model to use a picture in a company publication and then sell it to a manufacturer of calendars. For whatever use you anticipate, you should secure permission. Two sample releases are shown in Figure 11-6.

Copyright

The simplest way to avoid infringing on copyright laws is to request permission of the original author for any substantial reprinting you wish to do. On January 1, 1978, the copyright law experienced its first major revision since 1909. In general, it enhances the position of authors by extending the length of copyright provisions and making wholesale copying much more difficult. The advent of duplicating machines had much to do with these changes. Teachers, for example, are limited as to the number of pages of a text they may copy, the number of uses they may make of a specific book, and the number of copies they may distribute, and there are limitations on any charges they may assess students.

The key phrase in copyright is "fair use." This term seeks to define conditions under which materials may be reproduced or included in other works. "Fair use" is not specific, however, and each case—if it comes to court—will be decided on its own merits.

For example, it may make a difference whether or not the use of the

In consideration for value received, receipt whereof is acknowledged, I hereby give (name of firm or publication) the absolute right and permission to copyright and/or publish, and/or resell photographic portraits or pictures of me, or in which I may be included in whole or in part, for art, advertising, trade or any other lawful purpose whatsoever.

I hereby waive any right that I may have to inspect and/or approve the finished product or the advertising copy that may be used in connection therewith, or the use to which it may be applied.

I hereby release, discharge and agree to save (name of firm or publication) from any liability by virtue of any blurring, distortion, alteration, optical illusion or use in composite form, whether intentional or otherwise, that may occur or be produced in the making of said pictures, or in any processing tending towards the completion of the finished product.

Date _____   Model _____

                                        Address _____

                                        _____

Witness _____

a. A sample model's release.

Publication Consent Agreement

In consideration for value received, receipt whereof acknowledged,

I hereby give (name of author) the absolute right and permission to copyright and/or publish

or to have copyrighted or have published the information about me contained in the attached manuscript. I understand that the manuscript will undergo editing prior to any publication and I consent to the use of the information in revised or edited form without first seeing the revised or edited manuscript.

I also hereby waive any right to inspect and/or approve not only the final edited-for-publication versions, but also any advertising copy that may be used in connection therewith.

Date _____   Signature _____

                               Address _____

Witness _____

b. A suggested form for writers' use.

Figure 11-6 Two sample releases.
Courtesy: *Writer's Digest*

printed material is for profit. The nature of the copyrighted work is another factor. So is the amount and substantiality of the portion excerpted, and the effect the use may have on the market for original work.

The "amount" and "substantiality" will vary. A few lines from an article, however, would not normally infringe on copyright laws. The entire magazine, including all the other articles, could be used as a measure against the few lines quoted. As much as a page of a large book might be used—or even more under some circumstances—without getting advance permission, but again, the character of the material and its relation to the work as a whole could be factors. It is not safe, for example, to assume that some number like 250 words or 26 lines will be safe.

All materials cited should be properly acknowledged, whether or not permission has been requested.

The basic idea behind all the copyright provisions is that a person's work is his or her own and that this person is entitled to appropriate compensation for its use. This applies not only to written materials but to artwork, photography, trademarks, and other tangible results of creativity. So practitioners must be wary of lifting the works of others and should be certain that their own work is protected.

A few years ago, in a much-publicized case, the Roman Catholic Archdiocese of Chicago was ordered to pay over $3 million in damages to a composer who claimed churches in the archdiocese had illegally photocopied hymns he'd written. And some famous authors have settled out of court on charges that they lifted prose from other, lesser-known writers.

Authors have also been a little nervous about one phrase in the copyright laws that allows publications and institutions to retain the copyright rather than the author, if the work can be construed as "made-for-hire," meaning that it was done under the aegis of, or while in the employ of, or even at the direction of, someone other than the creator. Research done in commercial laboratories has long been subject to such restrictions, as have documents produced by writers in government offices. Just how far this practice will be carried is moot. Some magazines now have authors sign forms transferring all rights to them under a "made-for-hire" umbrella, and a few universities have looked at the legal ramifications of work produced by their faculties. Public relations firms could also be involved—when a staff member develops a written work while on the job, for example.

An even more complicated current issue is the whole question of videotaping programs off the air. PR persons might be involved when someone tapes one of their creations and shows it elsewhere; or they could tape something themselves—say, a newscast—to make a point with management or their stockholders. Even though a lot of this is done, and even though the taping is not done for profit, and even though policing may be extremely difficult, the fact remains that the practitioner should get permission for taping and replaying any program. Each network has a person in charge of granting permissions, and local stations may be approached through their station managers.

Contracts

Ordinarily, contracts are drawn up with the help of an attorney, but certain documents in current use by public relations and advertising firms become so familiar that the users forget they are dealing with actual contracts. When a media buyer in an advertising agency purchases time or space, he or she initiates a contract. When you agree to give a printer your brochure to print, you enter into a contract. You do this with many suppliers—photographers, artists, free-lance writers, models, typographers, film producers. Use standard forms for these transactions and read the contracts from time to time, just to be certain you know what they say. Even though you can't conduct all your day-to-day business on the level of a multinational corporation, it doesn't hurt to have simple contracts that spell out what you expect from the supplier and what the supplier can expect from you.

Miscellaneous

The admonitions given in this chapter merely scratch the surface. The public relations practitioner should be familiar with postal regulations (what may be mailed, what governs classes of mail, what constitutes a mail lottery), the tenets of the Federal Trade Commission (particularly relating to consumer interests such as false product claims, incorrect research studies, improper advertising, and counteradvertising), the strictures of the Federal Communications Commission, the guidelines of the Securities and Exchange Commission (discussed in Chapter 13), and the laws of his or her own state. If involved in political counseling, the practitioner should also be familiar with national and state regulations governing the source and expenditure of funds.

Keep in mind, too, that the public relations person not only could appear in court as a defendant but might also be a witness. Practitioners' testimony may be used in cases where they have involvement as participants or advisors, or where their expertise in communication might be utilized.

Because public relations law is fluid, owning a desk copy of a law book is not sufficient. Practitioners should keep up with current cases that seem to have implications for their communication efforts or for their client firms. Even publicity itself may some day receive the same sort of scrutiny that advertising has been getting in terms of First Amendment free-speech protection.

PROFESSIONALISM

Ethical business practices and knowledge of the law are two more adjuncts of the move toward professional status.

Three of the marks of a profession is that it has an accepted body of knowledge, a prescribed course of studies, and some form of certification by an authoritative third party. On the basis of those criteria, some argue that public relations is not and never will be a profession.

G. J. Meyer, corporate vice-president of external relations for the Mc-Donnell-Douglas Corporation, writes:

Clearly the claim of public relations to professional stature is infinitely weaker that that, say, of nursing. It is probably weaker than that of, say, insurance brokerage. If I am professional, my mailcarrier is, too.[14]

Frank Wylie, director of public affairs at California State University in Los Angeles, contends that public relations will never be a profession until it establishes accepted courses of graduate work and sets up a system for licensing.[15]

Writing in the *Dallas Morning News*, Clarence Walton thinks public relations has the potential for professionalism, if members can define its educational preparation and reverse the trend of assimilation by advertising agencies.[16]

Proponents insist accreditation must come first, followed by professional stature. There are some efforts to influence curriculum offerings; to standardize areas of expertise; to place more emphasis on research, issues, counseling and management; and to get more practitioners to take the two-day exam that leads to accreditation.

This exam includes an oral session with questions posed by local accredited peers, and a six-hour written examination covering a broad range of public relations topics, including in-depth case problems. To qualify for the examination, a person must have been in the PR field a minimum of five years. Successful candidates are allowed to add the letters A.P.R. (Accredited in Public Relations) after their names. Some PRSA chapters conduct refresher courses for those taking the exam, and a fee is paid by the applicant to cover costs of preparing study and test materials and for the grading of the responses by a private firm.

Although he sees many things to be accomplished by practitioners, author Allen H. Center feels that public relations is now regarded as an "emerging profession" with "almost all of the requisites—except licensing" in place.[17]

Even the most sanguine observers, however, admit that viewing practitioners in the same light as physicians and attorneys is many years ahead.

CHAPTER HIGHLIGHTS

- Only experience in the field can teach PR people what things cost, what real deadlines are, and how to deal with the frustrations of the practice.
- Although a lot of personal qualities may be helpful in public relations, the essential characteristics are organizational ability, judgment, communication skills, tolerance, understanding, creativity, integrity, leadership, broad knowledge, and patience.
- Women are entering public relations in record numbers, but there are more male than female counselors. Salaries have increased, although women's salaries still lag behind men's.
- A college degree (ordinarily, but not necessarily, in journalism or public

relations) and some internship experience have become the norms for PR education.

- Those seeking PR jobs should research the target companies or organizations; work hard and systematically at locating opportunities; draft a well-written, effective résumé and cover letter; and perform well during the interview.

- The two main types of PR jobs are the internal public relations director (who has the advantages of being more familiar with that company and more available) and the private counselor (who brings objectivity, a wider variety of experience, and, perhaps, some specialized skills).

- Fees and charges vary according to experience and locality but are usually based on a set retainer fee, hourly or daily charges, or the cost of a specific project.

- Ethics in public relations are guided by the PRSA Code and by the practitioner's own conscience and experience.

- The legal areas that most concern PR persons are libel, privacy, and copyright.

- The move toward professional status for public relations, although not applauded by all practitioners, is an attempt to give greater stature to the field and is accompanied by research, advice on curriculum, and accrediting exams.

NOTES

[1]*Profile '85*, IABC Foundation.

[2]Leo J. Northart, "Editor's Notebook," *Public Relations Journal*, May 1984.

[3]B. G. Yovovich, "Skills Needed, Status Growing," *Advertising Age*, January 5, 1981.

[4]Dennis L. Wilcox, quoted in "The Employees: What Do They Really Want?" *Public Relations Journal*, July 1978.

[5]James A. Files, "Order in the House," *Public Relations Journal*, March 1984.

[6]James B. Strenski, "Ten Criteria for Selecting PR Counsel," *Public Relations Quarterly*, Fall 1977.

[7]Don Bates, "Public Relations at Large," *Public Relations Journal*, March 1984.

[8]Robert A. Parker, "Harold Burson Discusses Potholes Lurking on the Public Relations Path," *Communication World*, November 1983.

[9]Jim Montgomery, "The Image Makers," *Wall Street Journal*, August 1, 1978.

[10]Robert Phelps and E. Douglas Hamilton, *Libel: Rights, Risks and Responsibilities* (New York: Macmillan, 1966); author's adaptation.

[11]Edwin L. Gasperini, "New Shift in the Libel Law," *Public Relations Journal*, December 1974.

[12]David Zucchino, "Publish and Perish," *Washington Journalism Review*, July 1985.

[13]Bill Francois, "Law and the Writer," (copyright) *Writer's Digest*, January 1973.

[14]G.J. Meyer, "The P.R. Circus," *Communicator's Journal*, November/December 1983.

[15]Frank Wylie, letter in *pr reporter*, April 27, 1981.

[16]Clarence Walton, "A Look at 3 Emerging Professions," *Dallas Morning News*, August 4, 1981.

[17]Allen H. Center, "The State of the Art: Part III," *Public Relations Journal*, October 1983.

SUGGESTED READINGS

ARONOFF, CRAIG E., and OTIS W. BASKIN, *Public Relations: The Profession and the Practice.* St. Paul, Minn.: West, 1983.

CHAMBERLIN, BILL F., and CHARLENE J. BROWN, *The First Amendment Reconsidered.* New York: Longman, 1982.

GILLMOR, DONALD M., and JEROME A. BARRON, *Mass Communication Law*, 3rd ed. St. Paul, Minn.: West, 1984.

GLASSMAN, DON, *Writers' and Artists' Rights.* Washington, D.C.: Writers Press, 1978.

LACZNIAK, GENE R., and PATRICK E. MURPHY, eds., *Marketing Ethics.* Lexington, Mass.: Lexington Books, 1985.

MERRILL, JOHN C., and RALPH D. BARNEY, eds., *Ethics and the Press: Readings in Mass Media Morality.* New York: Hastings, 1975.

NELSON, HAROLD, and DWIGHT TEETER, *Law of Mass Communication*, 4th ed. Mineola, N.Y.: Foundation Press, 1982.

OVERBECK, WAYNE, and RICK D. PULLEN, *Major Principles of Communication Law*, 2nd ed. New York: Holt, Rinehart & Winston, 1982.

PEMBER, DON R., *Mass Media Law*, 2nd ed. Dubuque, Ia.: Brown, 1981.

POLKING, KIRK, and LEONARD S. MERANUS, eds., *Law and the Writer.* Cincinnati: Writer's Digest, 1985.

ROTMAN, MORRIS, *Opportunities in Public Relations.* Lincolnwood, Ill.: VGM Career Horizons, 1983.

SANFORD, BRUCE W., *Synopsis of the Law of Libel and the Right of Privacy.* Cleveland: Baker Histetler and Patterson, 1977.

SCHRAMM, WILBUR, and CLIFFORD CHRISTIAN, *Responsibility in Mass Communication.* New York: Harper & Row, 1980.

SIMON, MORTON J., *Public Relations Law.* New York: Appleton-Century-Crofts, 1969.

SPIVACK, JANE F., ed., *Careers in Information.* White Plains, N.Y.: Knowledge Industry, 1982.

ZUCKMAN, HARVEY L., and MARTIN J. GAINES, *Mass Communications Law in a Nutshell*, 2nd ed. St. Paul, Minn.: West, 1982.

AEJMC Journalism Quarterly. Columbia, S.C.: University of South Carolina.

Columbia Journalism Review. New York: Columbia University.

Editor and Publisher, New York.

IABC News, San Francisco.

pr reporter. Exeter, N.H.: PR Publishing Co.

Public Opinion Quarterly. New York: Columbia University.

Public Relations Journal. New York: Public Relations Society of America.
Public Relations News, New York.
Public Relations Quarterly. New York: Columbia University.
Public Relations Review. College Park, Md.: University of Maryland.
Quill. Chicago: Society for Professional Journalists.

EXERCISES

1. Compile your own résumé—either chronological or functional—using guidelines in this text and materials you may find in your library or placement office.
2. Select a public relations position in town (whether there is an opening or not) and prepare a cover letter for that job to accompany your résumé.
3. Make a list of business practices you consider unethical and state why.
4. Talk to a person in your community who is accredited in public relations and get his or her comments on the value of such accreditation.

CASE PROBLEMS

1. A public relations director for a corporation that produces a major line of sporting goods has had his stories rejected consistently by one of the top outdoor magazines. The PR person suspects this rejection is due to the magazine editor's belief that the stories serve a commercial purpose, even though the practitioner has been careful not to include any overt references to brand names. To break this editorial barrier, the public relations director continues to write the articles but pays a free-lance writer a modest fee to submit these features under that writer's name. The articles are accepted, convincing the practitioner that his suspicions and conduct were justified. What do you think?
2. A PR consultant in an East Coast state has a falling out with the candidate he's handling—a man running for the House of Representatives. At the candidate's request, the practitioner quits the account. A week later, this same consultant is asked to join the staff of his previous employer's opponent for the House seat. He accepts, bringing with him the files from the earlier assignment. Hearing of this, the state chapter of the Public Relations Society of America says such behavior may be unethical and promises an investigation. The consultant protests that he was really dismissed from the previous account for no other reason than a personality conflict, and that he was entitled to take with him the results of his labors. How would you view this situation?
3. As the public relations director in a medium-sized company that manufactures appliances, you are under the direct supervision of the vice-president for communications. You get along well enough with your boss,

although you've never considered him a role model. One day, while he is away on a trip, he asks you to go into his office and find some papers and then call him with the information. While you're looking for these papers, you uncover evidence that the vice-president has been doctoring his expense account to the tune of more than $1,000 a year. What do you do, if anything?

4. The news editor of a college alumni magazine came across a news items regarding two physicians who had graduated from his institution. Both had the same last names and lived at the same address and had graduated the same year. He assumed they were husband and wife and set the story in type that way. As the magazine was being printed, his veteran secretary said she didn't think either of the physicians was married. In checking, the editor discovered they were brother and sister. He phoned the brother, explaining what had happened, and the brother at first said the magazine could run the item if it printed a retraction in the next issue. Later he called to say that he had discussed this with his sister and that she felt the story would be embarrassing and didn't want it run. The editor argued that 20,000 copies of that page had already been run and that throwing them away would be very costly. He contended that no real harm would be done and that the retraction in the subsequent issue should straighten things out. The physicians still said they would feel better if it didn't run at all. What should the editor do?

5. The utility company that you represent as public relations director was very much involved in a recent flood in your town. Not only were company members working professionally to restore service but they were also active as volunteers in the cleanup phase. You decided to do a brochure about their contributions and took photos to illustrate the flood damage and aftermath. Among the pictures was one of an old woman seated outside her ruined home in which her aged husband had drowned. She was hysterical, and a utility employee was attempting to comfort her. You feel the photo has great appeal, both because of its content and because it shows one of the utility company's employees on the scene. Would you use it or not? Defend your decision.

12

PUBLIC RELATIONS IN THE BUSINESS WORLD

The most common application of public relations skills occurs in the multi-faceted business world. Each of these assignments is just a bit different, and no formula can cover all problems or anticipate all situations. The public relations constants, however, remain solid research, thorough planning, imaginative execution, and faithful evaluation.

In this era of conglomerates and multinational firms, business seems to have become more and more complicated. And yet, some things never change. The aim continues to be the efficient production of a quality product or service that will attract and satisfy consumers and result in a profit for the company.

To achieve this aim takes a variety of departments and individuals, from competent technical help to quality control, and from aggressive sales staffs to creative advertising. Public relations also has its role.

TOUGH YEARS FOR BUSINESS

During the past two decades, the image of business has slipped, although it has now recovered somewhat from the darker days of the 1960s and 1970s. Some of this criticism may be deserved, but much of it stems from public ignorance about business or a failure by business to communicate its message. A 1982 survey by *Public Opinion* magazine revealed that Americans felt large corporations were less responsive to their needs than government was—and government received only a one-third vote of confidence! The severest critics have often been those who once supported business—college graduates, opinion makers, managerial and professional people, and the affluent.

Pollster Lou Harris said a decade ago that "American business is in trouble with the American people."

To the extent that this has improved, public relations practitioners can accept some share of the credit, and they accomplished this, not with tricks or mirrors, but by wise counsel and solid communication. Their research showed, for example, that the American people overestimated corporate profits by ten times what they actually were, that they were largely unaware of the federal restrictions on business, and that they didn't realize that half the new businesses that open up are gone within two years. Many of the misconceptions remain, but business is gaining some ground, largely because it has taken the initiative in stating its case. Some "born-again" business leaders have been more outspoken, and many corporate PR campaigns have been more sensitive to the problem.

Fortune magazine (January 7, 1985) did a cover story on the nation's most admired firms, and the least admired. IBM led the list of most admired, followed by Coca-Cola, Dow Jones, and 3M—but this could change. As a subhead points out, attitudes toward a firm like Union Carbide can change overnight. How and why these companies scored well or poorly is not examined, but key ingredients in their success appear to be strong leadership, well-defined goals, a firm social conscience, lack of crippling internal dissension, and a means of professionally communicating their corporate selves. Those who fell among the least admired often suffered because of their inadequate response to striking workers, their environmental lapses, or their financial misadventures. Even the most astute public relations cannot overcome such corporate failures.

In the 1970s, American business withstood a serious recession, a decline in productivity, a loss of world industrial dominance, and an increased reliance on domestic oil. Some of those ills have subsided, but new ones have taken their places—the national trade imbalance, a collapse of the farm economy, greater foreign competition, and a work force that needs retraining. Productivity has improved, but the economy has been slower. All these factors are represented in the public image of industry and in the public relations problems corporations must face.

CORPORATE SOCIAL RESPONSIBILITY

More emphasis has been placed upon the necessity for companies to demonstrate social concern, and the types of problems and pressures have multiplied. Most of these still center on safety, community leadership, support for the arts and humanities, fair treatment of employees, and freedom from suspect financial and political activities. Business sometimes complains that Americans expect too much of its corporate leaders, asking them to do everything from creating jobs to sustaining the elderly. If anything, under the Reagan administration, more initiative has been required of business in the solution of social difficulties.

Clearly, a new "public–private partnership" is emerging, as both sides and the general public reach a better understanding of the issues and the magnitude of the tasks. We are coming to understand that the phrase "the private sector" includes much more than corporations and businesses. In addition to profit-making enterprises, it embraces a rich mosaic of not-for-profit organizations such as educational and research organizations, labor unions, hospitals, museums, religious institutions and community service organizations.[1]

To pick up the slack created by federal withdrawal in some areas, business must commit to the notion of responsibility, prepare to act immediately, and be ready to extend the cooperative hand to a variety of causes. This means not only financial aid (which could reach $5 billion annually) but also the sponsorship of appropriate programs, the providing of community leadership, and research into the ills and needs of society—along with the traditional manufacture of quality goods and services, the creation of jobs, and the maintenance of high ethical and moral standards.

In the area of philanthropy, our tax structure limits amounts that can be contributed tax-free by corporations, and future laws may constrict this further, thus removing part of the reason for generosity. Currently, corporations account for less than 10 percent of philanthropic giving. A majority of corporations (most of them small) give nothing, and the larger companies average between 1 and 2 percent of their before-tax profits. There is room for improvement here, and enlightened corporate policy, encouraged by practitioners who see the value of such largess, can do much to aid the image of American business.

These contributions extend to other countries when multinational corporations are involved. Here, it is not only money that is required, but also a little imagination. Avon Products, for example, provides scholarships to French housewives seeking to return to school, presents awards to Women of Achievement in Japan, and works with Partners of the Americas in Mexico to improve living and working conditions. It is also careful about using local vendors whenever this is feasible.

Obviously, while performing these good deeds here and abroad, the corporation must insist on the highest internal standards, not only for products but also for employees. Some of this striving for excellence has been tarnished in the past by charges of illegal campaign contributions, interference in the internal affairs of other nations, abnormally high profits, failure to respond to consumer complaints (especially those about safety and environmental hazards), misleading advertising, and insensitivity to employee needs. Even the thoughtless statements of chief executives have come to haunt corporations, and the increase in white-collar crime (or, at least, the increase in the *detection* of white-collar crime) has reinforced the notion that all business cares about is the bottom-line dollar. In 1985, nearly half the major defense contractors were under criminal investigation by the government; many banks were charged with fraud against depositors, or with irresponsible management, or with conspiring to "launder" money from

Figure 12-1 Corporations may also add their voices on national and international issues. Courtesy: U.S. Corporate Council on South Africa

suspect sources; other companies were cited for tax evasion, mail fraud, labor mischarges, and similar misdeeds.

A *Fortune* article asks:

> Is there a problem with inadequate auditing standards? Are the people who commit crimes victims of a corporate culture that encourages illegality? Are the penalties what they should be?[2]

Whatever the causes and results, these lapses make one more area of concern for the PR person.

SPECIAL PROBLEMS

In the late 1970s, Nestlé Company found itself the target of an extensive boycott fueled by an organization called the Infant Formula Action Coalition, and containing such powerful opponents as Dr. Benjamin Spock.

> That the infant formula issue is complex, both sides agree. It involves arguments about breast feeding versus formula; the ethics of providing formula samples to doctors and health clinics for free patient distribution; differing interpretations of infant mortality statistics, and even the imposition of Western values on Third World nations via marketing techniques.[3]

This crisis lasted five years; cost Nestlé millions of dollars (although it did not significantly affect the company's profitability); tied up five full-time and ten part-time employees who responded to queries, developed position papers, and provided speakers; and became what company officials described as a "public relations nightmare" that intimated the firm was responsible for the deaths of Third World children. Nestlé ultimately came to terms with its critics, instituted some marketing reforms, and agreed to limitations on promotion enacted by the World Health Organization.

The A.H. Robins Company, maker of the Dalkon Shield, an intrauterine birth-control device, used a $4 million international advertising campaign urging women who use such devices to visit their physicians. Despite this effort, and despite the fact that the Dalkon Shield's manufacture was halted in 1974 (but the product was not recalled), Robins was the target of almost 1,500 lawsuits by women or families who claimed that illness or death resulted from use of the shield. Out-of-court settlement of half these lawsuits has already cost the corporation approximately $300 million.

Continental Illinois National Bank, the major lender to American corporations, is the most striking example of banks that have experienced trouble. Millions in bad loans, coupled with firings and forced retirements, nearly brought the bank to its knees. Conventional wit said the only difference between the Titanic and the Continental was that the Titanic had a band. While keeping its doors open, Continental recognized the need for a colossal public relations effort to win back consumer trust.

Citibank also survived the bad publicity generated by a former executive who blew the whistle on what he described as questionable foreign-exchange practices involving the manipulation of foreign currency, especially the French franc.

Other financial institutions haven't been as fortunate, and the demise of a number of institutions adversely affected by the agricultural crisis has caused banks and savings and loan companies to beef up their promotional

Our Credo

WE BELIEVE THAT OUR FIRST RESPONSIBILITY IS TO THE DOCTORS, NURSES, HOSPITALS,
MOTHERS, AND ALL OTHERS WHO USE OUR PRODUCTS.
OUR PRODUCTS MUST ALWAYS BE OF THE HIGHEST QUALITY.
WE MUST CONSTANTLY STRIVE TO REDUCE THE COST OF THESE PRODUCTS.
OUR ORDERS MUST BE PROMPTLY AND ACCURATELY FILLED.
OUR DEALERS MUST MAKE A FAIR PROFIT.

•

OUR SECOND RESPONSIBILITY IS TO THOSE WHO WORK WITH US—
THE MEN AND WOMEN IN OUR PLANTS AND OFFICES.
THEY MUST HAVE A SENSE OF SECURITY IN THEIR JOBS.
WAGES MUST BE FAIR AND ADEQUATE,
MANAGEMENT JUST, HOURS REASONABLE, AND WORKING CONDITIONS CLEAN AND ORDERLY.
EMPLOYEES SHOULD HAVE AN ORGANIZED SYSTEM FOR SUGGESTIONS AND COMPLAINTS.
SUPERVISORS AND DEPARTMENT HEADS MUST BE QUALIFIED AND FAIR MINDED.
THERE MUST BE OPPORTUNITY FOR ADVANCEMENT—FOR THOSE QUALIFIED
AND EACH PERSON MUST BE CONSIDERED AN INDIVIDUAL
STANDING ON HIS OWN DIGNITY AND MERIT.

•

OUR THIRD RESPONSIBILITY IS TO OUR MANAGEMENT.
OUR EXECUTIVES MUST BE PERSONS OF TALENT, EDUCATION, EXPERIENCE AND ABILITY.
THEY MUST BE PERSONS OF COMMON SENSE AND FULL UNDERSTANDING.

•

OUR FOURTH RESPONSIBILITY IS TO THE COMMUNITIES IN WHICH WE LIVE.
WE MUST BE A GOOD CITIZEN—SUPPORT GOOD WORKS AND CHARITY,
AND BEAR OUR FAIR SHARE OF TAXES.
WE MUST MAINTAIN IN GOOD ORDER THE PROPERTY WE ARE PRIVILEGED TO USE.
WE MUST PARTICIPATE IN PROMOTION OF CIVIC IMPROVEMENT,
HEALTH, EDUCATION AND GOOD GOVERNMENT,
AND ACQUAINT THE COMMUNITY WITH OUR ACTIVITIES.

•

OUR FIFTH AND LAST RESPONSIBILITY IS TO OUR STOCKHOLDERS.
BUSINESS MUST MAKE A SOUND PROFIT.
RESERVES MUST BE CREATED, RESEARCH MUST BE CARRIED ON,
ADVENTUROUS PROGRAMS DEVELOPED, AND MISTAKES PAID FOR.
ADVERSE TIMES MUST BE PROVIDED FOR, ADEQUATE TAXES PAID, NEW MACHINES PURCHASED,
NEW PLANTS BUILT, NEW PRODUCTS LAUNCHED, AND NEW SALES PLANS DEVELOPED.
WE MUST EXPERIMENT WITH NEW IDEAS.
WHEN THESE THINGS HAVE BEEN DONE THE STOCKHOLDER SHOULD RECEIVE A FAIR RETURN.
WE ARE DETERMINED WITH THE HELP OF GOD'S GRACE,
TO FULFILL THESE OBLIGATIONS TO THE BEST OF OUR ABILITY.

Johnson & Johnson

Figure 12-2 When Johnson & Johnson faced its first Tylenol crisis, it turned to its credo for guidance.
Courtesy: Johnson & Johnson

materials to indicate their own strength. Again, public relations, in the form of printed materials, speeches, and corporate advertising, has been essential.

Business crises come in all sorts of guises. They may come in the form of sex discrimination, with its attendant corollaries of advancement, comparable pay, even sex-based actuarial tables, which, women claim, bias benefits and premiums in favor of men. They may involve personal behavior of chief executives, including their perceived attitudes on social issues. They may even revolve around advertising. Pizza Hut, for example, withdrew a television commercial in South Carolina that showed a condemned man eating pizza as his final meal, because a recently electrocuted prisoner in that state had specifed pizza as a last request. And various companies and institutions have been convinced they should remove from their promotional efforts certain symbols of ethnic groups that these groups found offensive.

Takeovers and mergers have become prime concerns for managers and their PR aides. More than ten mergers took place every working day in 1985, partly owing to a more liberal antitrust attitude, partly to shore up existing businesses, and partly to create new ones. There have also been an increasing number of hostile takeovers, requiring a PR response in the battle for survival. Companies have mobilized towns to avert such maneuvers. Gerber did this in Fremont, Michigan, and Phillips displayed a strong defense against rumored moves by a Texas oilman to invade its Bartlesville, Oklahoma, domain. Standard Oil, Chevron, Texaco, Mobil, and other oil companies have been targeted for takeover, as have been the Hilton Hotels and even CBS. Few major corporations can afford to relax their promotional or financial strategies.

Every industry may also suffer particular problems: deregulation in the airline industry; slender margins in the supermarkets; quality versus cost in the automotive field. Not only did Coca-Cola have to fight the Pepsi challenge and the results of its experimentation with the New Coke, but it was also subject to attack by the Sugar Association (which claimed Coca-Cola was using corn syrup in its Classic version, rather than beet or cane sugar) and its own bottlers, some 40 of whom sued to get the Atlanta-based firm to reveal its century-old formula for the world's top beverage.

Each company attempts to solve its problems in its own way. Phillips, for example, keeps a low profile, earning plaudits from the media for the availability of information and executives. Mobil, battered by a television documentary and various print sources, went on the offense, earning quiet praise from some other industry members but reaping increased negative publicity from its media targets. Philip Morris, frustrated by the consistent news indicting smoking, struck back with its own magazine, a four-color quarterly mailed free to 150,000 people. The inaugural issue featured articles on tobacco farming, New York architecture, female tennis stars, the Southwest, and a Vatican exhibit sponsored by Philip Morris. Critics called it "another PR attempt."

Procter & Gamble, once almost immune from media criticism, fielded so much adverse publicity for its "heavy-handed operation of news conferences" that it revamped its PR department, with one segment charged with the responsibility for media inquiries and the other in charge of publicity and special events. Kodak's public relations department operates under the "one-voice" dictum, which ensures that all its 100 employees professionally engaged in communications speak with a single voice. That theory survived a severe test in 1982 when the company was able to stall inquiries about its new disc camera until it could be unveiled at a New York news conference that attracted 370 people, followed by seven regional conferences in the United States and 40 abroad. At the New York meeting, those in attendance were invited to use the camera, photographing models, and the results were later mailed to them.

Sometimes the public relations touches require a lot of thought and coordination, as with the Kodak news conference; sometimes they are merely commonsense responses. Piedmont Aviation, which bucked the deregulation tide by focusing on service to some of the smaller communities, faced a problem when an advertised nonstop flight from Charlotte, North Carolina, to Los Angeles had to refuel in Oklahoma City on its maiden flight because the long-range 727 scheduled for the trip was not ready and a shorter-range version had to be used. Piedmont's president issued letters of apology to all passengers, along with $50 in cash for those in first class and $20 for those who flew coach.

COMPETITION

Competition is nothing new in business. Few industries today have the luxury of ignoring their competitors. If they don't face rivalries from other American firms, they must compete with foreign products.

Japan is a case in point, especially in the area of electronics and automobiles. Many observers feel this is the result, not solely of cheaper labor, but of the differing attitudes of Japanese and American workers. Factory employees in the United States are viewed as possessing superior advanced skills (although they don't match up with the Japanese on basic skills), and as having more personal ambition and initiative. In other areas, however, from company loyalty to reliability, critics view Japanese workers as better. The Japanese workweek is longer, productivity higher, and labor costs about half. The answer to this imbalance can't be found in restrictions alone but must also include a response from American workers—a response promoted in part by internal public relations.

Competition within this nation is also serious business. There are fierce struggles within the appliance industry, apparel, automobile tires, discount chains, and even in greeting cards, which Hallmark has long dominated. A dozen smaller computer companies battle giants like Wang and IBM. Hershey Chocolate, once comfortable and complacent, was displaced by Mars and had to fight back. Hershey poured money into advertising and created new products, including candy for adults that is less sweet than the kiddie brands. Mars positioned its products as "sweet snacks" and paid $5 million to get M&Ms and Snickers named official snack foods for the Olympics in Los Angeles in 1984. The two firms are still slugging it out, toe to chocolate toe.

Another bitter contest rages among the nation's hamburger chains, especially McDonald's, Burger King, and Wendy's. What we see is the advertising, but many marketing and public relations ploys are also at work.

> McDonald's has "thanked" American communities with more than a dozen national programs, far more than any of its competititors. These range from supporting the Ronald McDonald houses—homes-away-from-home for parents of terminally ill children—to developing and promoting McDonald's All American High School Band and the All American High School Basketball Game, building the swimming pool for the Los Angeles Olympics, sponsoring gymnastic events, backing a gospel-singing contest, promoting seatbelt safety, sponsoring double-dutch-jumprope league tournaments, funding the fight against muscular dystrophy, and providing major support to the United Negro College Fund.[4]

There are also local projects spearheaded by McDonald franchisees, who are reminded that the company stresses "quality, service, cleanliness and value."

Burger King and Wendy's aggressively pursue the fast-food leader, experimenting more with alternate food items and tying their PR campaigns to their advertising efforts. Wendy's, for example, capitalized on the popularity of Clara Peller's "Where's the beef?" and sent her on tour through three dozen major American cities and onto the stage of virtually every network talk show. Burger King also used media tours to supplement its comparison advertising, and, although it hasn't caught McDonald's, it can't be upset by its strong annual growth rate. The leader, however, has never been complacent, introducing McNuggets and the McStop truckstop restaurants, and also marketing franchisee ideas, like the Big Mac, the Egg McMuffin, and the McSnack units.

Just as torrid is the conflict among soft-drink companies, with Coca-Cola and Pepsi as the main event, and 7-Up and Dr. Pepper in the prelims. With soft drinks taking over as the nation's premier beverage, and with the world as an active market, the stakes are high. Even 1 percent of the market is worth $300 million in sales. Coke typically runs ahead of Pepsi by 5–6 percentage points, and 7-Up and Dr. Pepper virtually tie with about a fourth each of Pepsi's share. The best other competitors can do is approach a 2 percent share of market.

The two giants slug it out in other product areas, simultaneously making it tougher on other brands, like Squirt and Tab and Sunkist Orange.

Advertising is their prime weapon, but Coca-Cola and Pepsi are also active in a variety of public relations ventures, from corporate sponsorship to the funding of international projects.

PRODUCTIVITY

> One of the most difficult problems facing the public relations professional is how to help management *increase the productivity* of its operations, which has been declining in comparison with that achieved by other nations with important industries. Many factors involved in this have been cited: export of American technology; less room for technological improvement than had been the case several decades ago; union work rules that interfered with efficiency; more restrictive safety and environmental laws in the U.S. than elsewhere, etc.[5]

Increased automation is regarded as one solution to the productivity dilemma, especially since younger workers adapt more readily to the new technology. Also, information is available more quickly, and computers make it much easier to monitor productivity and profit. Some people react against the scientific advances, however, and some human problems also have yet to be solved.

Many economists feel American business has turned the corner, spurred by a new generation of executives who are determined to raise industrial output. There are leaner operations, increased research and development, and more aggressive marketing—aided by public relations programs. PR also assists directly in the problem, encouraging supervisors to meet with employees and supplying them with materials and training to motivate workers. Practitioners have also supported the notion of more hands-on management, involving employees' input and giving them a greater stake in productivity, and they've tried to remove some of the fears created by more mechanized plants and offices.

WHAT ELSE CAN PUBLIC RELATIONS ACCOMPLISH?

Philip Lesly, author and president of the Chicago PR firm that bears his name, sees a fourfold responsibility for public relations in the business sector:

1. To sense trends in public attitudes and determine where they are headed
2. To help the organization accommodate these trends and bring it into confluence rather than conflict with its publics and their attitudes
3. To develop programs and policies to achieve that confluence
4. To help create the future attitude climate in which the organization will function[6]

Another cogent argument for the value of public relations in business is the fact that business leaders often select as subordinates people whose backgrounds and experience mirror their own. That makes criticism and evaluation more difficult. The public relations person brings to this situation another viewpoint, a more sensitive public viewpoint.

In this age of new channels of communication and more complex systems for delivering messages, the professional is invaluable. There is less room for the amateur communicator in business. Accompanying the increase in complicated tools is the decline of writing abilty among the masses and the need for a person expert in this skill.

Surveys show that corporate management has become more reliant on the PR function and more impressed with what it can do. Most business leaders see public relations as expanding its corporate role. They also list PRSA, the field's professional society, in the top ten of the most important business organizations. PR no longer suffers from the subordinate status once accorded that vocation. One reason is that business is able to see results that, although sometimes intangible, are nevertheless real.

> Public relations is aimed at maintaining the legitimacy of a company or industry, a perception by the public that the company or industry is operating in the public interest and is serving a social need.[7]

More and more emphasis is being placed upon accountability, and not only on government agencies and private charities, but also on corporations. Each business also has its constituencies to whom it is responsible. William Batten, chairman of the New York Stock Exchange, listed seven of these:

1. *Government*—for complying with tax & regulatory laws.
2. *Shareholders*—for managing efficiently, distributing profits responsibly.
3. *Employees*—for fair management practices, providing satisfactory working conditions and benefits.
4. *Customers*—for well-made products and useful services at reasonable prices.
5. *Suppliers*—for fair treatment and prices.
6. *Community*—for paying taxes and participating in local activities.
7. *General public*—"which expects some benefits to flow from the mere fact of the existence of the corporate form in our society."[8]

In all these areas, public relations is a key factor. It can help a small firm win plaudits for its involvement in charitable work, or it can aid a major city, like Detroit, in recovering from economic disaster.

As noted earlier, PR is no panacea. There are problems it can't eradicate, and there are practitioners who are inept, shortsighted, even dishonest. Some public relations persons share the blame with company presidents in scandals involving bribery of government officials, illegal payments to foreign governments, bid rigging, falsification of documents, and other crimes.

HOW TO WEAR A SAFETY BELT

YOU CAN BE BOTH SECURE AND COMFORTABLE IN YOUR CAR.

It's been proved over and over that safety belts at least double your chances of escaping death or serious injury in a severe accident.

But the freedom of movement allowed by the newer front safety belts has bothered some people. How can the safety belt hold you securely if it appears to have almost no tension?

The fact is, the shoulder belt is designed to restrict your movement only in an emergency. In normal situations, you can lean forward or to the side with little pressure from the shoulder belt.

In an emergency, the belts lock up to hold you in place. The inertial reel makes this possible. That's a mechanism as simple and reliable as gravity (as you can see in the accompanying diagram). Inertial reels have been used since the 1974 model year for the shoulder belt in many GM cars. They allow you complete freedom of movement in normal driving. You can turn easily to check traffic or reach to the glove compartment.

Adjusting your shoulder and lap belt. Even the slight tension you feel from the inertial reel is adjustable so there is almost no pressure. Pull the shoulder belt far enough away from you so that, when you let it go, it comes back flat against your chest. Then pull down slightly on the shoulder portion, about one inch, and let it go again.

Safety experts suggest allowing no more slack on the shoulder belt than absolutely necessary for comfort. Lap belts should be adjusted snugly as low on your hipbones as possible—not higher where they might damage internal organs in a crash.

How the inertial reel works. *Your shoulder belt is designed to allow freedom under normal conditions, but to lock automatically and restrain you in a collision.*

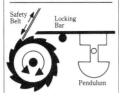

Ratchet Mechanism

Under normal conditions, *the pendulum and locking bar are in their rest positions. The reel which holds the safety belt is free to rotate. As you lean against it, the belt unreels.*

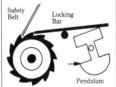

Ratchet Mechanism

In emergencies, *such as a collision from any direction, the pendulum tilts, forcing the locking bar to engage the ratchet. The reel locks and the safety belt restrains you.*

In a collision, lap/shoulder belts, worn properly, distribute the force across the large, strong bones of your hips and torso. Perhaps most important, belts help keep you from being thrown out of the vehicle in an accident.

What if you are pregnant? The American Association for Automotive Medicine says the dangers of being unbelted in a collision during pregnancy are far greater than the slight chance of injury caused by wearing the belts.

Other advantages of belts. By holding you in a proper driving position, the lap belt provides a feeling of control, keeping you in place on rough or curved roads or in an emergency maneuver. Some people even find that the added support makes driving easier on their backs.

Next time you drive, please take a moment to buckle up. Remember, the safety belt is an effective system to help protect you, and it's already part of your car.

This advertisement is part of our continuing effort to give customers useful information about their cars and trucks and the company that builds them.

Chevrolet • Pontiac
Oldsmobile • Buick
Cadillac • GMC Truck

Figure 12-3 A public service ad that ties nicely to the product. Reproduced courtesy of General Motors Corporation

---

Happily, these people are a minority. Still, there are other lapses, underlining the fact that practitioners are human.

The PR consultant for a computer firm that was operating under the supervision of a federal bankruptcy court thought he'd demonstrate that the firm hadn't lost its sense of humor, so when he provided press kits to the media, he enclosed a price list ($1.19 for the news release; $1.69 for the black-and-white photo of the company's new computer). No reporter or editor thought it was funny; most felt it was outrageous.

One truck-rental firm had its public relations firm circulate to the media a stack of internal memos from and news clippings about a competitor, accompanied by a letter impugning the safety record of this competitor. Most editors considered this practice unethical and rejected the information.

PUBLIC RELATIONS AND MARKETING

Marketing is a term that characterizes all the activities necessary to move a product from a manufacturer to a consumer. This involves product research, product development, branding, pricing, packaging, transportation, sales and distribution, advertising, and other factors—including public relations.

Of late, public relations efforts in marketing have intensified, owing partly to the effects of consumerism and to the saturation concerns about advertising. Marketing managers are beginning to realize that the customer's (or retailer's) attitude about a manufacturing firm may color his or her view of that company's product. If customers know and trust the corporation, they are more likely to trust the product. This kind of positive environment also makes things easier for the sales force, preparing the way for them as they make their calls.

Public relations practitioners may also be invaluable in marketing research, blending their skills with those of the research division. They are also likely to be less heavy-handed in preparing copy for print material or the media. And the PR professional is even more likely to have promotional ideas than is the advertising manager or agency.

In an article in the *Public Relations Journal*, Daniel S. Roher lists ten ways that public relations can help sales. In synopsized form, these ways are:

1. *Prospect for new markets.* A PR media campaign could narrow the prospect field to the most promising customers, saving expensive research and advertising efforts.
2. *Reach peripheral markets.* It is much more economical, for example, to reach an ethnic market via publicity than it is to try to buy ads in all the newspapers catering to that group.
3. *Provide third-party endorsement.* Prospects may be skeptical of advertising or sales literature, but the implied endorsement of a disinterested third party—the media—may enhance credibility.
4. *Obtain new sales leads.* Stories in newspapers and magazines often generate leads, and sometimes the publications themselves promote such inquiries.
5. *Pave the way for sales calls.* If the prospect has some information on the product or company, it makes the selling easier.
6. *Establish your company as a principal source of information.* When editors or news directors are looking for information in certain fields, they turn to those firms that have established themselves as leaders or experts in that specific industry. Obviously, larger companies are in better shape to perform this service, but smaller companies with solid reputations in lesser-known areas may also score.

7. *Help sell "minor" products.* Products with a small margin of profit may not be able to afford extensive advertising. Editorial efforts could supplant the ads.
8. *Obtain publicity for principal executives.* Magazine and newspaper interviews, feature stories, speeches, and television appearances—all these things help humanize a company by focusing on its key personnel.
9. *Stretch your promotional dollar.* Once an article is published, the company may order and distribute reprints, thus extending the value of the promotional piece.
10. *Make more effective use of sales literature.* Professionals in the PR field can merchandise new literature as well as products. They can obtain coverage for the brochures and booklets themselves.[9]

To this array of reasons, one might also add the factor of economy—publicity being cheaper than advertising—and the ability to get deserving stories placed where ads may not appear, such as on the front page of many papers.

Marketing executives, once doubtful about the value of public relations, are now more uniform in their praise of its potential. They also employ PR techniques far more than in the past. This expanded relationship argues for more familiarity on the part of practitioners with economic theory and practice. PR people usually appreciate popular concerns and trends and the means of communicating successfully in varied environments, but they may be weaker when it comes to divining the economic forces at work and the marketing strategies required to effectively move products and services.

All the techniques indigenous to public relations are also precepts of good marketing—research, planning, implementation, communication, evaluation. PR sets the stage for the sales team and serves as a conscience to the production staff. It can ease internal tensions and prepare external product acceptance. Public relations is part of the team.

> Ideally, everyone in an organization from top management to receptionists and messengers should be trained to develop marketing awareness. That is, not only people in the traditional sales functions, but anyone with public contact can contribute something to the marketing process in the most savvy organizations.[10]

The "promotion" aspect of business, which was once considered a poor cousin of the advertising function, now takes more planning and enjoys a bigger budget. Soft-drink manufacturers, for example, although still assigning a major portion of their budgets to advertising, have increased expenditures in areas like sweepstakes, personal tours, and sponsorship of the arts. A firm that produces alcoholic beverages spends thousands annually on printed materials dedicated to the preservation of endangered wildlife. Blue Ribbon Rice organized a high school band competition in the Houston area. A pharmaceutical company put on a conference for teenagers on sex and pregnancy.

A sports-equipment manufacturer developed a "golf swing analysis center" that provides computerized diagrams of golf swings for a nominal fee (more than half of which is donated to charity), making money with the service while promoting its own products.

To promote a polystyrene foam poster board, the manufacturer conducted a contest to determine the most creative use of the product, and General Foods encouraged youngsters to trade in proof-of-purchase seals for athletic equipment. Du Pont used a series of fishing tips on radio to call attention to its fishing line, and computer companies equip educational institutions with models of their latest units.

Not all PR efforts are appreciated, however, Although the public relations campaign for the Cabbage Patch dolls has been called "one of the greatest publicity coups of all times," resulting in an unprecedented run on the product, the PR firm that masterminded the program was fired from the account a year later. Cited as reasons were everything from economics to personality conflicts, but the dismissal again underlined the fact that nothing is certain in public relations, not even the rewards of success.

MANAGEMENT APPROVAL IS ESSENTIAL

Regardless of the originality or practicality of the PR plan, nothing significant will happen without the blessing and cooperation of the chief executive officer and other key company officials. That's why bringing these people in on the campaign and convincing them of the efficacy of public relations is always an initial step. Most progressive CEOs, recognizing the need for improved PR, have upgraded this function, according it more authority and a fairer share of the budget.

Beyond this understanding and cooperation is the key role the company president and/or chairperson play in any PR effort. Corporate leaders are almost invariably the chief spokespersons for the industry. When they are good at this task, things usually run a bit smoother; when they're not, the PR department may have to make up this ground. To help achieve an ideal executive performance, the practitioner must first understand the mind and philosophy of the boss or client, must appreciate what sort of administrator this person is or would like to be, what the person's strengths and weaknesses are, and how well the executive will adapt to the PR role. An educational primer in media relations, community awareness, social responsibility, internal sensitivity, and other functions may be necessary. A closed managerial style may require alteration; an open style may need to be modified.

Periodic surveys by publications like *pr reporter* indicate increasing involvement by corporate leaders, with nine out of ten CEOs taking part in PR planning sessions, or speaking to groups, lobbying, holding media conferences, or interesting themselves in consumer affairs. This trend, although helpful, doesn't relieve the practitioner of responsibility.

Despite business executives having developed reputations as men of action, they are embarrassingly uninformed about the social environment in which they live and move. They give evidence of having a need not to know about matters of consequence to them—and to us. . . . Social environment here refers not only to the publics (domestic and foreign) that corporations serve, but to the whole human, interpersonal webwork that forms our corporations themselves, as well as our society-at-large, which has a future to be shaped.[11]

Obviously, the professional public relations person can provide invaluable counsel in helping executive officers to grasp some of these public issues and can also encourage a more outspoken posture on those that affect the corporation or require a strong voice. Company officials may decry the lack of public understanding about business, and they may chafe at government regulation, and they may not trust the intent of the media, but these personal perceptions don't alter reality. The practitioner has to convey to the CEO a public view, one that is open, honest, and convincing. The executive should then be able to translate these lessons into a posture and image that reflect well on the corporation. Practically speaking, this training may, in many instances, require continual coaching to help the CEO develop a more relaxed, less jargon-punctuated rhetorical style. The CEO has to learn how to persuade rather than command, to explain rather than dictate.

In the political arena, which business leaders formerly tried to ignore or manipulate, chief executive officers are also more active—raising funds, providing endorsements, campaigning, becoming more vocal on issues, and even running for office or accepting government appointments. Despite the danger in such alliances and behavior, the trend does give further credence to the notion that corporate officers are ready and willing to go public.

Some CEOs earn special plaudits for their concern with social issues. Environmental protection is the pet project of conservative businessman Robert Anderson, founder of Atlantic Richfield; real estate magnate Harold Willens tries to woo other corporate presidents to support arms reduction; and Control Data's chairman focuses that corporation's efforts on providing jobs and training for the disadvantaged. Public relations staffs are heavily involved in these causes, sometimes taking their lumps, but generally finding that good works pay off—and good leadership makes good works happen.

Nothing is sacred, however, in the business world, and nothing is certain. Executives may ride the crest for a while, enjoying media celebrity status and reveling in employee adulation, only to have all this disappear in a crisis. United Air Lines chairman Richard Ferris, a former pilot, had the affection of his myriad crews and the admiration of shareholders and the financial media. A strike in 1985 tarnished that image quickly among employees, although he retained the respect of investors and airline competitors. In such cases, public relations may soften the difficulties, but it is rarely able to reverse all the negatives.

Much attention is given to the communication role of the PR professional, but a less obvious and equally important function is the advice and assistance the practitioner provides the chief executive. Professionalism in the skills areas is expected of PR people, but they must also make the boss (or client) look good.

DEALING WITH CRITICS, CRISES, AND CONSUMER ADVOCATES

Compared with the 1960s and 1970s, the decade of the 1980s witnessed a decline in enforcement of consumer protection laws. Rather than easing the responsibilities of corporations, this alteration made it more important than ever that companies examine their consciences on consumer and environmental issues, taking appropriate steps to curb any illegalities in their businesses while also addressing the general need for corporate accountability. Not every company has responded to this obligation, a complacent attitude some PR experts consider shortsighted. They insist that business is still not beloved by the populace, meaning that any ignoring of its social duty is risky. The consumer advocates, federal critics, and investigative reporters remain active and pose a threat to any industry not conducting itself responsibly.

Some public relations people prescribe multiple solutions to consumerism pressure, including the improvement of product quality and expansion of services, increased cooperation with nonprofit groups, and the establishment of firms' own regulatory committees, along with consumer-affairs departments.

Monsanto Company, for example, voluntarily cleaned up chemical waste dumps to which it had contributed, even though, legally, no guilt had been proven. Many corporations have recalled products as soon as problems were determined and before any government pressure was applied. Customer complaints are also handled rapidly by the most savvy firms, preventing things from becoming any more serious.

Of course, as always, preventive public relations is better than reactive public relations. Enough crises will occur even when you are prepared, so it's best to do as a matter of course those things that display an honest concern for the public good.

COMMUNITY RELATIONS AND PUBLIC AFFAIRS

Each firm or institution in a community is expected to be a good citizen. This translates into providing jobs for local workers, making local purchases of goods and services, providing leadership in community affairs, contributing funds to local causes, and supplying backing to community concerns—religion, education, athletics, and other areas.

The more public relations practitioners know about a town or city, the better they will be able to interpret its needs. The practitioner should aid management in developing a "community profile," which would catalog information on the cultural, sociological, political, and economic structures in

Figure 12-4 Different audiences are addressed in these publications—children (and their parents), employees, and shareholders and prospects.
Courtesy: Union Pacific Railroad; Standard Oil Company; reproduced with permission of AT&T

the community. The company officials must know who the real leaders are in the city, and where the real power lies. They must also understand needs and problems.

A single firm or institution can't be all things to all people. That is why many organizations concentrate on certain areas. A dairy may focus on youth programs by sponsoring athletic teams and summer camps. A utility may channel its efforts into cultural programs by donating art, underwriting operatic performances, and providing space for displays and meetings. An insurance company in Boston hosts a Shakespeare festival; a midwestern telephone company provides "loaned executives" to nonprofit institutions to help them in fund-raising or management chores; a Detroit manufacturer supports financially the local recycling organization.

Here are some other corporate efforts to sustain the "good citizen" status:

- Kellogg's fund-raising campaign for the refurbishing of the Statue of Liberty, and the listing of contributors in subsequent advertising in *USA Today*.
- Elanco's creation of a speech contest and lecture tour in cooperation with the Young Farmers Associations in 24 states, with the aim of encouraging these youngsters while informing other Americans of the agricultural crisis.
- Trailways Corporation's development of a program to publicize the plight of missing and runaway children, while providing them with free rides home.
- Sponsorship of a series of conferences by Atlantic Richfield Company to help improve relationships and cooperation between private industry and non-profit firms in major ARCO communities.
- Campus visits by Phillips Petroleum Company staffers who discuss public relations with journalism and communication students.

- One-year subsidization by Enron of a magazine on the fine arts in America.
- "Southern California Water Watch," a persuasive PR effort created by Burson-Marsteller for Metropolitan Water District of Southern California to sell conservation to consumers.
- A rope-skipping contest introduced by United Technologies Corporation, among their many community programs.
- Coca-Cola lends support and furnishes awards annually at the Houston Livestock Show and Rodeo.
- A number of organizations, like Philip Morris and the American Railroad Foundation, conduct contests for the best ideas or programs about their industries.
- Almost every major corporation has some ties to education—funding, scholarships, support of faculty fellows, donation of equipment, grants for research. Others may offer transportation or job training to those not enrolled in college. Still others, like General Motors, reach out to the handicapped, the secondary-school student, the underemployed, those struggling in the fine arts, and men and women engaged in health-related research.

One method of corporate involvement gaining support these last several years is the sponsorship of athletic contests or tournaments. Events like the Indianapolis 500 have long enjoyed the partnership of firms that can tie into that sporting scene. The Virginia Slims tennis tournament for women also relates to that company's target audience, as do the affiliations of track-shoe manufacturers with track meets. We have marathons, golf tourneys, and cross-country skiing. The Olympics corralled an impressive list of corporate sponsors, but you'll also find companies lending their names to Frisbee competitions, dog shows, and hula-hoop contests.

Every firm that sponsors these events, whether it's Texaco and the Metropolitan Opera or Volvo's tennis tournament, must make certain the event is appropriate and fundable, and that it reflects well on the sponsor.

The same sort of logic is applied to charitable giving—or it should apply. Many corporations give very little, and some that donate with regularity may do so unscientifically. The best-organized firms have committees and directors and staff people to sort out the appeals.

Public Affairs

There is more to community relations than contributions, sponsorship, and membership. In the last decade, the whole notion of "public affairs" has blossomed in corporate America. One study indicated that 60 percent of the companies with public-affairs departments today didn't have them ten years ago. Some use the term to embrace all external public relations; others narrow public affairs to community and government activites, along with, perhaps, their broader social programming.

> With a highly literate and educated population, with modern technology and communication, with continuing high hopes and expectations, the number and pressure of issues will inevitably create the need for effective public relations/public affairs responses. Thus, we can expect staff specialists and consul-

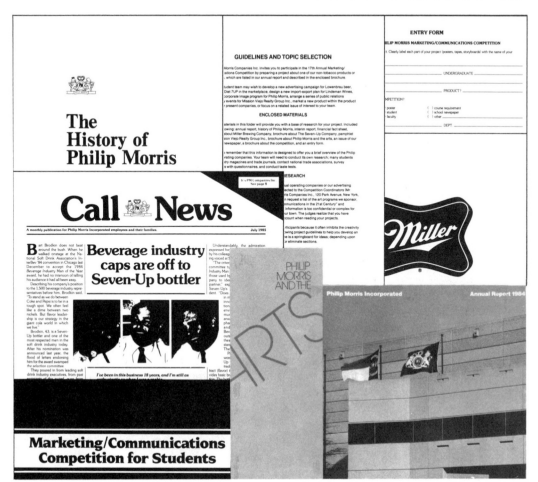

Figure 12-5 Philip Morris is among the corporations that conduct cash award competitions to college students.
Courtesy: Philip Morris Companies Inc.

WORKING WITH THE INNER CITY

Some industries have made it their special crusade to address problems of the inner city, tackling urban blight, housing decay, high unemployment, lack of job training, even health care. Corporations have invested in minority businesses, providing both funds and counseling, and they've helped encourage other companies to locate in or near the depressed areas.

Control Data's president, Bill Norris, articulated the company philosophy, which starts with the conviction that government has not done a good job in meeting the needs of the country, especially in the areas of employment, productivity, education, and health. Control Data doesn't give much in direct contributions to those in need but prefers to support causes that work toward alleviating such problems.

Norris preaches that "business can't operate in a sick society" and that business must have "the prospect of a reasonable return" before it commits its resources. To that end, Control Data has built half a dozen plants in decaying neighborhoods and has found this to be not only socially beneficial but also good business. It has taken its lumps, too, and members of the financial press have often criticized the wisdom of its programs. When the firm invested in computer-based education for the disadvantaged, some activists accused it of making a profit at the expense of the poor. But Control Data has persisted, sometimes working with other corporations, in attempts to reduce both urban and rural poverty.

Norris has the reputation of being very direct. Says one junior executive, "He expects people to be prepared. He tells you he doesn't want you to get him more later, but to get him more earlier."

This directness also applies to his dealings with the media, to whom he gives an average of one interview a week—with nothing off the record. However, he is also not above suggesting that a newspaper run an editorial to correct an erroneous impression a previous article made, and he once brushed off a feature writer from a national magazine, telling this writer he wasn't really prepared for the confrontation and would get back to the person later—which he did.

In St. Louis, a consortium of businesses, residents, potential investors, and elected officials pooled their talents to restore Hyde Park, a 66-square-block district in the city's inner core. They faced negative publicity about the dangers in that area, high interest rates for investors, a shrinking population, and an abundance of homes in terrible shape.

> The community relations program was guided by six-month public relations and marketing support objectives, updated at least every three months. Elements include media relations and media events; collateral materials (graphic identity, fact sheets, information kits, stationery, brochures, reprints, direct mail, exhibits and displays); special projects (Information Center activities, speakers' bureau, slide show, public relations training for volunteers, and promotion of neighborhood attractions through walking tours, concerts, barbecues and other events).[12]

In little over a year, the Hyde Park Partnership could point to overwhelming media response, thousands of visitors, sales completed or pending on 17 pieces of property, renovation started on threescore houses, and the prospect of doubling the $7 million in housing development funds it had garnered.

Figure 12-6 Materials used in Enron's traveling exhibit had a unified look and feel to them.
Courtesy: Enron Corp.

tants to become more oriented toward issue identification, with functional managers formulating responses based on their knowledge of the complexity of the enterprise.[13]

Some observers see public affairs as more *externally* driven than public relations, with more of a futurist outlook, with more concern for issues, and with more formulation of programs instead of reactions to crises. There is no neat division between public affairs and public relations, and the distinctions will remain clouded for some time to come, but whatever the terminology, the fact is clear that extra attention is being given to the cultivation and education of the more proximate publics.

In some instances, such contact and communication are relatively simple; in other cases, quite complicated. Corporations dealing with large Hispanic or Asian populations must contend with language barriers, cultural differences, a preference for graphics, perhaps, or a whole new set of communication channels. Companies with numerous branches find it difficult to coordinate their diverse programs and to educate their individual local managers to company goals and policies. And even corporations with exceptional leverage in their home-office cities must walk carefully. Even Kellogg Company, whose name is synonymous with Battle Creek, Michigan, had to work at reducing cries of intimidation when the cereal giant threatened to move its headquarters unless the city and township merged their governing bodies. Although the 2-to-1 vote in favor of Kellogg's proposal was gratifying, it was achieved at the cost of some bitterness. There are times when you have to make a stand, but corporations would prefer to just make friends.

The projects involving business are many, from driver education to drug rehabilitation, and from safety exhibits to playground equipment. All have the motive (in addition, it is hoped, to some altruism) of presenting the company to its constituent publics in a favorable light.

There are other methods, too, of gaining community acceptance.

Each method has its merits and demerits.

A *speakers' bureau* can be an excellent community-relations tool, but it may be a headache for the PR person. It means recruiting speakers, locating assignments, and then matching both. It can involve considerable scheduling, some expense, and multiple complaints. Some speakers, for example, become more popular than others—either because of ability or because of topic. They end up carrying a disproportionate share of the load. Sometimes an organization wants to pay a speaker. Does the speaker get to keep the fee, or does it go to the bureau? If one person is paid, will this create a problem among the other speakers? Before practitioners commit themselves to any such program, they should be certain they have weighed the risks.

These speakers, once trained, have to be promoted, their appearances publicized, and some follow-up made after each engagement. Smith Kline & French, for example, not only files clippings on each speaking engagement but also requires reports from the speakers, including a rundown on questions asked by the audience.

Memberships, if paid by the company, should be selfishly selective. It may be in the firm's interest to have an employee as a member of Rotary or Kiwanis or the Downtown Development Club or a local country club. Little benefit to the firm, however, may be derived from employee attendance at a Little Theatre Reading Society or a church bowling league. If the employee pays his or her own fees, that's another matter.

Company-sponsored members should feel an obligation to attend meetings, to represent their firm properly, to make periodic reports to the company, and to aspire to elective office within the civic organization.

The public relations director, incidentally, must be careful in the way he or she allots time. Only the more important organizations should be chosen, along with those for which the PR person has a special affinity or concern. In many organizations, members with public relations expertise are overworked. They seem to be the only ones who know how to organize an event, write a citation, edit a club newsletter, prepare an annual report, produce news releases, or even direct skits. Practitioners should be willing to tackle some of these chores, but they can't afford to get bogged down in club minutiae to the detriment of their regular jobs.

BUSINESS AND THE MEDIA

For the past quarter century or more, there has been a love-hate relationship between the nation's business firms and the nation's media. In the role of mediator has been the PR practitioner. The conflict has arisen because of what corporations may perceive as an investigative bias in the media, and the media's resentment of what they see as more sophisticated methods of controlling the free flow of information.

A CBS special that ran on Christmas a few years ago featured commentators Dan Rather, Mike Wallace, and Geraldo Rivera, and a roster of corporate executives. One thing that emerged clearly from this discussion (titled "Business and the Press") was that people like Rather and Wallace see PR people—the good ones—standing between them and top management, and willing to do almost anything to protect the image they have created. Rather called it "fogging the issue" and reminded viewers how much practitioners were paid for this type of service.

Not all of this is paranoia. Surveys conducted by the American Management Association reveal that nearly half the PR people polled had, at some time, withheld information from the media. This same research shows a wide disparity between media and business in terms of perceived availability, bias, openness, and cooperation. Other studies depict the "media elite" as being dissatisfied with the existing social order, holding such views as that America's heavy use of natural resources is immoral, that our economic policies are a cause of Third World poverty, and that our foreign policy is structured to

Figure 12-7 Phillips Petroleum issues a helpful glossary of technical terms for the media; Standard Oil Company offers case studies to universities; Mobil provides a different view of some energy-related stories. Courtesy: Phillips Petroleum Company, Standard Oil Company, Mobil Oil

protect American business. The media traditionally view business as having the greatest influence of any leadership bloc, whereas business may feel the same way about the media, especially television, citing case after case to "prove" media antagonism.

The very nature of television news may contribute to the problem. People are in a hurry; time segments are short; editing is a must. This results in judgments that are fallible, or versions that are incomplete.

Even more significant is the fact that neither side understands the other well enough. Reporters are often weak on the nuances of business and may even feel a bit hostile toward the corporate world. Business executives may not be convinced of the strict protection afforded the First Amendment freedoms, and they are largely ignorant of the professional aspects of the journalist's work. Obviously, anything—from meetings to mailings—that can bridge this mistrust would be helpful.

Some firms do this well. When Tylenol introduced its new tamperproof package via a 30-city press teleconference, the company president complimented the media on their avoidance of "panic or scare" stories and said the "coverage was responsible and accurate." And Delta Airlines execs expressed their gratitude for upbeat media treatment of their appreciative employees' gift to the company of a new $30 million Boeing 767. It might be argued that these stories were both hard news and that the persons responsible for working with the media handled things efficiently and professionally. Those two qualities are always beneficial.

Many corporate officers are now schooled in working with the media, especially the electronic media. They are taught the principles of the interview and subjected to grilling by people simulating print and television reporters. Colleges and universities are encouraged to incorporate more communications theory and practice into their business curricula. And both counselors and internal PR directors are spending more time bringing CEOs up to speed on media relations, stressing everything from availability to composure.

Important as the media are, they still constitute only one target audience for business PR.

DIRECTORS AND SHAREHOLDERS

Chapters 9 and 13 deal with directors and shareholders in some detail. Directors, of course, merit special attention. It is wise to send them copies of all significant printed materials, including the more important news releases, and to ensure that they receive VIP treatment at all company functions. Since, presumably, these men and women are on the board because of their ability to advise management, they should be given every opportunity to participate. Typically, some will be active and influential, and others will miss meetings, or, when they do attend, will have little to offer. Both kinds of directors must be treated equally, however, at least publicly.

Shareholders, as mentioned in the next chapter, are also special friends and should receive some of the "family" treatment that the general public does not receive. This means periodic mailings, invitations to company events, and other courtesies.

DEALERS, DISTRIBUTORS, AND SUPPLIERS

Again, some acknowledgment must be made of the special relationship that exists between the company and its dealers, distributors, and suppliers. Ordinarily this communication function will be performed by the departments most directly affected—marketing, sales, or purchasing. The public relations office, however, can serve a strong auxiliary role by helping to sense problems and offer solutions, preparing printed materials and other communications, remaining aware of the importance of these people, and seeing that management shares this awareness.

Suppliers—those who provide goods and services for the company— should be dealt with fairly and honestly. Nothing harms a public relations image faster than a reputation for favoritism or under-the-table dealing. It is smart business practice to have open bidding on all contracts. It is also wise to trade with local suppliers whenever possible. Firms who continually buy their supplies from distant locations soon lose their community support. Besides, aiding the local economy also helps the corporation.

Dealers and distributors of the firm's manufactured goods need to be kept informed and enthusiastic. This is accomplished through mailings and meetings. Both the public relations and advertising departments or counselors may have a hand in preparing materials for these people.

GOVERNMENT

Robert Crandall, in an article in the *Saturday Review*, stated that:

> . . . until as recently as a decade ago, the word *regulation* was applied almost exclusively to the government's attempt to control prices and licensing in such fields as transportation, electrical and gas utilities, communications, and gas production. Today, such agencies as the Civil Aeronautics Board, the Interstate Commerce Commission, and the Federal Communications Commission have this role.
>
> But the 1970s have witnessed the growth of a new form of regulation that involves health, safety, and environmental protection. In less than ten years, Congress has created a federal bureaucracy employing 80,000 people, with the mission of protecting consumers or workers from harm. Among the most important of the new agencies, and their dates of creation, are:
>
> - The Environmental Protection Agency (EPA), 1970
> - The National Highway Traffic Safety Administration (NHTSA), 1970
> - The Occupational Safety and Health Administration (OSHA), 1970
> - The Consumer Product Safety Commission (CPSC), 1972

- The Office of Surface Mining Reclamation and Enforcement (in the Department of the Interior), 1977

At least another 15 lesser agencies or offices have also been created, and many existing organizations—such as the Federal Trade Commission—enjoy greater authority.[14]

Several problems arise out of such regulations. The cost and labor involved in processing and accommodating the regulations is one result. Another is the increasing strength of pressure groups, many of which are small but well organized and vocal. Industry complains that it has to do such things as file Environmental Impact Statements on the consequences of the location and erection of an industrial plant, whereas objectors to the plant have no need to file any statements about the environmental or economic consequences of their actions.

Management and its public relations arm have to make every effort to concur with federal and state regulations. Failure to do so may be costly and is certain to garner negative publicity. This doesn't mean that they can't continue to work for changes in the restrictions or that they must collapse in the face of any pressure group. What it does mean is that the public relations person must add a whole new lexicon of information to his or her professional experience.

INTERNAL PUBLIC RELATIONS

PR, like charity, begins at home. You can't expend your best efforts on creating a public image while ignoring those problems closest to you. Not only is this unfair, it is also unwise. Your best spokespersons should be your own staff and employees. You may publish an ad boasting of great things you are doing, but if your employees' public conversations belie these claims, the effect is blunted.

Basically, employees want three things: *security*, *opportunity*, and *recognition*. Effective public relations doesn't stop here, it must begin here.

Every employee wants some guarantee that his or her job is not in constant jeopardy. In the past, some employers felt that fear was the best way to ensure efficiency and loyalty. They discovered it was not. The worker must feel secure, although not complacent, in order to function at a high level.

Few employees will settle for an endless rut. They prefer a chance to advance, to be transferred to another division or locale, or to somehow alter or improve their situation. This syndrome doesn't decrease with age. Employees in their forties start envisioning themselves at 60 and wonder if they want to be at the same old stand. They would like to have some options.

The final employee requisite, recognition, lies more within the PR area and is the easiest and cheapest need to supply. Outstanding employees should be noticed, thanked, and rewarded. When employees constantly perform above average, or devote their free time to community projects, or devise a new system for the company that saves labor and money, and then never hear a word from the front office, they are discouraged. The alert PR person can make the boss look good by staying on top of such deserving situations, then reminding the chief executive, or even drafting notes for his or her perusal and signature.

The public relations person is also likely to be involved in the programs that honor service or retirement. Although these may become routine to the practitioner, they are usually important to the recipient. Most programs start with pins for five years of service and then graduate to pen sets or more expensive items for longer service. Innovative firms have come up with a variety of awards, from appliances to vacations. Even appearing in the company publication may provide a thrill to some honorees.

What employees complain about most is communication. Even in quite sophisticated firms, they may gripe that no one tells them anything. That is why there should be a planned program of internal communication, one that is attractive and invites their reading or listening.

After all, communicating with employees should be a fairly easy task. For the better part of the week, they are involved with work—either on the job or coming and going. The PR person has some control over this audience and a chance to impart corporate views. The secret is to be able to combine a management outlook in an employee's context. Anything heavy-handed or propagandistic will fail.

Relations with Management

As with everything else in business, good internal relations start with management. The chief executive officer must be committed to programs that encourage and reward employees, that are attuned to their needs and concerns. Studies show that attitudes toward top management affect production, absenteeism, turnover, and safety. The worker wants to know that the boss is a problem solver, able to administer and delegate, that he or she truly cares about subordinates, and that changes that affect the worker will be speedily communicated.

Employees have many misconceptions about chief executives, caused partly by distance. One of the functions of the PR person is to bridge this distance by humanizing the boss, by advising him or her on internal relationships, and by implementing and monitoring an effective communication network.

One of the latest business buzz words is "corporate culture," which really defines the environment or climate within a company. Leaders set the tone but employees are full participants, sharing in the goals of the corporation. Only when employees perceive that these goals will also benefit them will they work hard to achieve company objectives.

This all means that managers must back off a bit from the administrative/financial outlook and consider the people side of the industry. Companies that have achieved these relationships also find that the bottom line improves. For one thing, executives who are involved get to know the employees; they hear things, learn things. And the employees perform better.

Again, the practitioner may be the catalyst.

Administrators have different styles. Some are shy, some too agressive. Some like to parcel out tasks; others dislike surrendering any authority. Some hesitate to exercise their power; others love to. The trick seems to be distinguishing between firmness and fear. A handful of American executives enjoy being viewed as mean and tough; this strokes their egos. Occasionally, they succeed despite these character deficiencies—perhaps because they have subordinates (or PR people) who can smooth over the rough spots. A leader may be strong without being dictatorial, and considerate without being naive.

The public relations professional works with many classes of administrator, and some adaptation is required. The practitioner tries to understand the personality of the CEO, accommodating programs to that style when possible, but reminding the leader of risks and error when conduct threatens internal order.

Communication

Management pronouncements are not nearly as effective as those communications that move upward from employees to the executive suite then back down again. Participatory communication results in higher involvement and credibility. In almost any survey of corporate staff members, the deficiencies in communication are at or near the top of the complaint list. Some executives feel that many details are none of the employees' business; some don't want to share; some are merely thoughtless or inept.

Most employees would like to get more information from their immediate supervisors; they have a feeling that the message is detoured somewhere, or deliberately halted. They may appreciate printed materials issued from the public relations office, but they would still prefer to get their news from those who manage their specific sections.

Many situations are bizarre. A plant is rumored to be closing, and no one at that plant has been informed of any management plans. Stories emerge in the media about an oil company selling off one of its hotel properties. The company hotly denies the rumor and says it has, in fact, just named a new manager. But the manager, then in Florida, hadn't been told.

Without question, PR can assist in these areas, beginning with the counseling of executives on proper communication techniques. The practitioner may also speed up the routing of internal communication, may send employees copies of news releases distributed to the media, may periodically check staff attitudes and opinions, and may augment or improve communication materials and channels. PR people may go even further, involving employees in research of issues or in social programs. Workers may be encouraged to express their concerns, not only through the old question box, but also via face-to-face meetings with executives.

There are any number of ways to improve the dissemination of information, but first, the company leadershp must be committed to an open, sharing attitude, and the means for circulating data and directives should be efficient.

Internal Publications

Although internal publications have traditionally fallen under the public relations aegis—and most still do—there is a trend toward separate departments for corporate and internal publications. These divisions are, of course, closely coordinated with the PR area but may function independently.

That is only one change occurring in company publications. Slowly—very slowly—editors are achieving more autonomy and are feeling freer to publish stories that would have been censored ten years ago. Much of the reason for this gradual shift comes from the more open stance of other publications, including religious newspapers, school newspapers, and the press in general. If the company magazines are to garner any sort of credibility, they must be more candid, even occasionally critical, and less self-serving.

In most instances, members of management support the internal newsletter or magazine and may feel they have the right to use its columns to present company policy and philosophy. Bucking this concept is difficult, but it is beginning to happen.

Chapters 7 and 8 detail content and graphic aspects of company publications, stressing that today's internal/external magazines feature a wider variety of stories, less heavy-handedness, more contemporary topics, occasional outside writers and photographers, larger size and bolder design, and items (like contests) that involve readers.

Studies show that employees value readability, regularity, and believability even more than content and appearance, and the worker prefers features on corporate plans, policies, and other job-related stories to those announcing anniversaries, birthdays, and engagements.

In addition to the internal magazine, newspaper, or newsletter, most companies publish a variety of other printed materials, from information manuals to presidential addresses. These, too, should invite readership via appearance and content.

More and more companies are issuing employee annual reports, slanting the copy and illustrations to internal interests. Nestlé, Nabisco, Kroger, and Getty are among the firms adopting this communication technique, expanding on the philosophy of management, responding to often-asked questions, or, like Munsingwear, informing workers about what's *right* with the organizaton.

Figure 12-8 Corporate communication is a billion-dollar industry, but the key element is still good PR personnel.

Many firms also broadcast local and national news at set times (usually around noon) over the company intercom system. Others use closed-circuit television to keep employees abreast of both external and internal news. And more and more firms are placing small daily newsletters at tables in the company lunchrooms. These newsletters capsulize important current events and also list significant company news.

Besides these communication tools—and others, such as bulletin boards and training films—the public relations officers try to encourage and arrange personal contacts among different company echelons. They realize that the credit union or athletic teams or in-house educational courses can help bring people together. Even better are regularly scheduled meetings of employees and management, with informal and unfettered exchange of ideas, complaints, and suggestions. If key executives won't make time for this kind of activity, the public relations director, while trying to change their minds, must establish such contacts. This is the only way he or she can learn what employees are thinking and thus advise management as to policy.

The creative PR person is constantly considering new ways to inform employees: internal telephone lines by which employees can dial a number and get recorded company information, a special annual report for employees alone, sessions for spouses of employees to update them on the firm's activities:

> One big division of General Electric operates a "hot line" for employees who have questions, worries, or wrongdoing to report. More than 100,000 calls were re-

ceived and answered last year. New England Telephone operates a similar kind of system called "Private Lines." The employee can remain anonymous and can challenge management even in such highly sensitive areas as discrimination and dishonesty. All questions are answered promptly, either by the Private Lines staff or by company officials.

Dow Chemical and American Airlines open pages of their company publications to employees' criticisms and questions. Embarrassing letters are published—accusations of management featherbedding, sham in labor relations, stupid supervisory practices. The official responses don't always satisfy the critics, but there is no doubt that the criticisms are heard, sometimes loud and clear. I know of no evidence that critics, when they give their names, are penalized.

Delta Airlines holds regular meetings in different locations with its 28,000 employees. After supervisors and foremen have been excused, top officials ask the workers, "What's bothering you?" Questions can be submitted anonymously by card. All queries are answered on the spot or posted on bulletin boards as soon as possible after a meeting.

Polaroid Corporation, with about 12,000 nonunion employees, has a hearing procedure for workers who feel they have been wronged by their superiors. The judges are workers elected from the ranks; the complaintant can have someone else act as counsel; and if the complaintant loses and is not satisfied with the judgment, he can turn next to an arbitration procedure.

A division of Xerox Corporation employs an ombudsman to investigate cases of wrongdoing. If the ombudsman cannot rectify the problem himself, he presents the facts to a senior executive who can. IBM has two systems—one called "Open Door" and the other "Speak Up!"—for bringing employee complaints to the attention of top management investigators.[15]

Some managers even use the rumor mill to get out information, leaking items to certain people they know will pass the information on. There is danger in this, but the circulation is rapid and packs its own kind of credibility. Some managers praise gossip for its educational value to new employees, its possiblility of sounding the alert on problem people and areas, and its obvious speed.

Rumors may also be destructive and require action.

Combatting Rumors

Rumors can be damaging to company morale, posture, and image. They may, of course, affect various publics, but most of them seem to center internally. Word gets around that Christmas bonuses have been canceled. Someone says that an entire department is being phased out. Rumors about safety hazards cause a rash of pseudo-illnesses.

According to an article in *The New York Times*, in order for a rumor to get started, the facts themselves must be ambiguous and the matter must be important.

When such false rumors surface, the PR person should first try to identify the source. Next he or she should attempt to cast doubts on the story while assembling facts that prove its inaccuracy.

Some firms have rumor clinics or rumor hotlines, or they meet with employee leaders periodically to discuss and dispel rumors. Some find ways to infiltrate the grapevine themselves and cut off rumors as soon as they start. Others use company publications to correct misapprehensions, or, if the rumor is more general, they take out ads in local or national newspapers.

Countering rumor with truth is still the best method. Several airlines have a policy that, whenever a disaster strikes, there should be an immediate investigation, followed by a quick and full disclosure of the facts. When Motorola was sued by employees over applications given to new employees, it immediately released all details to the media, and it also kept its own employees informed of both sides of the issue as the case progressed.

CORPORATE ADVERTISING

Eight out of ten PR people have some control (frequently an approval role) over image advertising, and nearly two-thirds of the ad themes are generated by the public relations professionals rather than an advertising agency. Participation is certain to grow stronger and budgets are certain to grow larger in the years ahead.

There is a lot of dull and boring corporate advertising around, but not as much as in the past. Some ads still talk down to the reader, still make ridiculous claims, still embrace "safe" themes. Others, however, report real news or tackle tough issues.

Kennecott Copper, meeting environmental criticism head on, ran a series of ads a few years ago with the theme "Mining is beautiful." The four-color ads showed examples of the ways in which Kennecott had actually enhanced the landscape.

U.S. Steel, making use of large and bold headlines and occasional illustrations, created a series on employee involvement in civic affairs, from working with Boy Scouts to playing with the local symphony. The slogan read, "We're involved."

Metropolitan Life got years of mileage out of the theme, "We sell life insurance. But our business is life." The print and television messages tackled some tough subjects in a no-nonsense way—venereal disease, drug education, learning disabilities, and day-care centers.

Other insurance firms—Liberty Mutual and State Farm, for example—discuss safety topics in their corporate advertising, often explaining what they are doing to help make vehicles safer or to eliminate drunken drivers.

ITT used corporate advertising to underline its open recruitment policies and practices, particularly with regard to minorities and women. These ads not only substantiated the company's progressive image but also sparked hundreds of job inquiries.

IBM plugs some of its TV fare; Rockwell International calls attention to its role in building the space shuttle; and U.S. Steel promotes the need for investment capital.

Few of the ads are really controversial.

> The objective of most corporate advertising today is neither to change society nor secure changes in government regulations or laws. Companies simply want to be better understood among those publics that they think are important to them in the hope that they will be more supportive of the company. The support may take many forms, from buying stock, selling them material or equipment, purchasing products, lending them money, to recommending them as a place to work as well as sometimes, when necessary, supporting them on social issues.[16]

Corporate advertising also serves an internal function. Employees like to work at a firm that has recognition; it gives them a certain status with neighbors and friends. Employees may also be featured in ad campaigns. Banks have done this to humanize their transactions, and railroads have employed this medium to bolster morale among far-flung workers.

MORALE AND THE SPECIAL INTERNAL PUBLICS

Morale is hard to categorize, but its effects are visible. When morale is low, productivity erodes, absenteeism increases, loyalty fades, turnover accelerates, and even things like petty theft soar. The size of many corporations contributes to this condition, but it isn't the whole story.

Besides good communication, the employee wants his or her grievances noted and satisfied, and rewards or congratulations accorded after some company accomplishment. Workers want to understand procedures, especially those that affect them, and they must be free of constant concern about company and job stability. They want to be part of the team.

Their supervisors must know how to lead, how to suggest change without criticizing, how to compliment when warranted, how to listen. There are special challenges in the motivation of the veteran employee, or the worker who is suffering burnout, or the person who has a dull job, like staring at a monitor all day. To succeed at this level, you have to know your people and what they want, and you have to be able to build a structure around what you have rather than forcing people into slots they can't successfully fill.

Some firms devise innovative methods of improving morale. The Hyatt Orlando fills the year with programs, from the familiar picnics and awards banquet to talent shows, departmental quiz shows, and theme parties. A major insurance company schedules periodic lunchtime entertainment, including some big-name stars. Employees-of-the-Month not only get the honor at some institutions, they also get a cash award. Other firms have experimented with allowing employees themselves to set the criteria on which evaluation will be based.

After the forced breakup of our national phone system, AT&T moved from promoting long distance to meeting competition for the $20 billion spent yearly on this service. One advantage it had was its superior number of

Figure 12-9 U S West Direct, one of the new companies formed after the breakup of AT&T, uses appropriate themes and graphics to match its title.
Courtesy: U S West Direct

employees. The company decided to use them. Working with their public relations staffs, the AT&T execs held rallies across the country to kick off their campaign, trained employees (using methods like role-playing sessions), and supplied them with packets of information. These workers talked

HAY

:30 TV COMMERCIAL   U S WEST DIRECT

ANNCR: A hundred years ago, our Yellow Pages started helping people in the West.

RANCHER: My cattle are stranded. I've got to get some feed up there.

ANNCR: And though we were the only Yellow Pages in town, we worked to be the best we could be.

RANCHER: Thanks boys.

ANNCR: At U S West Direct, we still believe in that tradition.

MODERN RANCHER: I have to get some feed to my cattle today.

ANNCR: We publish the West's complete Yellow Pages.

To help more people find what they're looking for.

U S West Direct.

Publisher of the West's best...

Yellow Pages.

Figure 12-9 *(continued)*

to their friends and neighbors, staffed booths at shopping centers, delivered literature door to door, handed out buttons and bumper stickers, and even held area open houses. The message was "CHOOSE AT&T," and the results, which must be shared with other company efforts (like advertising and familiarity), speak for themselves.

Morale is not just a personnel matter, and not merely a concern for the

---

IT PAYS TO CHECK OUT COMPLAINTS

A major railroad maintains its own fire department, which is located in the shop area in the yards of its headquarters town. These men and women train regularly and are able to respond immediately to any problem. In the 36 years of the fire department's existence, only one fire has required any city help. As a consequence, the railroad's insurance premiums are $100,000 lower than they might otherwise be.

Via the grapevine, the public relations director picked up the rumor that the firefighters were unhappy and thinking of quitting. Why? He was told that their passes on the trains, which once were plush perks, no longer meant much since the curtailment of passenger service.

Feeling that this might not be the whole story, the PR director checked further and found that what these people really wanted were jackets.

As a result of his investigation, the public relations director not only secured the jackets but also arranged to have the firefighters paid overtime for their drills, and he arranged for each of them to have a private parking space.

Result? Not only did nobody quit, but a lot of people tried to sign up to become firefighters.

---

chief executive officer. Everyone at every level is involved, and this includes the public relations staff, which must monitor attitudes and spot problem situations, advise employers and clients, organize and evaluate special events, and design the tools to reach the worker.

Every era brings new areas of concern. The work force is different today from what it was half a century ago. Employees want work that fulfills them, interests them. They want to provide some management input. They are remaining beyond the normal retirement age in some instances, dropping out early in others. Two groups that have visibly altered, and that pose challenges for the PR person, are the working woman and the union member.

Female Employees

The number of women who are employed in this country now exceeds the number who stay at home. Well over 40 million American women hold paying jobs. Some work because they need the money to stay even with rising prices; others want a change or professional satisfaction. The phenomenon of working wives has affected everything from mealtime hours to family size to purchasing power. It has also affected public relations, where a new consciousness needs to be developed. Discrimination, intentional and unintentional, remains a problem in business. It is not only the question of who makes the coffee—it is the larger question of salary levels, promotion standards, management's assumptions about female interests and capabilities, and a fair amount of overt sexism.

Public relations directors and counselors, male and female, have an educational role to perform here. This begins with their own commitment to equality and the resolution to make this commitment part of their daily communication.

At the moment, many arguments are being waged over such subjects as equal pay for equal work, opportunities in traditionally male jobs, the nature of "comparable" work, harrassment, sexist management decisions, and a host of other grievances. Even bosses who try to be fair struggle with their concerns about reprimanding females, and they claim that men speak a different language from women, that they are more willing to take risks than are their female counterparts, and that they are more skillful at office politics. All these contentions are controversial, and most women would find them acculturated traits that will change over a period of time.

Practitioners can't solve all these issues, but they can remain sensitive to female concerns and counsel employers on their conduct and policies. There must be procedures for the review of sexual-harassment charges, followed by disciplinary action when warranted. A company has to compensate and promote on the basis of accomplishment and should recruit without discrimination. If these or other issues are ignored, the PR staff, along with the rest of the company, will have both internal and external difficulties to handle.

As a corollary to the hard-won feminist gains, researchers now observe a male backlash that affects both the domestic and business scenes. Practitioners are just beginning to learn how to cope with this problem.

Labor Unions

In dealing with labor, the practitioner must be completely conversant with legal aspects of the relationship. This is a sensitive area and one in which the motives of the public relations person could easily be suspect. Every negotiation should be handled with tact and candor.

The ideal situation occurs when management and labor trust each other, even though they may have differences. As an arm of management, the PR professional must accept the role of the union, must not interfere in its affairs, must not discredit it in communications, must inform members of matters concerning them, and must counsel management to deal swiftly and fairly with complaints.

As mentioned in Chapter 14, unions, too, have their obligations. The key to a good working relationship is a real understanding of each other's problems and a willingness to deal with them openly and sympathetically. This is the kind of attitude the PR person should promote.

Some employers, however, can't hide their hostility toward unions. One thing they should consider is that, if unions continue to weaken and cease to be a political or industrial force, the temptation to scrap the gains of the past half century may be strong. For a variety of reasons, not the least of which is a just balance of concerns, the practitioner must strive to discourage any attempts to eliminate legitimate labor organizations.

Many corporations are more enlightened on labor relations and have extended a cooperative hand to unions. General Motors workers are consulted on plans for new subcompact cars. Firms like Chrysler, Eastern Air Lines, and Uniroyal have seats reserved on their boards of directors for union members. Some CEOs argue that unions serve a function by negotiating instead of quitting and that good unions are responsible for increased productivity.

In most situations, however, there remains an adversary relationship between unions and management. Much of this may be unavoidable, since the two sides have differing views on the profit structure, but it is still good PR to try to come to terms with labor demands, if possible.

Today's unions, diminishing in power, have turned to some new tactics, finding that it is harder and harder to win a strike. Some of these methods involve more sophisticated attempts to influence public attitudes, and they also include union efforts to affect the sale of product or stock.

Another trend to watch in unions is the increased number of women in the ranks of labor. Half the total increase in membership in the last two decades has been female, and today, one out of every three union members is a woman. Women have also risen to high posts in several national and local labor organizations.

Experts represent both parties in management–labor disputes, and the public relations practitioner is rarely a member of the negotiating team. This doesn't mean the PR person shouldn't possess such skills. In *The Art of Negotiating*, author Gerard Nierenberg calls negotiating "an essential public relations skill." He bolsters this thesis with a discussion of certain expertise associated with public relations in areas like research and communications.[17] Whether involved or not, the practitioner has a stake in any employee matter and must be prepared to deal with it within the limits of his or her mission.

CHAPTER HIGHLIGHTS

- Although public attitudes toward business have improved somewhat, the negatives still outweigh the positives, making public relations an absolute necessity.
- Both because it is right and because the federal government has made it more critical, industry must develop and support social programs. Corporations must also hold themselves accountable to the public.
- Business crises come in all sorts of guises, from product safety to financial manipulation. Public relations inevitably becomes involved.

- Competition has helped increase PR budgets in some industries that traditionally pour their resources into advertising.
- Public relations adds a necessary human dimension to financially oriented management, and it can support the marketing efforts through publicity and publications.
- Cooperation and approval of management are required in order to make any PR plan work.
- Techniques for responding to activist pressure include avoidance of direct confrontation, focusing on the big picture, beating them to the punch, dividing their leadership, concentrating on the "alert 10 percent" of the populace, blending emotion and logic, and sticking with realistic terms.
- Every firm or institution is expected to be a good citizen, which accounts for the growth in public affairs in the past decade. Activities include everything from philanthropy to event sponsorship.
- The gap between business and the media has widened in recent years, but the most successful companies somehow find a way to live with reporters and editors.
- Business has many special audiences, including directors, stockholders, dealers, distributors, suppliers, the government, and its own internal audiences.
- Internal public relations relies on open and enlightened management, an effective communication system, well-conceived publications, and, in some instances, corporate advertising.
- Morale is a function of management, but practitioners can influence this area through counsel, research, and proper communication.
- Special audiences, like female workers and union members, may require increased expertise on the part of the PR person, who should be advising management and monitoring relations between the executive level and these groups.

NOTES

[1]Louis C. Williams, "Who's Serious About Corporate Responsibility? (Or 187 Ways to Amuse a Bored Cat)," *IABC Journal*, Vol. 11, No. 4 (1982).

[2]Carol J. Loomis, "White-Collar Crime," *Fortune*, July 22, 1985.

[3]Leah Rozen, "Nestlé Curtails Worldwide Consumer Ads for Formula," *Advertising Age*, April 23, 1979.

[4]Rich Blake, "Burger Wars," *Public Relations Journal*, September 1985.

[5]*PR News*, Case Study #1785 (July 26, 1982).

[6]Philip Lesly, quoted in Charles A. Nekvasil, "Can Public Relations Do the Impossible?" *Industry Week*, January 22, 1973.

[7]James A. Little, past president PRSA, in a 1982 speech to the Southern Arizona Chapter of PRSA in Tucson, Arizona.

[8]William Batten, as reported in *pr reporter*, February 16, 1981.

[9]Daniel S. Roher, "A Public Relations Primer for the Marketing Manager," *Public Relations Journal*, September 1973.

[10]Phyllis Weiss Haserot, "Developing a Marketing Mindset," *The Executive Female*, May/June 1985.

[11]Allan Cox, "Where Executives Fall Short," *Advertising Age*, October 25, 1982.

[12]Peg Dardenne, "Community Relations: Rx for a Neighborhood in Decay," *Public Relations Journal*, February 1984.

[13]Kerryn King, "The Coming Revolution in Public Relations/Public Affairs," *Public Relations Journal*, October 1984.

[14]Robert Crandall, "Is Government Regulation Crippling Business?" *Saturday Review*, January 20, 1979.

[15]David W. Ewing, "The Corporation as Public Enemy #1," *Saturday Review*, January 21, 1978.

[16]Tom Garbett, "What Companies Project to Public," *Advertising Age*, July 6, 1981.

[17]Gerard I. Nierenberg, quoted in excerpts from his book (*The Art of Negotiating*), *tips* and *tactics*, a *pr reporter* supplement, Vol. 19, No. 14 (June 29, 1981).

SUGGESTED READINGS

ANSHEN, MELVIN, ed., *Managing the Socially Responsible Corporation*. New York: Macmillan, 1974.

BLAKE, GARY, and ROBERT W. BLY, *How to Promote Your Own Business*. New York: New American Library, 1983.

CLOSE, ARTHUR C., and STEPHANY J. FREEDMAN, eds., *National Directory of Corporate Public Affairs*. Washington, D.C.: Columbia Books, 1984.

D'APRIX, ROGER, *Communicating for Productivity*. New York: Harper & Row, 1982.

DICKSON, DOUGLAS N., ed., *Business and Its Public*. New York: Wiley, 1985.

GOLDMAN, JORDAN, *Public Relations in the Marketing Mix*. Lincolnwood, Ill.: NTC Business Books, 1986.

HELM, LEWIS M., RAY ELDON HIEBERT, MICHAEL R. NAVER, and KENNETH RABIN, eds., *Informing the People*. New York: Longman, 1981.

KINCAID, WILLIAM M., JR., *Promotion: Products, Services and Ideas*. Columbus, O.: Merrill, 1981.

KOENIG, FREDERICK W., *Rumor in the Marketplace*. Dover, Mass.: Auburn House, 1985.

LAMB, ROBERT, WILLIAM ARMSTRONG, and KAROLYN MORIGI, *Business, Media and the Law: The Troubled Confluence*. New York: Columbia University, 1981.

NOWLAN, STEPHEN E., DIANA R. SHAYON, et al., *Leveraging the Impact of Public Affairs*. Philadelphia: Human Resources Network, 1984.

PETERS, THOMAS J., and ROBERT H. WATERMAN, JR., *In Search of Excellence*. New York: Harper & Row, 1982.

Public Relations Business. New York: Larami.

REDDING, W. CHARLES, *The Corporate Manager's Guide to Better Communication*. Glenview, Ill.: Scott, Foresman, 1984.

STANLEY, RICHARD E., *Promotion*. Englewood Cliffs, N.J.: Prentice-Hall, 1977.

YARRINGTON, ROGER, *Community Relations Handbook*. New York: Longman, 1983.

EXERCISES

1. Select a publication aimed at business (*Fortune, Business Week, Barron's,* or any of a hundred others) and synopsize and critique the general content.
2. Design a brief survey on attitudes toward business, and poll a portion of the student body at your institution. This may be done as a classroom project.
3. Find two examples of corporate advertising you like and two you dislike. Explain why. (These may be print or electronic ads.)
4. Based on your reading or experience, what corporate public-affairs programs do you feel have been the most successful?
5. Analyze the communications and morale at the place where you are currently employed, or at a place where you were once employed.
6. Using your local paper, determine whether its attitude toward business is friendly or hostile. Cite at least three examples to support your contention.

CASE PROBLEMS

1. As the result of a canceled defense contract, Enterprise Industries must lay off approximately 300 people from its 1,200-member work force. Nearly all the personnel affected are members of the company union. All other avenues have been pursued without results, and it appears that the 300 employees must be let go for an indefinite period. Not only will this affect those laid off, but it will also have an effect on the rest of the company and on the relatively small community (32,000 people) in which Enterprise Industries is located. As the public relations director, you are asked to design a plan for the most effective way to break the news. Assume that those to be dismissed will be the ones with the least seniority, except in a few key positions. Write to the management your recommendations, which should contain:

- Timetable for dissemination of news. Who will hear it, and in what order?
- How will the news be communicated? Meeting? Memo? Letter to homes? Individual conferences? Through supervisors?
- Synopsis of message to be given to employees.
- Message for employees not being laid off.
- Anything further that can be done for employees laid off?
- How will you notify community leaders? Jot down ideas on what the president should say to them.
- How will you notify the media? Press conference? News release? Sketch out the content of the news release.
- Any longer-range plans the company might consider?

2. Looking at your own community, come up with two community projects that might be created, sponsored, or funded by local companies or corporations. How would you match these needs with the right company? How would you approach the company? How would the company get anything from this relationship? What problems could arise?

3. The CEO of Kiddie Clothes, an apparel manufacturer in Louisville, Ohio, receives an early morning call from the local media informing him that a 4-year-old Louisville boy, who had received one of Kiddie Clothes Company's T-shirts as a birthday present, accidentally came in contact with his mother's tanning machine, which was on. The shirt burst into flames, and the little boy was seriously burned. He is now at a local hospital.

   The father of the child happens to be the administrative assistant to and a close friend of the governor, a politically ambitious man who plans a run at the Senate next year. Once the governor learned of the incident, he called an immediate news conference and vowed he would find the responsible parties and see that they were punished. Furthermore, he intended to see that Kiddie Clothes T-shirts were withdrawn from all retailers' shelves across the country. That's what prompted the media call to the manufacturing firm.

   The CEO said he would check on this immediately and get back to the reporter. He then calls you, his public relations director, and lays the problem on you.

   The first thing you do is check out the details. Among other things, you discover that there is confusion in the media (and among members of the general public), which associate the T-shirt with sleepwear, which it isn't. (There are legal requirements about the use of nonflammable materials in such sleepwear). Your engineers inform you that, at the temperature generated by that tanning machine, anything that comes in contact with it, from paper to tweed, would most likely catch fire. You also find out that a couple of your salespeople who had called into the office from their posts more than 500 miles away were told of the event and have already spread the story. You report these findings to the CEO.

   "I don't know what to do," he says. "They are definitely wrong in blaming us, and any recall not only would be nearly impossible, but would also cost us several million dollars. Besides, it might reflect on our other product lines. What do you think we should do?"

   In detail, give your response, keeping in mind the consequences of any decision you make, the timing, the cost, and other factors.

13
FINANCIAL
PUBLIC RELATIONS

As with so many other areas of our society, even the terms used to describe financial public relations have changed. For one thing, many specialists now prefer and use "investor relations." Techniques have also been updated, and the jargon that long characterized the marketplace has now become part of the PR scene. Both the language and the practice—and the nature of the subject—make this a specialized area, one that requires training and concentration that only a small percentage of practitioners possess.

For one thing, the investor relations professional must have a working knowledge of economics, be attuned to the psychology of shareholders and analysts, and be conversant with the body of law and learning associated with the financial community.

A basic way to comprehend these topics is to begin with a study of the financial pages of your local newspaper, or, better yet, with the more extensive coverage given financial transactions in *The Wall Street Journal*.

On these financial pages you will find lists of companies offering their stock to the public, allowing them to share in both the burdens and the profits of corporations and government bodies. Some are listed under the New York Stock Exchange (called the "Big Board"); some are listed under the American Stock Exchange (or AMEX), which is less prestigious; and others are grouped under "Over the Counter" (or OTC) stocks, which include companies not currently eligible for listing on the larger boards. There are also lists of federal stock and bond offerings, municipal bonds, and other items.

What these lists convey, among other things, are the current prices being asked and offered for certain stocks. If Hilton Hotel shares are listed at $65, those who bought them at less have realized a profit. They may continue to keep their money in Hilton and receive periodic dividends, or they could sell, take the gain, and possibly invest it elsewhere. If they paid more than the current value of the stock, they may opt to sell before things get worse or hold on, hoping for an upturn.

As far as financial public relations is concerned, the focus is on informing actual and potential shareholders about a specific company. Even the best public relations practitioners can't promise an increase in the value of stock under their professional aegis. Many factors cause stock prices to go up and down, and no amount of publicity, five-screen extravaganzas, plant tours, or colorful brochures can protect a company whose profits are declining.

There are approximately 30 million shareholders in the United States, and each of them has a right to information that affects his or her holdings, no matter how small. The little old man with two shares must be given the same consideration as the powerful banker with 10,000 shares. Forget this principle and you're in trouble.

As mentioned earlier, investor relations are not as simple as calculating profit and loss, or reading columns in the financial section. Shrewd analysts look at performance, potential, the quality of management, and the possibility of some complication, like the scarcity of a necessary raw material or the likelihood of a crippling strike. Practitioners do the same sort of research in order to anticipate the queries of the experts and satisfy the expectations of the shareholder. Computers make much of this faster and easier. Still, many financial practitioners continue to merely go through the motions, organizing the requisite meetings and circulating the requisite printed material. Some approach their work more scientifically, attempting to define the intrinsic value of a stock.

Michael Seeley, president of Investor Access Corporation, preaches the doctrine of "valuation":

> By bringing the concept of finance and value-based strategic planning together with investor relations, we'll offer a powerful perspective from which to make those decisions that magnify shareholder value. And the effectiveness of traditional financial communication vehicles—everything from analyst presentations to corporate advertising—will be measureably enriched.[1]

Translating this doctrine into investor relations, Seeley suggests such things as the publication of an annual report without profit-and-loss statements, or one that shows the highest and lowest earnings along with an explanation of what the company did to enhance long-term profitability. He further proposes alterations in reporting procedures and accounting methods and encourages practitioners to break away from their regular routine.

Most commentators admit that change of some sort is inevitable. Annual meetings will rely more and more on teleconferencing; reports will assume new forms; analysts will be reached electronically, rather than via print or in person. Information will be dispensed more rapidly and have more immediate effect. New challenges will come in the form of deregulation of certain industries, and increase in mergers and takeovers, and the varied effects of government on business. Through all of this, public relations will continue to be important, because there has been no letup in the requirement to communicate.

Even though the practice of financial public relations can be one of the more complicated aspects of the profession, the tenets upon which effective work is based are relatively simple. Financial public relations is "a *planned, organized* communications effort to gain *deserved* recognition for publicly held corporations, implemented to permit *fair evaluation* of securities in the market place *at all times.*"[2] The practitioner is expected to be honest, accurate, and prudent. He or she should also be knowledgeable in this specific phase of communication, have the ability to convince and motivate others, and have the planning skills that can be translated into immediate action.

In financial public relations, several primary audiences must be considered:

- The company's executives
- The company's employees
- The shareholders
- The prospective shareholders
- The security analysts
- Financial publications
- The Securities and Exchange Commission

Unlike the communication of much other news, such disbursements of information in the financial field may not be merely good public relations; they may be legally required.

GOING PUBLIC

Although financial public relations is not limited to publicly held companies—that is, companies with outside shareholders—most firms that are privately owned or closely held do little in this area. For the PR person, the real task begins after a company has "gone public."

"Going public" means that the company is moving from a private type of ownership to an offering of its stock for sale to those who wish to purchase it. There is a formal ritual to this procedure. Wise administrators involve the financial public relations counsel in the beginning of this program and work with them as closely as they work with the attorneys.

When a company goes public, five periods are involved:

1. Preregistration (no time limit)

2. Registration
3. Preeffective (usually about 40 days)
4. Effective
5. Posteffective (usually about 90 days)

The *preregistration* period can be any time from the founding of the company until it files for a change in status with its own state and the Securities and Exchange Commission. The state appeal involves a request to amend the company charter.

Registration merely serves as a colon—a punctuation mark—between the closely held and the publicly held status.

During the *preeffective period*, which may encompass a month and a half, the applicant is not supposed to do any selling of its securities except within the limits of the "prospectus" or the preliminary "red herring" (see Figure 13-1).

This prospectus, a document available to analysts and prospective investors, contains information about the company, its products, its financial status, its inventory, its officers, their salaries and stockholdings, and dozens of other relevant items. It must be scrupulously honest in its preparation, since these data are compiled to inform astute readers about the actual condition of the firm and to advise them on the wisdom of purchasing these securities at their asking price. The prospectus is individually numbered, and each recipient is catalogued.

A good rule, in fact, for both the preeffective and posteffective periods is "last year's scrapbook." If you did something in previous years, it may be safe to repeat it. If not, be wary.

The company may not further tout its stock via special advertising campaigns, expensive brochures, parties, or similar extravagances. The SEC frowns on such activities. Everything the potential shareholder needs to know should be in the prospectus.

The *posteffective* period is one in which the newly offered stock is being sold. This may occupy approximately 90 days. When all the stock is sold— even if fewer than 90 days have elapsed—you may feel free to return to your normal business routine without fear of censure. Be certain, however, that *all* the stock is sold and that some is not still floating around the country.

What Can a PR Person Do during the Preeffective Period?

During the preeffective period, many things can be accomplished:

- Preparation of a company profile
- Identification of company spokespersons
- Counseling of spokespersons
- Aiding in establishment of policies

2,500,000 Shares

Common Stock

Commercial Federal Corporation (the "Corporation") is offering shares of its common stock ("Common Stock") to be issued upon conversion of Commercial Federal Savings and Loan Association (the "Association" or "Commercial Federal") from a federal mutual savings and loan association to a federal stock savings and loan association and the Corporation's acquisition of all of the Association's capital stock pursuant to the Association's plan of conversion (the "Plan"). The conversion of the Association to stock form, issuance of the Association's stock to the Corporation and offer and sale of the Common Stock by the Corporation is herein referred to as the "Conversion." The shares of Common Stock are being offered to account holders of the Association as of September 30, 1981 and September 30, 1983, members of the Association as of November 10, 1983 and members of the general public subject to certain priorities and maximum and minimum purchase limitations described in this Prospectus. The Corporation has the discretion to reject orders received from members of the general public in whole or in part.

All subscription rights are nontransferable and will expire at 5:00 p.m., Central Time, on December 14, 1984 unless extended by the Corporation until as late as January 7, 1985. Any shares not purchased in the Subscription Offering will be sold in a Public Offering, which is to be completed within 45 days of the Subscription Offering, as extended up until February 21, 1985. If the Conversion is not completed within 45 days after the last day of the Subscription Offering, as extended by the Corporation, which would be February 21, 1985, and the Federal Home Loan Bank Board consents to an extension of time to complete the Conversion, subscribers will be given the right to increase, decrease or rescind their subscriptions. If the Conversion is not completed within 45 days after the last day of the Subscription Offering, as extended, and the Conversion period is not extended, or the Conversion period is extended up to May 22, 1985, all funds held will be promptly returned after completion of the original or extended date together with accrued interest, and all withdrawal authorizations will be terminated. Subscription rights are exercisable by returning the accompanying order form along with full payment (or appropriate instructions authorizing withdrawal from a savings account of the Association) for all shares for which subscription is made. Funds received will be placed in a special escrow account, will earn interest at the savings account passbook rate and amounts authorized for withdrawal will continue to earn interest at the applicable account rate until the Conversion is completed, postponed or terminated. All shares not subscribed for in the Subscription Offering are expected to be sold to the public through an underwritten public offering. See "The Conversion—Public Offering." **The total number of shares to be issued in the Conversion may be significantly increased or decreased to reflect market and financial conditions at the time of the Public Offering.**

The Corporation will pay a fee of 4.5% of the actual purchase price per share to broker-dealer firms registered as such under the Securities Exchange Act of 1934 whose broker representatives assist subscribers and purchasers in the Subscription Offering and whose name is entered on the subscriber's order form.

There is no public market for the Common Stock and there can be no assurance that a public market for the Common Stock will develop. The Corporation will apply to have the Common Stock quoted on the National Association of Securities Dealers Automated Quotation ("NASDAQ") System.

THESE SHARES HAVE NOT BEEN APPROVED OR DISAPPROVED BY THE SECURITIES AND EXCHANGE COMMISSION, THE FEDERAL HOME LOAN BANK BOARD OR THE FEDERAL SAVINGS AND LOAN INSURANCE CORPORATION NOR HAS SUCH COMMISSION, BOARD OR CORPORATION PASSED UPON THE ACCURACY OR ADEQUACY OF THIS PROSPECTUS. ANY REPRESENTATION TO THE CONTRARY IS A CRIMINAL OFFENSE.

	Maximum Subscription Price(1)	Estimated Expenses(2)	Estimated Maximum Net Proceeds(3)
Per Share	$10.75	$1.61	$9.14
Total	$26,875,000	$4,028,750	$22,846,250

(1) As required by federal regulations, the Maximum Subscription Price has been determined on the basis of an appraisal of the estimated pro forma market value of the Corporation by Kaplan, Smith & Associates, Inc., a financial consulting firm, and is the amount to be paid for each share at the time of subscription. The actual price is expected to be within the range of $8.00 to $10.75 per share and will be the same as the public offering price. If the actual purchase price is $8.00 per share, the aggregate price would be $20,000,000, the estimated conversion expenses would be $3,740,000 or $1.50 per share and the estimated net proceeds to the Corporation would be $16,260,000 or $6.50 per share. If the actual purchase price is less than $10.75 per share, the difference will be refunded or the withdrawal authorization reduced, unless it is requested on the Subscription Order Form that the difference be applied to the purchase of additional whole shares of Common Stock. The Corporation may not increase the aggregate price above $26,875,000 or decrease the aggregate price below $20,000,000 without a resolicitation of subscriptions.

(2) Includes estimated printing, legal, accounting, appraisal, commissions paid to brokers in the Subscription Offering and other expenses incurred in connection with the Conversion, including an estimate of the underwriting discount for selling unsubscribed shares in the public offering. See "Use of Proceeds."

(3) Does not include net proceeds to the Corporation if the Underwriters exercise in full a 30-day overallotment option to purchase up to an additional 15% of the shares to be sold in the Conversion or the possible increase or decrease in the number of shares to be sold in the Public Offering to reflect any changes in the appraised value of the Corporation after the date hereof. See "The Conversion—Number of Shares to be Issued."

The date of this Subscription Prospectus is November 23, 1984.

Figure 13-1 The prospectus should contain all the information a prospective investor needs to know.

Courtesy: Commercial Federal Savings and Loan Association

- Determination of relations with the financial community
- Building of lists
- Preparation of miscellaneous forms

The *company profile* is, in effect, a case statement about the firm. It contains information on management, marketing, raw materials, production, distribution, transportation, and other business segments. Its purpose is to provide readily accessible details about the company to securities analysts, the financial media, customers, government agencies, and others who may require such information. It also serves as the foundation for various communication materials, such as brochures, speeches, films, presentations, and slide series.

The profile should be updated frequently and should contain no materials that have not already been published. For the company spokespersons alone, you may want to circle certain items in their copies and write beside them the agreed-upon responses. Such a practice is not deceptive. It is important that these people act in concert and that each is not giving his or her version of a central fact.

The spokespersons may be any number of key executives within the organization, but it is best to keep the number small. This group may include the president, the financial officer, and a few key vice-presidents. Ordinarily, the public relations director would not be included, and the outside counsel should never act as a company spokesperson. Other company personnel may channel information to these few people, but they should not themselves respond to queries from outside sources.

Although he or she doesn't speak for the principals, the public relations counselor should advise the spokespersons. Along with the briefings provided by attorneys and accountants, the PR person should supply counsel on matters affecting the corporate image. Among these would be a clear understanding of what sort of information should be released and a list of cautions concerning actions that could be detrimental to the institution's reputation.

There may be occasions when the financial public relations consultant will disagree with the company attorney. More often than not, the PR consultant backs down. However, unless there is clearly a legal danger represented by some proposed action, PR consultants should hold their ground. This means that consultants must be both experienced and prudent and that they must be able to articulate their ideas. Lawyers tend to err on the side of conservatism, but at times a more aggressive posture may be advisable.

Another important "preeffective" activity is the long and complicated matter of establishing relationships with the financial world. The PR consultant's job is to discover the key people in the major brokerage houses, the analysts who will make a market for this particular stock. The big brokerage houses have specialists in certain areas—such as petroleum, metals, heavy industry, and entertainment. The proper analyst must be identified and listed. Such lists must be updated constantly, since change is a way of life in financial circles. The more you learn about these people, the stronger your approach will be.

At the same time, you will be compiling a much smaller list—the members of the financial media—such as *The Wall Street Journal*, Reuters, Dow Jones, PR Newswire, AP, UPI, *Barron's Weekly*, your local financial editors, and magazines like *Fortune* and *Forbes*.

Both lists are extremely important, since you may have to act immediately on the release of some vital information and will not be able to take time to search around for names, titles, and correct spelling.

This 40-day waiting period also provides an opportunity for the preparation of *miscellaneous materials* that will be of use to the company spokespersons. These include:

1. A brief checklist to help the spokesperson capsulize key company information for ready response to queries.
2. A "Relationship Review Form," which contains data on each analyst firm, its visits, phone calls, and correspondence. These forms should be easily retrievable prior to an analyst's call or visit.
3. An "Analyst Contact Form," which would be used by the spokesperson to record all communications with each analyst. On one side might be the roster of usual topics—earnings, new products, manufacturing data, and the like. Beside each there should be a box to check if the analyst inquires about this item. The reverse side of the sheet is for other comments. When these forms are completed, copies should be circulated among other spokespersons to help them prepare for similar interviews. Copies should also go into the file of that particular analyst firm. If there seems to be a pattern to the inquiries about a certain topic—say, inventory—then this could be a clue that a rumor is circulating regarding that subject and should be checked out.
4. A similar form is the "Press Inquiry Form," which is used to keep track of media contacts and should receive treatment nearly identical to that of the Analyst Contact Form.

These documents are essential if the spokesperson is to keep accurate records of what was said. They may serve as protection later in case of an investigation, and collectively, they provide insights into trends and problems.

Obviously, other things are also happening during this period, and they could involve the PR staff. All parties involved—company officials, underwriters, attorneys, accountants, and others—will no doubt meet periodically to plan strategy and check progress of the stock. Some company spokespersons may go on the road to meet key analysts and investors. And once the effective date has been reached, a "tombstone" (or straight type) ad will be placed offering the stock.

In the past, the underwriting company usually handled the "going public" news release, but today, this is often a company responsibility.

As you might imagine, some events occur that don't fit neatly into the general SEC rules. During the preeffective period, for example, when the firm offering the stock is supposed to keep a low profile, what if some significant thing happens, like the awarding of a major government contract? Should the company release this congenial information or not? Most observers would say the details should be released. Should business and financial editors get a copy of the prospectus along with the news release, or is this touting? Again, most experts would consider this allowable.

Once considered a somewhat rare and narrow application of public relations, investor relations has grown rapidly. In the mid-seventies, the number of firms going public ᴐunted to about $1\frac{1}{2}$ per week. A decade later, the number jumped to 18 per week. These moves may bring improved liquidity and an improvement in borrowing potential, but they can also be expensive, cause expanded scrutiny by authorities, and impose pressure to sustain growth. The entire routine of doing business is altered. Because of these drawbacks, some executives counsel against following the "going public" trend:

> Sometimes selling stock in a public offering is an ego trip in search of a bit more respect at the bank or at cocktail parties. Sometimes it's for the delight of multiplying the latest over-the-counter quote by the number of shares you hold. Whatever the reason, taking your company public usually is a bad idea and usually isn't necessary.[3]

What concerns informed critics most is the paper work, the formality, the dangers of takeover, and other problems that plague the larger firms. For the small company, even the public relations budget could be an eye opener. Costs of counsel, printed materials, and miscellaneous items might range from $30,000 to well over $100,000 in the initial year.

THE SECURITIES AND EXCHANGE COMMISSION

The act of going public also sets up a new kind of relationship with the Securities and Exchange Commission, a government agency created to supervise compliance with the Securities Acts of 1933 and 1934. These acts cover many areas but focus on the requirements of distributing information, from the first steps of going public to the routine of releasing subsequent data.

The Securities and Exchange Commission has considerable power, including the right to enjoin or suspend trading, or initiate proceedings against a broker-dealer or a guilty management team. It should be noted that the SEC's sanctions may be only part of the punishment for infractions. Individuals may also sue for the violation of their rights under federal law.

GLOSSARY FOR GOING PUBLIC

Going public.   When a company sells securities to the public for the first time, requiring the company to file a registration statement with the Securities and Exchange Commission under the Securities Act of 1933. The process is also often called the "initial public offering" or IPO.

SEC.   The U.S. Securities and Exchange Commission, established by Congress to administer federal securities laws.

Blue sky laws.   Various states' securities laws, enacted to protect investors against securities frauds.

Over-the-counter market (OTC).   A market for those securities not listed on an exchange, where buying and selling is done over the telephone, rather than in the auction-type market found on exchanges.

Bid and asked.   The quoted prices for trading in the over-the-counter market. The bid is the highest price someone is willing to pay; the asked is the lowest price at which someone will sell.

All-hands meeting.   A meeting of all the parties involved in preparing the registration statement: company management, company counsel, the underwriters, underwriters' counsel, and accountants.

Due diligence.   A reasonable investigation conducted by the parties involved in preparing a registration statement to confirm that the statements contained therein are true and that no material facts are omitted.

Quiet period.   The period between the time a company reaches an understanding with the underwriters regarding the intent to go public and 90 days after commencement of the offering, so called because of the restrictions on publicity.

Waiting period.   The period between the date the registration statement is initially filed with the SEC and the date it is declared effective.

Prospectus.   The document or brochure, used as the selling document in an offering, that discloses pertinent information regarding the issuer.

Red herring.   A preliminary prospectus, circulated during the waiting period, which bears a legend in red ink stating that the registration statement has not yet become effective.

Road show.   A tour by a company's executives during the waiting period, for the purpose of making presentations to analysts and underwriters.

Tombstone.   An advertisement announcing an offering of securities and indicating where a copy of the related prospectus may be obtained.

Closing.   A meeting at the conclusion of an offering for the purpose of exchanging documents and the proceeds from the offering.

Form S-1.   Most commonly used form used in registering securities in an initial public offering.

Form SR.   A report required to be filed after an initial public offering which explains how the proceeds of the offering were used.

Form 10-K.   A report required to be filed with the SEC annually in compliance with the 1934 Act (Note: must be mentioned in annual report).

Form 10-Q.   Quarterly report, containing primarily unaudited quarterly financial information, required to be filed with the SEC in compliance with 1934 Act.

SOURCE: Adapted from "Strategies for Going Public," Deloitte, Haskins & Sells, 1983. Courtesy of *IABC Communication World.*

The Securities and Exchange Commission comprises three divisions:

- *The Division of Corporate Finance,* composed of attorneys, accountants, and securities analysts, who process reports, check disclosure, and can institute proceedings against offending firms.
- *The Division of Trading and Markets* also deals with corporations and seeks enforcement of existing laws.
- *The Division of Corporate Regulations* is responsible for monitoring the investment companies.

The SEC does not, and will not, set guidelines to cover every possible procedure. It cannot really define *materiality*, for example. Consequently, it operates case by case. Frustrated executives sometimes clamor for more specific directions, but if they were imposed, these same executives might find them unwelcome. Once a guideline is established, there might well be a series of attempts made to circumvent the particular language used. Then another guideline would be called for. So the commission prefers to set general guidelines in some areas, trusting the individual organization to operate within the spirit of the law. This may seem dangerously vague, but it actually works pretty well. Most cases that call for SEC sanctions demonstrate, upon close inspection, that they are clearly contrary to the principles of fair and equitable treatment of all stockholders.

In 1975, an Advisory Committee on Disclosure proposed a number of changes to the Securities and Exchange Commission. Some proposals remain under advisement; some were discarded as being too inhibiting; some have been incorporated into procedure, in part or in whole. Still, these are not written down like the Ten Commandments; they are more like guidelines.

In 1977, in order to control the alleged bribery of foreign officials by American firms seeking foreign markets, the SEC passed an act requiring corporations to come up with a series of internal procedures providing "reasonable assurance" that responsible company officers are aware of all financial arrangements and have accurately recorded them. Prison sentences and $10,000 fines await offenders.

Overseas entanglements are only one of the new concerns of the Securities and Exchange Commission. With the creation of new types of investments (money-market funds, zero-coupon bonds, and others), the tripling of shares traded, electronic registration of securities, and round-the-clock international trading, rules have to be simplified at the same time that enforcement multiplies. Foreign clientele hold at least 10 percent of the stock offered on the New York Stock Exchange, and their activities are encouraged but also require surveillance. Shrewd American investors are aware of hiding places abroad for their funds and also know how to take advantge of time differences to manipulate financial deals. The increasing number of bank failures has prompted the SEC to tighten regulations on holding companies, and the proliferation of "insider" information has produced an expanded range of potential liabilities.

Stockwatch and Sanctions

Among the surveillance techniques utilized by the Securities and Exchange Commission is a procedure called "stockwatch." This means that the SEC officials keep an eye on daily trading, looking for radical moves of stock. A sudden spurt up or down may cause the SEC to suspend trading for that day—or for an indefinite period. It wants to find out what is causing this fluctuation.

"Stockwatch" also includes the scrutinizing of financial filings, reports, and the financial press. The SEC may also act on tips from brokers or others whose suspicions are aroused. Despite such vigilance, it cannot uncover every irregularity. As one top analyst puts it, "They spear the fish that come to the top."

A sudden spurt in trading might indicate manipulation, or a takeover, or a careless leak of information. It could also be just a coincidence; if it is, the company still must prove this to the SEC's satisfaction.

All this points out that financial public relations is a sophisticated profession with many risks for the careless or inept practitioner. It is a phase of PR in which decimal points, precise dates, and even the unfortunate choice of words can lead to financial losses or federal penalties.

The Securities and Exchange Commission has acted against offending firms in some classic cases.

Often cited is the Texas Gulf Sulphur case (1965), in which the discovery of a major copper field in Canada was thoughtlessly leaked to a trade journal. Stockholders who inquired were told that there might be nothing to the exploration, that not many such ventures succeeded, and that nothing was certain at that point. Company news releases similarly played down the find. Less than two weeks later, Texas Gulf Sulphur announced the magnitude of its discovery. In the interim, several TGS executives and their friends had loaded up on shares while other stockholders, unaware of the copper bonanza, had sold or traded their stock. Many in the latter group took private action against the company, and the guilty executives were also tried under federal statutes.

Although legal arguments in this case were voluminous and complex, the principal fact that emerges is that *you must disclose material information immediately.* A corollary is that you obviously cannot profit via inside information.

The Merrill Lynch case centered on the distribution of some key information on Douglas Aircraft to certain large fund managers without its being disclosed to others. Merrill Lynch found itself prohibited from conducting its business for a substantial period of time. The SEC also ruled against the fund managers who had accepted and acted upon this private information. This was the first time the SEC had gone against receivers of inside information. The moral here is that you are also liable if you *accept* information that should really be made public, and then privately profit by it. Even the financial public relations consultant can be caught in this trap, as was seen in a 1986 case involving the incumbent president of PRSA.

In fact, a succession of cases indicates an extension of responsibility for profiting on insider information. What started as a principle involving executives and brokers now extends to accountants, attorneys, public relations officials, and, more recently, journalists.

A *Wall Street Journal* columnist, R. Foster Winans, admitted to leaking confidential information from upcoming columns to investors, allowing them to benefit from the subsequent gains in nearly two dozen stocks. Other media, including CBS, have been investigated to determine whether or not reporters or executives may have purchased or liquidated stock prior to programs praising or damaging an industry.

In recent years, SEC charges of insider trading have been made at the rate of one every couple of weeks, a dramatic increase over the one-a-year pace since the inception of the commission.

- A former deputy director of defense and former LTV Corporation chairman, Paul Thayer, was accused of telling friends about acquisition plans involving firms on whose boards he sat.
- Four investors were sued by the SEC because of alleged profiteering on a deal that never took place, involving the purchase of the Aladdin Hotel-Casino in Las Vegas by Johnny Carson and the National Kinney Corporation. Among the accused were the entertainer's brother-in-law and his attorney's father-in-law.
- In November 1984, the SEC moved against a Citibank vice-president and others, declaring that they had illegally obtained advance knowledge of a McGraw-Hill acquisition of a computer-system firm. (Citibank was not cited in the charge.)

An "Insider Trading Sanctions Act" signed into law in 1984 made things tougher on those who benefit from tips, specifying that the penalty for such action could be up to three times the profit realized.

Just as public relations and investor relations people can be charged with insider status, so, too, can they be subject to prosecution for other violations of SEC regulations.

Practitioners were reminded in the 1971 *Pig 'n Whistle* v. *Financial Relations Board* that they must make a sincere and reasonable effort to determine if information supplied to them by an employer or client, and subsequently used in a news release, is accurate and complete. Pig 'n Whistle, a restaurant franchiser then in receivership, was accused of issuing releases that eliminated material facts and included misleading statements.

In 1984, the Howard Bronson public relations firm was reprimanded by the Securities and Exchange Commission for "false and misleading statements of material facts made in connection with the offer and sale of unregistered securities of a foreign issuer. . . ."

Although cases involving insider trading or the distribution of false data may be complicated in their details, the principles are often fairly clear, even to a layperson. Something just doesn't smell right. The notions of fairness, equal access, and freedom from deception have been violated. Beyond that general feeling of shakiness, there are also some guidelines to help potential investors and practitioners.

In terms of investing, for example, when could a company official (including an investor relations director) feel safe in purchasing stock?

- If the executive regularly purchases stock and buys his or her usual amount, there will be no questions.
- If the executives act within 30 days of a quarterly report, annual report, publication of quarterly operating results, proxy statement, or other widely disseminated information, he or she may also be considered faultless.
- And, obviously, it is safe to buy additional stock when the market for these securities is relatively stable.

Disclosure and Materiality

As far as news releases are concerned, the key words are *disclosure* and *materiality.*

Disclosure means the prompt release of information that would have a market effect on the value of the stock. This information must be complete, accurate, honest, and timely. Disclosure is demanded whenever there is something "material" to report.

Materiality is difficult to define with absolute accuracy. Quarterly and annual financial results certainly constitute materiality. So do mergers, stock splits, important contracts and awards, lawsuits, expansion plans, labor problems, marketing difficulties, and a host of other items. Even a change in key personnel could be material.

When a highly respected executive moved from Motorola to Fairchild and the market dropped ten points for Motorola and went up 20 points for Fairchild, that was materiality!

A good test for materiality is to ask yourself whether you would buy or sell shares if you possessed this information. If the answer is affirmative, then disclose.

One safe rule of thumb is, *When in doubt, disclose!* It is a lot better to have a premature release than to permit a rumor to circulate and damage your firm.

A recent development in financial news releases is an increase in stories that predict a future event. Many investor relations professionals have been schooled in the dangers of such releases but are a bit more courageous in circulating anticipated activities such as a future dividend change, or the proposed addition of key personnel, or the initial discussion period of merger negotiations. There is always the problem of a crisis canceling the expected event or of the SEC regarding an advance notice as misleading, but advocates point out that these stories also allow for added control and give the impression that a company plans well ahead.

HOW FINANCIAL NEWS IS RELEASED

The financial PR person's job is to see that material information is released promptly. The public must be informed.

But suppose you abide by all the rules and the financial media fail to print your story? You may have to explain this to the SEC, and you may even be expected to take out a paid advertisement if the information was not disseminated in any other way.

Failure to get stories printed also causes complaints at home. Newspapers like *The Wall Street Journal* cannot print every release they receive, particularly during certain times of year, so they may decide on the basis of a firm's total sales volume. This leaves the PR person with the difficult chore of calling clients who have just experienced the largest quarter in their history and telling them that their figures failed to impress the *Journal*.

Mail delivery of a news release containing material information is not considered adequate. Trade magazines, because of their long deadlines and staggered schedules, are not sufficient for disclosure. Even the prestigious *Barron's Weekly* does not meet disclosure standards.

Disclosure of material information must be *immediate*. This means simultaneous release to the major wire services and *The Wall Street Journal*. Even used alone, the *Journal* fulfills disclosure requirements—*if* it prints your story.

The safest way to proceed is to notify all pertinent members of the financial press at the same time. This routine is often reminiscent of World War II films. Many PR firms synchronize the watches of persons assigned to call the various media. Calls will be placed at exactly the same time and identical information dictated.

These calls would be made to the Dow Jones & Company wire (sometimes called the "Broad Tape"), Reuters, the *New York Times, The Wall Street Journal,* United Press International, Associated Press, and the PR Newswire. The PR Newswire is a contractual service for which you pay, at so much a word.

If you live in the Midwest, you should call the regional office of *The Wall Street Journal* in Chicago rather than the New York office. Ditto for the West Coast and other regions. Circumventing the regional office makes them look bad, makes you look dumb, and endangers future relationships.

Stories should also be delivered (by hand) to your local newspaper (the financial editor), to local wire services, and, in some cases, to local TV and radio stations. These deliveries should be timed to coincide with the national phone calls. If you delay, the financial wires will already have moved the story into your local newspaper office, and this damages your hometown credibility.

The PR Newswire will run your story as you dictate it (since you are paying the cost), but other outlets may cut you short after you have given them the particulars they want. They may need only the sales and earnings figures and won't hang around to hear the statement from the company president.

When you are reading figures over the phone, the most acceptable method is as follows: "$25,400,503" is read as, "Dollars, twenty-five million, four hundred thousand, five hundred and three." The media sources will normally read back the story to see that they have it right. Listen!

Remember that all these people are busy professionals and will not react favorably to any incomplete, confused, or inaccurate transmission of news. Get it right—then call! Be prepared with more data than the release contains. You may go for months without having anyone ask you about "shares outstanding" or "depreciation allowance," and then some member of the media will query you on this point. This is no time to stumble around; you must have all the details readily available.

Finally, after disseminating the news immediately as outlined above, you may also wish to call *Barron's* or *Standard & Poor's* or *Moody's Investors Service,* but a release mailed to these periodicals will normally suffice.

One reminder. The company executive and the financial PR person usually have to experience only one crisis situation before they become more prudent in their conversation. The vice-president who, in chatting with a media representative or a financial analyst, lets something material slip will find that this calls for immediate disclosure to everyone. At times the erring executive and the visitor might solemnly agree not to circulate this item, but this is a riskly bargain. It is safer to get the story out.

Executives should also be schooled in scheduling such important meetings as the annual meeting at times that allow stories to coordinate with opening and closing hours at the New York Stock Exchange. They should also keep an eye on members of their firm who may be investigating merger possibilities, and, in particular, they should learn to be careful with material information and to refrain from making premature releases. Media representatives or analysts who are persistent should be informed, politely, when such details may be expected.

The SEC may check releases to see if the bad news about certain companies is circulated with the same alacrity as the good news. Corporate officers admit they are often too eager to supply the positive items, like the emergence of new products, but less concerned about negative items or controversial matters.

Writing the Financial News Release

The financial news release shares most points in common with the regular news release as discussed in Chapter 6. There are, however, some major differences.

Overall, the mood and concept are different. This is not the place to be clever, to insert catchy leads, or to dress up quotes. The object of a financial news release is clarity and completeness. Don't worry about repeating words or phrases if they are needed for clarification. Stick to workable, familiar formulas for listing data. Remember that the readers are really interested only in the firm's sales volume, its net income, and the earnings per share— and in any other items that influence these three things, either now or in the future.

Do not list your own name as the person to contact, as you do in the normal release. The contact person should be one of the company spokespersons. You do not want to be placed in the position of answering additional questions from the media that go beyond the scope of the release and beyond your authority.

Financial news releases are pretty straight, even dull, by other release standards. You begin with the statement concerning the reason for the release—the publication of an annual or a quarterly report, the annual meeting, a speech by the president, or whatever. Then, if financial data are included, you get right to them.

The way such details are normally cited is sales or income (or other gross figures as in the case of banks, utilities, and other specialized reports), net earnings, and earnings per share. If one of this trio is significant enough to deserve a lead, you may alter the listing.

Each of these figures is compared with the figure for the same period in the preceding year. When doing this, be sure you give the closing date for the information cited, since not all companies compute their quarters and years on the same basis. And be consistent in reporting dates. If you compare 1987 with 1986, do this throughout. Don't reverse the dates and compare 1986 with 1987. Here is an example of how a paragraph in a quarterly report might look:

> For the first quarter ended March 31, 1987, Acme Industries reported net sales of $34,554,408 compared with net sales of $29,832,101 for the quarter ended March 31, 1986. This represents an increase of nearly 16 percent.
>
> Net earnings for this same period were $1,144,516, compared with net earnings of $953,444 for the first quarter of 1986, an increase of 20 percent.
>
> Earnings per share moved to 37¢ for the quarter ended March 31, 1987, an increase of 17 percent over earnings per share of 32¢ for the comparable quarter last year.

In the reporting of subsequent quarters, you would want to include cumulative statistics in the same fashion. For example:

> Cumulative figures for the first three quarters ended September 30, 1987, show net sales of $88,101,933 compared with net sales of $79,494,005 for the comparable nine-month period in 1986.

Reporting procedures generally start with the current quarter's figures and then give the cumulative figures. You may omit percentages of gain or loss, but these are frequently helpful.

Following the financial data, you would add any information, including executive quotations, that would augment or explain the figures. Remember that this is not the place to tout or exaggerate. After a bad quarter, the president cannot be quoted as saying, "'Although things didn't turn out well in the last three months, I think we're going to have a great fourth quarter." If you already have evidence that things will improve considerably the next quarter, you may want to indicate some optimism, but be cautious. It is best to give out the bad news quickly and honestly, explain it if you can, and then stop—unless things have already begun to turn around. What you must avoid is trying to disguise unfavorable data with false hopes or promises.

Figure 13-2 indicates the way a story moves from the quarterly report stage, via news release, to publication.

Since national and local media also have their own financial editors and writers, some business news will result from investigative reporting as well as from the traditional PR release. Many view this as a healthy improvement.

As with all other media relations, the PR persons should be helpful and cooperative with the financial reporter, guarding, however, against any premature disclosure. The practitioner should also watch for distortions in the publishing of information, whether conscious or unconscious.

Financial press relations, then, seems to resemble two lawyers talking to one another more than it does two communicators. It is probably wise to think this way and to keep such relationships on an extremely professional level.

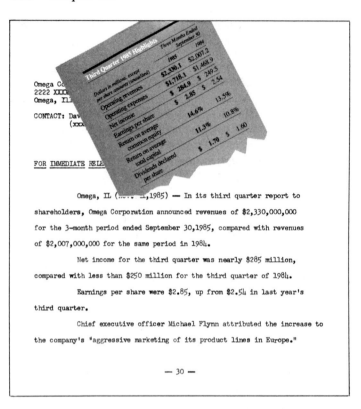

Other Communication

The news release is only one tool of communication for the practitioner. Others were mentioned as part of the "going public" phase; there are also the quarterly and annual reports and a variety of other printed materials, from speeches of the CEO to feature articles. All of these need to reflect these changing times.

> The key to promoting capital information today is an investor relations strategy that packages management as the corporate message, supplementing the corporate profile and Securities and Exchange Commission–mandated information. Recast annual reports, staid quarterly reports, perfunctory analyst meetings, half-hearted disclosures and other traditional investor relations techniques no longer suffice.[4]

Additional financial audiences, more overseas activity, and the competition for attention all dictate a more concise and more skillfully produced content that will upgrade the normal means of communication. This calls for both public relations ability and financial acumen.

More attention is also being paid to subgroups within the largely anony-

Figure 13-3 Proxy statements allow for absentee shareholder voting.
Courtesy: BellSouth Corporation

mous body of investors. Some of these shareholders may be speculators, portfolio managers, or people searching for undervalued assets; others are local citizens, people who follow a certain industry, or those who own a few shares they've inherited. Modern communication strategy suggests devising programs to accommodate certain differences in the aims and attitudes of these investor publics.

Analysts, for example, obviously need more detailed information than does the average investor. They also want access to management, responsible projections, and less wordy reports. Investors obviously want clues to earning potential, stability, and proven performance reflected in published documents. Both groups want more explanation than exposition.

Whatever the group, the essential elements in communicating financial data involve fact finding, planning, honesty, and professionalism.

And how do you know if you are doing a good job?

Depending on your objectives, the checklist for measuring your progress may include:

- Number and type of requests for business press interviews, especially as industry representative.

- Number of articles published about the company in the business and trade press.
- Number and types of requests for annual reports, quarterlies, and other financial data.
- Number of published research reports.
- Number of requests for analyst interviews with management.
- Number of appearances at professional societies and business seminars.
- Analyst attendance at meetings for your company.
- Price/earnings and trading volume relative to market and competition.
- Stock price movement versus competition and market.
- Stock ownership changes, by type of owner and geographic area.[5]

Overall, communications have improved, at least for the individual investor, partly out of concern for such activities as hostile takeovers or consumer complaints, but also because of a more personal attitude toward the shareholder. This manifests itself in the quality of the writing, in the number of publications, and in innovations like Braille reports and audio tapes for the blind and collect-call phone numbers for added information.

THE QUARTERLY REPORT

Reports to shareholders are issued every quarter, although the annual report sometimes replaces the fourth-quarter report. These quarterly reports are generally brief statements of the activities of the past three months, plus a cumulative look at the year to date. The president's message will be short and the figures compact.

The quarterly report normally matches current figures with those of the comparable period the preceding year and may also give sets of cumulative figures for the year to date. Most are designed to fit into a #10 envelope or smaller and may not exceed four small panels of copy. Others could be more complex, contain more detail, and, in a few instances, even include copy more common to annual reports. There are rarely any elaborate graphs or illustrations.

Like the annual report, the quarterly report fulfills an SEC requirement for "periodic" reports.

THE ANNUAL REPORT

Section 10k of the Securities Act of 1934 requires the publication of an annual report. Section 8k requires the publication of periodic reports such as quarterly reports and news releases.

Annual reports have been around a long time, but in the early years they were very elitist, not very regular in their publication dates, and not too accurate. Today the number of reports mailed annually to some 30–40 million stockholders is approaching 200 million copies.

These reports must include certain specific financial data, but they still allow room for a good deal of creativity, particularly in the selection of graphics. A number of good books are available on producing the company annual report. It is also advisable to collect annual reports for a variety of companies to see how they treated the required elements.

In addition to satisfying the SEC requirements, the annual report often has the characteristics of a promotional brochure. It is used for upgrading internal morale, for marketing products, and for establishing name identification. Some annual reports actually lobby for political and economic causes or help prepare shareholders for such corporate events as mergers.

A few annual reports parody popular magazines like *People, Playboy,* and the *New Yorker*; and Seven-Up once scented its report with lemon. Humor is rare, however. It frightens executives. The most common complaint of critics is that annual reports are dull and unoriginal. They all begin to look alike, regardless of the nature and scope of the company. One designer accused these publications of creating in the reader a sense of "terminal déjà vu."

Exceptions stand out.

Potlatch invariably captures attention with illustrations that dramatize the forest-products industry. Quaker Oats often features the homey touch of rural landscapes, and both Grolier and Tonka focus on that most appealing of subjects, children. Sharp photography rescues some reports, and crisp writing saves others. A Parker Drilling Company report carried these words on its cover: "THE FIRST HALF OF 1980 WAS LOUSY." This is a far cry from other publications that attempt to make losses read like gains. There are reports from hospitals, foundations, nonprofit organizations, trade associations, colleges and universities, athletic franchises—from large corporations and from struggling mini-industries.

Diebold Inc. of Ohio distributes its annual reports to its automated-banking-machine salespersons as sales tools. MacMillan Bloedel Ltd., a Vancouver firm specializing in forest products, lists nearly 80 percent of its 24,000 employees in the annual report. H.J. Heinz issued an annual report devoted to the recreational activities of its employees. United California Bank's annual report one year promoted its home state, and Armco Steel Corporation's report for the same year used one of the minor stockholders for a cover photo. Wheelabrator-Frye of New Hampshire published 200,000 copies of a second annual report for children—in comic book fashion and extolling the virtues of capitalism while criticizing the increasing interference of government.

The annual report may begin with a theme—a new plant, an anniversary, a new corporate symbol, record growth, or some other idea around which the report may be structured.

A few companies have featured their participation in trade shows, giving them a fresh setting for product photos. For Delta Drilling Company, cartoons about oil by Patrick Oliphant were the theme. Bendix showcased its technological advances, and the Bechtel Group discussed the company's involvement in global needs. Banks may detail an anniversary, a new facility, a financial philosophy.

Emhart began televising its annual report via satellite to half a hundred major commercial stations and to its own offices over closed-circuit television. Print media were supplied with pertinent graphs and data. Other variations include minority reports from utility shareholders and the widely read annual letter by Berkshire Hathaway's articulate president, Warren Buffet.

Planning the Annual Report

Practitioners should plan to devote some time to thinking about the report and collecting the data. It works best if they can work closely with the chief executive, seeing the relative importance of things through this executive's eyes rather than gathering details piecemeal, department by department, and then trying to make their own evaluations.

The investor relations field is full of horror stories relating to the cost or production of annual reports. Among the more common complaints are these:

- The entire process is begun too late.
- Key executives who must approve copy are not available.
- Few executives read anything until it's already in type.
- Too many people get to review the product, and they have too many diverse, often minuscule, corrections.
- Photos are often a tribute to executive ego rather than reader interest, and too much time is wasted on these illustrations.
- There is too much copy for the format.
- The budget is too small.

Those charged with the production of annual reports usually begin their work at least seven or eight months in advance of publication, gathering the material they can, lining up departmental contributors, getting approval for the theme, scheduling the photos, and performing other tasks that can be accomplished while the final figures are being compiled and audited.

However the annual report is handled, it will be costly. Depending on the scope, size, color, number printed, and other factors, the production of these reports can cost anywhere from 50 cents each to $3 or more.

That is another reason why care should be exercised. Errors cause problems with shareholders and regulating bodies. They are also expensive, even when you catch them before publication. This means you should avoid changes as much as possible. Get things right the first time instead of

Figure 13-4 Even similar companies exhibit variety of design in annual reports. Courtesy: Ameritech; Pacific Telesis Group; NYNEX; Southwestern Bell Corporation; reproduced with permission of AT&T

making changes in the galley proofs, page proofs, and even after the piece is printed.

Start early enough to make overtime work at the printer's unnecessary. Use machine-set headlines instead of hand-set headlines. Figure your color properly so that you aren't paying for multiple press runs for a single page. In fact, on short runs, you might question the advisability of using any color at all. Order your paper early, particularly in this time of paper shortages. And see if you can't use a self-cover stock rather than the heavier paper.

In addition to these technical reasons for delays and higher costs, there are also philosophical ones, as indicated by Richard A. Lewis in his book *Annual Reports* (see Figure 13-5).

In summary, plan ahead. Accomplish as much ahead as possible, and don't experiment with typesetters who have never done this kind of work before. The annual report is ordinarily a rush job, and you need all the help you can get.

Several paper companies and printers supply planning pages and documents to aid in the planning of reports. Included are schedule sheets, worksheets, and dummy publications.

CORPORATE REPORT CAPSULES

"From a publishing standpoint, the annual report is the most amateurish job undertaken by corporate management," says the public relations director of a large diversified company. Many executive traits tend to make it so: "Management wants stilted language—the annual report is a monument to corporate gobbledygook," says another executive. "Management gets literary and self-conscious," comments a third, "but they avoid detail and they don't say anything." Clearance is another major stumbling block: "Fighting an annual report through an executive committee of a major corporation is a bloody battle," says a veteran of the experience. Worst of all, top management is often unhappy at the result.

Why does the annual report, which costs so much money and takes so much time and effort, end up being such a disappointing document so often? Here are the most common reasons:

1. The chief executive offer does not assign the project to a man in whom he has confidence. As a result, this man is the victim of all the conflicting opinions of people who outrank him.

2. The chief executive doesn't get involved early in the planning stages. Instead he often makes hasty, expensive and ill-conceived changes at the last minute.

3. The writer of the text doesn't complete the first draft in time for careful consideration by top management.

4. The text is written on time, but the key executives put off reading it until there is a crisis.

5. The accountants don't deliver the book on time, causing an impossible squeeze between the time the figures are delivered and the book must be mailed.

6. After the design is set and the type is in galley form, a new group of people—such as lawyers, directors, assorted vice-presidents and possibly the president's wife—start making a whole series of comments with no understanding of the basic concept on which the annual report was developed.

7. The chief executive panics at the last minute, especially if Number 6 has occurred. The copy is hastily rewritten and released only because the deadline has arrived. The resulting compromise almost guarantees a very mediocre report.

Most of these problems could be prevented at the outset if it is admitted that an annual report can really speak for only one man—the one who runs the company. He must be close to the project at the outset, and must delegate its execution to someone who has his complete confidence and backing. Increasingly, the annual report project is going to the new, stronger communications chiefs being designated at corporations. These people often have the title of vice-president of corporate communications. Sometimes it is efficient to bring in an outside consultant, the weight of whose experience can be added to that of the company man in charge. What must follow—developing a schedule, gathering the creative ingredients, and following the report through to its final stages—can then go ahead with a minimum of conflict.

Figure 13-5
SOURCE: Excerpted from Richard A. Lewis, *Annual Reports* (Zurich, Switzerland: The Graphis Press, 1971)

Contents

Typically, an annual report includes the following:

Figure 13-6 Both photography and artwork are featured in annual reports.
Courtesy: Triad and Robert Tanenbaum, and Brockway, Inc.

- The cover
- Financial highlights
- Table of contents
- The president's letter
- Exposition
- Financial statements
- Notes to the financial statements
- Summary of statistics
- Graphs and charts
- Management profiles

There may be other sections and, in longer reports, even an index. Let us look at each of these categories briefly.

The Cover

The aim of the cover is to gain attention, to state the theme, to get the reader into the report. It may be a large photo, an embossed logo, a pop-art design, or an oversized set of figures. Whatever it is, it should be both attractive and appropriate (see Figure 13-7).

Figure 13-7 Annual report covers are often distinctive and original.
Courtesy: Amfac, Inc.; Triad and Robert Tanenbaum; United Telecom; Geisinger Foundation; Brockway, Inc.; Potlatch Corporation; The Coca-Cola Company; The LTV Corporation

Financial Highlights

Placed normally toward the front of the report, the financial highlights constitute an easily read synopsis of the company's operation, comparing the current year with the preceding year (see Figure 13-8).

FINANCIAL HIGHLIGHTS		
	1987	1986
Net sales	$1,827,669,000	$1,590,949,000
Earnings before income taxes	$ 253,910,000	$ 214,791,000
As a percent of sales	13.9%	13.5%
Net earnings	$ 141,696,000	$ 120,403,000
As a percent of sales	7.8%	7.6%
Return on stockholder's equity	21.8%	21.2%
Earnings per common share	$4.44	$3.76
Dividends per common share	$1.58	$1.47
Cash, time deposits & marketable securities	$ 187,867,000	$ 90,396,000
Capital expenditures	40,781,000	31,213,000
Working capital	499,288,000	418,442,000
Number of stockholders	41,364	42,468
Number of employees	29,200	29,700

Figure 13-8

Table of Contents

A table of contents may be included in longer reports but is unnecessary in shorter versions.

The President's Letter

The president's letter represents a specific, reflective look at the company's present and future and is frequently written by the chief executive personally. It is, in fact, a good idea to turn this chore over to the president, since he or she is the person with the overall view of the firm's operations. The PR person may be called in on the rewrite. This works better than having the practitioner initiate the copy and then seek the president's approval. Typically this letter consists of one or two pages, but some annual reports have woven this letter through the entire text. There are many ways to take away from the stilted look of most presidents' letters (see Figure 13-9).

Exposition

Few guidelines are available for the exposition section. It is used to tell readers about the company, its products and services, and its stand on social issues. This is often the most colorful and pictorial aspect of the report. Its length varies with the message to be conveyed (see Figure 13-10).

The exposition section features employees or customers or the product

Figure 13-9 Letters from corporate CEOs take many forms and set the tone of the annual report.
Courtesy: The Standard Oil Company

Figure 13-10 The expository pages are often entertaining.
Courtesy: The LTV Corporation; Amfac, Inc.; Marriott Corporation; United Telecom; Potlatch Corporation; RJR Nabisco, Inc.

line. It is characterized by crisp copy and excellent graphics. It may look to the future or the past; it may focus on the energy crisis or poverty; it can explain how a product works or why a problem arose. Planners are locked into other annual-report requirements, but this section allows for expansion and insight, and even a bit of boasting.

Financial Statements

The financial statements consitute the vital section of the annual report, and although there is more similarity than variety among reporting firms, the financial statements can vary to a degree. Some companies include six or eight tables; others carry only two or three. The most important items are these:

- The *balance sheet*, which shows the relationship of total assets to total liability, plus shareholder equity.
- The *statement of income and retained earnings*, which provides the results of the company's operations for the fiscal period, including principal sources of income less principal costs, net income, and amounts retained and distributed to stockholders.

These pages can be very dull, but some thoughtful selection of type, open arrangement, tint blocks, and other graphic ideas can make for easier reading.

The financial statements are not the responsibility of the financial PR consultant. The company's accounting firm, working with its fiscal officers, pulls this material together. These statements are ordinarily the last thing compiled in the report, so the wise PR person has everything else ready—the president's letter, exposition, cover, photos—and can then deliver the dummy to the printer as soon as the accountants furnish the figures. Since the financial statements will resemble the preceding year's statements in terms of layout, the person preparing the report can allow the proper space for them and then just insert the new figures.

Notes to the Financial Statements

Any of the items included in the financial statements that require further explanation are covered in the notes. These could be nonrecurring items, such as losses resulting from lawsuits or collection of back taxes or uninsured mishaps. Detailed breakdowns on income, taxes, long-term debt, and other matters may also be included.

It is well to note here that all type used in annual reports must be 10 point or larger. In the past, these notes were often in agate type and beyond the reading ability of some of the older stockholders. When the SEC added this 10-point requirement, it altered many annual-report formats, particularly those that were in a graphic rut.

This section also contains the accounting firm's affidavit.

Summary of Statistics

The summary of statistics consists of comparison tables for periods of five, ten, 15, or 20 or more years and may encompass sales, earnings, taxes, capital expenditures, number of employees, plant growth, and so forth.

Graphs and Charts

The inclusion of graphs and charts is helpful not only for the casual reader but also for the intense reader who wants an overview of the company. There is no need for these to be only bar graphs or simple line charts. All sorts of symbols are possible—segmented dollar bills, piles of coins, varying size of products, pie charts, and so on (see Figure 13-11). These graphs and charts may also show sales offices, overseas oil-drilling sites, number of employees, depreciation, property additions, amortization, and many other items.

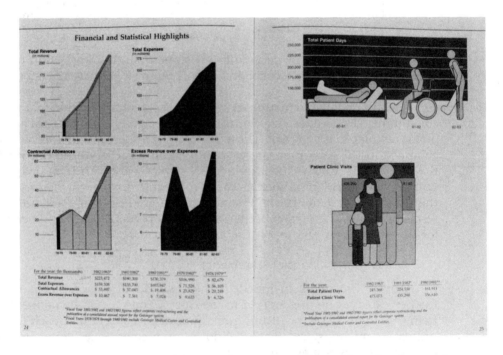

Figure 13-11 Pie charts and bar graphs are often replaced by other forms of graphics.
Courtesy: Geisinger Foundation

Management Profiles

Not too long ago, management teams were portrayed stiffly and unimaginatively in a series of "mug shots." This rogue's gallery then gave way to a stolid circle of executives staring up from a conference table. Even these had some value, at least for the analysts and salespeople who could jog their memories before making a call. Modern designers favor unusual groupings, informal poses, and work situations. This helps to humanize the company officers—and the company (see Figure 13-12). This portrait section is often accompanied by a longer list of executives by title.

Some firms have moved from the magazine format to newspaper ads for their annual reports, and others combine both of these methods. Large corporations with substantial overseas interests produce annual reports in a number of languages.

New officers elected in 1982 were, left to right: Dennis T. Terwilliger, Controller; Robert M. Kuhn, Vice President, Finance and an Armstrong Director; Paul C. James, Vice President, Research and Development; Richard B. Twickler, Vice President, Manufacturing; and Philip J. Durosko, Vice President, Consumer Affairs and Product Reliability.

For Armstrong people in 1982, the Company's growing strength as a competitor paid off in stable employment, a new three-year contract and the spirit of being on a winning team.

Figure 13-12 Portraits of officers in annual reports take many forms but most tend toward more informal poses. In this Armstrong Rubber Company report, newly elected officers are grouped with shots of employees.
Courtesy: The Armstrong Rubber Company

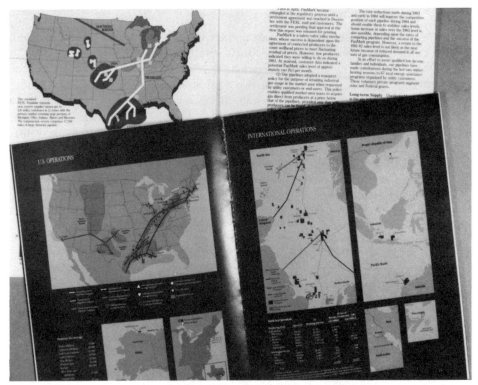

Figure 13-13 Maps are part of the annual report graphics for many corporations.
Courtesy: Panhandle Eastern Corporation; Texas Eastern Transmission Corporation (based on its 1983 annual report and its pipeline systems at that time)

THE SECURITIES-ANALYST PUBLIC

Besides communicating with the shareholders and the financial media, the investor relations director has a number of other assignments. Advising management is one of these, as is the organization of special events (plant tours, stockholders' meetings, analyst meetings, speeches, and the like). Still another duty is that of working with the securities analyst.

Although all publics are important in financial public relations, the securities analysts form a special group, which requires individual and expert attention.

Some two-score-plus autonomous societies make up the Federation of Financial Analysts, and these individual societies are located in the major U.S. cities. However, one-third of the nearly 13,000 members live or work in New York. Two-thirds of the members of the federation work for broker-dealers. The remainder may be employed by mutual funds, banks, investment trusts, insurance companies, corporate trusts, universities, hedge funds, pension funds, and even by wealthy individuals. The objectives of each differ, and so do the requirements for reaching them.

Most of all, however, the financial PR person should be familiar with the analysts who are key to the success of his or her client's stock. This may narrow down to six or eight persons. The research director in any brokerage house can inform the practitioner about house specialists, and these become the practitioner's contacts. Making a few good friends in this select group is advisable, because they may then pass along what is being said about the firm. When a big news item develops, the financial PR person may notify these key people after the normal channels of dissemination have been used.

The Federation of Financial Analysts can also provide a roster, and members are coded by specialties. The *Red Handbook of Security Dealers* includes similar information. Names must be spelled properly and the list revised regularly, since turnover is high.

The client company should have an "open-door" policy for securities analysts, financial reporters, and shareholders. The same information must be available to all these groups. They need to understand the company and be able to evaluate both management and potential.

Analysts come from various backgrounds. They might be business-school graduates, but they could also be attorneys, engineers, teachers, scientists. Some rise from the sales force. Diligent analysts can be like ferrets. They will ask probing questions and try to dig beneath the company sales pitch: "I would rather tour facilities than see pictures," states one New York analyst. "And when I tour, I like to visit the men's room or get deliberately lost in the warehouse. That way I can sometimes discover things not visible in the programmed tour. The analyst must be both sharp and devious—in the good sense."

What analysts do with the information they obtain is study it for significant trends, making their conclusions part of their personal advice to investors or part of reports circulated by their parent firms. E.F. Hutton may issue more than 50,000 copies of a single report, and Dean Witter Reynolds sends out more than 2,000 different reports annually.

Analysts try to follow certain companies, and they earn their reputations by being right in their predictions at least half the time. Even without that strong a batting average, they may still succeed—if they can attract clients to their companies.

What analysts seek from corporate publications or spokespersons is a candid look at the current situation, an assessment of the future, a view of management depth, an insight into company strategy, and conclusions about how a corporation may do in terms of competition. They are impatient with hype or complexity and admire the corporations that extend themselves to proffer information that goes even beyond the legal requirements.

In general, what the analyst is seeking is a deeper treatment of the generally available data. This enables the analyst to be more intelligent in

Figure 13-14 Securities analysts come from varied backgrounds and may scrutinize your company from diverse viewpoints.

advising others. In addition to the sales volume, net earnings, and earnings per share mentioned earlier, the analyst may wish to know such things as cost of sales, taxes, gross volume, gross profit, depreciation, and average number of shares outstanding. A new plant story may spark questions from analysts on dollar and physical volume, length of construction time, new capabilities, and even the price line. A dividend-increase story may cause them to ask *why*. And they may be looking for subtle things, including the competence of management.

"Earnings and balance sheets don't run a company; people do," concludes an analyst from Boston.

The spokespersons should be honest and blunt in response to analyst queries. Leave the judgment making to them. And don't promote, speculate, or show preference.

Analysts obviously prefer to meet with management rather than with the PR person unless the latter is also part of the management team. The PR person may still insist on being around, particularly if he or she is doubtful about the competence of the spokesperson.

Analysts are contacted by both the written and spoken word. The financial public relations person reaches them (and other publics) as frequently as practical. Material disseminated should have some real value and should not be mere puffery. Both the analyst and the SEC will notice whether or not you are as diligent about communicating bad news as you are about communicating good news.

Among the categories in the "written word" are the annual report, the quarterly statement, interim reports, the newsletter, the fact book, reprints of speeches, advertising, releases to the general press, articles in financial publications, pieces in the business section of the press, and other publicity.

The "spoken word" covers phone calls, special meetings, field tours, interviews, plant visits, and radio and television, as well as attendance, by invitation, at analyst society gatherings.

Many financial analysts are not members of the national society, and some cities do not have the requisite 35 members to form a chapter. Still, the chance to meet with this audience on a local or a regional basis is worthwhile. Even more coveted is the opportunity to address a meeting of the New York analysts. The federation always issues the invitation, although a company may request the interview. If successful, the company will receive a three-page list of guidelines that spell out the very formal procedures governing this meeting.

At the regional or local or New York meetings, a lavishly mounted presentation can't really make up for bad news. Practitioners should think carefully about appearing before such bodies until they have a success story to tell. When they do have such a story, the facts themselves will serve better than an expensive extravaganza with film, slides, and elaborate handouts.

Because of the difficulty of scheduling New York appearances, many companies settle for the regional financial presentations, holding these as often as quarterly, sometimes tied to their quarterly earnings reports. The locale could be company headquarters or a convenient hotel/motel, and the audience may be a mix of analysts, the financial media, and area shareholders. Often the program features a slide show or some audiovisual adjunct to the oral and printed data, especially if the audience is large. Sometimes the intended audience is surveyed in advance to solicit questions that will make up the agenda, and again after the meeting to help with evaluation.

THE SHAREHOLDERS' MEETING

The shareholders' annual meeting requires the same careful attention accorded other special events mentioned in Chapter 9. It may, in fact, be the most important meeting of the year. Some major companies spend as much as $350,000 on this meeting, and the average cost for such events among the major companies is between $5,000 and $10,000.

Shareholders' meetings vary. Most are held in the same cities (usually the company's home-office site) every year; some rotate among a number of cities; a few deliberately select inconvenient locales to discourage mass attendance. Ordinarily, the chief executive officer would be in charge of the meeting, or at least present, but there have been occasions when the CEO has delegated this authority to others.

The format of the meetings also differs, but a typical meeting might begin with registration of the shareholders. They might present admission cards to gain entrance and be issued badges to complete the security check. Each shareholder would receive one vote per a certain predetermined number of shares owned.

The group then gathers in a meeting room where a report is presented, questions solicited, a slate of officers presented and voted upon, and other business taken care of. Sometimes this is done in a matter of minutes; on other occasions, it may take hours.

After that, there may be a luncheon or a special presentation, or the shareholders may merely depart.

Some companies are devising ways to add spice to the annual meeting, to take it out of the dull routine. An article in the *Corporate Communications Report* features a roundup of ways to put "pep in the annual meeting," including these innovative ideas:

- W.R. Grace & Company blended a tour of historic sites in Lexington and Concord with their Boston meeting, and made their Los Angeles meeting unique by offering a Mexican-style meal prepared by a newly acquired restaurant subsidiary.
- Wometco Enterprises, Miami, attracted shareholders with the offer of a free first-run movie, complete with complimentary popcorn and pop.
- Norton Simon, Inc., and Masco Corporation handed out nominal gifts from their own product lines.
- 3M Company utilized a large video screen behind the head table to give the presentation more visibility and impact.
- Some companies hold stockholder meetings at resorts; some hold two meetings—one legal and one informational, at different times of the year.[6]

Most companies try to run a tight meeting, providing shareholders with an agenda and trimming the length of speeches. They also protect against disruptions by making sure that they have tight security, attendance checks, and strict rules for recognition and speaking, and by limiting questions and offering gifts or a film as a finale to prevent long sessions.

Shareholder concerns may center on financial policy, directors' salaries, corporate social conduct, or a range of other topics. In recent years, these interests often take the form of "shareholder resolutions," presented to the membership for consideration and support. Churches may instigate a resolution regarding a corporation's Third World policies or its trade with South Africa. Conservative stockholders continue to press for discontinuing business dealing with Communist countries. There are members seeking to put a stop to arms arrangements with Arab nations, or to investigate drug testing abroad, or to demand more environmental awareness in this country. Companies like Nestlé, Control Data, and Pfizer have all been targets of complaints, and shareholder resolutions work their way into the annual meeting or the proxy statements for action by the membership.

Disruptions are considered in the planning stage, and so are other abnormal events, like illness or death of attendees. Because of the advanced ages of some shareholders, a few corporations keep ambulances stashed discreetly near the meeting site. And probable tensions are sometimes defused by moving the annual-meeting locale to a less volatile area.

Once satellite communication becomes more common for shareholder meetings, a whole new range of problems will arise—cost, selection of receiving sites, technical difficulties, increased impersonality, and other exigencies. However, the system also has obvious advantages, and many firms are investigating this alternative.

Besides the legal necessity of scheduling annual meetings, companies find other positive reasons for such gatherings:

1. The annual meeting is the most effective medium (indeed, the only one) for face-to-face contact with a large group of individual shareholders.
2. A well-run, imaginative annual meeting reflects positively on a company's openness and investor relations style and helps fulfill the company's obligation to be responsive to the owners of the business.
3. The annual meeting can provide a convenient platform for a major corporate announcement or policy statement, such as a quarterly earnings announcement or a (chief executive officer) speech, which can be reprinted and distributed widely.
4. . . . the annual meeting offers a convenient opportunity for communications with non-shareholder audiences and can serve as the springboard for all sorts of side meetings (with directors, company operating group executives, and perhaps their wives, analysts, bankers, local press, etc.).[7]

A FINAL WORD ON FINANCIAL PR

As in other areas of public relations, there is constant change in the practice of investor relations. Satellites not only carry meetings, they also (through the Financial News Network, for example) telecast business and financial news to subscribers—or to anyone with a home dish. Research has been speeded up by computers and their ability not only to process new data but to tie into existing programs.

Among other uses, this rapid method of research may be helpful in categorizing and convincing shareholders in the face of a hostile takeover. Loyalty and trust are two main deterrents to the raiders who seek to assume control of an industry, and communication with shareholders on a regular and personal basis helps engender these traits. The number of takeover attempts is on the increase in the 1980s, and even when they are unsuccessful, they are costly and often depress the stock of the firm under attack. Even solid corporations like Phillips Petroleum, McGraw-Edison, Walt Disney Productions, and others have suffered. The government has failed to do anything about the raider maneuvers; the average shareholder seem uninterested; and the imperiled firm is left to its own devices, primarily strategic, in combatting the takeover.

Arbitrageurs, or professional speculators, stand by, ready to move in on merging companies. "Greenmailers" who own large blocs of a corporation's stock threaten to stage a takeover unless their stock is purchased at a premium. There are tender offers and sealed bids and proxy fights and other efforts that are proper or mischievous. Companies may be lost, stocks may tumble, and jobs may be wiped out. Even though economics dominates these affairs, the PR person has an important role—advising management, constructing the messages, working with the media, informing and convincing shareholders, suggesting gambits to meet the competition.

Local or Distant?

Do you need a financial public relations office in New York—or in one of the other major markets, such as Chicago, Boston, or San Francisco?

That depends on a lot of things. Size, for example. A General Motors can't settle for Detroit financial public relations counsel alone. It needs either a combination of local and New York or New York alone.

But what about the companies that are much smaller than General Motors? Can they be handled out of Cleveland or Kansas City or Denver?

Often the answer is yes.

True, the New York firms have the advantage of proximity to the market and to the major financial media. They may have better connections and a larger staff of experienced personnel.

The local firm, however, knows the client better, is more readily available in a time of crisis, and can attend to regional needs more satisfactorily. Besides, there is sometimes a benefit in relative isolation; you don't fall victim to every Wall Street rumor.

Perhaps the best arrangement—if you can afford it—is the pairing of local- and major-market expertise.

Evaluating Results

Because of its very nature, financial public relations is quite intangible—even more intangible than regular PR. In tough times, it may be the first to feel the budget ax. This warns practitioners that they should take steps to measure the results of all programs.

The simplest—and least helpful—method of evaluation is the cataloguing of your own activities, such as the number of releases mailed, letters sent, analysts contacted, and hours spent on behalf of each client.

An improvement on this is an analysis of response, such as column inches in business papers and magazines, attendance at the annual meeting, visits by analysts, and comments on the annual report.

The most reliable way to judge effectiveness is by having goals spelled out in advance and then measuring the results against these goals. Perhaps you want to broaden the geographical market for your stock and you actually accomplish this. Or you want a specific analyst to take an interest in your company and he or she does. These checkpoints are the most significant.

CHAPTER HIGHLIGHTS

- Investor relations practitioners cannot and should not promise an increase in the value of a company's or a client's stock based on their efforts alone.

- IR specialists must anticipate the queries of analysts and shareholders and come up with honest and appropriate responses.

- Primary audiences for financial public relations messages are company executives and employees, current and prospective shareholders, analysts, the financial media, and various regulating bodies.

- When a company goes public, five periods are involved: preregistration, registration, preeffective, effective, and posteffective. Each has its time limits and legal restrictions.

- While waiting for the green light from the SEC, a company going public may identify spokespersons, establish policies, build lists, establish contacts with the financial community, and prepare a number of documents and forms.

- The Securities and Exchange Commission oversees and regulates trading activities, including the general guidelines for investor relations. Stockwatch is one of their watchdog programs.

- In financial communication, disclosure and materiality are the key considerations, meaning that anything that will affect the value of a stock should be promptly publicized.

- The financial news release is usually terse, factual, accurate, and complete, and it is released simultaneously to all the principal media.

- Required by law, the quarterly and annual reports of public corporations are the main, but not the sole, means of communicating with their various audiences. There is a sameness to many of these publications, but even with the restrictions, there is room for innovation.

- Securities analysts, whose backgrounds may differ widely, help make the market for stocks and are treated as an important public, being reached by the written and spoken word. Special meetings are held for this group, and company spokespersons try to accommodate them within legal limits.

- Ingenuity may also be demonstrated by the program at the annual shareholders' meeting, which may feature a film, a meal, or a congenial locale. Some firms are turning to satellite meetings.

- Trends affect the nature of investor relations, which may be centered on either coast but which can be practiced anywhere.

NOTES

[1] Michael Seeley, "Investor Relations at the Crossroads," *Public Relations Journal*, April 1983.

[2]Harrison T. Beardsley, "Problem Solving in Corporate Financial Relations," *Public Relations Journal*, April 1978.

[3]Michael J. Cudahy, CEO of Marquette Electronics, "Going Wrong by Going Public," *Fortune*, December 24, 1984.

[4]Richard J. Coyle, "Management Is the Message," *Public Relations Journal*, April 1983.

[5]Joseph J. Graves, "Communicating in the Financial Community." Courtesy *Communicator's Journal*, January/February 1984.

[6]Corpcom Services, Inc., *The Corporate Communications Report* (New York: November 1977).

[7]*The Corporate Communications Report.*

SUGGESTED READINGS

BUDD, JOHN F., JR., *How Video Can Vitalize Financial Reporting.* New York: Corporate Shareholder Press, 1983.

GRAVES, JOSEPH J., *Managing Investor Relations: Strategies and Techniques.* Homewood, Ill.: Dow Jones-Irwin, 1984.

The SEC; The Stock Exchanges and Your Financial Public Relations. New York: Hill and Knowlton, 1983.

EXERCISES

1. Select a local firm and get a copy of its quarterly or annual report. You may also use a report from any corporation outside your area, or check for a copy of such a report at your local library. Using the information contained in this report, write a financial news release.

2. Select a local or regional firm and outline your ideas for its annual report, including theme and possible illustrations.

3. Using as sources *The Wall Street Journal, Business Week, Fortune, Barron's Weekly*, or other publications, write a 100-word report on some stock you think might be worth considering. Explain why.

CASE PROBLEMS

1. A closely held company that has been in the same family for over 100 years decides to go public in order to secure additional capital for expansion. To this point, the firm has managed pretty well with a strong marketing department and a local ad agency. Write a proposal to the president of this company, a man who has never been impressed with the validity of any form of public relations, and convince him why he should hire you as his investor relations person.

2. You handle financial public relations for a company that manufactures various forms of athletic equipment. Located in a city of 100,000, your

firm, Champion Inc., employs 4,000 people, making it the city's largest employer. After a couple of profitable years as a public corporation, Champion learns a fast-food conglomerate is contacting shareholders in an attempt at a takeover. In a subsequent board meeting, the president asks for your advice in combatting this raid. What suggestions do you have insofar as procedures go? What would you do to garner local support? How would you reach shareholders, and with what general message?

3. As the financial public relations director for Apex Steel, a public corporation, you are called into the president's office and told that Apex has just completed a merger with Gate Steel Corporation. "President Ryan of Gate and I decided we wouldn't announce this right away," says the Apex chief executive. "We'd like the announcement to coincide with our Apex annual meeting, which is only six weeks away. That's why I called you in. I want you to start working on the announcement."

    What do you say to the Apex president? What do you do about the situation?

4. Palmeston Aircraft, a nationwide manufacturer of executive jets, will celebrate its fiftieth anniversary as a company next year. Max Palmeston, founder and president, wants the annual meeting to be different. The firm, located in Cleveland, has traditionally merely notified stockholders, held the required meeting, provided a box lunch, and dismissed the gathering. For this golden anniversary celebration, Palmeston has budgeted $50,000. What the president wants from you, as his public relations consultant, are some thoughts on how to spend this money. He wants your idea for a theme for the meeting, a new way to present the annual report, a program for the meeting itself, and perhaps some gifts or prizes.

    Write Palmeston a memo with your suggestions.

14

PUBLIC RELATIONS FOR GOVERNMENT, UNIONS, TRADE ASSOCIATIONS, AND THE MILITARY

The applications of public relations skills and experience extend far beyond the business world. The profession affects nearly every aspect of society, from missionaries to media. Few enterprises would dare proceed without some form of public relations.

In this chapter and the next, we look at a sampling of public relations in action, concentrating not on the principles we've already studied, but on the differences that characterize each new responsibility.

PR IN GOVERNMENT

Although the art of political public relations may not be a common assignment for the general PR practitioner, it is a useful laboratory subject to employ the skills we have discussed. Nearly every aspect of the public relations repertoire comes to play in the political arena. Besides, beginning PR employees are finding increasing opportunities in government and politics.

Even though government service has its pleasant side, a lot of headaches are associated with elective and appointive office, and with the jobs that support and sustain officials. The public view of politicians is rarely a friendly one, although individual exceptions are made. Members of Congress are criticized as being too susceptible to pleas of lobbyists, and the judiciary is portrayed as soft on criminals. Those who staff departments at the federal or state level are characterized as slow, inefficient, indifferent, and overpaid.

Part of the problem is that the average citizen doesn't understand how government works or how complicated it has become. At the local, state, and federal levels, practitioners must be aware of how laws are made, amended,

Figure 14-1
Campaigns to "get out the vote" are also part of the government process.

and rescinded, and how the committee structure works every step of the way. They must know the personalities involved, the issues, the opposition, and the mood of both the legislators and the nation.

Dollar amounts are staggering, with the federal debt being explained in distances to the sun and in highways paved with currency in order to make the concept manageable. Relationships are interwoven at numerous levels, making it difficult to ascertain just who will benefit or lose as the result of certain government actions. Some ideas are so entrenched that they are nearly gospel.

Making things even more difficult for the public relations person in this era are the suspiciousness of citizens, their growing reluctance to fund programs, and an increasing withdrawal by the public from international responsibility. Another handicap is the tendency to lump political philosophy into conservative or liberal camps. Most Americans fit neither extreme, but rather think of themselves as moderates who split their allegiance on certain issues. They may have favored intervention in Grenada and supported the Equal Rights Amendment, may have advocated both tighter pornography laws and the SALT II treaty.

In the mid-eighties in America, liberals had a siege mentality, and one of the often-prescribed remedies was public relations.

> Liberals insist there is nothing wrong with their values, which center on a powerful and activist federal government committed to a fair society and a growing economy. But many liberals warn that they must learn from Reagan and improve their public relations skills. One goal is to place more emphasis on image instead of relying entirely on abstract ideas or programs to impress voters. [1]

Democrats are portrayed as split, adrift, and leaderless, and there has been much talk of "the way back." Republicans have their own party divisions, ranging from righteous ultraconservative candidates to hopefuls more in the mainstream. Target audiences must include born-again Christians, emerging women's groups, ethnic blocs (where they exist), a growing middle class, a dissident blue-collar work force, and a new business elite.

In this maze the practitioner operates, but always within the constraints of sensible public relations, paying attention to research, planning thoroughly, communicating wisely, evaluating constantly. What may appear on the surface as true in politics can be deceptive. PR professionals are alert to the strength of the independent voter. They know that many programs labeled liberal also have widespread support, and they are conscious that a "mandate" for one candidate may be more of a rejection of his/or her opponent than an embracing of the winner's total philosophy.

Government Bodies

There are two ways to view government bodies—as an insider wishing to influence the citizenry, or as a citizen trying to gain the attention of government. Both approaches require and employ PR expertise. Incumbents and their public relations consultants are leaders and communicators, or they should be. The work of both requires honesty, creativity, and patience. And their successes and failures are generally public knowledge.

Government at all levels needs to let its constituents know what it is doing. A new agency needs to be introduced; a new tax measure must be explained; support must be rallied for an administrative program; news about benefits or dangers must be communicated. With its sprawling organizational system and vast clientele, government has a bigger job than any conglomerate. And it must perform this job under the watchful and critical eyes of both peers and taxpayers.

The term *public relations* is rarely used in government circles. Instead, we see titles like information specialist, public affairs officer, public information officer, communications chief, and other euphemisms. Congress, which controls expenditures for a federal "publicity" effort, is suspicious of PR, and the public sector seems reluctant to use tax dollars to support functions labeled as public relations.

Despite such roadblocks, the number of people engaged in government public relations (regardless of title) has been escalating for years. Hundreds of millions of dollars are spent by the federal government to communicate its programs, and even state expenditures for public relations may run into the millions. The Department of Agriculture alone has more than 3,000 agents whose roles are primarily communication and PR.

Government is conducted, of course, at various levels, and the smaller subdivisions—such as a local weed-control board—may not have funds or personnel to mount a PR campaign. They are subject to whatever understanding they can generate through periodic and gratuitous media coverage and, perhaps, occasional publications, speeches, and open meetings. As the size of the government unit grows, so does the responsibility, and so does the likelihood of professional help. The mayor may have an administrative assistant whose primary function is public relations, and the county board or corps of engineers or welfare agency could have a communications specialist. Some of these posts are civil-service jobs; others share the characteristics of civilian employment. All of them are likely to be subject to certain regulations regarding budget, conduct, and image. Government practitioners are apt to be more wary, since they operate under the constant public challenge to their very existence. People are less likely to applaud the need for PR in government, despite the obvious magnitude of the task and the certain self-interest involved.

The roles of the PR person in government and his or her counterpart in industry are similar in skills but different in environment.

The government practitioner serves as counsel (although usually with less authority than the PR person in business), represents his or her employer at public functions, drafts speeches, writes news releases and brochures, conducts meetings, arranges press briefings, plans tours for constituents, answers correspondence, writes and produces films and slide shows (a major government tool), acts as a liaison between government agencies, and performs other duties ranging from advertising to editing.

The difficulties of practicing public relations under government auspices are many. To cite a few:

1. Citizens resent the use of tax dollars for PR.
2. Vested interests complain about any publicity that runs counter to their desires.
3. The media stress the public's "right to know," whereas many government officials seek to hold back certain actions from public scrutiny.
4. The image of the government employee is low, causing problems in morale and recruiting.
5. There are insufficient means for securing citizen input and involvement.
6. Agencies of government compete with each other for funding and personnel.
7. Clearance checks are required for much material.
8. The structure of government inhibits the collection and approval of information.

9. There is considerable political infighting, which affects programs.
10. There is insufficient research supporting many government communications.

Because of these and other difficulties, the practitioner in government circles is more likely to keep a low profile, is less likely to experiment, and is careful not to make too many waves.

Communicating Government

The practitioner could have a limited role in political public relations. Perhaps he or she is producing pamphlets for an agricultural department on crop rotation or approved insecticides. Or handling hometown releases and photography for visitors to a senator's office. Or engaging in research prior to launching a new directive.

Increasingly, however, the practitioner is becoming involved in high-level consultation and policymaking. Effective press secretaries, many of whom come out of media backgrounds, are credited with enhancing the image and, consequently, the power of certain legislators. Their staffs, working with constituents or through the media, seek to influence not only the reelection process but also the course of specific legislation.

President Reagan used a variety of methods to gain support for his tax-reform package, including personal appearances, lengthy published reports, congressional pressure, direct-mail appeals, and even judicious leaks. When a senator endorses one side in a controversial issue, he or she makes certain the citizens in his or her state are given the reasons for this behavior. This may mean news releases, news conferences, some carefully selected local platforms, a shoring up of political alliances, and other tactics organized and structured by the public relations staff.

Elected officials, if they are smart, don't leave the PR efforts until some day of reckoning; they are constantly active. Their PR staffs may be involved in finding jobs or information, serving as guides, making requested contacts. Some Washington offices get well over 10,000 letters a week, many from voters who want help or favors. Answering these is a staff function, and the problems range anywhere from farm closures to Medicare benefits. Congressional representatives may be asked to speed a reunion with an overseas bride, garnishee a check of a philandering serviceman, check into the loss of a Social Security payment, or vote against a certain bill. Congressional aides may supply photographs of names on the Vietnam Memorial, forward pamphlets on gardening, suggest restaurants and hotels in the nation's capital, or manage a hot line in their offices to field complaints and suggestions. Some legislators make it a practice to call constituents periodically, just to chat, and they circulate questionnaires to get voter input.

Although most of this communication is appreciated, the government always has to be careful about circulating information. The action may be regarded by recipients as hype. That's why the character and frequency of such communication must be professionally handled. Politicians want to keep their names before the public, but not in a way that suggests lavishing money on self-aggrandizement. Agencies, too, have to choose audiences carefully and update them periodically, but without an overt display of presumed expense. One of the targets of Reagan administration cutbacks, for example, was the government-publication budget. Subordinates were advised to weed out materials that served very little purpose. The Environmental Protection Agency, acting on that dictum, warehoused more than 3 million copies of 200 brochures. The Office of Management and Budget claimed that the moratorium on films, tapes, and printed materials saved the government over $100 million in just one year.

The danger here is that the story may not be told. Critics—especially those within the media—accused the Reagan administration of stonewalling on information, except where release served its purpose. Leaks, they charged, were used as much as or more than scheduled news conferences. In particular, reporters complained about bureaucratic secrecy, lack of access to certain agencies, and the overclassification of government documents. Some members of Congress sided with the media, agreeing that restrictions on coverage of the Grenada invasion and hostage negotiations were unnecessary.

Although admitting that President Reagan possessed a style that adapted well to public communication, reporters groused that he held far fewer news conferences than his predecessors and that the conferences he did hold were too controlled, too choreographed. Still, the president somehow managed to bypass this criticism, taking his case directly to the public and creating more confidence in the office and in the future of the country. Part of this was accomplished by bold acts—such as the forcing down of the Egyptian plane carrying hijackers who killed an American—and an even greater part was the result of Ronald Reagan's ability to reach the mind of the average citizen.

The success of various individuals and departments under Reagan varied. Problems in Labor, Interior, Agriculture, and the Environmental Protection Agency, among others, were largely due to actions or comments of the department supervisors, demonstrating that, in government, it's virtually impossible to present a positive image across the entire breadth of an administration.

Recent American presidents have had varied success with their public relations programs. Kennedy was relaxed and effective and was able to present an urbane, charismatic image. Lyndon Johnson didn't do nearly as well, even though he spent considerable time on public relations. Johnson often carried public-opinion polls around with him for ready reference or display. Richard Nixon's public relations had peaks and valleys, ending in disaster. Gerald Ford did quite well but was never able to completely alter the questioning attitude about his capability for the job. Carter suffered vicariously, through his appointments and, perhaps, because of his low-key style. In a real sense, the PR problems of presidents differ very little from those in other areas of society.

What does differ is the extent and amount of criticism of the PR function in government, simply because it exists.

Columnists love to present totals in terms of expenditures or personnel handling federal public relations: Six and a half million dollars is spent by the Agriculture Department for PR; Transportation's budget for public relations is $1.5 million; and the Pentagon lists nearly 1,100 full-time practitioners and a commensurate budget. They single out specific posts, like an international visitors' office that mails periodically to a list of 30,000 foreign "bureaucrats," or specific publications, like pamphlets on mulch.

It's relatively easy to take shots at these largely defenseless targets, and some may deserve the barrage. However, others serve a real function. The brochure on mulch, for example, which costs 4 cents to produce, is sent to over three-quarters of a million Americans annually who request this information. Without the brochure, someone would have to take time to respond to these letters, and the cost would be far higher.

Even so, argue dissenters, having public relations in government is dangerous, because it's the responsibility of these practitioners to present their agencies in a favorable light, thereby making it more difficult to trim budgets and reduce programs. The Defense Department is often cited, with the contention that it is the role of its "apologists" to present reasons for larger and larger financial commitments to the military. This department, and other arms of government, insist PR is absolutely necessary in order for them to make a case for their relative value in the face of so much opposition.

WORKING IN POLITICS

Even though some government PR positions may not offer the latitude (or the salaries) of their civilian counterparts, they can evoke a pleasure of their own. The ability to influence public policy is one agreeable challenge, as is the opportunity to affect an extremely broad constituency. Some government PR efforts are pressure-packed, like the presidential press secretary's responsibility; others may be unnaturally calm, like the writing and production of certain pamphlets.

The important thing to remember in this field is that the overall impression must be one of efficiency, economy, openness, and genuine public concern. These factors can be employed in two ways:

1. Explanation to the public of vital information
2. Intervention by the government in matters affecting consumer interests

An aide to a congressman, for example, would serve as a conduit for constituent opinion to his or her employer while conveying to these constituents the positive image of the congressman's activities. The aide's duties would entail speechwriting, news releases, media contacts, and correspondence, as well as the arranging of meetings, handling of voter queries and complaints, scheduling of Washington visits for hometown voters, and such other resonsibilities as periodic campaign chores prior to the upcoming elections.

In a department concerned with health or welfare, a person with a PR title might spend time traveling, speaking, inspecting local units, and cementing local ties. Or the PR person might have lobbying duties on Capitol Hill or be charged with disseminating news releases or publications or the creation of visual aids. Because this department has more than its share of visitors, escort service could occupy the PR person full time, as could circulation of information on grants and subsidies.

At the local level, mayoral assistants could find themselves much more valuable. This assistant could represent the mayor at public functions, assist with speeches, organize press conferences, meet with small groups, advise the mayor on sensitive matters, collect public-opinion samples on policy, and perhaps even manage city programs relating to such things as sports or entertainment.

In short, what the PR person in government tries to do is be responsive to public demands and needs while projecting a favorable image of individuals or programs, and while rendering more lucid the myriad details of governing.

COMMUNICATING IN D.C.

Washington is a major media center—second only to New York—with more than 1,000 newspaper representatives, half that number of radio and television reps, and nearly 1,000 magazine representatives and photographers.

A third of Washington's million-plus population work for the government, and most of the remainder are there because of the government. Despite periodic resolutions to cut back on employees and agencies, the numbers continue to increase in both categories. This makes contact more and more difficult. Add to this the proliferation of paperwork, which causes business to spend "an estimated 130 million person-hours filling out more than 5,000 different forms," according to former Secretary of the Treasury William Simon.

Among the federal workers are at least 20,000 people whose responsibilities are in the PR area, and who are employed by agencies, organizations, or elected officials. Often, initial contact may be made with them.

Experts say that local media have more influence on Congress than national media have—a point practitioners should remember. And along with these local stories and editorials, calls and letters from constituents rank as most influential, followed by national media, official government publications (including the *Congressional Record*), and congressmen's own staff research.

When business, through its executives and its public relations personnel, must communicate with Washington and weave its way through the bureaucracy, the techniques used differ very little from good PR practice anywhere. The presentation is expected to be thorough and professional.

Strong, factual data, delivered in a timely fashion and backed by logical and analytical arguments, should be the basis of any appeal to government agencies. A little implied pressure doesn't hurt either, as long as it is not couched as an overt threat.

PR people find most government officials to be reasonable men and women who will listen to thoughtful reasoning. They should be approached that way, and not with hostility or suspicion. This is true whether you are dealing with Congress, a state legislature, or a county board.

Some tips provided by those who deal daily with government bodies include these points:

- Be honest, factual, concise, and comprehensive in your presentation.
- Use the language of the layperson.
- Know your target audience and understand that arm of government.
- Stay in touch on a regular basis; don't contact your representative only when there is a problem.
- Be friendly, reasonable, cooperative, thoughtful, and realistic.
- Allow ample time to set up meetings, and have them at the convenience of the representative.
- Work closely with the media to get your point of view to the public.
- Read, talk, listen, so you can be attuned to trends and changes.
- Keep your own clients or management informed, and counsel them whenever the situation demands it.
- Give credit to legislators who have been helpful.
- Employ professionals when the situation warrants it.

Obviously, the practitioner should be conversant with the principal sources and documents that are germane to his or her mission. This list includes the *Congressional Record, Congressional Quarterly*, Library of Congress, National Archives, U.S. Government Printing Office, the *United States Government Manual, Congressional Directory, Public Information Guide, Directory of Information Resources in the United States, Statistical Abstract of the United States*, the *Federal Register*, various other government publications, and the Federal Information Centers located in 36 major American cities.

Besides these resources, there are many valuable publications, and certain magazines—like the *Public Relations Journal* and the *Washington Journalism Review*—include articles and guides to government relations. The *WJR Directory of Selected News Sources* (August 1985) gives, for example, phone numbers for special-interest groups and press offices, along with a detailed listing of news sources, from aerospace to telecommunications.

For those equipped to search databases electronically, much of the desired information can be quickly punched up, using Nexis, Lexis, PR Newswire, Legi-Slate, Cendata, and other services.

Just as the legislators have to be careful in their expenditures for communication, so do those trying to influence government. The money may be committed, but it shouldn't *look* like an onslaught of dollars. Defense Department contractors, who reportedly spent $140 million to convince federal decision makers to use their firms, were severely criticized by Congress, and legislation was filed to prevent such PR expenses from being used as tax deductions.

Another caution. While wooing legislative officials at all levels, the practitioner can't ignore the growing power of citizen groups that have turned some of their attention from government to the private sector. Even though their mandate may be self-imposed, such groups have to be reckoned with as a political force, and public affairs specialists have designed programs to meet this new challenge.

Whether working *for* the government or appealing *to* the government, such public relations chores are sensitive and, frequently, subtle. Much of the news Americans get out of Washington, for example, comes as the direct result of news releases from congressional PR people. Three-fourths of this country's newspapers have no Washington correspondents of their own, so they simply accept the "canned" releases from the nation's capital.

At this point, of course, the ethics and professionalism of the PR person dispensing such news must come into play. If he or she performs at a high level, the public is being served admirably; if not, then more fuel is added to the controversy about the public relations influence in governmental affairs.

The Press Secretary

The epitome of the PR challenge is found in the post of presidential or Congressional press secretary. This person is under constant pressure, since even the smallest activity of the boss may make news or cause controversy. Perhaps more than in any other communication situation, the media expect candor—and they don't always get it.

During President Richard Nixon's regime, constant complaints were made about deceptions practiced on the media, ranging from lies and half-truths to evasions and "no comment" replies, all from press secretaries. No presidential aide is free from such criticism, but some fare better than others. Concerning the Reagan administration, a columnist wrote:

> Every president has a lot of PR machinery, but what has given this one particular strength as a media force is the skill with which he projects himself, not as a head of government but as a neighborly guy who doesn't like government any more than you do.[2]

The way in which any president "projects himself" is attributable in part to his press secretary. The two must work closely together, must virtually think alike. The press secretary job, especially since the advent of television, is a highly visible post.

> National exposure is the path to power in this country, and that fact alone has enhanced the role of press secretary in public life. No matter that he cannot say anything unless the president or his key advisors want him to say it. No matter that he enjoys this instant celebrity status totally at the whim of the man who selected him in the first place, the president. The title is enough to confer immense power on a man.[3]

A quick check of some names validates that contention. James Haggerty, Pierre Salinger, Bill Moyers, Ron Ziegler, Ron Nessen, Jody Powell, and Larry Speakes became familiar figures by virtue of this post. It's the only White House office readily available to the media, and the pipeline to the public for the president's ideas and programs. It can be a touchy responsibility, for, although the press secretary must first be loyal to the president, he must also be conscious of the needs and rights of a free press. George Reedy, press secretary to Lyndon Johnson, referred to his job as a "transmission belt" of presidential ideas, and also stressed that the press secretary should be the primary advisor to the president on media matters, since other advisors are often isolated from this segment of society.

Former Carter press secretary Jody Powell revealed some of his frustrations in *The Other Side of the Story* (William Morrow & Co., Inc., 1984), castigating some reporters for their poor research or lack of objectivity and suggesting that the same sort of scrutiny that attends political figures should also be applied to media stars. Much of the problem, Powell asserts, results from the pressure "to be interesting," which leads to exaggeration and distortion instead of restraint and research.

PRESIDENTIAL PROBLEMS

Despite the unusually smooth manner in which President Ronald Reagan uses the media, especially television, there are many negative factors that a press secretary must deal with. Comments made when the president thought he was off the air, misstatements about policy issues, moments of a rare irritation—these cause concern and require explanation. There have been the hostage confrontations; the Iranian arms deal; queries about irregularities in the backgrounds of administration team members; the fallout from remarks made by advisors, like Meese and Watt; and even criticism surrounding the purchase of expensive china by the First Lady. Each provides its own challenge.

The list of problems is varied.

In 1980, President Reagan and his press secretary, James Brady, were shot. The George Washington University Medical Center became a virtual command post for two weeks, serving hundreds of reporters and federal officials with constant updates and bulletins and features.

Less frenzied but also a media event was the 1985 scare over the tumor in the president's colon. Spokesman Larry Speakes was kept busy responding to questions about the president's fitness to return to the job, and Republication politicians wondered what this would mean in the 1986 congressional races and to the fortunes of George Bush in 1988.

Far less traumatic but an even better example of a PR problem was the flak over Reagan's visit to a Nazi graveyard in Bitburg, Germany, in the spring of 1985. World War II veterans and American Jews protested the plan as soon as it was revealed, but the president refused to alter his schedule. Even the American Legion, long a supporter of Reagan, was angered by the Bitburg episode.

Michael Deaver, who left the White House soon after this incident to start his own PR firm, took a lot of the heat. When it was revealed that Deaver's advance crew spent time in Germany purchasing personal BMWs, the suggestion was made that they ignored their more important screening duties. Art Buchwald and Gary Trudeau both lampooned Deaver and associates, and members of Congress begged the president to reconsider.

Experts theorize that, had Reagan changed his itinerary early, all criticism would have ceased. The president decided to make the best of the blunder, however, and somberly toured both Bitburg and the concentration-camp site at Bergen-Belsen. At Bitburg the president said, "Some old wounds have been reopened, and I regret this very much, because this should be a time of healing," and at Bergen-Belsen, he closed his remarks with an echo of the Jewish cry, "Never again."

As aides predicted, Ronald Reagan weathered this error, no great thanks to the help of his staff, but largely because of his own popularity and the failure of the opposition to cast him in the image of a callous, insensitive leader.

All these incidents demonstrate that, in political public relations, little is certain. Circumstances and human failings interrupt the most carefully laid plans.

The presidential press secretary must always be conscious of the fact that the chief executive is the most powerful person in the world, even with the limitations of office. Every word and every action has meaning. Each president brings a different style and personalty, from the shy, cerebral conduct of Jimmy Carter to the more open and engaging behavior of Reagan and Kennedy. Each, therefore, presents a different challenge to the press secretary, who must also work to see that the total administration speaks with "one voice," as Reagan adherents claim theirs does.

Press secretaries may not be the only ones involved in public relations. Larry Speakes may appear at the podium with Reagan commentary, but others, like Michael Deaver and Stu Spencer, have had their own effect. Deaver was praised and blamed for his "manipulation of the media," accomplished by planting stories over lunch with reporters, carefully staging events to get maximum coverage, minimizing bad news with simultaneous release of good news, and even ensuring most favorable placement of the president during picture sessions. Deaver is also credited with changing the image of the First Lady from that of a cold, doting wife with no concept of cost control to a person who could laugh at herself, perform, and also dedicate time to helping handicapped children and fighting drug abuse. Spencer, a professional campaign manager who spent over 20 years advising Reagan, was one of those reponsible for creating the "citizen politician" image of the president.

Reporters on Capitol Hill have their favorites among the press secretaries, usually based on their availability and their knowledge of media needs. Howard Baker's press secretary, Tom Griscom, was respected by Washington reporters, who measure others by Griscom's standards. They cited Griscom's candor, accessibility, fairness, and knowledge. Qualities not admired are evasiveness and attempts to color or control the news. A senior fellow at the Brooking Institution insists that his research shows press secretaries *can't* control the news; they're too busy doing other things. Stephen Hess wrote:

> The hypothetical time sheet of the press officers I observed might have the following allocation: Responding to reporters' inquiries, 50%; keeping informed and working on agency business, 25%; and initiating materials and events, 25%. . . . I observed no press officer, outside of the White House, who spent most of his time staging events or initiating material even as innocuous as handouts.[4]

THE PROFESSIONAL LOBBYIST

The term *lobbying* usually has negative connotations, but for good or evil, lobbying is a fact of life in American politics. It takes its name from the practice of cornering legislators in the congressional lobbies and subjecting them to arguments, pleas, even bribes. It's not an overstatement to contend that government is able to function largely through the input of lobbyists. After all, the best congressmen and congresswomen—the most brilliant, hard-working, speed-reading, super-efficient overachievers—will be completely familiar with only a fraction of the legislation on which they may vote. Their support is influenced by the bill's sponsors, party loyalties, their own inclinations, constituents' pressures, and, to a considerable degree, lobbying.

It is no sin to listen to lobbyists. Much data can be garnered this way. The politicians should, however, listen to both sides of a controversial issue.

Today's lobbyists are different. Many are former incumbents, some lawyers, some business leaders, some public relations people. Nearly everyone concedes that public relations training and attitudes are beneficial. The methods are different, too. Smoke-filled rooms still exist, but they are few. So are gifts and favors beyond what the law allows. The most powerful weapon the modern lobbyist wields is the ability to gather and summarize data. The role is that of an educated advocate, a teacher, rather than a sinister manipulator.

In Washington, D.C., there are more than 7,000 registered lobbyists, and probably an equal number of unregistered lobbyists. Their expenses are estimated to be over $1 billion annually. Individual states have their own registered lobbyists, who number several hundred even in the least-populated states. Nationally, lobbyists represent postal workers, milk interests, gun owners, higher education, banking, insurance, oil, labor unions, and thousands of other specialties, including conservative and liberal politics. At the state level you find people lobbying for elementary and secondary schools, utilities, disarmament, health, and dozens of other interests. Some lobbyists act on their own and may represent several clients; others could be members of firms that employ 100 or more. They not only stage their own events, they also buy myriad tickets to other events, many of them fund raisers. They could be arguing against the elimination of wine and beer advertising or for the imposition of tariffs, against the enacting of a tax-reform package or for more energy decontrol.

Lobbying isn't confined to American interests. Foreign governments spend billions in attempts to influence federal actions and public opinion. Japan normally leads in expenses, but countries like Ireland, Indonesia, and Korea also spend millions annually. Many of these dollars go to consultants who are supposed to help foreign companies and governments pick their way through the D.C. maze. They could be representing Australian meat exporters, Central American arms requests, or Saudi Arabian petrochemical interests. Familiar names like James Symington, Frank Mankiewicz, and William Colby pop up in this context.

Whatever the specific job, the lobbyist lives on reputation and credit. He or she is careful not to use up this credit, which is why many supply details but back away from asking for a direct commitment.

Lobbyists are also advised not to hold grudges, not to count scores of who voted favorably and who did not, and not to take any credit for success but accord this to the elected officials.

Lobbying should occupy the professional year-round. There are fences to be mended, friends to make, positions to be researched, members to be pacified, favors to be returned.

The professional lobbyist is well regulated. Most states have fairly elaborate registration and reporting procedures, and even rules about when and where the lobbyist may visit legislators. The amateur lobbyist—and this may often define the PR person—should be aware of such limitations and should be as vigilant about the regulations as the pro.

THE PROFESSIONALS

As with any occupation, there are inevitably a few firms or individuals whose reputations as lobbyists rise above the crowd.

A former assistant secretary of commerce under Jimmy Carter, Jerry Jasinowski became chief lobbyist for the National Association of Manufacturers. As the son of two former members of Congress, Thomas Boggs of Patton, Boggs & Blow, a lobbying law firm, knew his way around Washington. Anne Wexler and Nancy Reynolds, chairman and president of Wexler Reynolds Harrison & Schule, are two of the growing number of successful female lobbyists. Reynolds is a close friend of the Reagans; Wexler was senior political advisor to Geraldine Ferraro in 1984. Gerald Lowrie (American Bankers Association) and Ray Denison (AFL-CIO) are among the busiest lobbyists in the nation's capital. Burson-Marsteller continually makes news by signing on people like Sheila Tate, formerly Nancy Reagan's press secretary, and Patrick Griffin, once secretary for the minority in the Senate.

The best known of the political lobbyists is undoubtedly Robert Gray, who heads the company that bears his name. A former campaign advisor to Ronald Reagan and former Hill and Knowlton exec, Gray operates his agency, composed of nearly 200 consultants and support staff, in a renovated electrical plant in Georgetown appropriately dubbed the Power House. He confesses he hires people on the basis of whom they know and cultivates a wide variety of aquaintances, from CIA director William Casey to members of the Cabinet. After only two years of existence, Gray & Company billed over $11 million in 1983. Fees range from $350 an hour to retain Gray himself to $40 an hour for secretarial assistance.

Stressing the communications and public relations aspects of lobbying, Gray & Company handles well over 100 clients, including Estée Lauder, the International Brotherhood of Teamsters, Mutual of Omaha, Stroh Brewery, Warner Communications, Western Union, the National Broadcasting Company, Motorola, the Korean and Canadian embassies, and dozens of other organizations, from tobacco to trucking. Gray made a case for increasing aid to Turkey, helped a Saudi Arabian prince publicize a campaign to feed hungry children, and took on the task of improving Haiti's image.

Besides relying on direct contact with legislators, Gray's staffers may also visit the representative's district and orchestrate a flood of mail on an issue. They do their homework, maintain their contacts, keep the pressure on. All this is accomplished by using the most sophisticated research methods available and by applying both sales and PR techniques.

The greatest asset a firm like Gray & Company offers is "access," the ability to reach the right person with the right message in the shortest period of time. Even with this capability, Gray, like any other practitioner, cannot promise success every time. He may not be able to deliver on a defense-contract proposal and can't even guarantee that his friend and former boss, Ronald Reagan, will appear at your annual convention.

Critics complain that firms like Gray & Company are merely peddling their influence and their connections, but Robert Gray insists they are only utilizing their communications skills to bring about a desired result for a client.

Said Gray in an article in *Communication World* (February 1984):

> The government official is part of an audience, like any other—requiring very specific access efforts. The artful marshaling of facts into opinion is the essence of the twin discipline of government [relations] and public relations.

Gray, whose firm assumed industry leadership after only three years' existence, considers himself a businessman who happens to be in public relations, and he sees lobbying as merely part of that job.

"If our professional obligation is to deliver information pertinent to our clients' interests to all concerned parties, we cannot avoid lobbying," he told the *Communication World* author.

Periodically, there is talk of placing even stricter limits on lobbying. Some states have initiated bills requiring detailed listing of expenses spent on lobbying, sometimes for expenses as low as $250. At the federal level, proposals have been made for broader disclosure statements. Lobbyists find themselves in the unusual position of lobbying against threats to their livelihood, or, at least, to their method of doing business.

This pressure emphasizes the requirement of PR skills.

> . . . legislative lobbying is an involvement with public opinion. Public opinion is reflected in the actions of legislators at national, state, county and township levels, actions that can affect the way a company does business. Therefore, legislative lobbying becomes, directly or indirectly, wanted or unwanted, a branch of the public relations function. . . . Properly handled and approached sensibly with clear-cut objectives in mind, lobbying will remain the brainchild of public relations. Neglected, lobbying becomes the stepchild of public relations and ineffective.[5]

The essential quality that a lobbyist should have is the ability to communicate. Along with this virtue should go resourcefulness, honesty, accuracy, and availability. Lobbyists should know the association, individual, or company they represent; they should know where all essential information is available; they should know the law; and they should know their contacts.

Writing in *Association Management*, S. John Insalta responds to the question about what you do with information after you have acquired it. He suggests that all cataloging systems seem to have four steps to them:

1. *Logging:* Keeping records of bills and their progress.
2. *Analyzing:* Scrutinizing each bill, comparing it with current legislation, anticipating its effect, looking for dangerous clauses, watching for language variations.
3. *Coding:* Marking bills in terms of their importance and whether or not they need to be reported to your membership or employer. A brief synopsis also helps.
4. *Retention:* A system for storing bills conveniently, with easy retrieval for current legislation.[6]

PACs, PRESSURE GROUPS, AND POWER

Closely associated with some lobbying efforts are the activities of Political Action Committees, which contributed 44 percent of the money raised by House candidates in 1984 and 23 percent of the money raised by Senate hopefuls. Overall, contributions totaled well over $100 million, causing some observers to fret about the increasing chance of legislative influence by special interests.

At the top of the list of corporate PAC spenders are organizations representing the oil and aircraft industries, manufacturers of automobiles, cigarettes, and computers, and a number of financial institutions. But the expenditures of these companies are often dwarfed by those of associations representing realtors, medicine, education, and labor. The American Medical Association disbursed over $2 million, hoping to find some support in its efforts to curtail Reagan cuts in health-care programs. Another PAC representing municipal employees, motivated by the same opposition to administration deletions, spent over $1 million in 1984. Contributions cut across political lines, focusing on officials with key committee posts or a strong chance of reelection or a commitment to a specific cause.

Despite periodic listings of those who receive PAC money, and despite increasing citizen pressure to limit or eliminate such funds, PAC activities are difficult to curtail. Incumbents who benefit from these gifts are reluctant to cut off a funding source at a time when campaign expenses are escalating. A number of Sunshine Acts do focus attention on sources of campaign funding, but even so, money, legal and illegal, manages to find its way into candidates' coffers. Then, too, an increasing number of charges are being leveled against candidates for improper use of donated funds. Some recipients have used the money to purchase cars, pay their house and utility bills, buy clothes, and even secure football tickets.

Although laws may change, the current limits on contributions to federal candidates and committees specify the following:

- The limit on annual gifts by an individual to federal candidates and committees is $25,000.
- A person may contribute up to $1,000 per candidate (or cause) per election (primary, runoff, or general).
- Up to $20,000 a year may be contributed to a national party, and up to $5,000 to a state party or PAC.
- Expenses for items like parties, tickets, and other items may count against the $1,000 limit. Even volunteer hours can be charged if they occur during the volunteer's regular working day.
- Small, unincorporated businesses may also contribute up to $1,000 in money or services for a candidate or committee.
- Corporations as such cannot make direct contributions to campaigns, but individual members of the corporation may give to PACs within the limits already specified.

If a corporation or organization does form a PAC, this new entity must be registered immediately with the Federal Election Commission, and it should have a set of bylaws, executive support, specific goals and restrictions, and a simplified way to reach potential donors.

In the future, PACs will continue to receive the same sort of negative treatment accorded them by candidate Gary Hart in 1984, but they will have as many supporters as detractors. Even the media, usually in a watchdog role, have their own PACs. Some 31 PACs, primarily broadcasting or cable TV companies, spent over $1.5 million on candidates and causes in 1984.

Pressure Groups

Circumstances occasionally create what some people have called "momentary majorities," pressure groups that arise around a specific issue or belief, usually a social concern. These coalitions may be composed of a number of single-issue groups that focus on abortion, the environment, tax legislation, equality for women, or other subjects. They may be short-lived or possess considerable staying power. Sometimes they are formally organized into a lobby; at other times, the group is loose-knit but may be able to mount an effective letter-writing campaign or even a mass demonstration.

Numbers aren't always important. As stated in Chapter 2, a very small pressure group can wield considerable influence. Part of this success can be attributed to learning how to deal with the media, how to communicate ideas or grievances. Three or four people may be able to stall a freeway or get a traffic light erected or close down an offending theatre.

Figure 14-2 Many PR persons are engaged in citizens' groups to benefit their communities. Communication skills are always welcome.

The public relations practitioner may be involved with these groups as either a leader-participant or a defendant. The practitioner may be joining them or combatting them. Either course requires a lawyerlike approach to the responsibility. As in other aspects of public relations, a solid background in the issues is essential. You will find that the person who can logically and skillfully display the facts has a definite advantage.

Power

As mentioned earlier in this text, the most effective way to communicate is via the established power structures. You want to persuade those who are able to bring about solutions. This is not always easy and not always pleasant, but it is the road to success.

Power structures may not be easy to identify, even when their effect is evident. Political leaders can be in the grip of their supporters or at the mercy of stronger, larger groups of legislators. Business leaders may be superficially impressive but personally powerless. Less-visible business leaders may exert considerable influence; so might a spouse or an associate. On occasion, a professional person or an educator or a vocal housewife can be a power source. So can groups with permanent status (like the Elks or American Legion or League of Women Voters) or with temporary status (like "Save our Children" or a city's centennial committee).

Power is also volatile. Yesterday's heroes may be discarded and new faces take over. People like Clint Eastwood, Tina Turner, Jane Fonda, Eddie Murphy, and Mother Theresa may share the spotlight temporarily with Ronald Reagan and Pope John Paul II. Dan Rather and Jerry Falwell may compete for attention with Ralph Nader and Edward Kennedy. Lee Iacocca of Chrysler headed a 1985 list of those most influential in the private sector. The list included people such as Henry Kissinger, who manages to remain highly visible, and newcomer Peter Ueberroth, whose Olympics television exposure made him an instant celebrity. Publications vie in predicting the next generation of superstars—Diane Sawyer, for example, or Steven Jobs of Apple, or Mayor Henry Cisneros of San Antonio. Some of these names may fade, and others will flourish.

Government is normally perceived as having the most power, followed by big business, television, financial institutions, and lobbyists. Advertising earns some votes, along with other media, labor, the military, education, the professions, and organized religion. Many groups are much smaller and much more easily defined.

Isolate these power structures, discover how you can reach them with the most effective messages, get them working for you. If you can't enlist their active support, perhaps you can neutralize them. If you can do neither, your situation is virtually hopeless. Without *some* power structure behind you, you can't effect change. There are large communities where no one would think of pursuing any civic, business, or social aim without the blessing of the power structure.

Whether such a situation is good or bad is moot. It exists; it must be dealt with; and the PR person has all the tools to do the best job.

THE CANDIDATE, THE CAUSE, THE CAMPAIGN

Everyone should work in politics at one time or another, either as a candidate or as a volunteer. The office may not be important, but the experience will be. Among other things, it provides new respect for even the weakest officeholder. You begin to appreciate what it takes to attain those positions and to keep them. Moreover, you get an insight into what a delicate system democracy is and how unreasonable and fickle the electorate can be. The experience is more valuable than a semester in political science.

Oscar Ameringer called politics "the gentle art of getting votes from the poor and campaign funds from the rich, by promising to protect each from the other."

A bit cynical, perhaps, but a reminder that most Americans do not, at present, have a high regard for their own political system. They may revere it in the abstract but suspect it in the concrete.

This is a lesson to keep in mind when handling PR chores for political candidates or causes. The problem is not usually competition; it is ignorance, frustration, and apathy. Despite our advanced communication techniques, many voters go to the polls woefully uninformed about office seekers or legislation. Others, either confused or indifferent, rarely bother to vote at all.

Politics has other discouraging aspects: ignorance of the issues, general apathy (which is often more significant than any other factor), the increasing focus on single issues, the polarization of certain segments of America, the persistence of myths about the ways in which campaigns are won and lost (many of them two decades old), and the most discouraging conclusion of all—that incumbents and big spenders normally prevail.

In 1982 and again in 1984, less than 3 percent of the incumbent House candidates and merely a handful of incumbent senators lost. Exposure, free mail privileges, subsidized broadcasting facilities, free telephone service, free travel, low-cost printing, and a host of research and writing services (all funded by taxpayers) are available to the incumbent. The "ins" also have a 2-to-1 advantage in raising money, so it takes a horrendous blunder or a constituent uprising to unseat a person already established. Add to this the hundreds of thousands of dollars it takes to mount an effective federal campaign, and it's a marvel that anyone is willing to campaign against a veteran.

Because of the prominence of television as a political decision maker, those who do run had better be able to handle this medium. James Michener, in a *TV Guide* article, theorized that it would be almost impossible for a bald-headed man to be elected president, and others contend that Abraham Lincoln, our most highly respected chief executive, wouldn't make it to the top today because of his appearance and thin voice.

Political public relations has virtually become a science, with specialists who move from campaign to campaign. Unless the practitioner stays with the political scene, it becomes much more difficult to move into a campaign and then out again. Many advertising agencies that once handled many campaigns are pulling back because of this specialization, and because of the time campaigns take, and because of monetary risks. In the future, political PR work is certain to become even more specialized.

Relations with the Candidate

Despite the rash of books asserting that successful candidates are plastic creations of their PR masters, there is a limit to what public relations can accomplish. In the end, candidates generally win or lose on their own. The experts never really succeeded in stopping Richard Nixon's upper lip from sweating. They couldn't cure Lyndon B. Johnson of his TV-prompter addiction. Jimmy Carter's smile intruded on his most serious moments. Despite his youth and good looks, Gary Hart was unable to project charisma, largely because his style is not naturally demonstrative. Walter Mondale was never able to convince voters they should replace Ronald Reagan. Ghostwritten speeches still have to be delivered; media questions must be answered; personal encounters must be adroitly managed. What the candidate is or isn't often shines through, regardless of the advice, expertise, and makeup skills of others.

Perhaps Reagan defeated Mondale on the basis of performance, not personality, as Andrew Kohut, president of the Gallup Poll, insists, but the contrast in personalities didn't hurt. Many times it is more important than the message.

What Can the PR Person Accomplish?

Money isn't everything, true, but there must be a certain amount of it available if anything is to be accomplished. Even if you volunteer your services, you can't make an impression without some realistic expenditures. The PR person who accepts a client on a paying basis must also decide very early how much time he or she can afford to spend in terms of the proposed budget. If a candidate for sheriff allocates $2,500 for his race, you can only offer minimum services. A senate hopeful with a budget of $500,000 will demand more effort—and deserve it.

Practitioners should not take on as a client someone with whom they disagree completely and for whom they have no respect. To do so is to court disaster. Once an agreement has been made, however, the PR person, like the attorney, should represent the client as effectively as possible until a decision is reached. Only in cases of illegality, conflict of interest, or irreconcilable differences should the practitioner seek to sever the relationship.

Once the arrangement has been made, the PR person should get to know the candidate in depth—strengths, weaknesses, background, friends, enemies, issues the candidate feels strongly about.

Limiting issues is a sensible idea. Candidates should be informed on all key issues but should not really try to push more than three or four. If candidates attempt to be expert on every issue, they will only confuse the voter. What the PR person should be looking for are the candidate's ideas that have strong communication potential.

Senator Gary Hart's press secretary during the 1984 campaign was Kathy Bushkin, a young woman who earned the respect of the political media for her candor and efficiency. When Hart's campaign started, her job was to try to get as much coverage as possible; later, she had to try to put the lid on media intrusion. In a *Wall Street Journal* article (April 10, 1984), she compared managing a planeload of reporters to "taking a tour of 100 high-school students to Europe." Not only did she have to brief the senator and provide information to the media, she also had to track down lost luggage and find phones for reporters. She stressed honesty and prudence as key traits when working with the media.

These qualities are echoed by Francis O'Brien, who performed a similar function for the Ferraro campaign. O'Brien convinced the vice-presidential candidate to wait and release all the tax information on her husband at once rather than submit it piecemeal as it became available. The resultant press conference, plagued by delays and a faulty sound system, found Geraldine Ferraro facing the media alone, sans charts or family, a strategy suggested by O'Brien. The press secretary also advised her to set no limits on the conference but to let reports ask questions as long as they wanted to. The result, although not perfect, did establish Ms. Ferraro as a strong person who could handle the vice-presidential job.

Again, the candidate must have the tools, but the practitioner can hone them.

CAMPAIGN '84 AND BEYOND

Many political observers dubbed the 1984 presidential campaign "boring," but, from a PR standpoint, it had its moments. True, Reagan's nomination was a foregone conclusion, and most of the convention betting was also on Mondale. Except for the nomination of Geraldine Ferraro as the Democratic vice-president candidate, there were few surprises.

But some topics intrigued practitioners:

- After the initial reaction to the naming of Ms. Ferraro had abated, experts began to ask questions about how Mondale should treat his running mate. It was a touchy situation. He couldn't be patronizing, indifferent, or domineering. There would be no hugging or kissing. The media insisted on writing about items of little import—like how Ms. Ferraro would be addressed, should she win—and many of them jumped eagerly on the financial woes of the candidate's husband. The Democratic vice-presidential candidate proved herself a tough campaigner, able debater, and resilient person.
- Walter Mondale's endorsement by AFL-CIO, although welcome in terms of potential votes, also hampered the Democratic hopeful by lending credence to the contention that he was a pawn of special interests.
- By calling Gary Hart "a candidate of tinsel and public relations," Walter Mondale did little to win the hearts and votes of practitioners.
- Although Mondale was given an edge on at least one of the presidential debates, his triumphs did him little good and barely affected the relative ratings.
- A new term surfaced in this campaign—the notion of "spin," which is the twist adherents put on a story when talking to reporters. Both sides, for example, tried to put their spin on the television debates, demonstrating why their candidate had won. Since most people don't know who won until someone tells them, this tactic could be important.
- If the failure to appear more decisive in the debates didn't hurt Mr. Reagan, neither did the series of misstatements—like the joking comment about starting to bomb Russia in five minutes, made while testing a mike; or the evasive quip when asked if he felt that the Rev. Martin Luther

Figure 14-3 For centuries the political cartoon has been a part of the political process in America.
Courtesy: Tom Flannery, *The Baltimore Sun*

King had ties to the communists ("Well, we'll know in about 35 years, won't we?"); or the reference to the rebels in Nicaragua as "freedom fighters." Walter Mondale was never able to make these items, or similar gaffes, serve as evidence that President Reagan was not a leader.

- Another term used in this campaign was "telectorate," to describe the millions of voters who would choose a president based on a TV image, much as they tune to their favorite talk show.

- Reagan strategists claim they varied very little from the game plan, and then only when responses to the Democrats were necessary. Mondale-Ferraro planners, however, seemed to be trying various approaches in the hope that something would catch on. The Republican team had a simpler job, working with an incumbent president who was able to use television well, and focusing on a single upbeat message.

- One of the spinoffs of a campaign that was not too exciting was that journalists complained their material had less than the usual readership, and they reportedly began to talk like coaches late in the campaign, telling themselves they'd have to wait until next time, until 1988.

Filing for Office

Filing presents an opportunity for news. If the office is important enough, the political consultant might opt for a news conference, scheduling it for a time when the widest audience can be reached. The accompanying news release should give details of the candidate's background, the candidate's reasons for running, and some of the things the candidate would hope to accomplish if elected. A good current photo should be included.

Some candidates, concerned because news conferences were becoming too common, devised other ways to reach the media. One person running for clerk of courts visited each news desk personally, carrying a news release and coffee and doughnuts, which he gave to the reporters, explaining that he didn't want to trouble them to come to another conference but didn't want them to miss out on the traditional coffee and doughnuts. It was different enough to be very effective.

Some Basics

The PR consultant shouldn't have to worry about or be involved in fund raising. All he or she should know is how much the campaign will have to spend and whether or not the person in charge of this activity is both capable and honest. It would also be to the consultant's advantage to know the current federal and state laws that apply to campaign fund raising and expenditures. In general, these may revolve around:

- Limitations placed on per-person gifts
- Reporting of funds and deadlines for these
- Strictures against corporate gifts
- Disclaimer procedures

Strict accounting procedures are essential. It is easy to lose track of funds and, in the heat of the contest, to overspend. The wise candidate lives within the established budget and doesn't commit funds until he or she has them in hand. The practitioner should be conscious of the many campaign expenses, ranging from media to travel and from headquarters costs to filing fees, which must be figured in the budget.

Organization can be another vital factor in winning. Putting together a group of people that can effectively garner support takes time. Again, this is not a job for the PR consultant, but rather for the candidate and the campaign manager. What they should be looking for are people who represent varied interests and geographical areas, people who will work hard and remain loyal. These people must be given something to do and not be merely listed on a roster. So it takes planning and thinking to match volunteers with needs.

Personal campaigning might become a concern of the PR consultant, particularly if he or she is part of the campaign strategy team. It is essential that the candidate be visible, but it is equally important that the most be made of his or her time. Can the candidate afford to attend a coffee reception where only six are present? Or take time to hand out leaflets in a supermarket? Should the candidate spend more effort on producing decent television spots and less on canvassing neighborhoods? These are the kinds of decisions the campaign staff must make. They want the voters to know the candidate is alive but don't want to exhaust him or her in proving this.

A good compromise might be to visit key areas where the election could be won or lost, and then work in brief visits to other areas wherever possible. It is true that the candidate feels better, psychologically, when busy, so even the poorly attended coffee may be all right on a slow day. And this coffee may also provide a platform for a news release with much wider effect.

THE POLITICAL PRESS

There have been many complaints about excessive media influence on politics. This criticism wasn't confined to Nixon and Agnew; it has issued from various sources, including the media themselves. On a national level, this could be true, although the alternatives to such occasional errors are worse than the problem. Few careers have been ruined by an overzealous press. Most disasters are brought upon the candidate by his or her own mistakes or misdemeanors.

One problem is the penchant of the press to make a contest out of every race. It's the old white-hat-versus-black-hat romance. Candidates get labeled as conservative or liberal when they may be neither. There is a great deal of stereotyping in the place of understanding. Issues are made simplistic, and viewpoints are capsulized into representative slogans. The complicated personality feels trapped in these easy identifications.

Perhaps the greatest problem in dealing with the political reporter is the limitation of time and space. Major policy statements may be cut to one paragraph or 30 seconds. There are issues that require an hour to define but must be conveyed in a brief news segment. Candidates may be phoned at night and, as the radio station bleeper pulses in their ears, are expected to respond briefly and instantaneously to the most diverse and intricate questions. There are queries that shouldn't be made and can't be answered. And yet, candidates feel that they dare not confess ignorance or refuse to respond. They let go instead with the more banal and abstruse replies, hoping they won't get into any trouble. Or they prepare a series of glib answers that provoke laughter but fail to reveal their true convictions.

The time-space frame is something the PR person must live with. There is no likelihood that this will change. The BBC may devote half its long newscast to a housing-development scandal or a candidate's platform, but our network news assumes that its audiences will not sit still for such extended coverage. It fills the 30 minutes with myriad news stories, leaving the longer treatments for documentaries, specials, or public broadcasting.

There are murmurs of dissatisfaction with Washington journalists who sometimes pool stories rather than doing the digging on their own, and who are seen to have an influence not always warranted by their circulation. These men and women can be caustic and unforgiving, as they were with Richard Nixon and as they've sometimes been with George Bush. It can be argued that the fault may more properly lie with the politician and not the media, but a little blame is to be shared by both sides. Sometimes the political figure deliberately lies, misleads, or distorts—or sometimes disappoints the media by not being what they assume he or she is. Another explanation for the problem, beyond that of personalities, is the failure of those in charge, including so-called public relations counselors, to do their jobs well.

These antagonisms and errors are not confined to national offices and national media; they can exist at every level. And at every level, solid public relations efforts can help establish credibility and confidence in a candidate, and can bring about smoother media relations.

Writing the political news release is not very different from writing any kind of release. All the points mentioned in Chapter 6 also apply here. The writer must be accurate, objective, and available; he or she plays no favorites and tells no lies.

A good rule to follow is to include something the media cannot ignore. Many political news releases are repetitive and unimaginative. Their authors may regard them as hard-hitting statements, but they produce only yawns in the city room. Original ideas or original ways of stating them make good copy. Strong positions on controversial issues also sell. A story can be made out of an important endorsement, a tie-in to a national issue, or even the schedule of the candidate's appearances. Acceptance of these stories depends partly on their merit and partly on the competition for space.

Some practitioners write many advance stories when things are quiet, and they later key these stories to the candidate's public appearances. This can be efficient and also enables the candidate to evince some variety.

It always looks better if the news release bears the address of the candidate's office rather than that of a public relations firm. The media know the stories are the work of a professional, but it is not good form to advertise this fact. Let the candidate serve as the spokesperson. The PR counselor should be virtually invisible.

Making the candidate available for TV and radio interviews, taping his or her comments, providing timely responses to current issues—these are also part of media relationships. The trick is to give service without getting in the way.

It is often tempting to candidates to make a direct attack on an opponent, particularly where they feel certain of their ground or when a devastating phrase pops into their minds. On these occasions, the consultant should exercise caution. And, if someone has to be quoted, try to give the attack to another member of the organization, sparing the candidate the need to look cruel and unfair. In most cases, it is best to forget about such tactics altogether.

The reverse of this situation may also involve PR expertise. Your candidate may be the target of abuse and you must respond. Remember you are a gentleman or a lady and don't get into a mud-slinging match. If you can, try to turn the jibe back on the originator.

Those who are involved in political public relations must also be aware of the guidelines for the media they serve—not only the general news-release guidelines, but also the special ones that cover political reporting.

Editors and news directors often devise rules to ensure equal treatment for candidates; to distinguish between newsworthy campaign stories and repetitious puffery; and to provide balance, accuracy (like the correct crowd estimates), and credibility (as with polls commissioned by suspect sources). Limits are also set by many media as to the amount of advertising that will be accepted, and even on the content, once the campaign draws to a close. The PR person needs to be familiar with every guideline.

Other Writing Assignments

Many other kinds of writing assignments could be tossed at the PR counselor. This depends, of course, on how much money is involved and how big a staff has been assembled. Speechwriting would be the most likely chore, and it can be a demanding one if the candidate is active. Correspondence is another routine that may take time, particularly correspondence of a sensitive nature, such as fund raising or media contacts. Brochures and printed materials could also be assigned, although the advertising agency is likely to have a larger role in this aspect. The political writer may also tackle public-service announcements, summaries of issues, and special-interest mailers.

One frustration inherent in such writing is the possibility of interference by volunteers, many of whom are totally unfamiliar with public relations techniques. Without creating enemies, the PR adviser should insist on some sort of autonomy, or, at least, limited review.

President Reagan employs half a dozen chief speechwriters, with most of them having logged time as reporters, editors, or television producers. In sessions with these writers, the president outlines his ideas, often suggests the theme, and also contributes a few pertinent anecdotes. The speechwriters confidently toss in catchy one-liners in the conviction that, in a formal presentation, Ronald Reagan will deliver expertly.

The president's style is friendly, almost confidential, and contrasts sharply with the oratorical fireworks of a Rev. Jesse Jackson or the ringing imagery of a Mario Cuomo. Each man requires a different kind of speech and, perhaps, a different kind of speechwriter.

Having a public relations sense is an excellent trait for a political speechwriter, since the memorable phrase may also provoke a negative reaction. Many candidates have later wished they could retract a sentence or two. Wise candidates have others check over the material, not with the idea of neutering it but with the aim of guarding against any unfortunate errors. A State of the Union address by a president may occupy months of writing and revisions and could go through several dozen hands.

POLLS

Polls were examined in Chapter 3, but it is well to recognize that politics can account for many surveys. Candidates want to know what kind of chances they have before they announce; they want to know how they are doing vis-à-vis the opposition; they want to test issues or identify weaknesses; they may even use survey input to help them write their campaign theme and literature.

Overall, national political polls have been remarkably accurate. Local and regional polls have enjoyed less-spectacular success, and some of these have been grossly in error. The unfortunate thing about an inaccurate poll is that it may instantly dry up support for the candidate assumed to be behind. If this occurs at a critical time, it may be too late to correct.

Candidates faced with commenting on an adverse poll have a tough job. Many use the old cliché, "It's the poll in November that counts," and others unearth a poll of their own that disagrees with the glum reading. The best response might be to acknowledge that the candidate is a bit behind but is working hard to overtake the opposition. In the long run, however, despite claims that trailing generates enthusiasm from workers, it is usually better to be ahead. That also generates enthusiasm from everyone, including the electorate.

Research and polls find their way into campaigns for other reasons than finding out who is winning or losing. There are the "A versus B" comparisons, of course, but polls also test the popularity or dangers of issues, probe for trends that could upset a candidate, and even collect opinion on the wording of key statements. Statistics come into play in many campaigns, with both sides taking the same figures and forging them into political ammunition. While President Reagan was pointing at the fact that more Americans were at work in 1984 than two years earlier, the Democrats were emphasizing that more than 8 million Americans were still unemployed. The president also utilized census statistics to combat the claim that his tax programs favored the wealthy.

On two scores, the media provoke polling controversy. One involves the penchant for prophecy, especially the practice of trying to be the first to project a winner. Although some of this has been curtailed, the predictions of winners and percentages remain television fixtures. Broadcasting and print also do their own polling and report their findings at key stages during a campaign.

The second critical aspect of polling and the media concerns their use of stories based on polls, a topic covered in Chapter 3. Cautions applied by the media could be summed up in the admonition to check all data, to balance them against other polls or against known information, and to stifle any temptation to overinterpret figures.

Despite the flaws and the fussing, two out of three American voters believe the polls.

CAMPAIGNING FOR CAUSES

In addition to handling personalities, the PR counselor might be called upon to promote legislation in a particular election. These causes are rarely easy.

The counselor is hired because passage appears difficult and help is required. More often than not, the cause will start behind in the polls and the PR campaign must turn public opinion around.

One of the difficulties is that many issues are clouded and complicated. If supporters could sit down over coffee with every constituent, they might be able to convince them of the proposition's logic. However, campaigns are tied to mass-communication methods and have to get the message across in the space and time allotted.

Research is the key again. A thorough job of analyzing the legislation, anticipating the opposition, and focusing on the points that will get across well to the average voter is the starting point. Then advisors must determine how they are going to package these persuasive messages. They may have to settle for themes that are less important but also less complicated than the central idea.

More and more issue campaigns are certain to arise as pressure groups mount and resources dwindle. Public relations help will be more in demand to help secure passage of school bonds, or hand-gun-control legislation, or funds to bolster public transporation, or to work for or against restrictive tax legislation.

MISCELLANEOUS POLITICAL CONSIDERATIONS

Handling political PR is a fast track and is not normally a good place to start in the profession. Things happen fast; a decision may make or break a campaign; the practitioner can become totally involved, with little time for other duties. Besides the obvious chores of media relations, speechwriting, and strategy planning, the PR person may have to shore up a weary candidate, respond quickly to an opponent's sally, or even be in charge of staging a major event, like a convention. However, politics is also a heady experience, and many practitioners thrive on the challenge.

LABOR UNIONS

Overall, labor unions have not fared well in public relations terms. For many years, messages were primarily internal, and few people outside the movement read union materials or listened to the unions' periodic broadcasts. Too often the stories that made news were negative stories. Part of this was attributable to labor's suspicion of public relations as solely a management tool; the unions' own PR staffs, if they had any, were likely to be composed of men who rose through the ranks rather than people selected for their training and expertise. Gains were accomplished through pressure, negotiations, and political maneuvering. Few PR programs were inititated except for those aimed at membership or at politicians.

Moreover, scandals and charges of gangsterism sapped union strength, and disparate views of members eroded party loyalties. Under the Reagan administration, union power slipped even further. Many businesses were taking stronger stands against unions, often refusing to budge from positions on salaries and fringe benefits, and firms that did not have unions were being counseled on how to avoid having their shops unionized. They were advised, for example, to pay more, honor job commitments, respect seniority, promote from within, and institute internal procedures for hearing grievances.

Some good results of these hard days have come about in unions' public relations as attempts to improve their image have led to the employment of more trained personnel, the institution of programs to win public support, and a conscious effort to establish a working person's point of view. Mass media are used more frequently, and the messages are less heavy-handed and more designed to influence the uncommitted.

But the process is slow. Much of the old rhetoric and many of the old tactics remain, and PR professionals who are trying to alter these approaches run into considerable opposition. Some unions have adapted more quickly than others. Some labor unions, for example, have discovered that there are other places where they can contribute their money besides politics. A few sponsor chairs at universities or underwrite courses. One midwestern union presented a fountain—paid for and built by a labor union—to a univeristy celebrating its centennial. The same union provides the impetus each year for a vast celebration surrounding Labor Day, involving music, parades, exhibits, balloon rides, and other events. Crowds total over 100,000.

In some ways, the PR person in the labor movement shares a role not unlike that of any association communicator. The magazine, news releases, and lobbying tasks are part of his responsibility. (In this instance, "his" is probably quite accurate, since there are few women engaged in labor PR.) Membership would also be a concern, as would the problem of getting union members to attend meetings. Special events—labor schools, family picnics, even sessions convoked for voting purposes—would involve the PR person or staff.

Union PR people may also serve as spokespersons for their members and will be especially active during strikes or negotiations. Recently, they have also been involved in campaigns to bring back former members who have left the union. In 1970, union members represented over 27 percent of all wage and salary workers; by 1985, that figure was less than 19 percent. To help swell the ranks once again, some unions have turned to the providing of financial services, like credit cards, insurance, and retirement programs. Organizers are also more active, and they will work with the practitioners, who should have input on strategy and on promotional campaigns.

ASSOCIATIONS

At the national level, various associations employ public relations staffs, both to enhance their image and to increase membership. If large enough, the associations may augment their in-house personnel with outside counsel.

This category includes groups whose size and purpose vary widely. Large organizations—such as the American Medical Association or the American Meat Institute—are generally headquartered in major cities and would probably have a branch office in Washington, D.C. Smaller national associations—the Association of Operating Room Nurses, for example—would headquarter in a somewhat smaller city and employ professional counsel to see to their public relations interests.

On a regional, state, and local level, associations also have PR programs, although of a more modest kind. A state teachers' association might locate a public relations office in the state capital and combine lobbying with the other duties. A regional office would seek a central locaiton.

Since the effectiveness of any organization depends to a considerable degree on its size, the recruiting of members is an important facet of the PR effort. Invariably there will be an internal magazine, sometimes a very elaborate printed piece. It may well be supported by advertising from members or suppliers. And a national (and perhaps regional) conference is probably part of the picture. The home office will attract members by appealing to their self-interest—the lobbying on their behalf, the chance to exchange ideas with people having similar occupations, and the opportunity to receive periodic materials relating to their specialties. Recruiting will be by mail, by phone, and sometimes in person. Local chapters would be expected to corral those in their community whose trade or profession makes them eligible. At the same time, they would be urging national membership on them.

Theoretically, members are united by a common bond of occupation or hobby or concern. Although these ties do exist, members also have other traits that divide them into camps—age, geography, religion, education, sex, and other uncommon denominators. Consequently the leadership can't count on a knee-jerk reflex to its pronouncements and policies. Members may have to be wooed and won just as much as outsiders.

Washington and New York are home to about a sixth of the nation's roughly 40,000 associations, and Chicago serves as headquarters for about 2 percent of the remainder. Membership in associations nearly matches this country's total population, and almost 400,000 people make up the staffs of these organizations, which have budgets approaching $10 billion. About half the associations have public relations programs, but that number is increasing. Public relations is also one of the areas most criticized by members; they feel it is inadequate.

> Association public relations is different from commercial public relations in several ways. The public relations practitioners must be able to work as comfortably with the volunteer members of an association as with the paid full-time staffers. Sensitivity and discretion are essential. The counselor who aligns himself with a volunteer board of directors, as opposed to working with the staff, is doomed to failure. And vice versa.
>
> Another reason for a different approach with association clients is that association presidents and committee heads change frequently. . . . As a result, changing priorities must be accommodated and new committee members educated regarding campaign objectives and methods.[7]

Lobbying, which we have already discussed, would be a function of nearly all associations. If their own staff members were not directly involved, they would have a paid lobbyist on the scene. Their goal would be to introduce or support legislation favorable to their membership and to oppose legislation considered detrimental. Their techniques would be those of any lobbyist, but size and money would have a major effect on their ability to succeed.

The public relations practitioner employed by an association could also have a role in training members in that specialty, organizing schools and seminars, preparing literature to update skills, and providing visual aids—such as films and slides—that can be viewed at local meetings. At the same time, this practitioner may be working with the membership to improve conditions in the industry or enhance acceptance of the product or service.

More and more, analysis is part of association PR activities, giving stronger emphasis to research and also enhancing the position of the practitioner, giving this person more of a voice in management. Another recent innovation is the increase in cooperative efforts among associations, especially when an issue unites them. These temporary mergers add strength and save money.

> Too many association managers and elected leaders still do not understand public relations and what it can do for an association. They measure good public relations by the number of press releases issued. Many public relations people are relegated to "firefighting" roles and are kept outside the policymaking process. Yet successful associations recognize that public relations is best used when integrated at the highest level of management.[8]

Groups like the American Library Association and the National Potato Board sponsor their own weeks, complete with brochures, posters, awards. A group of dental-gold manufacturers formed an association to combat the use of other minerals in dental work, and numerous associations are interested in the environment. There's Rotary and Save the Whales and insurance salespeople and disabled veterans. The American Forest Institute inserted an eight-page supplement in *Time*, and the American Hotel and Motel Association employed direct mail to promote advertising in its trade journal. The International Association of Chiefs of Police uses a telecommunications network of more than 1,000 terminals to broadcast messages simultaneously, and the American Management Association broadcasts a weekly video newsletter to members.

All these efforts are intended to interest, educate, and mobilize members, or to enhance the image and interests of the association. Like other segments of society, associations have also experienced a credibility gap and a competition for attention, and this undoubtedly accounts for the renewed emphasis on public relations, along with augmented budgets, more sophisticated techniques, and more-experienced counsel.

Margaret Lord, a private counselor, suggests ten ways to improve association credibility, including the coordination of communications; a more open attitude toward divergent views; the courage to speak up; the need for accuracy, honesty, and prudence; the willingness to confess error; the use of proper internal channels; and the requirement of constant evaluation.[9]

THE MILITARY

Although some critics lament the use of tax dollars to promote the viewpoint of the military, it seems clear that an adequate PR program is a necessity for the military, as it is for business. There is a story to be told here, sometimes a controversial one, and in the interests of balance, pubic relations personnel should be allowed to develop a professional response. In the past, those charged with PR for the service were largely involved in developing hometown releases and escorting dignitaries around the camp or base. Today's duties are a bit broader.

Military PR personnel have a variety of titles, including those of Public Information Officer (PIO) and Public Affairs Officer (PAO). Each military unit is likely to have its own specialist—sometimes a person with education or background in media, and sometimes a person who merely shows aptitude for this line of work. Hometown releases and tours are still on the agenda, but these men and women will also be advising, initiating, and supporting a long list of activities.

Recruiting is one important activity. In this regard, it is interesting to note the changes in the approach to young people. It is no longer feasible to merely suggest that "your country needs you." Advertising and promotion rely much more heavily on the career opportunities, the educational training,

Figure 14-4 All of the armed services have sophisticated advertising and public relations campaigns to attract recruits.

the foreign adventure, or the up-tempo attitude. The United States Marine Corps, faced with campaigns like these, took its own tack, declaring that it was interested only in "a few good men" and stressing the masculine appeal of the Marine Corps. These national advertising campaigns are, of course, the brainchildren of ad agencies, not staff PR personnel. Additions to the advertising barrage, such as printed materials, publicity, and special events, might, however, be more in line with PR activities. Air-force recruiting alone employs more than 150 advertising and public relations specialists, and, like other branches of the military, the air force also works with ad agencies.

Relationships with the media are also a priority. Some specialists consider this the major theoretical problem they face, the constant pressure to satisfy the "public's right to know" while preserving what they feel ensures security. In this dilemma, the public-affairs officers must often convince superiors that cooperation with the media is a necessity, and at the same time, they have to convince the media that certain items are classified. It's a tightrope.

Unhappiness over the media blackout during the invasion of Grenada resulted in the convening of a media–military relations panel by the Department of Defense. This so-called Sidle Panel (named for its chairman) produced a series of recommendations designed to ease tensions between the two groups. Among its proposals was a greater involvement of public affairs personnel during the planning stages of any operation.

This conflict of loyalties sometimes causes the PIO or PAO to be perceived by the media as overprotective and by his or her peers as insufficiently cautious. Many military personnel have had little contact with the media, and they complain that reports publicize only the negative aspects of their work. Some senior officers see this as symbolic of a political attitude rather than an open review of the facts. They admit good press is necessary to the successful conduct of any war, but they're not sure how that would work in a free society. Commodore Jack Garrow, the Navy's chief of information, stated:

> We're never going to get to the point where there'll be harmony. The country requires an aggressive press corps just as it requires an aggressive military. If we ever get to the point where the press is tame, we'll be in deep trouble.[10]

More often than not, television news is singled out by the military for more criticism than the print media. In particular, "60 Minutes" is a target, and there was a time when the Pentagon, miffed by the way that CBS program portrayed its efforts, put a ban on its officers granting interviews.

MILITARY CRISES FEW BUT SERIOUS

Much of military public relations is routine, even predictable. A lot of the activities are reactive, although military PR has been more aggressive in recent years, especially in areas that affect recruiting or funding. Still, because of a traditional emphasis on planning, a generally low profile, and an avoidance of many civilian public relations activities, practitioners in the armed services lead a little more controlled existence.

Except when something goes wrong!

Military problems are often front-page news, and the PR officers are subject to scrutiny from politicians, the media, superior officers, and the public.

Twenty years ago, a U.S. Air Force bomber malfunctioned and jettisoned a nuclear device off the coast of Spain. Air-force professionals were prepared for such an accident. News releases had already been written (in English, Spanish, Italian, and German) to cover any emergency, including one that reassured civilians that the device was unarmed. Despite that, media descended on the area, and the local PIO had to hastily set up tents, requisition typewriters and telephones, determine limits of access, issue press passes, and establish a routine for briefing. Besides the media, local officials and other miltary personnel had to be informed, and there was even a clause in the plan barring communist media. Surprisingly, the plan functioned extremely well—until officials in Washington panicked and sent in higher-ranking personnel who knew little of the circumstances but took over direction of the operation. Information was reduced to a trickle, so reporters began picking up on rumors from civilians, and the situation deteriorated. Until the device was found, the bad press continued. The lesson learned here was that, if the local PR people are doing the job, there should be no interference.

Even so, that sort of confusion continues to repeat itself. When a workman dropped a wrench into a missile silo and punctured a fuel tank, setting off an explosion, the media wanted to know if that missile warhead (which was missing for several days) had been armed. The official line was to refuse to confirm or deny such questions, and in this instance, President Reagan affirmed that stance. Since then, however, the policy has been altered, allowing for confirmation when danger or possibility of panic exist.

There have been well-publicized trials of military personnel who have been accused of everything from striking a superior officer to admitting homosexuality, to using drugs, to stealing military secrets. Many of these have featured civilian lawyers (like F. Lee Bailey) who have managed to tarnish the military image while winning their cases. Often the media get heavily into the scene, as they have when protesters crossed the designated line at the Strategic Air Command, or when "60 Minutes" looked into a case at the same base involving the grounding of a pilot whose urinalysis test showed the presence of drugs. When SAC refused to cooperate with "60 Minutes" and when the specimen used to substantitate the charges was not traceable with certainty to the pilot, military credibility suffered.

Strategic Air Command PR specialists host 7,000 distinguished visitors annually, and they mail out 15,000 different news releases and submit an average of 130 feature ideas to magazines. All these laudatory activities are sometimes torpedoed by a single negative incident.

Although not a military agency, NASA experienced one of the worst tragedies and subsequent PR fiascos in January 1986. *The Wall Street Journal* headlined a critical news story thus: NASA, ONCE A MASTER OF PUBLICITY, FUMBLES IN HANDLING SHUTTLE CRISIS.

Granted, this disaster was unusual, being witnessed by millions, who began asking questions before the space agency had an opportunity to research and react. Even so, NASA blundered by restricting the information available to the media; it impounded weather reports, issued conflicting statements from different officials on safety and operating methods, and held off on a press conference until five hours after the explosion, allowing all sorts of rumors to circulate.

The situation was aggravated by the departure six weeks earlier of agency administrator James Beggs, who was indicted on fraud charges related to his previous post at General Dynamics Corporation. The new acting administrator had been on the job only a week before the explosion of Challenger.

Some PR professionals observed that NASA, basking in a series of spectacular, error-free launches, seemed unprepared for any sort of bad news. Veteran practitioners know that crises are always possible and should be anticipated and planned for. They suggest that, in the military, these matters be handled at the lowest feasible level, and that those involved learn to speak with a single voice.

Whereas, the military once issued only printed releases, sometimes clumsily written, and accompanied them with occasional photos, the modern PR practitioner makes greater use of audio- and videotapes. Some of these are timely; some are of general interest—like a spot on Olympic athletes in the service. The National Guard circulated films on training units overseas to cable outlets, the Armed Forces Network, and more than 100 selected television stations. A record album featuring the best Army Reserve bands was mailed to more than 1,000 radio stations. News tapes may focus on Native Americans in the military, on innovations in training, or on the quality of military medicine.

Media people are invited to tour stateside or international facilities, and the military also launches its own tours, including one in 1985 centering on a female physician astronaut. Speakers who may address clubs or school assemblies are furnished with kits, speeches, and visual aids. Brochures that these people distribute are written in lay terms. There are special mailings to high school newspaper editors; essay contests for high school students; free kits on how to display the American flag.

Internally, the military relies heavily on official documents and frequent meetings, but it also publishes hundreds of newspapers and newsletters. Many of these are fairly bland, covering award ceremonies, safety drives, and other regular topics. Items that could be detrimental to morale (racial tensions, drug use, community conflicts, and others) may be edited out. Not every service paper fits this description, and publications like the *Army Times*, *Navy Times*, and *Air Force Times* certainly venture into the controversial. Military personnel often check these publications to find out what is going on in their branch of service. With a combined circulation of over 300,000 and advertising revenues in excess of $24 million, these papers can afford to be independent. The average military editor cannot.

Besides the newspapers and bulletin boards and tours and speakers' bureaus and closed-circuit television programs, military PR people face their own special problems. With units stationed everywhere, shouldn't there be more emphasis on learning languages? What about the ill feelings caused when vehicles rumble through a Central American village, spewing dust on the hanging laundry? How can the air force stop the defection of pilots to commercial airlines? How do you service all these requests for color guards? How do you quiet critics who learn that test pilots were killed while performing maneuvers designed to provide photos for an engine manufacturer's annual report? How do you simply perform satisfactorily as a citizen in your own community?

One aspect of community-affairs programs is an outreach into local problems. Military personnel—particularly reserve units—have been in evidence at disaster sites, such as floods or tornadoes; they have furnished trucks and supplies, picked up stranded persons via helicopter, helped move library books, provided toys for orphans, supervised summer camps, built playgrounds. Not only do these acts constitute good public relations, they also put into practice some of the tools the military employs best—manpower and organization.

Every plan for a field exercise, disaster, emergency, or actual war situation includes the PR function— everything from the setting up of reception centers for media to fill-in-the-blanks advance release forms.

Although the military makes its share of gaffes, it is probably one of the best PR planners. In San Antonio, for example, where many high-ranking officers have retired, the Fifth U.S. Army Headquarters keeps updated biographical sketches and maintains constant liaison with area hospitals in case of the illness or death of one of these personages. Once death seems imminent, local units are alerted to stand by for escort duty, color guard, rifle squad, and coffin bearers. Press briefings are called to provide exact details of the funeral and burial.

The military even has plans for relocation of its communication facilities in case of emergency. As you might imagine, these specify what will be loaded first, where and how they will move, and the manner in which the new operation will be set up. Much of this is classified information.

Instead of being a routine job, one defined by carefully worded directives, the military PR post can be as varied and exciting as any other communication assignment. Besides all the duties mentioned above, the PIO or PAO might be supervising a radio station or contributing to its programming, providing an interpreter or explaining local customs, or editing brochures covering everything from the role of NATO in Europe to the methods of opening a savings account in a foreign bank. Fulfilling these functions may be a layperson or a member of the military.

CHAPTER HIGHLIGHTS

- Government public relations comes under constant taxpayer scrutiny and, partially because of this, often bears different titles. However, the field is growing.
- Communicating government is ongoing and should be open, comprehensive, and not heavy-handed.
- Dealing with Washington media requires experience, as does testifying before and appealing to legislative bodies. Both take patience, honesty, and common sense, and both require adequate research. Numerous guides can help pave the way.
- The press secretary has a vital job and must reflect the views of the elected representative. The most respected press secretaries earn plaudits for their candor, availability, and professional knowledge of media needs.
- Lobbying can be part of the PR job, or public relations may be part of the lobbyist's tools; the two disciplines work together. Although lobbying may have an image problem, it remains an essential part of American government. All lobbyists work under restrictions.
- Restrictions are also imposed on Political Action Committees and other pressure groups and power blocs, but these entities continue to increase. As consumer strength advances, more pressure groups will arise, and power structures periodically shift from one center to another.
- Many trends in American politics affect the practice of campaign public relations. Single-issue blocs, apathy, old campaign methodology, the influence of television—all dictate strategy. Regardless of these things, the candidate remains the most important item, and a good PR program will not elect a candidate who fails to project a positive image. However, capable practitioners may aid candidates in their speeches, their television appearances, and their media relations, and their overall planning. They may even be responsible for the advertising themes.
- Polls should be professionally handled and can serve a variety of purposes, from counting potential votes to testing potential issues.
- Practitioners are rarely asked to work on safe issues; they normally inherit controversial ones, and these campaigns require the same research and restraint common to candidate races.

- After many years of attempting to conduct public relations in a somewhat amateurish manner, labor unions have turned to more sophisticated techniques and trained personnel. Their programs are beginning to resemble those of industry.

- Some 40,000 associations in America have PR needs, but only half of them have programs. Activities range from membership drives and lobbying to publications and special events.

- Like other areas of government, the military has to practice PR in a more subdued manner. Still, its range of activities has broadened, and its practitioners, military and lay, have become more professional.

NOTES

[1]Kenneth T. Walsh, "Battered Liberals Dream of Comeback," *U.S. News & World Report*, July 8, 1985.

[2]Christopher Matthews, "Washington Diarist," *The New Republic*, January 24, 1983.

[3]Ron Lovell, "Keepers of the Flame," *The Quill*, February 1981.

[4]James E. Roper, "An Inside Look at Government Press Officers," *Editor & Publisher*, October 6, 1984.

[5]"The Lobbyists," *Broadcasting*, February 24, 1985.

[6]S. John Insalta, "Government Relations at the State and Local Level," *Association Management*, Part IV, August 1965.

[7]Amelia Lobenz, "Problems & Opportunities," *Public Relations Journal*, February 1985.

[8]Edith A. Fraser, "Association Public Relations: The State of the Art," *Public Relations Journal*, October 1981.

[9]Margaret P. Lord, "10 Ways to Improve Your Association's Credibility," *Association Management*, February 1981.

[10]Andrew Radolf, "The Military Sounds Off," *Editor & Publisher*, December 1, 1984.

SUGGESTED READINGS

ABZUG, BELLA S., *Gender Gap: Bella Abzug's Guide to Political Power for American Women*. Boston: Houghton Mifflin, 1984.

BLUMENTHAL, SIDNEY, *The Permanent Campaign*. New York: Simon & Schuster, 1982.

CHAGALL, DAVID, *The New Kingmakers*. New York: Harcourt Brace Jovanovich, 1981.

Congressional Yellow Book and Federal Yellow Book, directories. Washington, D.C.: The Washington Monitor, 1986.

DICK, JANE, *Volunteers and the Making of Presidents*. New York: Dodd Mead, 1980.

DOMINGUEZ, GEORGE, *Government Relations: A Handbook for Developing and Conducting the Company Program*. New York: Wiley, 1982.

DREW, ELIZABETH, *Politics and Money: The New Road to Corruption*. New York: Macmillan, 1983.

FRENCH, BLAIRE ATHERTON, *The Presidential Press Conference: Its History and Role in the American Political System.* Lanham, Md.: University Press of America, 1982.

GABY, DANIEL M., and MERLE H. TREUSCH, *Election Campaign Handbook.* Englewood Cliffs, N.J.: Prentice-Hall, 1976.

GOLDENBERG, EDIE N., and MICHAEL W. TRAUGOTT, *Campaigning for Congress.* Washington, D.C.: CQ Press, 1984.

GREENFIELD, JEFF, *Playing to Win: An Insider's Guide to Politics.* New York: Simon & Schuster, 1980.

HAYES, MICHAEL T., *Lobbyists and Legislators: A Theory of Political Markets.* New Brunswick, N.J.: Rutgers University Press, 1981.

HREBENAR, RONALD, J., and RUTH K. SCOTT, *Interest Group Politics in America.* Englewood Cliffs, N.J.: Prentice-Hall, 1982.

Hudson's Washington News Media Contacts Directory. Bethesda, Md., 1986.

JAMIESON, KATHLEEN HALL, *Packaging the Presidency: A History and Criticism of Presidential Campaign Advertising.* New York: Oxford University Press, 1984.

LEVITAN, SAR A., and MARTHA R. COOPER, *Business Lobbies: The Public Good and the Bottom Line.* Baltimore: Johns Hopkins University Press, 1984.

LIPSET, SEYMOUR MARTIN, and WILLIAM SCHNEIDER, *The Confidence Gap: Business, Labor and Government in the Public Mind.* New York: Free Press, 1983.

LUSTBERG, ARCH, *Testifying with Impact.* Washington, D.C.: U.S. Chamber of Commerce, 1985.

MANDEL, RUTH B., *In The Running: Women and Political Candidates.* New Haven, Conn.: Ticknor & Fields, 1981.

MARTEL, MYLES, *Political Campaign Debates.* New York: Longman, 1983.

MAUSER, GARY A., *Political Marketing: An Approach to Campaign Strategy.* New York: Praeger, 1983.

MEADOW, ROBERT G., *Politics as Communication.* Norwood, N.J.: Ablex, 1980.

MERKEL, MURIEL, *The Labor Union Handbook.* New York: Beaufort, 1983.

PARKINSON, HANK, *Winning Your Campaign.* Englewood Cliffs, N.J.: Prentice-Hall, 1970.

POWELL, JODY, JERRY terHORST, and GEORGE REEDY, *Three Press Secretaries on the Presidency and the Press.* Lanham, Md.: University Press of America, 1983.

RIVERS, WILLIAM L., *The Other Government.* New York: Universe, 1982.

SABATO, LARRY, *The Rise of Political Consultants: New Ways of Winning Elections.* New York: Basic Books, 1981.

SCHMIDT, JOSEPH F. NAGEL, ed., *The Public Affairs Handbook.* New York: AMACOM, 1982.

SCHWARTZMAN, EDWARD, *Political Campaign Craftsmanship: A Professional's Candid Guide to Campaigning for Public Office.* New York: Van Nostrand Reinhold, 1984.

SIMPSON, DICK W., *Winning Elections: A Handbook in Participatory Politics.* Chicago: Swallow, 1981.

SPERO, ROBERT, *The Duping of the American Voter: Dishonesty and Deception in Presidential Television Advertising.* New York: Lippincott & Crowell, 1980.

VERMEER, JAN PONS, *"For Immediate Release": Candidate Press Releases in American Political Campaigns.* Westport, Conn.: Greenwood, 1982.

The Washington Lobby, 4th ed. Washington, D.C.: *Congressional Quarterly,* 1982.

EXERCISES

1. Take an upcoming campaign in your state or city and list what you feel are the strong points and weak points of the opponents in a single race.

2. Thinking back over the past several years, list three political ads that you recall, either favorably or unfavorably, and state what you feel were the good or bad points of each.

3. Assuming you had $25,000 to spend on your own campaign for city council in your community, how would you allocate these funds? Be specific as to the media, the general dates and times, and the reasons for your selections.

4. If you had to reach the various power structures in your own community, where would you start? How many power structures—or powerful individuals—can you identify?

5. You are the lobbyist for the insurance industry in your state. Who would some of your contacts be? What kind of legislation would you be likely to propose or to work against? How do you think you should be paid?

6. Interview a military recruiter to determine how effectively this person does the job, what materials are used, and what the overall campaign focuses on.

7. Get a union paper or an association newsletter and analyze the content for appeal, propaganda value, interest, and presumed intent.

8. Assume you are the press secretary for one of *your* congressional representatives and that the two of you are discussing plans for the ensuing year. What strategies would you suggest? What specific programs would you try to initiate?

CASE PROBLEMS

1. An air-force unit finds itself stationed outside the same German town this unit's World War II counterparts bombed to near oblivion. The citizens of this rebuilt community can't seem to shake the resentment for the destruction, and this has an effect on community relations. There have been numerous fights, prices seem to be higher to service personnel, and military people complain about everything from rudeness to police harassment. For their part, the German citizens contend that the service people are arrogant, rowdy, too free with their money, and totally oblivious to the culture and history of the town. As the base PAO, you are charged with devising a program to ease tensions. Let's have your recommendations.

2. As PR director for the Electrical Workers Union, Local 2500, you are faced with a problem involving the company retirement fund. In the past, the

company contributed 75% of the cost of this fund. Because of the tight economy and a couple of bad years, it proposes to pay only 25% of future costs, leaving employees to make up the difference or to reduce their retirement benefits. The company has, however, acceded to wage demands, and offered a 3% increase in salaries across the board. This proposition has the support of younger union members, who make up two-thirds of the company's work force. They are reluctant to strike when jobs are hard to find and are inclined to settle for what they can get and worry about retirement later. Senior workers, however, consider this proposal a severe blow and want to fight it to the limit. To further complicate things, the local community, which is experiencing a recession, is not too sympathetic to either the raise or the clamor for reinstatement of the pension contributions. As PR director, you have your work cut out for you—with union members, the community, and management. What strategies will you use for each target audience? What specific things will you do to satisfy or neutralize each?

3. In this calorie-conscious age, the purchase of white bread has declined considerably. Consumers consider it fattening and unhealthy. You represent the American Bakers Association, and this organization wants to turn Americans back to this staple. Assuming you are new on this job, what things would you try to do in your first year? What sort of theme would you develop to accomplish the bakers' mission? Describe the internal/external publication you would produce, in terms of audience and content. Would you use advertising? How? Do any special events suggest themselves? What would your goals be, and how would you evaluate results?

4. There has never been a female member of your city council, even though women make up 55% of the population in your town of more than 200,000. Mildred Jones files for the council and hires you as her PR consultant. She is single, 32 years old, holds a master's degree in English and political science, taught school for eight years, and is now enrolled in law school. She is a good speaker, although somewhat pedantic, has a pleasant appearance, and is very bright. She also has a temper, is impatient, and can be abrasive. What sort of problems can you expect to encounter? How will you counsel Ms. Jones on handling them? What themes will you emphasize in the campaign? What media strategies would you employ?

5. Edward Ney, President of Young & Rubicam, told the Association of National Advertisers that a law should be passed banning spot television for political campaigns because "this medium is basically incapable of doing justice to the subject and is susceptible to ingenious mischief." He went on to say that the 30-second TV commercial was appropriate for marketing chewing gum but was "dangerously insufficient for the serious exposition of vital national issues or for a really thorough view of a candidate's ability."

Walter Staab, president of SFM Media Service Corporation, disagrees. He points out that the 30-second spot is a "single-selling-idea medium" and that the candidate has control over it, as against, for example, the television debate. He argues that if the candidate has five ideas to discuss, he can use five 30-second commercials. He adds that newscasts often give less than 30 seconds to a candidate's views and that they may appear out of context, and that television debates can take any direction, even leaving the candidate with only 30 seconds to summarize his position. He believes that the 30-second spot may be the sole means for an unknown to reach a mass audience, and that there is more open discussion and less manipulation in political commercials than in product spots.

Consider too, audience reaction to longer programs like political debates or half-hour expositions on political philosophy. Hyped-up contests like presidential debates may gain audience approval, but what about local duels?

Write a 1,500-word essay on this subject, citing and defending your views, and using examples if possible.

15

NONPROFIT, COMMUNITY, CELEBRITY, AND OTHER FORMS OF PUBLIC RELATIONS

Practitioners often find themselves in different areas of public relations because of training, preference, availability, or luck. Many PR people aim for spots in corporations or head for an eventual career in a consulting firm; others know they want to labor in nonprofit organizations, tie themselves to athletic programs, explore international opportunities, or help publicize the rise of entertainment figures. There is room for all sorts of specialization, and every post comes with a unique set of problems and a different professional style.

A handful of these opportunities are explored in this chapter.

EDUCATION

Within the broad category of education are vast differences: grade and high schools, private and public universities, military schools and academies, church-related institutions and technical colleges. All have somewhat diverse problems and audiences.

All education suffers from a certain amount of misunderstanding. Some parents expect the schools to not only educate but also inculcate all the manners and morals they were unable to instill at home. High school principals get calls from irate mothers wondering why their daughters didn't come right home from school. Nuns field complaints about youngsters' not going to church on Sunday. College professors are blamed for students' poor study habits.

Elementary and Secondary Schools

The nature of education also makes for confusion. Admittedly, educators make errors, get caught up in teaching fads, or become slaves to unyielding routines. Most difficulties, however, stem from the educators' failure to communicate or the parents' and public's failure to appreciate.

Universal education accounts for many problems. Fifty or 75 years ago, a high-school diploma was relatively rare. Today we insist on this document. Naturally, we are going to be working with more uneven talent. In addition, all of society adopted a more liberal stance toward discipline, beginning perhaps in the 1960s or earlier. The schools happen to be the scapegoats for trends beyond their control.

Public schools in smaller towns have their own form of problems, including disciplinary actions, recruiting of teachers, and location of sufficient resources. Larger city school systems cite these areas of concern:

- Consolidation and the closing of school buildings
- Integration, busing, and related activities
- Finances—tax revolts, spending lids
- Complaints about teaching and about grades on college entrance exams
- Weather-related decisions
- Legislation that affects curricula, scheduling, and other areas
- Lack of understanding and support by parents and community

Superintendents, who would probably list communicating with the board of education as their prime public relations goal, also add some modern concerns, like "latchkey children," youngsters (some 60 percent of them in many urban areas) who have both parents working and come home to an empty house; the cost of programs necessitated by handicapped or exceptional students; the proliferation of drugs; and even the drain some public systems sense as the result of students' opting for private schools.

Protests by fundamentalists who wish to set up their own educational structures often involve the public-school authorities in lawsuits or confrontations. Along with these unpleasantnesses come complaints about sensitive topics, like sex education and the teaching of religion (including school prayers), and the ever-present attempt to influence the selection of textbooks. Some lists of prohibitions by critics are long: They are against any implied criticism of our form of government; criticism of parents in the classroom; attempts to ignore the existence of a Supreme Being; any support of ideas dangerous to national security; endorsement of compulsory charity or welfare; and even such specific items as role playing as a teaching tool.

One guide to parents' groups suggests:

> Contact other parents from your school when you find or hear of something objectionable so they too can complain. Keep those teachers on their toes. Let them know you are there and WATCHING![1]

While this sort of scrutiny is going on, taxpayers are also hardening their attitudes on paying for education:

> This antitax, antispend syndrome could not have caught the public schools at a worse time. On the one hand, they confront expenditure pressures spawned by court mandates and by the impact of inflation on their procurement and personnel costs. On the other, they enounter the resistance to increased funding epitomized by the rash of tax and expenditure limitations surfacing on all sides. Even in those states where voters are not mandating it, officials are using their powers to slow down increases in expenditures.[2]

Throw in the criticism of teachers, which hasn't abated, and you have a demanding role for the practitioner. Periodically we read of teachers who are not prepared for the classroom, who can't promote discipline, who can't even spell very well. Scores in the Scholastic Aptitude Tests are presented as evidence of the decline in good teaching. To further complicate things, many teachers are leaving the profession, victims of the lack of citizen support, the increasing problems of handling students, and the salary structure, which, in constant dollars, has been falling for a dozen years or more. Futurists foresee a teacher shortage within the decade.

Even though some of the dissatisfaction has leveled off, the PR person faces a variety of challenges and should have not only the requisite skills but also a firm commitment to education and the citizen responsibilities it entails. Planning for public-school public relations should be given the same priorities accorded building plans and lesson plans.

Typically, the PR person for a public-school system would work directly under the superintendent, with, perhaps, some direct or indirect ties to the elected school board. Duties would include periodic news releases, internal communication, arranging for radio and TV interviews, contact with principals, organization of meetings, lobbying with local or state legislative bodies, development of communication tools, speechwriting and public speaking, civic memberships, community relations, and intraschool relationships. Some PR persons even find themselves involved in yearbook counseling and the design of printed programs.

The audiences they seek to influence include students, faculty, staff, school-board members, parents, politicians, the media, former students, neighbors, and the general public. The tools vary from correspondence and posters to news releases and school functions.

Many systems have an internal-external newsletter, similar to that used by business firms. Subject matter covered might be news about teachers, special projects initiated by students, synopses of regulations such as winter-closing data, honors won by students or faculty, legislative news affecting education, retirements, curriculum, and statistical facts about enrollment. Some public relations projects are also covered, such as the periodic visits of a superintendent to various schools, or the cafeteria lunches that a principal regularly enjoys with members of the student body.

Many school systems also have a regular slot on local radio and television, discussing problems, introducing new ideas, responding to questions from listeners. The PR person may brief those appearing on issues and possible questions.

Relations with the elected school board could be a major duty of the school-system PR person. School boards invariably make news, and the news is frequently controversial. There are confrontations with irate taxpayers, teacher firings, personality conflicts. Since such meetings are public, there is little the PR person can do once the meeting has started, but he or she can confer in advance with members and also help to set their remarks in perspective after the fact.

Humanizing the superintendent could be another PR job. If this official already possesses gifts of a social nature, the job is relatively easy. When the superintendent is aloof, shy, or arrogant, the job is more difficult. Whatever the superintendent's personality, the PR person must help him or her to communicate more effectively.

Private schools are somewhat less affected by public pressures and, according to periodic Gallup polls, enjoy a higher reputation than their public counterparts. Still, they have their own problems. Money is a major one. Tuition, which may be quite high, still doesn't cover costs, forcing schools to mount fund drives for scholarships, equipment, and endowment. Teachers' salaries usually approximate those in the public schools, even though they may be slightly behind, and the diminishing federal programs and complaints about religious instruction are among the other headaches.

Many private high schools now have their own PR staffs, and these people are wearing many hats, covering regular and athletic publicity, editing publications, staging events, building alumni lists, and helping raise funds. Elementary schools would rarely have such programs, but a diocese or other religious jurisdiction might provide a communication link for all the institutions it encompasses.

Colleges and Universities

Higher education, although more isolated from parental displeasure, has its own set of crises.

Funding usually leads the list. Private colleges and universities face the problems of continually increasing tuition and competition for the charitable dollar. Public institutions are challenged by taxpayer reluctance and tight budgets.

Close behind comes the whole question of who shall govern. Students have assumed more authority as a result of the campus riots in the 1960s, but the compulsion to demonstrate has waned. Students remain concerned about relevance and about academic conduct, but confrontations are fewer and less volatile. Faculty members have been more active politically, organizing into bargaining units and lobbying legislators and other constituents.

Faculty and student grievances often conflict with the traditional roles of regents and administrators.

There are also massive parking problems, debates about the merits and demerits of the tenure system, concerns about declining enrollments, questions as to the relevance of the curriculum, complaints about teachers who don't teach, struggles with alumni and townsfolk about campus speakers, insipid cafeteria menus, and four-letter words in the student journals.

College public relations offices, looking ahead, foresee their efforts being channeled toward admissions, development, and image programs, with a likely decline in publicity and some of the less meaningful PR exercises. Like other levels of education, money remains a prime concern. College execs complain about deteriorating structures they haven't funds to repair, about the departure of underpaid faculty for industry posts (faculty salaries have been running behind inflation for a decade), about the need to pare programs, reduce student aid, delay equipment purchases, curtail travel, and reduce institutional activities to the minimum. As a consequence of this cash crunch, tuition has risen everywhere, although a wide disparity in the cost of an education remains. In 1985, students at the Massachusetts Institute of Technology faced tuition of $11,000, and Stanford broke past the $10,000 annual mark. Many state colleges and universities remained below $1,000— but the average tuition increase that year was 8 percent.

In terms of public relations, a corollary to these tuition boosts has been more scrutiny of programs and institutions by prospective students, invoking the need for greater emphasis on methods to enhance the status and image of the schools. Administrators have also had to strengthen their relationships with government as aid programs are further eroded, and even at public colleges, where admission standards have been more liberal, requirements for entry have been narrowed, meaning that some 20,000 applicants who might have once been admitted will be screened out each year. Colleges and universities are pushing for fewer, better students.

Because the supply of such students is necessarily limited, recruiting has become more competitive, and many institutions have turned to more sophisticated marketing strategies in order to keep pace. Goals are set, recruiting staffs expanded, events multiplied, publicity focused on admissions, and advertising directed toward attracting new students more than any other educational purpose. Bumper stickers invite seniors to explore certain campuses, and well-produced television spots extol the benefits of specific institutions. Printed materials are the products of experienced editors and designers, and special events go far beyond the loosely organized open house.

Besides increasing tuition and boosting numbers, higher education must continually cultivate sources of funding, whether state, federal, or private. Although these tasks are in the province of the board, the development office, and trustees, the PR director inevitably has an important role—

providing the groundwork for solicitation, backup during a campaign, lobbying, promotion, and assistance with all pertinent phases of fund raising.

Other college and university problems are many and varied. In 1984, Yale University faced a lengthy strike by 1,500 clerical and technical employees, which attracted widespread faculty and student support and media attention, and which crippled such campus functions as food service and janitorial duties. Even though teachers' strikes have been an activity of secondary schools rather than higher education, college professors have become more combative in their struggle for salary increments, teaching conditions, and a share in governance. Collegiate PR directors may have to cope with the misdeeds of students and faculty, the complaints of alumni about everything from a losing football season to a public policy statement by the president, the incursions of legislative or trustee committees, and the lack of understanding by members of the university family. Sometimes the crisis is major, as when a highly visible administrator resigns; sometimes it's minor, as when the local paper, given a list of campus activities ranging from a symphony concert and high-level symposium to a new noncredit course in motorcycle maintenance, decides to headline the latter. Schools with sectarian backgrounds may be defending themselves with increasing frequency from those critics who contend that the emphasis on traditional religious beliefs is either compromised or moribund.

Target audiences include faculty, staff, students, alumni, media, the local community, corporate and individual donors, special groups ranging from the legislature to church synods, and, of course, the trustees. More than half the trustees are from business or the professions, and most are elected (or appointed) through the political process or through balloting among alumni. Good boards can make any decent institution successful, so they must be carefully chosen, educated, and employed.

The College Communications Structure

The typical campus organization in the public relations area consists of officers responsible for PR, for alumni relations, and for development. On a small campus, one person could wear all three hats. At larger institutions, each of these specialties may employ several persons. It is not unusual to find student recruitment and job placement also included.

The alumni secretary may be in charge of the alumni publication, will certainly run such alumni affairs as homecoming, and will supervise the activities of alumni clubs across the nation. In fact, anything that has the word *alumni* in its title probably involves the alumni secretary.

Fund raising is the chief responsibility of the development officer. This may be segmented into annual giving (largely by alumni), business solicitation, federal grants, and foundation appeals. Special individual appeals would also be included, and perhaps wills and bequests.

Working as a team member with both these officers is the public relations director, who may have a news-bureau director, publications director, and others working under him or her. Among the PR director's charges would be news releases, publications, special events, community relations, multimedia and other visual tools, and internal campus relations. Some PR directors are also lobbyists, and a number enjoy faculty status in communications departments.

Programs for parents could involve several departments, including PR, and so might presentations to community leaders.

The PR director should be considered part of the university's top planning boards. Unless he or she has the confidence of the administration and the opportunity to participate in decision making, there is little room to operate effectively. The new PR director may have to earn such trust and should make this a top priority.

College public relations remains one of the most variable and interesting versions of the profession. Salaries today, although still a bit below the average for industry, are more competitive. Median salaries for all collegiate PR directors are close to $30,000, with the chief public relations officers at larger universities averaging $40,000 annually. A few positions offer compensation considerably higher than this figure.

Besides the categories of elementary, secondary, and higher education, there are also PR posts in nontraditional schools, in professional educational associations, and in government agencies that have education as a responsibility.

PUBLIC RELATIONS IN THE HEALTH SCIENCES

Public relations is something of a latecomer to medicine and related health fields, and, in these areas, it still has not achieved the status accorded PR in the corporate arena. Rarely are practitioners situated at the top management level. Salaries run behind those found in higher education and far behind those in industry, with median compensation at about $26,000.

Although numerous PR problems are peculiar to health-related specialties, many of them can be reduced to the concern over costs.

In St. John, Mich., the local hospital runs a laundry business. An Easton, Md., hospital gives refunds if a patient's hot meal is served cold. In Los Angeles, a medical center has started an alcohol-and-drug-abuse unit. In Houston, hospitals belonging to a for-profit health-care chain offer new parents a free infant's car seat with each delivery.

All these efforts are aimed at raising more money for hospitals by attracting new business. In the Reagan era of deregulation, the nation's 5,800 general hospitals have become a financially troubled industry.[3]

Figure 15-1 Materials for editors are a main element in promoting National High Blood Pressure Month.

From 1965 to 1985, health-care costs as a percentage of the gross national product nearly doubled, causing a shift in the way companies offer medical benefits and creating new organizations composed of employer, employee, and insurance companies. Patients are spending less time in the hospital, resulting in a decline in the occupancy rate—more financial bad news. The current trend is toward health-care chains, a grouping of several hospitals under a corporate structure. Over a third of America's hospitals are now part of such chains.

Growth may help with the financial stress, but it makes things no simpler for public relations. Size compounds some of the complaints about impersonal treatment and indifferent staff members. Even the notion of some hospitals being organized "for profit" counteracts the samaritan myth that has long dominated the image of medicine. The terminology itself reflects this change, with hospitals discussing "positioning" and "market share."

There are responses to such complaints, but hospitals have not done an adequate job of providing them. Citizens need to be made aware of the effect of malpractice suits and insurance, government regulation, rising utility bills, salary increases, patient demands, and other variables. Good PR can help, but it doesn't always get a chance to operate.

Since the cost issue seems to be a no-win situation, many hospital managers simply react to each barrage by not responding. This is sometimes an effective tactic for dispensing with the situation at hand, but it does little to banish the issue. Unless individual hospitals aggressively tackle the cost-of-care issue head-on and do so in the public arena, the tide of regulations, activists, reviewing agencies and adverse legislation will rise.[4]

The public relations director has to understand the reasons for high costs and be able to interpret them for the public. Timely and accurate news releases help, as well as informative printed materials and, where applicable, advertising. Some hospitals go the extra mile in supplying data, organizing exhibits in shopping malls, taking slide programs to service clubs, sponsoring an active speakers' bureau.

Along with the promotional efforts, hospitals continue to engage in attempts to find cost-saving remedies, but complications also multiply. Insurance companies, for example, offer incentives to patients who opt for surgery outside the hospital, and other alternative means of health care further erode the occupancy rates. To protect themselves, more and more hospitals are creating or purchasing health maintenance organizations (HMOs), establishing smaller surgical centers, and even getting into the insurance business. They are also concentrating more on marketing, sometimes to the detriment of public relations, and are learning to share services and equipment, a practice long scorned by ambitious medical staffs.

Those engaged in hospital work are all responsible for public relations. Each nurse, aide, receptionist, physician, pharmacist, and gift-store volunteer makes an impression on patients and visitors. One of the PR director's responsibilities is to see that these contacts are positive. These personnel must be reminded that most people come to hospitals under some sort of stress, and this requires extra effort to make them feel at ease. A cold demand

---

HEART TRANSPLANT ALWAYS NEWS

Even though at least 50 hospitals in the United States have had heart transplants performed by their surgeons, the operation continues to be a major news story.

The procedure, first used in 1967 by Dr. Christian Barnard, has been enhanced in recent years by the development of cyclosporine, but it remains a high-risk operation, and the public continues to have an interest in its success and in the longevity of the patient. Only health items like cancer, abortion, and test-tube babies seem to have an equal effect.

On occasion, the heart transplant has been performed without ceremony in some new area, and without anticipating the resultant news interest.

In the spring of 1985, a hospital in a major midwestern city was the scene of its first heart transplant. No prior notification was given to the media. In fact, the story broke when a friend of the recipient's family phoned a local televison station. Its crew was on the scene almost immediately but was turned away by the hospital's security officers, who, like most of the staff, were unaware of the operation. Even the PR staff was not briefed until the following morning.

By that time, the phones were busy and reporters were camped in the lobby. The public relations director suggested an immediate news conference. Fortunately for the hospital, the surgeon responsible for the operation was impressive and articulate. He fielded the usual questions about the procedure, and the PR staff supplied media with vital statistics on the recipient, the medical team, and the length of time the operation took. The hospital also issued a release reminding the public of its other firsts in the state—kidney transplant, bone-marrow transplant, cornea transplant.

The day after the operation, two of the three local stations broadcast live from the hospital. The next day, following a second press conference, the hospital PR staff began giving condition reports at 11 A.M. and 4 P.M., primarily to accommodate media deadlines. Reporters wanted to know what the patient had to eat, who visited her, what she said, when she would walk.

The public relations staff continued to impose some limitations on access by the media, handling photographs themselves in the early stages. When the donee was able to walk outside the intensive care unit, local cameramen were alerted and had their first pictures.

Newspaper stories featured the patient, individuals on the team of physicians, details of the operation, a rundown on other recipients and how they were doing, a story on the 18-year-old boy whose heart was used in the transplant, diagrams of the procedure, articles on cost (this operation was performed without charge), and periodic progress reports. The patient eventually returned home, but each time she returned to the hospital for heart biopsies, the results of these tests were released to the media.

This incident reveals one of the major difficulties in the field of health-related public relations. Medical staffs are often reluctant, for professional and legal reasons, to give advance notice of a newsworthy event. In fact, they may sometimes be ignorant of the interest that could develop. On the other hand, the PR person(s) would like sufficient time to properly organize media coverage. The ideal solution is a close working relationship between the two professions. Short of this, the PR staff should have an emergency procedure it follows routinely, whenever any news story erupts.

SOURCE: Compiled from a report by Carla Merritt, April 30, 1985. Courtesy: Carla Merritt.

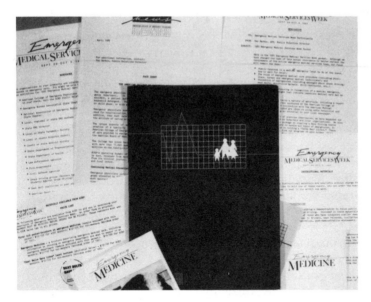

Figure 15-2 The press kit on Medical Services Week provides fact sheets, releases, illustrations, feature material, and other resources.
Courtesy: American College of Emergency Physicians

for cash in advance or a long litany of questions is not a helpful introduction. Neither is secrecy about a patient's condition, or an explanation that humiliates the worried parent or spouse. There are ways to be courteous without seeming impatient, and ways to inform without acting pompous. These little touches make a difference. The nervous visitor (or patient), who will more deeply resent a slight, will also more amply reward a friendly gesture.

Good internal public relations is the starting place for any hospital campaign. The staff must know the facts and develop a team spirit. This may be accomplished by solid communication, using all media, from publications to slide shows. Of course, the administration must be committed to this idea of partnership or it won't work. Traditionally there has been a hierarchy of positions in hospitals, and breaking this down, even a little, is difficult.

The staff physician rates top billing in hospital circles. The public relations director must be able to function with such professionals to anticipate their needs, earn their confidence, and interpret their contributions.

That is why doctors must be sold on the validity of public relations and convinced that it offers them more good than harm. They might, in fact, become adept themselves at the PR function, applying its tenets in their own daily relationships and learning to communicate with all those they contact.

The nursing profession has made considerable strides in upgrading the status of its members. Continuing education is encouraged; periodic seminars and conventions are well attended; both prestige and income have been enhanced. The nurse is a key public relations person in any hospital. To many patients, she or he *is* the hospital. Competence, compassion, and congeniality are virtual requirements. The nurse and the attendant aides can do wonders in breaking down the feeling of impersonality. Many hospitals have public relations training programs for nurses, and their own conferences usually include sessions on this skill.

Public relations impinges upon the nursing profession in another way. Because of the shortage of nurses nationwide, recruiting campaigns have been stepped up, including those sponsored by the National League of Nursing, which relies heavily on publicity generated by the media it contacts; the American Nursing Association also serves as a reporting resource.

Physicians and Practitioners

Competition is often the spur to public relations, and the nation's physicians find themselves turning more and more to techniques that will give them an edge in their practice or a boost to their reputations. To promote themselves, doctors may cut prices of some standard services, issue a periodic newsletter, even send cards and flowers to patients. Advertising is becoming more common, as the physician population grows three times faster than the general population. Most ads are hardly flamboyant, but even the mention of medicine in a commercial way is anathema to some. So is the hiring of public relations specialists for fees as high as $5,000 a month. These professionals may arrange for appearances of physicians on talk shows or other programs, may crank out news releases on their behalf, may establish them as experts in a specialty, or may even encourage and help them write books to increase their visibility. Often, the relationship between physician and PR person is kept secret.

> Even though they may hire press agents, physicians are aware that the practice is at odds with medicine's traditionally conservative image and is condemned by many leaders in the profession. Another reason for the paradox of secret publicity is that doctors would prefer the public to think they're featured on TV and radio and in newspaper and magazine stories because they're recognized as experts. Public knowledge that it's because of a hard-working press agent defeats the purpose.[5]

The doctor also knows that, especially in that field, publicity works better than advertising, because it's clear that advertising has been bought, whereas the publicity appears genuinely objective. The use of PR specialists is especially common when a new medical technique requires coverage, or a clinic faces competition, or a physician, for reasons of ego, wants to rise above his or her colleagues.

Critics argue that doing good work provides all the publicity a physician needs and that self-promotion often leads to misleading information. Those who employ public relations counter with the reminder that the world has changed and that public relations is a legitimate communication device, with a real value for the public. In any event, the trend is producing PR firms that focus on physician clients.

Other Medical Considerations

Next to the staff, the patient forms the most exacting public. Few people *elect* to enter hospitals; most *must* go there. They are captive consumers. Consequently, the possibility for resentment or discomfort is high. The food tastes strange, the rules seem calculated to destroy sleep, and the days drag. These feelings cannot be eliminated completely, but a little thought and planning can reduce their strength. Open communication, sunny dispositions, little personal touches—these deftly turn away wrath.

The public relations practitioner in this situation must be prepared for emergencies, since the hospital is sure to have them. There could be natural disasters such as fires or floods, or personal disasters such as malpractice suits, complaints about equipment or costs, or structural defects. There could be challenges like those faced by hospital PR staffs when important individuals, like President Ronald Reagan or Rock Hudson, are admitted for treatment. The media may descend on the locale, requiring space, telephone lines, and periodic briefings.

These instances, of course, are unusual, but the request for information on patients is not. Hospitals have their own rules about the release of such items, and most hospitals require the patient to sign a form permitting such disclosure. Often the nature of an illness or an operation is not given, but when the person is important, it is nearly impossible to conceal the facts.

Hospitals are very sensitive about bad publicity. They are also cautious about any practices that could result in lawsuits. Therefore you will find that most hospital public relations directors treat news rather conservatively. They may be at the opposite end of the promotional spectrum from the sports publicist. They would issue fewer releases, spend time on internal and community relations, help raise funds, work on printed and visual communications, coordinate volunteer efforts, and attend a considerable number of staff meetings.

RELIGION

To some, the marriage of religion and public relations may smack of hypocrisy. They conclude that any strong faith should be able to sell itself without the artificial injection of communication techniques. Opponents of this view like to speculate that Christ would have used television if he were traversing the earth today. Neither of these convictions is very productive. We don't know what Christ, or any religious leader from the past, might do with today's media. And it is fruitless to argue against merging the spiritual with the material, because this has become a way of life.

Few individual churches have their own public relations director or staff, but most synods, dioceses, educational centers, and other overall organizational structures do employ such professionals. These professionals may be responsible for printed communication, perhaps with the exception of the sectarian newspaper; radio and television shows and commercials, many of which are first-rate; publicity to local and national media; and special church events, including seminars and conferences. The PR persons may also have a strong advisory role in dealing with the hierarchy or other administrators, and they could be involved in training sessions in communication for the clergy.

During the last two decades, the changes in all churches have caused dissension and conflict. This is a necessary adjunct of such developments. Some traditionalists felt that all they had once believed in was being destroyed; more liberal members of the congregation berated their priests and ministers for moving too slowly. Scriptural translations were modernized and simplified, and more emphasis was given to community, as against personal, piety. These alterations, plus many physical differences—from music to language—presented various churches with the danger of a split allegiance.

To further complicate matters, attendance at services fell off in all denominations, with less than half this nation's population admitting to regular churchgoing. With the young, in particular, formal religious practice seemed to have lost its appeal, and churches made a massive effort to recover this dwindling audience. There was also debate about the social responsibility of churches. Should the clergy and religious people be in picket lines? Should the sermons contain exhortations about school integration and unfair labor practices? Must spiritual leaders become activists?

These disputes—and many more—came at a trying time for all churches. With declining congregations combining with inflation to create staggering financial woes, the ministry was pulled in many directions. Assembling a public relations program to deal with these pressures requires tremendous skill.

Some encouraging aspects have arisen in recent years, from the viewpoint of religious leaders. Gains in church membership have been modest, barely keeping pace with population increases, but the erosion seems to have halted. About 60 percent of Americans are now attached to some church. More than a fourth of those now enrolled in seminaries are women. And contributions are running far ahead of inflation. There has also been a gradual return to church by young people, a trend that may be the result of a more conservative outlook. Gallup polls show that Americans consider religion a major influence on their lives, even though their confidence in the ability of faith to solve their problems had declined.

But a spate of new problems, or new areas of activity, has also arisen. Catholic bishops have issued a pastoral letter on nuclear arms control, and some members of the clergy have deliberately trespassed on military property to call attention to the nuclear-freeze movement. The Interfaith Center on Corporate Responsibility, a New York–based amalgam of 18 different denominations, purchases stock, attends annual meetings, and proposes stockholder resolutions on everything from racial justice and equal employment to investments in South Africa. The group also encourages boycotts of certain products for what the center feels are social injustices. Locally, ministerial unions may push for better police relations with minority communities, or may lobby the state legislatures on matters considered morally sensitive. Several organizations (National Conference of Christians and Jews, Anti-Defamation League, Catholic League for Religious and Civil Rights, and so on) keep a watchful eye on discrimination in precept or practice, and others have been created to respond to a certain felt need, from school prayer to tuition grants.

Some of these movements attract opposition. Perhaps the two sides of the abortion issue, often interwoven with sectarian principles, get the most headlines, but opponents of the Moral Majority's influence on our political life are also active. Sometimes millions are poured into media campaigns to proclaim or protest beliefs. Internally, too, there are divisions. Southern Baptists, for example, America's largest Protestant denomination, are split on Biblical interpretation, the ordination of women, and how extensively the church should be embroiled in politics. Roman Catholics argue about female priests, birth control, celibacy, and a liberation theology reflected in political activism by priests and nuns in Central America, the Philippines, and elsewhere.

Then, too, public relations opportunities are inherent in ecumenism, a product of the early 1960s. Catholics continue to meet with Anglicans and Lutherans to discover a middle ground, and mergers among branches of Baptist, Lutheran, and Presbyterian churches are under discussion. Differences have not faded, but hostilities have declined measurably.

At the same time that churches are condemning the excesses of the media, especially television, their ministers are turning with greater frequency to these same media. Over $1 billion is involved in religious communication annually, with television, radio, books, and spectaculars using most of that budget. James Orsen Bakker, evangelist, declares:

> We believe in Christian television because Christian television is a real picture of the body of Christ standing together. You couldn't do this without millions of people all over the country standing together. When we stand together, things begin to happen.[6]

Most denominations do some TV work, but Christian evangelists, often assisted by PR staffs, make the most use of the electronic media. Bakker alone airs his show five days a week over almost 1,200 cable and regular broadcast stations and uses his own TV network to reach into all 50 states, via satellite, for 24 hours of every weekday.

This sort of coverage makes up for what religious leaders see as the lack of news about religion provided by regular news channels. Many editors and news directors try to follow religion as a topic but get lost in its complexities, its rivalries, and the confusion caused by the general public ignorance about varied beliefs. The Moonies and the Moral Majority make headlines, but the everyday activities fail to excite readers, viewers, and listeners.

Other devices used by those charged with PR responsibilities are parish newsletters, videocassettes, magazines, even comic books. In Europe, Videotext is used by a number of denominations for instruction, direct mail, and fund raising. Advertising is on the increase, and some of the best ads produced annually have a religious message. Fund raising, too, is getting more professional, with specialty firms organizing parish drives to replace the weekly exhortations from the pulpit. Organizations like EVCOM (Evangelism/Communication), a national interdenominational service, host training sessions to make pastors better communicators, and many major church groups schedule their own educational seminars to assists ministers in relating to congregations and media.

If the public relations function had not entered into this religious sphere, conditions would be virtually hopeless. Communication attitudes prevalent 50 years ago just wouldn't work today. Everything has changed, and nothing has changed more than religion—at least in its externals. The "Good News" is still the "Good News," but it is packaged in much more sophisticated ways to reach a much more sophisticated congregation.

As with other areas of PR, religion has its own peculiar set of concerns, and Cutlip and Center's *Effective Public Relations* identifies five of them:

1. *The intangible nature of many religious activities.* This makes the more bizarre activities more attractive, as far as publicity is concerned. The ordinary service may seem old hat and dull, but you can make news with locker-room Masses, Jesus freaks, speaking in tongues, and other, less-familiar practices.

2. *The sacred nature of religion, requiring a dignified approach.* Although every church is becoming much more informal, there is still the concern about taking photos during services, writing about spiritual matters in mundane terms, and even treating any religious subject lightly. The accusation of blasphemy is less frequently heard (or worried about), but few communicators dare to depart from the rather stiff portrayal of belief and ritual.

3. *The task of showing the practical value of religion.* Today's citizens want to know what something will do for them. They demand this of products, of educational curricula, and of government programs. They apply the same test to religion, and the churches must come up with answers that meet the needs and aspirations of this generation. Abou Ben Adhem, who was unfamiliar with God but loved his fellow man, seems a decent enough approach to many Americans. They have to be sold on the redeeming qualities of faith.

4. *Interpreting programs that follow traditional patterns.* There is much less conformity, even in the more structured religions, than outsiders

---

SOUND: STREET NOISES

DON: Thanks for taking time out of your busy schedule, Mr. Christ.

  C: Sure, I'm glad to do it.

DON: Oh, by the way . . . do you mind if I call you Jesus?

  C: Oh no. Actually, I'd prefer that.

DON: Uh huh.

  C: As long as you don't do it just when you're angry. For example, what's your name?

DON: Don Richman.

  C: Well, how would you like it, Don, that if every time someone slammed their finger in a door, they said, "Oh, Don Richman!"?

DON: Yeah, I can see what you mean. Now that you're a superstar, is this a promotional tour you're on?

  C: I've noticed a lot of people thinking that . . . they, they just don't matter and I'm trying to show 'em that I love them.

DON: And you think because you love them that they should think that they matter?

  C: Well, you see, these people think that no one loves 'em . . . but I do. And I'd like them to share my love with other people.

DON: How is your father taking your superstar status?

  C: Well, I think now he's pretty proud of me.

DON: Uh, what are your future plans now?

  C: Just the same thing, keep on lovin'.

DON: I know you're busy, and I really appreciate your spending this with me here.

  C: Hey, no, that's all right . . . I'm not just here with you right now. I'm, as a matter of fact, right now I'm helping a guy change a tire in San Diego.

DON: This thought shared with you by Lutherans, Presbyterians, and Disciples of Christ.

Figure 15-3 This innovative 60-second radio spot was written by Don Richman and produced for Bill Huie and the TRAV Agency by Chuck Blore & Don Richman Incorporated.

suspect. Even a hierarchical organization like the Roman Catholic Church is much more disparate than it appears. It is virtually impossible for the Pope, for example, to gain universal Catholic acceptance for any of his pronouncements. Relatively recent encyclicals on labor and marriage found Catholic zealots at both extremes. The PR challenge here is to be able to make these apparently rote activities visible as the innovations they may be.

5. *Knowing at what level to project ideas.* Every PR person can identify with this dilemma, since each communicator who seeks to reach diverse audiences experiences the same problem. Even a basic tool like the sermon finds the minister, priest, or rabbi questioning whether the intellectual content is over the head of some or too basic for others. Religion classes face this, too, and so does all printed material aimed at laypersons.[7]

Figure 15-4 An ecumenical message prepared by EVCOM and the United Church of Christ. Courtesy: EVCOM and the United Church of Christ

Professionals—and volunteers who assist on a parish level—may do much to alleviate the problems, but the most successful religious entities in all faiths remain those who involve members on a personal basis, show concern for the needs of parishioners, and offer meaningful liturgies and sermons.

NOT-FOR-PROFIT PUBLIC RELATIONS IN OTHER SOCIAL AGENCIES

There are innumerable nonprofit organizations, and each of them relies on communication in order to survive.

For a newcomer wishing to break into public relations, this may be an excellent place to start. Salaries, particularly beginning salaries, may be modest, but there will be opportunities for newcomers to involve themselves in a variety of projects and a chance to meet with many influential volunteers.

Most nonprofit organizations have built-in public relations problems. There is a constant need of funds, and it is difficult to recruit and retain staff members. These institutions may also be working in areas that have their own sensitivities—drug abuse, battered children, the Rape Line, alcoholism, marriage counseling, prison reform, poverty. In some of these areas it is impossible to do enough. As a result, the work always lags behind. When funds are short, the work lags even further behind. But the criticism doesn't stop.

Risks are inherent in many programs designed by health-care, volunteer, and nonprofit institutions. Much of the work is experimental. Sometimes the failures are spectacular and result in poor public relations. A work-release program for prisoners may function perfectly for years, but then one felon breaks parole and mugs someone, and the subsequent publicity may sink the whole scheme. When a halfway house looks for a location in a residential neighborhood, the citizens affected rise up in protest. They approve the idea, but not in *their* neighborhood. There are periodic stories (and continual rumors) about welfare cheaters driving Cadillacs or purchasing expensive cuts of meat at supermarkets. Even the term *welfare* has come to have a negative connotation.

Part of this onus stems from the puritan work ethic in America. Despite evidence to the contrary, many Americans regard poverty as primarily the result of laziness. They are convinced that anyone who wants to work, can work. The statistical data about children, the aged, the handicapped, and the husbandless mothers who make up the largest segment of the welfare rolls have little effect. Critics concentrate on the recipients who seem healthy and capable.

Because of this phenomenon—and the constant need to appeal for funds—some social workers become very defensive. They feel humiliated and inferior, even though they are in one of the most laudatory professions. Part of the PR program must be directed toward the elevation of their self-esteem. Such factors as strong internal communication, periodic meetings, intelligent supervision, and congenial surroundings help establish good morale. Unless the worker has a positive attitude toward his or her job, the public relations program will show an immediate decline.

Paramount among the concerns of not-for-profit social agencies is the funding of their programs. With government cutbacks reducing aid from that source, and with foundation assets receding, these institutions have had to turn directly to corporations and private donors. They've also had to trim services and personnel. Even the cost of direct mail, a mainstay for some types of not-for-profit agencies, has risen a minimum of 50 percent in the last several years.

Amid these financial negatives, these same agencies must reckon with a larger group of older citizens; the burden of health costs; the increase in

Figure 15-5 Even if the practitioner has no regular nonprofit account, he or she is likely to be involved in such work as a volunteer.

illegitimate births, single-parent families, divorce, and other domestic ills; a changing value system that confuses donors; and unemployment, especially among those who already suffer from other problems.

Besides the financial woes and the demands for services, not-for-profit agencies are subject to increased scrutiny and accountability along with more and more competition from other agencies.

If there is any good news in this scenario, it may be that not-for-profit institutions have to rely to an even greater extent on the skills of professional practitioners. With the aid of these people, agencies are becoming better communicators, more responsible, and more successful fund raisers. Salaries have moved up commensurately.

Volunteers are also an integral part of the charitable labor force. The Girl Scouts need den mothers; the Salvation Army needs people to manage the Christmas kettles; the Red Cross needs drivers. The PR practitioner must know how to attract and hold such people.

Surveys indicate that volunteers offer their services primarily because they want to be useful, because they are interested in the organization, or because they have strong religious convictions. These same motivations keep them going. If they do terminate their association, it may be because their schedules no longer permit it, because they have moved, because the project has been completed, or because their original reasons for joining have disappeared.

To keep good volunteers, the practitioner and administration must communicate, must utilize personnel, and must thank and reward those who give their time.

In addition to raising funds from external publics, the nonprofit institution needs to conduct an ongoing program of public relations to convince

---

THE BIGGER THEY ARE . . .

In the last couple of decades, numerous stories have been related to the accountability of nonprofit institutions. Some have involved fraud, some mismanagement, some merely a failure to report. As a result of widespread publicity and the tightening of standards by associations that monitor nonprofit appeals, charitable groups have been much more conscious of the need to share information on programs and finances. Occasionally this works a hardship, as when a smaller organization, strapped by startup costs, has to conform to the same reporting standards as those imposed on veteran institutions. Overall, however, not-for-profit enterprises concede that the scrutiny is valuable.

When an institution with high visibility, like Boys Town, becomes the object of negative publicity, the story just refuses to go away.

In March 1972, a local Nebraska weekly published a special, well-researched section headed, "BOYS TOWN—AMERICA'S WEALTHIEST CITY?" The stories revealed that the home for boys was netting over $17 million annually after all expenses were paid, and that its endowment was well in excess of $200 million. There was no hint of illegality, but the institution's failure to be up front about its condition (instead of sending appeal letters pleading impending poverty) and its declining enrollment were brought into question. So was the "inertia" of its programs.

It took Boys Town several weeks to respond. New policies were inaugurated, including an open door to the media and a formulation of creative ways to use the accumulated funds. Every one of the more than 15,000 critical letters was answered, and regular news conferences were held to keep reporters abreast of the rapidly developing changes.

An institution for hearing disorders and a high school for youngsters living in Omaha's depressed areas were built with the aid of Boys Town money. So was a research institute on the Boys Town campus, and two other research labs (which studied causes and cures of delinquency) were begun on either coast. Replacing the larger institutionalized dormitories were smaller, family-type cottages, and girls were allowed on campus for vocational studies. Satellite homes were established in other cities.

Boys Town recovered both its image and its success at fund raising. A new administration not only told the story aggressively, it developed realistic long-range goals and modernized the character of care. New films depicting this fresh approach were made and received wide acceptance. A made-for-television film was shot in 1985, the first such feature on the home in decades.

Because of the initial stories, however, Boys Town will remain under public surveillance. Every resignation, every firing, every complaint by employees receives coverage. The failure to renew research contracts with a couple of universities studying youthful behavior became headlines, and even comments by disgruntled former staffers were accorded feature treatment.

This sort of attention is the price of fame and the result of a national demand for accountability.

these publics of the continuing need and to assure them that their money is being wisely spent. It is not enough to merely crank up this effort annually, just prior to campaign time. Public relations must be year-round. Commercial institutions must prove themselves socially, and social institutions must prove themselves commercially. The public has to believe that they are efficiently run. This calls for accountability in reporting, and also revelation of some of the more dramatic uses of the funds.

These same publics may need convincing about new programs. Should they support a home for unwed mothers? Should their contributions be used to pay bail money for a political dissident? Are their hospital donations going to help provide abortions?

One important public that should not be overlooked is that composed of recipients of the services. This may be a sensitive group. There could be a temptation to feel superior to those who are benefiting from the public's largesse. Such an attitude is fatal to good public relations. The supplier of the services should be patient, understanding, available, and able to keep a confidence.

Let us take a brief look at some of the activities that those engaged in public relations efforts for nonprofit institutions might perform.

The American Cancer Society conducts "The Great American Smoke-out" annually. This is an attempt to get smokers to give up smoking on a particular day—with an eye, of course, to a more permanent cessation.

In addition to national publicity and advertising, local Cancer Society chapters establish goals and their own extensions of the total campaign. A state, for example, might have as its quota the enlisting of 50,000 smokers who would sign pledge cards promising abstinence on that single day.

What did this involve in terms of public relations?

- *Letters* are mailed to all major industries in each chapter's community, asking them to enlist smokers to take the pledge.
- *Volunteers* are organized to circulate pledges.
- *Contests* are stimulated among firms and departments within firms to see who can secure the most pledges.
- *Decals, buttons,* and other gimmicks are used. One button shows a frog and reads, "Kiss me—I don't smoke."
- *Publicity* is generated in local media and internal company publications.

Figure 15-6 The American Cancer Society uses buttons and decals with a lighthearted message to support its annual Smokeout Day.
Courtesy: American Cancer Society

There are also posters, crisis centers established in company locations, a special drive for executive smokers, and a drawing for a cold turkey for those who pledged.

Each one of the items above involves the public relations person. He or she has to handle printing, training of volunteers, securing of contacts within companies, production and delivery of news releases, supervision of contests (in some instances), and the running of a constant check on pledges to see how these are working out.

The public relations director for the American Red Cross has a number of areas to oversee, from lifesaving and military contacts to blood programs.

In some areas there is competition for blood, with private clinics paying donors. Since the Red Cross does not pay donors or charge for blood (the patient is charged a fee for administering it), its services are sometimes confused with those of the clinic where charges are made.

This may call for meetings with the clinic personnel to see what can be done to make the services more distinct. It may also call for publicity and printed materials emphasizing the difference.

Red Cross PR persons could find themselves in a disaster area responding to media questions about Red Cross involvement or even the extent of the destruction. They could be organizing a dance for teens or designing a brochure on adult-education classes.

In recent years, the Red Cross, facing the deficits other nonprofit organizations also fear, cut its national staff nearly in half and introduced a policy of having employees compete with newcomers for positions. Internal morale suffered, but industry praised the Red Cross administration for its "lean and mean" look.

A United Way Fund Campaign entails all kinds of public relations challenges, from the way agency requests for money are handled to the mountain of materials that must be produced to support solicitors.

All these items would be prepared by the public relations staff, and kits would have to be put together for the media, for various levels and kinds of volunteers, and for key staff members.

In addition, the PR people would be scheduling showings of the campaign film, arranging interviews on local talk shows, sending out news releases, arranging for report meetings, promoting the speakers' bureau, and performing dozens of other tasks.

The PR person for Big Brothers–Big Sisters could be publicizing the need for books in this organization's book drive and recruiting volunteers to collect them.

At a Jewish Community Center, the PR director may be arranging a film schedule, organizing a conference on brotherhood, and directing the installation of an exhibit of Middle East artifacts.

The PR director at a public television station is busy with the annual television auction to raise funds. He or she may be recruiting prominent people to answer a bank of phones; publicizing the need for donated gifts; promoting the auction via posters, news releases, and on-the-air spots; and arranging to thank all participants.

The National Association to Prevent Blindness launched a special campaign designed to warn car owners about the dangers of explosion from storage batteries when a car is being jump-started by another vehicle. Their efforts included warning stickers under the automobile hood; speeches to civic groups, professional people, and safety organizations; news releases and camera-ready features; and drop-in advertisements.

No two jobs are alike in nonprofit public relations. These posts offer variety because there is a lot to be done and few people to do it.

How do you break in?

Here is one area where experience may be easier to obtain. Such institutions thrive on volunteers; many use interns. The PR student can volunteer for on-the-job training, and his or her services will be welcomed. From here—if the student performs well—it may be a simple step to a full-time post upon graduation.

COMMUNITY PUBLIC RELATIONS

Within communities, staff PR people and consultants may be employed at a variety of tasks. These professionals may be instrumental in attracting industry, preserving historic monuments, assisting the celebration of an event, or changing the image of a locale.

When General Motors announced in 1985 that it would accept bids for the location of a new $5 billion Saturn car-production plant, a score of governors, aided by public relations staffs and consultants, made presentations. When Massachusetts faltered economically in the mid-1970s, it did a little self-analysis and marketed itself as a high-tech area, reversing its unemployment picture within a decade. Aspen, Colorado, once the King of the Hill in skiing circles, found itself overtaken by other areas, like Vail, and had to muster PR assistance to not only promote the town but convince local residents they should fix up their properties and alter their sometimes arrogant attitudes toward tourists. Omaha, Nebraska, used a series of novelty mailings to tour operators to generate business, mailing spice jars, for example, with the slogan, "Big City Spice, Small City Price." Indianapolis, Indiana, cultivated its cab drivers, dubbing them "goodwill ambassadors," and asked pilots of planes landing in that city to announce some of the activities available. Many communities also issue special publications, sponsor events to attract visitors and garner publicity, send their executives to target market areas, and advertise in national journals.

Goals vary. Some communities and states are after new businesses to locate there, others push for increased tourism, and still others merely seek to reverse a negative image or to correct a local attitude.

Subdivisions within a city may also have their PR functions. The police department, for example, often has a community relations division, and some cities have hired firms that specialize in public relations for law-enforcement agencies. Police officers themselves are more conscious of their need to work within the community and to earn the respect and trust of citizens. This result not only helps combat crime, it also aids the department when the subject of budget arises. Police departments in central Illinois, concerned about the quality of their officers' reports, hired an English professor to teach writing skills to them. Some cities also open community relations branches in poorer, high-crime areas, to blunt some of the hostilities and anxieties.

CELEBRITIES

Some practitioners would deny that press agents for celebrities really merit the PR designation. It is true that their efforts are fairly narrow, centering primarily on publicity, and that their behavior does not always meet the standards set down by organizations like the Public Relations Society of America. At best, this form of PR is highly suspect and earns some of the more cruel epithets, of which "flack" may be the kindest.

The major role for such a person is to gain favorable space and time for a client or clients. One firm may represent several clients—actors and actresses, musicians, athletes, popular figures on the lecture circuit, authors, artists, and others. It is also possible that one person, as agent for the celebrity, might combine business management with public relations.

In this capacity, the PR person issues releases about his or her clients, which usually have news value only because celebrities invariably make news. If a starlet sprains an ankle on the set of a film, or is seen at a nightclub with a new boyfriend, or announces that she has found God, these become the substance of news releases, features, and interviews. Myriad columns are replete with such trivia, and many magazines cater to this curiosity about such headliners. The PR person would try to stimulate editorial interest in the client rather than write such items himself or herself and might spend much more time setting up publicity angles than in producing copy.

Arranging tours and appearances would be another task, and these activities would usually by preceded by visits to newsrooms and news conferences. The advance person will have press kits available, and these could be either routine (with photos and biographical data) or elaborate (with tapes, film clips, mats, brochures, and the like). Although obviously propagandistic and uncritical, this information can prove valuable to those writing stories or fashioning local printed programs.

Celebrities may also rely on their PR aides for advice, particularly advice that will keep them in the limelight. Some of this reliance results in manufactured events, activities that showcase the personalities. Charitable work could be part of this, as could bizarre behavior at social functions. Today the

Figure 15-7 Agents for entertainment figures are always anxious to have them showcased on high-rated TV series like *Entertainment Tonight.* Robb Weller and Mary Hart appear on the nightly syndicated program. Copyright © 1985 by Paramount Pictures Corporation. All rights reserved. Courtesy: *Entertainment Tonight*

media are more suspicious (but sometimes still amused and tolerant) of publicity stunts. In the past this was less true, and agents had their clients doing all sorts of things to generate coverage:

> More than a decade ago, the historian Daniel Boorstin worried that we had gone from the celebration of heroes—people who had actually achieved something—to the celebration of celebrities—people well known simply for being well known. It was a keen insight, but it has hardly any slowing effect on the ways of the press. We seem to celebrate celebrity even more these days, for the flimsiest of reasons and for ever shorter spans of attention.[8]

Dr. Ruth Westheimer was transformed from a therapist with a late-night radio show in New York to a national celebrity, all through public relations efforts. A single press release led to the phenomenon of stints on every major talk show; features in *People, Newsweek, TV Guide,* and other magazines; and books, tapes, T-shirts, and other items. She gave her name to a board game, pitched typewriters and soft drinks, and is being touted for the international market.

Pia Zadora, backed by her millionaire husband, made a name for herself before she made a single movie. Despite claims of critics that her acting, singing, and dancing skills were minimal, Zadora used posters, billboards, public appearances, and feature billing in *Penthouse* to create a "sex kitten" image that was good for column after column of publicity. Charges that her husband's wealth bought awards and noteriety brought swift denials, but Pia was one of those named when reporters discussed those who became famous for being famous. The system isn't new; actresses from Jean Harlow to Marilyn Monroe were packaged and marketed. Pia made a couple of bad films, played nightclubs, made albums. For a while, her photo seemed to be everywhere, and even though she had no artistic successes, her name and persona are definitely familiar, even if this hype has not achieved stardom.

When Michael Jackson and his family began their Jacksons Victory Tour across America, they were in the capable hands of promoter "Chuck" Sullivan, who won out over several others for management rights. Not only did Sullivan have responsibility for items like media coverage; he also had to worry about stadium rental, security, transporting two huge stages, the functioning of electrical equipment, props, an expanded staff, local legal requirements, and even meals served on proper china for the performers. To get the show on the road, Sullivan had to come up with more than $12 million, including $500,000 in insurance premiums to protect fans against injury and the Jacksons against illness.

Press agents may always try to emphasize the positive in marketing their famous clients, but they can also have responsibility for handling less upbeat news. A PR spokesman for actor Steve McQueen revealed to the media the removal of the star's lung to prevent the spread of cancer and was later to brief reporters regularly on McQueen's condition until the actor's death.

Even after death, in the case of music idol John Lennon, the hype doesn't stop. Commemorative items were soon on the market, and the nation's newspapers featured a photo a week after his demise showing mourners gathered in Colorado's Garden of the Gods and facing a starry burst of light, as if they were greeting Easter morning. Elvis Presley's hometown remains a place of well-orchestrated pilgrimage. And the PR aide for Rock Hudson fielded a lot of criticism when it was revealed that he had created the touching "final words" supposedly uttered by the dying star and later read at a Hollywood AIDS benefit by Burt Lancaster.

Illness and death, of course, are not the only unfavorable items celebrity publicists must contend with. Famous people get into fights, divorce their spouses, are arrested on drug charges, battle with studios, renege on contracts, overindulge, or make asinine comments. During the height of the mid-1970s gasoline shortage, singer John Denver was criticized by his Aspen neighbors for erecting a gasoline tank on his property. Responding to PR pressure, he took it down. Later, he was in trouble again for shooting with a BB gun, but not seriously injuring, a trespassing dog that was nipping at his dog.

With celebrities, problems can come in big or small guises, from news of a film great hassling a waitress to squabbles over advertising contracts. Hiring stars to tout products can be expensive. Bill Cosby is paid more for representing some products than are the executives who manufacture the stuff. It also costs extra to tie these celebrities into exclusivity, and there is no guarantee that the person will do any more for the commercial than attract initial attention. John Wayne didn't score well in pushing headache remedies, and there have been dozens of other mismatches. The endorsement scene isn't confined to film or television headliners; vice-presidential candidate Geraldine Ferraro reportedly received half a million dollars for her controversial appearance in a Diet Pepsi spot, and golfing veteran Arnold Palmer has been associated for years with Pennzoil. Although arrangements for these stars are more the province of the management and advertising functions, PR personnel might be involved in ascertaining that the project is in keeping with the carefully crafted image of the celebrity.

There are hazards to this business. Many stars have colossal egos and are hard to work with. The popularity of a notable may be short-lived. And the demands of time and travel could be extensive. Top publicity agents, however, earn fat salaries. And if this appeals to them, they have the vicarious thrill of association with the famous or near-famous.

THE SPORTS PUBLICIST

Americans have always been interested in sports, and the advent of television and the introduction of sports magazines have intensified this interest. Whereas a few major sports used to occupy our attention, the range of choices today is vast and loyalties are diverse. Consider the offerings on television. Football, basketball, and baseball are standbys, but golf, boxing, and tennis share time with auto racing, bowling, wrestling, soccer, and even jai alai.

Each sport competes for audience and dollars. Sports publicists are employed to see that their particular organizations get a fair share of both. In the past, some of their chores were handled by the local sports reporter, and these people still provide a major impetus for attendance. Particularly when a home team is involved, the sportswriter and sportscaster may usually be counted upon to assume some partisan publicity coverage. Even then, however, the PR person has the job of making athletes available for interviews, compiling statistics, producing brochures, issuing news releases, taking photos or arranging for them to be taken, sending materials ahead to bolster road-game attendance, answering correspondence from fans, planning special events (Kiddies' Day, Ladies' Day, Band Day), helping individual athletes with their public relations efforts (opening supermarkets, conducting sports clinics, addressing banquets), speechwriting, community relations, and league activities. These items may only scratch the surface; the PR job ranges from that of collegiate publicist to that of front man for a major-league team.

Some critics—the irrepressible Howard Cosell among them—think this nation lavishes too much attention on sports to the detriment of more serious matters. Cosell also laments the role-model function assumed by athletes and their dominance of the sports media, whether or not they have any broadcasting talent or journalistic training. This complaint may be accurate, but it flies in the face of an America that wants to believe in this fantasy realm. Consequently, many of those who labor in sports PR struggle to keep the myth alive.

It can be a tough job. Some athletes are deliberately abrasive with the media. Others, like basketball notables Larry Bird and Moses Malone, are reluctant to say anything, and team and personal publicists have to mollify an angry press. As in other areas of public relations, sportswriters sometimes view the practitioner as a detriment to getting any story. In an *Advertising Age* article on sports columnist Stan Hochman of the *Philadelphia Daily News*, Hochman describes his attempts to interview the Philadelphia Eagles' owner while the "PR guy [does] a flamenco dance of despair behind us."[9]

Some athletes, like John McEnroe, manage to stir up controversy wherever they go; others, like Pete Rose, invariably appear as charming citizens worthy of imitation; still others, like Larry Holmes, have their ups and downs with the media and the public. Like politicians, the individual athlete often takes any strategy out of the public relations person's grasp, making points or making enemies, regardless of the practitioner's efforts. "Sports is growing closer and closer to the field of entertainment and our sports figures are becoming celebrities," says David Falk, senior VP of ProServ, which is increasingly adding entertainment figures to its client portfolio.[10]

Case in point: Mary Lou Retton. This diminutive Olympic star parlayed her winning smile and competitive spirit into endorsement contracts for nine major corporations, each worth between $100,000 and $200,000 a year over a three- to four-year period. Some $35 million in air time was purchased in a single year to display the gymnast's ability to sell everything from Wheaties to Eveready Energizer batteries. The commercials are only one aspect of the teenager's regimen. As a corporate spokesperson, she makes personal appearances, makes speeches, visits with the media. She co-wrote a book on her young life and gave her name to an exercise album. Throughout all these endeavors, Ms. Retton had to retain both her perspective and her spontaneous image in order to keep her fans and her contracts. Personality and public relations combined to make this possible.

Other Olympic winners weren't so fortunate. Fame brought few financial rewards to Carl Lewis, Greg Louganis, and Alberto Salazar. Former swimming champion Mark Spitz, winner of seven gold medals in 1972, experienced a brief flurry of commercial success, then faded, partially owing to his outspoken criticism of sports. A dozen years later, Spitz came under new management, which was determined to use public relations to upgrade the athlete's image and to make him more marketable. Olympic cyclists did cash in to a degree on endorsements of bicycles, but other opportunities haven't come their way.

Any star usually has chances to represent products associated with that particular sport—Nicklaus with clubs, Navratilova with rackets, Ewing with basketball shoes. Once the image slips, however, the opportunities dissipate.

Individual athletes aren't the only problems facing publicists in sports. Sports information directors for colleges and universities constantly deal with stories of illegal recruiting, coaching dismissals, athletes' academic mishaps, drugs, point-shaving, under-the-table payoffs, alumni unrest, and internal dissension. Some have had to explain to a naive public incidents of drunken driving, theft, rape, even death. Former players emerge to charge their alma maters with everything from supplying cars to failing to provide an education. Even the good news has its difficulties, as SIDs for tournament or bowl-bound teams will attest. In the pro ranks, there are player and umpire strikes, sudden shifts in team location, fat salaries, drugs, and other problems to contend with. Hockey fans, not the most tepid rooters, are becoming increasingly alarmed at the mayhem on the ice. Baseball fans grouse about the slow pace of the game or the callousness of owners.

Sports publicists can't work miracles. They can't force people to support a losing effort; they can't silence an irresponsible owner; and they can't police the private lives of players. They can, however, enhance the possibilities of a Heisman candidate or expose the human side of a crusty manager. They may even help save the franchise from moving or assist in attracting a new one to a community.

It helps, of course, to have an athletic background, and many former sports heroes with communications credentials gravitate to this field. But it's even more important to be professionally adept and to have a style and interest that adapt easily to this more flamboyant form of public relations.

PR AND THE ARTS

Audience and patrons may be the two most important target groups for public relations in the arts. Because of these twin needs, PR staffs not only are common to prominent institutions like the Metropolitan Opera but will also be found with museums, theatres, symphonies, ballet troupes, and other entities in smaller communities.

Many practitioners choose this line of work because of their interest in the art form. Their efforts may be directed toward building audiences for a performance; generating publicity; producing printed materials; directing special events, like teas, luncheons, previews, fairs, and auctions; and participating in the fund-raising process. Some have responsibility for the featured performers, who may be tempermental or uncooperative, and other practitioners may be charged with promoting a touring exhibit or a concert.

Membership drives occupy staff time every year and provide the base for subsequent funding of operations. Periodic capital campaigns are launched to handle construction, renovation, endowment, and other major needs. Some art galleries sell books and rent art to help defray costs. Others sponsor film series or lavish banquets. All these activities are intended to support some aesthetic endeavor, since art, by its nature, appeals to a limited segment of any community. Helping to broaden and focus the appeal is a public relations function.

The Children's Museum in Indianapolis dispatched a traveling exhibit to spread the word about its offerings; so did the Children's Museum in Denver, which also circulates a newspaper nationwide, publishes books, and, in cooperation with a supermarket chain, imprints shopping bags with games and puzzles that plug the museum. The Seattle Museum, to call attention to an exhibit of antique armor, dressed a man in medieval garb and had him ride through the city streets. The Detroit Symphony scheduled some of its concerts in shopping malls. All these activities are attempts to introduce new people to the pleasures of the arts.

Doing public relations for this type of organization requires some special knowledge. Even though the target audiences may sometimes be small, they are usually knowledgeable, so the practitioner must understand and be able to accurately interpret the art form. Human relations skills are also essential, since the practitioner must relate well with both artists and patrons, and it wouldn't hurt to have some instructional sense, because much of what has to be done in the arts is educational.

Salaries vary by the size of the organization and other factors, but overall, financial compensation is not a major incentive for those who choose this route. They are drawn more by the special nature of the work.

PR AND THE MEDIA

Although the purpose of the media is communication, it was many years before the media realized that they needed specialists within their industry to develop their own image. Many of these people now have the title of "promotion director" rather than "public relations director," and their duties are somewhat limited.

Community relations is one major aspect of their work. Not only do they endeavor to participate in civic enterprises, they also seek to involve local citizens and organizations in their programming or crusades. A newspaper may run a number of charitable funds and promote these through its pages. Television stations may conduct telethons for the same purpose. These must also be organized and publicized.

Promoting regular programs or features is also a responsibility. Television stations try to drum up viewers for certain programs, using publicity, advertising, and their own air time. You see billboards calling attention to radio and TV stations, probably concentrating on musical tastes or news teams. Mixed in with commercials for products will be station "promos" inviting listeners and viewers to tune in to some upcoming offering. The newspaper works at increasing circulation and readership. Newspapers may front-page some teaser lines about inside features or call attention in a daily paper to something that will appear in their Sunday edition.

Readers and viewers and listeners become the basis for advertising rates, so their numbers are important. The various promotion departments may pull together visual presentations that will be shown to advertisers and their agencies. These could be portable exhibits that would be carried to the corporate offices or ad agency board room, or they could be cocktail-party extravaganzas like those produced by TV networks and stations to announce programs for a new season.

Publicity about programs and personalities is dispensed liberally for networks and local outlets, and there are occasional events—a station-sponsored athletic event or a black-tie awards banquet—that fall into the PR or promotional province.

With the increasing criticism of the media, particularly television, this PR function has the added responsibility of monitoring citizen input and responding to complaints about sex, violence, or even programming options. Preempt NBA basketball or a "Dallas" episode in order to present a news special or a presidential conference and you are certain to field a switchboard full of dissenters. The reasons must be communicated to the public, using the station and other media.

Some stations also issue program logs, monthly publications that include listings and features. Educational channels may offer such a publication as part of a subscription fee, and these stations would also focus on fund raising, as against commercial television's freedom from this necessity.

The media, like other institutions, also celebrate anniversaries, conduct open-house events, and host dinners and similar affairs. Special documentary programs or enlarged commemorative newspaper editions may be used, together with professional seminars, awards, and even gimmicks like buttons or bumper stickers.

Crisis public relations is also familiar to media PR people. Strikes are not uncommon, and there are mechanical interruptions, protests about programs (like the 1985 flareup over the "Cagney and Lacey" episode on abortion), even shareholder uprisings. Media practitioners must continually remind readers, listeners, and viewers about the benefits provided by their services.

Each generation brings its own set of concerns. Radio worried for a long time about the inroads created by television; now TV networks are casting frightened glances at the revolution in videocassettes, a phenomenon that has replaced cable television as their primary fear. Newspaper owners fuss a lot about television, about the cost of newsprint, and about direct advertising, which steals some of their retail revenue.

With a few exceptions, PR staff members in the media are not often lumped with top management. Salaries, too, are not equivalent to those of senior editors, anchorpersons, station managers, or even sales and advertising execs.

MISCELLANEOUS

The PR applications described above hardly exhaust the possibilities in the profession. Many book publishers have PR staffs. So do racetracks, prisons, shopping centers, legal firms, architects, fast-food restaurant chains, service clubs, and investment houses. Every application possesses its own peculiar set of rules, not vastly different from the general principles we have enunciated, but with its own twists and its own audiences. Public relations for art galleries is apt to be intellectual and selective, whereas the promotion of restaurant patronage could be slick yet homey. The racetrack PR person would have to learn a whole new jargon, just as would the professional publicizing science or medicine.

- Most large libraries have PR staffs—to increase traffic, inform citizens, improve service. They may organize and work with Friends of the Library, supervise book sales or auctions, help design printed materials, visit schools, or work closely with industry.
- Supermarkets use their PR talent to produce internal publications, represent their interests in legislative bodies and civic organizations, devise programs to improve morale, assist with promotions to boost sales. One super-

market chain, seeking to ease the frustrations of waiting in checkout lines, arranged to show silent commercials on overhead TV sets by the register. Stores often cooperate with local churches, schools, and nonprofit organizations to assist with fund drives or special events.

- In the travel industry, airlines, cruise lines, bus lines, and major travel agencies, among others, employ PR personnel or firms. Midway, in Chicago, had a PR staff back as far as World War II. Duties in this industry might involve a slick in-flight magazine (although many of these are now handled by specialists), arrangements for press conferences for notables on tight schedules, smoothing the way for troubled passengers, handling community relations when conflicts arise over noise or other concerns, and taking care of the crises, large and small, from weather to crashes, that might cause problems.

- Organizations created to serve a specific purpose—such as help for the hungry of the world or a certain portion of the world, like Ethiopia or Bangladesh—need a great deal of public relations assistance. The message has to be communicated to millions, largely through the media, but it must also be done in a way that does not exploit the victims and does not alienate potential donors. Arranging concerts and special events may accompany the creation of printed materials, TV specials, and an abnormal amount of correspondence.

- Agriculture, which has had limited contact with the PR function, is now much more aware of the need to get its story told. Techniques vary from ads and lobbying to tractorcades and town-hall meetings. More success has been experienced in areas affected by rural problems, but the message must eventually get to the more populous urban areas.

- Even the dogcatchers in Columbus, Georgia, take a four-week course in public relations, to teach them how to relate better to dog owners!

With a few exceptions, experience in one PR field translates pretty well into another field. You must learn a new industry, new guidelines, a new list of audiences—but the skills and tools are likely to be quite similar.

INTERNATIONAL PUBLIC RELATIONS

There are two kinds of international public relations: The practitioner represents either an American firm abroad or a foreign firm in the United States. On occasion, an American PR firm may represent a foreign nation in its own part of the world.

In every case, the general PR principles apply, except that they must be modified to meet the standards, customs, pace and expectations of the foreign country or client. The PR person goes by a nation's rules, knowing there will be a lot of uncertainty and a lot of restrictions. In England, the practitioner may find the press unyielding and antagonistic. Nations exhibiting considerable internal stress, as in Africa and Latin America, force the practitioner to keep a low profile.

Besides the requisite public relations skills, the PR person serving abroad could benefit from a generalist background, including some working knowledge of the language and life-style of the host nation. He or she might also be attuned to the way in which Americans are viewed. Do these people see the United States as aggressive, flaunting its wealth, demanding all sorts of concessions? Or do they see us as efficient, humane, and cooperative? That viewpoint will greatly influence the shaping of PR policy.

At least a third of the American firms doing business abroad employ American counsel; some of them are augmented by foreign counsel—for

---

MULTINATIONAL SOCIAL RESPONSIBILITY IS GOOD BUSINESS
By William J. Corbett, APR

All fair-minded people believe that most multinational or transnational corporations make great contributions to the national development of their host country.

From the transfer of technology to consumer consciousness-raising, multinationals make an impact wherever they venture. When multinationals are concerned about the society and environment of their host country, they can make an even stronger impact for the common good. The welfare of the host country and its citizens, and the success of the corporation are compatible goals, and public relations, as a profession, has an important role to play in ensuring good corporate citizenship.

How can public relations creatively fill this role of ensuring good corporate citizenship? I'd like to offer a few suggestions:

Conduct a social audit on your client or company and its subsidiaries in each country and location.   Until you do an audit, it is difficult to know where you are and where you are going.

Work with local governments or groups to support areas of broad social concern.   Understand that critics of business do not necessarily have to remain your enemies. My company years ago started formal dialogues with consumer activists in one European country. This outreach proved so successful that it is now extended to many other countries.

Make corporate charitable contributions.   Although a longstanding American tradition, corporate charity is not so common in many other countries. At Avon we have required our local management to seek out and support worthwhile charitable projects. Local management, responsible for the bottom line—for turning a profit each year—are occasionally resistant. Our company policy holds that even in poor business years and even when a local company fails to make a profit, charitable contributions are a long-term investment in a host country and its people.

Create your own community events to promote corporate identification. An example of an Avon public relations program which promotes corporate goodwill while encouraging good works is our Women of Achievement awards in Japan. The award singles out those women who have contributed significantly to the status of women and to society in general. And in Europe we give scholarships to housewives all over France who are seeking to return to the work force.

Seek opportunities to work with like-minded groups or agencies. Last year we brought together a Washington-based organization with one of our subsidiaries. The result: Avon Cosmetics of Mexico today funds four excellent programs under the aegis of Partners of the Americas. The projects are varied, but they all help to improve living conditions in needy communities in Mexico by increasing agricultural production, generating additional sources of income, and improving health and nutrition.

Foster a climate of readiness to help. You can help make available key personnel and company facilities for local activities. This helps build bridges to the community; it presents your company in a positive light while providing tangible benefits to the local community.

Encourage the use of local vendors and suppliers. This will help the local economy. And in the long run, it is good business since most countries limit your import on ingredients and components. Many countries are now also insisting that any new company undertake an export commitment. Local suppliers can help you to achieve that goal.

Public relations must act as watchdog of the corporation to make sure that it lives up to its social responsibility. It must, through watchfulness, be sure its products are top quality. There are no second class customers in the world and products rejected by the government of one country, if a good reason is provided, should not be "dumped" in another country where standards are either less stringent or non-existent. By insisting on its own high standards, a multinational can help boost the industry's level of excellence in the host country.

Urge your clients and companies to appoint a local board of directors or advisory committee of respected local citizens. Make a bold social statement and include qualified local women and others who may thus far be excluded from leadership positions. Such a board can help establish your credibility and allay suspicion of foreign multinational corporations. Its advice can even make government and public relations much easier.

SOURCE: Excerpted from a speech given by William J. Corbett, now vice-president Communication of the American Institute of Certified Public Accountants, at an International Public Relations Symposium on "Communications and Development" held in Trinidad and Tobago. Reprinted with permission from *IABC Communication World*, October 1984.

better media contacts, translations, knowledge of local customs, connections with local governments, and a superior knowledge of local marketing. These are the same reasons foreign firms employ PR people in the United States, to become better acquainted with the vast and complicated American society, and to learn how to succeed in a competitive media world.

At least half of America's *Fortune* 500 firms spend heavily on public relations abroad, staffing offices in dozens of foreign nations, or making use of local agencies in more than 40 countries. Much of this expansion followed World War II, augmenting marketing efforts that were considerably older.

The reasons for an increase in international public relations are many—diplomacy, security, cultural exchange, and, especially, economic advantages. Many multinational firms in this country receive nearly half their revenue from foreign markets, including a growing market in the South Pacific. That latter fact accounts for the fact that Burson-Marsteller, the world's largest PR agency, has offices in Japan, Hong Kong, Malaysia, and Singapore. Like others doing business abroad, Burson-Marsteller quickly learned that numerous adjustments must be made in this arena. Rep. Leon Panetta says:

> We're lazy when it comes to understanding other cultures. It's not stressed in our educational system. It's not stressed when we go abroad because we always figure there's someone there who can speak English. But from a security point of view, from a business point of view, Americans must learn to relate to other people on the same basis that we relate to each other.[11]

Between 4 and 5 million American businessmen travel abroad annually, and the majority of them are at a cross-cultural disadvantage. Books and articles are full of their faux pas, like a mistranslation by the Parker Pen Company that told Mexican readers its ballpoints had contraceptive properties, and a realization by General Motors that, in South America, Nova means "doesn't go." Americans learned it was considered boorish to pat an Arab on the back, that striped ties in England weren't a good idea because they mocked regimental or school colors, and that a nod of the head in Bulgaria means "no." Small gifts are virtually expected in Japanese business deals but taboo in China. In Mexico, you inquire about the family, but in Saudi Arabia, this is in poor taste. There's a lot to learn besides language!

More than a third of all Americans who relocate abroad return home prematurely because the culture shock is too much for them. That includes PR types as well as others.

Although language isn't the only barrier, it is an important one. Businessmen point out that, when the Japanese come here, they speak English, but we don't reciprocate in their country—largely because language doesn't have sufficient emphasis in our schools. Even when an American has a working knowledge of a foreign language, company execs find local translators more reliable than academically trained Americans. The costs of our shortcomings are high. To translate a single manual for an American product may run well over $50,000.

As indicated above, the prime motivation for more international access, and for improved international public relations, is an economic one. Trade deficits have dominated the international marketing scene for America for nearly a decade. A steady decline in our trade balance amounts to billions in dollars and thousands in jobs lost. The disparity cuts across industries— clothing, steel, agriculture, even electronics. The strong dollar accounts for some of the problem, but we have also been outhustled by some of the most successful trading nations. Where the United States has done well, good public relations and strong advertising have usually helped.

Pizza Hut wisely moved its franchise within pubs in Great Britain, and Chase Manhattan aggressively promoted electronic banking to move ahead of competition. "A-Team" dolls, aided by the popularity of the series there, have scored big in South Africa. Marlboro learned to change the rugged outdoor image of its ads in the Far East, substituting a modern cowboy who appeared more prosperous, and American manufacturers of jeans have had to cut back their sexy approach in many foreign countries. American promoters also

---

COCA-COLA IS UNIVERSAL

Being the world's largest manufacturer of soft drinks has many marketing benefits, but it's not without problems. People expect Coca-Cola to be everywhere. The company's president, Donald R. Keough, once lamented that American tourists wrote letters of complaint to the Atlanta-based firm because they didn't find Coke in a trio of Swiss chalets—the only three out of hundreds in that small country that didn't stock the brand.

Traveling Americans are used to seeing signs for Coca-Cola all over the earth, even in some of the most remote areas. The drink travels well, is aided by the involvement of local bottlers, and is helped even more by the ambassadorial intent of its marketing team.

Coca-Cola is a major advertiser, here and abroad, but it also makes efficient use of public relations skills.

Each new country presents a different problem. Sometimes it is the translation of a slogan that doesn't mean the same thing in the new language; sometimes it's a cultural barrier that must be overcome.

The firm's entry into the Soviet Union was preceded by meetings with Russian officials, both in this country and in theirs. The introduction was gradual, starting with shops catering to tourists and the diplomatic corps, but with an eventual goal of 275 million new consumers. Publicity had to

Figure 15-8 Coca-Cola makes its presence felt in China.
Courtesy: The Coca-Cola Company

meet with the expectations of the Soviet media, and the overall promotional tactics were conservative by American standards.

Getting back into China after an absence of 40 years was another sort of challenge to Coca-Cola's marketing and public relations personnel. They moved slowly, schooling themselves in Chinese culture; supporting research for a monumental history of China, one that was applauded by the Chinese; and by attending the twice-yearly Canton Export Commodities Fair and purchasing everything from tea to handicrafts—which later appeared in corporate offices.

In April 1981, Coca-Cola chairman Roberto Goizueta cut the ribbon at the first Coca-Cola bottling plant in China, near Beijing. Again, the original target audience was composed of tourists (some 6 million of them), but the eventual consumer market was vast. Advertising was limited to a few signs and a single billboard, but the sight of the many travelers drinking Coke had its own effect. The soft-drink giant also sponsored the Beijing telecast of the Asian Zone World Cup Volleyball Preliminaries in Hong Kong, an event that culminated in a much-celebrated victory by the Chinese team over South Korea.

Even the translation of the famous name worked. The symbols "ke-kou-ke-la" can mean "it can make your mouth happy."

Just to show nothing ever goes off without a hitch, the grand opening was supposed to conclude with a toast by chairman Goizueta with an immediate segue to a tape of Aretha Franklin singing the Coca-Cola theme, "Have a Coke and a Smile." Instead, the confused audience heard Beethoven. What had been neglected was the necessity for a Chinese spokesperson to return the toast. The music was stopped, the toast delivered, and Aretha Franklin's rendition boomed forth.

Foreign markets have other benefits besides potential sales. The Beijing factory, for example, is seen as a technological model, a symbol of Western efficiency, and one that helps train young Chinese workers. The presence in Russia, even though limited, is a happy response to the notion that all Western ways are somehow decadent and corrupting.

Then, too, although publicity may be minimal in some of the foreign nations Coke serves, its claim to markets in more than 155 countries helps its image in the United States and elsewhere.

change their attitudes about being prompt for appointments, talking too much, and drinking and eating certain items. Adjustments must be made to make a decent impression, and this pertains not only to the selling of products but to the recruiting of industry, the appeal to tourists, and the search for investors. One of the first things Americans realize is that a foreign perception of our country may not match our own. Their versions of our TV anchorpersons may be communicating a totally different image of America. Similarly, our impression of the nature of other nations is also likely to be affected by what we read, hear, and see, and can often be guilty of a narrow focus.

The Soviet Union dominates America's political thinking, and we dominate that of the Soviets. Even though our two governments may operate under constant tension, average citizens in both countries—but especially in Russia—have a curiosity, even a grudging respect, for each other. Moreover, leaders in the Soviet Union are mastering Western public relations tactics.

> Mr. Gorbachev's emergence as an urbane, effective communicator of the Soviet party line should not obscure the fact that the sharpening of Soviet PR skills has been going on for years. He is just the newest, and certainly the most visible and potent, of the new breed of Soviet spokesmen.[12]

The Japanese are just beginning to regard public relations as having a positive connotation, a management function. Previously, partly because of their reluctance to open up to strangers, Japanese businessmen used PR primarily as a means of neutralizing unfavorable publicity.

Hill and Knowlton opened a public relations office in Beijing, China, early in 1985, primarily as a means of guiding its American clients through the intricacies of Chinese culture and politics, and to help it use China's massive newspaper and radio network and its growing television audience.

For years, public relations has been regarded with suspicion in countries like France and Italy, but the more sophisticated modern practitioner is starting to dispel many of these prejudices. Both countries have witnessed the effectiveness of public relations in handling union problems, lobbying, media relations, crisis situations, and competition.

DEVELOPING INTERNATIONAL PUBLICITY FOR A COMMUNITY

Although development of good media relations is just one of several aspects of public relations practice, it is still an extremely important one, both when an organization is unexpectedly in the news and when it seeks media help in introducing a new product, service, or activity. An unusual instance of the latter was a campaign conducted in 1982 to publicize *Altos de Chavon*, a new village created from what had been in 1975 a 400-foot-high, jungle-covered bluff. It overlooks the estuary of the Chavon River and, in the distance, the Caribbean Ocean, is located 75 miles from Santo Domingo in the Dominican Republic portion of the Island of Hispañola, and was designed to become a local and international center for the arts.

The village is owned by the Altos de Chavon Foundation, which is sponsored by *Gulf & Western Industries* (G&W), big NYC-headquartered conglomerate. Creating the village was an appropriate undertaking for G&W, which has substantial business interests in the Dominican Republic and therefore its people and their culture. It was built, largely of regional stone, by Dominicans under the guidance of artisans from around the world, according to the concept and plans of Roberto Copa, a noted Italian designer and architect.

Although many of the village's facilities were operative in 1981, it would not be until 1982 that all of its potential attractions would be ready for full-scale promotion. To handle the publicity aspects of that effort, the Foundation, in November 1981, retained *Morton Dennis Wax & Assocs.* (MDW&A), NYC. (MDW&A, founded in 1956, had had extensive experience in handling publicity for artists, art galleries, and pop music performers and had established excellent contacts with the media interested in their activities.)

Such contacts were valuable in helping MDW&A carry out its assignment and Altos de Chavon provided some highly distinctive material with which to work. The architecture is appropriately that of a European Renaissance village of the time of Christopher Columbus, who was the first European to visit Hispañola. The buildings actually appear that old and are highly photogenic. Among them are a church, arts and crafts workshops, a school of design, museums, restaurants, both elegant and simple, shops, a small inn (there are many resort hotels for tourists in the general area), and a 5,000-seat amphitheater built in the traditional style of ancient Greece (but with an ultramodern sound system).

The School of Design, opened in 1982, is a two-year college of the visual arts. It is operated in affiliation with NYC's well known *Parsons School of Design*. An activity of the Altos de Chavon School that particularly lends itself to publicity in selected media is an artist-in-residence program through which 20 three-month residencies a year are available, on a competitive basis, to "accomplished professionals." They live and work in the village; there are exhibits of their work; and their presence adds an extra dimension to the community.

MDW&A's President *"Mort" Wax* points out that the publicity challenge was to reach several diverse publics, those interested in: serious art; crafts; pop/rock or classical music; archeology (the preColumbian Taino Indians who had then inhabited the island had a culture dating back thousands of years); and vacationing or sight-seeing. In addition, Altos de Chavon's need to attract people from many countries dictated that publicity include countries in Asia, Europe, and South America where the principal languages were other than English.

To handle such a variety efficiently, the project was broken down into four component parts and each was assigned to a specific account executive with expertise in it. Wax himself supervised the entire activity.

Illustrating the diverse audience it was aimed to reach is this list of magazines to which *a kit* describing Altos de Chavon was mailed: *Life*; *Time*; *Newsweek*; *Harper's*; *Better Homes & Gardens*; *Ladies Home Journal*; *Town & Country*; *Where*; *National Geographic*; *Horizon*; *Museum*; *American Artist*; *Today's Art & Graphics*; *Camera Arts*; *Portfolio*; *Architectural Digest*; *Dance*; *Diversion*; *People, Places, and Parties*; *Temas*; *Travel*; *Travel & Leisure*; *American Way*; *Mainliner*; and *TWA Ambassador*.

Although the kits all had the same cover with a spectacular aerial color photo of the community, their items each varied according to the interests of the editors to whom they were sent. All contained background information and a brochure. But the releases were tailored for the publication and clippings, reprints, and photos taken within the village, were similarly selected.

Personal contacts were made with art columnists and such specialized publications as *Art World*, *Forum*, *Portfolio*, and *ARTgallerySCENE*. . . .Food editors and restaurant critics were informed about the village's five restaurants. . . .Releases were translated into the appropriate languages for use by art editors in the major cities of such countries as Argentina, Brazil, France, Germany, Italy, and Japan.

Extensive efforts were made in advance of the August 1982 opening of the amphitheater. In some cases, MDW&A's contacts with pop artists led to their appearances. One, for example, was *Carlos Santana*'s group, which shared the very important opening-week billing with singer *Frank Sinatra*.

Information about all activities during the year was duly conveyed to the appropriate media. This included schedules of art exhibitions, advance information about upcoming amphitheater appearances, and stories about artists, such as those in residence, and performers.

A study of *releases and other materials* issued during the year shows how potentially newsworthy details were worked into them. *Examples* follow.

A brief general announcement that Altos de Chavon was "at long last, complete" mentioned that five German expressionist painters had been among the artists in residence during the previous winter.

A release about the artists in residence revealed that their living quarters "with all basic comforts are provided at no cost and that, while they pay their daily living expenses, it is possible to live quite economically at Altos."

One story sent to photography editors characterized Altos de Chavon as "Location Paradise in the Sky" and a unique setting for commercial and film producers and fashion photographers.

Another release described the virtues of the village as a meeting place for small groups, the inn having nine double rooms, each with a spectacular view.

The publicity efforts earned coverage of amphitheater performances in all the well known *music-trade papers* and many others. A spectacular success was a five-page cover story in *Performance*, which describes itself as The International Touring Talent Weekly. In addition to 14 color photos interspersed in the text, both inside and outside covers carried Altos de Chavon pictures.

Stephen D. Kaplan, Altos de Chavon's Arts Director, has high praise for MDW&A's efforts. He cites such items as: special help with the Spanish-language press; excellent publicity for the School of Design; an "important" article in the *NY Times Travel Section*; "beautiful coverage" by American Airlines' American Way; success of an exhibition; the *Performance* cover story; and a special issue of the *ARTgallerySCENE*.

SOURCE: Case Study No. 1834, "Developing International Publicity for a Community," Vol. XXXIX, No. 34 (August 29, 1983). Courtesy of *Public Relations News*, Denny Griswold, editor.

More than half the world's nations have employed American public relations skills at some time. Why?

- To understand the United States better
- To handle special events, like fairs or exhibits

- To gain access to various levels of government
- To use media more effectively, including both advertising and publicity
- To perform a variety of services not available in their countries
- To provide advice in areas unfamiliar to them
- To build tourism
- To attract industry and investments
- To polish or change an image

Conditions make international public relations a demanding profession. The tools are likely to be less sophisticated in Third World countries, for example, and governments may also impose a considerable list of restrictions governing any form of communication. In a *Public Relations Journal* article, Cornelius Pratt made some suggestions for practitioners based on his field research in West Africa in the summer of 1984. A synopsis of his advice contains these suggestions:

- Reorient traditional Western principles on social responsibility to the socio-economic and political structure of the Third World environment.
- Get firsthand experience with the culture and the value system of the society in which your foreign operation will be conducted.
- Get an inside view of the political system.
- Do not take things for granted. Methods found useful in public relations in the West may not yield similar success in the developing nations.
- Demonstrate an enthusiasm to adapt to the host nation's value system, even if only in the short run. Nothing brings about the hostility of Third World citizens more than a display of a holier-than-thou attitude.[13]

Keep in mind, too, that other countries are developing their own practitioners. Ireland, with a relative handful of PR agencies, offers a one-year course in public relations for those interested; Australia, which looks to both Great Britain and the United States for PR trends, notes that its majority percentage of women entering the profession mirrors the other two nations; Canada's first public relations graduates received their degrees from Mount Saint Vincent University in Halifax in 1981. Some Third World countries send their students abroad to master communications skills, expecting them to return to their homelands and enter public relations or the media.

An International Public Relations Association spans some 64 countries and has over 750 members. The association publishes a quarterly journal (*IPRA Review*), holds periodic meetings, and attempts to supervise standards internationally. In addition, there are organizations like International Public Relations (IPR) Group of Companies, with 86 offices in 41 countries, and the foreign branches of some of America's largest PR firms. These sources, as well as government agencies, multinational corporations, college courses, travel, and the growing number of specialized publications, help interested persons learn more about international PR.

In reality, the action is everywhere, in all the hundreds of applications of public relations in this country and around the world. No professsion in America offers more variety or challenge, more opportunity to effect change, more openings for diverse talents.

But public relations is not a textbook subject; it is an experimental social science that has to be practiced to be learned.

That's why this book ends here.

CHAPTER HIGHLIGHTS

- Elementary and secondary schools list finances, discipline, recruiting, consolidation, integration, and lack of understanding among their problem areas. Criticism arises in areas such as teaching the basics, sex education, and taxes.

- Higher education wrestles with increasing costs, internal unrest, competition for the best students, and greater ties to the local community.

- In the health sciences, costs are again a concern, with skyrocketing medical and hospital bills creating numerous PR headaches. This version of pubic relations requires special sensitivity, an ability to work with people who have their own jargon, and a strict code of ethics.

- With a positive shift toward religion now taking place, practitioners in religious institutions are faced with debates on social justice, ecumenism, female participation, even competition from fundamentalist groups. More visible than ever before, America's churches have become sophisticated in the use of media but must still contend with the intangible, sacred, sometimes other-worldly aspects of faith, along with the difficulty of reaching a diverse audience and of interpreting programs that follow traditional patterns.

- Funds, recruiting of volunteers, and the problem of communicating social needs dominate not-for-profit PR. Private sources have to make up for the loss of government programs, and volunteers have to be relied on to provide much of the necessary staffing.

- To attract industry and tourism, many communities support public relations programs, sometimes using staff members, sometimes employing private counselors.

- Press agentry, a form of PR disdained by many professionals, is nevertheless a prominent adjunct of celebrity public relations, with the publicist serving as everything from a media rep to a personal aide. Temperament, travel, and lack of predictable behavior are among the shortcomings; money and the chance to hobnob with the famous or near-famous are the plus factors in celebrity public relations.

- The growing profession of sports PR often attracts ex-athletes who may or may not have appropriate backgrounds, and they must contend not only with occasionally difficult personalities but with a field riddled with complaints about drugs, excessive salaries, illegal payoffs, and other problems.

- Both the arts and the media employ PR specialists to reach their specific audiences. Goals may be membership, attendance, and financing in the arts; the media are after readers, listeners, viewers, and a certain amount of community support.
- Many other fields, from airlines to agriculture, include a PR function.
- Half the nations in the world have used American PR firms to help them attract industry or investment, bring tourists to their shores, get the attention of the U.S. government, or perform other chores. Successful practitioners must be able to adapt to foreign customs and culture.

NOTES

[1] Parental guidelines in a Minnesota community.

[2] L. Laszlo Ecker-Racz, *Today's Education*, September/October 1978.

[3] Abigail Trafford, *U.S. News & World Report*, March 18, 1985.

[4] Frank L. Riggs, "Team PR: Financial Manager, PR Director Explain Costs to Public," *Hospital Financial Management*, May 1979.

[5] Ronna Kabatznick and Janice Hopkins Tanne, "Press Agents: More and More Doctors Are Hiring Them," *Medical World News*, November 8, 1982.

[6] Kevin McManus, "Evangelist Jim Bakker's Earthly Success," *Advertising Age*, July 22, 1985.

[7] Scott M. Cutlip and Allen H. Center, *Effective Public Relations*, 5th ed. (Englewood Cliffs, N.J.: Prentice-Hall, 1978), p. 484. Adapted and annotated by this author.

[8] Edwin Diamond, "Would You Welcome, Please, Henry and Liv and Jackie and Erica!" *Columbia Journalism Review*, September/October 1975.

[9] Kevin McManus, "Coaxing Words from the Celtics' Bird," *Advertising Age*, January 21, 1985.

[10] Thomas L. Moore, "Business Office Becomes New Playing Field," *Advertising Age*, October 31, 1985.

[11] Don Oldenburg, "Focus: Bridging Cultural Gaps," *The Washington Post*, August 2, 1984.

[12] Jack Bernstein, "PR Scores for Soviets," *Advertising Age*, April 8, 1985.

[13] Cornelius Pratt, "The African Context." Reprinted with permission from the February 1985 issue of the *Public Relations Journal*. Copyright 1985.

SUGGESTED READINGS

CENTER, ALLEN H., and FRANK E. WALSH, *Public Relations Practices: Managerial Case Studies and Problems*. Englewood Cliffs, N.J.: Prentice-Hall, 1985.

COOPER, PHILIP D., *Health Care Marketing: Issues and Trends*, 2nd ed. Rockville, Md.: Aspen Systems, 1985.

Dos and Taboos Around the World. Janesville, Wisc.: Parker Pen Co.

FIELDS, GEORGE. *From Bonsai to Levi's*. New York: Macmillan, 1984.

FISHER, HEINZ-DIETRICH, and JOHN MERRILL, eds., *International Communications: Media Channel-Functions*. New York: Hastings House, 1970.

GERBNER, GEORGE, and MARSHA SIEFERT, *World Communications*. New York: Longman, 1984.

GORDON, GEORGE N., and IRVING A. FALK, *The War of Ideas: America's International Identity Crisis*. New York: Hastings House, 1973.

HALPERN, BURTON M., *Tell it to the World: A Guide to International Public Relations*. Jerusalem: Gefen Books, 1982.

JOHNSON, RAYNOLDS, *International Public Relations: A Survey*. Dubuque, Ia.: Kendall/Hunt, 1971.

KOBRE, SIDNEY, *Successful Public Relations for Colleges and Universities*. New York: Hastings House, 1974.

KOTLER, PHILIP, and KAREN F.A. FOX, *Strategic Marketing for Educational Institutions*. Englewood Cliffs, N.J.: Prentice-Hall, 1985.

KREPS, GARY L., and BARBARA C. THORNTON, *Health Communication*. New York: Longman 1984.

KURTZ, HAROLD P., *Public Relations for Hospitals*. Springfield, Ill.: Thomas, 1969.

LAHAV, PNINA, ed., *Press Law in Modern Democracies*. New York: Longman, 1985.

MERRILL, JOHN C., *Global Journalism*. New York: Longman, 1983.

MOWLANA, HAMID, *Global Information and World Communication*. New York: Longman, 1986.

RECK, W. EMERSON, *The Changing World of College Relations*. Washington D.C.: CASE, 1976.

Religious Public Relations Handbook. New York: Religious Public Relations Council, 1976.

ROGERS, HENRY C., *Walking the Tightrope*. New York: Morrow, 1980.

EXERCISES

1. Attend a local school-board meeting and make note of the issues discussed. Compare your views with subsequent media coverage.

2. Bring to class and critique one of the following:
   a. Hospital newsletter or magazine
   b. Church bulletin or newsletter
   c. Brochure from local arts organization

3. Write a cover letter to accompany the viewbook or recruiting brochure from your college or university. This letter will have an audience of high school seniors. Considering the collegiate options they have and the doubts and questions they may have, be certain your letter responds to *their* needs.

4. Select a current celebrity and see how many references you can find to this person in a single week (newspaper stories and columns, magazines, TV appearances, etc.). Based on these items, what sort of image is being presented?

5. In your immediate area, locate a PR person or program whose function would fall under the not-for-profit heading. Interview this person on the rewards and frustrations of that particular assignment.

6. What foreign countries do you feel have done a good job of public relations in the United States? Why?

7. If you have traveled to a foreign country, what cultural differences impressed you most? If you haven't traveled outside the United States, select a country you'd like to visit, give your impressions of what it would be like, and try to ascertain how you arrived at these conclusions.

CASE PROBLEMS

1. A popular professor at the university for which you are PR director has been denied tenure because the small amount of publishing she has done was considered insufficient. After this semester, she will be terminated. Students who like this teacher organize a protest, carrying signs outside the university. With a few exceptions, however, the faculty has been supportive of the decision. A local women's group charges that a double standard has been used to work against this female faculty member and threatens to mount a lawsuit. The campus chapter of the American Association of University Professors, of which she was a member, will conduct a routine examination of the whole affair. "Defuse this situation," the president tells you. Is there anything you can do?

2. A group of Brazilian businessmen will be visiting your community for three days, looking it over as a possible site for a new electronics plant. As public relations director for the regional Industrial Develoment Authority, you are responsible for preparing materials and planning events. Keeping in mind that other communities with similar characteristics will also be bidding for this plant, what kind of special activities would you plan? What materials would you supply? What local people would you involve? Draw up a plan for the entire three days for submission to the chairman of the IDA.

3. You are the public relations counselor hired by a small, 200-bed hospital in Cody, Wyoming. Because of the town's size and remoteness and the modest salaries, the hospital has been having difficulty recruiting physicians and nurses to its staff. Where would you look for prospects? What kind of a pitch would you make to them? What kind of media would you use?

4. How would you handle these situations when dealing with a foreign country?

   a. Your company wants to introduce an instant porridge to Scotland, a country that represents a strong porridge market but that also prides itself on making that product from scratch. What could you do to help break down this resistance?

b. Your American firm in an Arab country employs several dozen American women who, in this hot climate, often wear shorts and halter tops when off duty. You get numerous complaints from local authorities about what they consider is scandalous attire. You want to accommodate the locals, but, on the other hand, it is also hard to recruit and retain female personnel in this country. What will you, as public relations director, advise management to do?

c. You've been employed to do public relations for an emerging African nation that wants to attract tourists to the country. You are supposed to brief the head of the tourist department on America and Americans, and on opportunities and obstacles this country might expect. What are some of the things you would cover with the tourist-department head?

APPENDIX

CODES AND STANDARDS

PRSA: Code of Professional Standards

ASNE: Statement of Principles

PUBLIC RELATIONS SOCIETY OF AMERICA

This Code, adopted by the PRSA Assembly, replaces a similar Code of Professional Standards for the Practice of Public Relations previously in force since 1954 and strengthened by revisions in 1959, 1963 and 1977.

DECLARATION OF PRINCIPLES

Members of the Public Relations Society of America base their professional principles on the fundamental value and dignity of the individual, holding that the free exercise of human rights, especially freedom of speech, freedom of assembly and freedom of the press, is essential to the practice of public relations.

In serving the interests of clients and employers, we dedicate ourselves to the goals of better communication, understanding and cooperation among the diverse individuals, groups and institutions of society.

We pledge:

To conduct ourselves professionally, with truth, accuracy, fairness and responsibility to the public;

To improve our individual competence and advance the knowledge and proficiency of the profession through continuing research and education;

And to adhere to the articles of the Code of Professional Standards for the Practice of Public Relations as adopted by the governing Assembly of the Society.

CODE OF PROFESSIONAL STANDARDS FOR THE PRACTICE OF PUBLIC RELATIONS

These articles have been adopted by the Public Relations Society of America to promote and maintain high standards of public service and ethical conduct among its members.

1. A member shall deal fairly with clients or employers, past and present, with fellow practitioners and the general public.

2. A member shall conduct his or her professional life in accord with the public interest.

3. A member shall adhere to truth and accuracy and to generally accepted standards of good taste.

4. A member shall not represent conflicting or competing interests without the express consent of those involved, given after a full disclosure of the facts; nor place himself or herself in a position where the member's interest is or may be in conflict with a duty to a client, or others, without a full disclosure of such interests to all involved.

5. A member shall safeguard the confidences of both present and former clients or employers and shall not accept retainers or employment which may involve the disclosure or use of these confidences to the disadvantage or prejudice of such clients or employers.

6. A member shall not engage in any practice which tends to corrupt the integrity of channels of communication or the processes of government.

7. A member shall not intentionally communicate false or misleading information and is obligated to use care to avoid communication of false or misleading information.

8. A member shall be prepared to identify publicly the name of the client or employer on whose behalf any public communication is made.

9. A member shall not make use of any individual or organization purporting to serve or represent an announced cause, or purporting to be independent or unbiased, but actually serving an undisclosed special or private interest of a member, client or employer.

10. A member shall not intentionally injure the professional reputation or practice of another practitioner. However, if a member has evidence that another member has been guilty of unethical, illegal or unfair practices, including those in violation of this Code, the member shall present the information promptly to the proper authorities of the Society for action in accordance with the procedure set forth in Article XIII of the Bylaws.

11. A member called as a witness in a proceeding for the enforcement of this Code shall be bound to appear, unless excused for sufficient reason by the Judicial Panel.

12. A member, in performing services for a client or employer, shall not accept fees, commissions or any other valuable consideration from anyone other than the client or employer in connection with those services without the express consent of the client or employer, given after a full disclosure of the facts.

13. A member shall not guarantee the achievement of specified results beyond the member's direct control.

14. A member shall, as soon as possible, sever relations with any organization or individual if such relationship requires conduct contrary to the articles of this Code.

Figure A-1

SOURCE: Courtesy, Public Relations Society of America

American Society of Newspaper Editors

A Statement of Principles.

PREAMBLE

The First Amendment, protecting freedom of expression from abridgment by any law, guarantees to the people through their press a constitutional right, and thereby places on newspaper people a particular responsibility.

Thus journalism demands of its practitioners not only industry and knowledge but also the pursuit of a standard of integrity proportionate to the journalist's singular obligation.

To this end the American Society of Newspaper Editors sets forth this Statement of Principles as a standard encouraging the highest ethical and professional performance.

ARTICLE I - Responsibility

The primary purpose of gathering and distributing news and opinion is to serve the general welfare by informing the people and enabling them to make judgments on the issues of the time. Newspapermen and women who abuse the power of their professional role for selfish motives or unworthy purposes are faithless to that public trust.

The American press was made free not just to inform or just to serve as a forum for debate but also to bring an independent scrutiny to bear on the forces of power in the society, including the conduct of official power at all levels of government.

ARTICLE II - Freedom of the Press

Freedom of the press belongs to the people. It must be defended against encroachment or assault from any quarter, public or private.

Journalists must be constantly alert to see that the public's business is conducted in public. They must be vigilant against all who would exploit the press for selfish purposes.

ARTICLE III - Independence

Journalists must avoid impropriety and the appearance of impropriety as well as any conflict of interest or the appearance of conflict. They should neither accept anything nor pursue any activity that might compromise or seem to compromise their integrity.

ARTICLE IV - Truth and Accuracy

Good faith with the reader is the foundation of good journalism. Every effort must be made to assure that the news content is accurate, free from bias and in context, and that all sides are presented fairly. Editorials, analytical articles and commentary should be held to the same standards of accuracy with respect to facts as news reports.

Significant errors of fact, as well as errors of omission, should be corrected promptly and prominently.

ARTICLE V - Impartiality

To be impartial does not require the press to be unquestioning or to refrain from editorial expression. Sound practice, however, demands a clear distinction for the reader between news reports and opinion. Articles that contain opinion or personal interpretation should be clearly identified.

ARTICLE VI - Fair Play

Journalists should respect the rights of people involved in the news, observe the common standards of decency and stand accountable to the public for the fairness and accuracy of their news reports.

Persons publicly accused should be given the earliest opportunity to respond.

Pledges of confidentiality to news sources must be honored at all costs, and therefore should not be given lightly. Unless there is clear and pressing need to maintain confidences, sources of information should be identified.

These principles are intended to preserve, protect and strengthen the bond of trust and respect between American journalists and the American people, a bond that is essential to sustain the grant of freedom entrusted to both by the nation's founders.

—adopted by the ASNE board of directors, Oct. 23, 1975.

Figure A-2

SOURCE: Courtesy of the American Society of Newspaper Editors

INDEX